Bayview

ZAGAT
2014

San Francisco Bay Area Restaurants

LOCAL EDITOR
Meesha Halm
STAFF EDITOR
Cynthia Kilian

Published and distributed by
Zagat Survey, LLC
76 Ninth Avenue
New York, NY 10011
T: 212.977.6000
E: feedback@zagat.com
www.zagat.com

ACKNOWLEDGMENTS

We're grateful to our local editor, Meesha Halm, who is a Bay Area restaurant critic, cookbook author and editorial consultant. We also sincerely thank the thousands of people who participated in this survey – this guide is really "theirs."

We also thank Anne Bauso, Corrie Davidson, Andy Dolan, Jon Fox, Karen Hudes and Toby Nathan, as well as the following members of our staff: Aynsley Karps (editor), Brian Albert, Stephen Bassman, Sean Beachell, Maryanne Bertollo, Reni Chin, Larry Cohn, Nicole Diaz, Kelly Dobkin, Jeff Freier, Alison Gainor, Michelle Golden, Justin Hartung, Marc Henson, Anna Hyclak, Ryutaro Ishikane, Natalie Lebert, Mike Liao, Vivian Ma, Molly Moker, James Mulcahy, Polina Paley, Josh Siegel, Albry Smither, Amanda Spurlock, Chris Walsh, Jacqueline Wasilczyk, Art Yagci, Yoji Yamaguchi, Sharon Yates, Anna Zappia and Kyle Zolner.

ABOUT ZAGAT

In 1979, we asked friends to rate and review restaurants purely for fun. The term "user-generated content" had yet to be coined. That hobby grew into Zagat Survey; 34 years later, we have loyal surveyors around the globe and our content now includes nightlife, shopping, tourist attractions, golf and more. Along the way, we evolved from being a print publisher to a digital content provider. We also produce marketing tools for a wide range of corporate clients, and you can find us on Google+ and just about any other social media network.

The reviews in this guide are based on public opinion surveys. The ratings reflect the average scores given by the survey participants who voted on each establishment, while the text is based on quotes from, or paraphrasings of, the surveyors' comments. Ratings and reviews have been updated throughout this edition based on our most recent survey results. Phone numbers, addresses and other factual data were correct to the best of our knowledge when published in this guide.

JOIN IN

To improve our guides, we solicit your comments – positive or negative; it's vital that we hear your opinions. Just contact us al **nina-tim@zagat.com.**

Contents

Ratings & Symbols

	Name	Symbols		Cuisine		Zagat Ratings			
						FOOD	DECOR	SERVICE	COST

Area, Address & Contact	**Tim & Nina's** ◗ *Seafood* **Embarcadero** | 999 Mission St. (The Embarcadero) | 415-555-7233 | www.zagat.com	▽ 23 | 9 | 13 | $15
Review, surveyor comments in quotes	Open "more or less when T and N feel like it", this bit of unembellished Embarcadero ectoplasm excels at seafood with Asian-Argentine-Albanian accents; while the "surly" staff seems "fresh off the boat" and the view of the garbage barges is "a drag", no one balks at the "beneficent" "bottom-feeder prices."	

Ratings   **Food, Decor** & **Service** are rated on a 30-point scale.

26	–	30	extraordinary to perfection
21	–	25	very good to excellent
16	–	20	good to very good
11	–	15	fair to good
0	–	10	poor to fair

▽   low response \| less reliable

Cost   The price of dinner with a drink and tip; lunch is usually 25% to 30% less. For unrated **newcomers,** the price range is as follows:

I $25 and below   E $41 to $65

M $26 to $40   VE $66 or above

Symbols

◗   serves after 11 PM
Ⓢ   closed on Sunday
Ⓜ   closed on Monday
⌿   cash only

Maps   Index maps show restaurants with the highest Food ratings and other notable places in those areas.

San Francisco Bay Area at a Glance

WINNERS:

- **Gary Danko** (Food, Service, Most Popular)
- **Sierra Mar** (Decor)

SURVEY STATS:

- 1,495 restaurants covered
- 17,505 surveyors
- In our recent Dining Trends Survey, San Francisco Bay Area respondents reported that they eat 2.2 dinners out per week, spending an average of $41.87 per person for dinner, which is $1.34 more than the national average.
- When presented with a choice of dining irritants, surveyors selected noise as the most irritating, with 74% of diners saying they avoid restaurants that are too loud.
- Sixty-eight percent of Bay Area participants typically make restaurant reservations online, and 52% will not wait more than 30 minutes at places that don't take reservations.
- A whopping 81% of Bay Area surveyors typically split the bill evenly among them when dining in a group.

OUT OF THE ASHES: The year's biggest restaurant story was the closure of Alice Waters' legendary **Chez Panisse** and upstairs **Chez Panisse Café** following a devastating fire. Happily, the Berkeley icons have been restored and reopened, poised to continue their fourth decade leading the locavore movement.

TRENDS: Pop-up restaurants and food trucks have been putting down roots with first-time brick-and-mortar outposts including **B. Patisserie, Curry Up Now, El Huarache Loco, Hillside Supper Club, Juhu Beach Club, Marrow** and **20th Century Café.** Sustainable, local and organic are the buzzwords at Mexican newcomers **El Gusano, Nido, Padrecito** and **Rosa Mexicano,** while artisanal chocolate is sweetening the dessert scene at cacao-bean specialists **Charles Chocolate, Chocolate Lab** and **Dandelion Chocolate.** To wash it all down, the cocktail crews at **Hi Lo BBQ, MKT** and **Trick Dog** are punching things up with . . . punch.

HOT NEIGHBORHOODS: The Mission kept sizzling with arrivals including **Kronnerburger, The Palace, Trick Dog** and **20 Spot,** but with openings such as **The Mill** and **Wine Kitchen,** it's little wonder NoPa (North of the Panhandle in the Western Addition) has been dubbed The New Mission. Across town, the Embarcadero heated up with new ventures from top toques including **Coqueta** (Michael Chiarello), **Hard Water** (Charles Phan) and **Seaglass Restaurant** (Loretta Keller).

MOST SEARCHED ON ZAGAT.COM: Boulevard, Michael Mina, Delfina, Spruce, Redd, French Laundry, Prospect, Seven Hills, One Market, Frances

San Francisco, CA
September 24, 2013

Meesha Halm

KEY NEWCOMERS

Bravas Bar de Tapas, Café Lucia, Chalkboard Bistro & Wine Bar, The Parish Cafe

Empire

Napa

Sonoma

Fairfield

Sir & Star

Novato

Pizzalina

Odalisque Cafe

Belcampo Meat Co.

Richmond

Concord

Pittsburg

Martinez

Juhu Beach Club

Ramen Shop

Berkeley

Sausalito

Oakland

San Francisco

Alameda

San Leandro

San Ramon

Dublin

PACIFIC OCEAN

Daly City

San Francisco Bay

Hayward

Union City

Fremont

Millbrae

San Mateo

Redwood City

Palo Alto

Mountain View

Santa Clara

San Jose

Half Moon Bay

OAKLAND

El Gusano

Duende

Marrow

Tribune Tavern

Miss Ollie's

Forge

Nido

Lungomare

La Balena Cucina Toscana

Katsu

Los Gatos

Seaglass Restaurant

Capo's

Coqueta

Hard Water

Mason Pacific

Roka Akor

Rosa Mexicano

B. Patisserie

Aquitaine

Hakkasan

MKT

M.Y. China

The Cavalier

The Corner Store

The Mill

20th Century Cafe

South at SFJAZZ

Wine Kitchen

Rickybobby

Roku

1601 Bar & Kitchen

Padrecito

Kronnerburger

Hi Lo BBQ

20 Spot

Trick Dog

Chocolate Lab

Roxy's Cafe

Hillside Supper Club

Google

©2013 Google

Key Newcomers

Our editors' picks among this year's arrivals. See full list at p. 281.

BIG NAMES

Aquitaine
Capo's
The Cavalier
Coqueta
Duende/E
Hakkasan
Katsu/S
MKT
M.Y. China
Padrecito
Ramen Shop/E
Roka Akor
Rosa Mexicano
Roxy's Cafe
Seaglass Restaurant
Sir & Star/N
1601 Bar & Kitchen
South at SFJAZZ

NEIGHBORHOOD STARS

Belcampo Meat Co./N
The Corner Store
El Gusano/E
Forge/E
Hi Lo BBQ
La Balena Cucina Toscana/S
Lungomare/E
Mason Pacific
The Mill

Nido/E
Odalisque Cafe/N
Pizzalina/N
Rickybobby
Roku

POP-UP TO PERMANENT

Hillside Supper Club
Juhu Beach Club/E
Kronnerburger
Marrow/E
Miss Ollie's/E

WINE/BEER/SPIRITS

Hard Water
Tribune Tavern/E
Trick Dog
20 Spot
Wine Kitchen

SWEET SPOTS

B. Patisserie
Chocolate Lab
20th Century Café

WINE COUNTRY

Bravas Bar de Tapas/N
Café Lucia/N
Chalkboard Bistro & Wine Bar/N
Empire/N
The Parish Cafe/N

WHAT'S NEXT

Alta CA: Casual mid–Market Street entry from Daniel Patterson (**Coi**)

Box and Bells: Rockridge gastropub from James Syhabout (**Commis**)

Chez Spencer 2.0: Mission staple relocated in smaller quarters

The Company Bar and Kitchen: Michael Mina channels East India in SoMa

Fog City: Redo of the iconic Embarcadero diner with chef Bruce Hill (**Bix**)

Magnolia Brewery: Dogpatch taproom, whiskey bar and BBQ from
Dennis Lee (**Namu Gaji**) and Dave McLean (**Magnolia Gastropub**)

The Progress: A second, larger Fillmore Street restaurant and bar
from **State Bird Provisions**' Stuart Brioza and Nicole Krasinski

TBD: Yes, that's really the name of **AQ**'s SoMa cooking-by-fire spin-off

Tosca Café: Italian reboot of the iconic North Beach bar from April
Bloomfield and Ken Friedman (of NYC's **The Spotted Pig**)

Trou Normand: Tentative name of SoMa **Bar Agricole** offshoot

Most Popular

This list is plotted on the map at the back of this book. Places outside of San Francisco are marked as: E=East of SF; N=North; and S=South. When a restaurant has locations both inside and out of the city limits, we include the notation SF as well.

1. Gary Danko | *American*
2. Kokkari Estiatorio | *Greek*
3. Boulevard | *American*
4. French Laundry/N | *Amer./Fr.*
5. Slanted Door | *Vietnamese*
6. Acquerello | *Italian*
7. Evvia/S | *Greek*
8. Yank Sing | *Chinese*
9. House of Prime Rib | *American*
10. Delfina | *Italian*
11. Zuni Café* | *Mediterranean*
12. Bottega/N | *Italian*
13. Chez Panisse Café/E | *Cal./Med.*
14. Perbacco | *Italian*
15. Bouchon/N | *French*
16. Burma Superstar/E/SF | *Burmese*
17. Nopa* | *Californian*
18. A16/E/SF | *Italian*
19. Quince* | *Fr./Italian*
20. Frances | *Californian*
21. Chapeau! | *French*
22. Fleur de Lys | *Californian/French*
23. Tadich Grill* | *Seafood*
24. Absinthe | *French/Med.*
25. Wayfare Tavern | *American*
26. Cotogna | *Italian*
27. Hog Island Oyster/N/SF | *Seafood*
28. In-N-Out*/E/N/S/SF | *Burgers*
29. Alexander's/S/SF | *Japanese/Steak*
30. Auberge du Soleil/N | *Cal./Fr.*
31. Arizmendi/E/N/SF | *Bakery/Pizza*
32. State Bird Provisions | *American*
33. Scoma's/N/SF | *Seafood*
34. Flour + Water | *Italian*
35. La Ciccia | *Italian*
36. Ad Hoc/N | *American*
37. Osha Thai | *Thai*
38. Jardinière | *Californian/French*
39. Bistro Jeanty/N | *French*
40. Buckeye Rdhse./N | *Amer./BBQ*
41. Ajanta/E | *Indian*
42. Michael Mina | *American*
43. Amber India/S/SF | *Indian*
44. Aziza | *Moroccan*
45. R & G Lounge* | *Chinese*
46. House | *Asian*
47. Mustards Grill/N | *Amer./Cal.*
48. Village Pub*/S | *American*
49. Cheesecake/E/N/S/SF | *Amer.*
50. La Folie* | *French*

Many of the above restaurants are among the San Francisco area's most expensive, but if popularity were calibrated to price, a number of other restaurants would surely join their ranks. To illustrate this, we have added two pages of Best Buys starting on page 14.

---

* Indicates a tie with restaurant above

Visit zagat.com

Top Food Overall

29 | Gary Danko | *American*
28 | Erna's Elderberry/E | *Cal./Fr.*
| French Laundry/N | *Amer./Fr.*
| Sierra Mar/S | *Cal./Eclectic*
| Acquerello | *Italian*
| Cafe Gibraltar/S | *Med.*
| Kiss Seafood | *Japanese*
| Evvia/S | *Greek*
| Kokkari Estiatorio | *Greek*
27 | Chez Panisse/E | *Cal./Med.*
| Commis/E | *American*
| Terra/N | *American*
| La Forêt/S | *Continental/Fr.*
| La Ciccia | *Italian*
| Sushi Zone | *Japanese*
| Boulevard | *American*
| Chez Panisse Café/E | *Cal./Med.*
| Madrona Manor/N | *Amer./Fr.*
| Manresa/S | *American*
| Cucina Paradiso/N | *Italian*

Le Papillon/S | *French*
La Folie | *French*
Rivoli/E | *Cal./Med.*
Saison | *American*
Seven Hills | *Italian*
Cole's Chop/N | *Steak*
Meadowood Rest./N | *Cal.*
Tartine Bakery | *Bakery*
Benu | *American*
Local Mission Eatery | *Cal.*
Zushi Puzzle* | *Japanese*
Sushi Ran/N | *Japanese*
Ajanta/E | *Indian*
Fleur de Lys | *Cal./Fr.*
Atelier Crenn | *French*
Auberge du Soleil/N | *Cal./Fr.*
Redd/N | *Californian*
Keiko à Nob Hill | *Fr./Japanese*
House | *Asian*
Farmhouse Inn/N | *Cal.*

Top Decor Overall

29 | Sierra Mar/S
28 | Auberge du Soleil/N
| Erna's Elderberry/E
| Navio/S
| Ahwahnee Dining Room/E
| Garden Court
| Pacific's Edge/S
| Marinus/S
27 | Kokkari Estiatorio
| Gary Danko

French Laundry/N
Twenty Five Lusk
Farallon
Jardinière
Spruce
Waterbar
Roy's at Pebble Beach/S
Meadowood Restaurant/N
26 | Fleur de Lys
| Big Four

Top Service Overall

29 | Gary Danko
| Erna's Elderberry/E
28 | French Laundry/N
| Acquerello
| Benu
27 | Sierra Mar/S
| Terra/N
| Madrona Manor/N
| Coi
| Marinus/S

Chez Panisse/E
Manresa/S
Meadowood Restaurant/N
La Folie
Baumé/S
Kokkari Estiatorio*
La Forêt*/S
Fleur de Lys
26 | Auberge du Soleil/N
| Atelier Crenn

Excludes places with low votes, unless otherwise indicated; Top Food
excludes dessert-only spots

TOPS BY CUISINE

AMERICAN (NEW)

29 Gary Danko
28 French Laundry/N
27 Commis/E
   Terra/N
   Boulevard

AMERICAN (TRAD.)

26 Ad Hoc/N
   House of Prime Rib
24 Rutherford Grill/N
   Tarpy's Roadhouse/S
   Wayfare Tavern

BBQ (AMERICAN)

25 Buckeye Roadhouse/N
   Addendum/N
23 B-Side BBQ/E
   Wexler's
22 Bo's BBQ/E

BURGERS

24 900 Grayson/E
23 Pearl's Deluxe/E/N/SF
   Roam Artisan Burgers
   Super Duper/N/SF
   Mo's

CAJUN/CREOLE/SOUTHERN

26 Brown Sugar Kitchen/E
25 Brenda's
24 Broken Record
   Angeline's Louisiana Kitchen/E
   Picán/E

CALIFORNIAN

28 Erna's Elderberry/E
   Sierra Mar/S
27 Chez Panisse/E
   Chez Panisse Café/E
   Rivoli/E

CHINESE

26 Mingalaba/S
   Yank Sing
25 Z & Y
   Ton Kiang
24 R & G Lounge

DIM SUM

26 Yank Sing
25 Ton Kiang
24 Hong Kong Lounge
23 Koi Palace/E/S
   East Ocean Seafood/E

ECLECTIC

26 Della Fattoria/N
25 Celadon/N
   Willi's Wine Bar/N
   Va de Vi/E
24 Firefly

FRENCH

27 La Forêt/S
   Le Papillon/S
   La Folie
   Fleur de Lys
   Atelier Crenn

FRENCH BISTRO

27 Bistro des Copains/N
   Bistro Jeanty/N
   Chapeau!
26 Bouchon/N
25 K&L Bistro/N

INDIAN

27 Ajanta/E
26 All Spice/S
25 Chutney
24 Vik's Chaat Corner/E
   Saravana Bhavan/S

ITALIAN

28 Acquerello
27 La Ciccia
   Cucina Paradiso/N
   Seven Hills
26 Quince

JAPANESE

28 Kiss Seafood
27 Sushi Zone
   Zushi Puzzle
   Sushi Ran/N
   Keiko à Nob Hill

MED./GREEK

28 Cafe Gibraltar/S
   Evvia/S
   Kokkari Estiatorio
27 Chez Panisse/E
   Chez Panisse Café/E

MEXICAN

25 La Taqueria
   Loló
   Tamarindo Antojeria/E
   C Casa/N
   Don Pisto's

MIDDLE EASTERN

24 Saha
Dishdash/S
Kabul Afghan/S
23 Maykadeh
Helmand Palace

PERUVIAN

26 Piqueo's
25 La Costanera/S
Pasión
24 La Mar Cebicheria
Limón Rotisserie

PIZZA

26 Una Pizza Napoletana
Tony's Pizza
Pizzaiolo/E
Diavola/N
Pizzetta 211

SANDWICHES

26 Lucca Deli
4505 Meats
Fatted Calf/N/SF
Bakesale Betty/E
25 Saigon Sandwiches

SEAFOOD

27 Passionfish/S
26 Swan Oyster Depot
Hog Island Oyster/N/SF
Bar Crudo
Sotto Mare

SPANISH/BASQUE

26 Piperade
25 Contigo
Fringale
24 Zarzuela
ZuZu/N

STEAK

27 Cole's Chop/N
26 Press/N
Harris'
Alexander's/S/SF
House of Prime Rib

THAI

26 Sea Thai Bistro/N
25 Marnee Thai
24 Thep Phanom Thai
Basil
Lers Ros Thai

VEGETARIAN

26 Millennium
25 Greens
24 Gracias Madre
23 Udupi Palace/E/SF
22 Cha-Ya Vegetarian/E/SF

VIETNAMESE

26 Slanted Door
Thanh Long
25 Tamarine/S
Saigon Sandwiches
Crustacean

TOPS BY SPECIAL FEATURE

BREAKFAST

25 Brenda's
24 Bette's Oceanview/E
Willow Wood/N
Zazie
Venus/E

BRUNCH

27 La Forêt/S
Redd/N
26 Nopa
Zuni Café
25 Boulettes Larder

CHILD-FRIENDLY

25 Rosso Pizzeria/N
23 Super Duper/N/SF
22 Gott's Roadside/N/SF
Joe's Cable Car
21 Chow/Park Chow/E/SF

HOTEL DINING

28 Erna's Elderberry/E
(Château du Sureau)
Sierra Mar/S (Post Ranch Inn)
27 Madrona Manor/N
Meadowood Restaurant/N
(Meadowood Napa Valley)
Auberge du Soleil/N

OPEN LATE

26 Nopa
25 Ryoko's
Don Pisto's
Chutney
24 Broken Record

OUTDOOR SEATING

28 Sierra Mar/S
27 Madrona Manor/N
Cole's Chop/N

	Auberge du Soleil/N			Wolfdale's/E
26	Étoile/N	26		Slanted Door
		23		Waterbar

ROMANCE

28	Acquerello
27	Madrona Manor/N
	Fleur de Lys
26	Aziza
23	Gitane

WINNING WINE LISTS

29	Gary Danko
28	French Laundry/N
	Acquerello
27	Boulevard
26	Marinus/S

TRENDY

26	Nopa
24	Central Kitchen
	Hakkasan
	AQ
_	Trick Dog

WORTH A TRIP

28	Erna's Elderberry/E (Oakhurst)
	French Laundry/N (Yountville)
	Sierra Mar/S (Big Sur)
	Cafe Gibraltar/S (El Granada)
27	Chez Panisse/E (Berkeley)

VIEWS

28	Sierra Mar/S
27	Auberge du Soleil/N

TOPS BY OCCASION

Some best bets in a range of prices and cuisines for these occasions.

ANNIVERSARY DINNER

29	Gary Danko
27	Boulevard
	Manresa/S
	Meadowood Restaurant/N
	Fleur de Lys

	Starbelly
_	Fable

FIRST DATE

24	Locanda
	Betelnut
23	Comal/E
	Lolinda▽
_	Trick Dog

BRIDAL/BABY SHOWER

22	Garden Court
21	Rotunda
20	Lovejoy's Tea Room
_	Charles Chocolate
	Tout Sweet Patisserie

GRADUATION (BERKELEY)

27	Rivoli/E
	Ajanta/E
26	Riva Cucina/E
	Lalime's/E
23	Gather/E

BRUNCH WITH FRIENDS

25	Universal Cafe
24	Foreign Cinema
	Zazie
	Mission Beach Café
23	La Note/E

GRADUATION (STANFORD)

28	Evvia/S
24	Jin Sho/S
23	Tai Pan/S
	Fuki Sushi/S
22	St. Michael's Alley/S

BRUNCH WITH PARENTS

27	Redd/N
23	Absinthe
	Meritage/The Claremont/E
22	1300 on Fillmore
	Garden Court

HOLIDAY DINING

24	Navio/S
	Brasserie S&P▽
23	Murray Circle/N
21	Luce
20	Five/E

DINNER AFTER PRIDE

24	L'Ardoise
23	Canela Bistro & Bar▽
22	Destino

MEET FOR A DRINK

24 A16/E/SF
22 RN74
   15 Romolo
   César/E
‾| Trick Dog

SYMPHONY/ OPERA DINING

26 Jardinière
   Zuni Café
25 Rich Table
23 Absinthe
   Hayes Street Grill

TOPS BY DESTINATION

A selection of the best bets in a range of prices and cuisines near these points of interest.

AT&T PARK

22 American Grilled Cheese
   Twenty Five Lusk
21 Town's End Restaurant
20 Mijita
19 MoMo's

DOLORES PARK

27 Bi-Rite Creamery
   Tartine Bakery
26 Delfina
24 Izakaya Yuzuki
   Namu Gaji∇

FERRY BUILDING

26 Hog Island Oyster Co.
   Slanted Door
25 Boulettes Larder/Bouli Bar
23 Il Cane Rosso
22 Gott's Roadside

FISHERMAN'S WHARF

29 Gary Danko
23 Crab House
22 Bistro Boudin
21 McCormick & Kuleto's
   Alioto's

GOLDEN GATE PARK EAST & PANHANDLE

26 Nopa
   Koo
24 Ebisu
22 Magnolia Gastropub
   Pacific Catch

GOLDEN GATE PARK WEST

21 Sutro's at the Cliff House
20 Cliff House Bistro

   Java Beach Cafe
16 Park Chalet
   Beach Chalet

MOSCONE CENTER

26 Ame
24 Roy's
23 Super Duper
   Mo's
   Sanraku Metreon

SAUSALITO

27 Sushi Ran/N
25 Poggio/N
24 Fish/N
   Copita∇/N
23 Avatar's/N

UNION SQUARE

26 Campton Place
25 Farallon
23 Bourbon Steak
   Scala's Bistro
   Kuleto's

WINE COUNTRY (NAPA)

28 French Laundry/N
27 Terra/N
   Cole's Chop/N
   Meadowood Restaurant/N
   Auberge du Soleil/N

WINE COUNTRY (SONOMA)

27 Madrona Manor/N
   Cucina Paradiso/N
   Farmhouse Inn/N
   Bistro des Copains/N
26 Cafe La Haye/N

Best Buys Overall

Top-rated food $25 and under

1 Tartine Bakery | *Bakery*
2 Lucca Deli | *Deli/Sandwiches*
3 Mingalaba/S | *Burmese/Chinese*
4 4505 Meats | *Hot Dogs*
5 Downtown Bakery/N | *Bakery*
6 Pizzetta 211* | *Pizza*
7 Fatted Calf/N/SF | *Sandwiches*
8 Plow | *Californian*
9 Della Fattoria/N | *Bakery/Eclectic*
10 Bakesale Betty/E | *Bakery*
11 Cheese Board Pizzeria/E | *Pizza*
12 Brown Sugar/E | *Soul/Southern*
13 Refuge/S | *Belgian/Sandwiches*
14 Saigon | *Sandwiches/Viet.*
15 La Taqueria | *Mexican*
16 Gioia Pizzeria/E/SF | *Pizza*
17 Zachary's/E | *Pizza*
18 Arizmendi/E/N/SF | *Bakery/Pizza*
19 Brenda's | *Creole/Southern*
20 Addis Ethiopian/E | *Ethiopian*
21 Z & Y | *Chinese*

22 Blue Barn Gourmet/N/SF | *Cal.*
23 Ramen Dojo/S | *Japanese/Noodle Shop*
24 Craftsman & Wolves | *Bakery/Sandwiches*
25 Marnee Thai | *Thai*
26 Underdog | *Hot Dogs*
27 C Casa/N | *Mexican*
28 Boccalone | *Sandwiches*
29 Delica | *Japanese*
30 Addendum/N | *American*
31 Ike's/E/N/S/SF | *Sandwiches*
32 Little Star Pizza/E/SF | *Pizza*
33 Chutney | *Indian/Pakistani*
34 Orenchi Ramen/S | *Japanese*
35 900 Grayson/E | *Burgers/Cal.*
36 Broken Record | *Soul Food*
37 Grégoire*/E | *French*
38 Vung Tau/E/S | *Vietnamese*
39 Gracias Madre | *Mex./Vegan*
40 Bette's Oceanview/E | *Diner*

BEST BUYS BY CATEGORY

BAKERIES

27 Tartine Bakery
26 Downtown Bakery/N
   Bakesale Betty/E
25 Arizmendi/E/N/SF
   Craftsman & Wolves

BURGERS/HOT DOGS

26 4505 Meats
25 Underdog
24 900 Grayson/E
23 Pearl's Deluxe/E/N/SF
   Roam Artisan Burgers

BYO

25 Gioia Pizzeria/E
   Chutney
24 Grégoire/E
23 Cafe Citti/N
   Pakwan/E/SF

CHEAP DATES

25 Marnee Thai
24 Broken Record
   Tacolicious/S/SF
23 Angkor Borei
   Hawker Fare/E

DELI

26 Lucca Deli
23 Wise Sons Jewish Deli
21 Jimtown Store/N
20 Miller's East Coast Deli/N/SF
   Saul's Restaurant & Deli/E

DESSERT

27 Bi-Rite Creamery
26 Della Fattoria/N
25 Dynamo Donut
22 Emporio Rulli/N/S/SF
   Chile Pies

Best Buys excludes dessert-only spots

DINERS

24 Bette's Oceanview/E
   Fremont Diner/N
23 HRD
22 Gott's Roadside/N/SF
20 Sears Fine Food

HOLE-IN-THE-WALL

25 Chutney
23 A La Turca
   Shalimar/E/S/SF
22 House of Nanking
   Yamo

NOODLE SHOPS

25 Ramen Dojo/S
   Orenchi Ramen/S
22 Katana-Ya
21 King of Thai/E/SF
19 Hotei

SLEEPERS

27 La Taquiza/N
   Emilia's Pizzeria/E
26 Papito
   Truly Mediterranean
25 Sandbox Bakery

TAQUERIAS

25 C Casa/N
24 La Victoria Taqueria/E/S
   Tacolicious/S/SF
23 Taqueria San Jose/S/SF
   El Farolito/E/N/S/SF

TOP CHEF BARGAINS

25 Boccalone Salumeria
   Addendum/N
23 Hawker Fare/E
20 Mijita
 ⌐ Tout Sweet Patisserie

Visit zagat.com   15

CITY OF SAN FRANCISCO

Top Food

29 Gary Danko | *American*	Ichi Sushi | *Japanese*
28 Acquerello | *Italian*	Cafe Jacqueline | *French*
Kiss Seafood | *Japanese*	Michael Mina | *American*
Kokkari Estiatorio | *Greek*	Coi | *Californian/French*
27 La Ciccia | *Italian*	Chapeau! | *French*
Sushi Zone | *Japanese*	Sebo | *Japanese*
Boulevard | *American*	26 Piperade | *Spanish*
La Folie | *French*	Lucca Deli | *Deli/Sandwiches*
Saison | *American*	Harris' | *Steak*
Seven Hills | *Italian*	State Bird Provisions | *Amer.*
Tartine Bakery | *Bakery*	Quince | *French/Italian*
Benu | *American*	Una Pizza Napoletana | *Pizza*
Local Mission Eatery | *Cal.*	Tony's Pizza | *Italian/Pizza*
Zushi Puzzle* | *Japanese*	Kabuto | *Japanese*
Fleur de Lys | *Cal./Fr.*	Swan Oyster Depot | *Seafood*
Atelier Crenn | *French*	Delfina | *Italian*
Keiko à Nob Hill | *Fr./Japanese*	Aziza | *Moroccan*
House | *Asian*	Jardinière | *Californian/French*
Frances | *Californian*	Nopa | *Californian*
Range | *American*	Alexander's | *Japanese/Steak*

Top Decor

28 Garden Court	Quince
27 Kokkari Estiatorio	Sutro's at the Cliff House
Gary Danko	Bix
Twenty Five Lusk	Boulevard
Farallon	Hakkasan
Jardinière	Acquerello
Spruce	Coi
Waterbar	AQ
26 Fleur de Lys	25 Grand Cafe
Big Four	Cliff House Bistro

Top Service

29 Gary Danko	Quince
28 Acquerello	Michael Mina
Benu	Harris'
27 Coi	Alexander's
La Folie	25 Campton Place
Kokkari Estiatorio	La Ciccia
Fleur de Lys	Spruce
26 Atelier Crenn	Frances
Saison	Keiko à Nob Hill
Boulevard	Big Four

* Indicates a tie with restaurant above; excludes places with low votes,
unless otherwise indicated; Top Food excludes dessert-only spots

TOPS BY CUISINE

AMERICAN (NEW)

29 Gary Danko
27 Boulevard
Saison
Benu
Range

AMERICAN (TRAD.)

26 House of Prime Rib
24 Wayfare Tavern
Bix
Mama's on Washington
Chloe's Cafe

BAKERIES

27 Bi-Rite Creamery
Tartine Bakery
25 Arizmendi
Dynamo Donut
Craftsman & Wolves

BURGERS

23 Pearl's Deluxe
Roam Artisan Burgers
Super Duper
Mo's
In-N-Out

CALIFORNIAN

27 Local Mission Eatery
Frances
Coi
26 Jardinière
Nopa

CHINESE

26 Yank Sing
25 Z & Y
Ton Kiang
24 R & G Lounge
Hakkasan

FRENCH

27 La Folie
Fleur de Lys
Atelier Crenn
Keiko à Nob Hill
Cafe Jacqueline

FRENCH BISTRO

27 Chapeau!
25 Le P'tit Laurent
Bistro Central Parc
Fringale
24 L'Ardoise

INDIAN/PAKISTANI

25 Chutney
24 Amber India
23 Udupi Palace
Dosa
Roti Indian Bistro

ITALIAN

28 Acquerello
27 La Ciccia
Seven Hills
26 Quince
Delfina

JAPANESE

28 Kiss Seafood
27 Sushi Zone
Zushi Puzzle
Keiko à Nob Hill
Ichi Sushi

MED./GREEK

28 Kokkari Estiatorio
26 Campton Place
Zuni Café
25 Heirloom Café
Frascati

MEXICAN

25 La Taqueria
Loló
Don Pisto's
24 Gracias Madre
Mamacita

MIDDLE EASTERN

24 Saha
23 Maykadeh
Helmand Palace
À La Turca
22 La Méditerranée

PERUVIAN

26 Piqueo's
25 Pasión
24 La Mar Cebicheria
Limón Rotisserie
Mochica

PIZZA

26 Una Pizza Napoletana
Tony's Pizza
Pizzetta 211
Flour + Water
25 Ragazza

SEAFOOD

26	Swan Oyster Depot
	Hog Island Oyster Co.
	Bar Crudo
	Sotto Mare
25	Pesce

SPANISH/BASQUE

26	Piperade
25	Contigo
	Fringale
24	Zarzuela
23	Gitane

STEAK

26	Harris'
	Alexander's
	House of Prime Rib
24	Ruth's Chris
	Lark Creek Steak

VIETNAMESE

26	Slanted Door
	Thanh Long
25	Saigon Sandwiches
	Crustacean
24	Bodega Bistro

TOPS BY SPECIAL FEATURE

BREAKFAST

25	Brenda's
24	Zazie
	Mama's on Washington
23	Chloe's Cafe
22	Rose's Cafe

BRUNCH

26	Nopa
	Yank Sing
	Zuni Café
25	Boulettes Larder
	Universal Cafe

CHILD-FRIENDLY

23	Super Duper
22	Gott's Roadside
	Pacific Catch
	Joe's Cable Car
21	Chow/Park Chow

GOOD FOR GROUPS

28	Kokkari
26	Perbacco
24	Foreign Cinema
	Park Tavern
23	Lolinda∇

OUTDOOR SEATING

26	Hog Island Oyster Co.
24	Foreign Cinema
	La Mar Cebicheria
	Sociale
23	Lolinda∇

PEOPLE-WATCHING

27	Boulevard
26	Jardinière

	Nopa
24	Hakkasan
22	RN74

POWER SCENES

29	Gary Danko
28	Kokkari Estiatorio
27	Boulevard
	Michael Mina
24	Hakkasan

ROMANCE

28	Acquerello
27	Fleur de Lys
	Cafe Jacqueline
26	Aziza
23	Gitane

TRENDY

26	Nopa
24	Central Kitchen
	Hakkasan
	AQ
⎯	Trick Dog

VIEWS

26	Slanted Door
25	Greens
23	Waterbar
22	Epic Roasthouse
21	Sutro's at Cliff House

WINNING WINE LISTS

29	Gary Danko
28	Acquerello
27	Boulevard
24	A16
22	RN74

TOPS BY LOCATION

CASTRO/NOE VALLEY
27 La Ciccia
Sushi Zone
Frances
25 Contigo
Eiji

CHINATOWN
25 Z & Y
24 R & G Lounge
23 Oriental Pearl
Great Eastern
22 House of Nanking

COW HOLLOW/MARINA
27 Zushi Puzzle
Atelier Crenn
26 Lucca Deli
25 Umami
Capannina

DOWNTOWN
28 Kokkari Estiatorio
27 Fleur de Lys
Michael Mina
26 Piperade
Quince

EMBARCADERO
27 Boulevard
26 4505 Meats
Hog Island Oyster Co.
Slanted Door
25 Boulettes Larder/Bouli Bar

FISHERMAN'S WHARF
29 Gary Danko
24 Scoma's
23 Crab House
In-N-Out
22 Bistro Boudin

HAIGHT-ASHBURY/ COLE VALLEY
24 Zazie
23 Alembic
22 Magnolia Gastropub
Cha Cha Cha
21 La Boulange

HAYES VALLEY/ CIVIC CENTER
27 Sebo
26 Jardinière
Zuni Café
25 Brenda's
Rich Table

LOWER HAIGHT
24 Thep Phanom Thai
23 Indian Oven
22 Rosamunde Sausage Grill
Uva Enoteca
21 Little Chihuahua

MISSION
27 Tartine Bakery
Local Mission Eatery
Range
26 Delfina
4505 Meats

NOB HILL/RUSSIAN HILL
27 La Folie
Seven Hills
Keiko à Nob Hill
26 Sons & Daughters
25 Gioia Pizzeria

NORTH BEACH
27 House
Cafe Jacqueline
Coi
26 Tony's Pizza
Sotto Mare

PACIFIC HEIGHTS/ JAPANTOWN
28 Kiss Seafood
25 Pizzeria Delfina
SPQR
24 Tataki Sushi & Sake Bar
23 Roam Artisan Burgers

RICHMOND
27 Chapeau!
26 Kabuto
Aziza
Pizzetta 211
25 Burma Superstar

SOMA
27 Saison
Benu
26 Una Pizza Napoletana
Alexander's
Yank Sing

SUNSET
26 Thanh Long
Koo
25 Pasión
Arizmendi
Outerlands

Best Buys

Top-rated food $25 and under

1 Tartine Bakery | *Bakery*
2 Lucca Deli | *Deli/Sandwiches*
3 4505 Meats | *Hot Dogs*
4 Pizzetta 211 | *Pizza*
5 Fatted Calf | *Sandwiches*
6 Plow | *Californian*
7 Saigon | *Sandwiches/Viet.*
8 La Taqueria | *Mexican*
9 Gioia Pizzeria | *Cal./Pizza*
10 Arizmendi | *Bakery/Pizza*
11 Brenda's | *Creole/Southern*
12 Z & Y | *Chinese*
13 Blue Barn Gourmet | *Cal.*
14 Craftsman & Wolves | *Bakery/Sandwiches*
15 Marnee Thai | *Thai*
16 Underdog | *Hot Dogs*
17 Boccalone | *Sandwiches*
18 Delica | *Japanese*
19 Ike's Place | *Sandwiches*
20 Little Star Pizza | *Pizza*

BEST BUYS BY NEIGHBORHOOD

CASTRO
25 Ike's Place
23 Super Duper
22 Chile Pies
   Thai House Express
   La Méditerranée

DOWNTOWN
23 Super Duper
   Taqueria Can Cun
22 Henry's Hunan
   Emporio Rulli
   Katana-Ya

EMBARCADERO
26 4505 Meats
   Fatted Calf
25 Boccalone Salumeria
   Delica
23 Wise Sons Deli

MISSION
27 Tartine Bakery
26 4505 Meats
25 La Taqueria
   Arizmendi
   Craftsman & Wolves

NORTH BEACH
24 Tony's Coal-Fired Pizza
   Tacolicious
   Golden Boy
   Mama's on Washington
23 Taqueria San Jose

SOMA
24 Blue Bottle
23 HRD
   Pearl's Deluxe
   Super Duper
   Mo's

Best Buys excludes dessert-only spots

Visit zagat.com

City of San Francisco

| | FOOD | DECOR | SERVICE | COST |

Abbot's Cellar *American* ▽ 20 | 23 | 22 | $49

Mission | 742 Valencia St. (bet. 18th & 19th Sts.) | 415-626-8700 |
www.abbotscellar.com

It's the "closest to a British gastropub" you'll find in the Mission say
fans of this "trendy" Valencia Street New American from the Monk's
Kettle crew, where a "wide selection of unique beers" on tap and in
some 100 bottled varieties are offered in a stylishly rustic room decked
out in exposed brick and reclaimed woods; the seasonal menu is suds-
centric, and delivered with "helpful" service; P.S. the beer bottle–shaped
bathroom sink is a "nice touch."

Absinthe ●Ⓜ *French/Mediterranean* 23 | 23 | 22 | $49

Hayes Valley | 398 Hayes St. (Gough St.) | 415-551-1590 |
www.absinthe.com

A "touch of Paris" comes via this Hayes Valley brasserie that remains
a "favorite" with both "the symphony and opera" crowd and "hip young
diners", delivering "consistently strong" French-Med fare with service
that's "on point"; a "lively" bar area mixing "artisanal cocktails" appeals
to "high-energy" types, while others find "the low-lit atmosphere" in
the dining room "perfect for a romantic dinner."

Ace Wasabi's Rock-N-Roll Sushi *Japanese* 20 | 16 | 19 | $32

Marina | 3339 Steiner St. (bet. Chestnut & Lombard Sts.) | 415-567-4903 |
www.acewasabisf.com

"Always buzzing with groups" who are undoubtedly "enjoying
themselves", this "scene" is "still a trendy hangout" for the "young
Marina" crowd; it's "not the most authentic Japanese restaurant"
in town, and the noise-sensitive shout "bring earplugs", but "patient"
servers and "above-average" "midpriced sushi" seal its status as
a "party spot."

Acquerello ⓍⓂ *Italian* 28 | 26 | 28 | $107

Polk Gulch | 1722 Sacramento St. (bet. Polk St. & Van Ness Ave.) |
415-567-5432 | www.acquerello.com

For "sumptuous dining" "with all the perks", this "romantic", "extraordinarily refined" Polk Gulch classic is in "a league of its own", proffering "superb", "imaginative" Italian tasting menus complemented by
an "amazing" 100-page wine list and "impeccable" "formal service"
that leaves the "moneyed crowd" feeling "pampered"; an "elegantly
peaceful" former chapel setting and touches such as "footstools for
purses" further make it "worth every penny" when "you really want
to impress someone."

AK Subs Ⓧ *Sandwiches* 22 | 11 | 20 | $11

SoMa | 397 Eighth St. (Harrison St.) | 415-241-9600 |
www.aksubs.net

Subs piled high with "bundles of meat" and "fresh veggies" are suitable "for sharing" at this SoMa "super-friendly", affordable "simple"
"sandwich shop" fans deem "perfect for what it is"; you'll "get in and
get out" "quickly", even "during the big lunch rush from the nearby
tech startups", and breakfast is also served; P.S. open weekdays
only till 4 PM.

Alamo Square Seafood Grill *French/Seafood*
22 | 19 | 21 | $32

Western Addition | 803 Fillmore St. (Grove St.) | 415-440-2828 |
www.alamosquareseafoodgrill.com

French fare, including "fresh" fish cooked just "the way you like" and
served "with the sauce of your choice" by a "welcoming staff", keeps
this Western Addition bistro "crowded"; the daily "early-bird prix fixe"
delivers lots of "bang for the buck", compensating for "cozy" confines.

A La Turca *Turkish*
23 | 13 | 20 | $20

Tenderloin | 869 Geary St. (Larkin St.) | 415-345-1011 | www.alaturcasf.com

"Real-deal" Istanbul eats are on the "fantastic" menu at this "unassuming" spot that's "a little Turkey in the Tenderloin"; true, it's "not glamorous", but the "top-notch" fare, from "freshly made falafel" to "juicy
kebabs" and "amazing" baklava, comes in "generous" portions at "affordable" prices, and the "friendly" servers keep up a "brisk" pace.

Albona Ristorante Istriano *Italian*
24 | 18 | 25 | $46

North Beach | 545 Francisco St. (bet. Mason & Taylor Sts.) | 415-441-1040 |
www.albonarestaurant.com

"Distinctive", "delicious Istrian dishes" (i.e. a "palate-pleasing" blend of
Italian, Croatian and Slovenian cuisines) make this "unpretentious gem"
"very different from most North Beach spots" say supporters, who call
the "off-the-beaten-track" location "easy to miss but hard to forget";
"get ready to bump elbows" in the "small space", but "gracious" servers
who "make you feel like family" ensure a "totally lovely experience."

Alegrias, Food From Spain *Spanish*
22 | 18 | 22 | $35

Marina | 2018 Lombard St. (bet. Fillmore & Webster Sts.) | 415-929-8888 |
www.alegriassf.com

Recalling "a Madrid neighborhood hot spot", this "energetic" Spanish
"tapas tavern" in the Marina offers "authentic" decor and "reasonably
priced" small plates that "pack a lot of variety in a single meal"; it's
"like visiting a private home in Spain", with its "kind" and "genuine"
service adding to an experience that "will make you smile for sure."

The Alembic ❿ *Eclectic*
23 | 20 | 19 | $34

Haight-Ashbury | 1725 Haight St. (bet. Cole & Shrader Sts.) |
415-666-0822 | www.alembicbar.com

"Forgotten classic cocktails" pair with "inventive and new" "killer bar
bites" and "unusual" mains at this Eclectic "boutique" gastropub that
brings "a little uptown" to the "Upper Haight"; while the "small" drinks
may not be "priced accordingly", and the "witty" bartenders may cop
a "too-cool attitude", the "sexy, dimly lit" haute-saloon setting is "perfect for a first or 100th date."

Alexander's Steakhouse *Japanese/Steak*
26 | 25 | 26 | $92

SoMa | 448 Brannan St. (bet. 3rd & 4th Sts.) | 415-495-1111 |
www.alexanderssteakhouse.com

See review in South of San Francisco Directory.

Alfred's Steakhouse 🚫Ⓜ *Steak*
23 | 21 | 23 | $60

Downtown | 659 Merchant St. (bet. Kearny & Montgomery Sts.) |
415-781-7058 | www.alfredssteakhouse.com

"Deep leather booths", "bordello-red" decor and a "well-trained"
staff that's "been there forever" take you "back to the '50s" at this

"retro fabulous" Downtown steakhouse where the beef is "prepared precisely as requested" and "huge" martinis inspire "gin-induced good-old-boys camaraderie"; the "mandatory" "service surcharge" irks some meat mavens, but most maintain it's still a "much better deal than most."

Alice's *Chinese*

20 | 17 | 19 | $22

Noe Valley | 1599 Sanchez St. (29th St.) | 415-282-8999 | www.alicesrestaurantsf.com

For a "refreshingly fresh take on Chinese" chow – "healthy-tasting" fare full of "crisp" veggies – Noe Valley residents rely on this "really popular" neighborhood spot; the "pleasant" staff provides "quick service" in the "smallish dining room", and since the "fab" food is "priced right", it's a "longtime favorite" for takeout too.

Alioto's *Italian*

21 | 19 | 20 | $44

Fisherman's Wharf | 8 Fisherman's Wharf (The Embarcadero) | 415-673-0183 | www.aliotos.com

It may be "smack-dab in the middle of touristville" (aka Fisherman's Wharf), but this "nostalgic" "landmark" still seduces locals, who "get crackin'" with crab and other "dependable" Sicilian-inflected seafood; though some call it "a bit overpriced", most maintain it's "kept its mojo" thanks to "polite", "old-fashioned" servers and "fantastic views" of the "fishing boats and the Golden Gate Bridge."

Amber Dhara *Indian*

24 | 21 | 21 | $36

Mission | 680 Valencia St. (18th St.) | 415-400-5699

Amber India *Indian*

SoMa | 25 Yerba Buena Ln. (Market St.) | 415-777-0500 www.amber-india.com

See review in South of San Francisco Directory.

Ame *American*

26 | 24 | 25 | $77

SoMa | St. Regis | 689 Mission St. (3rd St.) | 415-284-4040 | www.amerestaurant.com

"Culinary enthusiasts" contend it's "worth dressing up" for a "special-occasion" meal at this "high-end" SoMa "destination" in the St. Regis where Terra owners Hiro Sone and Lissa Doumani proffer "gorgeously styled", "seriously delicious" (and "very expensive") New American cuisine infused with "Asian flavors" that's "graciously" served with an "over-the-top sake menu" and "exemplary wine list"; a "quiet", "minimalist" "Zen" setting that "feels like stepping into a meditation room" adds to the appeal of a "memorable evening."

American Grilled
Cheese Kitchen *American/Sandwiches*

22 | 16 | 19 | $14

NEW Mission | 2400 Harrison St. (20th St.) | 415-243-0107
SoMa | 1 S. Park Ave. (2nd St.) | 415-243-0107
www.theamericansf.com

Fromage fans "say cheese" at the thought of "refreshingly grown-up" "ooey-gooey grilled sandwiches" paired with "perfect" "smoky" tomato soup at these eateries that don't "break the bank"; there's "limited seating" indoors and out at the SoMa branch, which serves breakfast and lunch only, but stays open till the first pitch of SF Giants home night games, while the Mission outpost has extended hours.

Americano *Italian*

`20` `23` `19` `$43`

Embarcadero | Hotel Vitale | 8 Mission St. (Steuart St.) | 415-278-3777 | www.americanorestaurant.com

"Right on" the Embarcadero, with a "spectacular view" of the Bay Bridge, this "upscale" farm-to-table Italian inside the Hotel Vitale earns kudos for "creative" and "consistent" if "somewhat pricey" plates and servers who display "exactly the right amount of charm"; still, most surveyors stick to the "vibrant happy-hour scene", when "well-dressed" "law, financial and consulting types" mingle on the "lovely" "heated patio."

Amici's East Coast Pizzeria *Pizza*

`21` `16` `19` `$22`

AT&T Park | 216 King St. (bet. 3rd & 4th Sts.) | 415-546-6666
Marina | 2200 Lombard St. (Steiner St.) | 415-885-4500
www.amicis.com

For "East Coast pizza", this "no-frills" Bay Area chain is "as good as it gets" say fans of the "big" NY-style pies and their "crispy", "charred thin crusts" (available in reduced-carb and gluten-free versions too); there's also a "variety of delicious options for those not in the pizza mood", so while some find it a "bit expensive" given "what you get", most dig the "friendly" staffers and "comfortable", "family-friendly" atmosphere.

Anchor & Hope *Seafood*

`21` `21` `21` `$43`

SoMa | 83 Minna St. (bet. 1st & 2nd Sts.) | 415-501-9100 | www.anchorandhopesf.com

"Urban sophistication meets crab shack" at this "cavernous" "nautically themed" seafooder "tucked away" in a "converted garage space" in SoMa; "life-changing" lobster rolls and "really fresh" fish are matched by the "fantastic beer list" and "fun" "young" servers, but the "lively" ambiance is a bit much for some, who shout "the noise level is off the charts."

Anchor Oyster Bar *Seafood*

`25` `17` `22` `$37`

Castro | 579 Castro St. (bet. 18th & 19th Sts.) | 415-431-3990 | www.anchoroysterbar.com

"Why go to Fisherman's Wharf" ask fans of this "cute" vintage "oyster bar" with a "nautical motif" in the Castro that's a "pearl-in-the-ocean" for Boston clam "chowda" and "simple" seafood "so fresh you'll swear it was made by the Little Mermaid"; it's "fairly pricey" and "seating is tight", but the "super-friendly" staff and "limited" list of "local white wines" ensure the "hungry hordes" leave "happy as clams."

Andalu *Eclectic*

`21` `20` `19` `$35`

Mission | 3198 16th St. (Guerrero St.) | 415-621-2211 | www.andalusf.com
Even "Brussels sprouts taste unbelievable" at this "Mission hipster" where "tasty" Eclectic small plates come "at a fair price"; the "bright" "corner location" is "great for groups", and though it's "noisy" "like a train station" with "slow" service when "packed", it remains a "lively" "favorite" for "sharing tapas" while sipping "seriously delicious" sangria (and $5 margaritas on Taco Tuesdays).

Angkor Borei *Cambodian*

`23` `16` `21` `$24`

Bernal Heights | 3471 Mission St. (bet. Cortland Ave. & Kingston St.) | 415-550-8417 | www.cambodiankitchen.com

"Authentic Khmer cuisine" – from "exquisite vegetarian" dishes to "shrimply divine" seafood – is "beautifully prepared" at this "affordable" Cambodian that's "a real find" in Bernal Heights; it's "not much to look at" say some, but "endearing" servers and a "quiet atmosphere" add up to a "relaxed" experience.

Anzu *Japanese*   23 | 22 | 23 | $55

Downtown | Hotel Nikko | 222 Mason St. (O'Farrell St.) | 415-394-1100 | www.restaurantanzu.com

"Picture-worthy plates" including sushi and "nicely seared" steaks share the menu at this "elegant" Californian-inspired Japanese "hidden" "on the second floor" of Downtown's Hotel Nikko; it's "lovely" for a "well-prepared" if "pricey" dinner and "meticulously crafted cocktails" "prior to a show" at Feinstein's downstairs, and though some find the "hotel setting" "a bit impersonal", the "polite" service is "lovely."

Aperto *Italian*   22 | 17 | 22 | $36

Potrero Hill | 1434 18th St. (Connecticut St.) | 415-252-1625 | www.apertosf.com

"Housemade pastas" and "specials that change with the seasons" attract Italian enthusiasts to this "lovely" trattoria in Potrero Hill; a "homey" space that can get "a little cramped" is compensated by "always-pleasant servers", and since you can enjoy a "well-prepared meal without taking out a loan", locals just "wish every neighborhood could have a place like this."

AQ Restaurant & Bar Ⓜ *Californian*   24 | 26 | 22 | $58

SoMa | 1085 Mission St. (7th St.) | 415-341-9000 | www.aq-sf.com

"Creative to the max" is how fans describe this "stylish", upscale SoMa Californian "place of the moment" with both a "seasonal menu and seasonal decor", where chef-owner Mark Liberman is "like a biochemist at work" crafting "precisely prepared", "cutting-edge" dishes (think "deconstructed clam chowder"); "superb wine pairings" and a setting with "beautiful high ceilings" and "original brick walls" complete the "lively" scene.

🆕 Aquitaine *French*   - | - | - | M

Downtown | 175 Sutter St. (Kearny St.) | 415-402-5290 | www.aquitainesf.com

Owned by Laurent Manrique (ex Aqua, Fifth Floor), this Downtown boîte pays homage to his native Southern France, offering *grignoter* (bar snacks) and heartier midpriced Gascony-inspired small plates, along with a one-page carte des vins showcasing Southwestern and Basque bottlings; a bright-yellow Van Gogh-esque sunflower design on the awning beckons tipplers to the petite digs outfitted with red bistro chairs and a map of the namesake Aquitaine region on the wall.

Ariake Japanese Ⓩ *Japanese*   25 | 17 | 22 | $35

Outer Richmond | 5041 Geary Blvd. (bet. 14th & 15th Aves.) | 415-221-6210 | www.sfariake.com

"Generous cuts" of "brilliantly fresh" sushi plus a "variety" of "gorgeous" "specialty rolls" and cooked dishes seduce surveyors at this "cozy" (and often "packed") Outer Richmond Japanese where regulars "forget the menu" and allow "charming" chef-owner Jin Kim to choose for them; however, you really "can't go wrong with whatever you order", and best of all, prices "won't break the bank."

Arinell Pizza ⊄ *Pizza* | 23 | 8 | 15 | $8 |

Mission | 509 Valencia St. (16th St.) | 415-255-1303
Some of the "best NYC pizza" beckons "East Coast transplants" to these "gritty hole-in-the-wall" Mission and Berkeley walk-up siblings turning out "thin, greasy" "perfection" in an "authentic" "slice you can fold"; "loud punk music and a surly staff" complete the kit, which is a "great value" when a "craving" strikes.

Arizmendi *Bakery/Pizza* | 25 | 13 | 20 | $11 |

Inner Sunset | 1331 Ninth Ave. (bet. Irving & Judah Sts.) | 415-566-3117 | www.arizmendibakery.org Ⓜ⊄
Mission | 1268 Valencia St. (24th St.) | 415-826-9218 | www.valencia.arizmendi.coop
"Baked goods made with love" draw carbo-loaders to this "worker-owned co-op" with multiple Bay Area locations, where "made-from-scratch" items include arguably "the best scones in town" and "long lines" form for the "always awesome" daily vegetarian pizza with its "exquisite thin crust and interesting ingredients"; there may be "no decor to speak of" and "limited" seating, but the "food beyond compare" has fans shrugging "who cares?"

Arlequin Cafe *Mediterranean* | 20 | 18 | 17 | $19 |

Hayes Valley | 384 Hayes St. (Gough St.) | 415-626-1211 | www.arlequincafe.com
"Hidden away" in "bustling" Hayes Valley, the "delightful" patio is a "tranquil sanctuary" at this "casual" Med cafe next to "sister restaurant" Absinthe; "reasonably priced" "sandwiches, salads" and pastas are "prepared with love" by a "quick and courteous" staff, and the attached wine shop is an "added perk" when you want "excellent" vino.

A16 *Italian* | 24 | 21 | 22 | $47 |

Marina | 2355 Chestnut St. (bet. Divisadero & Scott Sts.) | 415-771-2216 | www.a16sf.com
Named after an Italian highway, this "always bustling" Marina "favorite" (with a new Rockridge outpost) attracts "young, upscale" patrons with "hearty" Southern Italian fare including "crisp", thin-crust pizzas from a wood-burning oven, "interesting" pastas, "amazing" meatballs and a "fabulous" Boot-focused wine list – all served "with a smile" by a "hip" staff; though it's often "noisy and crowded", advocates say a seat by the open kitchen is a "foodie experience"; P.S. lunch is served Wednesday–Friday.

Atelier Crenn ⓈⓂ *French* | 27 | 24 | 26 | $143 |

Marina | 3127 Fillmore St. (bet. Greenwich & Moulton Sts.) | 415-440-0460 | www.ateliercrenn.com
"The prettiest food" you may ever eat also "tastes amazing" say those "blown away" by this Marina culinary atelier, where "works of art" blending French cuisine and "molecular gastronomy" are "elegantly presented" on "unusual plates"; "personalized" service in the upscale-minimalist space can include a tableside visit from chef Dominique Crenn herself, and despite "expensive" tabs for "spartan" tasting menu portions, it's deemed a "brilliant dining experience."

	FOOD	DECOR	SERVICE	COST

Auntie April's *Soul Food*
▽ 24 | 15 | 20 | $14

Bayview | 4618 Third St. (Oakdale Ave.) | 415-643-4983 | www.auntieaprils.com

Expect to see "super-friendly" "local girl" "Auntie April herself" cooking the "authentic down-home soul food" at this "charming" "treasure" in Bayview; it's "decidedly downscale" and the commercial district neighborhood's somewhat "sketchy", but "huge portions" of "crisp" fried chicken and waffles that are "cooked just right" cause regulars to "rave" about this "solid budget choice."

Aziza *Moroccan*
26 | 22 | 24 | $59

Outer Richmond | 5800 Geary Blvd. (22nd Ave.) | 415-752-2222 | www.aziza-sf.com

Chef Mourad Lahlou offers a fresh Californian "spin" on Morrocan cuisine at this upscale Outer Richmonder where "inventive", "well-spiced" entrees are "a party for the palate", and even a "simple lentil soup soars" into "gourmet" territory; fans say "don't be fooled" by its "sleepy" location and point to "lovingly crafted" cocktails, "inviting" service and an "intimate" space, adding they'd "go back at the drop of a hat" – or for a "date"; P.S. closed Tuesday.

Baby Blues BBQ *BBQ*
21 | 16 | 19 | $25

Mission | 3149 Mission St. (Precita Ave.) | 415-896-4250 | www.babybluessf.com

"So many delicious choices" are offered at this Mission BBQ "gem" doling out "large portions" of "out-of-this-world", "Memphis-style" brisket, "juicy" ribs and "wonderful" sides ("don't miss the corn-bread") accompanied by "sweet, tangy, spicy" sauces; a "funky, fun atmosphere" and "shared tables" make one forget that "parking is a real pain"; though critics claim the relatively "expensive", "mediocre" 'cue "doesn't compare to Kansas City", the majority sighs "my God, it is delicious."

Bacco Ristorante *Italian*
23 | 20 | 23 | $42

Noe Valley | 737 Diamond St. (bet. Elizabeth & 24th Sts.) | 415-282-4969 | www.baccosf.com

"It's always delightful" at this "charming", "quiet" neighborhood trattoria set "in a lovely old building" – "a taste and feel of Italy right here" in "out-of-the-way" Noe Valley; "you can't go wrong" with anything on the "pretty darn authentic" menu, but they're "known for" "exceptional" housemade pasta, "daily risotto" and "regional Italian wines", graciously proffered by a "superb staff" that treats guests "like extended family."

Baker & Banker Ⓜ *American*
25 | 22 | 24 | $60

Upper Fillmore | 1701 Octavia St. (Bush St.) | 415-351-2500 | www.bakerandbanker.com

"Excellent breads" and "diet-busting" desserts "made on-site" (and sold at the adjacent "bakery/sandwich shop") begin and end "an amazing meal" at this "laid-back" neighborhood Upper Fillmore bistro where the eponymous husband-and-wife owners turn out "exceptional" New American dinners "worth" the "upscale" tabs; while the "homey" storefront with a "little wine bar in back" can get "loud" and "crowded", the "caring" service always "shines through."

| | FOOD | DECOR | SERVICE | COST |

Baker Street Bistro Ⓜ *French*

`21` `17` `21` `$37`

Marina | 2953 Baker St. (bet. Greenwich & Lombard Sts.) | 415-931-1475 |
www.bakerstreetbistro.com

"Unpretentious" and "delicious" Gallic fare is "a real treat" at this
"very romantic" Marina bistro where an "interior of the most Parisian
proportions" (i.e. "tiny") means the "tables are close together", but
"lovely" sidewalk seating and staffers with "a legit French accent" create a "hospitable" vibe; adding to the attraction, the *magnifique* "prix
fixe dinner", offered to "early birds" on weekends and until closing
weeknights, is undoubtedly "a bargain."

Balboa Cafe ● *American*

`20` `19` `20` `$36`

Cow Hollow | 3199 Fillmore St. (Greenwich St.) | 415-921-3944 |
www.balboacafe.com

From "socialites and politicos" to "frat boys and sorority gals", this
"convivial" "institution" in Cow Hollow (with a "more family-oriented"
Mill Valley sibling) is "all about the bar and the people"; the city "scene"
is "loud, loud, loud", while both offer a bistro setting and "solid" midpriced American fare including "beyond addictive" burgers plus "amazing" "classic cocktails" and a "welcoming staff", luring "regulars" to
"return time and time again."

Balompie Café *Salvadoran*

`23` `12` `16` `$15`

Bernal Heights | 3801 Mission St. (Richland Ave.) | 415-647-4000
Mission | 3349 18th St. (Capp St.) | 415-648-9199
www.balompiecafe.com

Order the "ripest platanos", "casamiento to die for" and "best pupu-
sas in town" at these "down-to-earth" Mission and Bernal Heights
Salvadorans where it's "too easy to overindulge"; service is "slow" and
the "decor is nothing special" ("half dive bar/half cafeteria"), but they're
"super cheap" and "great" for "hearty food and futbol"; P.S. "excellent
greasy Central American breakfast" is served until 10 AM.

Bar Agricole ● *Californian*

`22` `25` `22` `$51`

SoMa | 355 11th St. (bet. Folsom & Harrison Sts.) | 415-355-9400 |
www.baragricole.com

"Inventive", "locavore" dinners (and "not-to-be-missed" Sunday
brunch) "struggle for" "supremacy" with the "even better" "killer
cocktails" "hand-mixed" by "stylish bartenders" at this "stunning"
SoMa Californian "near the clubs" that's "so cool" "you kind of want to
hate it"; "portions are a bit small for the price", but service is "great"
and "you can't help but love" the "Zen" interior and "beautiful patio";
a chef change may not be reflected in the Food score.

Barbacco Ⓢ *Italian*

`24` `22` `22` `$42`

Downtown | 220 California St. (Front St.) | 415-955-1919 |
www.barbaccosf.com

They sure "know how to please the palate" at this "super-cute" "Italian
osteria", "little sister" to Perbacco next door, where "hearty pastas"
and a "divine" salumi selection are some of the "clever creations" that
Downtowners devour at the counter and "community tables"; add in
an "eclectic wine list" displayed "on an iPad" (a "fun" touch) and the
"contagious" "enthusiasm" of the "helpful" staff for additional reasons
why it's "so busy all the time."

	FOOD	DECOR	SERVICE	COST

Bar Crudo ⓜ *Seafood* — 26 | 19 | 20 | $44

Western Addition | 655 Divisadero St. (Grove St.) | 415-409-0679 |
www.barcrudo.com

"Sublime" fin fare featuring "innovative" "raw preparations" hooks
"trendy" "hipsters" at this Western Addition seafooder in a "minimalist" setting; the "fantastic beer list" offers "exciting" options to
accompany your "fabulous fish chowder" or "brilliant crudo", and
though service varies and "it's not cheap", the "happy hour is
a tremendous value."

Bar Jules ⓜ *American* — 24 | 19 | 21 | $44

Hayes Valley | 609 Hayes St. (Laguna St.) | 415-621-5482 |
www.barjules.com

"Always inventive" dishes listed on the chalkboard menu "look good"
and taste "even better" at this "casual" Hayes Valley "gem" where
Jessica Boncutter transforms the "freshest of ingredients" into "fantastic" New American fare; while some find it a bit "pricey", the
"charming" if "noisy" space draws "neighborhood" and "symphony
and opera" crowds jonesing for its "daily" specials.

Barney's Gourmet Hamburgers *Burgers* — 21 | 16 | 18 | $17

Marina | 3344 Steiner St. (bet. Chestnut & Lombard Sts.) | 415-563-0307
Noe Valley | 4138 24th St. (bet. Castro & Diamond Sts.) |
415-282-7770
www.barneyshamburgers.com

There's "a burger for every belly", from "honestly awesome" beef patties "dolled up dozens of ways" to "turkey, chicken" and "veggie" versions with "an obscene amount of toppings" at these "no-frills" chain
outposts that also serve "amazing" "old-fashioned" shakes and "curly
fries"; service can be "spotty" and the noise "overpowering" ("be prepared" for "kids and strollers"), but it's "well worth" the "reasonable
price", especially if you snag the "patio seating" at most locations.

Bar Tartine ⓜ *European* — 24 | 20 | 22 | $43

Mission | 561 Valencia St. (bet. 16th & 17th Sts.) | 415-487-1600 |
www.bartartine.com

It's "not just 'what's cooking?', it's 'what's fermenting?'" at this
Mission offshoot of the "worshiped" Tartine Bakery where chef
Nick Balla turns out "pickled vegetables" and other "delicious"
"European-meets-Californian" dishes, served up in a "warm, wood
interior"; it's "not for the food rigid", but "knowledgeable" staffers
help "pair" the offerings with "adventurous wine and beer" choices;
P.S. the adjoining sandwich shop (open Wednesday–Friday) features
some "rustic" baked goods.

Basil Thai Restaurant & Bar *Thai* — 24 | 19 | 21 | $29

SoMa | 1175 Folsom St. (bet. 7th & 8th Sts.) | 415-552-8999
Basil Canteen *Thai*
SoMa | 1489 Folsom St. (11th St.) | 415-552-3963
www.basilthai.com

Curry connoisseurs "Thai one on" at these midpriced SoMa siblings,
where "top-notch" Asian-inspired cocktails "whet your appetite" for
"beautifully presented" plates fans insist are better only "in Bangkok
itself"; the "cool" spaces "pleasingly blend Eastern elements" with an

"industrial aesthetic" and servers ensure you "feel more than welcome", but boy, it can be "loud."

The Beach Chalet Brewery & Restaurant *American*

| 16 | 21 | 16 | $31 |

Outer Sunset | 1000 Great Hwy. (John F. Kennedy Dr.) | 415-386-8439 | www.beachchalet.com

"It's all about the view" say those who "make the trek" to Outer Sunset to "ogle the ocean" from a "lovely old building" with "fantastic WPA murals in the lobby"; the consensus on the American fare is "decent but not memorable" and "service is shaky", but the "breathtaking" setting ("high-quality" "house-brewed" beer) "keeps people coming back."

Beast & The Hare Ⓜ *American/Californian*

| 23 | 19 | 20 | $36 |

Mission | 1001 Guerrero St. (22nd St.) | 415-821-1001 | www.beastandthehare.com

Since It's not your typical "meat and potatoes joint", "don't expect prime rib" at this "adventurous" Mission Cal-American where a "friendly" crew proffers "killer" bone marrow, "delectable homemade charcuterie" and the likes of a signature rabbit ragu complemented by an "eclectic" beer and wine selection; the "dark and cozy" digs "get absolutely packed at dinner", less so on brunch-only Sundays.

Bella Trattoria *Italian*

| 24 | 19 | 23 | $37 |

Inner Richmond | 3854 Geary Blvd. (3rd Ave.) | 415-221-0305 | www.bellatrattoriasf.com

"If you live nearby" (in the Inner Richmond), there's "no reason not to become a regular" of this "romantic" trattoria serving "perfectly prepared pastas, "luscious" "homemade" gnocchi and other "excellent" Italian fare at a "reasonable" price; no, it's not "glamorous", but "friendly service warms you up even when the fog rolls in."

Benu 🅩Ⓜ *American*

| 27 | 24 | 28 | $168 |

SoMa | 22 Hawthorne St. (bet. Folsom & Howard Sts.) | 415-685-4860 | www.benusf.com

"Fine dining at its edgy finest" is how devotees describe this "knock-your-socks-off" SoMa New American, where Corey Lee blends "French technique and Asian flavors" into "rock-star dishes" (stuffed Hokkaido sea cucumber, anyone?); though you may need an "expense account" to pay, "amazing" service ("the wine tasting alone is incredible") in a "Zen-like" space makes for an "outstanding culinary experience"; P.S. "go all the way" with the prix fixe menu, the only option Friday–Saturday, though à la carte is also available Tuesday–Thursday.

Beretta ◑ *Italian*

| 24 | 21 | 20 | $38 |

Mission | 1199 Valencia St. (23rd St.) | 415-695-1199 | www.berettasf.com

"Always a winner", this "lively", "always-packed" (reservations only for large groups) Mission "mad house" doles out "delicous artisanal pizzas", "exquisite" Italian small plates and "magical", "outstanding cocktails" that "steal the show"; "the noise can be out of control", but "when the food and drinks are this good, who needs to talk?" P.S. the gelato with EVOO and sea salt is "a must."

NEW Bergerac *Eclectic/Pub Food*
$-$ | $-$ | $-$ | M

SoMa | 316 11th St. (Folsom St.) | 310-869-3364 | www.bergeracsf.com

Craft cocktails are complemented by midpriced globally inspired bar fare at this SoMa restaurant and lounge in a bohemian setting replete with leaded windows, vintage furniture, a 25-seat bar and a warren of sitting areas where diners can socialize and snack; P.S. a separate nightclub, Audio Discotech, will be located upstairs.

Betelnut *Asian*
24 | 22 | 20 | $38

Cow Hollow | 2030 Union St. (bet. Buchanan & Webster Sts.) | 415-929-8855 | www.betelnutrestaurant.com

After a short-lived run as the restaurant Hutong, this "long-standing" Cow Hollow haunt is back, serving "innovative" Pan-Asian fusion small plates in a midpriced menu that includes greatest hits from both restaurants amid the original 1920s Asian beerhouse decor; everything about the joint is "a wow", including the "fun" ambiance and "twentysomething scene" fueled by "exotic" beers and cocktails in the "lively" bar.

B44 *Spanish*
21 | 18 | 19 | $40

Downtown | 44 Belden Pl. (bet. Bush & Pine Sts.) | 415-986-6287 | www.b44sf.com

Sitting "outside" on "quaint little" "pedestrian-only" Belden Place drinking "awesome" Iberian wines makes you "feel like you are in Barcelona" at this Downtown "paella paradise" serving "sensational" tapas and other "authentic Spanish cuisine"; "the tables are crammed quite closely together", but that only adds to the "festive" "buzz."

Biergarten Ⓜ *German*
21 | 20 | 18 | $18

Hayes Valley | 424 Octavia St. (bet. Fell & Linden Sts.) | 415-252-9289 | www.biergartensf.com

"What could be better than a brät and a beer on a sunny day" ask fans of Suppenküche's beer garden in a "converted bit of pavement" in Hayes Valley, where "big" mugs of brew and German pub food seem like "a good idea" (to "you and the 100 people ahead of you" quip some); service is "merely efficient", but communal tables with sun umbrellas and "lap blankets on a cool evening" assure it "does the trick."

Big Four ◑ *American*
24 | 26 | 25 | $62

Nob Hill | Huntington Hotel | 1075 California St. (Taylor St.) | 415-771-1140 | www.big4restaurant.com

Entering this "classy", "old-world" New American in Nob Hill's Huntington Hotel is "like stepping back in time" into a "private club" of "dark-wood" paneling say patrons who "start with a martini" amid the suited "bar scene" where a "pianist sets the tone", then head to the "quiet" dining room with banquettes and white linens; a "most attentive" staff and a menu of "old favorites" and "wonderful daily specials" lead diners to dub it "where adults go for real food."

Bi-Rite Creamery *Bakery/Ice Cream*
27 | 15 | 21 | $7

Mission | 3692 18th St. (Dolores St.) | 415-626-5600

NEW Bi-Rite *Bakery/Ice Cream*

Western Addition | 550 Divisadero St. (Hayes St.) | 415-551-7900 www.biritecreamery.com

The "salted caramel is out of this world, as are the lines" at this "beloved" Mission "ice cream institution" and bake shop (with a to-go counter at the Western Addition outpost), where "friendly", "laid-back" staffers scoop up "heavenly", "handmade" frozen treats in "unique" flavors that "will make you swoon"; "generous tastes" are offered to help choose, but those aiming for a quick exit "just go for a pint" or "try the soft-serve line" instead.

Bistro Aix *Californian/French* | 23 | 20 | 21 | $42 |

Marina | 3340 Steiner St. (bet. Chestnut & Lombard Sts.) | 415-202-0100 | www.bistroaix.com

Patrons "love" this "highly affordable" Marina "mainstay", a "hidden gem" whose "superb", "simple", seasonal Cal-Provençal fare (plus a "mean burger") and "well-selected" wines are proffered by "friendly, helpful" servers in a "refreshing" "rustic interior"; it's a "fave" for a "romantic date or small group of friends" – just be sure to "reserve in the back 'garden' if you want to talk, not shout", with your companions.

Bistro Boudin *Californian* | 22 | 20 | 19 | $20 |

Fisherman's Wharf | 160 Jefferson St. (Taylor St.) | 415-928-1849 | www.bistroboudin.com

Fisherman's Wharf bread buffs who "watch and smell" the "signature" sourdough being made at the city's "old favorite" head "upstairs" to this "semi-fancy" dining space, where "must-not-miss" clam chowder in a "gooey" bread bowl is served along with other "hearty", "basic" midpriced Cal fare; service is "efficient" but "limited" amid the "hustle and bustle" of "tourists" and some "locals" vying for the "beautiful" views "by the bay."

Bistro Central Parc M *French* | 25 | 21 | 24 | $43 |

Western Addition | 560 Central Ave. (Grove St.) | 415-931-7272 | www.bistrocentralparc.com

Regulars exchange "French-style cheek kisses" with the "fabulous" owner at this "friendly" bistro that's "a bit off the beaten path" in the Western Addition, serving "simple" yet "amazing" Gallic fare and "excellent" wines that won't "break the bank"; just "make sure" to reserve ahead for a "quiet", "romantic" dinner or "lovely" weekend brunch with "outdoor seating for sunny days."

Bix *American/French* | 24 | 26 | 23 | $61 |

Downtown | 56 Gold St. (bet. Montgomery & Sansome Sts.) | 415-433-6300 | www.bixrestaurant.com

Shimmy through a Downtown alley entrance to "soak up the Noël Coward mood" at this "elegant" American-French "supper club" likened to a "cruise ship from the 1940s", with its "art deco" bi-level space, "professional" staff in white jackets and "cool" live jazz nightly; a "top-notch" bar serves up "power martinis" while a "finely prepared" if "pricey" menu lets you "go big" (think steak tartare), all making for "a special night out."

Blowfish Sushi To Die For *Japanese* | 23 | 20 | 18 | $41 |

Mission | 2170 Bryant St. (20th St.) | 415-285-3848 | www.blowfishsushi.com

"Enjoy dinner with a side of anime" at these "fun, hip" Mission and San Jose outposts serving "creative sushi" and "exotic drinks" to a "younger crowd" that doesn't seem to mind the "noise"; fans who find it "overpriced" for "tiny" dinner portions go for the "daily lunch specials" "that won't kill your budget."

	FOOD	DECOR	SERVICE	COST

Blue Barn Gourmet *Californian* 25 | 19 | 19 | $15

Marina | 2105 Chestnut St. (Steiner St.) | 415-441-3232 |
www.bluebarngourmet.com

"Spectacular salads" full of "fresh organic" produce and "creatively concocted sandwiches" make a "hearty but healthy meal" at this "casual" Marina Californian (there's also a branch in Corte Madera) where eating your veggies is "a treat"; it's a "little bit pricey" and there's "limited seating" in the "crowded" space with "cute" barnlike decor, so some suggest "call ahead and order takeout", which also shortens the "long wait"; P.S. a Polk Gulch outpost is planned.

Blue Bottle Café *Californian/Coffeehouse* 24 | 17 | 19 | $8

Embarcadero | Ferry Building Mktpl. | 1 Ferry Bldg. (The Embarcadero) | 510-653-3394

NEW Mission | Heath Ceramics Factory & Showroom | 2900 18th St. (bet. Alabama & Florida Sts.) | no phone

SoMa | Mint Plaza | 66 Mint St. (Mission St.) | 510-653-3394

Blue Bottle Kiosk ⊘ *Californian/Coffeehouse*

Hayes Valley | 315 Linden St. (Gough St.) | 510-653-3394
www.bluebottlecoffee.net

Java junkies brave "crazy-long" queues to order "pricey" cups of "exquisite" "caffeine gold" from baristas who "make magic with coffee beans" at this cult chain; though a few "don't understand" the "extreme hype" and huff about the "hipper-than-thou" attitude, most maintain the "soul-satisfying" sips and "wonderful" pastries are "worth every minute" of the wait; P.S. some locations also serve a small menu of "fantastic" Californian breakfast and lunch fare.

Blue Plate *American* 24 | 19 | 21 | $40

Mission | 3218 Mission St. (bet. 29th & Valencia Sts.) | 415-282-6777 |
www.blueplatesf.com

It "still rules the Outer Mission" declare devotees who "hate giving away the secret" of this "neighborhood favorite" cooking "consistently delicious", "homey" American "comfort food with a modern twist" (and made with "seasonal local ingredients"); a "top-notch" staff and "lovely garden" setting are added bonuses at this "diamond in the rough."

Bluestem Brasserie *American/Steak* 19 | 21 | 19 | $51

SoMa | 1 Yerba Buena Ln. (4th St.) | 415-547-1111 |
www.bluestembrasserie.com

Between the "handsome bar area", "floor-to-ceiling windows" and "second-floor patio", this "swanky" brasserie with an "urban" ambiance is a "find" for "generous" cocktails and "solid" New American fare, including "great grass-fed" beef; though it's "a bit pricey", it suits SoMa suits ready to "shake on a deal" over a "long lunch", even if the "personable" service is sometimes "a little slow."

Bocadillos ⊠ *Spanish* 23 | 20 | 21 | $36

North Beach | 710 Montgomery St. (Washington St.) | 415-982-2622 |
www.bocasf.com

Proffering "far more" than the "delicious", "well-priced" sandwiches for which it's named, Gerald Hirigoyen's all-day "modern" tapas bar in North Beach is a "favorite" for "inspired" Basque "shared plates" and "Spanish wines"; despite "no reservations" and "tight" space, "friendly" servers "always seem to find room for you" at the "convivial bar" or "communal tables" and the "party atmosphere" guarantees "a good night out."

Boccalone Salumeria *Sandwiches* 25 | 15 | 20 | $14

Embarcadero | Ferry Building Mktpl. | 1 Ferry Bldg. (The Embarcadero) | 415-433-6500 | www.boccalone.com

"Melt-in-your-mouth" prosciutto, "to-die-for" mortadella and other "aged" salumi slices are served up in "meat cones" or stuffed into "toasties" at this Ferry Building shop where both "tourists and locals" (and fans of Incanto's Chris Cosentino) meet for "dried meats"; eating your "tasty little snack" at the bar feels like an "urban picnic" to some, who add that the staff is "happy" to help; P.S. closes 6 PM Monday–Saturday, 5 PM Sunday.

Bodega Bistro *Vietnamese* 24 | 13 | 21 | $28

Tenderloin | 607 Larkin St. (Eddy St.) | 415-921-1218 | www.bodegabistrosf.net

From "phantastic pho" to "French-inspired" Vietnamese fare to "Hanoi street food" "not found elsewhere", the eats are "amazing" at this "simple" Southeast Asian in the Tenderloin's "Little Saigon"; backers say it offers "better bang for the buck" than some competitors, and the "friendly" waiters "try very hard to please."

Boogaloos *Southwestern* 20 | 15 | 18 | $17

Mission | 3296 22nd St. (Valencia St.) | 415-824-4088 | www.boogaloossf.com

As "friendly to vegetarians, vegans and hipsters" as it is to everyday omnivores, this "trendy" Mission breakfast, lunch and brunch spot "housed in an old pharmacy" has "a line around the block on week-ends" for its Southwestern-influenced grub; fans swear the "unbeat-able biscuits and gravy" and other "delicious" options are "worth" the "ridiculous wait", though if you're "trying to chat", it can be "very loud and hard to hear."

Borobudur *Indonesian* 23 | 17 | 19 | $25

Nob Hill | 700 Post St. (Jones St.) | 415-775-1512 | www.borobudursf.com

Named for a Javanese Buddhist temple, this Indonesian is "a captivat-ing alternative" to other Nob Hill haunts, where devotees declare each "vibrant-tasting" dish "is better than the next", from "authentic" "apps and soups" to the "amazingly generous" *rijsttafel* (rice-table dinners); it's "a good way to sample lots of traditional dishes", and if the setting is merely "modest", "moderate prices" and "friendly" servers con-vince most to "recommend it."

Bottle Cap *American* 18 | 15 | 18 | $35

North Beach | 1707 Powell St. (bet. Columbus Ave. & Union St.) | 415-529-2237 | www.bottlecapsf.com

Surveyors are split on this midpriced North Beach American that "re-placed the long-standing Washington Square Bar & Grill"; fans like it for its "inventive" cocktails, "tasty" "comfort food" and "great" live music in an "airy" dining room, while the less-impressed dub the digs "sterile" and say "pleasant" servers don't make up for "mediocre" fare; undebatable is the "outstanding location" on Washington Square Park.

Bouche ● ◪ *Californian/French*   ▽ 24 | 19 | 21 | $49

Nob Hill | 603 Bush St. (Stockton St.) | 415-956-0396 |
www.bouchesf.com

Nob Hill locals seeking "a little bit of France" call this "trendy" Cal-French a "worst-kept secret" given the "hip" diners drawn to its "late hours" (till 1 AM Monday–Saturday) and "innovative" menu full of "big flavors" and "unusual combinations"; the "romantic" if "tiny" bi-level space includes some upstairs views "overlooking the kitchen."

Boudin Sourdough   21 | 17 | 18 | $16

Bakery *American/Sandwiches*

Downtown | 170 O'Farrell St. (bet. Powell & Stockton Sts.) |
415-296-4740
Downtown | 619 Market St. (bet. New Montgomery & 2nd Sts.) |
415-281-8200 ◪
Embarcadero | Embarcadero Ctr. | 4 Embarcadero Ctr. (Drumm St.) |
415-362-3330 ◪
Fisherman's Wharf | Pier 39 (Beach St.) | 415-421-0185
Parkside | Stonestown Galleria Ctr. | 3251 20th Ave. (Buckingham Way) |
415-564-1849
www.boudinbakery.com

The "intoxicating" aroma of "freshly baked" loaves "entices" "carb lovers" into this bakery/cafe chain for "delicious" sandwiches and other "affordable" American eats, like "out-of-this-world" "creamy clam chowder in a hollowed-out sourdough round"; the "casual" "cafeteria-style" spots get "crowded", but "friendly" servers keep things moving "quickly"; P.S. at the "touristy" Fisherman's Wharf location, "kids will be amazed" watching the "skilled" bakers make "awesome" loaves in "different shapes."

Boulettes Larder/Bouli Bar *American*   25 | 18 | 20 | $35

Embarcadero | Ferry Building Mktpl. | 1 Ferry Bldg. (The Embarcadero) |
415-399-1155 | www.bouletteslarder.com

A "high-end artisanal" New American menu "changes daily" at this "part gourmet take-out" shop, "part sit-down restaurant" at the Ferry Building – with outdoor seating and "a beautiful view of the bay" to boot – where the co-owners turn out some of "the best breakfast and lunch" items around, along with beignets at weekend brunch plus "delicious desserts" and "pre-cooked meals to take home"; it's a little "pricey", but an expansion means diners will have two options – daytime dining at the remodeled Larder, or lunch and dinner at adjacent new Bouli Bar, with a full liquor license.

Boulevard *American*   27 | 26 | 26 | $71

Embarcadero | Audiffred Bldg. | 1 Mission St. (Steuart St.) | 415-543-6084 |
www.boulevardrestaurant.com

"Year after year", chef-owner Nancy Oakes' "spectacular" "San Francisco mainstay" on the Embarcadero "never fails to impress" with its "bridge views" and belle epoque decor as backdrops for "superlative" "big, bold" American fare, "decadent desserts" and a "fantastic" selection of wines, all delivered by a "welcoming", "first-class" staff; there's a "lively" bar scene too and though it's "noisy" and "costs an arm and two legs", it's still the "gold standard" for "business" and "special occasions" and is itself "reason to have a special occasion."

CITY OF SAN FRANCISCO

FOOD | DECOR | SERVICE | COST

Bourbon Steak *Steak* 23 | 23 | 24 | $85

Downtown | Westin St. Francis Hotel | 355 Powell St. (bet. Geary & Post Sts.) | 415-397-3003 | www.michaelmina.net

You may have to "save up" to visit Michael Mina's "classy", "dimly lit" Downtown steakhouse in the Westin St. Francis, but the "excellent cuts of meat" "prepared to perfection", "epic wine list" (plus "mean" cocktails) and "first-rate staff" add up to an "experience" for "special occasions" or "business"; "when a restaurant serves you a trio of fries and dipping sauces instead of bread, it's already a win."

Boxing Room *Cajun/Creole* 20 | 20 | 21 | $42

Hayes Valley | 399 Grove St. (Gough St.) | 415-430-6590 | www.boxingroomsf.com

"Every day is Mardi Gras" at this "lively" Hayes Valley "ragin' Cajun"-Creole cranking out "killer", "NOLA-worthy" "Southern-fried goodness" (read: "heavy" and "spicy") with a "Californian sensibility"; the "modern" digs "do little to recall the Old South", but the staff's "hospitality" and a "sweeping bar" pouring "well-priced" wine and beer ensure "good times", plus "where else can you get alligator?"

NEW **B. Patisserie** *Dessert* ∇ 26 | 22 | 20 | $18

Pacific Heights | 2821 California St. (Divisadero St.) | 415-440-1700 | www.bpatisserie.com

Devotees "bless the day" this "delectable" Lower Pac Heights patisserie started baking up its "fabulous" croissants, macarons and "signature" Viennese-style kouign amann (which "alone is worth" the trip); a few "artisanal" sandwiches, "good strong French coffee" and a "cute" if "limited" capacity space draw "the ladies who lunch bunch", and while some say "b. ready to pay" for the treats, they admit "excellence has a price."

Brandy Ho's *Chinese* 20 | 15 | 17 | $25

Castro | 4068 18th St. (bet. Castro & Hartford Sts.) | 415-252-8000
Chinatown | 217 Columbus Ave. (Pacific Ave.) | 415-788-7527
www.brandyhos.com

Some prefer this Chinese duo's "original" Chinatown location, where "the decor needs serious updating" but you can "sit at the counter" and watch your meal "prepared in giant woks over huge flames", while others favor the more "modern" "Castro outlet"; regardless, the "consistent" "no-MSG" chow ranging "from mild to off-the-charts" hot will "satisfy" your Hunan "cravings" at an "affordable" price.

Brasserie S&P *Californian* ∇ 24 | 23 | 23 | $48

Downtown | Mandarin Oriental Hotel | 222 Sansome St. (bet. California & Pine Sts.) | 415-986-2020 | www.mandarinoriental.com

This FiDi brasserie with a tony Mandarin Oriental address offers a Californian menu of small plates and entrees including pastas, steaks and a raw bar; the casual space that replaced Silks is decidedly more toned down with a neutral palette and has floor-to-ceiling windows overlooking the plaza outside, plus a bar specializing in gin and tonics.

The Brazen Head ●⊄ *American* 20 | 19 | 21 | $38

Cow Hollow | 3166 Buchanan St. (Greenwich St.) | 415-921-7600 | www.brazenheadsf.com

Whether you're on "a first date" or having a "classic" cocktail with your spouse, you'll "feel like you're having an affair" at this "dark" and "clubby" Cow Hollow American with a "secretive" air (and "no sign outside"); a "solid" menu of "reasonably priced" American fare, like "sumptuous" steak and burgers, is "served late into the night" (until 1 AM), but "don't forget your cash", because they don't take credit cards.

Brenda's French Soul Food *Creole/Southern* 25 | 18 | 20 | $24

Civic Center | 652 Polk St. (bet. Eddy & Turk Sts.) | 415-345-8100 | www.frenchsoulfood.com

"If you miss NOLA, run", don't walk, to this "tiny" Civic Center "joint", where fans "line up" for "comfort Creole", from "super-creative" beignets to the "favorite" shrimp and grits, all served by a "hospitable" staff; known for "superb" Southern breakfasts and brunches at a "low" price, it's also open for dinner Wednesday–Saturday, though at times there can be a "longish wait"; P.S. breakfast served Sunday until 8 PM.

Broken Record ●🍴 *Soul Food* 24 | 14 | 17 | $18

Excelsior | 1166 Geneva Ave. (bet. Madrid & Naples Sts.) | 415-963-1713

"The secret is out" about this "laid-back" "dive bar" in Excelsior, where the "extraordinary" soul food cranked out by the "small kitchen" is a "wonderful surprise"; they don't "take plastic" for the "cheap" chow, and it's "crazy-crowded" on the "spacious" "outdoor patio", but the "good-natured staff" and an "impressive" "whiskey selection" soften the blow.

Brother's Korean Restaurant ● *Korean* 22 | 10 | 16 | $30

Inner Richmond | 4128 Geary Blvd. (bet. 5th & 6th Aves.) | 415-387-7991

The possible flavor combinations are seemingly "endless" at this "authentic" Inner Richmond Korean BBQ joint where you "compose your own dinner over glowing coals" in the grill at your table; prices are "reasonable", and even though the "minimalist" digs can be "crowded" and your clothes may "reek of garlic" and "smoke" ("don't go anywhere fancy afterwards"), fans insist the experience is "worth it."

B Star Bar *Asian* 25 | 18 | 21 | $28

Inner Richmond | 127 Clement St. (bet. 2nd & 3rd Aves.) | 415-933-9900 | www.bstarbar.com

"Fabulous" "fusion-y" Pan-Asian fare "bursts" with "huge flavor" at this "prettier younger sister" of Burma Superstar in the Inner Richmond, serving some of its sibling's "best" Burmese dishes without the "crowds" and "mile-long lines"; it also wins praise for "courteous" service, "reasonable prices" and "fancy" "soju cocktails", and though some sigh "the magic" of the original "is missing", it's "nice to be able to make reservations."

Bund Shanghai Restaurant *Chinese* ∇ 24 | 16 | 21 | $21

Chinatown | 640 Jackson St. (bet. Beckett & Kearny Sts.) | 415-982-0618

Fans who've discovered this Chinatown spot declare it their "new favorite" for "genuine" Shanghai fare, including dim sum, soup dumplings and other regional specialties, served in a basic space; even though it's not yet on tourists' radars, it "gets crowded" at lunch when "the FiDi types show up."

Bun Mee *Vietnamese*

20 | 16 | 17 | $14

Upper Fillmore | 2015 Fillmore St. (bet. California & Pine Sts.) | 415-800-7696 | www.bunmee.com

With "a perfect balance" of "tasty" meat and veggies "folded into warm, crisp baguettes", the "high-quality" banh mi served at this Upper Fillmore eatery are a "fancy-pants version" of those available at "your average Vietnamese" go-to; they might be a bit "more expensive", but it's a "delightfully retro" "little" cafe and the "expansive" menu of salads and "amazing" sides is served by a "friendly" staff.

Burger Bar *Burgers*

20 | 19 | 18 | $27

Downtown | Macy's | 251 Geary St., 6th fl. (bet. Powell & Stockton Sts.) | 415-296-4272 | www.burger-bar.com

"Build the burger of your dreams" with a "wide variety" of toppings at celebrity chef Hubert Keller's hamburger "heaven" inside the Downtown Macy's; "amazing" "milkshakes (alcoholic or otherwise)" and an "awesome view of Union Square" for those who "snag a window seat" add an "upscale" vibe, but critics complain the "touristy" chain is "a bit overpriced", especially in light of sometimes "slow service."

Burger Joint *Burgers*

19 | 15 | 17 | $15

Mission | 807 Valencia St. (bet. 19th & 20th Sts.) | 415-824-3494 | www.burgerjointsf.com

Fans frequent these Bay Area mini-chain links in the Mission and at San Francisco International Airport for a "quick-service", "solid burger" made from "high-quality" Niman Ranch beef and "cooked how you want it"; "good milkshakes and fries round out an inexpensive meal" that "beats the fast-food options."

BurgerMeister *Burgers*

20 | 15 | 17 | $16

Castro | 138 Church St. (bet. Duboce Ave. & 14th St.) | 415-437-2874
Cole Valley | 86 Carl St. (Cole St.) | 415-566-1274
North Beach | 759 Columbus Ave. (bet. Filbet & Mason Sts.) | 415-296-9907
www.burgermeistersf.com

"Big sloppy" burgers, "crisp fries" and "top-notch" milkshakes "hit the spot" at these "consistent" and "kid-friendly" Bay Area chain links; the Niman Ranch patties are "better than fast-food" versions and "reasonably priced" to boot, though some note "hit-or-miss" service and suggest you won't want to "linger" since there's "not much atmosphere."

Burma Superstar *Burmese*

25 | 17 | 20 | $26

Inner Richmond | 309 Clement St. (4th Ave.) | 415-387-2147 | www.burmasuperstar.com

"Bold" Burmese, like the "endlessly complex and addictive" tea-leaf salad, "will knock your socks off" at these "loud" siblings where "courteous" servers are "helpful" to newcomers "uninitiated" into the "exotic" menu; while it beats the "trip to Rangoon", expect "ridiculous" lines at the Inner Richmond original ("you don't have to wait as long" at the East Bay offshoots) and a "cramped", "simple" setting.

Burmese Kitchen   *Burmese*

22 | 12 | 20 | $20

Tenderloin | 452 Larkin St. (bet. Golden Gate Ave. & Turk St.) | 415-474-5569 | www.burmesekitchen.com

A "nice change" in a neighborhood dominated by Vietnamese spots, this Tenderloin Burmese offers a "big menu" that includes "all the classics" and "fine" service; the "casual" setting is "comfortable", and it's "cheaper and more centrally located" than other popular Myanmar eateries.

Burritt Tavern *American* | **20** | **23** | **21** | **$46** |

Downtown | Mystic Hotel | 417 Stockton St. (Sutter St.) | 415-400-0561 | www.burritttavern.com

Named after an alley in *The Maltese Falcon,* this "classy" Charlie Palmer project on the second floor of Downtown's "majestic" Mystic Hotel channels film noir with its "super-cool", "speakeasy"-like space, often filled with the strains of "excellent live jazz", where a "knowledgeable" staff serves upscale American dishes such as "meltingly tender" short ribs; P.S. the Food score may not reflect a chef change.

Butler & The Chef Bistro M *French* | **22** | **18** | **17** | **$22** |

SoMa | 155 S. Park Ave. (bet. Center & 3rd Sts.) | 415-896-2075 | www.butlerandthechef.com

Francophiles "squeeze" into "tiny" tables at this "cozy" SoMa bistro for "classic French" breakfasts and lunch; expect a "long wait" for your "delicious" coffee and "incredible" croque monsieur (especially "on the weekends"), and the "Gallic staff can be snooty at times", but with a location facing "darling South Park", it's "absolutely lovely nonetheless."

Butterfly M *Asian/Californian* | **23** | **23** | **21** | **$42** |

Embarcadero | Pier 33 (Bay St.) | 415-864-8999 | www.butterflysf.com

"Snag a window seat", because this Embarcadero eatery with a "delightful bay view" "never disappoints" with its "well-made" cocktails and "inventive" Cal-Asian cuisine served by an "attentive" staff; though a few find the tab "pricey" and note some "misses on the menu", at least the "excellent happy hour" is an "awesome" deal.

Cafe Bastille *French* | **19** | **17** | **18** | **$39** |

Downtown | 22 Belden Pl. (bet. Bush & Pine Sts.) | 415-986-5673 | www.cafebastillesf.com

Paris partisans longing for "the Left Bank" are willingly taken "captive prisoner" at this "charming" Downtowner that's "cozy" inside and "festive" outside, where tables line a "lively" pedestrian alleyway; "friendly" waiters with a "French accent" serve "basic" but "delicious" Gallic bistro fare that's a "treat" when you want a lot of "bang for the buck."

Café Bunn Mi ⊅ *Sandwiches/Vietnamese* | **23** | **15** | **18** | **$12** |

Inner Richmond | 417 Clement St. (6th Ave.) | 415-668-8908

Fans insist "you'll enjoy every bite" of the "hearty", "well-prepared" eponymous Vietnamese sandwiches at this Inner Richmond spot, which also serves pho and a "small selection of entrees"; the digs are basic and entertainment consists of a "TV playing sports", but the fare is "filling" and the "price is right"; P.S. cash only.

Café Claude ❂ *French* | **22** | **20** | **20** | **$42** |

Downtown | 7 Claude Ln. (bet. Bush & Sutter Sts.) | 415-392-3515 | www.cafeclaude.com

For an "authentic" experience "without having to exchange" dollars into Euros, Francophiles head for this "intimate" bistro "tucked away" in a Downtown alley; purists are "delighted" by the "simple" menu of "expertly prepared" "classic French" fare "expeditiously served" by waiters with "adorable" accents; "compatible" prices and "live jazz" Thursday–Saturday seal its status as a "romantic" "date spot"; P.S. a Marina location is in the works.

Café des Amis *French* 18 | 23 | 20 | $50

Cow Hollow | 2000 Union St. (Buchanan St.) | 415-563-7700 | www.cafedesamissf.com

You "could not ask for better ambiance" at this "beautiful", "bustling" Union Street brasserie that's crammed with a "good-looking" crowd and reminds some of "a Toulouse-Lautrec painting"; the service and "straight-up, well-executed" French classics are "mostly desirable", though a few say that "given the price, the experience is "missing" that certain je ne sais quoi.

Cafe Jacqueline Ⓜ *French* 27 | 20 | 22 | $51

North Beach | 1454 Grant Ave. (bet. Green & Union Sts.) | 415-981-5565

"Good things come to those who wait" insist Francophiles who "do not mind spending the entire evening" dining at this "romantic" "soufflé specialty house" in North Beach where "amazing" Madame "Jacqueline herself" is "still holding the fort in the back" with "a whisk and copper bowl" whipping up the nightly offerings to order; never mind that "service varies", just "share an entree" version "and of course one for dessert" – both are "out of this stratosphere."

Café Tiramisu *Italian* 22 | 19 | 21 | $40

Downtown | 28 Belden Pl. (bet. Bush & Pine Sts.) | 415-421-7044 | www.cafetiramisu.com

"One of the stars" of Downtown's "charming" Belden Place, this "reasonably priced" ristorante offers "classic" Northern Italian fare including "a wonderful array of desserts"; "go on a sunny day", "sit outside" and "try the house Chianti" for a "convivial" experience suggest supporters who appreciate "personalized" service by the "attentive" staff.

Cafe Zoetrope *Italian* 21 | 22 | 20 | $35

North Beach | 916 Kearny St. (Columbus Ave.) | 415-291-1700 | www.cafecoppola.com

"Don't be surprised" if you see owner Francis Ford Coppola himself "relaxing at one of the outdoor tables" of this "cute" North Beach Italian where you can order "pretty much any" of the filmmaker's wines to accompany midpriced fare such as "wonderful thin-crust pizza", "delicious" pastas and "dreamy" desserts; a "friendly" staff completes the "delightful" vibe.

Cajun Pacific Ⓢ Ⓜ *Cajun/Creole* ▽ 23 | 16 | 19 | $30

Outer Sunset | 4542 Irving St. (47th Ave.) | 415-504-6652 | www.cajunpacific.com

The "menu changes weekly" at this "tiny" Outer Sunset spot serving "tasty, comforting" Cajun and Creole staples in a "snug" space that some describe as "barely more than a pop-up"; grace notes such as "mismatched wine glasses" add to the "quirky vibe", and fans tout it for a "different kind of experience" – especially "on a foggy night"; P.S. open Thursday–Saturday only, so "reservations are an absolute must."

	FOOD	DECOR	SERVICE	COST

Campanula Kitchen & Bar *American*   ▽ 20 | 18 | 20 | $45

North Beach | 701 Union St. (Powell St.) | 415-829-7766 |
www.campanulasf.com

"Hidden" on a North Beach corner, this New American bistro from the owners of Frascati is "a cut above" its "old-line" neighbors and makes a "nice place to meet friends, share a few small plates" and enjoy "people-watching" through the "large windows"; the "gentle care" taken with the fare and "friendly", "helpful" staff help explain why it's a "neighborhood go-to" for those "in the know."

Campton Place *Californian/Mediterranean*   26 | 25 | 25 | $79

Downtown | Taj Campton Pl. Hotel | 340 Stockton St. (Sutter St.) |
415-781-5555 | www.camptonplacesf.com

Admirers report a "memorable" experience at this upscale Cal-Mediterranean on the Taj Campton Place's ground floor, thanks to "fabulous, over-the-top" tasting menus, including chef Srijith Gopinathan's "Indian-infused" Spice Route menu, an "incredible" journey from "amuse-bouche to dessert"; tabs are "very expensive", but you can expect "flawless" service in a "quiet", "intimate" space, and most agree it's worth it for a "special occasion."

Canela Bistro & Bar *Spanish*   ▽ 23 | 21 | 21 | $37

Castro | 2272 Market St. (bet. Noe & Sanchez Sts.) | 415-552-3000 |
www.canelasf.com

The Castro dining scene "is looking up" thanks to the "surprisingly delicious" fare at this Spaniard on Market offering "tip-top tapas" and entrees such as paella plus "interesting" domestic and Iberian wines including "lots of half bottles" – all at "reasonable prices"; the digs are "lovely", the service "friendly" and the owners are "wonderful hosts", while the spot gets props as a "nice break from traditional" options.

Capannina *Italian*   25 | 21 | 24 | $48

Cow Hollow | 1809 Union St. (Octavia St.) | 415-409-8001 |
www.capanninasf.com

"Generous portions" of "innovative" Italian eats are "made with love" at this "cozy" Cow Hollow trattoria, where "hospitable" waiters are "happy to explain every fantastic dish"; the tables might be "too close together", but it's still "homey enough to be your neighborhood hangout", and the "prix fixe three-course dinner before 6 PM" is a "great" deal.

NEW Capo's ⊅ *Italian*   - | - | - | M

North Beach | 641 Vallejo St. (Stockton St.) | 415-986-8998 |
www.sfcapos.com

Tony Gemignani (Tony's Pizza Napoletana) is the boss behind this midpriced cash-only Windy City–inspired pizzeria and whiskey bar in North Beach, serving various Chicago-style pies and other Italian classics; the storefront channels the vibe of a Prohibition-style speakeasy with a long banquette of tufted red-leather, exposed-red-brick walls and a wooden bar stocked with premium whiskeys.

Catch *Seafood*   21 | 21 | 21 | $39

Castro | 2362 Market St. (bet. Castro & 16th Sts.) | 415-431-5000 |
www.catchsf.com

"Fresh" fin fare (some swimming in "delectable" sauces) has surveyors declaring this "trendy" Castro seafooder is indeed "a catch"; the menu is "nothing fancy" and "not the cheapest", but a "great" cocktail list, "helpful" waiters who are "hotter than the food" and a "cozy" heated courtyard with an outdoor fireplace make it a "people-watching" paradise.

Catheads BBQ *BBQ*   ▽ 22 | 16 | 19 | $18

SoMa | 1665 Folsom St. (13th St.) | 415-861-4242 | www.catheadsbbq.com
Though some find the name "unappetizing", most find the "gourmet" Southern and Midwestern "comfort food" (pulled pork, ribs and brisket) at this SoMa BBQ "delicious"; "friendly" servers hand out victuals on "tin pie plates" and drinks in "mason jars" in a "small", counter-service space; P.S. you can also order 'cue by the pound.

⬛NEW The Cavalier *British*   - | - | - | M

SoMa | Hotel Zetta | 360 Jessie St. (Fifth St.) | 415-321-6000 | www.thecavaliersf.com
London's calling at this new British-themed brasserie in SoMa's Hotel Zetta from the folks behind Marlowe and Park Tavern, offering midpriced gastro-pub fare (fish 'n' chips, steak-and-oysters pot pie) along with Colony-inspired cocktails like a Pimm's Cup; the English hunting lodge meets '60s bohemia interior, with a warren of dining rooms, stokes the vibe with vintage dining-car touches and the all-day Blue Bar.

Central Kitchen *Californian*   24 | 22 | 22 | $60

Mission | 3000 20th St. (Florida St.) | 415-826-7004 | www.centralkitchensf.com
At this Mission sibling of Thomas McNaughton's Flour + Water, "fresh local" veggies (some plucked from the rooftop garden) are transformed into "fabulous", "simple but elegant" Californian dishes packing "exciting" flavor "combinations"; "casual" wooden tables combine with "industrial" touches in a partially outdoor space that works best "on a sunny day", and "friendly", "helpful" service helps encourage "repeat visits."

Cha Cha Cha *Caribbean*   22 | 19 | 18 | $27

Haight-Ashbury | 1801 Haight St. (Shrader St.) | 415-386-7670
Mission | 2327 Mission St. (bet. 19th & 20th Sts.) | 415-824-1502
www.cha3.com
"More or less an institution", this midpriced trio with two longtime SF locations and one San Mateo branch serves "some seriously deelish grub" by way of tapas seemingly "straight from the Caribbean" and made for washing down with rather "deadly" sangria; popular with "young" groups, the vibe's "loud and lively", service varies and there's "always a wait", but add in "kitschy" "Day of the Dead" decor, and it's a "trip south with no passport needed."

Chapeau! *French*   27 | 21 | 25 | $54

Inner Richmond | 126 Clement St. (bet. 2nd & 3rd Aves.) | 415-750-9787 | www.chapeausf.com
A "winner in every respect", this "warm, friendly" Inner Richmond French bistro has garnered a "loyal clientele" with its "fabulous", "beautifully presented" cuisine, backed by a "fine wine selection" and "congenial" service; "charming" chef/co-owner Philippe Gardelle "genuinely welcomes each diner" (and sends off ladies with "two kisses on the cheek") in the "bustling" yet "intimate" space, and "reasonable" prices (plus a "great-value" early-bird menu) are why many deem it "one of the best bargains in the city."

Charles Chocolate *Dessert*

FOOD	DECOR	SERVICE	COST
-	-	-	I

Mission | 535 Florida St. (bet. 18th & Mariposa Sts.) | 415-659-8770 | www.charleschocolates.com

This Mission chocolate store and cafe features artisanal chocolate confections – including fleur de sel caramels in an edible box – hot chocolate and snacks such as made-to-order s'mores, to be taken away or enjoyed on the patio; the biggest draw is the facility's exhibition kitchen, which allows visitors to watch the candy-making.

Chaya Brasserie *French/Japanese*

23 | 22 | 21 | $51

Embarcadero | 132 The Embarcadero (bet. Howard & Mission Sts.) | 415-777-8688 | www.thechaya.com

"French and Japanese" cuisines "come together" at this "stylish" hybrid on the Embarcadero with a "spectacular" Bay Bridge view; the "inventive" menu, from "fresh" sushi to more "eclectic" fare fashioned from the "highest-quality ingredients", may be "pricey" for "small portions", but "impressive" cocktails are served by a "knowledgeable" staff and there's an "awesome" all-evening happy hour in the "lively" bar.

Cha-Ya Vegetarian Japanese Restaurant ⌿ *Japanese/Vegan*

22 | 13 | 17 | $23

Mission | 762 Valencia St. (bet. 18th & 19th Sts.) | 415-252-7825

An "absence of pretension and meat" defines this Mission and Berkeley duo offering "expertly prepared" and "unusual" Japanese vegan and "vegetarian treats" that are "delicious and surprisingly filling"; though the "decor leaves a lot to be desired", and flavor-seekers find the fare "a bit bland", it's "popular with a young crowd" that goes for the "reasonably priced" "Zen experience."

Cheesecake Factory *American*

16 | 17 | 16 | $29

Downtown | Macy's | 251 Geary St. (bet. Powell & Stockton Sts.) | 415-391-4444 | www.thecheesecakefactory.com

With a menu that "competes in length with *War and Peace*", this "always packed" go-to dishes out "flavorful" midpriced American fare in portions so "gargantuan", many take their "scrumptious" signature cheesecake "home in a bag"; "long" waits and "over-the-top" decor deter detractors, who call the "calorific" eats "uninspired", but they're outnumbered by "crowds" of admirers dubbing it a "satisfying" and "fun" "family fave" with "friendly" service.

Cheese Steak Shop *Cheesesteaks*

22 | 12 | 19 | $11

Western Addition | 1716 Divisadero St. (bet. Bush & Sutter Sts.) | 415-346-3712 | www.cheesesteakshop.com

"Native Philadelphians" take a "trip down memory lane" at this "cheap" local chain, where the "hefty" cheesesteaks are as "authentic" as you'll find "this side of the Liberty Bell"; the "decor is lacking", but at least the "cheerful" servers are "fast" – a plus when getting your "gooey" "guilty pleasure" and Tastykakes "to go."

Chenery Park ⓜ *American*

23 | 20 | 23 | $41

Glen Park | 683 Chenery St. (Diamond St.) | 415-337-8537 | www.chenerypark.com

American "comfort food" "with a Cajun twist" is "made better" with "local ingredients" at this "upscale" "neighborhood find" in "unhip Glen Park"; the Tuesday Kids Club menu makes for a meal that "both

FOOD DECOR SERVICE COST

kids and parents will enjoy", and the "homey atmosphere" and "sincere" staff make it ideal for "date night" the rest of the week.

Chez Maman *French*
24 | 16 | 22 | $28

Hayes Valley | 401 Gough St. (Hayes St.) | 415-355-9067
Potrero Hill | 1453 18th St. (bet. Connecticut & Missouri Sts.) | 415-824-7166
www.chezmamansf.com

Francophiles get their "Paris fix" at this "casual" bistro known for its "easy, classic French brunch" and other "simple and delicious" fare including mussels ("a must to share"), steak frites and a "delicious" burger; the "charming" original Potrero Hill location is "intimate (read: small)" but some "sit at the bar and take in" the kitchen, while the newer, slightly larger Hayes Valley locale also has "few seats" and "long lines" plus "very European"-feeling "sidewalk seating."

Chez Papa Bistrot *French*
24 | 19 | 22 | $42

Potrero Hill | 1401 18th St. (Missouri St.) | 415-824-8205 |
www.chezpapasf.com

"Reminiscent of the fabulous bistros of Paris", from the "utterly charming" if "informal" setting to the "approachable" French fare (they perform "wizardry with mussels"), this "intimate" Potrero Hill spot is a relatively "affordable" option for "delicious" classics; it matters little that the "crowded" room can be "noisy", since the "authentic" Gallic staffers always ensure patrons feel "nurtured" "from start to finish."

Chiaroscuro 🆇 *Italian*
25 | 21 | 23 | $78

Downtown | 550 Washington St. (bet. Montgomery & Sansome Sts.) |
415-362-6012 | www.chiaroscurosf.com

"Mind-blowing" pastas made "the way a real Roman would" (chef-owner Alessandro Campitelli is a native) are highlights of the "creative" Italian menu at this "oasis" "in the shadow" of Downtown's Transamerica Pyramid; there are "no straw-wrapped Chianti bottles here", but instead "delightfully serene" (some say "stark") "modernist" decor that creates a "chic" setting for "fantastic food" and "great service"; P.S. dinner is now prix fixe only.

Chilango *Mexican*
∇ 22 | 14 | 20 | $21

Castro | 235 Church St. (bet. 15th & Market Sts.) | 415-552-5700 |
www.chilangorestaurantsf.com

"Too bad the secret is out" lament Castrolites "super-impressed" by the "jazzed-up" "Mexico City cuisine" prepared by a former Mexico DF chef at this "go-to" casual cantina; "don't let the looks fool you", despite "downscale decor" (and prices), "it's not your average taqueria" – the "handmade", largely "organic" dishes are "cooked to perfection" and the staff is "lovely."

Chile Pies (Sweet & Savory) *Dessert*
22 | 17 | 19 | $14

Castro | 314 Church St. (15th St.) | 415-431-9411
Chile Pies & Ice Cream *Dessert*
Western Addition | 601 Baker St. (Fulton St.) | 415-614-9411
www.chilepies.com

"Yummy pies" of both the "sweet and savory" varieties are the raison d'être of this "down-to-earth" Western Addition cafe and its Castro cousin, where after a "snack", aficionados indulge in "awesome" desserts featuring a "flaky" crust or turn their attention to the "extra-sinful" "pie shake"; it may be on the "expensive" side considering the "casual" setting, but the "really nice" staff is a sweet perk.

Chloe's Cafe ⊅ *American* 23 | 16 | 20 | $19

Noe Valley | 1399 Church St. (26th St.) | 415-648-4116

"Every neighborhood should have" a "perfect little" "brunch" spot like this Noe Valley nook cranking out "flavor-packed" "scrambles", "perfect" pancakes and other "unpretentious" American eats to a "cozy" handful of tables, including some "curbside" "in the sun"; "it's not cheap" for its ilk and there's "always a morning rush no matter the day, weather or time", but "once in", the staffers "do their best to keep a smile"; P.S. no dinner.

NEW Chocolate Lab ▥ *Dessert* ▽ 25 | 23 | 25 | $22

Dogpatch | 801 22nd St. (Tennessee St.) | 415-489-2881 | www.chocolatelabsf.com

"Delicious" smells greet you at this "cool" Dogpatch cafe from premier chocolatier Michael Recchiuti, known for his Ferry Building kiosk; in addition to "amazing" desserts (including "standout" affogato) and chocolates paired with beer, wine and "unique" teas, it also serves savory salads, charcuterie and more, including prix fixe dinners Tuesdays–Thursdays – aficionados insist it's "worth the detour"; P.S. there's also an adjacent retail shop, Little Nib.

Chotto *Japanese* 24 | 23 | 23 | $41

Marina | 3317 Steiner St. (bet. Chestnut & Lombard Sts.) | 415-441-2223 | www.chottosf.com

This "trendy" "late-night" izakaya attracts a Marina crowd with its "innovative" yet relatively "affordable" Japanese "small bites" (e.g. "bacon-wrapped mochi") and setting with handmade lanterns and barn-wood panels; the staff is "helpful", navigating offerings that are not for the "picky or bashful" plus an "excellent assortment of sake", which along with wine and snacks, is featured during happy hour.

Chouchou ▥ *French* 19 | 16 | 20 | $43

Forest Hills | 400 Dewey Blvd. (Woodside Ave.) | 415-242-0960 | www.chouchoubistrosf.com

A "welcoming" owner and his "caring" staff contribute to the "cozy" vibe at this "friendly" French bistro "in an unlikely spot" (Forest Hills); though it's "nothing fancy" and a few confess they "wouldn't cross town" considering the "uninspiring" interior and "crowded" confines, it's still a "nice neighborhood" spot for a relatively "reasonably priced" meal capped by a "phenomenal" tart.

Chow *American* 21 | 17 | 19 | $26

Castro | 215 Church St. (bet. 15th & Market Sts.) | 415-552-2469

Park Chow *American*

Inner Sunset | 1240 Ninth Ave. (bet. Irving St. & Lincoln Way) | 415-665-9912
www.chowfoodbar.com

Those "craving" "simple" "homestyle" American fare "chow down" at this "cozy" mini-chain of "comfort food favorites" where the "varied" menu caters to "a wide range of tastes"; "quirky" decor and "efficient", "friendly hipsters" for servers make it a "kick-back", "kid-friendly" option, even if the "bustling" spots "can be noisy at times."

	FOOD	DECOR	SERVICE	COST

Chubby Noodle 🈂️Ⓜ️⇆ *Asian* ▽ 24 | 13 | 17 | $22

North Beach | Amante's | 570 Green St. (bet. Columbus Ave. & Jasper St.) | 415-361-8850 | www.thechubbynoodle.com

"The novelty" of an "Asian-inspired" "pop-up" serving out of "the back" of a North Beach "neighborhood" bar is the hook at this shop from the team behind Don Pisto's, where cognoscenti home in on "delicious" "fried chicken, garlic noodles" and other cheap eats; the unconventional setup comes complete with "old-school bartenders" offering a "plentiful selection of your favorite alcoholic beverages."

Chutney ● *Indian/Pakistani* 25 | 14 | 15 | $16

Tenderloin | 511 Jones St. (O'Farrell St.) | 415-931-5541 | www.chutneysf.com

"Looks aren't everything" say fans of this Tenderloin Indian-Pakistani, a "casual" "walk-up-and-order type" joint where you take a number and wait for "huge" servings of "comforting" fare; service is "friendly", and "considering how cheap it is", some find the decor "actually quite nice."

Citizen's Band Ⓜ️ *American* 22 | 16 | 20 | $35

SoMa | 1198 Folsom St. (8th St.) | 415-556-4901 | www.citizensbandsf.com

"Offering no shortage of hipster appeal", this SoMa "neighborhood place" decorated with "old CB radios sitting on shelves" may look "like a diner", but the chef "seriously knows what he's doing", preparing "of-the-moment" American "down-home comfort food" (like "the crystal meth of mac 'n' cheese") for moderate tabs; "tight tables" make for a squeeze, but most are sweet on the staff and "desserts from Pinkie's."

Claudine 🈂️ *French* ▽ 22 | 18 | 20 | $37

Downtown | 8 Claude Ln. (Bush St.) | 415-362-1988

Franck LeClerc (Café Claude) and chef Bridget Batson (Gitane) team up at this "chic" "mini-bistro" on FiDi's dining alley; a change to an all-day menu of classic French fare (not reflected in the scores) makes it "perfect" for a "casual meal" or a "glass of wine" at the circular bar.

Cliff House Bistro *Californian* 20 | 25 | 21 | $41

Outer Richmond | 1090 Point Lobos Ave. (El Camino Del Mar) | 415-386-3330 | www.cliffhouse.com

"Wonderful, sweeping" ocean vistas and an art deco space with "lovely high ceilings" and "vintage" memorabilia shine at this "historic" cliff-hanger in Outer Richmond; steady service and "very good" Californian fare add to the allure, but most say you really "come for the view."

Coco500 🈂️ *Californian/Mediterranean* 24 | 20 | 23 | $49

SoMa | 500 Brannan St. (4th St.) | 415-543-2222 | www.coco500.com

"Foodies" "count on" "inventive" Cal-Med fare, like fried green beans and truffled flatbread (both "absolute musts" on the dinner menu), all "delivered with panache" by "friendly, efficient" servers at this SoMa bistro from Loretta Keller; the "young, hip crowd" "can be loud during prime time", and tables are "a little too close together", but its "relaxing atmosphere" and "civilized", "modern" space help earn its "favorite" status.

Coi 🈂️Ⓜ️ *Californian/French* 27 | 26 | 27 | $228

North Beach | 373 Broadway (Montgomery St.) | 415-393-9000 | www.coirestaurant.com

Daniel Patterson's "adventurous", "exquisitely prepared" tasting menus are a "journey worth taking" assert fans of this North Beach

Californian-French, where "seasonal" ingredients stand out in a "magical" "mélange of flavors and techniques"; service is "impeccable" while the "minimal" space is an "oasis of calm", and though it may be "outrageously expensive", many recommend it for a "special occasion" or just to "have your food mind blown."

Colibrí Mexican   23 | 19 | 21 | $37
Downtown | 438 Geary St. (bet. Mason & Taylor Sts.) | 415-440-2737 |
www.colibrimexicanbistro.com

"Not your typical Mexican restaurant", this "lively" Downtowner "manages to modernize" south-of-the-border bites with a "creative" menu of "upscale" "regional" dishes; "fantastic" guacamole is made "to your specifications", and "complex" cocktails are concocted from an "impressive" tequila selection (the "Macho Margarita" is "an epiphany"), and while service varies from "quick" to "slow", it's "always friendly."

Commonwealth American   26 | 20 | 24 | $63
Mission | 2224 Mission St. (18th St.) | 415-355-1500 |
www.commonwealthsf.com

"Some of the most thrilling food in the city" can be found at this "progressive" Mission New American, where the "wildly inventive", "beautifully composed" fare is available à la carte or in "highly recommended" tasting menus that foodies consider a "bargain" for the "quality" (plus $10 of each goes to charity); its "austere, industrial" digs may not inspire the same praise, but with "thoughtful wine pairings and "friendly, enthusiastic" service, most barely notice – and "get this, they have their own parking lot."

Contigo ⓂＭ Spanish   25 | 21 | 23 | $49
Noe Valley | 1320 Castro St. (24th St.) | 415-285-0250 | www.contigosf.com
"Go with a group of adventuresome eaters" or a hot "date" to this "convivial" Noe Valley "gem" turning out "tasty" "Catalonian-by-way-of-Californian tapas" (think "fatty slices" of imported jamón and "locally sourced" produce) and "great Spanish wines" shuttled by a "warm" staff; it's not cheap, and the "tiny" "modern" digs get "hectic", but regulars love to "sit at the bar" or retreat to the "sweet" garden patio.

NEW Coqueta Spanish   - | - | - | E
Embarcadero | Pier 5 (Washington St.) | 415-704-8866 |
www.coquetasf.com

Perched on the edge of Pier 5 with the San Francisco waterfront at its feet, this convival eatery from celebrity chef Michael Chiarello (Bottega) showcases contemporary regional Spanish tapas and *raciones* (family-style large plates); the marble-topped bar focuses on artisanal Spanish and Californian wines, loads of sherry and molecular cocktails such as frozen sangria, plus a variety of housemade gin and tonics, all of which can also be enjoyed in the glass-enclosed terrace or alfresco on the patio along the Embarcadero.

NEW The Corner Store American   ▽ 22 | 17 | 18 | $33
Laurel Heights | 5 Masonic Ave. (bet. Anza St. & Geary Blvd.) |
415-359-1800 | www.thecornerstore-sf.com

"Your neighborhood burger joint in a neighborhood that didn't have one", this "happenin'" new Laurel Heights spot has a "New York vibe" to go with the "very good", midpriced American food, "unique sodas" and "great beers"; the crowd's "young and hip" and the staff lends a "personal touch", making it a natural for a "casual meal."

Cotogna *Italian*   26 | 22 | 23 | $53

Downtown | 490 Pacific St. (Montgomery St.) | 415-775-8508 | www.cotognasf.com

Lindsay and Michael Tusk "elevate classic Italian dishes to another level" at the "popular" Downtown "little" sibling of next-door Quince, serving "exquisite" pastas, "mouthwatering" wood-fired pizzas and more, including "brilliant" family-style Sunday dinners, "at a fraction of the price" of its elder (and backed by an "affordable wine list"); a "gracious" staff works the "warm", "rustic" space, which can get "noisy", and it's become so "popular" that some say "good luck getting a reservation."

Crab House *Seafood*   23 | 19 | 20 | $41

Fisherman's Wharf | 203 Pier 39 (The Embarcadero) | 415-434-2722 | www.crabhouse39.com

"If you like crab or lobster" some say "look no further" than this "busy" Fisherman's Wharf seafooder, where the "delicious" crustaceans find their way into the signature garlic sauce as well as soups, salads and sandwiches; "friendly" servers work the "diner-style" space bedecked in seafaring paraphernalia, with "nice views of the bay" as a backdrop, and while a few find it "expensive" and "touristy", others tout it as their "favorite place to bring out-of-town guests."

Craftsman & Wolves *Bakery/Sandwiches*   25 | 24 | 23 | $15

Mission | 746 Valencia St. (bet. 18th & 19th Sts.) | 415-913-7713 | www.craftsman-wolves.com

Fans of this über-modern Valencia Street patisserie from William Werner "love" its "bold", "creative" and "beautiful" sweet and savory treats, including the "must-get" Rebel Within (a muffin with a sausage and egg center), which are lit and displayed like jewels; the slick space decked in "beautiful natural wood" has become a "hangout" for "stylish hipsters", and while some find it "expensive", most agree it's "given pastry a new reputation"; P.S. it also serves afternoon tea on weekdays (reserve a day ahead) and has an expanded savory menu and operating hours.

Credo *Italian*   20 | 19 | 22 | $38

Downtown | 360 Pine St. (bet. Leidesdorff & Montgomery Sts.) | 415-693-0360 | www.credosf.com

"Fun quotes all over the walls" and "trendy" "modern decor" create an "inviting environment" at this "usually busy" go-to on the Downtown dining scene; the "very personable staff" serves "consistently excellent Italian dishes" and "solid cocktails", and since "prices are reasonable for the Financial District", devotees who "have never been disappointed" declare they are "definitely coming back."

Crustacean *Asian/Vietnamese*   25 | 20 | 21 | $59

Polk Gulch | 1475 Polk St. (California St.) | 415-776-2722 | www.anfamily.com

"Home of the exalted roasted Dungeness crab and out-of-this-world garlic noodles" that are "worth having bad breath for a week", this Vietnamese-Asian fusioner on Polk Street "never fails" with its "finger-lickin'" fare "exploding with flavor"; it's a somewhat "fancy place with cloth tablecloths", but that doesn't stop "friendly" servers from "strapping a bib" on "crabaholics", who easily overlook "expensive" tabs.

Cupola Pizzeria *Italian/Pizza*   21 | 19 | 19 | $33

Downtown | Westfield San Francisco Ctr. | 845 Market St., 4th fl. (bet. 4th & 5th Sts.) | 415-896-5600 | www.cupolasf.com

Its "high-tech decor" "makes you feel like you're in Milan", but the "top-notch" "thin-crust pizzas" blistered in an "imported" oven are "authentic" "Naples-style" at this somewhat "pricey" "sleeper" under the Westfield Centre's dome; the "innovative" Italian eats and "personable service" are a "cut above", though aesthetes admit there's "no escaping" that you're "eating in a mall."

NEW Curry Up Now *Indian*   ∇ 21 | 12 | 16 | $14

Mission | 659 Valencia St. (18th St.) | 415-735-3667 | www.curryupnow.com

See review in South of San Francisco Directory.

NEW Dandelion Chocolate Ⓜ *Dessert*   - | - | - | I

Mission | 740 Valencia St. (19th St.) | 415-349-0942 | www.dandelionchocolate.com

Chocoholics can get a peek of the entire chocolate-making process at this Mission factory and cafe set in a former auto repair shop, before picking up some single-origin-bean bars or sampling daily pastries including brownies, hazelnut praline truffles and chocolate cake with Moroccan spices; several types of hot and iced chocolate drinks and smoothies made from the fruit of the cacao tree are also available.

NEW Dante's Table Ⓜ *Italian*   - | - | - | M

Castro | 544 Castro St. (bet. 18th & 19th Sts.) | 415-529-2797 | www.dantestable.com

Classic, casual Italian fare headlines this cozy Castro restaurant headed up by the team behind nearby Poesia, including reasonably priced salads, panini, pizzas and pastas, as well as specialty cocktails, wine and beer; Dante quotes and splashy murals by a San Francisco painter cover the walls in the main dining area, which includes plenty of tables and a long copper-topped bar (patio seating is planned).

Dante's Weird Fish *Seafood*   ∇ 22 | 18 | 20 | $29

Mission | 2193 Mission St. (18th St.) | 415-863-4744 | www.weirdfishsf.com

"Weird in a good way" is how Mission pescatarians sum up this "cute" seafooder whose original owner returned with his "fun and fresh" 'Seven Daily Sins' menu of daily fish specials, plus fish 'n' chips, tacos, vegan entrees and other "well-prepared" dishes; "lovely" service in a space with Galapagos-green walls add to the "character and charm."

Delarosa ◗ *Italian*   21 | 18 | 19 | $31

Marina | 2175 Chestnut St. (bet. Pierce & Steiner Sts.) | 415-673-7100 | www.delarosasf.com

"Always buzzing" with a "good-looking" "throng", this "happening" Marina Italian earns "brownie points" for its "affordable" menu of "scrumptious" "small plates" plus "super-thin" Roman pizzas (when in "doubt, just add burrata"); some aren't "big fans" of the mostly "communal tables" (either "fun or awkward, depending on the company"),

FOOD   DECOR   SERVICE   COST

but supporters are sold on the "young, fun staff", "creative" cocktails and "late-night" hours (until 1 AM).

Delfina *Italian*   26 | 20 | 23 | $48

Mission | 3621 18th St. (bet. Dolores & Guerrero Sts.) | 415-552-4055 | www.delfinasf.com

"After all these years" (since 1998), Craig and Anne Stoll's "sterling" Northern Italian in the Mission is "still the standard" for "simple and perfectly cooked" pastas and other "unfussy" but "divine" mains, matched by an "interesting wine list" and "polite", "real" service; there's a "hip crowd", but "waits" for the "too-close" tables "can be a drag", which is why those without a reservation often end up "seated at the bar" – or at their "amazing" pizzeria next door.

Deli Board *Deli*   ∇ 23 | 12 | 19 | $13

SoMa | 1058 Folsom St. (bet. Moss & Russ Sts.) | 415-552-7687 | www.deliboardsf.com

NEW 1058 Hoagie *Sandwiches*

SoMa | 180 Seventh St. (bet. Howard & Natoma Sts.) | 415-552-8984 | www.1058hoagie.com

"Fantastic handmade sandwiches" are the name of the game at this SoMa deli known for "amazing fixin's" and "some unique options" along with your traditional roast beef or turkey; service is "great" too – just be warned seating is limited and it closes after lunch, as does its mostly take-out sibling, 1058 Hoagie.

Delica *Japanese*   25 | 15 | 17 | $22

Embarcadero | Ferry Building Mktpl. | 1 Ferry Bldg. (The Embarcadero) | 415-834-0344 | www.delicasf.com

At lunch a "Japanese deli" with "lovely" bento boxes and "interesting salads" to "grab and go", come evening this "unassuming" Embarcadero spot offers diners "an unusual selection" of sushi that goes "beyond the California roll"; the staff is "helpful" and it makes for a "nice change of pace", though some say it's a little pricey for "small" portions.

Destino *Nuevo Latino*   22 | 20 | 21 | $42

Castro | 1815 Market St. (Pearl St.) | 415-552-4451 | www.destinosf.com

A "favorite spot for a celebration", this "warm" and "welcoming" Nuevo Latino bistro coddles the Castro crowd with "superb" ceviche and "delicious" South American tapas plus "wonderful wines" and cocktails that "perfectly" "complement" the meal; "super-patient" servers happily explain the "creative" menu, but if you want to hear them, opt for an "early meal", before the "happy" "young" crowd creates an "ear-splitting" din (if they're not at sibling Pisco Lounge next door).

Dixie *Southern*   ∇ 20 | 23 | 22 | $56

Presidio | 1 Letterman Dr. (Lyon St.) | 415-829-3363 | www.sfdixie.com

For "fine dining" in a "beautiful park setting with views of the Palace of Fine Arts", fans tout this "comfortable" American serving "sophisticated", "flavorful" Southern cuisine from chef Joseph Humphrey (ex Meadowood); the interior of the former Presidio barrack is "beautiful" and service is "prompt and courteous", and while a few grouse about "tiny portions and big prices", others tout the "incredible" five-course tasting menu as a "bargain."

Domo Sushi *Japanese* ▽ 27 | 20 | 22 | $30

Hayes Valley | 511 Laguna St. (Linden St.) | 415-861-8887 | www.domosf.com

This "intimate" Hayes Valley Japanese is so "teeny-tiny", "you can watch the chefs at work" as they prepare "exquisitely crafted sushi" and "put their own spin on things" with "surprising" "specialty rolls"; the "fabulous" cuts set "a new standard" say fervent locals, who also appreciate the "super-friendly staff" and "reasonable prices."

Don Pisto's ● Ⓜ *Mexican* 25 | 20 | 21 | $28

North Beach | 510 Union St. (Grant Ave.) | 415-395-0939 | www.donpistos.com

The Mexican fare at this North Beach spot is "as good as anything in the Mission" declare fans of its "authentic flavors" and "excellent" takes on street food; the "lovely" space with exposed-brick walls is overseen by a "pleasant" "hipster" staff, though there are sometimes "crazy waits" for weekend brunch, thanks in part to "bottomless mimosas and sangria."

Dosa *Indian* 23 | 23 | 21 | $39

Mission | 995 Valencia St. (21st St.) | 415-642-3672
Upper Fillmore | 1700 Fillmore St. (Post St.) | 415-441-3672
www.dosasf.com

Indian "as you've never experienced it" distinguishes this "moderately priced" duo delivering "innovative" fare, like "out-of-this-world" dosas "the size of your head" and other plates that "explode with flavor" (and so much spice you may want "lots of water" handy), all backed by "darn good cocktails"; Fillmore is "swankier", with "beautiful soaring ceilings" and "sultry" decor, while the Mission space is "more cramped", but both attract a "cult following" – luckily service remains "cordial despite being slammed", leaving most "everybody happy."

Dynamo Donut & Coffee Ⓜ *Coffeehouse* 25 | 15 | 20 | $8

🆕 **Marina** | 110 Yacht Rd. (Marina Blvd.) | no phone
Mission | 2760 24th St. (bet. Hampshire & York Sts.) | 415-920-1978
www.dynamodonut.com

"Insanely tasty" donuts, including the "favorite" maple bacon (a "no-brainer"), are "too good to be true" at this petite Mission bakery and its Marina kiosk, a "hipster destination" for "unsurpassed" sweets offered in "innovative", "daring combos", plus "strong, delicious" coffee poured by the "friendliest crew"; sure, it's "rather pricey", but fans swear "all hesitation melts away" after one bite.

E&O Asian Kitchen *Asian* 21 | 22 | 20 | $39
(fka E&O Trading Co.)

Downtown | 314 Sutter St. (bet. Grant Ave. & Stockton St.) | 415-693-0303 | www.eosanfrancisco.com

"One of the original 'fusion' restaurants – and still original", this recently refreshed, "cavernous" Pan-Asian "paradise" off Union Square continues to pack them in, especially for "tasty" "business lunches" or "large-group" dinners over shared "small plates" or entrees; it's a bit "pricey" for some, though "happy-hour" deals are popular in the dining room or "scene-y" downstairs lounge that serves "fantastic" "exotic cocktails."

	FOOD	DECOR	SERVICE	COST

Ebisu ⓜ *Japanese*

24 | 18 | 20 | $37

Inner Sunset | 1283 Ninth Ave. (Irving St.) | 415-566-1770 | www.ebisusushi.com

A "neighborhood place with citywide appeal", this "popular" longtime Inner Sunset Japanese (with a SFO offshoot) "still has them lining up for more" with a "diverse" array of "consistently high-quality" fare, from "expertly crafted rolls" and "delicate, artful sushi" to other "interesting" apps and grilled items, all at "reasonable" prices; "cheerful" servers work the "small", "family-friendly" digs, though the wait can sometimes be "unforgiving."

Eiji ⓜ *Japanese*

25 | 16 | 21 | $37

Castro | 317 Sanchez St. (bet. 16th & 17th Sts.) | 415-558-8149

The fish is "extremely fresh and flavorful", and the "nigiri melts in your mouth" at this midpriced Castro sushi bar, but some Japanophiles say it's the "authentic" "non-sushi dishes that shine", including the "sublime" "housemade" *oboro* ('silky tofu') "made right at your table" as well as the strawberry mochi (a "must"); you can "expect to wait awhile" for one of the "few tables" in the "cozy, intimate" space – but a "gracious", "delicious" experience ("like being in Japan") awaits.

El Farolito ● *Mexican*

23 | 8 | 17 | $10

Mission | 2779 Mission St. (bet. 23rd & 24th Sts.) | 415-824-7877
Mission | 2950 24th St. (Alabama St.) | 415-641-0758
Mission | 4817 Mission St. (Onondaga Ave.) | 415-337-5500
www.elfarolitoinc.com

"You'll never leave hungry" from these "authentic" taquerias that "don't skimp on anything", turning out "inexpensive" Mexican "comfort" food in "large portions", including "big, fat, juicy burritos"; the decor is "divey" and service can be a bit "rough around the edges", but "lines out the door at dinnertime" are "good indicators" that the grub "outweighs" all else; P.S. the Mission locales are "open late for post-drinking sustenance in the wee hours."

El Huarache Loco ⓜ🚭 *Mexican*

▽ 21 | 13 | 18 | $12

Bernal Heights | Alemany Farmers Mkt. | 100 Alemany Blvd. (Peralta Ave.) | 415-572-6832 | www.huaracheloco.com
See review in North of San Francisco Directory.

Elite Cafe *American*

20 | 20 | 19 | $42

Pacific Heights | 2049 Fillmore St. (bet. California & Pine Sts.) | 415-673-5483 | www.theelitecafe.com

"New Orleans–inspired dishes" including "obscenely delicious" biscuits are "the real deal" at this "wonderfully old-fashioned" American where "high-backed" booths are a "romantic" option; perhaps it's "a little pricey" ("this is Pac Heights" after all) and often "crowded", but fans affirm the "hospitality is worthy of the Big Easy."

Eliza's *Chinese*

22 | 17 | 16 | $24

Pacific Heights | 2877 California St. (bet. Broderick & Divisadero Sts.) | 415-621-4819

"Generous portions" of "fresh-tasting" Chinese chow are "elegantly presented" at this Pacific Heights Hunan haunt, where "quality ingredients" add up to an "excellent" meal; the "lovely" modern setting and "reasonable" prices make it "a favorite for those in the know" (lunch is an especially "amazing deal"), but idlers opt for "takeout" to avoid "the bum's rush" from the "fast" waiters.

Ella's American

| 21 | 15 | 18 | $25 |

Presidio Heights | 500 Presidio Ave. (California St.) | 415-441-5669 | www.ellassanfrancisco.com

Perfect for an "inventive" weekday breakfast or "fantastic" weekend brunch, "if not for a diet", this "homey" Presidio Heights cafe proffers "huge portions" of "crazy-good baked goods" and other "tasty" American "comfort food"; it's "totally worth the wait" gush groupies, but the less-impressed aren't "sure what all the fuss – and the gargantuan lines – are about"; P.S. no dinner.

El Metate Mexican

| 23 | 17 | 18 | $12 |

Mission | 2406 Bryant St. (22nd St.) | 415-641-7209

"Bargain bites" come in the form of "authentic, flavorful" *comida*, including "well-put-together" burritos that "rock", at this Mission Mexican; service is "quick" in the "sunny, mellow" digs, and there are "outdoor tables too."

Emmy's Spaghetti Shack Italian

| 21 | 18 | 19 | $24 |

Bernal Heights | 18 Virginia Ave. (bet. 29th & 30th Sts.) | 415-206-2086 | www.emmysspaghettishack.com

"Heaping helpings" of "steaming" spaghetti topped by "awesome" "giant" meatballs headline the "down-home" Italian eats "for cheap" at this "loud" Bernal Heights "hipster" haven with "creative", "funky" decor; the plates aren't "particularly special" say some, who declare they could "do better at home", but "super-friendly" servers and "stellar" cocktails contribute to the "fun" vibe.

Emporio Rulli Dessert/Italian

| 22 | 20 | 18 | $20 |

(aka Emporio Rulli Italian Caffe at Union Square)

Downtown | Union Sq. Pavilion | 333 Stockton St. (bet. Geary & Post Sts.) | 415-433-1122 | www.rulli.com

See review in North of San Francisco Directory.

Epic Roasthouse Steak

| 22 | 25 | 21 | $71 |

Embarcadero | 369 The Embarcadero (bet. Folsom & Harrison Sts.) | 415-369-9955 | www.epicroasthousesf.com

A "haven for carnivores", this Embarcadero steakhouse offers "dinosaur-size cuts" and a "deep wine list" (plus a "standout" brunch) in "beautiful" waterfront environs with "breathtaking" "panoramic views" of the Bay Bridge; service is "attentive", and if tabs are "expensive", "sitting outside on a pretty day is magical", and the "lively" (and comparatively "cheap") happy hour and "beer-burger-brownie deal at the upstairs bar can't be beat."

Eric's Chinese

| 22 | 16 | 18 | $23 |

Noe Valley | 1500 Church St. (27th St.) | 415-282-0919 | www.ericrestaurant.com

For "flavorful", if "somewhat Americanized Chinese" "without the hassle of Chinatown", Noe Valley-ites head to this "ever-popular" neighborhood "go-to"; it's "not fancy", but "welcoming" staffers, "reasonable" prices and a "homey" feel make it "just perfect" for a "low-key" meal.

Esperpento *Spanish*

22 | 16 | 18 | $26

Mission | 3295 22nd St. (Valencia St.) | 415-282-8867 |
www.esperpentorestaurant.com

"Authentic tapas", "killer paella" and "delicious sangria" "remind" traveler types "of Spain" at this "cozy" Mission "hole-in-the-wall"; the "colorful" space is a "little shabby", but "mostly friendly" service, "affordable prices" and a "lively atmosphere" ensure many "come back."

Espetus Churrascaria *Brazilian*

24 | 21 | 23 | $71

(aka Espetus Churrascaria Brazilian Steakhouse)

Hayes Valley | 1686 Market St. (Gough St.) | 415-552-8792 |
www.espetus.com

"Unapologetic" carnivores "with an endless appetite" "fast during the day" then "wear big clothes" to these "pretty pricey" Brazilian churrascarias in Hayes Valley and San Mateo; there's a "bountiful" buffet of "salads and side dishes", but beef buffs know not to "load up" before the "endless parade" of "delicious" "meat, meat and more meat" "served right off the skewer" by the "handsome" "wandering" staff.

Eureka Restaurant & Lounge *American*

21 | 19 | 21 | $41

Castro | 4063 18th St. (bet. Castro & Hartford Sts.) | 415-431-6000 |
www.eurekarestaurant.com

Southern style and "influences from New Orleans" "jazz up" the "upscale" New American "home cooking" at this "lively" Castro bistro with a "fabulous upstairs lounge" ("ask for a table" "by the window"); "cheerful", "attentive" servers seal its status as a "solid" spot "for a romantic date or cozy dinner with friends", and it even has an "upscale bar to boot."

NEW Fable M *American*

- | - | - | M

Castro | 558 Castro St. (bet. 18th & 19th Sts.) | 415-590-2404 |
www.fablesf.com

Expect an affordable menu of classics with a twist at this upstart sit-down restaurant in the Castro, including the likes of crisp-skinned chicken breast with butternut squash; the cozy interior takes its cues from storybooks, with playful antler chandeliers and bright tiles to mirrored walls with whimsical animal figures.

Fang *Chinese*

22 | 19 | 18 | $34

SoMa | 660 Howard St. (bet. New Montgomery & 3rd Sts.) | 415-777-8568 |
www.fangrestaurant.com

"Forgo the menu" and "put yourself" in owner "Peter Fang's hands" at this more "upscale" SoMa sibling of the "long-standing" House of Nanking; "you won't be disappointed" by the "large portions" of mid-priced "modern" Chinese chow, even if service can be "a bit stoic" – and at least you "don't have to wait on line" like at the Chinatown original.

Farallon *Seafood*

25 | 27 | 25 | $69

Downtown | 450 Post St. (bet. Mason & Powell Sts.) | 415-956-6969 |
www.farallonrestaurant.com

"Make sure you sit in the main dining room" to soak in the "weird and wonderful" undersea decor at this "bustling" Downtown seafooder; service is on par with the "excellent" food, and though dinner (especially with wine) "is not cheap", many feel such "grand dining" lives up to the tabs.

	FOOD	DECOR	SERVICE	COST

Farina Foccaccia & Cucina Italiana *Italian* | 22 | 21 | 20 | $59

Mission | 3560 18th St. (Dearborn St.) | 415-565-0360 | www.farina-foods.com

For "authentic Italian like your grandmother made (if she were from Liguria)", patrons point to this "hip" Mission hang turning out "deliciously done" pastas and "world-champion pesto" in a modern, "thoughtfully" decorated space with an "upbeat atmosphere"; some might niggle over "uneven" service and "noisy" conditions, and say it's "overpriced for what you get", but it's "usually very busy" nonetheless.

Farina Pizza & Cucina Italiana *Italian/Pizza* | ∇ 20 | 18 | 15 | $36

Mission | 700 Valencia St. (18th St.) | 415-565-1900 | www.farina-foods.com

"Learn what Italian pizza is about" at this Farina offshoot in the Mission slinging "authentic" Neapolitan pies (by a native pizzaiolo) and other dishes in a "casual", attractive setting with white-leather stools and a marble bar; on the downside, service gets mixed marks and some find it "a little pricey for pizza."

Farmerbrown Ⓜ *Soul Food* | 21 | 16 | 18 | $28

Tenderloin | Hotel Metropolis | 25 Mason St. (Turk St.) | 415-409-3276 | www.farmerbrownsf.com

Farmerbrown's Little Skillet ⌖ *Soul Food*

SoMa | 360 Ritch St. (bet. 3rd & 4th Sts.) | 415-777-2777 | www.littleskilletsf.com

Southern comfort fare "with all the trimmings" comes in "big portions" at this Tenderloin soul fooder where the likes of "amazing" chicken and waffles and a "weekend brunch buffet" plus "great cocktails" are delivered with "unrushed" service in a "hip and artsy atmosphere"; the SoMa take-out counter is expanding next door and will be offering sit-down dining.

Fatted Calf *Sandwiches* | 26 | 16 | 22 | $20

Embarcadero | Ferry Building Mktpl. | 1 Ferry Bldg. (The Embarcadero) | no phone Ⓢ Ⓜ
Hayes Valley | 320 Fell St. (Gough St.) | 415-400-5614
www.fattedcalf.com

"More of a specialty deli" and "high-end butcher shop" "than a restaurant" (get takeaway or settle for a seat on a bench), this "Valhalla of cured meats" sells "artisanal sandwiches" stuffed with "sublime" charcuterie, "to-die-for" meatloaf and more; "friendly" staffers are "extremely knowledgeable" about the "sustainably raised" fare, and added appeal comes from Butcher Happy Hours Wednesdays in Hayes Valley and the first Thursday of the month in Napa; P.S. it's also at the Ferry Plaza Farmer's Market Saturdays 7:30 AM-2 PM.

Ferry Plaza Seafoods Ⓜ *Seafood* | 22 | 18 | 19 | $32

Embarcadero | Ferry Building Mktpl. | 1 Ferry Bldg. (The Embarcadero) | 415-274-2561 | www.ferryplazaseafood.com

Extroverts who enjoy "interaction" with the "wonderful staff" "love sitting at the bar" at this "lively" Ferry Building seafooder, washing down their "impeccably fresh" fish, "spirit-warming chowder" and raw-bar bites with "delicious" wines at lunch and "early" dinners; the tab easily "adds up", but you can't put a price on the "unparalleled vista of the Bay Bridge."

	FOOD	DECOR	SERVICE	COST

15 Romolo ● *American*   22 | 21 | 21 | $26

North Beach | Basque Hotel | 15 Romolo Pl. (B'way) | 415-398-1359 | www.15romolo.com

Dispensing "killer cocktails" and "quirky" American bar bites, this "hidden", back-alley "escape" from "touristy" North Beach attracts a "late-night" crowd, while luring daytime diners with an "excellent" weekend "Punch-Drunk Brunch"; though service "takes awhile" and there can be "quite the scene", the "Barbary Coast" "saloon vibe", "great jukebox" and reasonable prices appeal when "with friends" or on "a first date."

Fifth Floor Ⓢ Ⓜ *American/French*   24 | 23 | 24 | $85

SoMa | Hotel Palomar | 12 Fourth St., 5th fl. (Market St.) | 415-348-1555 | www.fifthfloorrestaurant.com

A "special-occasion place" "hidden" away in SoMa's Hotel Palomar, this New French–New American is "firing on all cylinders" under chef David Bazirgan (ex Chez Papa Resto), who presents "creative", "complicated food prepared perfectly" and complemented by an "unparalleled" wine list; "friendly, well-informed" service and an "elegant setting" with "comfortable seating" further justify "expensive" prices, though shallower pockets hit the "busy bar" for the "burgers, bourbon and brew deal."

54 Mint Ⓢ *Italian*   22 | 21 | 21 | $43

SoMa | 16 Mint Plaza (Jessie St.) | 415-543-5100 | www.54mint.com

"Old-school Italian charm meets new-school decor" at this "real-deal" trattoria where "authentic", "elegant" Sicilian specialties and an "intriguing" wine list result in many a "happy camper"; hidden on a "tiny alley" in SoMa, the "jumping" joint may be a "bit on the loud side", but the "welcoming" owners and "warm" servers "take care of you like family", and there's also terrace and wine-cellar seating.

Firefly *Eclectic*   24 | 21 | 24 | $45

Noe Valley | 4288 24th St. (Douglass St.) | 415-821-7652 | www.fireflyrestaurant.com

A "longtime neighborhood favorite", Brad Levy's Noe Valley Eclectic still "enchants" with an "ever-changing menu" of "masterfully prepared" "upscale comfort food" – including fried chicken and gluten-free options – that's "inventive but not overwrought"; "friendly, unpretentious service" and a "charming", "homey" setting further explain how it "gets all the details right", and though not cheap, fans deem it an "excellent value" (especially its "bargain" Sunday–Thursday prix fixe).

5A5 Steak Lounge *Steak*   23 | 23 | 22 | $64

Downtown | 244 Jackson St. (Battery St.) | 415-989-2539 | www.5a5stk.com

Packing "a very trendy punch", this "modern" Downtown steakhouse "lounge" attracts a "cool" crowd with its "chic" "retro" design as a backdrop for "imaginative" starters and "real-deal" cuts of beef; "prompt", "accommodating" service and "killer cocktails" soften the sting of potentially "spending a small fortune."

Fleur de Lys Ⓢ Ⓜ *Californian/French*   27 | 26 | 27 | $101

Downtown | 777 Sutter St. (bet. Jones & Taylor Sts.) | 415-673-7779 | www.hubertkeller.com

Hubert Keller remains "at the top of the game" at his Downtown "flagship" presenting "outstanding" "three-hour"-long French-Californian prix fixes with "perfectly" paired wines in meals that display the "hands of a master"; patrons say "there's no more romantic" or prettier setting than the tented room where guests are "treated like kings and queens" "from reception to departure", and while you'll "pay for every bit of it", it remains the "standard" bearer for that "dream night out for any major celebration."

Florio *French/Italian*　　　21 | 21 | 21 | $46

Pacific Heights | 1915 Fillmore St. (bet. Bush & Pine Sts.) | 415-775-4300 | www.floriosf.com

"Comforting" French-Italian "brasserie cuisine" and "welcoming" service result in "clean plates and happy campers all around" at this Pacific Heights bistro; a "Manhattanish atmosphere" and "great bar scene" also help make it a "neighborhood favorite."

Flour + Water *Italian*　　　26 | 20 | 22 | $49

Mission | 2401 Harrison St. (20th St.) | 415-826-7000 | www.flourandwater.com

"Careful preparation" goes into the "amazing" wood-fired pies and "incredible", high-end pastas by chef Thomas McNaughton at this "lively", "industrial-chic" Italian standout in the Mission; quarters are "tight", the music's "loud" and the "difficult" rezzies and waits discourage some, but others say "go early on a slow night" and you might have a shot.

Foreign Cinema *Californian/Mediterranean*　　　24 | 25 | 23 | $49

Mission | 2534 Mission St. (bet. 21st & 22nd Sts.) | 415-648-7600 | www.foreigncinema.com

"Still packing them in", this "ultrahip" "Mission mecca" offers "inventive" Cal-Med fare in a "beautiful" courtyard where you can "enjoy the stars, both above and foreign" in films projected on the wall; despite the "gimmick", it "doesn't disappoint", whether for "strong cocktails" alfresco or dining "by the fire" inside, and the "cool" setting and "super" service make the experience "even more memorable"; P.S. "don't miss" brunch with "gourmet Pop Tarts."

4505 Meats Ⓜ *Hot Dogs*　　　26 | 16 | 21 | $15

Embarcadero | Ferry Building Mktpl. | 1 Ferry Bldg. (The Embarcadero) | 415-255-3094 🅿🚲

NEW Mission | 1909 Mission St. (15th St.) | 415-525-4239 www.4505meats.com

Butcher-in-chief Ryan Farr's Ferry Building "meat lover's mecca" and new large Mission outpost deliver the likes of "bacon-studded hot dogs" and "addictive" chicharrones that satisfy "anything a carnivore is craving"; there's "no seating" and tabs are relatively high, but "service is great" – just "come early to avoid the crowds"; P.S. the Ferry Building branch, which also offers "killer" burgers, is open Thursdays and Saturdays only, until 2 PM, while the butcher shop is closed Tuesdays.

Frances Ⓜ *Californian*　　　27 | 20 | 25 | $58

Castro | 3870 17th St. (Pond St.) | 415-621-3870 | www.frances-sf.com

"No wonder" reservations are "tough to score" say devotees of this "unassuming" "farm-to-table" Californian in the Castro where Melissa Perello "always does something spectacular" with her "fresh ingredients"; sure, there are "too many tables" crammed into "too small a space" (plus a few seats at the bar), but an "always attentive" staff and innovative "pay-what-you-drink" (per ounce) wine program offering "amazing deals" keep this "hidden gem" "everyone's favorite neighborhood restaurant."

Frascati *Californian/Mediterranean* | 25 | 20 | 23 | $55 |

Russian Hill | 1901 Hyde St. (Green St.) | 415-928-1406 | www.frascatisf.com

Atop "lovely Russian Hill" where you can "watch the cable cars pass by", this "intimate" "date-night" destination "couldn't be more charming" say admirers of the "well-conceived" Cal-Med menu and "thoughtfully curated" wine list; an "attentive" staff contributes to the "cozy" environment, so most give a pass to seating that's "a bit tight" and parking that's "a drag."

Fresca *Peruvian* | 22 | 18 | 19 | $36 |

West Portal | 24 W. Portal Ave. (Ulloa St.) | 415-759-8087
Noe Valley | 3945 24th St. (bet. Noe & Sanchez Sts.) | 415-695-0549
Upper Fillmore | 2114 Fillmore St. (Clay St.) | 415-447-2668
www.frescasf.com

"Save the plane fare to Lima" and get the "real Peruvian deal" at this "casual", "often crowded" trio, where "spectacular" ceviche shares the menu with "perfectly cooked seafood", "comforting lomo saltado" and "sweet" and "fruity" sangria; dishes are "reasonably priced" (especially during the "fabulous" weekend brunch) even if service is sometimes "slow."

Fringale *French/Spanish* | 25 | 19 | 23 | $52 |

SoMa | 570 Fourth St. (bet. Brannan & Freelon Sts.) | 415-543-0573 | www.fringalesf.com

Each "lovingly prepared" "dish is better than the one before" at this "classic" Gallic-Basque bistro "that will delight even the pickiest" Parisian with its "bang for the price" and "fantastic" wine list; "the only downside" is "snugly placed" tables squeezed into a SoMa space that's "a wee bit too small", but the "endlessly gracious" "French-speaking staff" establishes a "warm and welcoming" vibe.

Frjtz Fries *Belgian* | 20 | 17 | 16 | $17 |

Mission | 590 Valencia St. (17th St.) | 415-863-8272 | www.frjtzfries.com

"Delicious" frites with an "amazing sauce variety", plus bowls of mussels and "super-filling" crêpes add up to the "perfect balance of food and value" at this casual Belgian in the Mission; despite lags in service, it has a "great vibe" and opens early, so it's a "nice place for breakfast" too.

The Front Porch *Caribbean/Southern* | 22 | 17 | 19 | $33 |

Bernal Heights | 65 29th St. (bet. Mission St. & San Jose Ave.) | 415-695-7800 | www.thefrontporchsf.com

"When you crave real comfort food", this midpriced Southern–Cajun-Creole in Bernal Heights fits the bill, turning out "hipster soul food", like "legit" fried chicken and "spicy shrimp and grits", all served by "the friendliest" staff; sure, it can be a "little cramped", and "low tin ceilings and lots of talkative people don't go well together", but the "cheerful" vibe helps distract, and many leave with "no complaints"; P.S. nearby spin-off Rock Bar is at 80 29th Street.

	FOOD	DECOR	SERVICE	COST

Gamine *French*

24 | 17 | 23 | $40

Cow Hollow | 2223 Union St. (bet. Fillmore & Steiner Sts.) | 415-771-7771 | www.gaminesf.com

Regulars relish the "happy, easygoing vibe" at this "always bustling neighborhood bistro" serving up "enjoyable", "good-value" French food and wine in a "tiny" Cow Hollow locale; the "welcoming" owner may just "charm your socks off", though look out if you don't like a "loud" scene; P.S. reservations only accepted for six or more.

Garçon   *French*

22 | 19 | 21 | $45

Mission | 1101 Valencia St. (22nd St.) | 415-401-8959 | www.garconsf.com

It "feels like you're in a restaurant in Paris" sigh fans of this "quaint", not-too-expensive Mission bistro "with a West Coast twist"; a few find the menu "relatively standard", but "neighborhood" regulars return often for the "authentic" dishes, "divine" cocktails and "lively" atmosphere where "friendly French service" is "not an oxymoron."

Garden Court *Californian*

22 | 28 | 23 | $55

Downtown | Palace Hotel | 2 New Montgomery St. (Market St.) | 415-546-5089 | www.sfpalace.com

"Ooh-la-la" say those who love this "gorgeous" Californian in the Palace Hotel delivering one of the "most luxurious" Sunday brunches in town, as well as daily breakfast, lunch and Saturday afternoon tea; some balk at the prices and advise "it's not the finest dining experience", but "you may not notice as it's so romantic."

Garibaldis *Californian/Mediterranean*

24 | 22 | 23 | $50

Presidio Heights | 347 Presidio Ave. (bet. Clay & Sacramento Sts.) | 415-563-8841 | www.garibaldisrestaurant.com

"Always packed" with "well-heeled" Presidio Heights patrons, who "start the night" with a "fabulous" cocktail or "excellent" wine, this "clubby" "neighborhood institution" serves a "broad" "seasonal" menu of "creative" Cal-Med creations; it's "pretty pricey" say some, and "too noisy at times", but "expert" servers ("attentive without being overbearing") and "chic" "modern" decor add to the "understated elegance."

Gary Danko *American*

29 | 27 | 29 | $111

Fisherman's Wharf | 800 N. Point St. (Hyde St.) | 415-749-2060 | www.garydanko.com

"In a city of great restaurants", Gary Danko's Wharf-area "classic" is the "all-time favorite" – and once again voted No. 1 in the Bay Area for Food, Service and Popularity thanks to its "sensational", "personalized" New American prix fixe menus and "perfect wine pairings" (plus "the most impressive cheese cart"), all delivered "without a speck of pretentiousness" by a "smart, warm" staff that treats everyone "like royalty"; true, it "isn't cheap" and "reservations are difficult to get" in the "understated, tasteful" room, but for those with the bucks and the necessary "hours" to indulge, devotees urge "just put yourself in their hands, and you won't go wrong."

Gialina *Pizza*

25 | 17 | 21 | $30

Glen Park | 2842 Diamond St. (Kern St.) | 415-239-8500 | www.gialina.com

Devotees pilgrimage from "all over the city" to this "family-friendly" Glen Park pizzeria, a "small place that packs a big punch" with its

FOOD   DECOR   SERVICE   COST

"high-class" pies featuring "crispy", "almost crackerlike crusts" and lots of "inventive topping combinations", plus "memorable" salads and "lovely" wines; "service is friendly" and the space "cozy", just "go early" because it's "always crowded" with folks "begging for a table" (no reservations).

Gioia Pizzeria ⓜ *Californian/Pizza*   25 | 12 | 18 | $16

Russian Hill | 2240 Polk St. (Green St.) | 415-359-0971 | www.gioiapizzeria.com

"New York pizza" with a "thin crust" and "simple toppings" (as well as "magnificent" seasonal varieties) is the star at this duo that began with a Berkeley take-out shop offering what some call the "best pizza in the Bay Area"; its larger Russian Hill offshoot provides a Californian menu and "pleasant" sit-down service as well, with a following that's more "family"-based than fanatical.

Giordano Bros. *Sandwiches*   22 | 15 | 19 | $14

Mission | 3108 16th St. (Valencia St.) | 415-437-2767
North Beach | 303 Columbus Ave. (B'way) | 415-397-2767
www.giordanobros.com

"Sandwiches hit the spot every time" at this Mission and North Beach duo where the "Primanti's-style sammies" with "french fries and coleslaw in the middle" make transplants feel like they "never left Pittsburgh"; "lots of TVs for watching games" draw sports fans who appreciate service that's still generally "fast" even when there's a "packed house" during Steelers games.

Giorgio's Pizzeria *Pizza*   21 | 14 | 21 | $20

NEW **Downtown** | Crocker Galleria | 50 Post St. (Montgomery St.) | 415-837-1070 ⓢ
Inner Richmond | 151 Clement St. (3rd Ave.) | 415-668-1266
www.giorgiospizza.com

If you're "getting a little tired of all those designer pies", join Inner Richmond locals at this "solid" "family-friendly" spot that's just "like the pizza parlor you grew up going to" with "old-school" decor ("cheesy rubber grapes and red-checkered tablecloths"); or stop by the new Crocker Galleria branch for the same "classic, thin-crust" 'zas and "friendly" service that's bound to make it also a local "favorite."

Gitane ●ⓢⓜ *French/Spanish*   23 | 25 | 22 | $52

Downtown | 6 Claude Ln. (bet. Bush & Sutter Sts.) | 415-788-6686 | www.gitanerestaurant.com

"Low lights" and a "sexy ambiance" make for "a romantic evening" at this "youth-oriented" Spanish "hideaway" Downtown, where many "first dates" begin with "creative" cocktails at the "energetic" ground-floor bar before progressing to the "richly colored" dining area up-stairs for "interesting" and "delicious" Andalusian-inspired plates; it's not cheap, but service is "warm", and many agree it "adds much-needed spice" to the city.

Globe ● *Californian/Italian*   18 | 15 | 17 | $42

Downtown | 290 Pacific Ave. (Battery St.) | 415-391-4132

"Wear black" to blend in at this "dark", "spare" "Manhattan-style" space Downtown "famous for its late-night fare" (as well as "ample" weekday lunches); some "service industry" folks arrive "after their own shifts" to dine on the "dependable" Cal-Italian eats, creating a "friendly feeling all around", and though old-timers opine it's "not what it used to be", service is decent and prices won't break the bank.

Goat Hill Pizza *Pizza* 22 | 14 | 19 | $20

Potrero Hill | 300 Connecticut St. (18th St.) | 415-641-1440
SoMa | 171 Stillman St. (bet. 3rd & 4th Sts.) | 415-974-1303
www.goathill.com

"Amazing for kids" and anyone else craving a "quality" pie on a "perfectly cooked" "sourdough crust", this "inexpensive" Potrero Hill pizzeria – with a takeout- and delivery-only SoMa branch – is staffed by the "friendliest folks" around; it isn't "upscale", but the "budget"-minded attest you "can't beat" the "very popular" "Monday night all-you-can-eat" option.

Golden Boy ●◉⌑ *Pizza* 24 | 14 | 19 | $10

North Beach | 542 Green St. (Jasper) | 415-982-9738 |
www.goldenboypizza.com

"After a night out in North Beach", this "hole-in-the-wall" is a "lifesaver", serving "thick" slices of "square" focaccia pizza; it's just the thing to "soak up the booze" proclaim "partygoers" who "grab a slice" and "go" until 2:30 AM on weekends, but "it's pretty tasty sober too" attest regulars who snag a "barstool" and soak up the "funky", "friendly" vibe.

The Golden West ⓩ *Bakery/Sandwiches* ▽ 21 | 7 | 20 | $14

Downtown | 8 Trinity Alley (Montgomery St.) | 415-216-6443 |
www.theauwest.com

"Nothing beats the warm pastries" at this bakery/take-out shop from Dennis Leary (The Sentinel) tucked away in a Downtown alley that also serves up "perfect lunch" offerings, like a "variety of salads" and solid sandwiches; prices are "slightly more expensive than a typical deli" but fans find it "worth the extra dollar (or two)" for the "inventiveness and quality of ingredients"; P.S. open Monday–Friday only.

Good Luck Dim Sum ⌑ *Chinese* 21 | 5 | 10 | $10

Inner Richmond | 736 Clement St. (bet. 8th & 9th Aves.) | 415-386-3388 |
www.goodluckdimsum.com

"Ten dollars buys a feast" at this "no-frills", quick-serve Inner Richmond Chinese known for dim sum that "sells so quick it's all fresh"; there are no rolling carts, seating is limited and "don't expect friendly service", but "no place has lines out the door like it", proving the "consistently good" grub for "amazingly inexpensive" prices trumps all; P.S. closes at 6:30 PM.

Goood Frikin' Chicken *Mideastern* 20 | 11 | 17 | $18

Mission | 10 29th St. (Mission St.) | 415-970-2428

"Just like its name says", this "simple" Mission Middle Eastern "does chicken right", sending out "tender", "juicy" birds along with "tasty" bread and "delicious" sides, like hummus and mac 'n' cheese; service is "efficient" and prices low, and though there's "lots of space", many still recommend "getting takeout and enjoying it all at home."

Gott's Roadside *Diner* 22 | 15 | 17 | $19

Embarcadero | Ferry Building Mktpl. | 1 Ferry Bldg. (The Embarcadero) |
866-328-3663 | www.gotts.com

See review in North of San Francisco Directory.

	FOOD	DECOR	SERVICE	COST

Gracias Madre *Mexican/Vegan*

24 | 22 | 20 | $25

Mission | 2211 Mission St. (18th St.) | 415-683-1346 | www.gracias-madre.com

"*Gracias!*" cry devotees of this "organic" Mexican cantina in the Mission serving up affordable, "super-creative" vegan fare "without alienating omnivores" by being too "hippie-dippie"; it's "slow" at peak times and the "communal tables weird some people out", but regulars appreciate the "festive atmosphere", as well as the "to-die-for" nut-based desserts.

Grand Cafe *French*

20 | 25 | 20 | $47

Downtown | Hotel Monaco San Francisco | 501 Geary St. (Taylor St.) | 415-292-0101 | www.grandcafe-sf.com

"Majestic ceilings" and "gorgeous" "art nouveau decor" "whisk you across the pond" and to another era at this "elegant" bistro where the "varied" menu of "French favorites" has "flair"; "reliable" servers make it "perfect" for "pre- or post-theater" Downtown dining, and the "attractive" "bustling bar" is popular for more "casual" meals, though perfectionists sigh "if only the food matched decor."

Great Eastern ❶ *Chinese*

23 | 13 | 16 | $27

Chinatown | 649 Jackson St. (bet. Grant Ave. & Kearny St.) | 415-986-2500 | www.greateasternsf.com

"Skip the chow mein and get the real goodies" at this Chinese choice "in the heart of Chinatown" – like "wonderful seafood" selected from "big tanks" full of "live sea creatures" and during the day, "superb" dim sum (order it from the "brisk" waiters, since there are "no carts"); yes, it's "crowded" (even "Obama stopped in" in 2012) and decor is "minimal", but prices are "very fair" considering the "high quality."

Green Chile Kitchen *Southwestern*

22 | 19 | 18 | $19

Western Addition | 1801 McAllister St. (Baker St.) | 415-440-9411 | www.greenchilekitchen.com

Fans tout "the best posole outside of Santa Fe" and "fantastic" green chile stew at this "family-friendly" Western Addition Southwesterner that's "as close to New Mexican cooking" as you'll find hereabouts; a "casual" setup where you "order at the counter and seat yourself", it makes for a "well-priced" and "relatively fast" meal (preferably followed by some "damn tasty" pie).

Greens Ⓜ *Vegetarian*

25 | 24 | 23 | $44

Marina | Fort Mason Ctr., Bldg. A | Marina Blvd. (Buchanan St.) | 415-771-6222 | www.greensrestaurant.com

After more than 30 years, this Marina "granddaddy of vegetarian cuisine" "still has it", continuing to set a "gold standard" with "carefully prepared" dishes that "can convince even the most meat-inclined" to go to the "greens side"; service is "warm" in the "casually elegant" space, where "huge windows" offer "dramatic" bay views (especially at sunset), all leading fans to hail its "incredible staying power."

NEW Hakkasan ❶ *Chinese*

24 | 26 | 24 | $74

Downtown | 1 Kearny St. (Geary St.) | 415-829-8148 | www.hakkasan.com

"Artful" Chinese food (including "unusual but tasty" dim sum) that's "almost as seductive as the decor" goes with "amazing" cocktails and strong service at this new Downtown "power" place – part of a high-end international chain; while it strikes some as "excessively priced" and "pretentious" ("trying to be LA in SF"), others are smitten by the "clubby", "happening" scene.

Hamano Sushi *Japanese* ▽ 21 | 15 | 19 | $40

Noe Valley | 1332 Castro St. (bet. Jersey & 24th Sts.) | 415-826-0825 | www.hamanosushi.com

"What you go for is the sushi" say fans of this "low-key" Noe Valley Japanese that doles out "fresh fish" (including some "unusual cuts") and "interesting rolls", all for "affordable" prices; service is "friendly" too, now if only the "modest" space would undergo a "quick makeover."

Han IL Kwan *Korean* 24 | 15 | 17 | $27

Outer Richmond | 1802 Balboa St. (19th Ave.) | 415-752-4447

Among the "multitude of Korean restaurants" in the Outer Richmond, this one "takes the title" for "plentiful" portions of "amazing" eats, from "high-quality" barbecue to "varied" *banchan*; "you know" it's "authentic" since "tour groups come here by the busload", but they also "wipe out the seating", so "call ahead" to reserve and brace for variable service "depending on the crowd."

Hard Knox Cafe *Southern* 21 | 16 | 20 | $19

Dogpatch | 2526 Third St. (bet. 22nd & 23rd Sts.) | 415-648-3770
Outer Richmond | 2448 Clement St. (26th Ave.) | 415-752-3770
www.hardknoxcafe.com

"Rib-sticking" soul food – think "crisp" fried chicken and "guilt-inducingly good side dishes" "like grandma used to make" – "hits the spot" at this "friendly", "funky" "down-home" duo in Dogpatch and the Outer Richmond; calling it "nice for a change", most are "super-satisfied" with the "experience", down to the "unbeatable" price.

NEW Hard Water ● *Cajun/Creole* - | - | - | M

Embarcadero | Pier 3 (bet. Pier 7 & Pier 12) | 415-392-3021 | www.hardwaterbar.com

Unlike his popular Slanted Door Vietnamese restaurant and offshoots, Charles Phan's latest waterfront entry is an American whiskey bar specializing in New Orleans–inspired seafood-centric cuisine with Cajun-Creole touches along with raw-bar offerings and the chef's famous fried chicken; the compact dining room is dominated by a marble-topped horseshoe bar and a sky-high collection of backlit brown bottles that line the back wall.

Harris' *Steak* 26 | 24 | 26 | $72

Polk Gulch | 2100 Van Ness Ave. (Pacific Ave.) | 415-673-1888 | www.harrisrestaurant.com

"One of the few old-style steakhouses left", this Polk Gulch meatery provides "first-rate" cuts of beef "with all the trimmings" and "superb" martinis amid "gentleman's club surroundings"; there's "nothing cheap" on the menu, but the "efficient" staff "caters to your every need", so fans say it "stands the test of time."

Hayes Street Grill *Seafood* 23 | 18 | 23 | $51

Hayes Valley | 320 Hayes St. (bet. Franklin & Gough Sts.) | 415-863-5545 | www.hayesstreetgrill.com

"Always a very satisfying" experience, this "elegant" yet "understated" Hayes Valley venue allows the "super-fresh" fish to "shine" in "simple"

dishes that are nonetheless "exquisitely prepared"; "popular" with "concertgoers" who "overlook the dated decor" since the "professional" "staff knows how to make the curtain", it's been a seafood "stronghold" for more than 30 years.

Hayes Valley Bakeworks 🖼 American/Bakery ▽ 21 | 22 | 24 | $14

Hayes Valley | 550 Gough St. (bet. Fulton & Grove Sts.) | 415-864-2688 | www.bakeworkssf.com

Decorated with "retro rolling pins", this "bright, attractive place to stop in the opera house area" offers American breakfasts and lunches ("surprisingly good" pizza) as well as "sweet, delicious" pastries, gluten-free options and kombucha on tap; as it helps to train homeless and at-risk people with disabilities, it's an "admirable" enterprise all around; P.S. closes at 7 PM (5 PM Saturdays).

Heirloom Café 🖼 Californian/Mediterranean 25 | 21 | 22 | $50

Mission | 2500 Folsom St. (21st St.) | 415-821-2500 | www.heirloom-sf.com

"Up-to-date locavore food" offering "delightful combinations of flavors" is complemented by "incredible" wines "lovingly chosen" by the oenophile owner at this "cute" Mission Cal-Med; it's "a bit pricey, but worth it" say those who find it "fun to sit at a counter and see the chef at work" or "score a spot at the communal table."

Helmand Palace Afghan 23 | 16 | 20 | $35

Russian Hill | 2424 Van Ness Ave. (bet. Green & Union Sts.) | 415-362-0641 | www.helmandpalacesf.com

"Outstanding", "authentic" Afghan eats from "fabulous" pumpkin dishes to "lamb beyond measure" appeal to the globe-trotting gourmands drawn to the "wide choice" of "unusual" flavors offered at this "quiet" Russian Hill haunt; as for the setting, though "pleasant", "a palace it's not", but an "accommodating" staff and "very fair" prices make it a "neighborhood gem."

Henry's Hunan Chinese 22 | 11 | 18 | $22

Chinatown | 924 Sansome St. (bet. B'way & Vallejo St.) | 415-956-7727
Downtown | 674 Sacramento St. (Spring St.) | 415-788-2234 🖼
Excelsior | 4753 Mission St. (bet. Persia & Russia Aves.) | 415-585-8838
Noe Valley | 1708 Church St. (bet. Day & 29th Sts.) | 415-826-9189
SoMa | 1016 Bryant St. (bet. 8th & 9th Sts.) | 415-861-5808 🖼
SoMa | 110 Natoma St. (bet. New Montgomery & 2nd Sts.) | 415-546-4999 🖼
www.henryshunan.com

"When they ask you" "how hot", get "prepared to perspire" at these "hole-in-the-wall" Chinese chain branches, where the "distinctive" Hunan dishes "bursting" with "fresh ingredients" are "a cut above" the competition; there's "no atmosphere to speak of", but "what it lacks in charm it makes up" in the "efficiency" of the "friendly servers" and the "insanely reasonable" price.

NEW Heyday 🖼 Californian - | - | - | I

SoMa | 180 Spear St. (Howard St.) | 415-284-4515 | www.heydaysf.com

A former Chez Panisse chef crafted the small organic breakfast and lunch menu at this inexpensive Californian cafe, which also has roasted chicken to take home for dinner; the petite, stylishly decorated space has become a fast favorite among workers looking for fresh, from-scratch options in the Financial District.

NEW Hillside Supper Club *American*

- | - | - | M

Bernal Heights | 300 Precita Ave (Folsom St.) | 415-285-6005 | www.hillsidesupperclub.com

After using the space as a pop-up, two of the folks behind the former Bernal Supper Club have dropped anchor in this Victorian Bernal Heights storefront where they're serving up Italian-influenced, seasonal American eats at moderate prices; large arched windows overlook Precita Park, and the updated interior features mason jar light fixtures and a zinc-topped bar stocked with sustainable wines and craft beers.

NEW Hi Lo BBQ *BBQ*

- | - | - | M

Mission | 3416 19th St. (bet. Mission & San Carlos Sts.) | 415-874-9921 | www.hilobbqsf.com

Slinging self-styled Northern California BBQ, this Mission joint from Scott Youkilis (Maverick, Hog & Rocks) brings locally sourced meat and purist-defying touches to classic picnic fare (e.g. the ribs, links and brisket platter for two) and sides, with cocktails and suds to wash it down; the airy, two-level space is both slick and smokehouselike, with decor touches including charred-cedar planking and polished-wood communal tables.

Hog & Rocks ◗ *American*

22 | 20 | 21 | $37

Mission | 3431 19th St. (San Carlos St.) | 415-550-8627 | www.hogandrocks.com

"Oysters, oysters and more oysters" keep seafood lovers happy at this "popular" "high-end pub" in the Mission while "excellent ham" and "creative" cocktails are some of the other specialties on the New American menu of fairly sophisticated small and large plates; communal tables and "friendly" staffers add to the "hoppin' vibe", especially during happy hour when the "half-shell goodies" are even more "reasonably priced."

Hog Island Oyster Co. & Bar *Seafood*

26 | 18 | 20 | $36

Embarcadero | Ferry Building Mktpl. | 1 Ferry Bldg. (The Embarcadero) | 415-391-7117 | www.hogislandoysters.com

The "freshness cannot be beat" at this Ferry Building "must" known for its "fantastic" oysters, "awesome" clam chowder and "first-class" grilled cheese; expect "long lines", a "busy" atmosphere (especially at happy hour) and a bill that "depends on your appetite", but go ahead and "have a dozen with some bubbles and enjoy the view"; the branch at Napa's Oxbow Market gets a lot of "love" too.

Hong Kong Lounge *Chinese*

24 | 15 | 16 | $25

Laurel Heights | 3300 Geary Blvd. (Parker Ave.) | 415-668-8802
Outer Richmond | 5322 Geary Blvd. (bet. 17th & 18th Aves.) | 415-668-8836 | www.hongkonglounge.net

Lines rivaling "the Great Wall" suggest this Outer Richmond dim sum option (with a Laurel Heights offshoot) is "one of the best", serving a "stunning variety" of "superb" dumplings delivered "directly from the kitchen to your table"; "quality" Chinese dinners, including "bargain"

FOOD | DECOR | SERVICE | COST

"prix fixe" options, add to the possibilities – as long as you can overlook sometimes "not so nice" staffers.

Hotei *Japanese*
19 | 14 | 18 | $23

Inner Sunset | 1290 Ninth Ave. (bet. Irving St. & Lincoln Way) | 415-753-6045 | www.hoteisf.com

"Gorgeously fresh" "sushi from Ebisu", its sibling across the street, joins forces with "Japanese noodles" that chase away the "cold" "foggy days" at this Inner Sunset eatery; though the "cozy" room can get "crowded" and a few find the fare "hit-or-miss", most "highly recommend" the "robust" ramen and "fabulous" soba at "bargain prices."

The House *Asian*
27 | 16 | 22 | $44

North Beach | 1230 Grant Ave. (bet. Columbus Ave. & Vallejo St.) | 415-986-8612 | www.thehse.com

Some of the city's "top" Asian-fusion fare can surprisingly be found in North Beach at this "small" but "mighty good" "eclectic" stalwart that "continues to impress" with its "phenomenal" "high-caliber" cuisine ("especially the melt-in-your-mouth sea bass"), creatively presented along with an "amazing" sake and wine list; the "cramped and noisy" setting is "maybe not the best romantic date-night choice", but fans attest it offers some of the best "food and value" in the city.

House of Nanking *Chinese*
22 | 9 | 14 | $24

Chinatown | 919 Kearny St. (Columbus Ave.) | 415-421-1429 | www.houseofnanking.net

"They have a menu, but I'm not sure what for" say regulars of this "no-frills" Chinatown "hole-in-the-wall", who advise allowing the "Soup Nazi-ish" servers to "decide what you should eat" from the cheap array of "killer" Chinese chow; prepare to "line up along the sidewalk" before being seated at a "cramped" table and "bumping elbows with strangers", but – "love it or hate it" – "it's all part of the experience."

House of Prime Rib *American*
26 | 22 | 25 | $55

Polk Gulch | 1906 Van Ness Ave. (Washington St.) | 415-885-4605 | www.houseofprimerib.net

"Succulent" "prime rib and fixin's are second to none" at this "SF original for red-meat lovers" in Polk Gulch, a "true time capsule" that "does one thing exceedingly well" (and even "serves you seconds"); though expensive, it delivers "unbeatable value", "old-school charm" and "entertaining" service to go with its "oh-so-satisfying" eats, making it "always a favorite" for fans.

HRD Coffee Shop ☒⇄ *Diner/Korean*
23 | 8 | 22 | $11

SoMa | 521 Third St. (bet. Bayshore Frwy. & Brannan St.) | 415-543-2355 | www.hrdcoffeeshop.com

NEW HRD Smokin Grill Ⓜ *BBQ/Korean*

North Beach | 532 Green St. (bet. Grant Ave. & Stockton St.) | 415-402-0528 | www.hrdsmokingrill.com

"Bazillions of local workers" flock to this "cramped", "no-frills" Korean diner in SoMa for "awesome fusion" breakfast eats such as kimchi burritos and more "everyday plates"; further enticements include prices that are "rock-bottom ridiculous" and staffers who are "friendly

FOOD | DECOR | SERVICE | COST

even in the craziest of lunch rushes", and though it closes at 3 PM (2 PM Saturdays), its new North Beach outpost is open for (only) dinner and brunch.

Hunan Home's Restaurant   *Chinese*

21 | **13** | **19** | **$25**

Chinatown | 622 Jackson St. (bet. Beckett & Kearny Sts.) | 415-982-2844 | www.hunanhomes.com

Connoisseurs of "homestyle" Hunanese "develop a habit" at this "reliable" Chinatown Chinese (and its Los Altos and Palo Alto offshoots), thanks to "generous" servings of "freshly made" fare and "fabulous" sauces from "not spicy" to "really hot" (if you're "feeling strong", say "make me sweat"); though the "dated decor" has detractors, service is "a cut above" what you'd expect "in this price range" (i.e. "cheap").

Ichi Sushi 🗷 *Japanese*

27 | **19** | **22** | **$44**

Bernal Heights | 3369 Mission St. (Godeus St.) | 415-525-4750 | www.ichisushi.com

"Some of the best and most distinctive sushi" can be had at this minnow-sized Japanese seafooder in Bernal Heights that racks up "long" lines for its artfully presented, "super-fresh", sustainably sourced fish and nightly omakase offered at "reasonable prices"; P.S. the restaurant plans to relocate across the street (3282 Mission) and offer more seating plus an expanded menu (including hot dishes and a full bar), while installing a new seafood-centric concept in the original space.

Ideale Restaurant   *Italian*

25 | **18** | **23** | **$43**

North Beach | 1315 Grant Ave. (Vallejo St.) | 415-391-4129 | www.idealerestaurant.com

"Superb" Roman *cucina,* from "excellent" antipasti to "flawless" risotto and "homemade pasta", is "as authentic as it gets" at this "unpretentious" eatery with an "extensive" wine list; the price is "reasonable" say fans who are "transported" from North Beach "to a little trattoria in Italy" by the "homey" setting and "welcoming" "staff."

Ike's Place   *Sandwiches*

25 | **12** | **18** | **$12**

Castro | 3489 16th St. (Sanchez St.) | 415-553-6888

Ingleside | Cesar Chavez Student Ctr., SFSU Campus | 1650 Holloway Ave. (19th Ave.) | 415-841-0369 🗷

www.ilikeikesplace.com

"Ginormous" sandwiches that are "hot" and "toasty" "heaven on a bun" take subs "to a new level" at this "well-hyped" Castro-ite with branches around the bay; it's "not really a sit-down place" (the "hipster clientele" usually heads to "Dolores Park") and "insanely long lines" can stretch "round the block", so "call ahead" or "order online" to "breeze past the starving masses" and "collect" your "pricey" "prize" from the "upbeat" staff.

Il Cane Rosso   *Italian*

23 | **12** | **15** | **$22**

Embarcadero | Ferry Building Mktpl. | 1 Ferry Bldg. (The Embarcadero) | 415-391-7599 | www.canerossosf.com

"Exceptional sandwiches, salads" and rotisserie chicken comprise the "satisfying" bill of fare at this "small", "casual" Italian cafe in the Ferry Building, where the counter service can be "slow", but the prices always equal a "bargain"; "snagging a table" can be "stressful", so "if the weather's nice, take it outside" and "swoon" over the bay view.

	FOOD	DECOR	SERVICE	COST

Il Fornaio *Italian*

18 | 19 | 18 | $43

Downtown | Levi's Plaza | 1265 Battery St. (Greenwich St.) | 415-986-0100 | www.ilfornaio.com

"Always packed" with folks digging into "dependable" Italian fare, this "busy" chain pleases with its "wonderful bakery" goods, regional specials and "comfortable surroundings" for "dates, business meetings or family dinners"; service is "generally good" and prices "fair", and while the "food isn't magical" it usually "hits the spot."

Imperial Tea Court *Tearoom*

18 | 20 | 19 | $23

Embarcadero | Ferry Building Mktpl. | 1 Ferry Bldg. (The Embarcadero) | 415-544-9830 | www.imperialtea.com

A "calm oasis" amid the "bustle of the Ferry Building" with an even "more picturesque" Berkeley branch, this "Zen" tearoom twosome is the "perfect place" to "slow down" with a pot of "exotic" tea from an "impressive selection"; the "small" menu includes "incredible" dim sum and (at Berkeley) "excellent handmade noodles", and oolong enthusiasts who aren't "in a hurry" are rewarded with a "lovely" experience.

Incanto *Italian*

25 | 22 | 24 | $58

Noe Valley | 1550 Church St. (bet. Duncan & 28th Sts.) | 415-641-4500 | www.incanto.biz

Plying "cuts of meat" "most people don't think of eating", Chris Cosentino's "Dante's Inferno"-themed Noe Valley "nose-to-tail" ristorante is a "treat" for "adventurous carnivores" and "swineophiles", while those preferring something "more traditional" can stick to "rustic Italian" fare such as "spectacular salumi" and "top"-notch "handmade pastas"; "charming" servers "know what to suggest", including "flights" from the "exclusively Italian wine list", and all things considered, it doesn't cost an "offal" lot.

Indian Oven *Indian*

23 | 18 | 21 | $28

Lower Haight | 233 Fillmore St. (bet. Haight & Laussat Sts.) | 415-626-1628 | www.indianovensf.com

"Indescribably delicious" Indian eats, from "divine" curries to "beautifully prepared" meats, "never fail to please" Lower Haight habitués at this "surprisingly lovely" location with a "bright and airy" dining room; it's perpetually "packed", especially "on weekends", but a "friendly" staff that "showers you with attentive service" means most "can't wait to go back."

Indigo   *American*

20 | 19 | 22 | $48

Civic Center | 687 McAllister St. (Gough St.) | 415-673-9353 | www.indigorestaurant.com

Guests are "pleasantly surprised" by the "well-prepared" prix fixe dinners with "well-chosen" wines at this "deep-blue" New American near the Civic Center; it's smoothly run and "less expensive" than some other pre-show options, and while perhaps "not outstanding", usually "quite acceptable."

In-N-Out Burger   *Burgers*

23 | 14 | 21 | $9

Fisherman's Wharf | 333 Jefferson St. (Leavenworth St.) | 800-786-1000 | www.in-n-out.com

"Burgers and fries made fresh on the spot" set apart this "well-priced" California-born chain, the "best thing goin'" when it comes to "quality" fast food served by a "proud" team; just "don't forget the secret code" ("get it animal-style") and be prepared for a line, as fans "would drive many miles and happily wait for a double-double and chocolate shake."

Isa *French*

24 | 20 | 21 | $47

Marina | 3324 Steiner St. (bet. Chestnut & Lombard Sts.) | 415-567-9588 | www.isarestaurant.com

There's "lots to love" at this "lively" "small-plates palace" in the Marina, including "terrific" French nibbles, "great" wines, an "enthusiastic staff" and "dark", intimate digs that are ripe for "date night"; though some feel that the "volume-to-price ratio" isn't high, others say that costs are "reasonable", and even better with happy-hour (nightly) and prix fixe (Sunday–Thursday) deals; P.S. sitting "on the covered back terrace" is "nothing short of magical."

Izakaya Sozai *Japanese*

23 | 17 | 16 | $35

Inner Sunset | 1500 Irving St. (16th Ave.) | 415-742-5122 | www.izakayasozai.com

Purists are "blown away" by the "traditional" "small plates" – like "staggeringly good" yakitori and "exceptional" ramen in a "delicious porky broth" – at this "cozy" Inner Sunset Japanese that also pours "amazing" sakes; prices are moderate, and though you'll likely have to "wait outside" for a seat in the "tiny" space, connoisseurs claim the "friendly owner" has captured "the true spirit of izakaya."

Izakaya Yuzuki *Japanese*

24 | 18 | 21 | $43

Mission | 598 Guerrero St. (18th St.) | 415-556-9898 | www.yuzukisf.com

This izakaya in the Mission from owner/Osaka native Yuko Hayashi specializes in "authentic Japanese dishes"; "don't expect a quick, cheap meal", but do leave time to "sample lots of amazing little bites", shochu, beer and sake at the walnut bar surrounded by calligraphy-style paintings and other simple adornments.

Izzy's Steaks & Chops *Steak*

22 | 19 | 22 | $45

Marina | 3345 Steiner St. (bet. Chestnut & Lombard Sts.) | 415-563-0487 | www.izzyssteaks.com

A "dimly lit" "throwback" to a previous era, this "inviting" Marina steakhouse (with a "not to be overlooked" San Carlos branch) caters to meat mavens with "huge portions" of "fantastic" chops, "terrific" "old-style" sides and a "well-priced wine list"; though "a bit pricey for everyday", budget-watchers call it a "way-better value" than the "bigger names", and "professional waiters" help create a "relaxing" vibe.

Jackson Fillmore Trattoria Ⓜ *Italian*

21 | 14 | 19 | $40

Upper Fillmore | 2506 Fillmore St. (bet. Jackson St. & Pacific Ave.) | 415-346-5288 | www.jacksonfillmoresf.com

"Home away from home" for Upper Fillmore habitués, this "itty-bitty" "neighborhood hot spot" "rolls on year after year" serving Italian fare such as "excellent" "fresh pastas" at "reasonable" tabs; "the atmosphere" alone "is worth the price of admission" say regulars, who "sit at the bar" for "very personal service", but "would it kill them to spruce up the joint" inquire critics, who sometimes wish it weren't so "loud" and "crowded."

CITY OF SAN FRANCISCO

	FOOD	DECOR	SERVICE	COST

Jai Yun *Chinese* ▽ 23 | 11 | 15 | $82

Chinatown | 680 Clay St. (bet. Kearny & Montgomery Sts.) | 415-981-7438
"A smorgasbord of meticulously prepared dishes" comes from "innovative" chef-owner Nei Chia Ji at his Chinatown joint where guests "come with an open mind", choose one of three or so "prix fixe small-plate dinners" and sample "delicacies not found on most Chinese menus"; just "be prepared for a very long dinner", service that's "good, not great" and an "expensive bill" (it's "worth every penny").

Jardinière *Californian/French* 26 | 27 | 25 | $79

Civic Center | 300 Grove St. (Franklin St.) | 415-861-5555 |
www.jardiniere.com
"Lovely and celebratory", this Civic Center "delight" by Traci Des Jardins "remains the gold-standard for pre-opera dining", providing an "extraordinary" French-Californian menu based on "pristine" ingredients, served in a "grand" bi-level setting; as the staff is "tops" and the wine list "sparkles", expect to pay a "small fortune" for the experience (or go for the less costly Monday night prix fixe or bar menu in the lounge).

Jasper's Corner Tap & Kitchen *American* 19 | 17 | 20 | $33

Downtown | Serrano Hotel | 401 Taylor St. (O'Farrell St.) | 415-775-7979 |
www.jasperscornertap.com
"Helpful" staffers dish up a mix of "standard pub fare" and "innovative" American eats (the "famed burger" is "really good") at this affordable Downtown that also serves plentiful beers and cocktails, including a Negroni on tap; the two-tiered space isn't big on decor, but the front bar appeals to sports fans and has a "friendly vibe."

Java Beach Cafe *Sandwiches* 20 | 19 | 20 | $12

Outer Sunset | 1396 La Playa St. (Judah St.) | 415-665-5282
Outer Sunset | 2650 Sloat Blvd. (45th Ave.) | 415-731-2965
www.javabeachcafe.com
Folks "enjoying a day at the beach" like to "chill" at these "cute little" Outer Sunset cafes over coffee, sandwiches and salads; it can be "hard to get a table", though the service is "pretty fast – even when they're swamped"; P.S. the Sloat Boulevard branch closes at 8 PM.

Joe's Cable Car *Burgers* 22 | 16 | 18 | $20

Excelsior | 4320 Mission St. (Tingley St.) | 415-334-6699 |
www.joescablecar.com
"Awesome burgers" are "what it comes down to" at this "kitschy" Excelsior diner where "Joe himself" "grinds his own fresh chuck daily" for some of the "highest-quality" patties in town; he's a "great host" who "makes sure every customer is happy", but he can't cheer up wallet-watchers unprepared to "pay more than $10" for beef on a "paper plate."

John's Grill *Seafood/Steak* 21 | 22 | 20 | $46

Downtown | 63 Ellis St. (bet. Market & Powell Sts.) | 415-986-0069 |
www.johnsgrill.com
"More than a bit old-fashioned", this "dark" Downtown surf 'n' turfer is "fabulous" for dining "before or after the theater" while soaking in some "history" ("Sam Spade might have bent his elbow" at the bar); the staff is generally "accommodating", and even if some find the food "good, not great", most agree the experience is "well worth the price."

	FOOD	DECOR	SERVICE	COST

Just Wonton ⓜ *Chinese*   ▽ 20 | 7 | 16 | $15

Outer Sunset | 1241 Vicente St. (bet. 23rd & 24th Aves.) | 415-681-2999

"Customize" your own "inexpensive and filling meal" via a "wide variety" of "delicious wontons" at this Outer Sunset Chinese "hole-in-the-wall"; rice and noodle dishes "do not disappoint" either, and the staff is "friendly" too.

Kabuto ⓜ *Japanese*   26 | 15 | 19 | $43

Outer Richmond | 5121 Geary Blvd. (bet. 15th & 16th Aves.) | 415-752-5652 | www.kabutosushi.com

"Amazing", "extremely fresh" sushi, both "traditional" and "totally original", reels seafood fanatics into this "tiny" Outer Richmond Japanese "that knows its fish"; "adventurers" who sample the "imaginative" creations of the "talented chefs" or order the "oh-my-gawd" omakase are "rewarded" with a "unique experience", so few fret about the "long wait" to be seated in the "casual", "minimalist" dining room.

Kappou Gomi ⓜ *Japanese*   ▽ 28 | 20 | 22 | $44

Outer Richmond | 5524 Geary Blvd. (bet. 19th & 20th Aves.) | 415-221-5353

"Adventurous" eaters "cannot go wrong" at this "low-key" Outer Richmond "jewel" proffering an "enormous menu" of impeccably presented", "home-cooked" "delights you won't find outside of Japan" ("there's no such thing as sushi here", but "sublime sashimi" is served); solid service and "reasonable prices" are two more reasons fans "wholeheartedly recommend" it for an "out-of-the-ordinary" experience.

Kasa Indian Eatery *Indian*   21 | 14 | 18 | $14

Castro | 4001 18th St. (Noe St.) | 415-621-6940
NEW Polk Gulch | 1356 Polk St. (Pine St.) | 415-931-3991
www.kasaindian.com

"Atypical" Indian eats, such as "amazing" "kati rolls" ("like Indian burritos") and "tasty" Thali dinners, attract a following to this "cheap and cheerful" Castro-ite with a new Polk Gulch sibling; "portions could be bigger", but the "trendy" "young" patrons are partial to the "hipster" staff's use of "organic" "local" ingredients; P.S. "you might catch" their "cool purple truck" at locations around the Bay Area.

Katana-Ya ● *Japanese*   22 | 11 | 15 | $18

Downtown | 430 Geary St. (bet. Mason & Taylor Sts.) | 415-771-1280

"Get your ramen on" at this "hole-in-the-wall near Union Square", where "gigantic bowls" of "amazing", "chewy" Japanese noodles in "rich" broths (plus sushi that some deem "delicious" and others find "forgettable") are sold for "cheap prices"; "packed" quarters with a "line out the door" means "the staff expects you to get in and out" – "which is fine" by most folks.

Kate's Kitchen ⌿ *Southern*   ▽ 23 | 16 | 20 | $15

Lower Haight | 471 Haight St. (bet. Fillmore & Webster Sts.) | 415-626-3984 | www.kates-kitchensf.com

If you "get the large stack" of "hearty" pancakes, "for the love of God, split it", because the "amazing" Southern breakfasts and lunches come in "very generous portions" at this Lower Haight "friendly" "hipster hangover" haunt with "cute" "checkered tablecloths"; "be prepared to wait" "on weekends" and don't forget to "bring cash", because it "doesn't disappoint" when you want "cheap" chow.

Katia's Russian Tea Room ⓂRussian   ▽ 20 | 16 | 21 | $31

Inner Richmond | 600 Fifth Ave. (Balboa St.) | 415-668-9292 |
www.katias.com

Katia herself "oversees the kitchen", concocting "authentic" (and otherwise "hard to find") Russian "comfort food" (think "excellent borscht"
and "great blini") at this casual "little" midpriced Inner Richmond
"jewel"; the formal tea service requires advance reservations, but expect the owner to "provide very attentive care" when you arrive.

Keiko à Nob Hill Ⓜ French/Japanese   27 | 24 | 25 | $129

Nob Hill | 1250 Jones St. (Clay St.) | 415-829-7141 |
www.keikoanobhill.com

For "sublime food" in an "elegant", "old-world setting", well-heeled
diners trek to this "absolutely amazing" Nob Hill sleeper where chef
Keiko Takahashi (ex El Paseo) turns out Japanese-influenced French
tasting menus showcasing "some of the most delicious, innovative
and beautifully prepared dishes" around; the "excellent" staff offers
"spot"-on wine pairings from the "impressive" list, and while it's all
"worth the price", there's also a "less-formal bar area" offering izakaya à la carte options.

Ken Ken Ramen ❶ Japanese/Noodle Shop   ▽ 21 | 18 | 18 | $22

Mission | 3378 18th St. (bet. Capp & Mission Sts.) | 415-967-2636 |
www.eatkenkenramen.com

"A tiny kitchen" whips up some of "SF's finest ramen" at this Japanese
noodler in the Mission that originated as a pop-up; it can get "packed",
but the vibe is "casual", service "quick" and tabs are low; P.S. Sunday
brunch and curry at lunch are also served.

Khan Toke Thai House Thai   21 | 22 | 20 | $30

Outer Richmond | 5937 Geary Blvd. (bet. 23rd & 24th Aves.) | 415-668-6654
Guests head to this "grand old Thai" in the Outer Richmond for a "fine
array of family-style dishes" along with "authentic" atmosphere (you
take off your shoes and sit on the floor); prices are moderate, though
some would like to see quicker service.

Kiji Sushi Bar & Cuisine Ⓩ Japanese   ▽ 25 | 19 | 20 | $41

Mission | 1009 Guerrero St. (bet. Alvarado & 22nd Sts.) | 415-282-0400 |
www.kijirestaurant.com

"One of the best-kept secrets" in the Mission is this "sexy-looking"
Japanese whose "creative", "delectable" (and mostly sustainable) sushi comes at "a reasonable price"; "friendly, knowledgeable servers"
and a "wide range of sake" only add to its allure.

Kingdom of Dumpling Chinese   22 | 6 | 13 | $16

Parkside | 1713 Taraval St. (bet. 27th & 28th Aves.) | 415-566-6143 |
www.kingofchinesedumpling.com

This "tiny" Parkside "hole-in-the-wall" "charms the tongue" with
"darn-good dumplings" and other "cheap and delicious" Chinese eats;
just "don't expect service or decor" or fast in-and-out, as there are often "huge waits" – though "takeout is quick and easy."

King of Thai Thai   21 | 12 | 17 | $14

Downtown | 184 O'Farrell St. (bet. Powell & Stockton Sts.) |
415-677-9991 ❶

(continued)

King of Thai

Fisherman's Wharf | Anchorage Sq. | 2800 Leavenworth St. (bet. Beach St. & Lincoln Hwy.) | 415-346-9555 ●
Inner Richmond | 346 Clement St. (5th Ave.) | 415-831-9953 ●
Inner Richmond | 639 Clement St. (bet. 7th & 8th Aves.) | 415-752-5198 ●⇄
North Beach | 1268 Grant Ave. (Vallejo St.) | 415-391-8222 | www.kingofthainoodlehouse.com ●
Outer Sunset | 1507 Sloat Blvd. (bet. Everglade & Havenside Drs.) | 415-566-9921 ⇄
Outer Sunset | 1541 Taraval St. (bet. 25th & 26th Aves.) | 415-682-9958 ●

"Hungry students with a light wallet" and other penny-pinchers "shocked" at the "unbeatable" prices flock to these "casual" eateries in SF and Alameda, where "large" portions of "very tasty Thai noodles" and "spicy" curries come "amazingly fast"; there's "no ambiance whatsoever", so some favor "takeout", but they're undoubtedly "convenient" when you have a "late-night" "craving" (most are open nightly until at least 1 AM).

Kiss Seafood ⊠ Ⓜ *Japanese*   28 | 17 | 25 | $81

Japantown | 1700 Laguna St. (Sutter St.) | 415-474-2866

The "easy-to-miss entrance" is like a "special portal to Japan" gush groupies of this "very traditional" and "very expensive" Japantown "find" where an "adorable" "husband-and-wife" team "work in harmony" proffering "extremely fresh" sushi along with "divine", elegantly presented omakase dinners; "don't come if you're in a rush" or sans reservations, as there are "only 12 seats", and expect to see the chef doing "all the sashimi and cooking right in front of you."

Koh Samui & The Monkey *Thai*   21 | 21 | 19 | $30

SoMa | 415 Brannan St. (bet. Ritch & 3rd Sts.) | 415-369-0007 | www.kohsamuiandthemonkey.com

"There are no monkeys" at this "hip", midpriced SoMa stop, just "wonderfully fresh", "artful Thai food" ("try the pumpkin curry") including "excellent vegetarian options" plus "cocktails infused with flavors like lemongrass, basil and ginger"; despite sometimes "slow service", it's a "cool"-looking choice for "groups" and "happy-hour deals."

Kokkari Estiatorio *Greek*   28 | 27 | 27 | $59

Downtown | 200 Jackson St. (bet. Battery & Front Sts.) | 415-981-0983 | www.kokkari.com

"Opa!" cheer fans of this "still-hot" Downtown taverna that remains the place to "get your Greek on" amid the "power" lunch and dinner crowd feasting on "the best lamb this side of Mount Olympus" and other "spit-roasted marvels" served in a "stylish", "energetic" setting; whether you "sit at the bar" or "by the fireplace", there's "warm", "expert" service, all adding up to a "magnificent experience" that requires you "open your wallet" wide, but leaves diners with "big smiles."

Koo Ⓜ *Asian*   26 | 19 | 22 | $43

Inner Sunset | 408 Irving St. (bet. 5th & 6th Aves.) | 415-731-7077 | www.sushikoo.com

An "excellent selection of sushi and grilled dishes", many with "inventive" Asian-fusion twists, is what's on offer at this Inner Sunset site

FOOD | DECOR | SERVICE | COST

with "fast, friendly service" and "pleasant decor"; if you don't grab the "early-bird special", "expect to drop some cash", but most find it "totally worth it", especially those who "sit at the bar and watch the chefs at work."

NEW Kronnerburger 🅼 Burgers — | — | — | I

Mission | Bruno's | 2379 Mission St. (bet. 19th & 20th Sts.) | 415-656-9871 | www.kronnerburger.com

A former Bar Tartine chef has found a semi-permanent spot for his burger pop-up inside Bruno's nightclub, where he slings his sought-after bone-marrow burger, crab patties and other snacks Sunday–Friday evenings; diners can enjoy the eats to go or along with cocktails, Miller High Life and craft beers in the retro-looking bar and lounge area.

Kuleto's Italian 23 | 21 | 21 | $48

Downtown | Villa Florence Hotel | 221 Powell St. (bet. Geary & O'Farrell Sts.) | 415-397-7720 | www.kuletos.com

Popular with both "out-of-towners" and locals "relaxing" "after a long day of Union Square shopping", this "fairly priced" Downtowner delivers "terrific" pastas and other Northern Italian fare in a "lively", "beautiful" setting featuring a historic carved-wood bar; "professional" servers please theatergoers with "time constraints", while those snagging "counter" seats facing the cooks claim it's "like watching the Food Channel" "in 3D."

La Boulange Bakery 21 | 17 | 18 | $16

Cow Hollow | 1909 Union St. (Laguna St.) | 415-440-4450
Downtown | 222 Sutter St. (Kearny St.) | 415-989-5010
Cole Valley | 1000 Cole St. (Parnassus Ave.) | 415-242-2442
Hayes Valley | 500 Hayes St. (Octavia St.) | 415-863-3376
Noe Valley | 3898 24th St. (Sanchez St.) | 415-821-1050
North Beach | 543 Columbus Ave. (bet. Green & Union Sts.) | 415-399-0714
Pacific Heights | 2043 Fillmore St. (bet. California & Pine Sts.) | 415-928-1300
Pacific Heights | 2325 Pine St. (bet. Fillmore & Steiner Sts.) | 415-440-0356
Russian Hill | 2300 Polk St. (Green St.) | 415-345-1107
SoMa | The Monadnock Bldg. | 685 Market St. (bet. New Montgomery & 3rd Sts.) | 415-512-7610 🅂
www.laboulangebakery.com
Additional locations throughout the San Francisco area

A "sweet little spot" for "big bowls of café au lait", "incredible" "open-face sandwiches" and "delicate" pastries, these "Parisian patisseries" with "friendly" "staffers" are "charmers" affirm Francophiles, who arrive "early" "on weekends" when they're "always crowded"; the chain's "expanding like crazy" (it was acquired by Starbucks), and though a few feel it was "better before the corporate makeover", most maintain it's still "*magnifique!*"

La Ciccia 🅼 Italian 27 | 17 | 25 | $50

Noe Valley | 291 30th St. (Church St.) | 415-550-8114 | www.laciccia.com

"If you can score a reservation, take it" urge devotees of this "out-of-the-way" Noe Valley "neighborhood gem" proffering "incredibly flavorful", "delightfully unique" Sardinian cuisine (including "killer pastas" and seafood); the married owners' "passion" comes across in the cuisine as a "welcoming" staff helps navigate the "brilliant", "reasonably priced" all-Italian wine list and "makes you feel at home" in the "tiny", albeit "crowded" digs; P.S. an enoteca spin-off, La Nebbia, is slated to open at 1781 Church Street.

La Corneta *Mexican*   22 | 13 | 18 | $12

Glen Park | 2834 Diamond St. (Kern St.) | 415-469-8757 ⌨
Mission | 2731 Mission St. (23rd St.) | 415-643-7001
www.lacorneta.com

"Don't let the line scare you away", it usually "moves fast" at this "no-frills", "pleasant" "cafeteria-style" Mexican quartet serving up "solid burritos" and such; what's more, everything comes in "large portions" and for "affordable prices", making it "a great value."

La Cumbre Taqueria *Mexican*   20 | 10 | 16 | $11

Mission | 515 Valencia St. (bet. 16th & 17th Sts.) | 415-863-8205
Some fans "wouldn't buy a burrito anywhere else" but this Mission ta-queria and its San Mateo twin, where "huge portions" go for "reason-able" prices in "hole-in-the-wall" digs; still, others concede they're "not outstanding", and suspect "the love just isn't there anymore"; P.S. the Valencia Street location is open late on weekends.

La Folie 🗷 *French*   27 | 25 | 27 | $110

Russian Hill | 2316 Polk St. (bet. Green & Union Sts.) | 415-776-5577 | www.lafolie.com

Roland Passot's "shrine" to French "gastronomy" is "anything but folie" declare diners "blown away" at his "chic" Russian Hill "special-occasion" "haven" proffering an "exquisitely prepared" "parade of plates" as "tasty" as they are "beautiful to behold (plentiful too)"; it's a "fabu-lous" "fine-dining" experience "from start to finish", enhanced by brother George's "compact wine list" and service that's "beyond com-pare", all making it worth the "beaucoup bucks"; P.S. the adjacent lounge serves a late-night bar menu.

La Mar Cebicheria Peruana *Peruvian/Seafood* 24 | 24 | 21 | $51

Embarcadero | Pier 1.5 (Washington St.) | 415-397-8880 | www.lamarcebicheria.com

"Sublime ceviche" headlines the menu of "world-class Peruvian" plates at "celeb chef" Gastón Acurio's "very popular" South American sea-fooder where "knowledgeable" servers navigate an "enchanting" Embarcadero setting; whether you drink "sophisticated" cocktails in the "gorgeous bar" or snag "outdoor seating" (the best for "killer" bay views), it's "so much fun", as long as "money is no object" and you're prepared to "embrace" the "loud", "high-energy" "scene."

La Méditerranée *Mediterranean/Mideastern* 22 | 17 | 20 | $23

Castro | 288 Noe St. (bet. Beaver & 16th Sts.) | 415-431-7210 | www.lamednoe.com
Upper Fillmore | 2210 Fillmore St. (bet. Clay & Sacramento Sts.) | 415-921-2956 | www.cafelamed.com

Devotees "dream about" the "simple" Middle Eastern–Med menu from "savory" "phyllo treats" to "great" "meze platters" at these "rea-sonably priced" "standbys" in the Castro, Upper Fillmore and Berkeley; they're "not the fanciest of restaurants", but they're "as popular as ever" thanks to "warm", "relaxed" service and "lovely" sidewalk seat-ing perfect for "people-watching."

	FOOD	DECOR	SERVICE	COST

L'Ardoise ✍Ⓜ *French*

24 | 20 | 24 | $49

Castro | 151 Noe St. (Henry St.) | 415-437-2600 | www.ardoisesf.com
"Imagine that you are in a French bistro in Paris" to conjure this "charming" place in the Castro with a "closet"-sized space and "amiable", "attentive service" that make it "ideal for dates"; as for the fare, it's "excellently prepared, beautifully plated", relatively "reasonably priced" and complemented by a "thoughtfully chosen, varied wine selection."

Lark Creek Steak *Steak*

24 | 22 | 23 | $58

Downtown | Westfield San Francisco Ctr. | 845 Market St., 4th fl. (bet. 4th & 5th Sts.) | 415-593-4100 | www.larkcreeksteak.com
"Sides and starters shine as brightly as the perfectly charred beef" at this "modern steakhouse" in Downtown's Westfield Centre, where a "comfortable atmosphere" and "impeccable service" make you "forget you're in a mall"; though it "can get expensive", "great deals" are offered at the "cool bar" during happy hour, for a "nice respite" "after shopping."

La Taqueria ⑂ *Mexican*

25 | 11 | 17 | $12

Mission | 2889 Mission St. (bet. 24th & 25th Sts.) | 415-285-7117
For over 30 years, this "true original" in the Mission has been churning out affordable, "consistently delicious" Mexican meals comprising "awesome tacos" and "amazing" burritos that disciples call "massive missiles of yummy goodness" (they're "traditional", so "they don't have rice"); "seating is scarce" in the "no-frills" environs, so prepare for "constant lines" – though "speedy service" keeps them moving.

Le Central ✍ *French*

21 | 19 | 21 | $45

Downtown | 453 Bush St. (bet. Grant Ave. & Kearny St.) | 415-391-2233 | www.lecentralbistro.com
The signature "cassoulet is first-rate" and the "people-watching" even better at this "friendly, busy" "Downtown mainstay" where all of the French bistro fare is "delicious"; a known place for a "power lunch", its location "a quick jaunt from Union Square" means it's "a nice respite from hectic shopping" too, while "fair pricing" makes it "worth a try" whatever the occasion.

Le Charm French Bistro ✍Ⓜ *French*

22 | 19 | 21 | $44

SoMa | 315 Fifth St. (bet. Folsom & Shipley Sts.) | 415-546-6128 | www.lecharm.com
Devotees agree that the "name fits" at this "charming" SoMa bistro where the "friendly", "attentive" staff "can recommend interesting wines" to complement the "rich", "terrific" staples, all available for "reasonable prices" (especially on the "inexpensive prix fixe"); adding to the attraction, an "evening of escargot and Chablis on the patio" is especially "delightful" on Thursdays, when live jazz is offered.

Le Colonial *French/Vietnamese*

22 | 24 | 21 | $53

Downtown | 20 Cosmo Pl. (bet. Jones & Taylor Sts.) | 415-931-3600 | www.lecolonialsf.com
Take "a romantic walk into an alley" for "beautiful French-Vietnamese" fare at this Theater District Downtowner with a "sensual atmosphere" recalling "pre-war Saigon"; those who deem it "pricey" suggest "make a meal of" starters or head for the lounge (with live music or DJs most nights), but wherever you perch, service is "helpful" and it's "delightful" "for groups" or "date night."

	FOOD	DECOR	SERVICE	COST

Leopold's *Austrian*
23 | 23 | 23 | $33

Russian Hill | 2400 Polk St. (Union St.) | 415-474-2000 |
www.leopoldssf.com

"Pretty girls" in dirndls deliver "fantastic", "hearty", "reasonably priced" Austrian fare with Italian twists at this "jovial" Russian Hill "gasthaus" where locals "chug down" "ice-cold" European brews from "boot-shaped glasses" amid Alpine "lodge decor"; the atmosphere is "really loud", but that's to be expected since it's like "Oktoberfest year-round" here.

Le P'tit Laurent *French*
25 | 21 | 24 | $39

Glen Park | 699 Chenery St. (Diamond St.) | 415-334-3235 |
www.leptitlaurent.net

"Big things" do indeed come in "little packages", as evidenced by this Glen Park bistro "find", where "skilled and charming" host-owner Laurent (he "runs a tight ship") and his "capable staff" deliver "consistently excellent" "classic" French fare and a "nice selection of wine" in a "tiny-triangle" of a setting; the "reasonable" price point, particularly on the Sunday–Thursday prix fixe, is a boon.

Lers Ros Thai *Thai*
24 | 14 | 18 | $27

Hayes Valley | 307 Hayes St. (Franklin St.) | 415-874-9661
Tenderloin | 730 Larkin St. (O'Sarrell St.) | 415-931-6917 ◑
www.lersros.com

Some of the "best Thai in the city" draws fans to these Tenderloin and Hayes Valley spots where "flavors that are robust" and "authentic" can also be "melt-your-face-off hot"; a minority complains about "noise levels", but regulars call it an "inexpensive" place to try "funky and assertive" specials like "rabbit, boar" and "alligator", along with the more "traditional" dishes on their "crazy-long menu"; P.S. the original Larkin Street locale is "open late."

Liberty Cafe Ⓜ *American*
22 | 18 | 22 | $33

Bernal Heights | 410 Cortland Ave. (bet. Andover & Bennington Sts.) |
415-695-8777 | www.thelibertycafe.com

This longtime "neighborhood anchor in Bernal Heights" offers a "consistent", "reasonably priced" American menu featuring the likes of "flaky, delicious" chicken pot pie; "friendly" service, a "homey" atmosphere, "delightful" outdoor seating and a "cottage in the back" that "serves as a bakery in the morning and a wine bar at night" are additional reasons it's deemed a "gem."

Limón Rotisserie *Peruvian*
24 | 18 | 19 | $33

Bayview | 5800 Third St. (bet. Armstrong & Bancroft Aves.) |
415-926-5665
Mission | 1001 S. Van Ness Ave. (21st St.) | 415-821-2134
Mission | 524 Valencia St. (bet. 16th & 17th Sts.) | 415-252-0918
www.limonrotisserie.com

"Fantastic" "flame-grilled" rotisserie chicken keeps these "lively" Peruvian outposts "always packed" with fans dipping their birds into a "trio of sauces" (the "perfect complement"); small plates including "to-die-for" ceviche and "delicious drinks" like pisco sours add to the "good value", whether at the Van Ness location with "basement" seating, the slightly more polished Valencia locale or Third Street, where there's free parking.

Little Chihuahua *Mexican*

21 | 15 | 17 | $14

Lower Haight | 292 Divisadero St. (bet. Haight & Page Sts.) | 415-255-8225
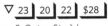 **Mission** | 581 Valencia St. (bet. 16th & 17th Sts.) | 415-355-9144
Noe Valley | 4123 24th St. (bet. Castro & Diamond Sts.) | 415-648-4157
www.thelittlechihuahua.com

"High-quality ingredients" and unusual fillings are the hallmarks of
these sustainably minded Mexican burrito-slingers that also pour
"amazing" sangria; the "quirky decor" and "big smiles" from the counter servers help make it a "go-to" for "casual, quick takeout", albeit
one with "slightly upscale" prices to match.

Little Nepal Ⓜ *Nepalese*

▽ 23 | 20 | 22 | $28

Bernal Heights | 925 Cortland Ave. (bet. Folsom & Gates Sts.) |
415-643-3881 | www.littlenepalsf.com

"Tasty, interesting" food with a "spicy" kick comes out with "consistent" quality at this small, "welcoming" Nepalese in Bernal Heights;
moderate prices and "kind, helpful" service are further perks, so locals
"love going and supporting" their "neighborhood" place.

Little Star Pizza *Pizza*

25 | 16 | 19 | $23

Mission | 400 Valencia St. (15th St.) | 415-551-7827
Western Addition | 846 Divisadero St. (bet. Fulton & McAllister Sts.) |
415-441-1118
www.littlestarpizza.com

"Heavenly deep-dish" Chicago-style pizzas with "flavorful" cornmeal
crusts and "tangy, chunky tomato sauce" are offered alongside "super-
crispy thin-crust" varieties at these "fair-priced" parlors; devotees call
it a "fun space", but because it's often "noisy" – and "no reservations"
lead to "long waits" – some just "grab" and "go."

Local Mission Eatery Ⓜ *Californian*

27 | 24 | 25 | $36

Mission | 3111 24th St. (bet. Folsom & Shotwell Sts.) | 415-655-3422 |
www.localmissioneatery.com

Everything is "fresh, unique and awesome" at this "hidden gem" in the
Mission (with a seafood spin-off, Local's Corner) serving everything
from "superb", "elegant" sustainably sourced Californian dinners and
"quick lunches" to "tasty" brunch and "amazing pastries" courtesy of its
partner bakery, Knead Patisserie, in the back; the "thoughtful, skilled"
service and a "cozy" setting filled with works from "local artisans" and a
cookbook "library" for browsing "embody" the same locavore spirit.

Local's Corner *Seafood*

▽ 26 | 23 | 24 | $41

Mission | 2500 Bryant St. (23rd St.) | 415-800-7945 |
www.localscornersf.com

"Super-fresh ingredients" go into the "limited menu" of locally sourced
seafood dishes at this "small", oyster-proud offshoot of the nearby Local
Mission Eatery; an "attentive" staff keeps the food coming morning till
night, so go with a group and "have a bite of everything" – or take a "killer
date with a good appetite"; P.S. Sundays are brunch-only.

Locanda ◑ *Italian*

24 | 22 | 22 | $50

Mission | 557 Valencia St. (bet. 16th & 17th Sts.) | 415-863-6800 |
www.locandasf.com

Proof that "everything the Stolls touch turns to gold", this "standout"
Mission osteria with a "distinctly Roma attitude" delivers "fantastic"

FOOD | DECOR | SERVICE | COST

pastas, "offal" and other Italian "goodness" along with "friendly" service just like "you'd expect from the Delfina crew", in an "action"-packed, "trendy" room; add in a "buzzing" "bar scene" with "magnificent cocktails", and "valet parking" ($12 charge), and little wonder "reservations are hard to land."

Lolinda ● *Argentinean/Steak* ▽ 23 | 24 | 22 | $56

Mission | 2518 Mission St. (21st St.) | 415-550-6970 | www.lolindasf.com
"The meats are the main event" at this "super-tasty" Argentinean steakhouse in the Mission boasting Californian touches like a wood-fired grill and small-plates menu; the "lively", upscale ambiance is enhanced by "good cocktails" and pleasant service, while the sprawling terrace with a retractable tented roof serves tableside bar bites and craft cocktails.

Loló ☒ *Mexican* 25 | 23 | 23 | $34

Mission | 3230 22nd St. (bet. Mission & Valencia Sts.) | 415-643-5656 | www.lolosf.com
Tiny and "very eclectic", this "neighborhood jewel" turns out "somewhat random but delicious" Mexican "small plates" made with local ingredients that are "just as spectacular" as the "funky decor" with its "colorful" walls and collection of "cute knickknacks"; "as with everything in the Mission, it's gotten a bit too popular" but the "friendly" staff and "great-value" offerings are "so worth it"; P.S. open until midnight Friday and Saturday.

L'Osteria del Forno ⊭ *Italian* 24 | 15 | 21 | $29

North Beach | 519 Columbus Ave. (bet. Green & Union Sts.) | 415-982-1124 | www.losteriadelforno.com
"Loyal neighbors" and savvy visitors alike happily "squeeze in" to this cash-only, "family-owned", "shoebox-sized" osteria "hidden" among "the shinier" North Beach "tourist traps" to enjoy "phenomenal", "paper-thin" pizzas, roasts and other "real-deal" Italian fare "like grandma used to make"; waits can be "obnoxious" and the "rushed" staff and "cramped setting" don't encourage lingering, but diners "begin to ooh and aah" when it "all comes to the table."

Lovejoy's Tea Room Ⓜ *Tearoom* 20 | 22 | 23 | $26

Noe Valley | 1351 Church St. (Clipper St.) | 415-648-5895 | www.lovejoystearoom.com
"Treat yourself" to an "*Alice in Wonderland* tea party" – "complete with fussy, flowery decor" and "mismatched antiques" – at this midpriced Noe Valley "hangout" built for "bonding over a good cuppa", some "real scones" and "finger sandwiches"; service is fit "for queens" but "make a reservation" as it's often "filled to the brim" with kiddy birthdays, "bridal showers and other events."

Lucca Delicatessen *Deli/Sandwiches* 26 | 16 | 22 | $16

Marina | 2120 Chestnut St. (bet. Mallorca Way & Pierce St.) | 415-921-7873 | www.luccadeli.com
"Family-owned and -run since forever" (1929), this "institution" sells "superb sandwiches", soups, salads and pastas (the ravioli are "amazing") alongside a "wide variety" of "imported Italian ingredients", all for "fair prices"; there's "zero" decor, but it's takeout-only anyway, and perfect for an "impromptu picnic" on the nearby Marina green.

	FOOD	DECOR	SERVICE	COST

Luce *American*

| 21 | 23 | 21 | $65 |

SoMa | InterContinental Hotel | 888 Howard St. (5th St.) | 415-616-6566 | www.lucewinerestaurant.com

"High ceilings and marble floors" distinguish this "smart", "elegant" New American in SoMa's InterContinental Hotel where "service is attentive but not rushed" and dishes with "fantastic flavor combinations" pair well with "interesting" wines; if a few diners wish it were even "better for the cost", most assure it will "definitely" "not fail to please."

Luella *Californian/Mediterranean*

| 23 | 21 | 23 | $44 |

Russian Hill | 1896 Hyde St. (Green St.) | 415-674-4343 | www.luellasf.com

Fans "love the quintessential San Francisco feel" and "friendly" service at this "casual" "jewel on Russian Hill", where the chef "treats ingredients with TLC" while executing his Cal-Med dishes; options including a weekday prix fixe with "great choices" that's "a steal" and Sunday kids' menus bring in regulars, and it's also "a fun place to take visitors", especially "with the cable car running outside."

Luna Park *American/French*

| 20 | 17 | 18 | $34 |

Mission | 694 Valencia St. (bet. 17th & 18th Sts.) | 415-553-8584 | www.lunaparksf.com

"Down-home" French–New American cuisine "with an edge" is served in an "energetic atmosphere" brimming with a "plethora of hipsters" ("dining and working") at this Mission "neighborhood joint"; some wish the midpriced menu had a little "more pizzazz" and the service a bit more speed, but the "cozy", "funky setting" ("booths hidden behind a curtain") makes it "worth the wait."

Lupa Trattoria *Italian*

| 23 | 17 | 23 | $39 |

Noe Valley | 4109 24th St. (bet. Castro & Diamond Sts.) | 415-282-5872 | www.lupatrattoria.com

"Everything's flavorful and fresh", including the "amazing" handmade pastas, at this "comfortable" neighborhood place for Roman food in the "heart of Noe Valley"; admirers say the cooking and the staff "remind me of Italy", and with "generous portions" for moderate prices, many "will definitely be back."

Machine Coffee &
Deli ☒ *Coffeehouse/Sandwiches*

| - | - | - | I |

Downtown | 1024 Market St. (6th St.) | 415-913-7370

This affordable Downtown shop owned by the Foreign Cinema folks features Four Barrel Coffee offered in presses, espressos and as hand-cast cups of single origin beans alongside a simple lineup of breakfast fare and baked goods; in-house smoked and roasted meats (overseen by next-door sibling Showdogs' resident charcutier, Peter Temkin) are destined for build-your-own sandwiches gilded with housemade sauces, fixings and breads.

Magnolia Gastropub &
Brewery ◑ *Southern*

| 22 | 20 | 18 | $29 |

Haight-Ashbury | 1398 Haight St. (Masonic Ave.) | 415-864-7468 | www.magnoliapub.com

"Hopsheads rejoice" at this midpriced Upper Haight microbrewery whose "insane" list of "fantastic beers" is complemented by "inventive", "delectable" Southern-inflected American bar snacks; "service is sometimes slow" (though mostly "friendly"), and it gets "over-the-top loud" inside, as it's "always packed"; P.S. a Dogpatch taproom and BBQ branch run by Dennis Lee (Namu Gaji) is slated to open at 2505 Third Street.

Mamacita *Mexican*

24 | 20 | 19 | $36

Marina | 2317 Chestnut St. (Scott St.) | 415-346-8494 | www.mamacitasf.com

"You'll be hard-pressed to leave anything on your plate" at this "trendy" Marina Mexican where the "wonderfully delicious tacos" and such are ferried by "chic" staffers; "ambient lighting, star-shaped chandeliers" and "tequila bottles backlit" behind the bar make for an atmosphere that could be dubbed "sex-Mex", but bear in mind that the "boisterous" vibe can turn "overwhelmingly loud" thanks to the "world-class margaritas."

Mama's on Washington Square ⓂﬞＮ *American*

24 | 16 | 19 | $22

North Beach | 1701 Stockton St. (Filbert St.) | 415-362-6421 | www.mamas-sf.com

"Your first bite justifies the long wait in line outside" this "charming" North Beach breakfast-and-lunch "institution" where the "home-style" American fare includes "awesome French toast" and a Monte Christo sandwich that's a "sinful delight"; "low costs" and decent service are additional reasons fans say it's "worth" the effort to squeeze into the "small", "tight space."

Mandalay *Burmese*

25 | 18 | 22 | $27

Inner Richmond | 4348 California St. (bet. 5th & 6th Aves.) | 415-386-3895 | www.mandalayst.com

Those who "don't want to wait two hours" for the popular Asian spots on Clement Street contend "the food is even better" at this "well-appointed", "reasonably priced" Inner Richmond "stalwart" where "tasty" Burmese dishes are brought by staffers who "treat everyone like royalty"; expect a bit of a line on weekends – while you used to be able to go "without a reservation", "those days are over."

Manora's Thai Cuisine ⓩ *Thai*

▽ 23 | 18 | 21 | $25

SoMa | 1600 Folsom St. (12th St.) | 415-861-6224 | www.manorathai.com

"Traditional Thai" fare is as "scrumptious" as it is "well priced", particularly the "great lunch deals", at this "friendly" SoMa spot that'll "make it as spicy as you want"; "fast", "gracious" service and "charming" digs also help explain how it's "succeeded this long" (since 1987).

Mario's Bohemian Cigar Store Cafe *Italian/Sandwiches*

19 | 16 | 20 | $20

North Beach | 566 Columbus Ave. (Union St.) | 415-362-0536

The "meatball sandwich is the way to go" at this congenial, longtime North Beach Italian that's ideal for a "quick meal or a latte" (but "no cigars"); a little "divey" with "good prices", it's a favorite "first-stop" for some out-of-towners – just remember the "outdoor seating is key."

Market & Rye *Deli/Sandwiches*

▽ 19 | 19 | 21 | $15

West Portal | 68 W. Portal Ave. (Vicente St.) | 415-564-5950

(continued)

(continued)

Market & Rye

Potrero Hill | 300 De Haro St. (bet. 16th & 17th Sts.) | 415-252-7455
www.marketandrye.com

"Excellent lunch and brunch options", including salads and "innovative sandwiches" on "amazing bread", make this new daytime-only
deli duo an "awesome addition" to West Portal and Potrero Hill; the
"cool vibe" and "friendly service" also appeal, though a few find it "a
bit pricey for a quick lunch."

MarketBar *American*

18 | 19 | 19 | $38

Embarcadero | Ferry Building Mktpl. | 1 Ferry Bldg. (The Embarcadero) |
415-434-1100 | www.marketbar.com

"Very pleasant for a late lunch" or happy hour, especially on the huge patio with some water views, this "bistro-like" locale in the Ferry Building is
a "solid option" for "tasty" American eats and "well-poured" drinks;
"lively" and moderately priced, it stirs up a "good scene on a sunny day."

Marlowe ⓩ *American/Californian*

24 | 19 | 22 | $41

SoMa | 330 Townsend St. (4th St.) | 415-974-5599 | www.marlowesf.com
Renowned for its market-driven, Cal-American "comfort food", including the "fabled burger", this "tiny", "bustling" SoMa bistro "not far
from the ballpark" is a "favorite" of the "young, hip crowd" from lunch
to late-night; it gets "insanely loud and cramped" at the communal tables, but "upbeat" staffers, "good vibes" and urban-casual decor "make
you feel like you're in Manhattan" (in a good way).

Marnee Thai *Thai*

25 | 15 | 19 | $23

Inner Sunset | 1243 Ninth Ave. (bet. Irving St. & Lincoln Way) |
415-731-9999

Outer Sunset | 2225 Irving St. (bet. 23rd & 24th Aves.) | 415-665-9500
www.marneethaisf.com

Though small, the "kitchens produce big flavors" at these Sunset Thais
turning out budget-friendly "classic" dishes, including some "you can't
typically get" such as "to-die-for" spicy "angel wings"; the digs may
look like "a hole-in-the-wall" on a "side street" in Bangkok, complete
with servers "yelling across the restaurant", but overall these "authentic" spots "set the gold standard" for local Siamese cuisine.

NEW Mason Pacific Ⓜ *American*

– | – | – | M

Chinatown | 1358 Mason St. (Pacific Ave.) | 415-374-7185 |
www.masonpacific.com

This cozy neighborhood bistro is quintessential San Francisco, with a
prime location (a big-windowed corner spot on the cable car line), a
moderately priced menu of New American standards, a well-curated
wine list and an impressive pedigree (alums from Delfina, RN74 and
others); the small but sophisticated space bordering Nob Hill and
Chinatown is outfitted with a white marble bar, tall tables along the
windows up front and banquette seating in the back room.

The Matterhorn Swiss Restaurant Ⓜ *Swiss*

∇ 22 | 21 | 22 | $43

Russian Hill | 2323 Van Ness Ave. (bet. Green & Vallejo Sts.) |
415-885-6116 | www.thematterhornrestaurant.com

"When you gotta have fondue" this "family-friendly" Alpine getaway
in Russian Hill is "a little piece of Switzerland" complete with a "great

wood-paneled interior" (meaning "kitschy, in a good way"); the staff is "friendly" and the "well-priced", "well-selected" wines are sure to complement the "cheesy comestibles."

Maven ● *American*   ▽ 18 | 23 | 19 | $36

Lower Haight | 598 Haight St. (Steiner St.) | 415-829-7982 | www.maven-sf.com

Customers commend the "beautiful" interior with "communal tables" at this Lower Haight American that also "shines" with its selection of "excellent craft cocktails"; while some dub the small plates "delicious", those put off by the "price-to-portion ratio" recommend the burger as "best bang for the buck."

Maverick *American*   24 | 18 | 23 | $44

Mission | 3316 17th St. (bet. Mission & Valencia Sts.) | 415-863-3061 | www.sfmaverick.com

"Prepared with an adult's palate in mind", the "inventive" American menu draws fans to this "sophisticated" but "not pretentious" Mission eatery (sibling of Hog & Rocks) that's "famous" for its "amazing fried chicken" and also offers a "killer brunch"; the "intimate" setting is overseen by "cool" staffers who know their way around the "well-planned wine list", so feel free to "leave the pairings" to them – they'll "never steer you wrong."

Maykadeh *Persian*   23 | 21 | 22 | $43

North Beach | 470 Green St. (bet. Grant Ave. & Varennes St.) | 415-362-8286 | www.maykadehrestaurant.com

Kebabs "grilled to perfection" and served with "warm, soft pita bread" are mainstays at this North Beach oasis that boasts a menu full of "fragrant", "rarified" Persian dishes served in "an attractive room" with a "traditional atmosphere"; the staff "takes great care of their customers", and it all comes at "reasonable prices to boot."

McCormick & Kuleto's *Seafood*   21 | 24 | 21 | $47

Fisherman's Wharf | Ghirardelli Sq. | 900 N. Point St. (Beach St.) | 415-929-1730 | www.mccormickandkuletos.com

"Fabulous views" of the bay stand out at this Fisherman's Wharf seafooder where the somewhat "expensive" fare is "enjoyable" if "not overly creative", and both the space and service help "accommodate large groups"; naturally it's pretty "touristy", but locals also head there for "dates" and "special occasions."

The Melt ⊠ *Sandwiches*   17 | 14 | 17 | $12

Downtown | 1 Embarcadero Ctr. (bet. Battery & Front Sts.) | 415-813-6062

SoMa | 115 New Montgomery St. (bet. Minna & Mission Sts.) | 415-691-6536

SoMa | 345 Spear St. (bet. Folsom & Harrison Sts.) | 415-813-6075 | www.themelt.com

Flip founder Jonathan Kaplan is "taking melts" "to a whole new level" at the outposts of this "quick-growing", high-tech chainlet where "miracle cookers" efficiently crank out soup-and-sandwich meals elevated by "interesting" "combos" (including dessert iterations); diners "on the run" "love" the goods, but despite an "upscale atmosphere" and "friendly service", some find prices a bit too "steep" for "bread and cheese."

Memphis Minnie's BBQ Joint *BBQ*

| 20 | 14 | 16 | $20 |

Lower Haight | 576 Haight St. (bet. Fillmore & Steiner Sts.) | 415-864-7675 | www.memphisminnies.com

Backers of the "hearty barbecue" at this Lower Haight stop call it "cheaper than flying to Memphis and every bit as tasty"; "portions are generous" and it's a "good value", though the "fast-food setting" makes some suggest getting your order "to go."

Men Oh Tokushima

| – | – | – | I |

Ramen *Japanese/Noodle Shop*

Outer Richmond | 5120 Geary Blvd. (bet. 15th & 16th Aves.) | 415-386-8802 | www.menohusa.com

Ladling out "arguably the best bowl of ramen you can get in San Francisco", these affordable Outer Richmond and Union City outposts of the popular Japanese ramen chain specialize in housemade Tokushima-style noodles and a rich made-from-scratch tonkotsu broth, paired with a variety of "super-delicious" traditional toppings; just be aware that seating is limited in the contemporary blond-wood accented settings.

Mescolanza *Italian*

| 23 | 18 | 24 | $35 |

Outer Richmond | 2221 Clement St. (bet. 23rd & 24th Aves.) | 415-668-2221 | www.mescolanza.net

"One of the best-kept secrets" in Outer Richmond, this trattoria offers up "knockout" Northern Italian eats including "homemade pasta" and thin-crust pizzas, all at "reasonable" prices; the "charming old-world service" and "decent wine list" bring in repeat customers who relish an "intimate" atmosphere that's conducive to "quiet conversation."

Michael Mina *American*

| 27 | 25 | 26 | $104 |

Downtown | 252 California St. (Battery St.) | 415-397-9222 | www.michaelmina.net

"Artful" New American menus ensure "an adventure each time" for fans of Michael Mina's Downtown destination, which also earns high marks for its "stylish" decor (in the former Aqua digs), "stupendous wine list" and "lovely" service; it's "definitely expensive" and often "noisy", but some can't get enough of the "buzzing" scene.

Mifune *Japanese*

| 18 | 13 | 15 | $20 |

Japantown | Japan Ctr. | 1737 Post St. (bet. Laguna & Webster Sts.) | 415-922-0337 | www.mifune.com

"Unpretentious" and "family-friendly", this "noodle joint" in Japantown's Japan Center fills its booths daily with regulars who slurp up its "house-made" udon and soba dishes and other "serviceable" staples; the staff can be somewhat "indifferent" and the "authentic" decor "hasn't changed" "in years", but "you can't go wrong" when you want to grab a "cheap", "fast" meal before heading to the nearby Kabuki Theater.

Mijita *Mexican*

| 20 | 14 | 16 | $19 |

South Beach | AT&T Park | 24 Willie Mays Plaza (3rd St.) | 415-644-0240

Embarcadero | Ferry Building Mktpl. | 1 Ferry Bldg. (The Embarcadero) | 415-399-0814
www.mijitasf.com

Fans lap up the "upscale" taqueria fare and refreshing "agua frescas" (and the tequila too) at this walk-in "lunch spot" from Traci Des Jardins

FOOD | DECOR | SERVICE | COST

(Jardinière) in the Ferry Building with outdoor seating where you can "watch the boats arrive", and its sit-down offshoot outside AT&T Park that offers a hidden entrance into the stadium; sí, "you can get cheaper" tacos elsewhere, but these are "miles above" most Mexican spots, thanks in part to the use of "super-fresh", mostly local ingredients.

NEW Mikkeller Bar ● Eclectic — | — | — | M

Tenderloin | 34 Mason St. (Turk St.) | 415-984-0279 | www.mikkellerbar.com

There's a whole lot brewing at this ambitious specialty beer bar in the Tenderloin, a co-venture of the famous self-described 'gypsy brewer' Mikkel Borg Bjergsø and Chuck Stilphen of The Trappist that boasts 40 hard-to-find international craft beers (including a slew of Mikkeller brews), along with another 100 in bottles; a small, midpriced upscale pub menu (think housemade sausage and smoked meats) is served all day in the minimalist Danish-looking digs anchored by a 30-seat, four-sided white oak bar and outfitted with antique streetlight fixtures from Copenhagen and whimsical artwork from Mikkeller's label artist.

NEW The Mill Bakery/Coffeehouse — | — | — | I

Western Addition | 736 Divisadero St. (Fulton St.) | 415-345-1953 | www.themillsf.com

Four Barrel Coffee and Josey Baker Bread join forces at this Alamo Square shop where the simple menu includes breads, toasts, treats and fresh coffee made with much attention to detail; the bright, airy space features white walls and blond wood, communal seating and tables for two in an open design that allows diners a peek into the kitchen while they wait.

Millennium Vegan 26 | 23 | 25 | $52

Downtown | Hotel California | 580 Geary St. (Jones St.) | 415-345-3900 | www.millenniumrestaurant.com

"Inventive" dishes "based on whatever gorgeous vegetable is picked and delivered that day" (plus "unbelievable" desserts) mean this "high-class" vegan Downtowner "lives up to all the raves"; "delicious" drinks and "delightful" service are further perks, so enthusiasts consider it worth the cost – and maybe even the "best vegetarian in the world."

Miller's East Coast Delicatessen Deli/Jewish 20 | 12 | 17 | $19
(fka Miller's East Coast West Delicatessen)

Polk Gulch | 1725 Polk St. (bet. Clay & Washington Sts.) | 415-563-3542 | www.millersdelisf.com

Polk Gulch mavens get their Jewish deli "fix" at this noshery (with a San Rafael twin) dishing out "to-die-for matzo balls", "chopped liver like mom used to make" and "big, tasty" sandwiches, all for "reasonable prices"; "service is inconsistent" and the decor is "mediocre", but for an "authentic New York" experience – or at least the "glimmer" of one – it's "worth it."

Mission Beach Café Californian 24 | 18 | 19 | $34

Mission | 198 Guerrero St. (14th St.) | 415-861-0198 | www.missionbeachcafe.com

Weekend noshers know to get to this Mission Californian "hangout" "early" to avoid "long waits" for its "fantastic brunch" starring "divine sweet maple bacon" and "huge mimosas"; at other times, "premium" lunches and dinners come for "midrange prices" (and end with "amazing" pies), while "kind, knowledgeable servers" make even a newcomer "feel like a welcome regular" whatever the meal.

Mission Cheese 🅼 *American*

22 | 17 | 19 | $24

Mission | 736 Valencia St. (bet. 18th & 19th Sts.) | 415-553-8667 | www.missioncheese.net

"Heaven on earth" for "cheeseheads", this "friendly little" Mission fromagerie highlights Sarah Dvorak's "carefully curated selection" of America's "finest" artisanal offerings alongside charcuterie plates and "really inventive" pressed sandwiches, plus an assortment of California wines and beers; the space is quite "spare" and the servings may "suffer from small-portionitis" but still, it's "always packed" and "for good reason"; P.S. cheeses are available for purchase.

Mission Chinese Food *Chinese*

22 | 8 | 15 | $25

Mission | 2234 Mission St. (bet. 18th & 19th Sts.) | 415-863-2800 | www.missionchinesefood.com

"Insanely creative" "Chinese-inspired" dishes "like you've never had before" are prepared with "amazing technique" and served at a "fast pace" (but also "with love") from inside Lung Shun Restaurant at Danny Bowien's kitchen that garners "lots of attention" and "massive" "hipster" crowds; the "decor has improved as their fortunes have risen" (it's "expanded to NYC"), though the place remains a "dive" – albeit a "charitable" one that donates 75 cents per entree to the SF Food Bank; P.S. closed Wednesdays.

NEW Mission Picnic *Sandwiches*

- | - | - | I

Mission | 3275 22nd St. (Valencia St.) | 415-735-3080 | www.missionpicnic.com

A small menu of gourmet sandwiches draws diners to this inexpensive Mission spot that opens for lunch and dinner (but frequently sells out early); the tiny space is decked out with colorful tiles and reclaimed materials – think tables made from doors and soda-bottle lighting – but if seating is short, Dolores Park is just steps away.

Mission Rock Resort *Seafood*

▽ 16 | 19 | 15 | $33

Dogpatch | 817 Terry Francois Blvd. (Mariposa St.) | 415-701-7625 | www.missionrockresort.com

"If you're a sucker for a good industrial view of San Francisco Bay" while indulging in an "oyster happy hour", then "look no further" than this Dogpatch seafooder; some cite "overpriced bar fare" and "MIA staffers", and feel its last "face-lift" takes away from its "cheap and funky" roots, but for others the "happening" vibe and "delightful" scenery more than compensate.

NEW MKT ● *Californian*
(fka Seasons)

- | - | - | M

SoMa | Four Seasons San Francisco | 757 Market St., 5th fl. (O'Farrell St.) | 415-633-3838 | www.mktrestaurantandbar.com

Tucked away on the fifth floor of the Downtown Four Seasons overlooking Market Street, this bar-centric restaurant (replacing Seasons) offers guests a more urban-chic setting for enjoying its signature steaks, along with a new slate of midpriced, shareable Californian plates; the dining room sports a subtle printing press theme, while the adjacent lobby lounge features low-slung seating and an L-shaped bar where the drinks include punches served in vintage bowls.

Mochica *Peruvian*   24 | 18 | 20 | $37

SoMa | 937 Harrison St. (bet. Merlin & Oak Grove Sts.) | 415-278-0480 | www.mochicasf.com

"Incredible ceviche" and other "interesting" Peruvian fare is sold for "reasonable" rates at this "small, lively" tapas spot with "simple but tasteful decor" "in a slowly gentrifying part of SoMa"; the "approachable wine list" is also "well priced", and "accommodating" service is another enticement.

Moki's Sushi & Pacific Grill *Japanese*   ∇ 25 | 19 | 23 | $32

Bernal Heights | 615 Cortland Ave. (bet. Anderson & Moultrie Sts.) | 415-970-9336 | www.mokisushi.com

Bernal Heights locals call this a "sushi restaurant for everyone" thanks to the "kid-friendly" items (chicken satay, fish 'n' chips, etc.) offered among the "fresh, delicious" rolls and other "high-quality" Japanese grill fare; decor that's described as "classy" "tiki", "great service" and "good prices" ensure it remains a go-to for a "night out" in the neighborhood.

MoMo's *American*   19 | 20 | 20 | $40

South Beach | 760 Second St. (King St.) | 415-227-8660 | www.sfmomos.com

Buzzing like "a beehive during baseball season", this South Beach "fixture" "across the street from AT&T Park" serves New American fare that's "nothing extraordinary" but "well prepared" nonetheless; surveyors split on value ("reasonable" vs. "a bit expensive for what it is"), while the majority pegs the service as "friendly and knowledgeable"; P.S. the energy is especially "electric" on the patio where fans "gather for a drink" and toast the Giants.

Morton's The Steakhouse *Steak*   23 | 21 | 22 | $80

Downtown | 400 Post St. (bet. Mason & Powell Sts.) | 415-986-5830 | www.mortons.com

"If you have a hankering for meat" you'll find steaks "well aged, well prepared and well served" at these Downtown and San Jose links in the upscale chain; "full of guys in suits", they're fairly "formulaic" with a "staid" menu – and you may think you "paid for the entire cow" – though folks who hit the bar before 6:30 PM or after 9 PM find "happy-hour heaven."

Mo's *American*   23 | 16 | 20 | $21

North Beach | 1322 Grant Ave. (bet. Green & Vallejo Sts.) | 415-788-3779
SoMa | Yerba Buena Gdns. | 772 Folsom St. (4th St.) | 415-957-3779 | www.mosgrill.com

"You can pay more and find fancier", but why do that ponder patrons of these "basic" North Beach–SoMa "institutions" serving up American fare like "super-fresh, tasty" burgers, "real strawberry" shakes and "killer" fries (plus "great" breakfast fare at Grant Avenue); add in "bargain" prices for "huge" portions, and it's a little piece of "heaven."

Moshi Moshi *Japanese*   ∇ 23 | 17 | 22 | $29

Dogpatch | 2092 Third St. (18th St.) | 415-861-8285 | www.moshimoshisf.com

With "creative rolls and an impressive drink menu" among its "extensive" Japanese offerings, this "neighborhood sushi joint" in Dogpatch comes "highly recommended"; "cozy" and "welcoming", it's a "favorite" for kicking back at the bar or on the patio.

Mozzeria *Pizza* ∇ 21 | 15 | 22 | $26

Mission | 3228 16th St. (bet. Dolores & Guerrero Sts.) | 415-489-0963 | www.mozzeria.com

The wood-fired pizza is "wonderful" and the Italian midweek specials "quite the steal" at this "terrific" Mission option with "unique", pleasant service by a mostly deaf staff; visitors say they "value the challenge of communicating fully in a new way" (iPad and pen and pad are available), as well as the "quiet" environs, but the food is why they "keep going back."

Muracci's Japanese Curry & Grill ⓩ *Japanese* 20 | 10 | 16 | $17

Downtown | 307 Kearny St. (bet. Bush & Pine Sts.) | 415-773-1101 | www.muraccis.com

"Filling, flavorful" plates of Japanese curry are "made with real care for the craft" at this inexpensive, "popular" Downtown joint that's mostly geared toward takeout ("go early or face a huge wall of people"); it's only open weekdays, but the Los Altos branch is open Saturdays and has more seating too.

NEW M.Y. China *Chinese* 19 | 21 | 18 | $40

Downtown | Westfield San Francisco Ctr. | 845 Market St. (bet. 4th & 5th Sts.) | 415-580-3001 | www.mychinasf.com

"It's like going to a Las Vegas restaurant" at this new Chinese by celeb chef Martin Yan in the Westfield San Francisco Centre, where the "noodles are freshly pulled in the kitchen for all to see", and the staff sets down "beautiful", "high-quality" dishes in a "gorgeous" setting (complete with a "giant bell in the bar"); while some find it a bit "steep" – citing "big hits and some little misses" on the menu – others would "recommend it to everyone."

My Tofu House *Korean* 23 | 13 | 17 | $23

Inner Richmond | 4627 Geary Blvd. (bet. 10th & 11th Aves.) | 415-750-1818

Soy boys (and girls) say the house specialty – a bowl of spicy tofu soup – at this "authentic" Inner Richmond Korean is perfect "comfort food" to "warm up your soul on a foggy night"; though the decor does it no favors and service gets mixed marks, "you'll understand why this small joint fills so quickly" when the "bibimbop, barbecued meats and pancakes" arrive; P.S. "no liquor" served.

Naked Lunch Ⓜ⇗ *Sandwiches* ∇ 24 | 11 | 19 | $20

North Beach | 504 Broadway (Kearny St.) | 415-577-4951 | www.nakedlunchsf.com

The "small" menu "changes daily" at this North Beach bar and restaurant that makes a "mad" fried chicken sandwich, among other affordable favorites with "great ingredients"; having recently expanded into the owners' former Txoko space, there's now more room to meet friends and chow down.

Namu Gaji Ⓜ *Asian/Korean* ∇ 24 | 22 | 21 | $33

Embarcadero | Ferry Building Mktpl. | 1 Ferry Bldg. (The Embarcadero) | no phone ⓩ⇗

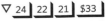

(continued)

Namu Gaji

Mission | 499 Dolores St. (18th St.) | 415-431-6268
www.namusf.com

A "revelation" in the Mission, this "top-notch" Korean–Pan-Asian by chef Dennis Lee impresses with "vibrant", "unusual combinations" ("excellent" tacos, "flavor-packed" fries) served by a "knowledgeable" team for moderate tabs; it's "teeny and noisy", but some find it "cozy", and the original stand at the Ferry Building (Thursdays and Saturdays) is much "loved" too.

Nettie's Crab Shack *Seafood*

20 | 18 | 19 | $37

Cow Hollow | 2032 Union St. (bet. Buchanan & Webster Sts.) | 415-409-0300 | www.nettiescrabshack.com

Fans say this "cute" Cow Hollow seafood "shack" offers an "excellent" selection of "oysters, crab and fish" served at some of the "sweetest real estate in the Marina" – "breezy" and "comfortable" inside with a lovely outdoor patio for "sipping and dipping"; while it's "not for the cheap", the "fun atmosphere" and "friendly service" are added values.

Nick's Crispy Tacos 🐷 *Mexican*

21 | 12 | 15 | $14

Russian Hill | Rouge Night Club | 1500 Broadway St. (Polk St.) | 415-409-8226

"Restaurant by day and club by night", this somewhat "surreal taqueria" in Russian Hill (think "red velvet booths" and crystal chandeliers) serves "uh-mazing" "Baja fish" and other tacos that regulars order "Nick's way" – with both a crispy and soft tortilla; critics decry the "fratty college bar" feel, especially on $2 Taco Tuesdays, but the "cheap" eats, "super-fun" vibe and "flowing pitchers of alcohol" "always draw a crowd."

Nihon ●🗵Ⓜ *Japanese*

▽ 21 | 20 | 17 | $45

Mission | 1779 Folsom St. (14th St.) | 415-552-4400 | www.nihon-sf.com

At this "quirky" bi-level Mission izakaya, "delicious" Japanese small plates are coupled with an "insane selection of whiskeys" (500 plus) that can be enjoyed by the pour or mixed into "inventive cocktails"; service can be "disjointed" and prices run on the "higher end", but thanks in part to a "laid-back" vibe in the modern digs ("quiet" dining on top and a downstairs bar with a "great atmosphere"), most don't notice.

903 Ⓜ *Japanese/Sandwiches*

▽ 24 | 20 | 23 | $28

Bernal Heights | 903 Cortland Ave. (Gates St.) | 415-678-5759 | www.eat903.com

"Homemade"-style food draws fans to this Bernal Heights cafe – a sit-down offshoot of cult favorite Sandbox Bakery – where chef-owner Mutsumi Takehara's "clever" eats include Asian-inspired bites like "delicious" Japanese-style sandwiches plus "amazing" fish tacos and other "super-fresh" dishes; wine and locally roasted Ritual coffee are also on offer in a "chill" space with picnic tables that some deem best for lunch or "families on the go"; P.S. closes at 3 PM Sunday–Tuesday.

Nob Hill Café *Italian*

22 | 16 | 20 | $35

Nob Hill | 1152 Taylor St. (bet. Clay & Pleasant Sts.) | 415-776-6500 | www.nobhillcafe.com

The "old San Francisco feel" – "cute", "quaint" and "great for a date" – is only part of the story at this "low-key" Italian "favorite" with a "basic" menu including "awesome gnocchi", "terrific pastas" and "thin-crust pizza"; the no-reservations policy and "reasonable prices" mean there's "always a wait", but the "wonderful atmosphere", complemented by a "friendly" staff, makes it "worth the hike to the top of Nob Hill."

Nojo *American/Japanese*

25 | 19 | 20 | $40

Hayes Valley | 231 Franklin St. (Hayes St.) | 415-896-4587 | www.nojosf.com

"Prepare yourself" for some "creative and unusual" dishes at this "fantastic" Hayes Valley American-Japanese where the likes of beef tongue and "pig jowl" are brought by servers who "know what's worth trying"; while a few find the yakitori skewers and small plates "on the pricey side", "groovy Zen decor" and a locale that's "convenient to the Symphony" tend to compensate.

Nombe *Japanese*

∇ 21 | 14 | 19 | $38

Mission | 2491 Mission St. (21st St.) | 415-681-7150 | www.nombesf.com

Serving "unique" Japanese street food and "steamy" bowls of ramen along with "carefully selected sakes", this "funky" Mission izakaya "hits the spot" at mealtime (including "excellent" late-night nibbles and weekend brunch); though an "odd" layout and somewhat "generic" decor don't win many fans, the generally "friendly" staff and moderate prices do.

Nopa ● *Californian*

26 | 23 | 24 | $48

Western Addition | 560 Divisadero St. (Hayes St.) | 415-864-8643 | www.nopasf.com

"Sublime", "ingredient-driven" Californian dishes, an "outstanding" bar and "personal" service in a "well-laid-out" bi-level space ("it's hypnotizing watching" the action "in the kitchen below") add up to a "stellar dining experience" at this "happening" Western Addition "winner"; what's more, it's "open late" and "not overpriced", so even if it "oozes hipster", it's a "top pick" for many.

Nopalito *Mexican*

24 | 18 | 20 | $29

Inner Sunset | 1224 Ninth Ave. (bet. Irving St. & Lincoln Way) | 415-233-9966
Western Addition | Falletti's Plaza | 306 Broderick St. (Oak St.) | 415-437-0303
www.nopalitosf.com

"Fairly priced" "classic Mexican" fare "done extremely well" draws fans to these Nopa offshoots, where regional dishes get a kick of "fresh, bright flavors" from "high-quality, organic ingredients"; the Inner Sunset location with patio seating offers a "much shorter wait" than at the Panhandle original, though both offer a "modern" setting "to catch up with friends" over "delicious" cocktails.

North Beach Pizza *Pizza*

20 | 12 | 17 | $19

Excelsior | 4787 Mission St. (bet. Persia & Russia Aves.) | 415-586-1400 | www.northbeachpizza.net
Haight-Ashbury | 800 Stanyan St. (Beulah St.) | 415-751-2300 | www.northbeachpizza.com
North Beach | 1462 Grant Ave. (Union St.) | 415-433-2444 | www.northbeachpizza.com
Outer Sunset | 3054 Taraval St. (bet. 40th & 41st Aves.) | 415-242-9100 | www.northbeachpizza.net

"Gooey mozzarella", "crunchy crusts" and "exotic toppings" are hallmarks of the pies at this "family-friendly" North Beach "pizza joint" and its offspring; "decent prices" and "accommodating" service keep the "old-fashioned" parlors "busy", but fans suggest "if it's crowded, take it home" – or opt for the "reliable" delivery.

North Beach Restaurant ● *Italian*   24 | 21 | 24 | $51

North Beach | 1512 Stockton St. (bet. Green & Union Sts.) | 415-392-1700 | www.northbeachrestaurant.com

"Fantastic, authentic" Tuscan fare (including "homemade prosciutto") and "real service from real old-style waiters" are the draws at this "classy, consistent" North Beach "old-timer" that insiders insist "hasn't diminished over the years"; "high prices" peeve the budget-minded, but for most it's "pure bliss" – especially if meals include the "excellent" house wine from the "owner's vineyard."

One Market ⊠ *Californian*   24 | 23 | 23 | $61

Embarcadero | 1 Market St. (bet. Spear & Steuart Sts.) | 415-777-5577 | www.onemarket.com

At this Embarcadero "splurge spot", "incredible" Californian fare with French influences is "graciously" presented by a "discerning" staff and complemented by the wares of "knowledgeable sommeliers" armed with a "top-flight wine list"; "comfy banquette seating" in an "attractive" room packs in the "business-lunch" and "special-occasion" crowds, and even though a few say it "tends to be noisy", the "perfect" "views over the Embarcadero" help justify its rep as a "go-to place to impress all."

Oola Restaurant & Bar ● *Californian*   21 | 18 | 18 | $42

SoMa | 860 Folsom St. (bet. 4th & 5th Sts.) | 415-995-2061 | www.oola-sf.com

"Open late for dinner", this SoMa hangout pleases with "tasty" burgers, babyback ribs and other Californian fare, along with a "great atmo-sphere"; while a few feel the lofty setting could use "a bit of updating" and more "attentive" service, especially considering the slightly upscale tabs, others like to hit the bar for tapas and nibble the night away.

Oriental Pearl *Chinese*   23 | 15 | 20 | $36

Chinatown | 760 Clay St. (Grant Ave.) | 415-433-1817 | www.orientalpearlsf.com

Diners encounter "dim sum extraordinaire" ("from a menu instead of carts") at this fairly spacious, two-floor Chinatown Chinese that's also known for Peking duck and other "fine entrees"; it's a bit "expensive" for the genre, though, and there can be "long waits" at peak times.

Original Joe's *American/Italian*   21 | 22 | 23 | $39

North Beach | 601 Union St. (Stockton St.) | 415-775-4877 | www.originaljoessf.com

Relocated to North Beach in 2012 after a fire at the Tenderloin original (opened in 1937), this "classic" Italian-American joint has fans de-claring it "was worth the wait" for "hearty", "honest" fare like "heaping plates of pasta" and "reasonably priced wine"; "tuxedoed waiters" and "red booths" abound for an "early-SF" vibe, and "young and old" crowds alike are "pleased" to have this "gem back in action."

Osha Thai *Thai*   22 | 21 | 19 | $28

Cow Hollow | 2033 Union St. (bet. Buchanan & Webster Sts.) | 415-567-6742

(continued)

(continued)

Osha Thai
Embarcadero | Hyatt Regency San Francisco | 4 Embarcadero Ctr., street level (Drumm St.) | 415-788-6742
Glen Park | 2922 Diamond St. (Bosworth St.) | 415-586-6742
Mission | 819 Valencia St. (bet. 19th & 20th Sts.) | 415-826-7738
SoMa | 149 Second St. (Natoma St.) | 415-278-9991
SoMa | 311 Third St. (Folsom St.) | 415-896-6742
www.oshathai.com

Osha Thai Noodle Cafe ● *Thai*
Tenderloin | 696 Geary St. (Leavenworth St.) | 415-673-2368 | www.oshathai.com

After Osha ⊠ *Thai*
Downtown | 432 Sutter St. (Stockton St.) | 415-397-6742 | www.afterosha.com

Most find this "relatively inexpensive" chain "convenient" and "satisfying" for its "variety" of Thai staples – including "killer" curries – delivered in a "clean, modern" setting complete with "wonderful" cocktails (the original Tenderloin location offers beer and wine only); generally "friendly" staffers add to the "happy" vibe; P.S. individual branches range from stylish sit-down eateries to "express" take-out stops.

O3 Bistro & Lounge ⊠ *Asian*   24 | 22 | 22 | $31
Civic Center | 524 Van Ness Ave. (bet. Golden Gate Ave. & McAllister St.) | 415-934-9800 | www.o3restaurant.com

A "handy" "pre-symphony option", this Civic Center Cal-Asian offers an "amazing" menu and "delicious cocktails", all served by a generally "helpful" staff in a "dark, cozy and sexy" space; add in moderate prices and a sweet "happy hour", and it's no surprise patrons vow to "keep going back."

Outerlands Ⓜ *American*   25 | 20 | 19 | $29
Outer Sunset | 4001 Judah St. (45th Ave.) | 415-661-6140 | www.outerlandssf.com

Helping to revitalize the Outer Sunset "one plate at a time", this "tiny" spot "out by the beach" racks up "long lines" for "rising star" Brett Cooper's "awesome", ingredient-driven New American meals and farm-to-glass cocktails; the "fabulous" "warm" "homemade breads" and "quaint" "driftwood decor" provide solace from the "cold outside" (where you can "wait a lifetime", particularly for weekend brunch), but fans still insist it's "one to seek out."

Out the Door *Vietnamese*   23 | 15 | 19 | $30
Embarcadero | Ferry Building Mktpl. | 1 Ferry Bldg. (The Embarcadero) | 415-321-3740
Upper Fillmore | 2232 Bush St. (Fillmore St.) | 415-923-9575 www.outthedoors.com

Offering the "same" "modern Vietnamese" "goodness" without "the hassle of its parent", the Slanted Door, this "less-expensive" offshoot in the Upper Fillmore allows fans to "spontaneously enjoy shaking beef" and other favorites (Asian and "American breakfasts" too), while its more "downscale take-out" sibling in the Ferry Building hawks lunches and "take-home" cooking "kits"; if the Bush Street location's "modern" decor isn't everyone's "cup of oolong", "friendly" service and "wine on tap" "warm things up."

	FOOD	DECOR	SERVICE	COST

Oyaji ⓜ *Japanese*   ▽ 23 | 17 | 18 | $40

Outer Richmond | 3123 Clement St. (bet. 32nd & 33rd Aves.) |
415-379-3604 | www.oyajirestaurant.com
It's one "big sushi party" at this "intimate" Outer Richmond Japanese,
where the chef-owner (a "real character") produces "delicately prepared" fish and "wonderful" izakaya specialties for midpriced tabs in
a "traditional" setting; regulars advise to amp up the fun, pour the *oy-
aji* ("old man") "a few drinks" and "let the good times roll."

Ozumo *Japanese*   25 | 24 | 21 | $61

Embarcadero | 161 Steuart St. (bet. Howard & Mission Sts.) |
415-882-1333 | www.ozumo.com
"Prepare to be wowed" at this "modern, cool" Embarcadero and
Oakland duo, where "remarkable" Japanese fare – including "incredible" delights from the robata grill and "fresh, creative" sushi – is sup-
plemented by an "extensive sake menu" and "attentive" service; "expect
to pay a premium" ("if you're on an expense account, go crazy"), but
fans promise it's "worth every single penny."

Pacific Café *Seafood*   23 | 17 | 24 | $34

Outer Richmond | 7000 Geary Blvd. (34th Ave.) | 415-387-7091 |
www.pacificcafesf.com
"Get there early" warn regulars of this "no-reservations" seafooder, a
"casual" Outer Richmond "classic", where "deliciously fresh, reliable"
fare ensures "long lines" to get in (not to worry, there's "free wine
while you wait"); the menu and decor "haven't changed since the
'70s", but a "welcoming" staff that's "worked there for years" and "fair
prices" keep locals "returning."

Pacific Catch *Seafood*   22 | 17 | 20 | $26

Inner Sunset | 1200 Ninth Ave. (Lincoln Way) | 415-504-6905
Marina | 2027 Chestnut St. (bet. Fillmore & Steiner Sts.) | 415-440-1950
www.pacificcatch.com
"Healthy" fin fare with a Pan-Pacific influence is the hook at this outpost of a small chain of "casual", "affordable" seafooders whose "simple preparations" "allow the fish to stand out"; "there isn't much to the
decor", but the staff "makes you feel at home" with its "attentive service", while it's also "welcoming to children."

NEW Padrecito *Mexican*   - | - | - | M

Cole Valley | 901 Cole St. (Carl St.) | 415-742-5505 | www.padrecitosf.com
Fans of this red-hot Cole Valley taqueria and cantina from the Mamacita
gang applaud its "really inventive", locally sourced Mexican food
("pork belly tacos!") showcasing made-to-order tortillas and produce
from the co-owner's family farm in Sonoma; the colorful bi-level dining
room gets "incredibly busy" and "loud", thanks to the downstairs bar
and its "great cocktails" made with premium mescal and tequila.

Pakwan *Pakistani*   23 | 9 | 14 | $16

Mission | 3180-3182 16th St. (bet. Albion & Guerrero Sts.) |
415-255-2440 ⏉
Tenderloin | 501 O'Farrell St. (Jones St.) | 415-776-0160
www.pakwanrestaurant.com
"Fragrant, scrumptious curries" and "soft, chewy naan" are "outstanding" and "cheap" at these "hole-in-the-wall" Pakistani Bay

Area mini-chain branches; you "order at the counter" (the "staff can be gruff") and "ambiance is negligible", so "just close your eyes", or better yet, get "your order to go"; P.S. they're "BYO – always a plus."

NEW The Palace 🅂Ⓜ *Californian*   – | – | – | E

Mission | 3047 Mission St. (Cesar Chavez St.) | 415-666-5218
Manny Torres Gimenez – a fine-dining vet (Nobu, Coi and Quince) with a knack for transforming holes-in-the-wall into cult restaurants (Mr. Pollo, Roxy's Cafe) – has taken over this old-school Mission beef palace and is turning out market-driven Californian steakhouse fare with Venezuelan touches; affordable tasting menus (with an à la carte option) are offered in a stripped-down setting, with just nine tables, BYOB and dinner served Wednesday–Sunday only.

Palio d'Asti 🅂 *Italian*   21 | 20 | 22 | $46

Downtown | 640 Sacramento St. (bet. Kearny & Montgomery Sts.) | 415-395-9800 | www.paliodasti.com
With its "heartwarming" Italian standards made from "quality ingredients", "professional service" and "upscale" Tuscan-inspired trappings, this FiDi trattoria is a "great choice" for a "business lunch" or a "special meal" in the city; "truffle dinners in the fall" and an "awesome happy-hour special" ($1 pizza) seal the deal.

Pancho Villa Taqueria ● *Mexican*   23 | 11 | 17 | $12

Mission | 3071 16th St. (bet. Hoff St. & Rondel Pl.) | 415-864-8840 | www.smpanchovilla.com
"Frequent lines" at this "cheap, fast" taqueria duo in the Mission and San Mateo attest to the "freshness and popularity" of its "better-than-usual" "Mexican standards" ("stomach-busting" burritos, "refreshing" agua fresca "with chunks of real fruit") that make up for an interior that's "nothing special"; a staff providing "speedy counter service" "tries very hard to accommodate."

Pane e Vino *Italian*   23 | 18 | 23 | $43

Cow Hollow | 1715 Union St. (Gough St.) | 415-346-2111 | www.paneevinotrattoria.com
"In a city filled with" "neighborhood Italian joints", this Cow Hollow trattoria is deemed "one of the better", with "unpretentious but delicious" Northern Italian fare, a "great wine selection" and an "affable staff"; though the "homey", "kid-friendly" space can get "crowded" and parking can be a "problem", fans say "bravo" to its overall "value."

Papalote Mexican Grill *Mexican*   22 | 12 | 17 | $14

Mission | 3409 24th St. (Valencia St.) | 415-970-8815
Western Addition | 1777 Fulton St. (bet. Central & Masonic Aves.) | 415-776-0106
www.papalote-sf.com
"Hipsters stream out the door" at this Mission and Western Addition taqueria duo serving "unusually interesting" and "non-greasy" Mexican fare including "fantastic" "burritos" and salsa that "alone is worth a trip" ("buy a jar to take home"); purists say they're "not really authentic", and since the no-frills spaces get "pretty cramped", regulars "phone in" and get their affordable grub to-go.

Papito *Mexican*

▽ 26 | 16 | 20 | $23

Potrero Hill | 317 Connecticut St. (bet. 18th & 19th Sts.) | 415-695-0147 | www.papitosf.com

"Inventive, French-influenced Mexican dishes" are a resounding "success" at this Potrero Hill sib of Chez Papa, a "tiny" storefront "surprise" run by a "friendly, entertaining" team; with "fabulous prices", a copper-topped bar and sidewalk seating as well, "there's no better place on a warm Saturday afternoon."

Parada 22 *Puerto Rican*

▽ 23 | 19 | 22 | $18

Haight-Ashbury | 1805 Haight St. (Shrader St.) | 415-750-1111 | www.parada22.com

This "adorable little" Haight-Ashbury storefront features a "super-friendly" staff serving "rib-sticking Puerto Rican comfort food done right" (including "red beans so good" fans "could swim in a tub of them"); "cheap prices" for "good-sized portions" washed down with a "half-pitcher of sangria" are the makings of a "good night."

Parallel 37 *American*

24 | 22 | 23 | $64

Nob Hill | Ritz-Carlton San Francisco | 600 Stockton St. (California St.) | 415-773-6168 | www.parallel37sf.com

At this New American in the Ritz-Carlton, new chef Michael Rotondo (ex Charlie Trotter's) shows a "passion" for seasonal and "sometimes unusual" ingredients in the "delicious, fresh" dishes and prix fixe menus that servers might skillfully "pair with" "interesting and delicious cocktails" from the central bar area; though the experience doesn't come cheap in the wood-decked, clubby setting, some "can't wait to go back"; P.S. the Food score may not reflect the chef change.

Park Chalet Garden Restaurant *Californian*

16 | 22 | 18 | $29

Outer Sunset | 1000 Great Hwy. (John F. Kennedy Dr.) | 415-386-8439 | www.parkchalet.com

Facing Golden Gate Park, this Outer Sunset hangout "welcomes all" with an "outdoor vibe" and "house-brewed beer" to accompany "tasty" midpriced Californian grub served by a "happy staff"; unlike the adjacent Beach Chalet, there's no water "view", still, sitting on the patio with the "ocean air in your face" is "heaven."

Park Tavern *American*

24 | 24 | 23 | $53

North Beach | 1652 Stockton St. (bet. Filbert & Union Sts.) | 415-989-7300 | www.parktavernsf.com

There's "a certain magic" to this "happening" "see-and-be-seen" North Beach tavern with "great views of the park" that's often "jammed" with "politicos", the "social" set and clientele "of all ages" "eating and drinking well" in the "cool"-looking space; the "imaginative", market-driven New American fare (including the famed "Marlowe burger") is delivered with service that's "always pro", and a late-night bar adds to the "lively" vibe.

Pasión *Nuevo Latino/Peruvian*

25 | 23 | 22 | $40

Inner Sunset | 737 Irving St. (bet. 8th & 9th Aves.) | 415-742-5727 | www.pasionsf.com

Chef Jose Calvo-Perez serves Nuevo Latino–Peruvian fare (including "delicious" ceviche and "fantastic" entrees) at this "imaginative" Inner Sunset offshoot of his father's Fresca chain; service is sometimes "slow", and the "energetic environment" with a bright, "beautiful" Inca-inspired mural can "get noisy", but admirers swear the "happy hour is a steal."

Pasta Pomodoro *Italian*   18 | 16 | 19 | $22

Laurel Heights | 3611 California St. (Spruce St.) | 415-831-0900
Noe Valley | 4000 24th St. (Noe St.) | 415-920-9904
www.pastapomodoro.com

"Friendly" staffers, "comfortable, inviting" decor and "uncomplicated", "inexpensive" Italian fare (including a "wide selection" to fix a "pasta craving") are the hallmarks of this "semi-fast chain"; it's popular with "families and friends", and though it sometimes looks "like a day-care center early evenings", it "can always be depended upon to please."

Patxi's Pizza *Pizza*   22 | 16 | 18 | $22
(fka Patxi's Chicago Pizza)

Cow Hollow | 3318 Fillmore St. (Lombard St.) | 415-345-3995
Hayes Valley | 511 Hayes St. (bet. Laguna & Octavia Sts.) | 415-558-9991
Inner Sunset | 822 Irving St. (bet. 9th & 10th Aves.) | 415-759-9000
Noe Valley | 4042 24th St. (bet. Castro & Noe Sts.) | 415-285-2000
www.patxispizza.com

Even displaced Chicagoans swear the "deep-dish", "decadent stuffed pizzas" at this Bay Area chain are "the real deal" (though some "prefer the thin-crust" pies); since they're "always packed" with "families", the ambiance "tends to be noisy" and "waits are long" (locals know to "call ahead" for "half-baked pizzas" to finish up at home), and while service can be "slow" and the "decor could use work", it's a "great deal" that's "totally worth the calories."

Pauline's Pizza 🅢 🅜 *Pizza*   22 | 14 | 19 | $27
Mission | 260 Valencia St. (Brosnan St.) | 415-552-2050
Pauline's Wines 🅢 🅜 *Pizza*
Mission | 260 Valencia St. (Brosnan St.) | 415-552-2050
www.paulinespizza.com

They've been "getting it right" for decades at this "family-friendly" lo-cavore pizzeria in the Mission offering "unusual toppings" ("the pizza-of-the-day is the way to go") and "fresh salads" harvested "from their own farm"; although it can "be kind of pricey" and "parking may be an issue", "carafes" of house wine quaffed in the no-frills main room or in the nearby vino bar help lessen the sting.

Pazzia 🅢 *Pizza*   25 | 15 | 23 | $34
SoMa | 337 Third St. (bet. Folsom & Harrison Sts.) | 415-512-1693

SoMa habitués "squeeze" into this "solid neighborhood Italian" for "standout" "thin-crust pizza", "wonderful housemade pastas" and other "authentic" fare accompanied by a "surprisingly affordable wine list"; while the "friendly" atmosphere generated by the staff and "charming owner" is part of the "attraction", regulars suggest asking for an "outdoor table" if it's "too noisy inside."

Pearl's Deluxe Burgers *Burgers*   23 | 12 | 19 | $13
SoMa | 1001 Market St. (6th St.) | 415-861-1605
Tenderloin | 708 Post St. (Jones St.) | 415-409-6120
www.pearlsdeluxe.com

"Fat and juicy" patties plus half-and-half combo side-order "frings, springs and spries" and a "large variety" of "sooo-good" shakes stand up to the Bay Area "burger craze" at these local chain links offering high-end ingredients and different sizes to suit "lighter and heartier appetites"; most agree "you get a lot" for the money (without the "foodie pretention"), and whether you hit a "small" location or a "roomy" one, the staff keeps the "traffic flow" moving.

Perbacco ⊠ *Italian*
26 | 23 | 24 | $57

Downtown | 230 California St. (bet. Battery & Front Sts.) | 415-955-0663 | www.perbaccosf.com

"Phenomenal pastas" and other "fabulous" Italian dishes served by a "professional" team "always exceed high expectations" at this "more upscale" FiDi sib to Barbacco next door; there's a "superb wine list" and a "nice energy" to the "lovely" space, though it does get "noisy", so "request an upstairs table for peace and quiet."

Per Diem ●⊠ *American*
▽ 20 | 23 | 20 | $37

Downtown | 43 Sutter St. (bet. Montgomery & Sansome Sts.) | 415-989-0300 | www.perdiemsf.com

FiDi folks feast on "terrific lunches" (or go for "girls' night or a date") at this American with a Cal-Italian accent (with items like cioppino, porchetta and pizzettas) and a nod to the Gold Rush era in the two-story space; some find the "service is best at the bar", where "amazing" drinks keep it humming after work; P.S. Saturday is dinner-only.

Pesce *Italian/Seafood*
25 | 18 | 24 | $43

Castro | 2223 Market St. (bet. Noe & Sanchez Sts.) | 415-928-8025 | www.pescebarsf.com

In the process of relocating to larger Castro quarters from its former Russian Hill home, this "casual" ristorante plans to continue offering its "Venetian inspired" seafood and "terrific" pastas served "tapas"-style and enhanced by cocktails and "wonderful wines"; the "attentive staff" and "friendly" vibe will also be making the move.

Pi Bar ● *Pizza*
▽ 21 | 17 | 19 | $20

Mission | 1432 Valencia St. (bet. 25th & 26th Sts.) | 415-970-9670 | www.pibarsf.com

"Authentic NY-style, thin-crust pizza" and a "small but stellar rotating beer selection" delivered with "friendly" service make this pie purveyor a "popular Mission haunt"; the "simple, casual" digs are "perfect for a post-work" stop, especially during "hap-Pi hour" when suds and a slice go for $6.24 (the clever price of $3.14 each); P.S. it also "opens at 3:14" PM.

Pica Pica Maize Kitchen *Venezuelan*
21 | 14 | 18 | $15

NEW **Castro** | 3970 17th St. (Hartford St.) | 415-525-3359
Mission | 401 Valencia St. (15th St.) | 415-400-5453
www.picapicakitchen.com
See review in North of San Francisco Directory.

Piccino *Italian*
24 | 23 | 22 | $36

Dogpatch | 1001 Minnesota St. (22nd St.) | 415-824-4224 | www.piccinocafe.com

Situated in "modern"-rustic "digs" in The Yellow Building, this Italian "gem" continues to draw Dogpatch "regulars" with its "superb" "thin-crust pizza", "imaginative salads" and "inventive small plates", all "made from the freshest ingredients"; servers who are "über-friendly" add to the "solid value", as does "sitting at the bar watching the magic happen" in the "bright, airy room."

Piperade *Spanish* | 26 | 23 | 24 | $56 |

Downtown | 1015 Battery St. (bet. Green & Union Sts.) | 415-391-2555 | www.piperade.com

Chef-owner Gerald Hirigoyen "brings the Basque dining experience to life" at this "delightful", "out-of-the-way" Downtowner featuring "rustic", "authentic" regional classics and "affordable" wines from the area, all delivered with a "level of hospitality" that "just keeps getting better"; the "exposed-brick" digs are "filled at lunch with business" folk, but the "cozy" ambiance works for a "date", dinner with "friends" or any occasion calling for "flavor" and a bit of "flair."

Piqueo's *Peruvian* | 26 | 18 | 22 | $37 |

Bernal Heights | 830 Cortland Ave. (Gates St.) | 415-282-8812 | www.piqueos.com

At this "neighborhood jewel" in Bernal Heights, chef-owner Carlos Altamirano creates "beautifully presented" midpriced Peruvian fare with a "modern flair" featuring "easy-to-share small plates" (called "piqueos" in Peru) including "amazing ceviche" plus entrees; it's "loud and crowded" and "can be hard to get into" but has a "sexy atmosphere" and the "staff is very knowledgeable", especially "about the wines."

Pizzeria Delfina *Pizza* | 25 | 17 | 19 | $29 |

Mission | 3611 18th St. (Guerrero St.) | 415-437-6800
Pacific Heights | 2406 California St. (bet. Fillmore & Steiner Sts.) | 415-440-1189
www.pizzeriadelfina.com

"Insanely good", "beautifully charred" Neapolitan-style pies with "innovative toppings" à la "Delfina proper" (its big sis) have fans of this Mission–Pac Heights duo vowing they "won't eat pizza anyplace else"; it's no "one-trick pony" though, also offering "delicious" salads, antipasti and wines as staffers efficiently "swim their way through the sea of hipsters" – while those averse to "long lines" and "loud music" order "ahead for takeout."

Pizzetta 211 *Pizza* | 26 | 15 | 19 | $25 |

Outer Richmond | 211 23rd Ave. (California St.) | 415-379-9880 | www.pizzetta211.com

"Thin-crust artisanal pizzas" with toppings such as farm-fresh "eggs, pancetta, butternut squash" and other locavore ingredients that change weekly make this bare-bones pizzeria "one of the great hidden secrets" of the Outer Richmond; diehards arrive "early" to "snag" one of the few seats, and "dress warmly" lest they be relegated to "eating outside."

Pläj *Scandinavian* | ∇ 24 | 23 | 25 | $55 |

Hayes Valley | Inn At The Opera | 333 Fulton St. (bet. Franklin & Gough Sts.) | 415-863-8400 | www.plajrestaurant.com

They "definitely kill it in the cooking department" at this "tastefully decorated" Hayes Valley spot highlighting seasonal ingredients in "inventive", "well-balanced" Scandinavian fare that "you'll never find anywhere else"; the service is "casual yet refined", the cocktails "wonderful" and the tabs not cheap but "not too terribly expensive" either, so tipsters tout "don't miss it before or after the symphony, ballet or opera."

The Plant Cafe Organic *Health Food*   22 | 19 | 18 | $26

Downtown | 101 California St. (Front St.) | 415-693-9730 🌀
Embarcadero | Pier 3 (bet. B'way & Washington St.) | 415-984-1973
Marina | 3352 Steiner St. (Lombard St.) | 415-931-2777
www.theplantcafe.com

"Tasty", "organic" Californian cuisine served "in a cool atmosphere" is the concept that keeps these crunchy cafes turning out "awesome" "housemade veggie burgers", "fresh vegetable juices" and other "affordable" clean-living staples; the staff can get "slammed during the lunch rush", but fans appreciate being able "to eat out with friends and not blow your diet"; P.S. the Embarcadero location's patio has "beautiful views of the bay."

Plouf *French*   22 | 16 | 18 | $41

Downtown | 40 Belden Pl. (bet. Bush & Pine Sts.) | 415-986-6491 |
www.ploufsf.com

"Feel like you're in Europe" at this "industrial"-chic Downtown seafooder, where Francophiles declare the "mussels and fries" ("prepared many different ways") "are the best this side of Belgium"; "the French waiters" can be "nonchalant" and the outdoor seating on Belden Place can get "jammed", but it's still a "go-to place" for a "romantic" tête-à-tête at a moderate tab.

Plow *Californian*   26 | 19 | 21 | $24

Potrero Hill | 1299 18th St. (Texas St.) | 415-821-7569 | www.eatatplow.com
"Delicious breakfast and lunch dishes" (including "amazing home fries" and lemon ricotta pancakes "to die for") made of "locally sourced ingredients" have daytime diners coming "early" to avoid a "torturous" wait at this Potrero Hill Californian cafe; while the nothing-fancy interior of reclaimed wood floors and oak-barrel tables belies the sometimes pricey tabs, "friendly service" and a no-pressure vibe help make this a "favorite" of the "young crowd."

Poesia *Italian*   23 | 20 | 22 | $46

Castro | 4072 18th St. (bet. Castro & Hartford Sts.) | 415-252-9325 |
www.poesiasf.com

"Handmade pasta" and other "homey Italian food" from the Calabria region pairs with "Italian cinema classics" "projected on the wall" at this "vibrant", "intimate" Castro osteria; while some feel the "portions are small" for the price tag and "tables are close together", the "friendly" staffers "really do treat you like part of the family."

Pomelo *Eclectic*   24 | 16 | 22 | $24

Inner Sunset | 92 Judah St. (6th Ave.) | 415-731-6175
Noe Valley | 1793 Church Street (30th St.) | 415-285-2257
www.pomelosf.com

With menus featuring "a variety of dishes" influenced by cuisines from "around the world", this Eclectic duo serves "fresh" "global" grub cosmopolitans consider an "awesome value"; service can be uneven at both the "microscopic" Inner Sunset outpost and the "noisier" Noe Valley locale, but diners like that they "can watch the chef cook" in the vibrant, sunny rooms' open kitchens.

Pork Store Café *American*   19 | 12 | 16 | $17

Haight-Ashbury | 1451 Haight St. (bet. Ashbury St. & Masonic Ave.) |
415-864-6981
Mission | 3122 16th St. (bet. Albion & Valencia Sts.) | 415-626-5523
www.porkstorecafe.com

At this "greasy-spoon" "breakfast-and-lunch" duo in the Haight and
the Mission, "hangover" sufferers forget "Saturday night sins" with
"huge" portions of "excellent-value", "diner-style" classics (and a
"make-your-own" "Bloody Mary bar"); despite "lightning-fast" service, there can be "long waits", so regulars "crawl out of bed early" to
get their pick of tables; P.S. the 16th Street location is open until
3 AM Thursday–Saturday.

Postrio *American*   23 | 22 | 21 | $62

Downtown | Prescott Hotel | 545 Post St. (bet. Mason & Taylor Sts.) |
415-776-7825 | www.postrio.com

Though some "miss the big restaurant" of its heyday, this "simple cafe"
Downtown still turns out "wonderful" "personal pizzas" and American
"bar food" with "friendly", "timely" service; while the tab can be "pricey",
it's a longtime "favorite" that works "for a quick bite" "after shopping" or
"pre-theater", but one can only "descend the stairs like a star" to the
"beautiful" "main dining room" for breakfast or private parties.

PPQ Dungeness Island *Seafood/Vietnamese*   24 | 13 | 19 | $31

Outer Richmond | 2332 Clement St. (25th Ave.) | 415-386-8266 |
www.ppqcrab.com

Those who like crab say this Vietnamese in the Outer Richmond "is the
place to go" for "delicious", "transcendent" takes on the crustacean;
while the faux-tropical space can get "quite crowded" and parking in
the area is about the "roughest in the city", fans applaud the relatively
"cheap" prices and service that can accommodate "large groups" in
the upstairs dining room.

Presidio Social Club *American*   19 | 21 | 20 | $41

Presidio | 563 Ruger St. (Lombard St.) | 415-885-1888 |
www.presidiosocialclub.com

"Tucked away in the trees in the Presidio", this "vintage" military bar-
racks turned "casual" American serves up a "time warp back to the
'20s" to go with the "quirky", updated renditions of "down-home" eats
presented on "mess hall plates" and "lovely old-fashioned cocktails"
poured into "circa-1954" glassware; service can be "slow" but "prices
are reasonable", and "you can't beat lunch on the outside deck on
warm, sunny days."

Prospect *American*   24 | 24 | 24 | $63

SoMa | Infiniti Towers | 300 Spear St. (Folsom St.) | 415-247-7770 |
www.prospectsf.com

If "creative food" and "well-made" cocktails are "what you crave",
this New American "casual sister" to Nancy Oakes' "more upscale
Boulevard" is "a likely prospect"; its "spiffy", warm "urban" decor, "impeccable service" and "yuppie crowd" are reflective of its locale in a
"tony" SoMa "high-rise", but if you've got an "expense" account,
"first-rate" dinners and "Sunday brunch" will "surprise and delight",
while the "robust bar scene" is HQ for "happy-hour" deals and drinks.

	FOOD	DECOR	SERVICE	COST

Public House *Pub Food* | 17 | 20 | 17 | $29 |

South Beach | AT&T Park | 24 Willie Mays Plaza (3rd St.) | 415-644-0240 | www.publichousesf.com

Boasting its "own entrance to AT&T Park", this mega gastropub offers a "vast" beer selection to accompany "elegant" "bar food" at moderate prices from chef Traci Des Jardins (Jardinière); it hits a home run for "pre-game festivities" (just "get there early" to avoid "the line"), but "even on non-game days", diehards "stop by for a pint" and to "watch sports on the telly."

Q Restaurant & Wine Bar *American*   20 | 18 | 20 | $29

Inner Richmond | 225 Clement St. (bet. 3rd & 4th Aves.) | 415-752-2298 | www.qrestaurant.com

"Quirky, quick and quintessentially yummy", this Inner Richmond American with a "youthful vibe" and "playgroundlike dining room" complete with "magnetic letters on the walls" is "comfort-food central", turning out the likes of "mac 'n' cheese, Tater Tots" and "BBQ ribs" for a "truly reasonable price"; service can be spotty, but devotees say this "funky" spot will "make you smile."

Quince ⊠ *French/Italian*   26 | 26 | 26 | $101

Downtown | 470 Pacific Ave. (bet. Montgomery St. & Pacific Ave.) | 415-775-8500 | www.quincerestaurant.com

Guests embark on a "gastronomic adventure" at this "outstanding" Downtown Italian-French by chef Michael and Lindsay Tusk, proffering "exquisite" food and service with a focus on "inspired" tasting menus featuring Northern Californian ingredients; "intimate", "elegant" and "very expensive but worth it", it's "at the top of the local game", providing "a total experience."

Radish *American*   ∇ 18 | 17 | 19 | $23

Mission | 3465 19th St. (Lexington St.) | 415-834-5441 | www.radishsf.com

"Bottomless mimosas" enhance the "awesome" brunches (served Wednesday–Sunday) at this sunny Mission hangout that's "hip and fresh" with "no attitude"; regulars also "like the burgers" among other "pretty good" eclectic American eats – including gluten-free options – for budget-friendly prices.

Radius Restaurant & Cafe ⊠ⓜ *Californian*   ∇ 23 | 17 | 21 | $46

SoMa | 1123 Folsom St. (bet. Hallam & Langton Sts.) | 415-525-3676 | www.radiussf.com

SoMa "locavores" embrace this sit-down dinner Californian (and its adjacent "quick-lunch cafe") on Folsom Street's emerging "Restaurant Row", where a "welcoming" staff ferries out "creative" and "delicious" cuisine and wine – all "sourced within a 100-mile 'radius' of the restaurant (hence the name)"; "prices are reasonable for the quality", and the rustic-industrial setting includes a patio.

Ragazza *Pizza*   25 | 18 | 21 | $33

Western Addition | 311 Divisadero St. (bet. Oak & Page Sts.) | 415-255-1133 | www.ragazzasf.com

A "nice respite" from the crowds at older sister Gialina, this "fantastic neighborhood spot" in the Western Addition turns out "the same" seasonally driven "wood-fired" pizza, pasta and sides at moderate prices; a "nice wine list" and "very friendly" crew are the "icing on the cake", just "don't go with too many people" as the "small" space lined with "old family photographs" "doesn't take reservations" (though they do on the patio for groups of seven or more).

Ramen Underground ⊄ *Japanese/Noodle Shop* ▽ 19 | 12 | 17 | $14
Downtown | 355 Kearny St. (Pine St.) | 415-765-9909

"Get there before the lunch rush" to nab a seat at this "tiny", cash-only Downtown ramen shop, serving up "delicious" bowls of noodles with a "wide range of toppings" (but you do "pay extra" for them); service is "ok" and portions are "decent", though the "busy" scene puts off those who feel it's "not that exceptional."

R & G Lounge *Chinese* 24 | 13 | 16 | $37
Chinatown | 631 Kearny St. (bet. Clay & Sacramento Sts.) | 415-982-7877 | www.rnglounge.com

"Excellent" salt-and-pepper crab is a "must" among a "first-rate" variety of dishes at this "superior", "locally famous" Chinatown Cantonese with a "nicer than usual" space (and "pricier" tabs as well); the servers do "hurry you along" to make room for the crowds, but you should bring your "out-of-town guests" and "make them happy" nonetheless – just "make sure you have reservations."

Range *American* 27 | 21 | 25 | $55
Mission | 842 Valencia St. (bet. 19th & 20th Sts.) | 415-282-8283 | www.rangesf.com

"Not the stereotypical Mission hipster restaurant", this New American run by a husband-and wife team has real cred, turning out "inventive", "flavorful" "foodie-styled" fare along with "some of the city's finest" "housemade cocktails" to a "mature" crowd; the "cozy" digs get "noisy", but service is "attentive" and fans call it "one of the best buys in town" making it the "go-to" spot for a "special" "but not outrageous" date night out; P.S. its Dogpatch bar, Third Rail, is slated to open in fall 2013.

Regalito Rosticeria *Mexican* 23 | 19 | 22 | $29
Mission | 3481 18th St. (bet. Lexington & Valencia Sts.) | 415-503-0650 | www.regalitosf.com

At this "authentic, high-quality" "gem" "in the heart of the Mission", "organic ingredients" make for "delicious, fresh Mexican" "rotisserie" fare that's more "sophisticated and subtle" than you might expect; the "cute place" can get crowded, but the "friendly" servers are most "accommodating", while prices are moderate; P.S. connoisseurs "check out" Pigalito Night on Tuesdays, when the menu features "a whole pig."

Restaurant LuLu *French/Mediterranean* 21 | 19 | 19 | $47
SoMa | 816 Folsom St. (bet. 4th & 5th Sts.) | 415-495-5775 | www.restaurantlulu.com

There's a "lively" "buzz" about this SoMa French-Mediterranean stalwart serving "homey", "hearty" "family-style" eats in a "noisy but fun" "cavernous room" with an "open kitchen", rotisserie and "wood-burning stove"; critics call out "pricey" tabs and uneven service, but most "enjoy being together" here, plus there's a "nice wine list" to boost the mood.

	FOOD	DECOR	SERVICE	COST

The Richmond ☒ *Californian* | 25 | 18 | 25 | $44

Inner Richmond | 615 Balboa St. (bet. 7th & 8th Aves.) | 415-379-8988 |
www.therichmondsf.com

"Fine dining for a terrific price" is on offer at this Inner Richmond
Californian with "gracious service" and a "friendly chef" who turns out
"quality" dishes from an ever-changing menu; "affordable" wines and
a prix fixe option make dinner in this "unassuming yet sexy little dining
room" seem like an "outstanding bargain", and regulars predict "you
will leave feeling glad that you came."

Rich Table *Californian* | 25 | 18 | 22 | $63

Hayes Valley | 199 Gough St. (Oak St.) | 415-355-9085 | www.richtablesf.com
The "imaginative", "seasonal" Californian food "explores new ground"
and "matches the hype" while "embodying the best of Bay Area cuisine" at this "amazing addition to the Hayes Valley 'hood" by chef/
co-owners Evan and Sarah Rich; a few cite "crunched seating" and
"variable" service, suggesting it got "too popular" too fast, though
fans say it delivers real "value" for a "brilliant dining experience."

NEW Rickybobby ☒Ⓜ *Pub Food* | - | - | - | I

Lower Haight | 400 Haight St. (Webster St.) | no phone |
www.rickybobbysf.com

The "genius" duo behind Broken Record now offers its signature
low-priced "dressed-up" pub grub (e.g. "incredible" lobster mac
'n' cheese and bacon burgers) at this snug Lower Haight haunt; the
decor features a taxidermied two-headed cow and there's a bar
stocking local wines and beer, but you'll usually need to "wait in
line with all the twentysomethings, smart phone in hand" to share
the "communal seating."

Ristobar Ⓜ *Italian* | 20 | 21 | 20 | $43

Marina | 2300 Chestnut St. (Scott St.) | 415-923-6464 | www.ristobarsf.com
A "terrific menu of small plates, pastas and pizzas" is topped off with
"great coffee and desserts" by owner/pastry chef Gary Rulli (Emporio
Rulli) at this "sophisticated" Marina Italian whose "beautiful" setting
"makes you feel like you're in Venice"; though some naysayers
knock it's "pricey for what it is", the service generally satisfies, fueling
a "lively" scene.

Ristorante Milano *Italian* | 24 | 17 | 23 | $45

Russian Hill | 1448 Pacific Ave. (bet. Hyde & Larkin Sts.) | 415-673-2961 |
www.milanosf.com

Gnocchi cognoscenti hope this "first-rate Northern Italian" in Russian
Hill "stays unknown" to a wider audience so they can continue to get
a table in the "tiny" dining room that fills up fast; "gracious" service,
"fabulous" "handmade pastas" and other classic dishes are the main
draws, and regulars contend that even "higher-priced" competitors
don't always "match" this "neighborhood standby."

Ristorante Umbria ☒ *Italian* | ▽ 21 | 17 | 19 | $35

SoMa | 198 Second St. (Howard St.) | 415-546-6985 |
www.ristoranteumbria.com

"Details" are important at this "sweet, old-school Italian" where the
"Umbrian cuisine" is "solidly executed" and "the owner glad-hands all
patrons"; some say service "can be abrupt", but most find this "loud,

"popular" SoMa spot "completely charming" and "perfect for lunch" or for dinner "before a show" at the nearby Yerba Buena Center or Metreon.

RN74 *French*

22 | **23** | **22** | **$64**

SoMa | Millennium Tower | 301 Mission St. (bet. Beale & Fremont Sts.) | 415-543-7474 | www.rn74.com

Oenophiles happily "jump aboard" Michael Mina's "swank" SoMa bistro done up like a "European train station" where the drama of the "revolving" "timetable board" advertising bottle "bargains" "nearly eclipses" the "solid", "high-ticket" New French fare; it's aces for a "client lunch" and "happy hour" is a "scream" (as in "loud") when the "beautiful people" and "tech" titans crowd in, but the vino, chosen with prowess by Rajat Parr and crew, is what really "makes it special"; P.S. the Food score may not reflect the arrival of a new chef.

Roam Artisan Burgers *Burgers*

23 | **17** | **18** | **$18**

Cow Hollow | 1785 Union St. (bet. Gough & Octavia Sts.) | 415-440-7626
NEW **Pacific Heights** | 1923 Fillmore St. (bet. Pine & Wilmot Sts.) | 415-800-7801
www.roamburgers.com

Patty partisans "go to sleep thinking about the burgers" at these Cow Hollow and Pac Heights dens dedicated to "sustainable" ingredients in their "juicy, grass-fed" beef, all-natural bison, "harvest turkey" and "amazing" veggie options gilded with "unique toppings" and washed down with "thick, delicious" shakes; you may have to "jockey for a table" at these counter-service spots, but connoisseurs "love" customizing their orders to taste, and for a "fair price" too.

Rocco's Cafe ⇗ *Italian*

24 | **18** | **20** | **$26**

SoMa | 1131 Folsom St. (7th St.) | 415-554-0522 | www.roccoscafe.com
"Big" plates of "hearty" Italian fare for modest prices make customers "mega-happy" at this "fast, friendly" longtimer in SoMa; warmed up by a photo-covered interior, the "unpretentious atmosphere" appeals for "filling" breakfasts as well as lunch, dinner and midweek happy hour.

NEW Roka Akor ● *Japanese*

- | **-** | **-** | **E**

Downtown | 801 Montgomery St. (Jackson St.) | 415-362-8887 | www.rokaakor.com

This high-profile robata grill and sushi specialist (with other U.S. and international branches) brings contemporary upscale Japanese fare (both raw and cooked) and plenty of eye candy to Downtown's Jackson Square; the ultramodern dining room is anchored by a central open charcoal grill where guests can watch the prime steaks and flown-in-fresh fish being prepared, while a subterranean lounge lures the bar crowd with house-infused shochu, whiskeys and seasonal cocktails plus late-night bar bites.

NEW Roku M *Japanese*

- | **-** | **-** | **I**

Hayes Valley | 1819 Market St. (Pearl St.) | 415-861-6500 | www.rokusf.com
The first brick-and-mortar restaurant from the team behind the JapaCurry truck, this izakaya-style pub on the edge of Hayes Valley offers a selection of "amazing" Japanese bar bites and other homestyle fare at "neighborhood prices" with sake and shochu to wash it down; the small storefront is modestly decorated with dark paneling and a wood bar.

	FOOD	DECOR	SERVICE	COST

NEW Rosa Mexicano *Mexican*
▽ 24 | 26 | 24 | $44

Embarcadero | 30 Mission St. (Steuart St.) | 415-874-4300 |
www.rosamexicano.com

"Completely packed" after work with folks downing pomegranate
margaritas, this "neat space" in the One Market building delivers tableside guac that "rocks" along with other "delicious" upscale Mexican
fare; the staff (and the "tequila selection") keeps it a "favorite" for
"large group dinners" (and business lunches), though some locals just
"don't understand why a NY Mex joint" should take hold in SF.

Rosamunde Sausage Grill ⌺ *German*
22 | 11 | 14 | $13

Lower Haight | 545 Haight St. (bet. Fillmore & Steiner Sts.) |
415-437-6851
Mission | 2832 Mission St. (bet. 24th & 25th Sts.) |
415-970-9015 ◐
www.rosamundesausagegrill.com

These link purveyors dispensing "delicious housemade sausages"
"blow your standard hot dog out of the water" insist fans who call
them "a SF must" and a "great value" too; at the original Lower Haight
"hole-in-the-wall", customers go "next door to Toronado" for a "cold
one to wash it down", while patrons of the roomier Mission outpost
sample "favorite German beers on tap"; the Oakland outpost is located
in Swan's Marketplace, a gourmet emporium in a historic building.

Rose Pistola *Italian*
21 | 19 | 20 | $47

North Beach | 532 Columbus Ave. (bet. Stockton & Union Sts.) |
415-399-0499 | www.rosepistola.com

"Solid" rustic Ligurian cuisine – "delicious" pastas, "good-quality" fish
and "thin-crust" pizzas from the wood-fired oven – plus "an active
bar" scene in an "open, comfortable space" still draw them in at this
North Beach Italian stalwart; though some say the tab is "kind of
pricey", service is "attentive" and many like to "linger" and "people-
watch", especially at one of the "outdoor tables" or window seats
facing Columbus Avenue.

Rose's Cafe *Italian*
22 | 19 | 20 | $32

Cow Hollow | 2298 Union St. (Steiner St.) | 415-775-2200 |
www.rosescafesf.com

"Union Street swells" often stop by this all-day cafe offering the kind
of "delicious" Italian eats and "welcoming feel" that make it a "neighborhood favorite"; a "popular" spot to "grab brunch with the girls"
(their signature "breakfast pizza" is not to be missed), it gets "crowded
on weekends" and the "outdoor seating" fills up quickly "when it's
sunny"; even so, reservations are accepted for dinner only.

Roti Indian Bistro *Indian*
23 | 18 | 21 | $30

West Portal | 53 W. Portal Ave. (bet. Ulloa & Vicente Sts.) | 415-665-7684 |
www.rotibistro.com

"Upscale yet friendly and casual", this Indian pair in Burlingame
and West Portal turns out "delicious" "traditional" fare as well as
more "innovative dishes", including abundant vegetarian options;
service is generally "accommodating" in the modern, warm-hued
settings, and while some find the tabs a bit "pricey", regulars say
portions are "huge."

FOOD | DECOR | SERVICE | COST

The Rotunda *American*

21 | 25 | 21 | $45

Downtown | Neiman Marcus | 150 Stockton St. (Geary St.) | 415-362-4777 | www.neimanmarcus.com

"After dropping a fortune" in the Downtown Neiman Marcus, shoppers head to this "elegant" in-store cafe with a signature "stained-glass ceiling" for "pricey" American standards including lobster club sandwiches and "huge popovers with strawberry butter"; service could "be more attentive" and it's "a mad rush during the holidays", but all considered, it's a "place to feel very special"; P.S. no dinner served.

NEW Roxy's Cafe 🅂🅼 *Eclectic*

- | - | - | M

Mission | 2847 Mission St. (bet. 24th & 25th Sts.) | 415-375-1185 | www.roxyscafe.com

At this small, nondescript Mission storefront, chef Manny Torres Gimenez (ex Mr. Pollo) presents market-driven Eclectic fare in affordable prix fixe meals and bigger-ticket tasting menus; expect Latin, Asian and Italian influences, and Gimenez's signature arepas, cheese- or meat-topped corn patties that are a nod to his Venezuelan roots.

Roy's *Hawaiian*

24 | 23 | 24 | $54

SoMa | 575 Mission St. (bet. 1st & 2nd Sts.) | 415-777-0277 | www.roysrestaurant.com

"Expertly prepared", "top-notch" seafood and "fruity" cocktails are some of the highlights at this SoMa link in Roy Yamaguchi's Hawaiian fusion chain, where a "courteous" staff "takes care of every detail" in the lofty, white-tablecloth setting; many agree the high prices are "justified by the quality of the food" – plus the prix fixe deals and "aloha hour" are a "real bargain."

Ruth's Chris Steak House *Steak*

24 | 21 | 23 | $66

Polk Gulch | 1601 Van Ness Ave. (California St.) | 415-673-0557 | www.ruthschris.com

"They know how to treat a piece of meat" at these Polk Gulch and Walnut Creek chophouse chain links providing "predictably great meals" in an "upscale" (some say "corporate") atmosphere with "sophisticated" service; sure, they're "expensive", but most agree the "wonderfully juicy steaks" are worth it.

Ryoko's ● *Japanese*

25 | 20 | 21 | $39

Downtown | 619 Taylor St. (bet. Post & Sutter Sts.) | 415-775-1028 | www.ryokos.com

For a "notorious, late-night" "basement sushi bar", this Downtown den puts out "fresh", "well-executed" fin fare, offering "great quality at the right price"; while it's probably "not the best sushi you ever had", it's an "energetic, fun, divey" spot for "after-clubbing munchies" (serving until 1:30 AM), plus there's a "DJ in the corner" some nights.

Saha Arabic Fusion 🅂🅼 *Mideastern*

24 | 21 | 23 | $43

Nob Hill | Carlton Hotel | 1075 Sutter St. (bet. Hyde & Larkin Sts.) | 415-345-9547 | www.sahasf.com

Guests say the "small-plate strategy is the way to go" (and give a nod to "staff recommendations" too) at this "haute" Middle Eastern option in the Carlton Hotel; the decor has a "fun", somewhat "hippie-chic" look with blown-glass lamps and Moroccan metalwork, though some are "not thrilled with the location" on the Nob Hill–Tenderloin border.

Saigon Sandwiches ⊘ *Sandwiches/Vietnamese* | 25 | 4 | 14 | $7 |

Tenderloin | 560 Larkin St. (bet. Eddy & Turk Sts.) | 415-474-5698 |
www.saigon-sandwich.com

"Lines run out the door" at this famed Tenderloin "hole-in-the-wall"
dispensing "ridiculously inexpensive" Vietnamese sandwiches featuring "crusty rolls" stuffed with "exactly the right ratio of ingredients",
including "tofu or meat", "chopped greens" and "tangy carrot-slaw";
it's "takeout only" and closes at 5 PM, yet devotees insist you'll get the
"best bang for your banh mi" at this "quick-service" spot.

Sai Jai Thai *Thai* | ▽ 24 | 13 | 18 | $15 |

Tenderloin | 771 O'Farrell St. (Hyde St.) | 415-673-5774 |
www.saijaithairestaurant.com

"Authentic Thai" is dished out at this no-frills stop on a "sketchy
block" in the Tenderloin, where fans find some of the most "flavorful"
cheap eats "in the city"; newcomers note: "these folks will make it
super-spicy if you ask" and deliver it with "friendly service" to boot.

Saison ⊠Ⓜ *American* | 27 | 22 | 26 | $322 |

SoMa | 178 Townsend St. (bet. 2nd & 3rd Sts.) | 415-828-7990 |
www.saisonsf.com

"A unique approach to dining" comes via Joshua Skenes' "fantastic"
tasting-menu-only New American eatery – now settled into its new
SoMa digs with only "18 seats" and an "open kitchen" – and "hard-
core" foodies insist "you can bet the house that it'll be mind-blowingly
good" "from the first inventive course to the last sip of wine from the
pairings", all delivered with "incredible service"; it's also "stratospheric" in price, though diners can indulge for less on an à la carte sa-
lon menu in the cocktail lounge; P.S. open Tuesday–Saturday only.

Salt House *American* | 22 | 20 | 20 | $49 |

SoMa | 545 Mission St. (bet. 1st & 2nd Sts.) | 415-543-8900 |
www.salthousesf.com

Like its "sister" shops, Town Hall and Anchor & Hope, this "hip" SoMa
boîte with its "delicious" New American eats is a go-to favorite for
"after-work drinks, a bite with friends" or date night; a "bustling" "bar
scene" can make it "incredibly loud" in the "cool" "old" brick-lined
room, but that's "all part of the appeal" to the "buzzy young crowd"
too buzzed to notice the variable service.

Salumeria Deli *Deli/Sandwiches* | - | - | - | I |

Mission | 3000 20th St. (Florida St.) | 415-471-2998 |
www.salumeriasf.com

This petite, old-world–style Mission deli from the Flour + Water team
sells spit-roasted meat, antipasti and fresh pastas, plus morning pastries, fresh cheeses and fancy meat-centric sandwiches built on
house-baked bread; it's primarily an affordable take-out spot (open
until 7 PM), but seating is available most days until about 4 PM (not
on Sundays) at communal tables on the patio that sits between it and
sibling Central Kitchen; P.S. a second Mission branch is opening.

Samovar Tea Lounge *Tearoom* | 20 | 21 | 20 | $25 |

Castro | 498 Sanchez St. (18th St.) | 415-626-4700
Hayes Valley | 297 Page St. (Laguna St.) | 415-861-0303

(continued)

(continued)

Samovar Tea Lounge

SoMa | 730 Howard St. (bet. 3rd & 4th Sts.) | 415-227-9400
www.samovarlife.com

"Fine teas from around the world" and an "inventive" yet "limited" eclectic menu "can be sampled" at this trio of "peaceful tearooms" perfect for "a meditative experience" or "afternoon date" (particularly in SoMa with its "urban spectacular" views of the Yerba Buena gardens); still, service is a bit "uneven", and while the tea is "properly brewed", even aficionados agree it's "pretty pricey for what you get."

Sam's Grill & Seafood Restaurant ⊠ *Seafood*

22 | 18 | 21 | $43

Downtown | 374 Bush St. (bet. Kearny & Montgomery Sts.) | 415-421-0594
"Consistently terrific seafood" is what you find at this circa-1867 "San Francisco treasure" with "the look and feel of a Spencer Tracy movie" – think "martinis, curtained booths" and "crusty" waiters in tuxes who are all "grizzled pros"; while tabs can be "pricey", some believe this "historic" spot still offers "the best value Downtown", plus "the bar pours good drinks" and best of all, it "feels like home."

Sandbox Bakery *Bakery*

▽ 25 | 16 | 21 | $12

Bernal Heights | 833 Cortland Ave. (Gates St.) | 415-642-8580 |
www.sandboxbakerysf.com

Fans "flock" to this "French bakery with a Japanese twist" in Bernal Heights for "sweet and savory snacks and pastries" plus "great coffee" and "unique" "bento-style lunch items"; though it "ain't cheap" for what you get and there's no indoor seating, sidewalk "benches" and a "nice staff" will "do just fine" for most; P.S. closes at 3 PM.

Sanraku *Japanese*

23 | 16 | 19 | $32

Downtown | 704 Sutter St. (Taylor St.) | 415-771-0803

Sanraku Metreon *Japanese*

SoMa | Metreon | 101 Fourth St. (Howard St.) | 415-369-6166
www.sanraku.com

"You're not going to get a lot of wacky rolls" but for "fresh", well-"crafted" sushi, "excellent bento boxes" and other "authentic Japanese" staples, washed down by some good sake, this "small", "crowded" Downtown spot and its larger SoMa Metreon sibling are "hard to beat"; both offer "reasonable prices" and "fast, courteous service."

San Tung *Chinese/Korean*

24 | 10 | 13 | $21

Inner Sunset | 1031 Irving St. (bet. 11th & 12th Aves.) | 415-242-0828 |
www.santungrestaurant.com

"Crunchy, sticky, lick-your-fingers" good, the "dry fried chicken wings" cause a commotion at this Inner Sunset "Chinese-Korean" "dive" that also offers "hand-pulled noodles" and other specialties; patrons endure "long lines", "slow service" and "dull" decor, but most say the "reasonable" prices for "heaven on a plate" make this place "worth the hassle."

Saru Sushi Bar Ⓜ *Japanese*

▽ 28 | 22 | 25 | $44

Noe Valley | 3856 24th St. (Vicksburg St.) | 415-400-4510 |
www.akaisarusf.com

Noe Valleyites dine "cheek by jowl" at this "tiny" Japanese offering "fresh, delicious" classic and nouveau sushi and a "carefully thought-out" sake list; the renovated room run by an "extremely friendly" staff juxtaposes traditional wood paneling with exposed-concrete walls decorated with monkeys (from whence the name comes).

Sauce ● *American*   22 | 17 | 22 | $44

Downtown | 56 Belden Pl. (bet. Bush & Pine Sts.) | 415-397-8800
Hayes Valley | 131 Gough St. (Oak St.) | 415-252-1369
www.saucesf.com

An "interesting menu" of American tapas and other "upscale comfort" food is served up by a "lovely" staff at this duo, where dining "outdoors under the lights and stars" in restaurant alley Belden Place can feel "very European" as long as the "weather cooperates" (there's also indoor space), while the "relaxed" Hayes Valley original offers "a good buy for pre-theater"; P.S. open daily until 2 AM.

Scala's Bistro *Italian*   23 | 22 | 23 | $49

Downtown | Sir Francis Drake Hotel | 432 Powell St. (bet. Post & Sutter Sts.) |
415-395-8555 | www.scalasbistro.com

"Memorable" seasonal Italian fare with some French touches gives "high satisfaction" to diners at this "bustling" bistro in Downtown's Sir Francis Drake Hotel, where patrons praise the "helpful" staff and warm "Tuscan atmosphere" inside the "classic, old SF" room; yes, "it can be noisy", still, the majority feels it's an "outstanding value" and "a breath of fresh air in the overpriced Union Square" area; P.S. the arrrival of a new chef is not reflected in the Food score.

Schmidt's *German*   22 | 19 | 20 | $28

Mission | 2400 Folsom St. (20th St.) | 415-401-0200 | www.schmidts-sf.com

"Casual" and "non-kitschy", this suds-centric German in the Mission from the owners of nearby Walzwerk dishes up a "limited menu" of "amazing sausages", "spaetzle", "apple strudel" and other usual suspects, along with a "killer" selection of Deutsch beers on tap; prices are "reasonable" for the "filling" fare served at "communal" tables in basic surroundings, but "be forewarned – when they say 'large beer', they mean it."

NEW Schulzies Bread Pudding *Dessert*   - | - | - | I

Hayes Valley | 364 Hayes St. (Gough St.) | 510-783-3464 |
www.schulziesbreadpudding.com

"Really different from your typical" frozen dessert specialist, this "undeniably adorable" Hayes Valley pudding parlor (a spin-off of the original SoCal original) features a classic ice cream shop look while showcasing a rotating menu of creatively flavored sweet and savory bread puddings ("so many to choose from!" – there are 108 varieties in rotation, both hot and cold), each whimsically named (e.g. Salted Caramel Sutra), scooped and capped off with free toppings by a "really friendly" staff.

Scoma's *Seafood*   24 | 20 | 22 | $49

Fisherman's Wharf | Pier 47 | 1 Al Scoma Way (Jefferson St.) |
415-771-4383 | www.scomas.com

"As reliable as the morning fog", these Fisherman's Wharf and Sausalito waterfront "favorites" serve "wonderful Italian-style seafood" to a mix of "locals and tourists" who keep them "popular and crowded"; though a bit "dated" and "not cheap", they're "friendly", "entertaining" and still "highly recommended."

NEW Seaglass Restaurant Ⓜ *Californian*

| − | − | − | M |

Embarcadero | Exploratorium | Pier 15 (The Embarcadero) | 415-528-4360 | www.seaglassrestaurantsf.com

Headed up by Loretta Keller (Coco 550), with assistance from master su-shi chef Sachio Kojima, this ultramodern sit-down restaurant in the relo-cated Exploratorium features midpriced locally sourced Californian fare inspired by the bay, including Monterey Bay Seafood Watch–approved fish and even sea-grape cocktails, along with kid-friendly eats; the glass-lined interior incorporates elements of the museum's exhibits, while an outdoor patio area beckons with its unobstructed waterfront views; P.S. open till 10 PM (as is the museum) Wednesday–Thursday.

Sears Fine Food *Diner*

| 20 | 15 | 19 | $23 |

Downtown | 439 Powell St. (bet. Post & Sutter Sts.) | 415-986-0700 | www.searsfinefood.com

"Little" "Swedish pancakes" served with warm maple syrup "melt in your mouth" at this Downtown "legend", where there's typically a "long line in the morning"; the interior is "nostalgic", though "a bit noisy", but service is "decent" and there's also a menu of "American diner food" that goes beyond breakfast, while tabs are "relatively light on the wallet."

Sebo Ⓜ *Japanese*

| 27 | 19 | 21 | $80 |

Hayes Valley | 517 Hayes St. (bet. Laguna & Octavia Sts.) | 415-864-2122 | www.sebosf.com

Self-proclaimed "sushi experts" say "if you love fresh fish" and pre-mium sake, this "traditional Tokyo-style" bar in Hayes Valley is quite a catch with its "inventive", "seasonal" seafood "you've never heard of before" that's "flown in daily from Japan" then fussed over "to bring out its maximum umami"; regulars sit at the counter to "watch them make art" that comes at "exorbitant prices"; P.S. closed Monday.

Sens Restaurant Ⓢ *Mediterranean/Turkish*

| 20 | 21 | 19 | $42 |

Embarcadero | Embarcadero Ctr. | 4 Embarcadero Ctr. (Drumm St.) | 415-362-0645 | www.sens-sf.com

"Reliable" Mediterranean "comfort food" and a "spacious setting" in the Embarcadero Center make this destination a "mainstay" for "busi-ness lunches", "group" dining and "alfresco happy hour"; but it's the "lovely" "views of the bay and Ferry Building" that make it a "cool place to hang out" and enjoy mezes and cocktails while being waited on by "accommodating" servers.

The Sentinel Ⓢ *Sandwiches*

| ▽ 23 | 9 | 18 | $13 |

SoMa | 35 New Montgomery St. (Stevenson St.) | 415-284-9960 | www.thesentinelsf.com

Lines run "long" at this SoMa "takeout-only" shop from Dennis Leary (The Golden West) cranking out "superb" morning pastries and "in-credible" "artisanal sandwiches" on "fantastic breads"; "they fre-quently sell out", but regulars "don't mind spending a little extra" for the "tastiest lunch you can get"; P.S. open weekdays only till 2:30 PM.

Serpentine *American*

| 23 | 21 | 21 | $40 |

Dogpatch | 2495 Third St. (22nd St.) | 415-252-2000 | www.serpentinesf.com

"Impressive creations" make this "trendy" New American "Dogpatch gem" (and Slow Club sibling) a "perennial brunch favorite", while it

	FOOD	DECOR	SERVICE	COST

also serves up "excellent" cocktails and "delicious" lunch and dinner fare with a focus on "local" and "sustainable" ingredients; fans "love the industrial feel" – "high ceilings and concrete" – as well as the "friendly" staff and "fair" prices, and despite the occasional menu "miss", most leave "full and happy."

Seven Hills ☒ *Italian*

27	21	25	$53

Nob Hill | 1550 Hyde St. (Pacific Ave.) | 415-775-1550 | www.sevenhillssf.com

Forget North Beach, Italophiles suggest you head to this "lively" trattoria on Nob Hill proffering "amazing pastas" (order "half portions" to "try as many as you can") and other "drop-dead delicious", "gorgeous" farm-to-plate cuisine, complemented by a wine list curated by two master sommeliers; servings can be "tiny" and seating "cramped", but any shortcomings are forgotten thanks to a staff that "really knows how to treat people."

Shalimar *Indian/Pakistani*

23	7	13	$16

Polk Gulch | 1409 Polk St. (Pine St.) | 415-776-4642

Tenderloin | 532 Jones St. (bet. Geary & O'Farrell Sts.) | 415-928-0333
www.shalimarsf.com

"Ignore the decor" (i.e. lack thereof) and "fast-food service" and relish the "insanely good" and "spicy" "cheap eats" at these outposts of an Indian-Pakistani chainlet that loyalists say puts its "imitators" to shame; a few balk at the "greasy fare" and "shabby digs" but others remind "you go here to eat, not hang out."

NEW Shorty Goldstein's ☒ *Deli*

-	-	-	I

Downtown | 126 Sutter St. (bet. Kearny & Montgomery Sts.) | 415-986-2676 | www.shortygoldsteins.com

Expect Jewish soul food (think matzo ball soup, brisket and pastrami) updated with a seasonal, sustainable angle at this Financial District deli from chef-owner Michael Siegel (formerly of Betelnut), who does all the smoking, brining, curing and pickling (and most of the baking) in-house; the storefront, which is simply outfitted with subway tile, exposed brick and a blackboard menu, is geared for takeout but has a long counter for folks who prefer to nosh on-site (note that the deli is open only Monday–Friday from 8 AM-4 PM).

Showdogs *Hot Dogs*

∇ 20	12	15	$13

Downtown | 1020 Market St. (Golden Gate Ave.) | 415-558-9560 | www.showdogssf.com

Dog lovers declare this upscale Downtown sausage shop slinging luxury "links" and "homemade" condiments is worth applauding "loudly"; sandwiches (e.g. "an excellent fried-chicken" one) and a "surprising range of hearty breakfasts" are also offered, and if tabs are "a little pricey", the "variety and creativity" plus a "great beer" selection make it "best" in show for grabbing a bite near the theater district.

NEW 1601 Bar & Kitchen ☒☒ *French/Sri Lankan*

-	-	-	M

SoMa | 1601 Howard St. (12th St.) | 415-552-1601 | www.1601sf.com

This upscale Sri Lankan–influenced French eatery from Brian Fernando (ex Le Papillon) offers adventurous diners midpriced, seasonally driven small plates that draw on the island's multicultural cuisine (which has

Indian, Portuguese, Dutch and British elements) mixed with modern French techniques and plating styles; the SoMa setting sets the stage with brightly hued batiks and potted plants, but despite the name, there's no hard alcohol served (just happy-hour specials and food-friendly wines and beer at the dark-wood bar).

Skool *Seafood* | 23 | 22 | 21 | $41 |

Potrero Hill | 1725 Alameda St. (De Haro St.) | 415-255-8800 | www.skoolsf.com

Located in Potrero Hill, this "secluded", "Japanese-influenced" sea-fooder gets "straight A's" for its "fresh", "innovative" eats and "great cocktails" ably served by an "informed" crew in a "way-cool" "modern" setting; "the only demerit is for an ocean-sized roar", especially during a "happy hour" attracting "a zillion young sweet things", but "reasonable prices" and a "beautiful patio" earn "extra credit."

Slanted Door *Vietnamese* | 26 | 23 | 22 | $53 |

Embarcadero | Ferry Building Mktpl. | 1 Ferry Bldg. (The Embarcadero) | 415-861-8032 | www.slanteddoor.com

"Tourists and regulars just keep coming and rightfully so", as Charles Phan's "longtime favorite" provides "extraordinary" "contemporary" Vietnamese cuisine in a "terrific" Embarcadero waterfront location; opinions vary on whether the "modern", "airy" space is "inviting" or too "noisy", and some feel the service can be "rushed", but most affirm the "pricey" tabs are worth it for such a "sensational" meal – "and the views of the bay aren't too bad either."

Slow Club *American* | 23 | 18 | 21 | $37 |

Mission | 2501 Mariposa St. (Hampshire St.) | 415-241-9390 | www.slowclub.com

"Mission cool" paired with "fresh" "local" ingredients from a "seasonal" New American menu characterize this "popular" "neighborhood" "go-to" in a "noisy" "industrial" space; "hipsters" come for the "not-too-pricey" fare, "solid brunch and "impressive" cocktails, while service is generally "knowing."

Sociale ◨ *Italian* | 24 | 22 | 23 | $51 |

Presidio Heights | 3665 Sacramento St. (bet. Locust & Spruce Sts.) | 415-921-3200 | www.caffesociale.com

Down a "side alley" in Presidio Heights, this "charming" "hideaway" serving "first-rate" "seasonal" "Northern Italian" fare is a neighborhood "favorite" for a "romantic dinner" or "catch-up time with good friends", particularly on the "secret patio"; the "tiny" dining room's "tight seating" means "you'll get to know your neighbors" and the tabs are "a bit pricey", but the "friendly" staff is "gracious and knowledgeable."

SoMa StrEAT Food Park *Eclectic* ∇ | 23 | 19 | 18 | $13 |

SoMa | 428 11th St. (Bryant St.) | no phone | www.somastreatfoodpark.com

With "about 10 food trucks at any given time", this "unique" SoMa hub proffers "awesome" eats in an "energetic, fun environment", complete with a beer-and-wine truck, trivia nights and DJ parties; the "diverse group" of vendors changes every day", so you can "try a different one each time" and have a taste of "San Francisco at its finest"; open daily but closed from 3–5 PM weekdays.

Sons & Daughters   *American*

26 | 21 | 23 | $137

Nob Hill | 708 Bush St. (bet. Mason & Powell Sts.) | 415-391-8311 | www.sonsanddaughterssf.com

The "brilliant" young chefs behind this "tiny" Nob Hill "gem" have "foodies" "purring with delight" over their New American "tasting menus" enlivened with "a dash of molecular gastronomy" and game-changing "wine pairings"; it's all "a bit precious" and prices have crept up while "portions" remain "microscopic", but the savvy staff is disarmingly "playful" and the open kitchen adds to the experience.

Sotto Mare ⊠ *Italian/Seafood*

26 | 16 | 21 | $35

North Beach | 552 Green St. (Columbus Ave.) | 415-398-3181 | www.sottomaresf.com

You'll find fish, pasta and "that's about it" at this "eccentric" yet "excellent" Italian seafooder in North Beach, which "looks like a dive bar" "full of neighbors" who sit "at the counter", the few tables or "outside when it's sunny" feasting on what may be the "best cioppino in the city"; overall, expect "good value" on "huge portions" of "simple", "fresh" fare along with "decent" service in an atmosphere that's "boisterous" "fun."

Source   *Pizza/Vegetarian*

∇ 24 | 14 | 20 | $20

Potrero Hill | 11 Division St. (De Haro St.) | 415-864-9000 | www.source-sf.com

"Really tasty veggie and vegan choices", including "heavenly" brick-oven pizzas, make this Potrero Hill locale a "sure bet" for those going meat-free – but carnivore pals will "rejoice" over the "exceptional quality" too; with "quirky" decor, "friendly" service and low prices, it's an easy option "for everyone."

🆕 South at SFJAZZ   *American*

- | - | - | M

Hayes Valley | SFJazz Ctr. | 201 Franklin St. (Fell St.) | 415-539-3905 | www.southatsfjazz.com

Charles Phan (the Slanted Door) jettisons his usual Asian cuisine and instead pays homage to jazz's Southern heritage with a compact, mid-priced menu of soul food–inspired small plates including fried oysters and entrees like gumbo at this stop located in the SFJazz Center; the sleek Lundberg-designed interior, outfitted with silver-gray tones, floor-to-ceiling windows and a glassed-in kitchen, also includes three bars that specialize in bourbon and New Orleans–inspired cocktails.

South Park Cafe ⊠ *French*

22 | 18 | 19 | $44

SoMa | 108 South Park St. (bet. Center & 3rd Sts.) | 415-495-7275 | www.southparkcafe.com

"Tucked away" in SoMa, this bistro "calls Paris to mind" with its "simple, affordable and authentic" "French cuisine" served in a "low-key" atmosphere that's "intimate enough to have a conversation"; service is just "adequate", but the lovely parkside location is a plus at this "old classic" that's still considered a "neighborhood gem."

Southpaw BBQ & Southern Cooking   *BBQ*

∇ 20 | 18 | 22 | $28

Mission | 2170 Mission St. (Sycamore St.) | 415-934-9300 | www.southpawbbqsf.com

Bringing good ol' "Southern food" to the Mission, this "delightful" upscale "great barbecue" joint and microbrewery decked out with vintage photos cranks out the likes of brisket, brined chicken and "ribs done right"; the vast "selection of sauces" boosts the flavor, and the all-American whiskeys, wines and suds add to the appeal.

Spice Kit ☒ *Asian* — 19 | 12 | 17 | $14

Downtown | 405 Howard St. (1st St.) | 415-882-4581 | www.spicekit.com

"Customizable" organic Californian takes on "traditional Asian street food" like banh mi draws FiDi and Palo Alto habitués to these affordable breakfast, lunch and dinner spots; the fare "isn't exactly authentic" and "takeout" is popular since there's scant seating, but the "concept" brings "culinary diversity" to the neighborhoods.

SPQR *Italian* — 25 | 19 | 22 | $55

Pacific Heights | 1911 Fillmore St. (bet. Bush & Pine Sts.) | 415-771-7779 | www.spqrsf.com

Fans insist "you should try" the "*fantastico*" Italian fare at this "urbane" Pac Heights sibling of A16 turning out "heavenly pastas" and other "soulful" yet "extremely creative" dishes and pouring "amazing" "lesser-known" wines; the "tiny" room gets "noisy", but service is "fine" and "sitting at the chef's counter" is a "reward" in itself.

Spruce *American* — 26 | 27 | 25 | $70

Presidio Heights | 3640 Sacramento St. (bet. Locust & Spruce Sts.) | 415-931-5100 | www.sprucesf.com

"Brilliant, assured cuisine", "elegant" decor (with "well-spaced" tables) and "professional" service create a "sophisticated" dining experience at this "popular", "high-end" farm-to-table New American in Presidio Heights; while the "extensive wine list" does get "pricey", casual customers appreciate the bar menu's "simply delicious" burger.

Starbelly *Californian* — 22 | 20 | 19 | $34

Castro | 3583 16th St. (bet. Market & Pond Sts.) | 415-252-7500 | www.starbellysf.com

"Creative drinks and rustic comfort food" are on order at this Castro Californian, where the menu includes "delicious pizzas" and "unique beers on tap", and the "back patio" is perfect for lunch "on a warm day"; though dissenters say service isn't always "on the ball", at least it's "well priced for the area."

State Bird Provisions ☒ *American* — 26 | 18 | 23 | $59

Western Addition | 1529 Fillmore St. (bet. Geary Blvd. & O'Farrell St.) | 415-795-1272 | www.statebirdsf.com

The "fabulous concept of dim sum–style service" for "super-creative", "delightful" American dishes is "completely realized" at this "absolute winner" by chef-owners Stuart Brioza and Nicole Krasinski in a "barebones" Western Addition storefront; "it's a challenge" to get a reservation (or a seat at the bar), and "can get really expensive if you have no self-control", but given the "refreshing" service, "electric" atmosphere and "unbelievable" food, first-timers "want to come back for more"; P.S. an expansion next door is planned.

St. Francis Fountain *Diner* — 19 | 20 | 17 | $16

Mission | 2801 24th St. (York St.) | 415-826-4210 | www.stfrancisfountainsf.com

"Hipsters" populate this all-day Mission "soda fountain" where "old-time charm" and "super-reasonable" prices come with "good ol' greasy" "addictive diner fare"; service is "usually courteous", and a "vintage candy counter" and "satisfying" veggie dishes are unexpected perks.

The Stinking Rose *Italian*   20 | 20 | 20 | $36
North Beach | 325 Columbus Ave. (bet. B'way & Vallejo Sts.) | 415-781-7673 | www.thestinkingrose.com

"Get your stink on" at this "kitschy" Cal-Italian in North Beach, where "they season their garlic with food" in dishes such as "40-clove chicken" and "even ice cream"; "friendly" service and "decent" prices add to the "unique experience" that bulb-lovers say both "locals and tourists" "must try at least once."

Straits Restaurant *Singaporean*   20 | 21 | 18 | $36
Downtown | Westfield San Francisco Ctr. | 845 Market St. (bet. 4th & 5th Sts.) | 415-668-1783 | www.straitsrestaurants.com

"Creative cuisine and a fun atmosphere" make this "beautiful" Pan-Asian restaurant-cum-lounge in the Downtown Westfield Centre (with Burlingame and San Jose siblings) the place where "the hip hang out" to sample the midpriced "small plates" and other fare on the "interesting" "Singapore-style" menu; the music can be "very loud" and the service "incredibly slow", but most appreciate the "strong drinks."

Straw *Californian/Sandwiches*   ▽ 20 | 19 | 22 | $24
Hayes Valley | 203 Octavia St. (bet. Lily & Page Sts.) | 415-431-3663 | www.strawsf.com

"Let your inner child out" at this affordable Hayes Valley Californian, where a "whimsical" carnival theme features a "Tilt-a-Whirl booth" and a "quirky", "upscale" take on "circus food" including a Bearded Lady sandwich, a "burger on a donut" and a "cotton-candy cocktail"; the "helpful", "efficient" staff adds to an experience fans declare "worth the line."

St. Vincent Tavern &   ▽ 21 | 20 | 20 | $51
Wine Merchant 🗷 *American*
(fka Heart Wine Bar)
Mission | 1270 Valencia St. (bet. 23rd & 24th Sts.) | 415-285-1200 | www.stvincentsf.com

The staff "knows the intense wine list front to back" and "can walk you through" an impressive beer selection too at this Mission tavern from David Lynch (former wine director for Quince) serving "strong, local" American plates to accompany the upscale drinks; "small and intimate", it's "great for a date", and those out to sample some revamped bar bites will "love the pickled eggs."

🅽🅴🆆 Sugoi Sushi *Japanese*   - | - | - | M
Mission | 1058 Valencia St. (Hill St.) | 415-401-8442 | www.sugoisushisf.com

This modern Japanese in the Mission wins "creativity" points for its affordable, modern twists on traditional Japanese cuisine – "delicious" sushi, omakase dinners, "new-style sashimi" and cooked small plates "bursting with flavor and freshness" – ferried by an "attentive" staff; the red-hued corner storefront (previously KFC and Spork) offers casual booth seating plus a six-person sushi bar that's stocked with premium sake and wine.

Sunflower Restaurant *Vietnamese*

23 | 13 | 19 | $19

Mission | 3111 16th St. (bet. Albion & Valencia Sts.) | 415-626-5022
Potrero Hill | 288 Connecticut St. (18th St.) | 415-861-2336
www.sunflowersf.com

"Locals already know and love" these Vietnamese "gems" with "to-die-for" pho and other "stellar" dishes, including "excellent vegetarian choices"; at the small, centrally located Mission original, there can be a "wait", while the Potrero Hill locale is deemed "more attractive", but "quick service" and "inexpensive" tabs appeal at both venues.

Super Duper *Burgers*

23 | 16 | 19 | $13

Castro | 2304 Market St. (16th St.) | 415-558-8123
Downtown | 721 Market St. (bet. 3rd & 4th Sts.) | 415-538-3437
Marina | 2203 Chestnut St. (Pierce St.) | 415-931-6258
SoMa | 783 Mission St. (bet. 3rd & 4th Sts.) | 415-882-1750
www.superdupersf.com

Patty partisans agree the "name not only describes the food, but the prices" and "super-fast" service at these "sustainable" Bay Area burger joints notable for their "organic" ingredients, "amazing" vegetarian variations and "homemade pickles"; though "industrial" in feel, they let you "subdue" "beefy" "guilty-pleasure" "cravings" without the guilt, plus you can "add alcohol to your milkshake", while "mini"-sized options and "choco-dipped" "soft serve" placate the "pint-sized" set.

Suppenküche *German*

23 | 18 | 19 | $32

Hayes Valley | 525 Laguna St. (Hayes St.) | 415-252-9289 |
www.suppenkuche.com

"From the pretzel to the schnitzel", this Hayes Valley hofbräuhaus serves "large portions" of some of the "the best German food around" backed by an "incredible beer selection", all "excellently priced"; "shoulder-to-shoulder crowds" make it "noisy as a rock concert" and sometimes "hard to get good service", but "das Boot" (a glass boot full of brew) makes fans say *"sehr gut!"*

Sushi Bistro *Japanese*

23 | 20 | 21 | $33

Inner Richmond | 431 Balboa St. (6th Ave.) | 415-933-7100
Mission | 2809 24th St. (Potero Ave.) | 415-282-2001
www.sushibistro.com

"A long, creative list of rolls" is offered at these Japanese siblings in Inner Richmond and the Mission serving "well-prepared" sushi that twists tradition with ingredients like jalapeño and wasabi aïoli; most agree you "get what you pay for", and when you factor in "friendly" service, it's no wonder these are "welcome neighborhood finds."

Sushirrito 🛂 *Japanese*

20 | 11 | 16 | $12

NEW **Chinatown** | 226 Kearny St. (Bush St.) | 415-544-9868
Downtown | 475 Sansome St. (Clay St.) | 415-393-9905
SoMa | 59 New Montgomery St. (Jessie St.) | 415-495-7655
www.sushirrito.com

"Gimmicky? yes", but the "burrito-sized" rolls (hence the name) "made to order" with quality ingredients like "fresh fish" and "local organic veggies" are "deliiiiicious" swear devotees of these quick-service, Japanese-inspired take-out shops with "lines out the door" for their "cheap eats"; choices are limited and frankly it's "way too much" food to finish, but "courageous" lunch-goers "try anyway"; P.S. hours vary by location.

Sushi Zone ⓈⱣ *Japanese*
27 | 14 | 19 | $34

Castro | 1815 Market St. (Pearl St.) | 415-621-1114 | www.sushizonesf.com

There's a "cult following" for this "extremely small" Castro Japanese where the "mustachioed genius behind the bar" turns out "very fresh" sushi and fusion-y rolls (like those with mango) in "good-sized" portions at prices that are "very reasonable"; a "ridiculously long sake list" adds to the appeal, but prepare for a "long wait" on the sidewalk or "neighboring bar."

Sutro's at the Cliff House *Californian*
21 | 26 | 22 | $52

Outer Richmond | 1090 Point Lobos Ave. (El Camino Del Mar) | 415-386-3330 | www.cliffhouse.com

You "can't beat the views (when the ocean isn't blanketed in fog)" at this "magnificent" Outer Richmond location where the "excellent" Californian fare, emphasizing seafood, is "beautifully presented" by a "helpful" staff; the "clean, bright" decor is "just fancy enough", and while the bill's "on the high side", it's "not overpriced for a landmark setting"; P.S. "if you can't get a window seat, a seat at the bar is the next best thing."

Swan Oyster Depot ⓈⱣ *Seafood*
26 | 13 | 22 | $35

Polk Gulch | 1517 Polk St. (bet. California & Sacramento Sts.) | 415-673-1101

"Just a food counter inside a fish market", this century-old Polk Gulch "institution" serves "the freshest seafood imaginable" until 5:30 PM; the "uncomfortable stool seating" is "as informal as the docks" but "the crew behind the counter" treats you "as one of their own", so while detractors say it's "not worth the price and wait", some supporters consider it "a strong contender for last meal on earth."

Sweet Woodruff *Sandwiches*
∇ 24 | 24 | 23 | $18

Nob Hill | 798 Sutter St. (Jones St.) | 415-292-9090 | www.sweetwoodruffsf.com

The "casual", quick-service offspring from the Sons & Daughters crew, this American in Lower Nob Hill proffers a rotating slate of "delicious" artisanal sandwiches, small plates and desserts; the tiny corner storefront is set up primarily for takeout, though with 11 stools lining the reclaimed-wood counter, it can be a "great lunch spot" too.

Tacko *Mexican*
22 | 18 | 18 | $16

Cow Hollow | 3115 Fillmore St. (bet. Filbert & Pixley Sts.) | 415-796-3534 | www.tacko.co

"Tack on over" to this Cow Hollow taqueria for an "oddball combination" of "Mexico and New England" that nonetheless "works beautifully", from its "lobster rolls" "as good as any you'd get in Bar Harbor" to chef-owner Nick Fasanella's "signature tacos" prepared his "way" with a "crispy shell"; the service and nautical decor earn mixed reviews, but moderate tabs and "buckets of margaritas" encourage patrons to keep "coming back."

Tacolicious *Mexican*
24 | 19 | 19 | $25

Embarcadero | Ferry Building Mktpl. | 1 Ferry Bldg. (The Embarcadero) | no phone ⓈⱮⱣ
Marina | 2031 Chestnut St. (Fillmore St.) | 415-346-1966 Ⱨ
Mission | 741 Valencia St. (18th St.) | 415-626-1344

(continued)

(continued)

Tacolicious

NEW North Beach | 1548 Stockton St. (Columbus Ave.) | 415-433-1800 ◗
www.tacolicious.com

Sceney yet "friendly", these "upscale" Bay Area Mexicans (siblings of
the original Thursday Ferry Building lunch stall) turn out "creative"
"twists on tacos" "from duck confit to skirt steak" boosted by "fine ingredients" and "amazing salsas"; margaritas pack a "punch" plus
there's a "mind-blowing tequila collection" at the Mission location's
adjacent bar, Mosto.

Taco Shop At Underdogs ◗ *Mexican*

| ∇ 24 | 15 | 19 | $14 |

Outer Sunset | 1824 Irving St. (19th Ave.) | 415-566-8700 |
www.underdogssf.com

"Tacos Nick's Way are a supreme bite of heaven" for fans of this Outer
Sunset Mex who "love going here to watch games, have a few drinks" and
chow down; it does get "packed", but the staff keeps the "quesadillas
loaded" and the margaritas "full-strength" even during the $1 Friday
deal (6–6:30 PM); P.S. two-buck Taco Tuesdays are another perk.

Tadich Grill ⊠ *Seafood*

| 24 | 22 | 22 | $46 |

Downtown | 240 California St. (bet. Battery & Front Sts.) | 415-391-1849 |
www.tadichgrill.com

"They define cioppino" at this "historic", "no-nonsense" Downtown seafooder (opened in 1849) where "anything off the grill is well done", wines
are "well priced" and the "surly" service should be taken with a "sense of
humor"; since it gets "busy" at peak times, vets advise "go for a late
lunch or early happy hour" and get a seat at the "entertaining" bar.

Taqueria Can Cun ◗⇲ *Mexican*

| 23 | 10 | 16 | $10 |

Downtown | 1003 Market St. (6th St.) | 415-864-6773
Mission | 2288 Mission St. (bet. 18th & 19th Sts.) | 415-252-9560
Mission | 3211 Mission St. (Valencia St.) | 415-550-1414

"Plump", "satisfying" burritos and "super" tacos are the main draw at
this "superb" taqueria trio offering "one of the best value meals in all
of SF"; the atmosphere is "no-frills" but late hours at the two Mission
locales still attract plenty of "hipsters", and the "cheap", "mouthwatering" Mexican fare wins over most everyone else.

Taqueria San Jose *Mexican*

| 23 | 13 | 17 | $11 |

Mission | 2830 Mission St. (24th St.) | 415-282-0203 |
www.taqueriasanjose1since1980.com

Taqueria San Jose No. 3 ⊠ Ⓜ *Mexican*

North Beach | 2257 Mason St. (Francisco St.) | 415-749-0826

High demand for the "great-value burritos" and "carnitas tacos" can
create "nightmare lines" at this bare-bones Mission Mexican stalwart
(with newer offshoots in North Beach and San Jose); decor and service
are not its strong points, so repeat customers advise figuring out your
order "before you reach the counter."

Tartine Bakery *Bakery*

| 27 | 15 | 16 | $16 |

Mission | 600 Guerrero St. (18th St.) | 415-487-2600 |
www.tartinebakery.com

It's not just a "corner bakery" – "it's a real experience" swears the
carb-craving crowd "flocking" at all hours to this unmarked "Mission

mecca" known for its "amazing" pastries, "massive" tartine sand-wiches and the "best croissants ever", along with country bread so sought-after ("reserve three days in advance or line up at 5 PM") the loaves "should be FDA regulated"; it's all served with "coffee in a bowl" and "a slice of oh-so-San Francisco attitude", and though seating is "sparse", the "precious" goods are deemed well "worth the calories" and "insane waits."

Tataki Canyon *Japanese*   24 | 18 | 19 | $33
Glen Park | 678 Chenery St. (Diamond St.) | 415-859-9383
Tataki South *Japanese*
Noe Valley | 1740 Church St. (bet. Day & 29th Sts.) | 415-282-1889
Tataki Sushi & Sake Bar *Japanese*
Pacific Heights | 2815 California St. (Divisadero St.) | 415-931-1182
www.tatakisushibar.com

"Snob-worthy", "responsibly acquired fish" and "creative rolls" (in-cluding "several vegan options") can be had if you brave "the waits to get in" at these "small", "modern" Japanese, with a Pac Heights loca-tion offering sushi, Noe Valley also serving robata grilled items and Glen Park adding ramen and other hot dishes to the mix; service re-views may vary and tabs are "a little pricey", but those who "go early" can "catch the happy-hour deals" and "sit down right away."

Tava Indian Kitchen Ⓢ *Indian*   - | - | - | I
SoMa | 163 Second St. (Natoma St.) | 415-543-8282 | www.tavaindian.com
See review in South of San Francisco Directory.

Terzo *Mediterranean*   25 | 23 | 23 | $49
Cow Hollow | 3011 Steiner St. (Union St.) | 415-441-3200 | www.terzosf.com
Regulars "order a lot of small plates to share" at this Cow Hollow Mediterranean where chef Mark Gordon "keeps whipping up delectable new dishes" that are "organic and seasonal"; prices can be "fairly high", but a "romantic interior" and "incredible servers" are in the package.

Thai House 530 *Thai*   22 | 16 | 19 | $19
Mission | 530 Valencia St. (bet. 16th & 17th Sts.) | 415-503-1500 | www.thaihouse530.com
Thai House Express *Thai*
Castro | 599 Castro St. (19th St.) | 415-864-5000
Tenderloin | 901 Larkin St. (Geary St.) | 415-441-2248 | www.thaiexpresssf.com ◗

"Solid", "super-cheap" Thai standards make this "efficient", family-run chainlet a "favorite before-the-bars haunt" in the Castro and Tenderloin, the latter open till midnight nightly; meanwhile, the swanky annex in the Mission offers more Pan-Asian options for the same "inexpensive" price point.

Thanh Long Ⓜ *Vietnamese*   26 | 16 | 20 | $49
Outer Sunset | 4101 Judah St. (46th Ave.) | 415-665-1146 | www.anfamily.com
You don't have to wait for "the arrival of Dungeness crab season" to "get down and dirty" with a "nutcracker and plastic bib" and "dig in" to "roasted" crustaceans and "amazing" Vietnamese-style noodles (smothered with enough garlic "to sink a boatful of vampires") at this "remote" Outer Sunset stalwart; for "frozen" seafood, it's pretty

	FOOD	DECOR	SERVICE	COST

"pricey", but "nice" drinks and "valet parking" help offset the variable service and sometimes "noisy" ambiance.

Thep Phanom Thai Cuisine *Thai* | 24 | 17 | 21 | $30 |

Lower Haight | 400 Waller St. (Fillmore St.) | 415-431-2526 | www.thepphanom.com

Presenting "phenomenally fresh and tasty" fare in a "small" "dimly lit" Lower Haight Victorian, this long-running Thai "never fails" to deliver a "more formal" Siamese dining experience ("not Westernized at all") "complete with authentically costumed" staff, "classically prepared dishes" and "traditional" decor; it "gets crowded" and as result "service can be spotty" but prices are reasonable.

3rd Street Grill ⊠ *American/Mexican* | 23 | 21 | 22 | $26 |

SoMa | 695 Third St. (Townsend St.) | 415-538-0804 | www.3rdstreetgrill.net

For a "quick lunch" in SoMa or a "delicious" burger or burrito "before or after the big game" at AT&T Park, this American-Mexican hybrid gets "two thumbs" up; it's "usually not too busy", and "great" service and reasonable tabs assure most "definitely would go back."

1300 on Fillmore *Soul Food/Southern* | 22 | 24 | 22 | $44 |

Western Addition | 1300 Fillmore St. (Eddy St.) | 415-771-7100 | www.1300fillmore.com

"Putting the soul back in soul food", this "dimly lit" "boîte" offers "refined" Southern-inspired eats amid "historical photos" that "embrace" the Western Addition's "jazz" tradition; sure, it's "somewhat pricey", but the "luxe" setting, "expertly crafted cocktails" and "charming" service make for a "glamorous" night out, especially when live music adds a "festive" touch on Friday nights and at the Sunday gospel brunch.

To Hyang Ⓜ *Korean* | ▽ 25 | 14 | 21 | $27 |

Inner Richmond | 3815 Geary Blvd. (bet. 2nd & 3rd Aves.) | 415-668-8186

It may fly under the radar, but this "no-frills" "real deal" in the Inner Richmond dishes out "amazing" affordable Korean fare and is "filled with locals" and avid eaters who love "exploring the unique dishes"; the menu's "not for the squeamish" and "when they say spicy, they mean it", but everything from the soy sauce and kimchi to the infused soju drinks is "housemade."

Tommaso's Ⓜ *Italian* | 24 | 17 | 21 | $32 |

North Beach | 1042 Kearny St. (bet. B'way & Pacific Ave.) | 415-398-9696 | www.tommasosnorthbeach.com

"Long before" there was a pizzeria "on every corner", this "old-school" North Beach Italian "institution" was firing up pies out of its "original wood-burning oven"; it's "not showy", just a "charmingly downscale" spot doling out Neapolitan "comfort food" at a "dockworker's price" by folks who "make you feel like family" – but "expect to wait" because there are "no reservations."

Tommy's Mexican Restaurant *Mexican* | 20 | 16 | 21 | $27 |

Outer Richmond | 5929 Geary Blvd. (bet. 23rd & 24th Aves.) | 415-387-4747 | www.tommystequila.com

"Delicious" margaritas "by the pitcher" and a "mind-blowing" "selection of sipping tequila" curated by "the original tequila ambassador", Julio Bermejo, make this "family-run" Outer Richmond Mexican featuring "authentic Yucatán favorites" ultra-"popular" with locals and fans from afar; something of a "neighborhood dive", it can get "very crowded", but servers who "are tops" and moderate prices help fuel the "fiesta."

Ton Kiang *Chinese*   25 | 14 | 18 | $29

Outer Richmond | 5821 Geary Blvd. (bet. 22nd & 23rd Aves.) | 415-387-8273 | www.tonkiang.net

"Order your heart out" at this "two-floor" Outer Richmond "institution" where a "dazzling" variety of dim sum is "served all day", joined by "Hakka cuisine" at dinner; "it's not the cheapest" and could use "sprucing up", plus there are "long" waits "weekend mornings", but for "delectable" Chinese food without the "drive to Chinatown", it's "the place to go."

Tony's Coal-Fired Pizza & Slice House *Pizza*   24 | 15 | 17 | $19

North Beach | 1556 Stockon St. (Union St.) | 415-835-9888 | www.tonyspizzanapoletana.com

"Now that's a slice of pizza" announce fans of renowned pizzaiolo Tony Gemignani's "take-out haven" offering single servings of his signature pies ("so many choices") to folks who "don't want to brave the crowds next door" at this famed North Beach 'za HQ; other "fast, great eats" include a mean "Chicago beef sandwich", but since there's no seating, most take their orders across the street to Washington Square Park.

Tony's Pizza Napoletana Ⓜ *Italian/Pizza*   26 | 18 | 20 | $29

North Beach | 1570 Stockton St. (Union St.) | 415-835-9888 | www.tonyspizzanapoletana.com

"It's hard to find a better pie" than those among the "great variety" of "award-winning" pizzas (Neapolitan-style, "Sicilian, Californian, Roman" even "gluten-free") that famed chef-owner Tony Gemignani tosses and cooks to a crisp in seven types of ovens at his "lively" "North Beach gem"; tabs are "somewhat pricey", but the "excellent wine list" and "friendly" servers help soothe after a "brutal" wait for a table.

Tout Sweet Patisserie *Dessert/European*   - | - | - | I

Downtown | Macy's | 170 O'Farrell St., 3rd fl. (Stockton St.) | 415-385-1679 | www.toutsweetsf.com

Top Chef: Just Desserts champ Yigit Pura's "lovely" patisserie perched on the third floor of Macy's Downtown sates sweets lovers and TV groupies with "precious pastries", "darn good tea" and a rotating menu of breakfast and lunch items; the fanciful treats are showcased in custom-made Italian display cases, available to go or eat-in at the ultramodern white-and-pink cafe with a "killer window view" where guests can "watch the action in Union Square."

Town Hall *American*   23 | 21 | 22 | $52

SoMa | 342 Howard St. (Fremont St.) | 415-908-3900 | www.townhallsf.com

"Not your grandmother's biscuits 'n' ham", the "upscale Southern-inspired" American eats (including "dessert to die for") at this "cozy" SoMa "tavern" keep it "always jam-packed" with "lotsa SF celebs and politicos" and "corporate" types knocking back "after-work drinks"; tabs are "kinda pricey" and things can get "noisy" both at the bar and the outdoor tables, but the "friendly and warm" staff stays "on top of things."

Town's End Restaurant & Bakery *American/Bakery*

`21` `16` `21` `$30`

Embarcadero | South Beach Marina Apartments | 2 Townsend St. (The Embarcadero) | 415-512-0749 | www.townsendrb.com
"Since way before" AT&T Park arrived nearby, this "terrific breakfast/brunch" Embarcadero "waterfront" spot has been turning out "reliable" American grub and "baked goods" (including "mini-muffins" arriving "as you sit down") that are "worth the calories" – and won't "break the bank"; the "relaxed" setting includes some outdoor seats, and the "attentive, happy" staff will "do anything to make you happy"; P.S. no dinner.

Trace ● *American* (fka XYZ)

∇ `22` `17` `22` `$54`

SoMa | W San Francisco | 181 Third St. (Howard St.) | 415-817-7836 | www.trace-sf.com
A "good option" in SoMa, this American in the W Hotel delivers small and large plates of "fresh, local food" for tabs that are a "bit on the expensive side", while offering a better "value" at breakfast and lunch; still, some find the "modern" setting too "sterile" and "loud", and recommend going when it's "not too busy."

Trattoria Contadina *Italian*

`24` `18` `22` `$40`

North Beach | 1800 Mason St. (Union St.) | 415-982-5728 | www.trattoriacontadina.com
"Out of the way" from "tourist-heavy Columbus" Avenue, this "cheerful" North Beach "classic" "is where the locals go" to enjoy "unpretentious", "old-school" Italian standards (including "housemade gnocchi" and "delicious pasta sauces") for "little money"; staffers provide "pleasant service", but since the "cozy" quarters can get "crowded", regulars say make a "reservation" or "eat at the bar to skip the wait."

NEW Trattoria da Vittorio Ⓜ *Italian*

`-` `-` `-` `M`

West Portal | 150 W. Portal Ave. (Vicente St.) | 415-742-0300 | www.trattoriadavittorio.com
Focusing on the Southern part of The Boot, this moderately priced West Portal Italian offers Calabrian pastas, pizzas, meats and bruschetta; there's table and banquette seating (plus a few outdoor seats for the rare warm evening) in the spacious yet intimate-feeling eatery, which is accented with brick, stone and a marble counter.

NEW Trick Dog ● *Eclectic*

`-` `-` `-` `I`

Mission | 3010 20th St. (Florida St.) | 415-471-2999 | www.trickdogbar.com
This late-night venture from the Bon Vivants cocktail and spirits consulting company features beer, wine and a craft cocktails list plus an affordable menu of Eclectic bar snacks; the converted Mission warehouse is decked out with industrial elements like cast-iron and vintage bric-a-brac, including a trick-dog piggy bank located behind the 100-year-old marble bar.

Tropisueño *Mexican*

`20` `18` `19` `$27`

SoMa | 75 Yerba Buena Ln. (bet. Market & Mission Sts.) | 415-243-0299 | www.tropisueno.com
"Taco shop by day, sit-down restaurant by night", this SoMa Mexican gets praise for its "homemade salsas", "fresh chips" and "chile-salt-

rimmed margaritas"; service is generally "convivial", so the wood-and-tile hacienda-style space is often "crowded", and if prices are "on the high end" for its ilk, it's "in an area that doesn't have much" else like it.

Troya *Turkish* 21 | 17 | 22 | $30

Inner Richmond | 349 Clement St. (5th Ave.) | 415-379-6000
Pacific Heights | 2125 Fillmore St. (bet. California & Sacramento Sts.) | 415-563-1000
www.troyasf.com

Kebabs are "juicy" and the vegetarian dishes "excel" at this midpriced duo serving "tasty" Turkish meze and larger plates in the Inner Richmond and at a "slicker" new Fillmore setting; service is generally "attentive" and the atmosphere pleasant, plus the Clement "happy hour is a deal."

Truly Mediterranean *Mediterranean* ▽ 26 | 8 | 17 | $12

Mission | 3109 16th St. (bet. Guerrero & Valencia Sts.) | 415-252-7482 | www.trulymedsf.com

Truly a gyro hero, this Mission hole-in-the-wall cranks out "fantastic", "cheap" Med–Middle Eastern eats including "super-tasty shawarma" and "died-and-gone-to-heaven" halvah; the helpful crew is "willing to mix it up if you have diet needs", and "late" hours (till midnight on weekends) and a location "within walking distance of many cool bars" make it easy to "grab dinner", but seating is scant, so many just "pop in" and "get it to go."

Tsunami Sushi & Sake Bar ●⊠ *Japanese* 22 | 21 | 19 | $40

South Beach | 301 King St. (bet. 4th & 5th Sts.) | 415-284-0111
Tsunami Sushi Panhandle ●⊠ *Japanese*
Western Addition | 1306 Fulton St. (Divisadero St.) | 415-567-7664
www.dajanigroup.net

"Delicious sake flights" pair with "fresh and tasty sushi" and "izakaya-style tapas" at this Japanese duo in Western Addition and South Beach, where "hipsters" fill the "chic" rooms, particularly during the "great happy hour"; though the upscale experience "comes at a price", it still fits the bill for "a lively date" or "catching up" with friends.

Turtle Tower Restaurant *Vietnamese* 21 | 7 | 13 | $13

NEW **Ingleside** | Cesar Chavez Student Ctr., SFSU Campus | 1650 Holloway Ave. (19th Ave.) | 415-338-7188 ⊠⊅
Outer Richmond | 5716 Geary Blvd. (Bryant St.) | 415-221-9890 ⊅
SoMa | 501 Sixth St. (Bryant St.) | 415-904-9888 ⊠
Tenderloin | 645 Larkin St. (Ellis St.) | 415-409-3333 ⊅
www.turtletowersf.com

"No-nonsense pho" – Vietnamese noodle soup that's "simple and soothing" with a "light, clean broth" – "fills you up without emptying your wallet" at these SF noodle shops (including a relocated Larkin Street branch); service is "quick", but these "go-to spots" still "get packed" with "experienced" slurpers who "come here in droves", meaning "you might end up sharing a table."

Twenty Five Lusk *American* 22 | 27 | 22 | $60

SoMa | 25 Lusk St. (Townsend St.) | 415-495-5875 | www.25lusk.com
"Sophisticated and sexy", this "chic", bi-level SoMa American has a rustic yet "dramatic" look with "floating fireplaces", as well as "fabu-

lous" cocktails and an "overall welcoming attitude" to go with the open kitchen's "beautifully presented, satisfying" food; all in all, it's a "memorable" choice whether you want to "celebrate something special" or just "spend some money with your honey."

NEW 20 Spot *American*

| - | - | - | M |

Mission | 3565 20th St. (bet. Mission & Valencia Sts.) | 415-624-3140 | www.20spot.com

This Mission lounge offers local brews and an extensive variety of wines by the bottle and by the glass plus a brief, midpriced menu of New American small plates; exposed brick, vintage chairs and lights, leather sofas and a long bar made from reclaimed wood give the little space a cool but cozy feel, and the lit sign outside honors the space's record-store past.

NEW 20th Century Café Ⓜ🚭 *Bakery*

| - | - | - | I |

Hayes Valley | 198 Gough St. (Oak St.) | no phone | www.20thcenturycafe.com

Inspired by the old-world patisseries of Vienna, Budapest and Prague, this retro corner bakery in Hayes Valley from pastry whiz Michelle Polzine (ex Range) offers sweets like tortes and coffee cake and also savories (think knishes and charcuterie) plus housemade ice creams; the cafe setting is filled with vintage details such as a copper cash register, a pressed-metal tile counter and marble tables.

2G Japanese Brasserie *Japanese*

| 22 | 20 | 21 | $38 |

Civic Center | Opera Plaza | 601 Van Ness Ave. (Golden Gate Ave.) | 415-292-9997 | www.2gjapanese.com

"Hidden inside the Opera Plaza complex", this "reasonably priced" Civic Center Japanese offers a "varied" menu ranging from "artistic" and "unusual dishes" to "beautifully prepared" "traditional" fare; "super-helpful servers" make it a "haven" for "symphony attendees" who need to catch the curtain, but less-rushed fin fanatics "make sure" to order the omakase and soak up the "ambiance."

Udupi Palace 🚭 *Indian/Vegetarian*

| 23 | 13 | 19 | $16 |

Mission | 1007 Valencia St. (21st St.) | 415-970-8000 | www.udupipalaceca.com

"Even carnivores love" the vegetarian fare at this "authentic" South Indian Mission and Berkeley duo, including "huge, spicy uttapams", "dosas packed with flavor" and other "truly delicious dishes"; "don't be fooled" by shabby exteriors, as these venues offer "fast" and "cheerful" service, a "family-friendly" environment and "unbeatable quality for the price."

Umami *Japanese*

| 25 | 23 | 21 | $42 |

Cow Hollow | 2909 Webster St. (Union St.) | 415-346-3431 | www.umamisf.com

Taking "sushi to a different level", this Cow Hollow Japanese "hot spot" turns out "amazingly fresh" and "inventive combinations" of raw fish as well as "Asian-fusion" specialties like "Kobe beef sliders" and "ahi tacos"; "daring cocktails" and the "cool interior" of "dark wood" and "dim" lighting stoke the "lively" vibe, while fans call the "wallet-happy" "sumo hour" (nightly 5:30–6:30 PM) offering discounted bites and "half-off" bottles among "the best in town."

FOOD | DECOR | SERVICE | COST

Umami Burger *Burgers*

22 | 17 | 18 | $22

Cow Hollow | 2184 Union St. (bet. Fillmore & Webster Sts.) | 415-440-8626 | www.umamiburger.com

Converts attest these Bay Area links in a "popular" LA chain "live up to its hype" serving "innovative, juicy burgers" in "amazing" "flavor combinations" with "housemade condiments" adding "another dimension"; the decor differs from location to location, and if "portions could be a little larger" for the price, wine and beer (and in Oakland, cocktails) compensate, so "come early to avoid a wait."

Una Pizza Napoletana   *Pizza*

26 | 16 | 17 | $31

SoMa | 210 11th St. (Howard St.) | 415-861-3444 | www.unapizza.com

"True Neapolitan" pies emerge from the central blue-tiled "imported" "oven-cum-altar" at this SoMa "church of pizza" presided over by NYC transplant Anthony Mangieri; "when he runs out of dough, no more for you", but if you're good with the "long waits", "crazy" prices and limitations – "no substitutions", "no meat", "no desserts" – "purists" praise the "sublime" pies as "the best" in town; P.S. open Wednesday–Saturday.

Underdog ⊄ *Hot Dogs*

25 | 15 | 20 | $15

Inner Sunset | 1634 Irving St. (bet. 17th & 18th Aves.) | 415-665-8881 | www.underdogorganic.com

"Cheap and tasty" franks are "handcrafted" from "organic" ingredients at this Inner Sunset "find" also offering "veggie-friendly" options (including "vegan sausages" and desserts); the staff is "friendly" and the atmosphere's "chill", but since it's "the size of a shoebox", regulars suggest "taking your dogs to the park."

Unicorn Pan Asian Cuisine ⊠ *Asian*

23 | 22 | 21 | $31

Downtown | 191 Pine St. (bet. Battery & Front Sts.) | 415-982-9828 | www.unicorndining.com

Situated "in the heart of the Financial District", this Pan-Asian favorite of the "business-lunch crowd" offers "creative interpretations of classic" dishes that are "beautifully presented" and served by a "friendly staff" in an "interesting" setting with glass sculptures, dark wood and "dim" lighting; "vegetarian options" are an added plus, as are "ample portions" and "reasonable prices."

Universal Cafe Ⓜ *American*

25 | 19 | 22 | $37

Mission | 2814 19th St. (bet. Bryant & Florida Sts.) | 415-821-4608 | www.universalcafe.net

"Fresh" ingredients "handpicked" "from local markets" assure the "outstanding" New American cuisine at this "down-to-earth" Mission "gem" is "on par" with nearby hot spots "but with less fuss" and at a "better price"; the "small, sunny front deck" and one of the "best brunches in the city" (including weekdays Wednesday–Friday) attract a "stylish" "crowd" of local "hipsters", and while the "vibe" is "friendly and enjoyable", there's sometimes a "long wait."

Uva Enoteca *Italian*

22 | 20 | 22 | $38

Lower Haight | 568 Haight St. (bet. Fillmore & Steiner Sts.) | 415-829-2024 | www.uvaenoteca.com

"Surrounded by bars and BBQ joints", this Lower Haight "diamond in the rough" offers a "small", midpriced Italian menu of "delicious" pizzas, salumi and "cheese plates", along with a "well-crafted wine list" that the "approachable", "knowledgeable" staff will help translate; "tables are a little close", but the "cozy" atmosphere is "great for a date" and the "justifiably well-known happy hour" and "bottomless Bellinis" at brunch are nice perks.

Venticello *Italian*   23 | 22 | 22 | $52

Nob Hill | 1257 Taylor St. (Washington St.) | 415-922-2545 | www.venticello.com

"Like dining in an exquisite home in a previous century", this "warm and cozy" Nob Hill "neighborhood gem" turns out Northern Italian cooking "just like mama's", including "homemade pastas" and "wood-fired pizzas" ferried by "charming" servers; all in all, it's a "very SF experience" with views out "the large window" of the "crooked street" and "cable cars going by", so "locals" "keep coming back again and again."

Walzwerk 🅼 *German*   21 | 15 | 17 | $28

Mission | 381 S. Van Ness Ave. (bet. 14th & 15th Sts.) | 415-551-7181 | www.walzwerk.com

Images of "Marx, Engels and Lenin stare down" from the walls of this "unusual" East German in the Mission offering up "the best of everything from behind the Iron Curtain"; the atmosphere may feel a bit "cold" and service can range from "dutiful" to "snooty", but "authentic" "tasty" fare like "sausages, schnitzel and sauerbraten" paired with "excellent imported beers" ensures many "leave happy."

Waterbar *Seafood*   23 | 27 | 22 | $58

Embarcadero | 399 The Embarcadero S. (Folsom St.) | 415-284-9922 | www.waterbarsf.com

Loyalists "looove the oysters" and other "fabulous" seafood at this Embarcadero eatery that's "gorgeous inside and out" with its "awesome view of the Bay Bridge" and "eye-drawing aquariums"; the "friendly" service and "lively" atmosphere suit a "long, leisurely lunch" or happy hour, though be sure to "bring moola" when you're out to "impress."

Waterfront Restaurant *Californian/Seafood*   21 | 23 | 20 | $51

Embarcadero | Pier 7 (Lincoln Hwy.) | 415-391-2696 | www.waterfrontsf.com

"Breathtaking" Bay Bridge "views from every table", both indoors and from the "tented patio", make this Embarcadero seafooder a "wonderful place to relax" and absorb the "beautiful setting"; the Californian fare is deemed "well executed" while service is "pleasant" if at times "uneven", and the "cost"-conscious "go for lunch" when the "same food" comes at "lower prices."

Wayfare Tavern *American*   24 | 24 | 23 | $52

Downtown | 558 Sacramento St. (bet. Leidesdorff & Montgomery Sts.) | 415-772-9060 | www.wayfaretavern.com

"Popovers are an addictive treat" and the fried chicken is "simply delicious" at this "consistently satisfying" FiDi American by Tyler Florence, staffed by a "hospitable" crew; while it's usually "bustling", the pubby "period decor" is "relaxing" (particularly upstairs), and even those who aren't "wowed" by the "pricey" food say it's a natural for "entertaining guests."

	FOOD	DECOR	SERVICE	COST

West of Pecos ⓜ *Southwestern*

▽ 19 | 18 | 19 | $31

Mission | 550 Valencia St. (bet. 16th & 17th Sts.) | 415-252-7000 | www.westofpecos.com

"Come and git it" at this new Mission "chuckwagon" from the Woodhouse Fish Company team, serving "tasty Southwestern fare" and "great margaritas" for "reasonable prices"; designed with saloon doors and adobe-style fireplaces, it has a "fun atmosphere" and "fast" service, all adding up to guests who "have a blast."

Wexler's Ⓩ *BBQ*

23 | 21 | 21 | $40

Downtown | 568 Sacramento St. (Montgomery St.) | 415-983-0102 | www.wexlerssf.com

"Not your typical BBQ joint with peanut shells on the floor", this "very modern" Downtown American furnishing "inventive seasonal cocktails" and comfort food that's both "sophisticated" and "offbeat" draws the "hip FiDi" crowd; "calling it 'barbecue' is a stretch" and "service is hit-or-miss", but the "awesome atmosphere" is smoking good "for drinks" or a "date"; P.S. their lunch truck is out back weekdays.

'Wichcraft *Sandwiches*

18 | 15 | 14 | $16

Downtown | Westfield San Francisco Ctr. | 868 Mission St., ground fl. (bet. 4th & 5th Sts.) | 415-593-3895 | www.wichcraftnyc.com

"Tom Colicchio knows how to make a sammich!" say fans of the celeb chef's Westfield Centre outpost with its "well-made", "creative sandwiches" and dreamy "sweet" "creamwiches" served in a "cafeteria"-style setting; cost-conscious types say the "NYC" transplant's relatively "high-end prices" for "small" portions just "don't cut it in SF", still, it's "not bad for a quick lunch while shopping."

🆕 The Willows ◑ *American*

- | - | - | I

SoMa | 1582 Folsom St. (12th St.) | 415-529-2039 | www.thewillowssf.com

The Sycamore crew brings affordable American cuisine (including sliders, sandwiches and those famous pork belly donuts) to SoMa, complete with the laid-back living room feel of its sister bar and restaurant; the casual establishment features pinball, pool, board games and a jukebox, and the dining rooms have table and banquette seating, plus a couple of semi-private nooks.

🆕 Wine Kitchen *American*

- | - | - | M

Western Addition | 507 Divisadero St. (Fell St.) | 415-525-3485 | www.winekitchensf.com

A duo of fine-dining chefs (who worked together at Commonwealth, Bar Tartine and Contigo) brings its fare to this casual Western Addition wine bar and restaurant offering a midpriced New American menu ranging from the de rigueur cheese plate to sophisticated small plates, all of which come with suggested pairings; the narrow digs include a living room-esque dining area and a long mahogany bar stocked with international and local wines, many of which are available by the glass or on tap.

Wise Sons Jewish Delicatessen *Deli/Jewish*

23 | 13 | 18 | $18

Embarcadero | Ferry Building Mktpl. | 1 Ferry Bldg. (The Embarcadero) | 415-787-3354 Ⓩ ⓜ
Mission | 3150 24th St. (Shotwell St.) | 415-787-3354 ⓜ

(continued)

CITY OF SAN FRANCISCO

(continued)

Wise Sons Jewish Delicatessen

NEW SoMa | The Contemporary Jewish Museum | 736 Mission St. (bet. 3rd & 4th Sts.) | 415-655-7887
www.wisesonsdeli.com

"Why did we have to wait so long?" wonder fans of this Mission brick-and-mortar offshoot of the "popular" Jewish deli pop-up (still operating Tuesdays at the Ferry Building) turning out "housemade" versions of "traditional" classics, such as "sublime pastrami" and "to-die-for" chocolate babka, "updated with locally sourced ingredients"; though a bit pricey, it's "always jammed", and only offers lunch, brunch and Friday night dinner, so expect "crazy" lines; the newest branch in the Contemporary Jewish Museum offers a pared-down, lunch-only sandwich menu and a walk-up window for non-museumgoers.

Woodhouse Fish Company *Seafood*   22 | 16 | 20 | $32

Castro | 2073 Market St. (14th St.) | 415-437-2722
Pacific Heights | 1914 Fillmore St. (bet. Bush & Pine Sts.) | 415-437-2722
www.woodhousefish.com

"Meaty" "crab" and "lobster rolls" "never fail" to please at this New England–style seafood duo in Pac Heights and the Castro where "flavorful, affordable" seafood ("who can beat $1 oysters on Tuesdays?") is served by a "cheery", "helpful" staff; the "low-key", "nautical"-themed joints are "popular with locals" and "there are no reservations", so "be prepared to wait."

Woodward's Garden 🚫Ⓜ *Californian*   24 | 16 | 21 | $53

Mission | 1700 Mission St. (Duboce Ave.) | 415-621-7122 |
www.woodwardsgarden.com

Despite being "almost under the freeway", this "little" "oldie but goodie" in the Mission is "still" a surprisingly "charming" and "quiet" place to enjoy a "casual" dinner "with close friends or a date"; the "creative" Californian cuisine (prepared right "in front of you" in the "open kitchen") is "matched by" an "excellent wine selection" and a "warm reception" that compensate for its "iffy" locale.

Yamo 🚫🚭 *Burmese*   22 | 7 | 13 | $11

Mission | 3406 18th St. (bet. Mission & San Carlos Sts.) | 415-553-8911
It "feels like you're in Rangoon" "sitting shoulder-to-shoulder, slurping housemade noodles" at this "quintessential hole-in-the-wall" in the Mission dishing out "cheap", "delicious" Burmese grub; service can be brusque but it's "quick", even so, there are "often long lines" and veterans sometimes "call ahead for takeout" to avoid them.

Yank Sing *Chinese*   26 | 18 | 20 | $38

SoMa | Rincon Ctr. | 101 Spear St. (bet. Howard & Mission Sts.) |
415-957-9300
SoMa | 49 Stevenson St. (bet. 1st & 2nd Sts.) | 415-541-4949
www.yanksing.com

"The carts roll by in rapid succession" ferrying "phenomenal" dim sum (including "delectable" dumplings and some "unusual offerings") at this Rincon Center brunch/lunch place and its smaller nearby branch tucked away in a SoMa alleyway; the food comes with "efficient" service and "refined surroundings" at "refined prices", and while there's "quite a wait at lunchtime", admirers assure it's "always a hit."

	FOOD	DECOR	SERVICE	COST

Yellow Submarine ⊄ *Sandwiches* — ▽ 23 | 13 | 17 | $11

Inner Sunset | 503 Irving St. (6th Ave.) | 415-681-5652

"Huge, delicious" "hot subs" ("a medium" easily equals "two meals") dressed with "awesome" "secret sauce" are the draw at this "venerable" Inner Sunset sandwich shop with low prices, "quick" service and a notable lack of decor; true, "there's not really anything healthy on the menu", but this place is a "solid" choice all the same.

Yoshi's San Francisco *Japanese* — 22 | 23 | 21 | $45

Western Addition | Fillmore Heritage Ctr. | 1330 Fillmore St. (bet. Eddy & Ellis Sts.) | 415-655-5600 | www.yoshis.com

See review in East of San Francisco Directory.

Yuet Lee ● *Chinese* — 20 | 6 | 11 | $27

Chinatown | 1300 Stockton St. (B'way) | 415-982-6020

Regulars say it "hasn't changed" since the '70s (when it opened) at this Chinatown "classic" still serving "authentic" Cantonese seafood for "reasonable prices"; the "decor is garish" and it can be "hard to find a seat", but service is "fast" plus it's open till 3 AM Friday–Saturday for a "late-night Chinese" fix.

Zadin *Vietnamese* — ▽ 20 | 20 | 21 | $30

Castro | 4039 18th St. (Hartford St.) | 415-626-2260 | www.zadinsf.com

"Significantly better than you'd expect" to find on this stretch in the Castro, this "quiet", "relaxing" spot turns out "great noodle soups" and an array of Vietnamese vittles (some "quite spicy") at "reasonable prices"; the fact that "nearly everything is gluten-free or can be made" so is a big perk for some, and the "delightful" atmosphere and "excellent" service have all around appeal.

Z & Y *Chinese* — 25 | 13 | 15 | $23

Chinatown | 655 Jackson St. (Wentworth St.) | 415-981-8988 | www.zandyrestaurant.com

"For those who like their food with lots of heat", this Chinatown dive doles out "incredibly authentic Sichuanese" cuisine that's "generous with the peppers", resulting in "tasty, spicy" dishes; it's "not much to look at" and service is nothing special, but the "good, honest food" makes up for it.

Zaré at Fly Trap ⊠ *Californian/Mediterranean* — 21 | 21 | 22 | $47

SoMa | 606 Folsom St. (2nd St.) | 415-243-0580 | www.zareflytrap.com

Chef-owner "Hoss Zaré brings his Persian culture to life" at this SoMa "gem" where some of the "most pleasant folks you're ever going to meet" proffer "memorable drinks" and "flavorful" Cal-Med meals elevated by the "interesting use of spices"; it's "noisy", but the "inviting" atmosphere and "hopping bar" attract regulars like flypaper, be it for "a first date, happy hour" or some "real food before a Giants game."

Zarzuela ⊠Ⓜ *Spanish* — 24 | 18 | 23 | $42

Russian Hill | 2000 Hyde St. (Union St.) | 415-346-0800

"I hope they stay here forever" sigh supporters of this "terrific neighborhood tapas place in Russian Hill" that's "right on the cable car line" and serves "authentic Spanish food" along with "first-rate" sangria; an "accommodating staff" and "good value" help compensate for the "no-reservations" policy in a room that's "small" and often "crowded", but still has "charm."

Zazie *French*

24 | 20 | 22 | $29

Cole Valley | 941 Cole St. (bet. Carl St. & Parnassus Ave.) | 415-564-5332 | www.zaziesf.com

"C'est magnifique!" exclaim locals about this "small" but "dependable" "slice of Paris in Cole Valley" that's open all day and "roaringly busy" at brunch – it's offered daily – when there can be "unbearably long" lines for a table (thankfully, there's a "warm and friendly" staff); another option is a "great-value", "delicious" French meal on the "magical" "outdoor patio", where Bring Your Dog to Dinner commences every Monday.

Zero Zero *Italian/Pizza*

24 | 20 | 21 | $37

SoMa | 826 Folsom St. (4th St.) | 415-348-8800 | www.zerozerosf.com

Neapolitan pizzas are "so in vogue" and this "swanky" SoMa Italian stands out with its "phenomenal" "thin-crust, flame-kissed" pies (including a "seasonal" option) plus antipasti and pastas courtesy of chef-owner Bruce Hill; crowded from brunch through dinner, "noise levels are high", but tabs are "decent" and service gets a nod, as do "terrific" cocktails; P.S. "build-your-own" sundaes are a hit with all ages.

Zuni Café ⓜ *Mediterranean*

26 | 21 | 23 | $53

Hayes Valley | 1658 Market St. (bet. Franklin & Gough Sts.) | 415-552-2522 | www.zunicafe.com

"Judy Rodgers' menus continue to delight" at this "eclectic" Med "legend" in Hayes Valley, where the brick-oven chicken (for two) with bread salad is the "stuff of dreams" and oysters at the zinc bar are "terrific"; while it can get "a bit frenetic" in the "quirky", "upscalish" two-story space, the staff keeps it "rolling" and the "atmosphere around dinnertime is always good."

Zushi Puzzle ⓩ *Japanese*

27 | 11 | 18 | $50

Marina | 1910 Lombard St. (Buchanan St.) | 415-931-9319 | www.zushipuzzle.com

Some of the "most unique and uniquely prepared seafood in the city" (including "killer sushi", sashimi and "hand rolls") "beckons" fin fans to this "funky little" Japanese joint in the Marina; it does "not have the decor of some of the hipper" spots, and service can be "robotic", but if your budget can withstand it, "sit at the bar" with the "fantastic" Roger Chong "at the helm" and "ask for the chef recommendations" – "you won't be disappointed."

EAST OF SAN FRANCISCO

Top Food

28 Erna's Elderberry | *Cal./Fr.*

27 Chez Panisse | *Cal./Med.*
Commis | *American*
Chez Panisse Café | *Cal./Med.*
Rivoli | *Cal./Med.*
Ajanta | *Indian*
Wolfdale's | *Californian*

26 Esin Rest. | *Amer./Med.*
Asena Restaurant | *Cal./Med.*
Pizzaiolo | *Italian/Pizza*
Wood Tavern | *Californian*
Bakesale Betty | *Bakery*
Cheese Board Pizzeria | *Pizza*
BayWolf | *Cal./Med.*
Riva Cucina | *Italian*
Brown Sugar | *Soul/Southern*
Prima | *Italian*
Lalime's | *Cal./Med.*

25 Burma Superstar | *Burmese*
Marica | *American/Seafood*

Dopo | *Italian*
Joshu-ya Brasserie | *Japanese*
Gioia Pizzeria | *Pizza*
Wente Vineyards | *Cal./Med.*
Oliveto Restaurant | *Italian*
Zachary's | *Pizza*
Chevalier | *French*
Arizmendi | *Bakery/Pizza*
Kirala | *Japanese*
Sasa | *Japanese*
Tamarindo Antojeria* | *Mexican*
Addis Ethiopian | *Ethiopian*
Artisan Bistro | *Cal./Fr.*
Haven | *Californian*
Trattoria Corso | *Italian*
Ozumo | *Japanese*
Va de Vi | *Eclectic*
Ike's Place | *Sandwiches*
Little Star Pizza | *Pizza*

24 À Côté | *Fr./Med.*

Top Decor

28 Erna's Elderberry
Ahwahnee Dining Room

26 Meritage/The Claremont
Wente Vineyards

25 Postino
Chez Panisse
Vic Stewart's

24 Bocanova
Picán
Skates on the Bay

Esin Rest.
Sasa
Comal
Ozumo
Lake Chalet
Rivoli
Chez Panisse Café
Haven

23 Yoshi's Oakland
Bridges Restaurant

Top Service

29 Erna's Elderberry
27 Chez Panisse
26 Wolfdale's
Chez Panisse Café
Esin Rest.
Commis

25 Rivoli
Asena Restaurant
Riva Cucina
Marica

24 BayWolf
Wente Vineyards
Lalime's
Vic Stewart's
Ajanta
Postino

23 Ruth's Chris
Prima
Meritage/The Claremont
Oliveto Restaurant

* Indicates a tie with restaurant above; excludes places with low votes, unless otherwise indicated

TOPS BY CUISINE

AMERICAN

27 Commis
26 Esin
23 Lark Creek
Flora
Rick & Ann's

CALIFORNIAN

28 Erna's Elderberry
27 Chez Panisse
Chez Panisse Café
Rivoli
Wolfdale's

CHINESE

23 Koi Palace
East Ocean Seafood
22 Shen Hua
Hong Kong East Ocean
21 Mayflower

FRENCH

25 Chevalier
Artisan Bistro
24 À Côté
Grégoire
23 La Note

INDIAN/PAKISTANI

27 Ajanta
24 Vik's Chaat Corner
23 Udupi Palace
Pakwan
Shalimar

ITALIAN

26 Pizzaiolo
Riva Cucina
Prima
25 Dopo
Oliveto

JAPANESE

25 Joshu-ya Brasserie
Kirala
Sasa
Ozumo
24 Ippuku

MEDITERRANEAN

27 Chez Panisse
Chez Panisse Café
Rivoli
26 Esin
Asena Restaurant

MEXICAN/PAN-LATIN

25 Tamarindo Antojeria
24 La Victoria Taqueria
23 Comal
El Farolito
Bocanova

PIZZA

26 Pizzaiolo
Cheese Board Pizzeria
25 Gioia Pizzeria
Zachary's
Arizmendi

SEAFOOD

25 Marica
24 Walnut Creek Yacht Club
23 East Ocean Seafood
21 Dead Fish
20 Skates on Bay

TOPS BY SPECIAL FEATURE

BREAKFAST/BRUNCH

25 Wente Vineyards
24 Bette's Oceanview
Venus
23 Mama's Royal
Rick & Ann's

CHILD-FRIENDLY

25 Zachary's
22 Lo Coco's
Pizza Antica
21 Barney's
Chow

OPEN LATE

23 In-N-Out
Top Dog (Berkeley)
22 Caspers Hot Dogs
Adesso
Fonda Solana

OUTDOOR SEATING

25 Wente Vineyards
24 À Côté
23 La Note
Gather
Comal

PEOPLE-WATCHING

27 Chez Panisse
24 A16 Rockridge
23 Comal
   Corners Tavern▽
22 Doña Tomás

ROMANCE

28 Erna's Elderberry
27 Chez Panisse
   Wolfdale's
26 Lalime's
25 Wente Vineyards

SMALL PLATES

25 Va de Vi
24 À Côté
22 Adesso
   César
   Barlata

TRENDY

25 Ozumo
24 Hopscotch▽
23 Comal
   Flora
22 Adesso

VIEWS

27 Wolfdale's
25 Wente Vineyards
23 Bocanova
   Meritage/The Claremont
21 Ahwahnee Dining Room

WINNING WINE LISTS

28 Erna's Elderberry
27 Chez Panisse
26 Prima
25 Va de Vi
24 À Côté

TOPS BY LOCATION

BERKELEY

27 Chez Panisse
   Chez Panisse Café
   Rivoli
   Ajanta
26 Cheese Board Pizzeria

LAKE TAHOE AREA

27 Evan's American Gourmet▽
   Wolfdale's
23 Dragonfly
   PlumpJack Cafe
19 Gar Woods Grill & Pier

OAKLAND

27 Commis
26 Pizzaiolo
   Wood Tavern
   Bakesale Betty
   BayWolf

WALNUT CREEK

26 Prima
25 Sasa
   Va de Vi
   Ike's Place
24 Ruth's Chris

Best Buys

Top-rated food $25 and under

1. Bakesale Betty | *Bakery*
2. Cheese Board Pizzeria | *Pizza*
3. Brown Sugar | *Soul/Southern*
4. Gioia Pizzeria | *Pizza*
5. Zachary's | *Pizza*
6. Arizmendi | *Bakery/Pizza*
7. Addis Ethiopian | *Ethiopian*
8. Ike's Place | *Sandwiches*
9. Little Star Pizza | *Pizza*
10. 900 Grayson | *Burgers/Cal.*
11. Grégoire | *French*
12. Vung Tao | *Vietnamese*
13. Bette's Oceanview | *Diner*
14. Vik's Chaat Corner | *Indian*
15. Southie | *American*
16. Bangkok Thai | *Thai*
17. Blue Bottle | *Cal./Coffee*
18. Dragon Rouge | *Vietnamese*
19. La Victoria Taqueria | *Mexican*
20. B-Side BBQ | *BBQ*

BEST BUYS BY NEIGHBORHOOD

ALAMEDA/EMERYVILLE
25| Arizmendi
24| Bangkok Thai
    Dragon Rouge Restaurant
23| East Ocean Seafood
    Pearl's Deluxe

BERKELEY
26| Cheese Board Pizzeria
25| Gioia Pizzeria
    Zachary's
24| 900 Grayson
    Grégoire
    Bette's Oceanview
    Vik's Chaat Corner
    Bangkok Thai
23| Udupi Palace
    Arinell Pizza

LAFAYETTE/WALNUT CREEK
25| Ike's Place
22| Cheese Steak Shop
    Caspers Hot Dogs
    Patxi's Pizza
    Bo's Barbecue

OAKLAND
26| Bakesale Betty
    Brown Sugar
25| Zachary's
    Arizmendi
    Addis Ethiopian
    Ike's Place
24| Grégoire
    Southie
    Blue Bottle
23| B-Side BBQ

East of San Francisco

À Côté *French/Mediterranean*　24 | 21 | 22 | $42
Oakland | 5478 College Ave. (Taft Ave.) | 510-655-6469 |
www.acoterestaurant.com
"California meets Provence" in the "excellent small plates" at this
"hopping" Mediterranean in Oakland's Rockridge area serving "French
food for real people"; thanks to a menu that "changes often", "eclectic" wine list and "amazing" cocktails, patrons "party in the front" or
"enjoy a quiet meal" in the "secluded" garden – either way, staffers are
"always on their game."

Actual Cafe *Californian*　22 | 21 | 20 | $15
Oakland | 6334 San Pablo Pl. (Alcatraz Ave.) | 510-653-8386 |
www.actualcafe.com
"Everything is fresh, including the attitude" at this "hip, scruffy, bike-
friendly" Oakland "neighborhood hang" where "lots of different types"
"mix and mingle" over Californian eats like "gigantically awesome"
salads, sandwiches, coffee, "fresh juices" and "homemade sodas" – all
"inexpensive" and served by an "unfailingly polite" staff; P.S. weekends
are "laptop- and cell phone–free", while there's "free live music" most
Saturday and Sunday nights.

Addis Ethiopian *Ethiopian*　25 | 18 | 22 | $21
Oakland | 6100 Telegraph Ave. (61st St.) | 510-653-3456 |
www.addisethiopian.com
"Come hungry" to "eat phenomenal food with your fingers" at this "authentic" Ethiopian that's like "Africa on Telegraph"; while the "decor is
a bit funky", "service is very friendly" and dishes like *kitfo* (minced,
seasoned beef) and tofu tibs are "top-notch" at "modest prices", plus
"they even serve African beer."

Adesso ●☒ *Italian*　22 | 19 | 21 | $33
Oakland | 4395 Piedmont Ave. (Pleasant Valley Ave.) | 510-601-0305 |
www.dopoadesso.com
Prepare for "a salumi celebration" at this "bustling" Italian "charcuterie lover's dream" (and Dopo sibling), where "Piedmont Avenue
hipsters" wash down "superb cured meat" with "atypical Italian
wines" and "imaginative mixologist-style cocktails"; heartier eaters bemoan "small plates" that are "a bit" on the "pricey" side, but
most happily "meet a friend for happy hour" and nibble away on the
"fantastic artisanal food."

Ahwahnee Dining Room *Californian*　21 | 28 | 23 | $58
Yosemite | Ahwahnee Hotel | 1 Ahwahnee Way (Village Dr.) |
Yosemite National Park | 209-372-1489 | www.yosemitepark.com
"After a day of hiking", visitors to Yosemite National Park sit down
to a meal that's a "real treat" in this "dramatic, iconic" hotel dining
room where the "baronial" setting with vaulted ceilings, a "huge
fireplace" and "majestic" window views recalls "Harry Potter at
Hogwarts"; a "professional" staff delivers the "truly good" Californian
fare, and if it's "pricey", it's also "a must for the experience"; P.S. "make
reservations", especially for the holiday Bracebridge dinner or
"busy" Sunday brunch.

	FOOD	DECOR	SERVICE	COST

Ajanta *Indian*

27 | 22 | 24 | $31

Berkeley | 1888 Solano Ave. (bet. Fresno Ave. & The Alameda) | 510-526-4373 | www.ajantarestaurant.com

"Dishes from various regions of India" are presented at this midpriced Berkeley "favorite", where a "changing menu" of "exotic, spicy goodness" includes "deeply flavored sauces", curries and tandoori vegetables redolent with "tantalizing" aromas; service that's "warm, fast and friendly" is led by "gracious" chef-owner Lachu Moorjani, who may "personally" take your order in the "pleasant, quiet" setting decorated with "artful" murals.

Amber Bistro ☒ *Californian*

23 | 20 | 22 | $39

Danville | 500 Hartz Ave. (Church St.) | 925-552-5238 | www.amberbistro.com

This "small bistro" and "watering hole" in Danville remains a "reliable" "local spot" for grabbing a "casual" Californian lunch or dinner washed down with "delicious cocktails"; "small plates", a "prix fixe dinner" and "great happy-hour deals" "keep the cost down", and while the room gets "very noisy" and "service is hit-or-miss", you can't beat the outdoor seating in summer.

Amici's East Coast Pizzeria *Pizza*

21 | 16 | 19 | $22

Danville | Rose Garden Ctr. | 720 Camino Ramon (Sycamore Valley Rd.) | 925-837-9800

Dublin | 4640 Tassajara Rd. (bet. Central Pkwy. & Dublin Blvd.) | 925-875-1600

www.amicis.com

See review in City of San Francisco Directory.

Anchalee Thai Cuisine *Thai*

23 | 21 | 23 | $25

Berkeley | 1094 Dwight Way (bet. San Pablo Ave. & 10th St.) | 510-848-4015 | www.anchaleethai.com

"Creative" eats come with "mouthwatering" presentations at this "unique, unassuming Thai" in Berkeley; modest tabs and "great service" make it versatile for a "date or family dinner", just "keep the party size small" because the "pleasant" dining room with exposed brick is "tiny."

Angeline's Louisiana Kitchen *Cajun/Creole*

24 | 20 | 22 | $28

Berkeley | 2261 Shattuck Ave. (bet. Bancroft Way & Kittredge St.) | 510-548-6900 | www.angelineskitchen.com

When "your inner Cajun" or Creole calls, answer with the likes of "crawfish étouffée", "amazing" fried chicken, "must-try" hushpuppies and "scrumptious beignets" at this Berkeley answer to NOLA that "could fry ice if they had to"; though the decor is "plain", prices are "reasonable", while "jazzy music" and "friendly service warm it up."

Arinell Pizza ⇗ *Pizza*

23 | 8 | 15 | $8

Berkeley | 2119 Shattuck Ave. (Addison St.) | 510-841-4035

See review in City of San Francisco Directory.

Arizmendi *Bakery/Pizza*

25 | 13 | 20 | $11

Emeryville | 4301 San Pablo Ave. (43rd St.) | 510-547-0550 | www.arizmendi-bakery.org

Oakland | 3265 Lakeshore Ave. (MacArthur Frwy.) | 510-268-8849 | www.lakeshore.arizmendi.coop

See review in City of San Francisco Directory.

| | FOOD | DECOR | SERVICE | COST |

Artisan Bistro Ⓜ *Californian/French* 25 | 20 | 22 | $50

Lafayette | 1005 Brown Ave. (Mt. Diablo Blvd.) | 925-962-0882 | www.artisanlafayette.com

Offering "just the right blend of amazing local, fresh cuisine and fabulous service", this Cal-French "treasure" "in a converted house" appeals to Layfayette locals seeking a "gourmet" meal at a "more affordable price"; an "inventive and oft-changing menu" keeps things interesting, but sensitive types advise "sit on the lovely patio, or bring earplugs."

Asena Restaurant Ⓢ *Californian/Mediterranean* 26 | 20 | 25 | $30

Alameda | 2508 Santa Clara Ave. (Everett St.) | 510-521-4100 | www.asenarestaurant.com

"Fresh ingredients, sublime flavors" and "mouthwatering" "home-made bread" make this midpriced Alameda Cal-Med a "beloved" "local staple" that "always knocks it out of the park" ("the lamb dishes are outstanding"); thanks to "old-school elegance", "warm and inviting owners" and staffers that "take you into their family", islanders claim they've "never had a bad meal here."

NEW A16 Rockridge *Italian* 24 | 21 | 22 | $47

Oakland | 5356 College Ave. (Manila Ave.) | 510-768-8003 | www.a16rockridge.com

See review in City of San Francisco Directory.

Asmara Restaurant Ⓜ *Ethiopian* ▽ 26 | 17 | 21 | $20

Oakland | 5020 Telegraph Ave. (51st St.) | 510-547-5100 | www.asmararestaurant.com

Become a "connoisseur of Ethiopian cuisine" while scooping up "delicious and inexpensive" specialties with injera bread that's "perfectly tangy and wonderfully textured" at this "friendly" Oakland "favorite"; some caution one room is "romantic" but the other is "cafeterialike", so for "intimate" dining "with your hands", choose accordingly (and don't miss the "addictive" "honey wine").

Bakesale Betty ⓈⓂ *Bakery* 26 | 12 | 21 | $13

Oakland | 5098 Telegraph Ave. (51st St.) | 510-985-1213 | www.bakesalebetty.com

Braving "crazy-long lines" is "worth it" at this "quirky", affordable Oakland bakery take-out place assure fans of its "incredible fried chicken sandwich", a "hefty, mouthwatering" "taste feast" topped with "jalapeño slaw"; "extremely friendly and efficient" staffers "crank out" the limited menu, including "unparalleled" chicken pot pies, "marvelous" strawberry shortcake and "cookies the size of your head"; P.S. open Tuesday–Saturday, 11 AM–2 PM.

Bangkok Thai *Thai* 24 | 20 | 21 | $18

Berkeley | 1459 University Ave. (Acton St.) | 510-848-6483
Emeryville | Public Mkt. | 5959 Shellmound St. (bet. Powell & 65th Sts.) | 510-601-1038
www.bangkokthaicuisine.com

When "Thai cravings" arise, locals head to this "reasonably priced" Berkeley Thai or its Emeryville sibling in the Public Market; both are "nothing fancy" inside (with fast food–style seating and "music videos" playing) but are "go-tos" for their "huge selection" on a menu "heavily laden with soups, curries and noodle dishes", plus some "vegetarian" options.

Barlata *Spanish*

| 22 | 17 | 19 | $35 |

Oakland | 4901 Telegraph Ave. (49th St.) | 510-450-0678 | www.barlata.com
Those "into Spanish food" head to this "lively" tapas bar in Oakland's "up-and-coming Temescal district", from the "owner of B44", that's akin to "being in Barcelona" with its "authentic" specialties – some "served in a can (*lata*)" – plus "superb drinks" and wines that "merit a tip of the hat"; it's "too loud" and a bit "overpriced" for a few, but the "happy-hour deals" are a "best bet."

Barney's Gourmet Hamburgers *Burgers*

| 21 | 16 | 18 | $17 |

Berkeley | 1591 Solano Ave. (Tacoma Ave.) | 510-526-8185
Berkeley | 1600 Shattuck Ave. (Cedar St.) | 510-849-2827
Oakland | 4162 Piedmont Ave. (bet. 41st St. & Linda Ave.) | 510-655-7180
Oakland | 5819 College Ave. (bet. Chabot Rd. & Oak Grove Ave.) | 510-601-0444
www.barneyshamburgers.com
See review in City of San Francisco Directory.

BayWolf *Californian/Mediterranean*

| 26 | 22 | 24 | $52 |

Oakland | 3853 Piedmont Ave. (Rio Vista Ave.) | 510-655-6004 | www.baywolf.com
Michael Wild's "spectacular" "Oakland dining institution" (opened in 1975) can still "be counted on every time" for "superb" seasonal Cal-Med "slow meals" – "the duck is a must" – paired with "interesting wines" that "won't break the bank"; it "may not be new or sexy", but the "aim-to-please staff" and "lovely" "converted home" setting with "enclosed front porch" "keep it in the game" "for business or special occasions."

Bellanico Restaurant & Wine Bar *Italian*

| 23 | 19 | 22 | $40 |

Oakland | 4238 Park Blvd. (Wellington St.) | 510-336-1180 | www.bellanico.net
"Robust", "developed flavors and attention to detail" mark the "inventive" Italian fare "prepared with respect and love" at this "jam-packed" Oakland "neighborhood trattoria" (sibling of SF's Aperto); service is "warm and welcoming", plus there's "always an affordable prix fixe option" – and "don't miss the wine flights."

Bette's Oceanview Diner *Diner*

| 24 | 18 | 20 | $20 |

Berkeley | 1807 Fourth St. (bet. Hearst Ave. & Virginia St.) | 510-644-3230 | www.bettesdiner.com
For over 30 years, this "retro-chic" "Berkeley landmark" has been dishing out its "exciting twist on nostalgic diner food" – like "gourmet scrapple" and "soufflé pancakes" – with "fast, pleasant service" at "fair prices"; there's a "long, long wait" for the "amazing", "hearty" breakfasts, but "your taste buds will thank you", so "bring the *Chron*, grab a cuppa joe and chill"; P.S. no dinner.

Bistro Liaison *French*

| 23 | 21 | 22 | $40 |

Berkeley | 1849 Shattuck Ave. (Hearst Ave.) | 510-849-2155 | www.liaisonbistro.com
There's "no jet lag" involved to savor "classic dishes prepared flawlessly" at this "little slice of France" in Berkeley "sans the French atti-

tude"; fans look past "hellishly tight quarters" for "heavenly" midpriced bistro fare served by "expert", "friendly" servers – and "the wine-club dinners are huge fun."

Blackberry Bistro *Southern*

| 21 | 16 | 18 | $20 |

Oakland | 4240 Park Blvd. (Wellington St.) | 510-336-1088 | www.theblackberrybistro.com

"Great breakfast eats" like "homemade biscuits", "crêpes", "tofu scramble" and vanilla-orange French toast are "standouts" at this "cozy yet hip" daytime-only Southern "neighborhood gem"; it can get "very busy" on weekends, and "limited space can lead to substantial waits", but "winning" service helps compensate; P.S. it's a "find for early Sunday brunch."

Blue Bottle Roastery & Coffee Bar *Californian/Coffeehouse*

| 24 | 17 | 19 | $8 |

Oakland | 300 Webster St. (3rd St.) | 510-653-3394 | www.bluebottlecoffee.net
See review in City of San Francisco Directory.

Bocanova *Pan-Latin*

| 23 | 24 | 22 | $41 |

Oakland | Jack London Sq. | 55 Webster St. (1st St.) | 510-444-1233 | www.bocanova.com

A "bright spot" in Jack London Square for a "relaxed and sociable meal", this "hip" "waterfront" Oaklander pleases the "beautiful crowd" with "excellent", "innovative" Pan-Latin shared plates, "incredible desserts" and "not-to-be-missed specialty cocktails"; the "attentive" staff also gets props, but it's the "sexy" setting, particularly the "lovely patio" where you can "watch the boats", that really "steals the show."

Boot & Shoe Service   *Italian/Pizza*

| 24 | 19 | 21 | $31 |

Oakland | 3308 Grand Ave. (Elmwood Ave.) | 510-763-2668 | www.bootandshoeservice.com

"Amazing" thin-crust pizza with "über-fresh" toppings and "unique" appetizers, washed down with "fantastic cocktails", justify the "long waits" at this "hip" "offshoot of Pizzaiolo" in Oakland, packed with "twenty- and thirtysomethings" who "don't seem to mind" the "way-too-loud" music or "communal tables"; P.S. besides having the "friendliest" staff, it now serves "awesome" weekend brunch plus breakfast and lunch.

Bo's Barbecue   *BBQ*

| 22 | 13 | 17 | $24 |

Lafayette | 3422 Mt. Diablo Blvd. (Brown Ave.) | 925-283-7133 | www.bosbarbecue-catering.com

"Don't go looking for atmosphere" (or "table service" for that matter) as this Lafayette 'cue joint is "all about the food" – such as the "best brisket around" – and an "excellent selection of beer and wine" "to match"; some say it's "inconsistent" and "pricier than it should be", but more consider it "a local gem."

Breads of India & Gourmet Curries *Indian*

| 20 | 16 | 18 | $25 |

Oakland | 948 Clay St. (10th St.) | 510-834-7684 🅢
Walnut Creek | 1358 N. Main St. (bet. Cypress & Duncan Sts.) | 925-256-7684 Ⓜ
www.breadsofindia.com
Patrons praise the "generous variety of breads from all over India", along with "tempting curries" and other dishes on the "changing daily

menu" at these East Bay subcontinentals; service varies, and the traditional decor is "nice" enough, but best of all there's a "small price tag"; the Berkeley location is temporarily closed after a fire.

Bridges Restaurant *Asian/Californian* | 23 | 23 | 23 | $46 |

Danville | 44 Church St. (Hartz Ave.) | 925-820-7200 |
www.bridgesdanville.com

"Still a great place to go", this Danville "old standby" that won fame in *Mrs. Doubtfire* appeals with its "delicious" "Asian-influenced" Californian fare ferried by "gracious and attentive" servers in a "contemporary" setting; added draws are a "terrific happy-hour menu" (5 PM till closing weeknights) with prices that "can't be beat", and a summertime patio with "live music."

Brown Sugar Kitchen Ⓜ *Soul Food/Southern* | 26 | 18 | 22 | $22 |

Oakland | 2534 Mandela Pkwy. (26th St.) | 510-839-7685 |
www.brownsugarkitchen.com

"Amazing fried chicken" and a "cornmeal waffle" so "ethereal" you almost "have to hold it down so it won't float away" are among the "down-home" fare with "nouveau flair" at this midpriced West Oakland Southern and soul food "paradise" from chef Tanya Holland; the "wait is insane but well worth it", though the 3 PM closing time leaves devotees longing for "longer hours."

B-Side BBQ Ⓩ Ⓜ *BBQ* | 23 | 19 | 21 | $21 |

Oakland | 3303 San Pablo Ave. (34th St.) | 510-595-0227 |
www.bsidebbq.com

Take a "quick trip to the Deep South" by way of this "affordable" West Oakland BBQ sibling of Brown Sugar Kitchen dishing out chef Tanya Holland's "flavorful, satisfying" brisket and ribs in "two styles" ("sweet and saucy" or jerk), plus "sinful" mac 'n' cheese and more, backed by "quality mixed drinks"; some find the "turnaround neighborhood" on the "sketchy" side, but a "friendly staff" helps put them at ease.

Bucci's Ⓩ *Californian/Italian* | 21 | 21 | 22 | $35 |

Emeryville | 6121 Hollis St. (bet. 59th & 62nd Sts.) | 510-547-4725 |
www.buccis.com

"Mama Bucci is almost always on hand to make it feel like home" at this "relaxed" Emeryville Cal-Italian, a "reliable 'go-to' place" for a "civilized lunch" or "last-minute" "dinner on a Friday night when you don't feel like cooking"; regulars rave about the "wonderful food", "knowledgeable and friendly staff", "spacious" "art-filled interior" and "oasis patio", confirming "it only gets better with time."

Bull Valley Roadhouse Ⓜ *American* | - | - | - | M |

Port Costa | 14 Canyon Lake Dr. (Reservoir St.) | 510-787-1135 |
www.bullvalleyroadhouse.com

A surprising culinary find at the end of a canyon road in Port Costa (look for the golden bull hanging over the entrance), this recently revamped historic East Bay hostelry lures locals and day-trippers with a midpriced American roadhouse menu updated with sustainably procured ingredients and served family-style; the saloonlike 1897 landmark digs feature Victorian furniture, period music and a bar slinging pre-Prohibition cocktails; P.S. open for dinner Thursday–Sunday and weekend brunch.

	FOOD	DECOR	SERVICE	COST

The Bureau 510 *American*

-	-	-	I

Emeryville | 5800 Hollis St. (Powell St.) | 510-595-1000 |
www.thebureau510.com

While burgers take top billing at this affordable Emeryville eatery, the breaded catfish fillet, banh mi and IPA onion rings are additional incentives to plan a return visit; inside, oversized windows and industrial fixtures – think slate-gray walls, natural-wood accents and hanging metal lights – combine to create an open, inviting atmosphere.

BurgerMeister *Burgers*

20	15	17	$16

Alameda | 2319 Central Ave. (bet. Oak & Park Sts.) |
510-865-3032
Berkeley | 2237 Shattuck Ave. (Kittredge St.) | 510-649-1700
www.burgermeistersf.com
See review in City of San Francisco Directory.

Burma Superstar *Burmese*

25	17	20	$26

Alameda | 1345 Park St. (bet. The Alameda & Central Aves.) |
510-522-6200
Oakland | 4721 Telegraph Ave. (bet. 47th & 48th Sts.) |
510-652-2900
www.burmasuperstar.com
See review in City of San Francisco Directory.

Cactus Taqueria *Mexican*

21	14	17	$13

Berkeley | 1881 Solano Ave. (bet. Colusa Ave. & The Alameda) |
510-528-1881
Oakland | 5642 College Ave. (Keith Ave.) | 510-658-6180
www.cactustaqueria.com

"Fresh Mexican" bites are "a real bargain" at this Berkeley and Rockridge "counter service" duo offering "extras most taquerias don't" – such as an "extraordinary selection of intriguing salsas" in bright, casual digs; expect a "loud" scene with "long lines and tons of kiddies", unless you "come after 7 PM."

Café Gratitude *Vegan*

19	18	17	$23

Berkeley | 1730 Shattuck Ave. (bet. Francisco & Virginia Sts.) |
510-725-4418 | www.cafegratitude.com

Backers of these "hippie-dippie" vegan and "raw-food" Berkeley and Santa Cruz outposts on a "mission" call their "nutritious" fare "creative" and "surprisingly flavorful", even if reactions to the "devoted" staff vary with patrons seeking "food, not dogma" quipping "I'd be grateful for lower prices"; likewise, "communal tables can be a blessing or a curse", but believers insist the experience will make you "feel like a better person."

Café Rouge *Californian/Mediterranean*

22	19	21	$40

Berkeley | Market Plaza | 1782 Fourth St. (bet. Hearst Ave. & Virginia St.) |
510-525-1440 | www.caferouge.net

"Carnivorous chomping" is the name of the game at this midpriced Fourth Street Cal-Med "known for" its "superior" organic meats including burgers "freshly ground at the on-site butcher shop" and "cooked to perfection"; clock-watchers say "service can be slow", but the oyster special is "a great deal", and outdoor seating offers "some of the best dog-watching in the Bay Area."

	FOOD	DECOR	SERVICE	COST

Camino *Californian/Mediterranean*   24 | 22 | 22 | $48

Oakland | 3917 Grand Ave. (Sunny Slope Ave.) | 510-547-5035 |
www.caminorestaurant.com

Chef/co-owner Russell Moore (ex Chez Panisse) is practically "out-Alice-ing" mentor Alice Waters at his "fairly simple" yet "utterly delicious" Cal-Med Oaklander where "almost everything" is cooked in a "huge fireplace", resulting in "marvelous flavors" and a "warm environment" to boot; though some are "underwhelmed" by service that "can be on or off" and communal "farm-table" seating, once dinner arrives, "the annoyances of life melt away"; P.S. closed Tuesdays.

Cancun *Mexican*   22 | 17 | 18 | $13

Berkeley | 2134 Allston Way (bet. Oxford St. & Shattuck Ave.) |
510-549-0964 | www.sabormexicano.com

"Great, fresh food, much of which the restaurant grows" at its Sonoma farm, helps set this Berkeley order-at-the-counter Mexican apart; "quality" ingredients that are "organic, with normal pricing", plus the "amazing salsa bar" mean it's "mobbed during peak hours."

Casa Orinda *Italian/Steak*   20 | 19 | 21 | $36

Orinda | 20 Bryant Way (Moraga Way) | 925-254-2981 | www.casaorinda.net

"Like walking into a spaghetti Western", this Orinda Italian steakhouse with Old West decor is the kind of "retro" "hangout" where "waiters remember repeat customers" and bartenders "make old-fashioned drinks" as families and an "older crowd" "chow down" on "hearty" prime rib and "dynamite Southern fried chicken"; some say it's "pricier than it should be", still most find it "as comfortable as an old bathrobe."

Caspers Hot Dogs *Hot Dogs*   22 | 12 | 20 | $8

Albany | 545 San Pablo Ave. (bet. Brighton Ave. & Garfield St.) |
510-527-6611
Dublin | 6998 Village Pkwy. (bet. Amador Valley & Dublin Blvds.) |
925-828-2224
Hayward | 21670 Foothill Blvd. (bet. Grove Way & Rex Rd.) | 510-581-9064
Hayward | 951 C St. (bet. Main St. & Mission Blvd.) | 510-537-7300
Oakland | 5440 Telegraph Ave. (55th St.) | 510-652-1668
Pleasant Hill | 6 Vivian Dr. (Contra Costa Blvd.) | 925-687-6030 ◑
Richmond | 2530 MacDonald Ave. (Civic Center St.) | 510-235-6492
Walnut Creek | 1280 Newell Hill Pl. (Newell Ave.) | 925-930-9154
www.caspershotdogs.com

You "can't go wrong" with the "old-school" franks at this East Bay "institution", where "the scene is pure '50s" and the grub comes "the way hot dogs should be served" – "with a snap to them" on "steamed buns" and "plenty of condiments" to pile on top; "old-time counter girls" who "call you 'hon'" add to a "classic" experience that's "well worth" the tiny tab.

César ◑ *Spanish*   22 | 20 | 20 | $36
(fka César España)

Berkeley | 1515 Shattuck Ave. (bet. Cedar & Vine Sts.) | 510-883-0222 |
www.cesarberkeley.com
César Latino *Pan-Latin*
Oakland | 4039 Piedmont Ave. (bet. 40th & 41st Sts.) | 510-985-1200 |
www.barcesar.com

This Berkeley tapas spot is a "Gourmet Ghetto mainstay", plying "imaginative" "small plates", "well-seasoned" paella and some "tasty wines" (its Oakland sibling purveys a Pan-Latin menu and "great cocktails"); service is "attentive", and the space is "festive" (if "noisy"), with such a "community" vibe you may "make new friends by the end of the meal."

Cha-Ya Vegetarian Japanese Restaurant ⊘ *Japanese/Vegan*

22 | 13 | 17 | $23

Berkeley | 1686 Shattuck Ave. (bet. Lincoln & Virginia Sts.) | 510-981-1213
See review in City of San Francisco Directory.

Cheese Board Pizzeria ⊠ *Pizza*

26 | 16 | 19 | $13

Berkeley | 1512 Shattuck Ave. (Vine St.) | 510-549-3055 |
www.cheeseboardcollective.coop

A "classic" in Berkeley's Gourmet Ghetto, this pizzeria from the worker-owned Cheese Board Cooperative serves "innovative, immensely flavorful" thin-crust vegetarian pies made with its own cheeses plus "seasonal ingredients"; there's only one menu choice ("whatever they decide to make that day") and some gripe that "seating can be hard to come by", but that doesn't stop fans from standing in the "long" (but "fast-moving") lines; P.S. "fantastic live jazz" daily is another plus.

Cheesecake Factory *American*

16 | 17 | 16 | $29

Pleasanton | Stoneridge Mall | 1350 Stoneridge Mall Rd. (Deodar Way) |
925-463-1311 | www.thecheesecakefactory.com
See review in City of San Francisco Directory.

Cheese Steak Shop *Cheesesteaks*

22 | 12 | 19 | $11

Alameda | Blanding Shopping Ctr. | 2671 Blanding Ave. (Tilden Way) |
510-522-5555
Concord | 3478 Clayton Rd. (Roslyn Dr.) | 925-687-6116
Berkeley | 1054 University Ave. (bet. San Pablo Ave. & 10th St.) |
510-845-8689
Lafayette | 3455 Mt. Diablo Blvd. (2nd St.) | 925-283-1234
Oakland | 3308 Lakeshore Ave. (bet. Lake Park Ave. & Trestle Glen Rd.) |
510-832-6717
Pleasanton | Gateway Square Shopping Ctr. | 4825 Hopyard Rd.
(Stoneridge Dr.) | 925-734-0293
San Ramon | Crow Canyon Crest Shopping Ctr. | 3110 Crow Canyon Pl.
(Crow Canyon Rd.) | 925-242-1112
Walnut Creek | 1626 Cypress St. (bet. California Blvd. & Locust St.) |
925-934-7017
www.cheesesteakshop.com
See review in City of San Francisco Directory.

Chevalier Ⓜ *French*

25 | 21 | 23 | $55

Lafayette | 960 Moraga Rd. (Moraga Blvd.) | 925-385-0793 |
www.chevalierrestaurant.com

It's "worth staying local" in Lafayette for "excellent classic French" cuisine from a "personable" chef-owner who's "genuinely excited to cook"; though wallet-watchers note it's "expensive", the "lovely" outdoor patio, "old-fashioned service" and "unstuffy atmosphere" make this a "special-celebration spot", and besides, "the prix fixe is a good value."

Chez Panisse ⊠ *Californian/Mediterranean*

27 | 25 | 27 | $85

Berkeley | 1517 Shattuck Ave. (bet. Cedar & Vine Sts.) | 510-548-5525 |
www.chezpanisse.com

Following a fire, Alice Waters' "inspired" "gastronomic shrine" in Berkeley is again welcoming acolytes who come for "simple" yet "exquisite" "seasonal" Cal-Med prix fixes that "let the ingredients shine" ("even their green garden salad is amazing"), delivered with "exemplary service"; there are "no new surprises" on the menu and the "unique Craftsman-style setting" remains largely the same, so while "the lack of choice" might still miff a few, most locavores insist the place "where it all started" remains "the gold standard"; P.S. scores do not reflect changes after reopening.

Chez Panisse Café ☒ *Californian/Mediterranean*   27 | 24 | 26 | $54

Berkeley | 1517 Shattuck Ave. (bet. Cedar & Vine Sts.) | 510-548-5049 | www.chezpanisse.com

Alice Waters' "unpretentious" upstairs "little sister still performs" as well as its lauded "farm-to-table" sibling downstairs, offering an "unbelievably good" "seasonal" Cal-Med à la carte menu (including "great" wood-fired pizza), "excellent" wines and "attentive but not intrusive" service at "more affordable" prices; the "homey" setting gets "crowded", but remains on the "bucket list" of everyone from casual lunch-goers to gastro-"tourists" looking to "get their food passports stamped"; P.S. scores don't reflect changes after a devastating fire.

Chop Bar *Californian*   24 | 20 | 22 | $29

Oakland | 247 Fourth St. (Alice St.) | 510-834-2467 | www.oaklandchopbar.com

"Comfort service" matches the "comfort food" at this "comfortable yet edgy" Californian that's "one of the hottest dinner spots in Jack London" Square; locals swear "they must have the cows in the back room, the ground beef tastes so fresh", while "reasonable prices", "wine on tap" and a setting with a garage-door front add to the "laid-back" vibe; P.S. open all day.

Chow *American*   21 | 17 | 19 | $26

Danville | 445 Railroad Ave. (San Ramon Valley Blvd.) | 925-838-4510
Lafayette | La Fiesta Sq. | 53 Lafayette Circle (Mt Diablo Blvd.) | 925-962-2469
www.chowfoodbar.com

See review in City of San Francisco Directory.

Christy Hill *Californian/French*   ∇ 23 | 24 | 23 | $60

Tahoe City | 115 Grove St. (Lake Blvd.) | 530-583-8551 | www.christyhill.com

"Amazing views" of the lake go on for miles at this "elegantly simple" Tahoe City "favorite" perched 100 feet above the water, with outdoor seating in the summer months and white linen–clad tables indoors; some prefer "the off-season when it's lower key", but throughout the year a "friendly" staff serves a solid Cal-French menu, and "wonderful" happy-hour discounts add to the "fantastic experience."

Comal *Mexican*   23 | 24 | 20 | $39

Berkeley | 2020 Shattuck Ave. (bet. Addison St. & University Ave.) | 510-926-6300 | www.comalberkeley.com

The ambiance is "unbeatable" at this "slightly upscale" Berkeley Mexican boasting a "fab" interior and "outstanding" patio with a fire pit, setting the stage for a "tasty", "different take" on south-of-the-border fare from chef Matt Gandin (ex Delfina); the staff is "good about explaining dishes", although a few report "rushed" service, while "awesome" margaritas and "out-of-this-world" cocktails fuel the "festive" (read: "loud") vibe and "hip scene."

Commis ☒ *American* 27 | 21 | 26 | $111
Oakland | 3859 Piedmont Ave. (Rio Vista Ave.) | 510-653-3902 | www.commisrestaurant.com
Oakland native James Syhabout's "incredible precision" results in "stunning", "deliciously inventive" New American prix fixes imbued with molecular gastronomy at his Lilliputian, high-end Piedmont Avenue flagship; despite "tiny portions" and "quiet", "spartan" digs ("the servers should be wearing robes"), acolytes insist all "pleasure points" get "hit", particularly if you opt for the "excellent" wine pairings and dine at the "chef's counter" overlooking the "talented kitchen staff" in action; P.S. Syhabout's Box and Bells, for casual eating and drinking, is in the works at 5912 College Avenue.

Corners Tavern *American* ▽ 23 | 22 | 22 | $38
Walnut Creek | Broadway Plaza Shopping Ctr. | 1342 Broadway Plaza (Main St.) | 925-948-8711 | www.cornerstavern.com
"Classic comfort food", "wonderful cocktails" and a "busy bar scene" are the hallmarks of this "cool", midpriced American gastropub in Walnut Creek where "attentive" service adds to the "lovely" vibe; while some report "loud" conditions in the "airy", antique-modern space, two garage doors open onto an outdoor patio that's "great" on a "warm summer evening."

Cottonwood *Eclectic* ▽ 20 | 21 | 21 | $38
Truckee | 10142 Rue Hilltop (Orelis Rd.) | 530-587-5711 | www.cottonwoodrestaurant.com
"Great upscale comfort food" (including a signature Caesar salad "made the way it should be") and a "nice view" "overlooking Truckee" make this midpriced Eclectic housed in a historic ski lodge "the place to come" for "rejuvenation" "after a day on the slopes" or for a relaxing meal on the deck in summer; casual environs and solid service help assure "everybody feels comfortable", while weekly live music adds to the "fun atmosphere."

Dead Fish *Seafood* 21 | 21 | 20 | $41
Crockett | 20050 San Pablo Ave. (Merchant St.) | 510-787-3323 | www.thedeadfish.com
"If you want a place with a view", this Crockett seafooder overlooking the Carquinez Strait fits the bill say aficionados who also go for the "satisfying", occasionally "inspiring" eclectic roundup of dishes, including its "famous" crab; "service is prompt", and though a few surveyors find the tabs "a bit pricey for what you get", the "patio is perfect" for soaking up the scenery.

Doña Tomás ☒ *Mexican* 22 | 18 | 19 | $36
Oakland | 5004 Telegraph Ave. (bet. 49th & 51st Sts.) | 510-450-0522 | www.donatomas.com
An "emphasis on fresh, seasonal ingredients" and a "modern twist – or two" add up to "flavorful", "well-prepared" Mexican plates (including "carnitas from heaven") at this Oakland "institution" where "friendly" (if "slow") staffers also offer up "tasty drinks"; sure, it gets "a bit crowded and noisy", and some find it "pricey" for the genre, but most

agree it's "worth the extra money" and recommend "eating outside if the weather is nice."

Dopo ⑤ *Italian*
25 | 18 | 22 | $39

Oakland | 4293 Piedmont Ave. (bet. Echo & Glen Eden Aves.) | 510-652-3676 | www.dopoadesso.com

Regulars rave about the "innovative Italian cuisine" at this midpriced Oakland "trattoria" (and Adesso sibling) that dishes out "delicate" "handmade pastas", "authentic pizza" and cured meats with flavors that "shine"; "uneven" service, "cramped quarters" and "no reservations" for fewer than six are a bit of "a downer", but "eating at the bar and watching the chefs work is great."

Dragonfly *Asian/Californian*
23 | 20 | 21 | $42

Truckee | Porter Simon Bldg. | 10118 Donner Pass Rd., 2nd fl. (bet. Bridge & Spring Sts.) | 530-587-0557 | www.dragonflycuisine.com

"Creative Asian-inspired Californian cuisine" (including sushi) draws fans to this second-floor Truckee stop, where regulars recommend "eating outside if you can" for "spectacular views of the mountains" and trains "coming and going over nearby Donner Pass"; it's not cheap, but realists remind "you get what you pay for."

Dragon Rouge Restaurant *Vietnamese*
24 | 19 | 22 | $25

Alameda | 2337 Blanding Ave. (29th Ave.) | 510-521-1800 | www.dragonrougerestaurant.com

Relocated to a "great space right on the waterfront", this "delightful, family-run" Alameda Vietnamese offers "inventive items" "with a Cali twist"; though "a bit pricey compared to places in Oakland's Chinatown", "distinct flavors", an "attentive staff", "surprise entertainment" and a "lively bar scene" make it a "local gem."

NEW Duende *Spanish*
▽ 23 | 24 | 25 | $53

Oakland | 468 19th St. (bet. B'way & Telegraph Ave.) | 510-893-0174 | www.duendeoakland.com

"Bright" flavors and a "big spirit" keep things "jumping" at this Oakland Spaniard from chef Paul Canales (Oliveto) and GM Rocco Somazzi, offering a selection of tapas and large plates including a *"fabulosa"* paella; service is "great", while the "hip" lofty space offers "communal tables", "microbrews" on tap, a "bodega" area that "doubles as a wine store" and occasional live music – and since it's "quite a scene", you'd best "make a reservation."

East Ocean Seafood Restaurant *Chinese*
23 | 17 | 19 | $24

Alameda | 1713 Webster St. (bet. Buena Vista & Pacific Aves.) | 510-865-3381 | www.eastoceanseafoodrestaurant.com

"Crowds line up" at this Alameda "family-run" "dim sum temple" serving "authentic and flavorful" "Cantonese" Chinese fare for "reasonable" prices; it's "often very busy" with "banquet-style" "parties on weekend nights", but the staff is so "helpful" that "even the pushcart servers can explain dishes in English"; P.S. dim sum served 10 AM–2:30 PM.

NEW Easy Creole ⑤ *Cajun/Creole*
- | - | - | I

Berkeley | 1761 Alcatraz Ave. (Ellis St.) | 415-347-5640 | www.easycreole.com

This brick-and-mortar location of a pop-up restaurant brings Cajun-Creole lunches and dinners to the Berkeley-Emeryville border with an

FOOD | DECOR | SERVICE | COST

inexpensive, changing menu including the likes of red beans, gumbo and even some vegan dishes, in a casual, cash-only cafe setting.

El Farolito *Mexican*
23 | 8 | 17 | $10

Oakland | 3646 International Blvd. (37th Ave.) | 510-533-9194 | www.elfarolitoinc.com

See review in City of San Francisco Directory.

NEW El Gusano *Mexican*
- | - | - | I

Oakland | 1015 Clay St. (11th St.) | 510-444-9676 | www.el-gusano.com

An offshoot from San Francisco's Tropisueño, this affordable Old Oakland Mexican plays the part of a taqueria by day (complete with salsa bar) and full-service hot spot at night, serving up authentically inspired, yet locally sourced classics; reclaimed wood accents create an inviting vibe, but the action is at the bar where Mexican movies are projected overhead and bartenders pour an array of tequila and mezcal-based cocktails that pay homage to its name ('the worm').

Emilia's Pizzeria 🅱Ⓜ🚫 *Pizza*
∇ 27 | 8 | 20 | $17

Berkeley | 2995 Shattuck Ave. (Ashby Ave.) | 510-704-1794 | www.emiliaspizzeria.com

"Light crust, very fresh" ingredients and "the right ratio of cheese" have pals of "East Coast–style pizza" phoning the instant this "small", "hard-to-find" Berkeley storefront opens to reserve a "time slot" for pickup; some gripe the "one-size" pies aren't worth the "rigmarole", but regulars counter "put the number on speed dial"; P.S. only eight seats and cash only.

Encuentro Cafe & Wine Bar 🅱Ⓜ *Vegetarian*
∇ 26 | 23 | 23 | $32

Oakland | 202 Second St. (Jackson St.) | 510-832-9463 | www.encuentrooakland.com

Even "meat eaters" won't feel they've "missed out" at this Jack London District vegetarian where the midpriced menu of small plates is filled with "satisfying" flavors and "seasonal ingredients"; a "friendly" staff that's "knowledgeable" about the "interesting" wine selection adds to the "all-in-all great experience."

Enoteca Molinari 🅱Ⓜ *Italian*
∇ 22 | 17 | 21 | $40

Oakland | 5474 College Ave. (Taft Ave.) | 510-428-4078 | www.enoteca-molinari.com

For a "pleasant dining experience", admirers tout this storefront eno-teca in North Oakland that "transports you to *Italia*" with a "focused" Italian menu and hospitality that both reflect "care and attention"; some quip that "you practically sit in the kitchen" of the "tiny" space, but fans insist that whether you go for a "glass of wine" or a "full sit-down" meal, it's "worth the squeeze."

Erna's Elderberry House *Californian/French*
28 | 28 | 29 | $101

Oakhurst | Château du Sureau | 48688 Victoria Ln. (Hwy. 41) | 559-683-6800 | www.elderberryhouse.com

Delivering a "superlative" dining experience as "inspired and com-manding as Yosemite's Half Dome" itself, this culinary "Brigadoon" just outside the park in Oakhurst "delights and surprises" travelers with "exquisite", locally sourced New French–Californian prix fixe dinners proffered in a "magical", "elegant setting" by a "prescient" staff that "makes you feel as if they've personalized the evening just for you"; PS. there's a "wonderful Sunday brunch" for guests who "stay at the château" next door.

Esin Restaurant & Bar *American/Mediterranean*

26 | 24 | 26 | $45

Danville | Rose Garden Ctr. | 750 Camino Ramon (Sycamore Valley Rd.) | 925-314-0974 | www.esinrestaurant.com

Curtis and Esin deCarion have created a "real East Bay favorite" with their upscale Danville New American–Med "jewel", a "go-to place for special occasions", thanks to "outstanding" "seasonal" menu items, "must-not-miss" desserts and "gracious", "surprisingly kid-friendly" service; the "strip-mall" location doesn't detract from the "wonderful atmosphere" in the lofty space, one more reason many "can't wait to go back."

Evan's American Gourmet Cafe *American*

∇ 27 | 24 | 26 | $59

South Lake Tahoe | 536 Emerald Bay Rd. (15th St.) | 530-542-1990 | www.evanstahoe.com

"Exquisitely prepared" New American plates that would be "wonderful for anywhere" are considered especially "priceless for Tahoe" at this "special-occasion" destination; staffers make diners feel like "invited guests" in the "intimate" converted cabin surrounds, so fans find it "worth the pricey tab."

Everett & Jones Barbeque *BBQ*

21 | 12 | 16 | $22

Berkeley | 1955 San Pablo Ave. (bet. Hearst & University Aves.) | 510-548-8261
Hayward | 296 A St. (bet. Flagg & Princeton Sts.) | 510-581-3222
Oakland | Jack London Sq. | 126 Broadway (bet. 1st & 2nd Sts.) | 510-663-2350 | www.eandjbbq.com

"Smack your lips and lick your fingers" – "they really know how to serve up some 'cue" in "delicious heaping abundance" at this BBQ trio; just beware that there's counter service and "no frills" at Berkeley and Hayward, while Oakland is slightly "more expensive" with "sit-down" service.

Five *American/Californian*

20 | 22 | 19 | $42

Berkeley | Hotel Shattuck Plaza | 2086 Allston Way (Oxford St.) | 510-225-6055 | www.five-berkeley.com

"Eye-popping decor", thanks to the "tasteful renovation" of an "elegant old hotel", creates a "lovely" "retro atmosphere" at this Berkeley Cal-American where "colorful, creative dishes" are served by a "polished" staff; the location makes it "one of the best places for before or after the theater", and it's "not noisy, as it used to be."

Flora *American*

23 | 22 | 21 | $43

Oakland | 1900 Telegraph Ave. (19th St.) | 510-286-0100

"Exotic cocktails" plus "fantastic attention to detail" in its "refined and confident" New American fare proffered amid "swanky" "art deco" decor make this "Uptown hipster" haven one of Oakland's "great" spots for a "date night"; "warm service" adds to the "romantic" vibe, and though it can get "too loud" and a bit "pricey", it's in a prime "location near the Fox and Paramount theaters."

Fonda Solana ● *Pan-Latin*

22 | 19 | 19 | $34

Albany | 1501 Solano Ave. (Curtis St.) | 510-559-9006
An Albany "late-night place", this Pan-Latin "hangout" draws a "lively crowd" for its "high-quality south-of-the-border" small plates topped off by "delish drinks"; bigger eaters moan "it costs a fortune to fill up", but "recession pricing" at happy hours (5–7 PM and 9 PM till close) and "courteous", "efficient service" let everyone "leave happy."

NEW Forge *American/Pizza*

– | – | – | M

Oakland | 66 Franklin St. (Jack London Sq.) | 510-268-3200 | www.theforgepizza.com
This artisanal pizza-and-beer hangout in Oakland's Jack London Square offers a sensibly priced menu starring thin-crust pies fired in the eponymous Italian oven plus American comfort classics like potato skins and wings; the converted warehouse digs feature burnt plywood floors, a high community table, flat-screen TVs and a spacious patio complete with fire pits – perfect for a Negroni on the waterfront.

FuseBox ▣ Ⓜ ⇄ *Korean*

▽ 26 | 19 | 25 | $28

Oakland | 2311 Magnolia St. (Grand Ave.) | 510-444-3100 | www.fuseboxoakland.com
"Wow, what flavors" say fans who find themselves "craving" the affordable, bar-style Korean food with "modern" (even "healthy") touches at this West Oakland option; the "bare-bones" interior is abetted by outdoor seating and sunny service, completing the "whole experience"; lunch is served Wednesday–Saturday, dinner Thursday–Saturday.

Gar Woods Grill & Pier ● *Californian*

19 | 23 | 20 | $41

Carnelian Bay | 5000 N. Lake Blvd. (Center St.) | 530-546-3366 | www.garwoods.com
"Lots of deck" and "endless views over Lake Tahoe" steal the show at this "fun" Carnelian Bay hangout that's ideal for downing "creative cocktails" in the summer; while the service and Californian fare take a back seat to the setting, the bar menu gets props as "probably better than the regular menu and less expensive" too.

Gather *Californian*

23 | 21 | 21 | $37

Berkeley | David Brower Ctr. | 2200 Oxford St. (Allston Way) | 510-809-0400 | www.gatherrestaurant.com
"Innovative combinations of the freshest local ingredients" "showcase" the Bay Area's bounty at this "very Berkeley" Californian, where you can "go whole hog" or "whole vegan" since many of the "well-prepared" mid-priced offerings (including the "exquisite" charcuterie) are meat-free; "eco-friendly" stylings are as expected, and though visitors disagree on service ("efficient" vs. "slow"), most agree it works "when you want to be healthy and feel good about your dining experience."

Gaumenkitzel Ⓜ *German*

▽ 21 | 17 | 20 | $23

Berkeley | 2121 San Pablo Ave. (Cowper St.) | 510-647-5016 | www.gaumenkitzel.net
"Hearty stews", spaetzle and other German dishes with notably "bright, clean flavors" are complemented by "fresh-baked" bread and desserts at this inexpensive Berkeley option; German wines and beers round out the offerings, while the fairly "spartan", "storelike" environs benefit from "prompt, friendly" service.

	FOOD	DECOR	SERVICE	COST

Gioia Pizzeria *Pizza* — 25 | 12 | 18 | $16

Berkeley | 1586 Hopkins St. (bet. McGee & Monterey Aves.) |
510-528-4692 | www.gioiapizzeria.com
See review in City of San Francisco Directory.

NEW Grand Lake Kitchen *Deli* — - | - | - | I

Oakland | 576 Grand Ave. (bet. Euclid Ave. & MacArthur Blvd.) |
510-922-9582 | www.grandlakekitchen.com

Grads of Park Tavern and Delfina are behind this Oakland deli just off
Lake Merritt doling out wallet-friendly salads, sides and "to-die-for"
made-to-order sandwiches featuring slices from 4505 Meats and artisanal breads that will "make you swoon", as well as choice craft beer
and wine; "friendly service" and a mix of counter and sidewalk seating
encourages locals to stick around and "chat", while a small grocery selection caters to picnickers and other to-go customers.

Grégoire *French* — 24 | 10 | 18 | $20

Berkeley | 2109 Cedar St. (bet. Shattuck Ave. & Walnut St.) | 510-883-1893
Oakland | 4001 Piedmont Ave. (40th St.) | 510-547-3444
www.gregoirerestaurant.com

Offering "off-the-wall" "tasty" fare, this oft "packed" North Berkeley and
Oakland French duo "wows" with "beautifully prepared" "gourmet fast
food", like "deliciously creative" sandwiches and "divine" potato puffs in
"small" digs best suited to takeout (albeit "upscale takeout"); though
some say it's "a little too expensive" for grub that you "eat out of a card-
board box", most agree it offers some of the "best" quick bites around.

Haven *Californian* — 25 | 24 | 21 | $55

Oakland | 44 Webster St. (Embarcadero W.) | 510-663-4440 |
www.havenoakland.com

"Heaven" is what acolytes rename this "adventurous entry into Daniel
Patterson's empire" (Coi, Plum) situated in Jack London Square where
chef Kim Alter works "magic in the open kitchen" conjuring a "divine",
"innovative" Californian menu; "snazzy" stonework-and-wood digs
plus mostly "attentive" service are boons, and though "your wallet will
be a lot lighter", you'll leave "happy"; P.S. "the best deal is the tasting
menu" – "you'll be dazzled."

Hawker Fare ⊠ *SE Asian* — 23 | 15 | 17 | $23

Oakland | 2300 Webster St. (23rd St.) | 510-832-8896 |
www.hawkerfare.com

Locals feel "blessed" by Commis chef James Syhabout's "street food,
not haute cuisine" at this "playful" Southeast Asian in Oakland, where
"organic produce", "pastured meats" and "impeccable technique" "elevate the humble rice bowl"; "expect to wait" in the graffiti-covered
storefront where you'll be "seated cheek-to-pierced-jowl next to people much hipper than you" shouting over the "blare of the hip-hop"
and other tunes – but it's all "inventive, cheap fun."

Home of Chicken & Waffles ● *Southern* — 19 | 14 | 17 | $18

Oakland | 444 Embarcadero W. (B'way) | 510-836-4446
Walnut Creek | 1653 Mt. Diablo Blvd. (California Blvd.) | 925-280-1653
www.homeofchickenandwaffles.com

For "chicken and waffles" like "mama used to make" served up with
"Southern hospitality", this pair is an East Bay "go-to"; decor is

"cute and cool", and they're "a post-bar-hopping staple" "for cheap eats, especially late at night" Friday and Saturday "when everything else is closed."

Homeroom ☑ *American* | 21 | 19 | 21 | $19 |

Oakland | 400 40th St. (Shafter Ave.) | 510-597-0400 | www.homeroom510.com

"Childhood comfort food comes of age" at this "retro schoolroom" look-alike in Oakland's Temescal, where "everyone from babies to hipsters" "keeps coming back" to try the many iterations of "tasty", "filling" "mac 'n' cheese like your mother never made" (goat cheese, Mexican, vegan and gluten-free among them); it's "tiny" and the line to get in "can be long", but it's "worth it" considering the "reasonable prices", not to mention "grown-up" concoctions like beer floats.

Hong Kong East Ocean | 22 | 19 | 15 | $33 |
Seafood Restaurant *Chinese*

Emeryville | 3199 Powell St. (Frontage Rd.) | 510-655-3388 | www.hkeo.us

The "spectacular view" at this "Hong Kong"–style Emeryville Chinese "overlooks the bay", and "the food is good enough to complement it" when "big family groups" order dim sum from the menu (since there are "no carts coming around"); just be warned, it "can be pricey" because "you're basically paying for the ambiance."

Hopscotch ☑ *American/Japanese* | ▽ 24 | 17 | 23 | $50 |

Oakland | 1915 San Pablo Ave. (bet. 19th & 20th Sts.) | 510-788-6217 | www.hopscotchoakland.com

"Don't miss the culinary experience" at this Uptown Oakland option serving "inventive" Japanese–New American dishes ("absolutely delicious" fried chicken, oyster combinations "like a sushi bar in a single bite") in a tiny retro diner setting; though a bit "pricey for the location", "marvelous" cocktails and "helpful" service make it quite "inviting", so "reservations are definitely recommended."

Hotel Mac Restaurant & Bar *American* | 22 | 22 | 21 | $41 |

Richmond | Hotel Mac | 50 Washington Ave. (Cottage Ave.) | 510-233-0576 | www.hotelmac.net

"Take your sweetie" to this "charming" historic Point Richmond hotel built in 1911 (think pressed-tin ceilings and lots of brass and wood) for "solid American" "fine dining" that's "elegant without being pretentious"; a "friendly staff", "adequate portions", "good specials" and a weekday "happy hour" that's "a steal" further make this a "hidden gem."

Ike's Place *Sandwiches* | 25 | 12 | 18 | $12 |

Oakland | 2204 Broadway St. (22nd St.) | 510-338-6789
NEW Walnut Creek | 1159 Locust St. (bet. Botelho Dr. & Olympic Blvd.) | 925-944-4755
www.ilikeikesplace.com
See review in City of San Francisco Directory.

Il Fornaio *Italian* | 18 | 19 | 18 | $43 |

Walnut Creek | 1430 Mt. Diablo Blvd. (bet. B'way & Main St.) | 925-296-0100 | www.ilfornaio.com
See review in City of San Francisco Directory.

Imperial Tea Court *Tearoom*
18 | 20 | 19 | $23

Berkeley | Epicurious Gdn. | 1511 Shattuck Ave. (bet. Cedar & Vine Sts.) | 510-540-8888 | www.imperialtea.com

See review in City of San Francisco Directory.

In-N-Out Burger ● *Burgers*
23 | 14 | 21 | $9

Oakland | 8300 Oakport St. (Edgewater Dr.) | 800-786-1000 | www.in-n-out.com

See review in City of San Francisco Directory.

Ippuku *Japanese*
24 | 23 | 21 | $41

Berkeley | 2130 Center St. (bet. Oxford St. & Shattuck Ave.) | 510-665-1969 | www.ippukuberkeley.com

"Live dangerously" at this "friendly" Japanese izakaya near the Downtown Berkeley BART station, where "two guys and a hibachi" reward "adventurous eaters" with "amazing" yakitori and other dishes featuring "various chicken parts" that might "challenge" your "comfort zone"; just "bring plenty of yen", as the fare and the "interesting" shochus and sakes that "go with them" can "add up quickly."

Italian Colors *Italian*
22 | 20 | 23 | $34

Oakland | 2220 Mountain Blvd. (Scout Rd.) | 510-482-8094 | www.italiancolorsrestaurant.com

"They recognize regulars" at this Montclair "hangout" where the "Italian comfort food" "is not gourmet", but is "a big step above pizza-parlor spaghetti"; the "friendly staff" is "accommodating with kids", and the "accomplished guitarist" Wednesday–Saturday nights is "a definite plus."

Jimmy Beans *Diner*
20 | 11 | 16 | $19

Berkeley | 1290 Sixth St. (Gilman St.) | 510-528-3435 | www.jimmybeans.com

Fans of this diner in a "weird" West Berkeley location say it serves "ordinary items made with panache and grace", including all-day breakfast ("don't miss the silver-dollar pancakes"); there's "no table service during the day" and the "funky setting" leaves something to be desired", but the $15 three-course dinners ($20 on Sunday) are "a great bargain."

Jim's Country Style Restaurant *Southern*
▽ 26 | 16 | 24 | $14

Pleasanton | 5400 Sunol Blvd. (Bernal Ave.) | 925-426-7019

Pleasanton "locals" have "been overeating" "forever" at this "classic homestyle family place" that dishes up "great" Southern fare "for the price"; it "isn't fancy", but "excellent breakfasts", "large portions" and "friendly" service mean it's "always packed" "on the weekends."

Johnny Garlic's *Californian*
19 | 17 | 19 | $29

Dublin | Hacienda Crossings | 4920 Dublin Blvd. (Hibernia Dr.) | 925-248-2347 | www.johnnygarlics.com

See review in North of San Francisco Directory.

Joshu-ya Brasserie *Japanese*
25 | 22 | 23 | $34

(fka Joshu-ya Sushi Bar)

Berkeley | 2441 Dwight Way (Telegraph Ave.) | 510-848-5260 | www.joshu-ya.com

Deemed "an exceptional restaurant" by its admirers, this Berkeley Japanese "keeps changing for the better", providing "exquisite" fish, "off-the-hook" seasonal selections and "creative fusion" dishes; regulars say the staff enhances the pleasant "neighborhood" atmosphere, and recommend the omakase as one of the "best deals" around.

Juan's Place *Mexican*   19 | 13 | 19 | $18

Berkeley | 941 Carleton St. (9th St.) | 510-845-6904

"Go with an empty stomach" to fill up on "large portions" of "old-fashioned" "Mexican comfort food" at this "funky, fun" "Berkeley tradition" since 1972; prices are "fantastic", and even if it's a little "divey", the presiding family brings a "caring" attitude.

NEW Juhu Beach Club 🅂🅜 *Indian*   - | - | - | I

Oakland | 5179 Telegraph Ave. (bet. 51st & 52nd Sts.) | 510-652-7350 | www.juhubeachclub.com

Top Chef alum Preeti Mistry's Oakland brick-and-mortar outpost of her popular pop-up showcases "delicious", affordable updated renditions of Indian street food and homestyle cooking with "complex" flavors that "go way beyond your average" subcontinental eatery (including slider-style sandwiches with masala fries); the colorfully painted storefront is filled with Bollywood images, monkey wallpaper and shelves lined with spice containers that store her house-ground blends.

King of Thai Noodles 🅞🅥 *Thai*   21 | 12 | 17 | $14

Alameda | 1635 Park St. (bet. Buena Vista & Pacific Aves.) | 510-522-8200

See review in City of San Francisco Directory.

Kirala *Japanese*   25 | 16 | 18 | $36

Berkeley | 2100 Ward St. (Shattuck Ave.) | 510-549-3486

Kirala 2 *Japanese*

Berkeley | Epicurious Gdn. | 1511 Shattuck Ave. (bet. Cedar & Vine Sts.) | 510-649-1384

www.kiralaberkeley.com

"Serious sushi and Japanese-food lovers" endure "epic" waits for "outstanding fresh fish", "amazing robata" and "even better" "udon dishes" at this "deservedly busy" "go-to place" for a "sublime dining experience" in Berkeley; "try coming when the doors open or two hours later" to avoid "standing in line"; P.S. get bento boxes and premade rolls to go at the takeout-only Epicurious Garden branch.

Koi Palace @ Dublin *Chinese*   23 | 18 | 15 | $33
(fka Koi Garden)

Dublin | Ulferts Ctr. | 4288 Dublin Blvd. (bet. Glynnis Rose Dr. & John Monego Ct.) | 925-833-9090 | www.koipalace.com

See review in South of San Francisco Directory.

La Boulange *Bakery*   21 | 17 | 18 | $16

Danville | 405 Railroad Ave. (Hartz Ave.) | 925-838-1200
Lafayette | 3597 Mt. Diablo Blvd. (Dewing Ave.) | 925-284-1001
Walnut Creek | 1348 Broadway Plaza (Main St.) | 925-274-1655
www.laboulangebakery.com

See review in City of San Francisco Directory.

Lake Chalet *Californian*   17 | 24 | 18 | $38

Oakland | 1520 Lakeside Dr. (bet. 14th & 17th Sts.) | 510-208-5253 | www.thelakechalet.com

With an "absolutely fabulous setting" in a "beautifully renovated boathouse" on Lake Merritt, diners just "wish the food and ser-

FOOD DECOR SERVICE COST

vice" were "as good as" the "spectacular location" of this Oakland Californian; "happy-hour prices are really great" though, so "go, enjoy the view", "have snacks, appetizers, drinks" and hope "they get their act together."

Lalime's *Californian/Mediterranean* — 26 | 22 | 24 | $52
Berkeley | 1329 Gilman St. (bet. Neilson St. & Peralta Ave.) | 510-527-9838 | www.lalimes.com

"First", and fans say "still the best", of the K2 restaurant group's ventures, this Berkeley Cal-Med is "a neighborhood gem if there ever was one", proffering a "changing menu" of "seasonal", "locally sourced" cuisine and "very good wines" in a "romantic" "Craftsman-style" "bungalow"; service "offered with genuine smiles" and "fun theme nights" keep them coming back, plus it's "relatively" affordable, making it a "go-to favorite" of locals who've been celebrating "special occasions" here "since it began": P.S. closed Monday–Tuesday.

La Méditerranée *Mediterranean/Mideastern* — 22 | 17 | 20 | $23
Berkeley | 2936 College Ave. (bet. Ashby Ave. & Russell St.) | 510-540-7773 | www.cafelamed.com

See review in City of San Francisco Directory.

La Note *French* — 23 | 21 | 20 | $26
Berkeley | 2377 Shattuck Ave. (bet. Channing Way & Durant Ave.) | 510-843-1535 | www.lanoterestaurant.com

"Sensational" "French countryside–inspired" breakfasts starring "creative" pancakes and omelets and "bowl-size café au lait" make this "affordable" cafe with a "charming" "Provence vibe" "renowned" in Berkeley; "get there early" to avoid the "long lines during the weekend" or come for dinner (Thursdays–Saturdays only) when it's less "crowded" and "noisy"; P.S. a "lovely garden" is open in good weather.

Lark Creek *American* — 23 | 21 | 22 | $44
Walnut Creek | 1360 Locust St. (bet. Cypress St. & Mt. Diablo Blvd.) | 925-256-1234 | www.larkcreek.com

"Delicious" Traditional American "comfort food" is made with "farm-fresh ingredients" and served with "verve" by a "caring staff" at this "classic standby" in Walnut Creek, whose "warm, welcoming" setting features an open kitchen inside and sidewalk seating out; though some feel prices are "on the expensive side", the "exceptional desserts" and "excellent" wines help keep it on the list of places "you can always depend on."

La Sen Bistro *Californian/French* — ▽ 23 | 16 | 20 | $35
Berkeley | 2002 Salvio St. (Galindo St.) | 925-363-7870 | www.lasenbistro.com

"Nobody seems to know about" this "small, cozy" Berkeley bistro that offers a Californian-French menu accompanied by "lovely" service; loyalists say it offers "great value" "for the money" and makes a "nice, quiet lunch place" or "great pre-theater option."

La Victoria Taqueria *Mexican* — 24 | 12 | 16 | $9
Hayward | 26953 Mission Blvd. (Sorenson Rd.) | 510-537-8700 | www.lavicsj.com

See review in South of San Francisco Directory.

Le Cheval *Vietnamese*

21 | 17 | 19 | $28

Berkeley | YWCA | 2600 Bancroft Way (Bowditch St.) | 510-704-8018 🛇
Oakland | 1007 Clay St. (10th St.) | 510-763-8495
Walnut Creek | 1375 N. Broadway (bet. Cypress & Duncan Sts.) | 925-938-2288 Ⓜ
www.lecheval.com

Regulars at the Walnut Creek outpost find it the most "comfortable" of this Vietnamese trio serving a "wide range of tasty dishes including clay pots", pho and banh mi at "reasonable prices"; the Berkeley outlet is best for a "quick lunch", while Oakland fans are "still impressed" with the original, reopened at its previous Clay Street address.

Little Star Pizza *Pizza*

25 | 16 | 19 | $23

Albany | 1175 Solano Ave. (Cornell Ave.) | 510-526-7827 | www.littlestarpizza.com

See review in City of San Francisco Directory.

Lo Coco's Restaurant & Pizzeria Ⓜ *Italian*

22 | 16 | 22 | $28

Berkeley | 1400 Shattuck Ave. (Rose St.) | 510-843-3745
Oakland | 4270 Piedmont Ave. (Echo Ave.) | 510-652-6222 ⑆
www.lococospizzeria.com

"Truly authentic", "reasonably priced" "Sicilian food" is the draw at this "lovely little Italian" pair with a "happy, bustling, warm atmosphere"; "homemade pasta and sauces" are "so good" you "want to cry", the pizza is like "grandmother used to make" and "the bread is out of this world", all leaving patrons "satisfied and full."

🆕 Lucille's Smokehouse Bar-B-Que ⚫ *BBQ*

- | - | - | I

Concord | Sunvalley Shopping Ctr. | 486 Sunvalley Mall (Contra Costa Blvd.) | 925-677-7427 | www.lucillesbbq.com

This lively Concord BBQ joint – the first Bay Area outpost of a Western U.S. chain – offers spicy smoked meats and budget-friendly Southern-style dishes, including an extensive kids' menu and gluten-free options, along with beer, wine and cocktails; the big, bright shopping center space has playful Americana-themed decor and offers plenty of seating for families and big groups, plus live music, weeknight happy-hour specials and several televisions for sports fans.

Luka's Taproom & Lounge ⚫ *Californian/French*

20 | 15 | 18 | $27

Oakland | 2221 Broadway (Grand Ave.) | 510-451-4677 | www.lukasoakland.com

Expect "comfort food" with Californian-French "flair" at this midpriced brasserie that's an "anchor" for the Uptown Oakland "hipster" "food scene"; there's a "classy beer selection" and the "Belgian fries with three different sauces" are a "must-have", but "the burger is what you come back for" – assuming you don't mind variable service and a "loud and lively crowd"; P.S. there's dancing to DJs Wednesday–Sunday.

🆕 Lungomare *Italian*

- | - | - | M

Oakland | 1 Broadway (Water St.) | 510-444-7171 | www.lungomareoakland.com

The latest from the Chop Bar folks, this coastal Italian on Oakland's waterfront is making a splash with midpriced Boot-inspired offerings including seafood, cured meats, wood-fired pizza and handmade pastas proffered by "knowledgeable" servers; early visitors say you can't beat the "great location", complete with outdoor patio and a large bar offering "great cocktails", a "well-chosen" wine list and local craft brews; P.S. an adjacent cafe serves coffee, morning pastries and lunch to go.

Mama's Royal Cafe ⊘ American

23 | 15 | 20 | $17

Oakland | 4012 Broadway (bet. 40th & 41st Sts.) | 510-547-7600 | www.mamasroyalcafeoakland.com

"You feel like you're in a '70s time warp" at this "funky", "longtime" Oakland "breakfast favorite" with "strong coffee", "generous servings" and waitresses who "call you 'hon'"; the "often local and organically sourced" chow is "still solid after all these years" (including the "shockingly delicious" home fries), adding up to a "good value" that's "worth" the "long waits"; closes 2:30 PM weekdays, 3 PM weekends.

Manzanita Lake Tahoe *Californian*

▽ 22 | 26 | 20 | $63

Truckee | Ritz-Carlton Lake Tahoe | 13031 Ritz Carlton Highlands Ct. (Highlands View Rd.) | 530-562-3050 | www.manzanitalaketahoe.com

"It's worth a trip on the gondola" to enjoy the "out-of-this-world" vistas from this Truckee restaurant/bar in the Ritz-Carlton, perched "halfway up the mountain" of the Northstar Resort; diners dub the price "quite fair" for the seasonal Californian fare served up by an "attentive" staff, though those "gorgeous views" are the main event.

Marica *American/Seafood*

25 | 20 | 25 | $40

Oakland | 5301 College Ave. (Bryant Ave.) | 510-985-8388 | www.maricafood.wordpress.com

"Shh, don't tell anyone" plead Rockridgers who are "blown away" by this "small" neighborhood "gem" serving some of the most "inventive" seafood "for the price" in the East Bay on its New American menu; add in "a cool, old wooden bar", a "friendly staff" and specials like "oysters for $1" and the "early-bird prix fixe", and it's no wonder it's a "local favorite."

NEW Marrow ⊠ American

- | - | - | I

Oakland | 325 19th St. (bet. Harrison & Webster Sts.) | 510-251-1111 | www.marrowoakland.com

The founder of the Jon's Street Eats food truck is behind this brick-and-mortar lunch-only New American in Uptown Oakland that serves sandwiches and other creations made from just one animal at a time, which means the creative, wallet-friendly menu changes daily; the tiny storefront has a few counter seats and an industrial feel, with big windows and paintings inspired by local sites.

Marzano *Italian/Pizza*

23 | 21 | 22 | $35

Oakland | 4214 Park Blvd. (Glenfield Ave.) | 510-531-4500 | www.marzanorestaurant.com

There are "so many great menu items" at this "neighborhood" Italian in Oakland, and it's "difficult to choose" among dishes such as antipasti, Neapolitan pies that taste like they were "shipped from Italy" and "hearty entrees" that are pulled from the "wood-burning pizza oven"; prices are "not bad at all", and the "delightful staff" adds to the appeal.

	FOOD	DECOR	SERVICE	COST

Mayflower *Chinese*

| 21 | 16 | 16 | $29 |

Union City | 34348 Alvarado Niles Rd. (Decoto Rd.) | 510-489-8386 | www.mayflower-seafood.com

See Hong Kong Flower Lounge review in South of San Francisco Directory.

Men Oh Tokushima
Ramen Ⓜ *Japanese/Noodle Shop*

| - | - | - | I |

Union City | 34308 Alvarado Niles Rd. (Decoto Rd.) | 510-477-9481 | www.menohusa.com

See review in City of San Francisco Directory.

Meritage at The Claremont *Californian*

| 23 | 26 | 23 | $58 |

Berkeley | The Claremont Hotel | 41 Tunnel Rd. (Claremont Ave.) | 510-549-8510 | www.meritageclaremont.com

The "breathtaking view" of the San Francisco Bay is hard to resist at this "lovely" Californian tended by a "warm, attentive" staff in Berkeley's Claremont Hotel; though it can be costly, diners say the "dressed-up food makes you feel special" while savoring "memorable" evenings and bountiful Sunday buffet brunches; P.S. no dinner Sunday–Monday.

Mezze *Californian/Mediterranean*

| 22 | 21 | 22 | $37 |

Oakland | 3407 Lakeshore Ave. (Mandana Blvd.) | 510-663-2500 | www.mezze.com

Regulars contend that "every neighborhood should have a place" like this Oakland "warm and welcoming" "Lakeshore District" Californian-Mediterranean "staple" with its "adventurous spirit", where there's "always something new, flavorful and exciting to try" from the "eclectic menu" with a "creative spin"; adding to the appeal, the budget-minded say the "the prix fixe" dinner option is a "good value."

🆕 Miss Ollie's ⓈⓂ *Caribbean*

| - | - | - | I |

Oakland | Swan's Market | 901 Washington St. (9th St.) | 510-285-6188 | www.missolliesoakland.com

Barbados-born chef Sarah Kirnon (ex Front Porch and Hibiscus) offers her signature fried chicken alongside other affordable Caribbean-inspired staples at this cafe in Old Oakland's Swan's Market, modeled after the one-stop shops of the West Indies and offering daily specials and a few regular à la carte items; the sunny "warehouselike" setting is filled with colorful paintings, piped-in Haitian music and communal picnic tables where diners sip the likes of ginger brew and ruby-tinged hibiscus punch; P.S. there's counter service by day and table service at dinner.

Moody's Bistro & Lounge ◐ *American*

| ∇ 23 | 17 | 21 | $44 |

Truckee | Truckee Hotel | 10007 Bridge St. (bet. Church St. & Donner Pass Rd.) | 530-587-8688 | www.moodysbistro.com

"Seasonal dishes" and "thin-crust" pizzas enhance the "flavorful" New American selection at this "comfortable" Truckee bistro offering "moderately priced" lunches and somewhat more expensive dinners; a "friendly" staff, wines on tap and frequent live music are further pluses.

Mua Lounge ◐ *American*

| 21 | 21 | 19 | $32 |

Oakland | 2442 Webster St. (bet. 24th & 26th Sts.) | 510-238-1100 | www.muaoakland.com

"From vegan to bone marrow", there are small plates for everyone at this "eclectic", midpriced American set in a refurbed Oakland car repair shop; "refreshing" drinks, "cool" service and a "funky", "industrial" atmosphere that's "always lively to loud" (with a DJ spinning) make it "fun for a younger crowd"; P.S. lunch on Fridays only.

Nama Sushi & Teriyaki Japanese ▽ 27 | 16 | 22 | $26
Walnut Creek | 1502 Sunnyvale Ave. (Main St.) | 925-932-9540

Fin fanciers say the chef "is a creative master when it comes to raw fish" at this "casual", always "busy" Japanese hidden in a Walnut Creek strip mall just off Highway 680; some belly up to the L-shaped bar for "awesome sushi", but there are also tables, and warm dishes including "great tempura" at "moderate" prices, all delivered with "great service."

Nan Yang Rockridge Burmese ▽ 22 | 17 | 23 | $25
Oakland | 6048 College Ave. (bet. Claremont & Harwood Aves.) | 510-655-3298 | www.nanyangrockridge.com

"Reliably delicious", "beautiful" dishes are filled with "delightful flavor combinations" at this midpriced Rockridge "neighborhood" Burmese; patrons suggest "ask Philip", the chef/co-owner, "to select your meal for you and he'll create a perfect balance" of "favorite" items like "garlic noodles" and "ginger salad", while those who find the "pleasant" setting a bit too minimal advise "get a seat by the window."

NEW Nido M Mexican - | - | - | M
Oakland | 444 Oak St. (4th St.) | 510-444-6436 | www.nidooakland.com

Run by a husband-and-wife team, this midpriced farm-to-table restaurant and bar near Oakland's Jack London Square offers a lineup of Mexican fare inspired by family recipes; the industrial-chic 'nest' filled with bird cages and shipping containers is walk-in only, but open all day with happy-hour deals on beer, margaritas and the vast tequila and mezcal selection.

900 Grayson Burgers/Californian 24 | 18 | 21 | $22
Berkeley | 900 Grayson St. (7th St.) | 510-704-9900 | www.900grayson.com

"Prepare to confess" after meeting the "Demon Lover", this "funky" Californian's "sinful" version of chicken and waffles from a menu of "classics with a twist", plus an "outstanding" burger; sure, the place is in the "hinterlands" of Berkeley, and Saturday brunch lines are "out the door", but it's "worth squeezing" in for such "comforting" fare and "warm", "efficient" service; P.S. closes 3 PM weekdays and 2:30 PM Saturday.

North Beach Pizza Pizza 20 | 12 | 17 | $19
Berkeley | 1598 University Ave. (California St.) | 510-849-9800 | www.northbeachpizza.net

See review in City of San Francisco Directory.

Ohgane Korean BBQ Restaurant Korean 22 | 16 | 16 | $26
Dublin | 7877 Amador Valley Blvd. (San Ramon Rd.) | 925-875-1232
Oakland | 3915 Broadway (40th St.) | 510-594-8300
www.ohgane.com

"Tabletop grills" make this East Bay twosome "a fun place to take newcomers" for Korean fare suggest fans who praise the "high-quality ingredients" and the wood-charcoal barbecue; service varies, but moderate prices add to the good feeling; P.S. the Oakland location has a "huge dining room."

Oliveto Cafe *Italian*
23 | 18 | 20 | $38

Oakland | 5655 College Ave. (Shafter Ave.) | 510-547-5356 | www.oliveto.com

When East Bay diners "miss Europe", this "little cafe" located "steps from the Rockridge BART" fits the bill with cappuccinos and "quick bites" from the "limited" but "satisfying" "locally sourced" Italian menu that's a cheaper "alternative to what's cooking at its big brother" upstairs; "people-watching" patrons appreciate that the "friendly" crew lets you "stay a long time", and early-birds chirp cheerfully for the "breakfast pizza."

Oliveto Restaurant *Italian*
25 | 23 | 23 | $57

Oakland | 5655 College Ave. (Shafter Ave.) | 510-547-5356 | www.oliveto.com

This "deservedly popular" Rockridge Northern Italian continues to reach "sublime heights" with chef Jonah Rhodehamel's "innovative", "locally sourced fare", especially when it's paired with "extraordinary" vino suggested by an "attentive" staff; while some say it's "high-priced", even those with "bridge-a-phobia" feel it's "worth a trip" on a "special occasion" or for its well-known "themed dinners" ("whole hog, tomato or oceanic").

Ozumo *Japanese*
25 | 24 | 21 | $61

Oakland | 2251 Broadway (Grand Ave.) | 510-286-9866 | www.ozumo.com

See review in City of San Francisco Directory.

Pakwan *Pakistani*
23 | 9 | 14 | $16

Fremont | 41068 Fremont Blvd. (bet. Adams Ave. & Washington Blvd.) | 510-226-6234 Ⓜ🍽

Hayward | 25168 Mission Blvd. (Central Blvd.) | 510-538-2401

www.pakwanrestaurant.com

See review in City of San Francisco Directory.

Pappo Ⓜ *American*
∇ 23 | 19 | 22 | $42

Alameda | 2320 Central Ave. (bet. Oak & Park Sts.) | 510-337-9100 | www.papporestaurant.com

"Expertly balanced flavors" from a "talented chef" who lets "the seasonal ingredients shine through" bring "big-city food" to "tiny Alameda" at this "intimate", "relaxed" New American; true, the "menu" is "small", but it's also "exciting" and "changes frequently", while service is "quietly efficient" and prices are "reasonable."

Pasta Pomodoro *Italian*
18 | 16 | 19 | $22

El Cerrito | 5040 El Cerrito Plaza (Fairmount Ave.) | 510-225-0128

Emeryville | Bay Street Mall | 5614 Shellmound St. (Bay St.) | 510-923-1173

Oakland | 5500 College Ave. (Lawton Ave.) | 510-923-0900

Pleasant Hill | 45 Crescent Dr. (bet. Contra Costa Blvd. & Crescent Plaza) | 925-363-9641

San Ramon | 146 Sunset Dr. (bet. Bishop Dr. & Bollinger Canyon Rd.) | 925-867-1407

www.pastapomodoro.com

See review in City of San Francisco Directory.

	FOOD	DECOR	SERVICE	COST

Patxi's Pizza *Pizza*
(fka Patxi's Chicago Pizza)

| 22 | 16 | 18 | $22 |

Lafayette | The Clocktower | 3577 Mt. Diablo Blvd. (Lafayette Circle) | 925-299-0700
NEW **Livermore** | 2470 First St. (bet. Livermore & Railroad Aves.) | 925-371-1000
www.patxispizza.com
See review in City of San Francisco Directory.

Pearl's Deluxe Burgers *Burgers*

| 23 | 12 | 19 | $13 |

Alameda | 2254 S. Shore Ctr. (Franciscan Way) | 510-864-1015 | www.pearlsdeluxe.com
See review in City of San Francisco Directory.

The Peasant &
the Pear Ⓜ *Californian/Mediterranean*

| 23 | 21 | 23 | $41 |

Danville | 267 Hartz Ave. (Diablo Rd.) | 925-820-6611 | www.thepeasantandthepear.com
Chef-owner Rodney Worth "gets it right", offering "unpretentious but excellent" "comfort food" for "reasonable prices" at this Danville Cal-Med; staffers make you "feel like they care", and the "intimate", "relaxed" vibe is "perfect for a first date", especially on the patio where there's "live music" Thursday–Saturday nights from April–November.

Pho 84 Ⓩ *Vietnamese*

| 23 | 16 | 20 | $20 |

Oakland | 354 17th St. (Webster St.) | 510-832-1338 | www.pho84.com
"Wonderful spices", "fresh ingredients" and meat that's "so very tender" make this Oakland Vietnamese "the place to go" for "authentic pho" and other specialties; although the decor is pretty basic, and there's "always a long line" at lunch waiting to "slurp up" a "great deal", staffers are largely "welcoming" (and dinner is more "leisurely and relaxing").

Pianeta *Italian/Mediterranean*

| ▽ 20 | 17 | 17 | $56 |

Truckee | 10096 Donner Pass Rd. (Bridge St.) | 530-587-4694
"Well-done" hearty specialties (such as housemade pasta) hit the spot on "a cold day" and are matched by a serious wine cellar at this Truckee Italian-Med with friendly service and a "warm, welcoming" old world–setting; sure, "you pay a little more" (it's in a "tourist area", after all), but "what the heck, you're on vacation" justify Tahoe travelers.

Piatti Ristorante & Bar *Italian*

| 21 | 21 | 21 | $38 |

Danville | 100 Sycamore Valley Rd. W. (San Ramon Valley Blvd.) | 925-838-2082 | www.piatti.com
"Enormous portions" of "tasty" Italian specialties "at good prices" assure "you can't go wrong" at these "vibrant" (if a bit "noisy") Bay Area chain outposts where dolce vita details include "fresh potted herbs on the table" (and, in Mill Valley, a "spectacular" water view); most agree it fits the bill for "business lunches" or celebratory dinners for "large parties", plus service is "fast and attentive."

Picán *Southern*

| 24 | 24 | 22 | $47 |

Oakland | 2295 Broadway (23rd St.) | 510-834-1000 | www.picanrestaurant.com
"Southern sassy meets Northern Californian" "urban chic", and the result is a "classy, sexy, high-end soul food" stop where "all of Oakland

feels at home" and the "fried chicken is so good", it's "just like mom never made"; though the chow is "not diet", fans will "happily eat veggies the rest of the week" to atone.

Picante Cocina Mexicana *Mexican*   22 | 16 | 19 | $17

Berkeley | 1328 Sixth St. (Camelia St.) | 510-525-3121 | www.picanteberkeley.com

"Watch them make corn tortillas right in front of you" at this "large, festive" "cafeteria-style" "Berkeley institution" with a "family atmosphere" and "consistently" "tasty" Mexican fare built with "quality ingredients"; it can be "noisy" with "lots of kids" and "long lines", but fans adore the "full bar", "quick service" and "ultrareasonable pricing", plus the "little outdoor garden" is "delightful" in nice weather.

Pizza Antica *Pizza*   22 | 17 | 19 | $26

Lafayette | 3600 Mt. Diablo Blvd. (bet. Happy Valley & Oak Hill Rds.) | 925-299-0500 | www.pizzaantica.com

See review in South of San Francisco Directory.

Pizzaiolo 🄍 *Italian/Pizza*   26 | 20 | 21 | $37

Oakland | 5008 Telegraph Ave. (bet. 49th & 51st Sts.) | 510-652-4888 | www.pizzaiolooakland.com

Most patrons visit this Oakland Italian for its "spectacular" "wood-fired pizzas" crowned with "delicious" and sometimes "unusual" toppings, but say "don't overlook" the "incredible salads" and other "sublime dishes" where the "fresh ingredients" "sing out" amid the "boisterous surroundings"; while service "varies" and some complain about the "price-to-portion ratio", most agree it's still "worth it"; P.S. "make a reservation" or "the wait" can be "intimidating."

Plum *Californian*   23 | 21 | 22 | $48

Oakland | 2214 Broadway (Grand Ave.) | 510-444-7586 | www.plumoakland.com

Daniel Patterson's "exciting" Oakland outpost "gets mobbed" for its "remarkably inventive" Californian small plates ably served by a "hipster staff" in a "snazzy" yet "casual" setting featuring "giant" photos of plums; fans love to "sit at the counter" and watch the chefs "create their masterpieces", which are "a bargain" compared to tabs at "sister Coi in SF", but a few ding the "micro-sized" meals and "uncomfortable" "hardwood" seats; P.S. the adjacent Plum Bar offers "nice" farm-to-glass cocktails, bar snacks, dinner and weekday lunch.

PlumpJack Cafe *Californian*   22 | 21 | 21 | $56

Olympic Valley | PlumpJack Squaw Valley Inn | 1920 Squaw Valley Rd. (Squaw Peak Rd.) | 530-583-1576 | www.plumpjackcafe.com

At this resort restaurant in North Tahoe's Olympic Valley, après-skiers chill out with seasonally focused Californian cuisine matched with a "huge", "reasonably priced" wine list; service is "friendly", and though tabs may be "expensive", the "young" crowd populating the "cozy", rustic digs and at the adjacent bar doesn't seem to mind.

Postino *Italian*   24 | 25 | 24 | $51

Lafayette | 3565 Mt. Diablo Blvd. (Lafayette Circle) | 925-299-8700 | www.postinorestaurant.com

"Intimate dining rooms" featuring exposed brick and fireplaces in "a lovely old building", as well as attractive "outdoor seating", make this

	FOOD	DECOR	SERVICE	COST

Lafayette "oasis" a "beautiful setting" for a "fantastic" "high-end, high-class" Italian meal; "attentive" servers and a "nice wine list" add up to an "overall good choice", particularly for a "date" or "special occasion."

Prima *Italian* | 26 | 23 | 23 | $49

Walnut Creek | 1522 N. Main St. (bet. Bonanza St. & Lincoln Ave.) | 925-935-7780 | www.primawine.com

A "perennial favorite", this "excellent" Walnut Creek Italian "continues to wow" with chef-owner Peter Chastain's "authentic, sophisticated" dishes and an "amazing" wine list (featuring bottles available at its next-door wine shop); dissenters call it "pricey" and "a little pretentious", but most agree the "excellent ambiance" with service to match helps make it a "lovely place" for "date night" or a "formal occasion."

NEW Ramen Shop ◐ *Japanese/Noodle Shop* | ▽ 24 | 21 | 22 | $34

Oakland | 5812 College Ave. (Birch Ct.) | 510-788-6370 | www.ramenshop.com

There's "a small menu but some creatively delicious offerings" at this ambitious new Rockridge ramen place from three Chez Panisse alums, producing "fabulous" Japanese noodles with "complex flavors" and touches like a "medium-boiled egg that will make your knees buckle"; modestly sized and decorated in light woods, the room gets "crowded" fast, so be prepared to "wait."

Restaurant Peony *Chinese* | 20 | 14 | 14 | $27

Oakland | Pacific Renaissance Plaza | 388 Ninth St. (bet. Franklin & Webster Sts.) | 510-286-8866 | www.restaurantpeony.com

"Ignore the ambiance" and "forget the service" (which can be downright "indifferent") because the "huge selection" of "spectacular" dim sum (and other Chinese specialties) is the real draw at this "popular" Oakland "extravaganza"; the weekend "crowds" are often "daunting" and some find the menu "a bit pricey" for what it is, but it packs 'em in all the same.

Revival Bar & Kitchen ◐Ⓜ *Californian* | 22 | 21 | 21 | $43

Berkeley | 2102 Shattuck Ave. (Addison St.) | 510-549-9950 | www.revivalbarandkitchen.com

"Local, sustainable", "snout-to-tail" cuisine "that holds up" against "the competitive Berkeley standard" makes for "perfect pre-theater" or late-night dining at chef-owner Amy Murray's "quirky but imaginative" Californian, where dishes star "seasonal ingredients" "prepared at the peak of freshness"; alas, it's sometimes "so noisy you can't hold a conversation", but "knowledgeable" staffers, a "cozy atmosphere", "decent prices" and "inventive drinks" keep it a "cool scene."

Rick & Ann's *American* | 23 | 17 | 19 | $25

Berkeley | 2922 Domingo Ave. (bet. Ashby Ave. & Rusell St.) | 510-649-8538 | www.rickandanns.com

Berkeleyites "keep coming back" for the "great American chow" made from "locally sourced", "high-quality" ingredients at this inexpensive, "family-friendly" joint that offers plenty of "healthy and unique options" for breakfast through dinner; there are often "long lines on weekends", but service comes "with a smile" and the "feel-good food for the soul" is "worth the wait"; P.S. no dinner Mondays.

EAST OF SAN FRANCISCO

| | FOOD | DECOR | SERVICE | COST |

Riva Cucina 🅢🅜 *Italian*
26 | 23 | 25 | $38

Berkeley | 800 Heinz Ave. (7th St.) | 510-841-7482 | www.rivacucina.com

"Perfetto" agree fans of this "hidden" "slice of Italy" "tucked away amid the warehouses of West Berkeley" that's a "casual place for serious" Emilia-Romagna–inspired cuisine with "a touch of locavore creativity"; the midpriced eats are delivered with "excellent", "personal service" in a "lovely", "peaceful" dining room, making this place "feel like a find"; P.S. closed Sundays and Mondays.

Rivoli *Californian/Mediterranean*
27 | 24 | 25 | $51

Berkeley | 1539 Solano Ave. (bet. Neilson St. & Peralta Ave.) | 510-526-2542 | www.rivolirestaurant.com

Even after "20 years", this "exceptional" Berkeley "favorite" "continues" to "delight", dishing up "exquisite" seasonal Cal-Med cuisine along with "good vibes"; factor in a "small" but "charming" setting overlooking a "lovely plant-filled courtyard" and "an attentive (but not overly so)" staff, and it's deemed one of the best "special-occasion restaurants" in the area – minus the usual high prices or "blaring music."

NEW Rosamunde Sausage Grill ⧸ *German*
22 | 11 | 14 | $13

Oakland | Swan's Mktpl. | 911 Washington St. (9th St.) | 510-338-3108 | www.rosamundesausagegrill.com

See review in City of San Francisco Directory.

Rudy's Can't Fail Café ● *Diner*
19 | 18 | 18 | $19

Emeryville | 4081 Hollis St. (Park Ave.) | 510-594-1221
Oakland | 1805 Telegraph Ave. (bet. 18th & 19th Sts.) | 510-251-9400
www.iamrudy.com

"Just what a diner should be", these "hipster hangouts" in Emeryville and Oakland are "open late", serve "solid", "homey" American grub all day long and are manned by an "indifferent", "tatted-up staff"; there's enough "kitsch decor" (including "funky Barbies") and "loud" music in the "punk rock–meets-playroom settings" to "keep kids of all ages entertained", and given the decent prices, many "can't fail to stop here" when they need a "greasy fix."

Rumbo Al Sur 🅜 *Pan-Latin*
19 | 20 | 20 | $38

Oakland | 4239 Park Blvd. (Wellington St.) | 510-479-1208 | www.rumboalsurrestaurant.com

"You just can't get a better margarita" say habitués who love the Pan-Latin drinks and food ("out-of-this-world" mussels) with a "good tang" at this "enjoyable" Oaklander featuring a wood-accented, group-friendly layout; service is "upscale" and tabs moderate (especially at happy hour), plus "Taco Tuesdays are a treat."

NEW Rustic Tavern 🅜 *American*
- | - | - | M

Lafayette | 3576 Mt. Diablo Blvd. (Oak Hill Rd.) | 925-385-0559 | www.rustictavernlafayette.com

One Market and Lark Creek alums are behind this moderately priced Lafayette restaurant specializing in seasonal New American cuisine and regional beer and wine; the open space has two-tops and larger tables for groups, as well as bar seating and a flower-lined outdoor seating area.

	FOOD	DECOR	SERVICE	COST

Ruth's Chris Steak House *Steak*

| 24 | 21 | 23 | $66 |

Walnut Creek | 1553 Olympic Blvd. (bet. Locust & Main Sts.) |
925-977-3477 | www.ruthschris.com

See review in City of San Francisco Directory.

Sasa *Japanese*

| 25 | 24 | 23 | $46 |

Walnut Creek | 1432 N. Main St. (Cypress Dr.) | 925-210-0188 |
www.sasawc.com

"Mouthwatering combinations" from an "interesting izakaya-style
menu" – plus "creative cocktails", a "superb" staff and "wow-factor"
decor – have turned this Walnut Creek Japanese into a "trendy hot
spot"; though some complain it's "noisy" and a little "overpriced", the
"exquisite presentations" and "creative" dishes, including "innovative" sushi, are sure to please; P.S. the plant-filled "outdoor" patio is
a "delightful" plus.

Saul's Restaurant & Delicatessen *Deli*

| 20 | 15 | 18 | $22 |

Berkeley | 1475 Shattuck Ave. (bet. Rose & Vine Sts.) | 510-848-3354 |
www.saulsdeli.com

"Authentic Jewish comfort food" like at a "real East Coast deli – only
better" (it's "taken up a notch with good Californian ingredients") –
means "you cannot go wrong" at this "old-fashioned" Berkeley
standby with "pleasant" service; since there's "something for everyone" including "the kids or grandma or grandpa", there's always a
"wait" on "weekends."

Shalimar *Indian/Pakistani*

| 23 | 7 | 13 | $16 |

Dublin | 7410 Amador Valley Blvd. (bet. Interstate 680 & Village Pkwy.) |
925-248-2746
Fremont | 3325 Walnut Ave. (Liberty St.) | 510-494-1919
www.shalimarsf.com

See review in City of San Francisco Directory.

Shen Hua *Chinese*

| 22 | 17 | 18 | $24 |

Berkeley | 2914 College Ave. (bet. Ashby Ave. & Russell St.) | 510-883-1777
Regulars say "some of the very best Chinese food in the East Bay" can
be found at this big Berkeley eatery delivering "fresh" fare and "good
service most of the time"; it's easy on the wallet too, and considering
the "large portions", you might "get two meals out of it."

Sidebar 🗷 *Californian/Mediterranean*

| 22 | 19 | 20 | $37 |

Oakland | 542 Grand Ave. (bet. Euclid Ave. & MacArthur Blvd.) |
510-452-9500

"Local, casual cuisine" attracts an "eclectic crowd" to this "hip"
Oakland gastropub dishing out Cal-Med fare and run by "veteran
folks" (from the shuttered Zax Tavern); though perfectionists find it
"predictably good but rarely outstanding", "inventive cocktails" and
"cool" service in a "comfortable" space with a U-shaped copper bar
add to the "value."

Skates on the Bay *American*

| 20 | 24 | 20 | $40 |

Berkeley | 100 Seawall Dr. (University Ave.) | 510-549-1900 |
www.skatesonthebay.com

While "the food's quite good" at this midpriced American with a "terrific location right on the water" in the Berkeley Marina (and lots of

seafood on the menu), it's the "breathtaking views of San Francisco and the bridges across the bay" that steal the show; though service can be "spotty", fans maintain this locale is "more than just a tourist trap", and is "popular for happy hour" and "special occasions."

Soi4 *Thai*   23 | 19 | 22 | $33

Oakland | 5421 College Ave. (bet. Lawton & Manila Aves.) | 510-655-0889 | www.soifour.com

"If this is Thai street food, then bring on more streets like it" praise proponents of the "unconventional but tasty" "Bangkok-style" dishes that are "attractively presented" at this "stylish/casual" Oaklander with large windows and "modern" decor; add in "gracious" servers who are adept at "explaining dishes like they cooked them themselves" to see why it's a "local favorite."

Soule Domain *American*   ∇ 24 | 24 | 24 | $52

Kings Beach | 9983 Cove Ave. (Stateline Rd.) | 530-546-7529 | www.souledomain.com

Tahoe travelers and locals say it's "always a treat to go back" to this "gem" hidden behind the Biltmore Casino, thanks to the chef-owner and his "knowledgeable staff"; the American fare and "great wine selection" make it a standout for the area, while the vintage "cozy" log cabin digs seem built for "fireplace nights."

Southie *American*   24 | 15 | 22 | $21

Oakland | 6311 College Ave. (bet. Alcatraz Ave. & 63rd St.) | 510-654-0100 | www.southieoakland.com

Whether for "breakfast, lunch or dinner", they're "slinging some great dishes" at this pint-size New American "Wood Tavern spin-off" in Oakland, including "incredible, original sandwiches" by day and small bites at night, plus "great beers on tap"; it "might seem a little pricey, but it's well worth it" for "good-quality" eats with a "warm and friendly" vibe.

NEW Stella Nonna *American*   - | - | - | I

Berkeley | 1407 San Pablo Ave. (Camelia & Page Sts.) | 510-524-3400 | www.stellanonna.com

Opened by local caterers operating under the same name, this San Pablo Avenue eatery offers classic American comfort food, including affordable small bites and sandwiches plus some entrees; the modern space, with polished concrete floors, high wood-beamed ceilings and a roll-up garage door, has plenty of table and bar seating, as well as a patio.

Sunnyside Lodge Restaurant *Seafood/Steak*   ∇ 18 | 24 | 20 | $40

Tahoe City | 1850 W. Lake Blvd. (Sequoia Ave.) | 530-583-7200 | www.sunnysideresort.com

A "beautiful view of the lake" rewards visitors at this slightly pricey Tahoe City "favorite" serving "decent" steak and seafood in congenial style; in the wintertime, two fireplaces warm up the après-ski set.

Tacubaya *Mexican*   22 | 14 | 16 | $17

Berkeley | 1788 Fourth St. (bet. Hearst Ave. & Virginia St.) | 510-525-5160 | www.tacubaya.net

"Sophisticated" Mexican fare draws noshers to this "cafeteria"-style "taqueria" (an "offshoot of Doña Tomás") tucked among

Berkeley's Fourth Street shops, where "fantastic fresh corn tortillas" provide "authentic flavor" and the "seasonal menu" makes "you feel like there's a chef in the kitchen, not a CEO"; the decor isn't much to look at, but "outdoor seating", "efficient service" and "super-cheap" tabs compensate.

Tamarindo Antojeria Mexicana 🗷 *Mexican* | 25 | 21 | 21 | $36 |

Oakland | 468 Eighth St. (bet. B'way & Washington St.) | 510-444-1944 | www.tamarindoantojeria.com

"Fine Mexican dining" in "a modern, trendy setting" brings Oaklanders Downtown for "fresh and flavorful" small plates that are "cleverly reinvented" with "depth", "complexity" and "gourmet ingredients"; the "small portions disappoint a little" "compared to the prices", but "caring" service plus "excellent margaritas" and a "great tequila selection" help to ease any shortcomings.

🆕 Tomo's Japanese *Japanese* | - | - | - | I |

Berkeley | 2026 San Pablo Ave. (University Ave.) | 510-981-8225 | www.tomosjapanesecuisine.com

At this casual but stylish Berkeley Japanese, former Yoshi's chef Tomo Owada serves up a simple selection of lunchtime rice bowls and bento boxes, plus a wider mix of sushi, seafood dishes and shareable small plates for dinner.

Top Dog *Hot Dogs* | 23 | 11 | 17 | $8 |

Berkeley | 2160 Center St. (bet. Oxford St. & Shattuck Ave.) | 510-849-0176
Berkeley | 2534 Durant Ave. (bet. Bowditch St. & Telegraph Ave.) | 510-843-5967 🌑
Oakland | 3272 Lakeshore Ave. (bet. Lake Park Ave. & Trestle Glen Rd.) | 510-419-0333
Oakland | Rockridge Shopping Ctr. | 5100 Broadway (Pleasant Valley Ave.) | 510-601-1187
www.topdoghotdogs.com

"Every type of sausage you can imagine" – "kielbasa", "Calabrese", "veggie", "chicken apple" and more – is "cooked perfectly and ready when you are" at these Berkeley and Oakland link specialists; there's not much in the way of decor, but the offerings make for "quick" and "delicious drunk food", especially since Durant Avenue is "open late."

Townhouse Bar & Grill 🗷 *Californian* | 22 | 19 | 22 | $39 |

Emeryville | 5862 Doyle St. (bet. 59th & Powell Sts.) | 510-652-6151 | www.townhousebarandgrill.com

"Hidden inside" a townhouse, this "semi-fancy" "favorite" in a former Emeryville "speakeasy" pulls off the "right balance of comfort and creativity", proffering "flavorful" Californian "comfort food" in "old-time" surroundings (think potbelly stove, wood beams and "brass chandeliers"); add in "friendly" staffers and a "nice outdoor patio", and no wonder most maintain "it's not just another place to grab a bite."

Trader Vic's 🅼 *Polynesian* | 18 | 23 | 20 | $44 |

Emeryville | 9 Anchor Dr. (Powell St.) | 510-653-3400 | www.tradervicsemeryville.com

Take "a mini tropical vacation" at this "truly timeless" Polynesian in Emeryville complete with "island atmosphere" and "fancy" "tiki drinks"; critics contending this "institution" is "past its prime" with merely "average" fare and service are missing the point that a couple of "old-

"fashioned" mai tais and "great pupus" still make for a "fun night" – plus there's a "spectacular" bay view; P.S. the Palo Alto branch has closed.

Trattoria Corso *Italian*   25 | 19 | 22 | $42

Berkeley | 1788 Shattuck Ave. (Delaware St.) | 510-704-8004 | www.trattoriacorso.com

Rivoli's "smaller, more casual" trattoria sister near the Berkeley Rep serves up "divine pasta" and other "rustic" Florentine-style *cucina* plus "top-rate" wines at "value prices"; while it gets "noisy" at times, a "friendly and patient" staff and "black-and-white Italian movies playing in the background" at the bar "overlooking the kitchen" add to the "charming atmosphere."

Trattoria La Siciliana 🖻 *Italian*   24 | 16 | 18 | $34

Berkeley | 2993 College Ave. (bet. Ashby Ave. & Webster St.) | 510-704-1474 | www.trattorialasiciliana.com

"Fairly priced" and "family-owned", this Berkeley Sicilian serves "unpretentious" fare that is "simple" and "beautiful", starting with the "delicious" bread and "oil dip"; the wait is "horrific", the "cramped quarters" are "always crowded" and "the kitchen is as slow as a Rome traffic jam" – i.e. it's a "real", "authentic" Italian "find"; P.S. "cash only."

T Rex Restaurant & Bar *BBQ*   18 | 16 | 17 | $30

Berkeley | 1300 10th St. (Gilman St.) | 510-527-0099 | www.t-rex-bbq.com

Berkleyites seeking a "primal meat-eating experience" frequent this "upscale BBQ" offering favorites like "beef brisket, babyback ribs" and "Southern fried chicken" in a "cavernous open space" with "a full bar and TV screens"; the "staff doesn't rush you" through the "comfort food at a comfortable price", and an "excellent happy hour" tops it off.

NEW Tribune Tavern 🖻 *British*   - | - | - | M

Oakland | 401 13th St. (Franklin St.) | 510-452-8742 | www.tribunetavern.com

Set in the historic Tribune Tower building in Downtown Oakland, this watering hole and gastropub from the folks behind the Grand Tavern and Chop Bar showcases moderately priced modernized British pub fare and a standout bar program that has a dedicated kitchen where the staff makes its own sodas, tonics, liqueurs, syrups and bitters; the sprawling dining room has a bygone-era vibe, thanks to the antique fixtures, pressed-tin ceiling tiles and marble bar, which also stocks local craft beer on tap and boutique California wines.

Trueburger 🖻 *Burgers*   21 | 12 | 17 | $14

Oakland | 146 Grand Ave. (bet. Harrison & Valdez Sts.) | 510-208-5678 | www.trueburgeroakland.com

Two Bay Wolf alums "focus on a single dish with such zeal, we all come out ahead" at this Oakland bastion of "juicy" burgers made from "freshly ground" meat ("vegetarian" options too) and served on buns that "beg to be squeezed"; an "epic" mural of the city distinguishes the space, and prices "won't break the bank."

Udupi Palace 🖻 *Indian/Vegetarian*   23 | 13 | 19 | $16

Berkeley | 1901-1903 University Ave. (Martin Luther King Jr. Way) | 510-843-6600 | www.udupipalaceca.com

See review in City of San Francisco Directory.

	FOOD	DECOR	SERVICE	COST

NEW Umami Burger *Burgers* — 22 | 17 | 18 | $22

Oakland | 2100 Franklin St. (21st St.) | 510-899-8626 |
www.umamiburger.com

See review in City of San Francisco Directory.

Uzen ⑤ *Japanese* — ▽ 24 | 14 | 19 | $33

Oakland | 5415 College Ave. (Manila Ave.) | 510-654-7753
"Restraint, balance and subtlety are the rules" at this "very bright, very small" but "oh-so-delicious" Oakland Japanese serving "impeccably fresh", "well-priced" sushi, "amazing" udon and other "traditional" dishes in a "stark, modern" setting; "selection is limited", but the "staff is attentive" and the "quality remains great."

Va de Vi *Eclectic* — 25 | 22 | 21 | $45

Walnut Creek | 1511 Mt. Diablo Blvd. (Main St.) | 925-979-0100 |
www.vadevi.com

"Graze your way through" your meal on "haute cuisine small plates" paired with "tempting wine flights" and delivered by "helpful" servers at this "hip" Eclectic Walnut Creek eatery offering a sophisticated "combination of flavors"; some gripe that the "tiny" "tapas" "add up fa$t!" and tables are a bit too "close" for comfort, but groupies gush that "sharing oohs" with your neighbors is "the best part."

Vanessa's Bistro *French/Vietnamese* — 23 | 19 | 21 | $36

Berkeley | 1715 Solano Ave. (Ensenada Ave.) | 510-525-8300 |
www.vanessasbistro.com

Vanessa's Bistro 2 *French/Vietnamese*

Walnut Creek | 1512 Locust St. (Bonanza St.) | 925-891-4790 |
www.vanessasbistro2.com

"Imaginative", "gorgeously presented" French-Vietnamese cuisine is "a tasty gourmet twist on home cooking" at this "family-run" East Bay duo (the Berkeley original and a recently relocated Walnut Creek locale) where a menu of mostly "small plates" "makes it easy to take advantage of the variety"; while service reviews are mixed, most applaud the "top-notch food at midrange prices."

Venus *Californian* — 24 | 19 | 22 | $32

Berkeley | 2327 Shattuck Ave. (bet. Bancroft Way & Durant Ave.) |
510-540-5950 | www.venusrestaurant.net

"Everyone leaves contented" at this "funky" Berkeley Californian, where "consistently delectable" dishes (including breakfast and a "crowd-pleasing brunch") are "put together with great care and integrity" using "organic, sustainable" and "seasonal" ingredients; granted, it gets "loud and crowded" in the "cozy" dining room, but "friendly" servers help compensate, as do a few "vegetarian options" and "moderate" prices.

Vic Stewart's Ⓜ *Steak* — 24 | 25 | 24 | $57

Walnut Creek | 850 S. Broadway (bet. Mt. Diablo Blvd. & Newell Ave.) |
925-943-5666 | www.vicstewarts.com

"It doesn't get much more romantic" than dining in a "private" compartment of an old "railroad parlor car" at this "standby steakhouse" located in a historic, circa-1891 "train station"; "a mainstay in Walnut Creek for many years", it's "a dazzling choice for carnivores", and while tabs are "quite expensive", service is "outstanding."

Vik's Chaat Corner *Indian*

24 | 11 | 14 | $14

Berkeley | 2390 Fourth St. (Channing Way) | 510-644-4432 |
www.vikschaatcorner.com

"Authentic South Indian snacks" and "stuff you won't see anywhere else"
are among the "delicious" "street food" at this affordable Berkeley quick-
service cafe; seats can be "hard to get" in the "warehouse" space with
"all of the charm of the Mumbai airport crossed with your school cafeteria", but the "small Indian grocery market" up front is a boon for home
cooks; P.S. 6 PM closing Monday–Thursday, 8 PM Friday–Sunday.

Vung Tau *Vietnamese*

24 | 18 | 18 | $25

Newark | 6092 Mowry Ave. (bet. Alpine St. & Cedar Blvd.) | 510-793-8299 |
www.vungtaurestaurant.com

See review in South of San Francisco Directory.

Walnut Creek Yacht Club   *Seafood*

24 | 19 | 22 | $42

Walnut Creek | 1555 Bonanza St. (Locust St.) | 925-944-3474 |
www.wcyc.net

Though this "popular" nautically decorated Walnut Creek spot is "miles
from any body of water", the seafood on its ever-changing menu is "so
fresh it almost bites you"; alas, it can get "very loud", but "a comfy
neighborhood vibe" and "friendly" service help make up for that.

Wente Vineyards,
The Restaurant at *Californian/Mediterranean*

25 | 26 | 24 | $59

Livermore | 5050 Arroyo Rd. (Veterans Rd.) | 925-456-2450 |
www.wentevineyards.com

It's tempting to "spend an afternoon" or evening dining on Cal-Med
fare and "sampling wonderful wines" at this "romantic" venue complete with a patio and set among "beautiful" vineyards in Livermore;
while the high-end food is "reliable" and service "helpful", the setting
is the most memorable part.

Wolfdale's *Californian*

27 | 23 | 26 | $59

Tahoe City | 640 N. Lake Blvd. (bet. Grove St. & Pioneer Way) |
530-583-5700 | www.wolfdales.com

North Shore diners say the "quality" Californian food, service and view
add up to an "outstanding experience" at this longtime dinner destination in Tahoe City; while it's on the "expensive" side, there's a "relatively cheap" happy hour; P.S. closed Tuesdays September–June.

Wood Tavern *Californian*

26 | 20 | 23 | $44

Oakland | 6317 College Ave. (bet. Alcatraz Ave. & 63rd St.) |
510-654-6607 | www.woodtavern.net

"Pick anything on the menu" and "you won't be disappointed" at this
"perpetually packed" Rockridge Californian that "lives up to all the
hype" with "divine" "gourmet comfort food" delivered by "respectful
servers" at a price that's "right"; sure, "the noise level requires texting
your dinner partner", but admirers are "too busy eating" to care.

Xolo   *Mexican*

∇ 23 | 18 | 18 | $13

Oakland | 1916 Telegraph Ave. (19th St.) | 510-986-0151 |
www.xolotaqueria.com

"Fast and fresh" Mexican fare is on offer at this "large", quick-service
taqueria (sibling to Tacubaya and Doña Tomás) in Oakland's Uptown

that redefines "what a burrito" (or a taco) "can be" with "unique" options; a few feel it's "pricey" for the grub, but the "cool vibe" and proximity to the Fox Theater make it popular for "after-concert."

Xyclo   *Vietnamese*

21 | 18 | 19 | $29

Oakland | 4218 Piedmont Ave. (bet. Entrada & Linda Aves.) | 510-654-2681 | www.xyclorestaurant.com

"Everything tastes bright" at this Oakland "neighborhood favorite" that "brings a fresh approach to Vietnamese cuisine" with its "creative dishes"; the modern decor with lots of warm wood "puts out a fancy vibe", yet the fare is still "affordable" and the place is "family-friendly", with a staff that's "very attentive."

Yankee Pier   *New England/Seafood*

19 | 16 | 19 | $35

Lafayette | Lafayette Mercantile Bldg. | 3593 Mt. Diablo Blvd. (bet. Dewing Ave. & Lafayette Circle) | 925-283-4100 | www.yankeepier.com

See review in North of San Francisco Directory.

Yoshi's Oakland   *Japanese*

22 | 23 | 21 | $45

Oakland | Jack London Sq. | 510 Embarcadero W. (bet. Clay & Washington Sts.) | 510-238-9200 | www.yoshis.com

Sushi and jazz "please all the senses" at this "sophisticated" duo of music venues in Oakland (a "landmark for good reason") and SF's Fillmore District ("gorgeous"); service is solid, and though a few find the "enjoyable" Japanese-inspired menu "pricey", most who take in the "vibrant" shows call the whole package "reasonable" for a "fun and different" night out.

Zachary's Chicago Pizza   *Pizza*

25 | 15 | 19 | $21

Berkeley | 1853 Solano Ave. (The Alameda) | 510-525-5950
Oakland | 5801 College Ave. (bet. Claremont Ave. & Grove Shafter Frwy.) | 510-655-6385
NEW **Pleasant Hill** | 140 Crescent Dr. (Boyd Rd.) | 925-602-7000
San Ramon | Crow Canyon Crest Shopping Ctr. | 3110 Crow Canyon Pl. (Crow Canyon Rd.) | 925-244-1222
www.zacharys.com

"Stuffed" or "thin-crust" pies that give "other pizzas inferiority complexes" pack the "crowds" into these Bay Area parlors despite their "basic" decor and somewhat "pricey" tabs; the "buttery, flaky" crusts topped with "zesty", "chunky" tomato sauce are "highly addictive", but "prepare for a wait" or "call ahead" and get it "to go."

Zatar   🅢 Ⓜ ⇄ *Mediterranean*

∇ 24 | 20 | 22 | $37

Berkeley | 1981 Shattuck Ave. (University Ave.) | 510-841-1981 | www.zatarrestaurant.com

"Fresh" ingredients including produce grown by the married chef-owners in "their own organic garden" contribute to the eclectic "Mediterranean-inspired" menu at this Berkeley charmer; at times service can be "a little slow", but the "small", "cozy place" with "enchanting decor" has moderate prices; P.S. open Wednesday–Saturday.

NORTH OF SAN FRANCISCO

Top Food

28	French Laundry | *Amer./Fr.*
27	Terra | *American*
	Madrona Manor | *Amer./Fr.*
	Cucina Paradiso | *Italian*
	Cole's Chop | *Steak*
	Meadowood Restaurant | *Cal.*
	Sushi Ran | *Japanese*
	Auberge du Soleil | *Cal./Fr.*
	Redd | *Californian*
	Farmhouse Inn | *Californian*
	Bistro des Copains | *French*
	La Toque | *French*
	Bistro Jeanty | *French*
26	Press | *American/Steak*
	Cafe La Haye | *Amer./Cal.*
	Cook St. Helena | *Italian*
	La Gare | *French*
	Hana Japanese | *Japanese*
	Fig Cafe & Winebar | *French*
	Ad Hoc | *American*

Picco | *Italian*
Diavola Pizzeria | *Italian*
Étoile* | *Californian*
Bouchon | *French*
Downtown Bakery | *Bakery*
Hog Island Oyster Co.* | *Seafood*
Jole* | *American*
Sea Thai Bistro | *Thai*
Fatted Calf | *Sandwiches*
Zazu | *American/Italian*
Della Fattoria | *Bakery/Eclectic*
Cafe Beaujolais | *Cal./French*
Scopa | *Italian*
Solbar | *Californian*
Pizzeria Picco | *Pizza*

25	Rosso Pizzeria | *Italian/Pizza*
	Central Market | *Cal./Med.*
	Harvest Moon Café | *Cal./Med.*
	Morimoto Napa | *Japanese*
	Marché aux Fleurs | *French*

Top Decor

28	Auberge du Soleil
27	French Laundry
	Meadowood Restaurant
26	Étoile
	Madrona Manor
	Farm
25	El Paseo
	Murray Circle
	Terra
	Farmhouse Inn

Rustic, Francis's Favorites
John Ash & Co.
Tra Vigne
Napa Valley Wine Train
Poggio

24	Dry Creek Kitchen
	La Toque
	Cole's Chop
	Press
	Solbar

Top Service

28	French Laundry
27	Terra
	Madrona Manor
	Meadowood Restaurant
26	Auberge du Soleil
	Farmhouse Inn
	La Toque
	Étoile
	Cucina Paradiso
	Bistro des Copains

La Gare

25	Marché aux Fleurs
	Cafe La Haye
	Ad Hoc
	Cole's Chop
	Redd
24	Fig Cafe & Winebar
	Central Market
	Albion River Inn Restaurant
	K&L Bistro

---

* Indicates a tie with restaurant above; excludes places with low votes, unless otherwise indicated

Visit zagat.com

TOPS BY CUISINE

AMERICAN
28 French Laundry
27 Terra
Madrona Manor
26 Press
Cafe La Haye

CALIFORNIAN
27 Meadowood Restaurant
Auberge du Soleil
Redd
Farmhouse Inn
26 Étoile

ECLECTIC
26 Della Fattoria
25 Celadon
Willi's Wine Bar
24 Willow Wood Mkt.
22 Flavor

FRENCH
27 Bistro des Copains
La Toque
Bistro Jeanty
26 La Gare
Fig Cafe & Winebar

ITALIAN
27 Cucina Paradiso
26 Cook St. Helena
Picco
Diavola
Zazu

JAPANESE
27 Sushi Ran
26 Hana Japanese
25 Morimoto Napa
Osake
19 Tex Wasabi's

MEDITERRANEAN
25 Central Market
Harvest Moon Café
Insalata's
Willow Wood
23 Hurley's Restaurant

PIZZA
26 Diavola
Pizzeria Picco
25 Rosso Pizzeria
Arizmendi
Redd Wood

SEAFOOD/STEAK
27 Cole's Chop
26 Press
Hog Island Oyster Co.
25 Willi's Seafood
Stark's Steak & Seafood

TOPS BY SPECIAL FEATURE

BREAKFAST/BRUNCH
27 Redd
26 Downtown Bakery
24 Willow Wood
Freemont Diner
22 Alexis Baking

CHILD-FRIENDLY
25 Rosso Pizzeria
Insalata's
24 Fish
Super Duper
22 Gott's Roadside

HOTEL DINING
27 Madrona Manor
Meadowood Restaurant
   (Meadowood Napa Valley)
Auberge du Soleil
Farmhouse Inn
La Toque (Westin Verasa Napa)

OUTDOOR SEATING
27 Madrona Manor
Auberge du Soleil
26 Étoile
25 Bistro Don Giovanni
24 Tra Vigne

PEOPLE-WATCHING
27 Redd
26 Picco
Bouchon
25 Morimoto
20 Spoonbar

QUICK BITE
26 Downtown Bakery
Hog Island Oyster Co.
Fatted Calf
Della Fattoria
25 Arizmendi

ROMANCE

- 27 Terra
- Madrona Manor
- Auberge du Soleil
- Farmhouse Inn
- 23 El Paseo

SMALL PLATES/TAPAS

- 26 Picco
- Jole
- 25 Willi's Wine Bar
- Willi's Seafood
- 24 ZuZu

TRENDY

- 27 Redd
- 26 Solbar
- 25 Morimoto
- Barndiva
- 22 Underwood Bar

VIEWS

- 27 Auberge du Soleil
- Farmhouse Inn
- 26 Étoile
- 23 Murray Circle
- 22 Brix

WINE BARS

- 27 Sushi Ran
- 26 Fig Café & Wine Bar
- Étoile
- 25 Willi's Wine
- 21 Oxbow Wine▽

WINNING WINE LISTS

- 28 French Laundry
- 27 Terra
- Cole's Chop
- Meadowood Restaurant
- La Toque

TOPS BY LOCATION

MARIN COUNTY

- 27 Sushi Ran
- 26 Picco
- Sea Thai Bistro
- Pizzeria Picco
- 25 Marché aux Fleurs

MENDOCINO COUNTY

- 26 Cafe Beaujolais
- 25 955 Restaurant
- Mendo Bistro
- 24 Albion River Inn Restaurant
- MacCallum House Rest.

NAPA COUNTY

- 28 French Laundry
- 27 Terra
- Cole's Chop
- Meadowood Restaurant
- Auberge du Soleil

SONOMA COUNTY

- 27 Madrona Manor
- Cucina Paradiso
- Farmhouse Inn
- Bistro des Copains
- 26 Cafe La Haye

Best Buys

Top-rated food $25 and under

1. Downtown Bakery | *Bakery*
2. Fatted Calf | *Sandwiches*
3. Della Fattoria | *Bakery/Eclectic*
4. Arizmendi | *Bakery/Pizza*
5. Blue Barn Gourmet | *Cal.*
6. C Casa | *Mexican*
7. Addendum | *American*
8. Ike's Place | *Sandwiches*
9. Sol Food | *Puerto Rican*
10. Fremont Diner | *Diner*
11. Avatar's | *Indian*
12. Cafe Citti | *Italian*
13. El Farolito | *Mexican*
14. Pearl's Phat | *Burgers*
15. Super Duper | *Burgers*
16. Betty's Fish/Chips | *British/Seafood*
17. In-N-Out | *Burgers*
18. Model Bakery | *Bakery*
19. Cheese Steak Shop | *Cheesestks.*
20. Gott's Roadside | *Diner*

BEST BUYS BY NEIGHBORHOOD

HEALDSBURG/ SANTA ROSA

- 26 Downtown Bakery
- 25 Ike's Place
- 23 El Farolito
- Betty's Fish & Chips
- 22 Cheese Steak Shop

LARKSPUR/SAN RAFAEL

- 25 Arizmendi
- 24 Sol Food
- 23 Avatar's
- 22 Emporio Rulli
- Barney's Gourmet Hamburgers

MILL VALLEY

- 24 Sol Food
- 23 Avatar's
- Pearl's Phat
- Super Duper
- In-N-Out

NAPA/YOUNTVILLE

- 26 Fatted Calf
- 25 C Casa
- Addendum
- 23 In-N-Out
- Model Bakery

North of San Francisco

	FOOD	DECOR	SERVICE	COST

Addendum 🅱️🅼 *American*   25 | 15 | 18 | $22

Yountville | 6476 Washington St. (bet. Mission St. & Oak Circle) |
707-944-1565 | www.adhocrestaurant.com

For "easy access" to gourmet "picnic" fare, fans of chef Thomas Keller
head to Ad Hoc's seasonal adjacent outdoor area to "dine by the garden" on boxed takeout from a brief, lunch-only American menu offering either "to-die-for" "crunchy fried chicken" or "tender, delicious
barbecue" plus "yummy" side dishes; though limited seating might
leave some "eating in their cars", most find the experience "wonderful
on a warm day"; P.S. open from early spring to late fall for lunch,
Thursday–Saturday only.

Ad Hoc *American*   26 | 21 | 25 | $68

Yountville | 6476 Washington St. (bet. Mission St. & Oak Circle) |
707-944-2487 | www.adhocrestaurant.com

"This is how family-style was meant to be" declare devotees of
Thomas Keller's "informal" yet "wow"-inducing Yountville American,
where an "efficient" staff serves "large" portions of "locally sourced,
simply prepared" dinner and Sunday brunch classics including "famous" buttermilk-brined fried chicken (also on alternating Mondays
and Thursday–Saturday at seasonal neighbor Addendum); though
the set menu offers "no choices", it's "usually so good you won't
care" and can focus instead on the "in-depth" wine list; P.S. closed
Tuesday and Wednesday.

Albion River Inn Restaurant *Californian*   24 | 24 | 24 | $50

Albion | Albion River Inn | 3790 N. Hwy. 1 (Albion-Little River Rd.) |
707-937-1919 | www.albionriverinn.com

Whether you "stay the night or head up to Mendocino town" afterwards, "by all means take a ride" on "the world's most scenic coastal
highways" to this "romantic getaway" in Albion that's a "win on all
fronts"; sure, the "drop-dead gorgeous oceanfront views" are what
"elevate" it to "an extraordinary experience", but the "wonderful"
Californian cuisine is "matched by warm, attentive service", an "extensive wine list" and an "amazing collection of single malts" (125 kinds).

Alexis Baking Company *Bakery*   22 | 13 | 17 | $18
(aka ABC)

Napa | 1517 Third St. (bet. 4th & School Sts.) | 707-258-1827 |
www.alexisbakingcompany.com

You're more likely to "run into locals" than tourists at this "wonderful
little" bakery/cafe in Napa that "keeps it simple" with a "unique take
on breakfast" ("best huevos rancheros ever"), daily lunch specials and
"off-the-charts" "homemade bread and pastries"; there's "no dinner",
and the service and decor is "chaotic" at best, but many deem it the
"best brunch place in town" providing you "get there before the crowds."

Alex Italian Restaurant 🅼 *Italian*   24 | 22 | 22 | $63

Rutherford | 1140 Rutherford Rd. (Rte. 29/St. Helena Hwy.) |
707-967-5500 | www.alexitalianrestaurant.com

Diners think they're "back in Italy" at this "upscale" sommelier-backed
Rutherford ristorante proffering "fresh", "creative" pastas and other

specialties from Liguria and Emilia-Romagna, "presented profession-ally" by an "attentive" staff; a "wondrous" wine list and a "charming" space add to the appeal, and "the crackling fireplace is a nice touch"; P.S. a chef change is not reflected in the Food score.

All Seasons Bistro Ⓜ *Californian* | 23 | 21 | 22 | $39 |
Calistoga | 1400 Lincoln Ave. (Washington St.) | 707-942-9111 | www.allseasonsnapavalley.net
"Tastefully prepared" plates offered in "charming" bistro environs make this Calistoga Californian a "pleasant" "place to escape", es-pecially since service is "friendly" too; the wine selection is "excel-lent" but you can also bring a bottle from the on-site retail shop (for a corkage fee).

Amici's East Coast Pizzeria *Pizza* | 21 | 16 | 19 | $22 |
San Rafael | 1242 Fourth St. (C St.) | 415-455-9777 | www.amicis.com
See review in City of San Francisco Directory.

Angèle *French* | 24 | 22 | 23 | $50 |
Napa | Hatt/Napa Mill Bldg. | 540 Main St. (5th St.) | 707-252-8115 | www.angelerestaurant.com
"It's hard to beat" the "amazing" ambiance "indoors and out" at this "posh little bistro" set in an old boathouse "on the banks of the Napa River" where "consistently good", midpriced, "upscale French comfort food", a "lovely" dog-friendly patio and a slightly "snooty" staff com-bine to "remind one of the South of France"; a bar pouring "excellent cocktails" and wines keeps it "crowded with locals."

Applewood Restaurant Ⓜ *Californian* | 24 | 22 | 24 | $51 |
Guerneville | Applewood Inn, Restaurant & Spa | 13555 Hwy. 116 (River Rd.) | 707-869-9093 | www.applewoodinn.com
Like a "cosmopolitan retreat among the redwoods", this Guerneville "Euro-style inn" "hits all the right notes" serving Californian fare in-cluding tasting menus delivered with "unpretentious" service that "ex-ceeds expectations"; though it's not cheap, a "romantic" "country" setting warmed by a "cozy fireplace" and an "approachable and excit-ing" wine list add to reasons most would gladly "drive back up to the middle of nowhere"; P.S. closed Monday–Tuesday.

Arizmendi Ⓩ *Bakery/Pizza* | 25 | 13 | 20 | $11 |
San Rafael | 1002 Fourth St. (bet. A St. & Lootens Pl.) | 415-456-4093 | www.arizmendi-sanrafael.com
See review in City of San Francisco Directory.

Auberge du Soleil Restaurant *Californian/French* | 27 | 28 | 26 | $88 |
Rutherford | Auberge du Soleil | 180 Rutherford Hill Rd. (Silverado Trail) | 707-967-3111 | www.aubergedusoleil.com
"Sitting on the deck looking out at the vines of Napa Valley as the sun sets" is a "world-class experience" attest fans of this "intimate" Cal-French in a "beautiful setting" with "gorgeous views of the vineyards" to go with its "refined" menu and "gracious" service; an "extensive wine list" further makes it perfect for "special occasions, especially romantic ones", though "lunch on the terrace" is also deemed "an indulgent treat."

	FOOD	DECOR	SERVICE	COST

Avatar's *Indian*

23 | 13 | 22 | $20

Larkspur | 574 Magnolia Ave. (Doherty Dr.) | 415-945-1808
Mill Valley | 15 Madrona St. (bet. Lovell & Throckmorton Aves.) | 415-381-8293 Ⓢ
Petaluma | 131 Kentucky St. (bet. Washington St. & Western Ave.) | 707-765-9775
Sausalito | 2656 Bridgeway (Coloma St.) | 415-332-8083 Ⓢ
www.enjoyavatars.com

Prepare to "wolf down" "exotic", "flavor-filled" Punjabi burritos, "incomparable" enchiladas and other "innovative Indian fusion cuisine" at these "budget-friendly" eateries tended by "the friendliest servers" who "guide you through the crazy fun menu"; sure, they're "spartan in atmosphere" (and Mill Valley has few seats), but since they're "exceptionally habit forming", most insist "you'll likely become a regular."

Azzurro Pizzeria e Enoteca *Pizza*

23 | 19 | 21 | $27

Napa | 1260 Main St. (Clinton St.) | 707-255-5552 | www.azzurropizzeria.com
The 'in' "place for pizza in Napa", this "local go-to" dishes "delicious" thin-crust pies complemented by a "nice selection of wines"; service is "fast" and prices are modest, so despite a "cool", "happening" vibe, it's still a "no-reservations" (except for large parties), "no-fuss" pick.

🆕 Backyard *Californian*

- | - | - | M

Forestville | 6566 Front St. (First St.) | 707-820-8445 | www.backyardforestville.com
Chefs Daniel Kedan and Marianna Gardenhire – a husband-and-wife team of wine country restaurant vets (Ad Hoc, p/30) – are behind this casual Californian in sleepy Downtown Forestville, where daily menus are inspired by local ranchers, farmers and vintners; the hacienda-style digs include a small rustic room filled with terrariums and planter boxes, but the most coveted seats are on the shady brick courtyard out front, particularly on weekends for Southern-style brunch or Wednesday evenings for family-style fried chicken dinners.

Balboa Cafe ● *American*

20 | 19 | 20 | $36

Mill Valley | 38 Miller Ave. (Sunnyside Ave.) | 415-381-7321 | www.balboacafe.com
See review in City of San Francisco Directory.

Bank Café & Bar *French*

▽ 23 | 18 | 20 | $39

Napa | Westin Verasa Napa | 1314 McKinstry St. (bet. 1st St. & Soscol Ave.) | 707-257-5151 | www.latoque.com
Ken Frank's casual, all-day French in the Westin Verasa Napa delivers "La Toque–quality" regional à la carte and prix fixe meals at prices that won't break the bank; the room's "nice ambiance" makes it a "great place" "to unwind at the end of the day", particularly if the more formal dining room "next door" "is not an option."

Bar Bocce *Pizza*

22 | 21 | 19 | $31

Sausalito | 1250 Bridgeway (bet. Pine & Turney Sts.) | 415-331-0555 | www.barbocce.com
Take a "micro vacation" at this "right-on-the-water" Sausalito hang offering a midpriced menu of "creative" sourdough pizza, "amazing salads" and "delicious" cask wine in "tiny" digs elevated by a fire pit-enhanced back patio and bocce court; sure, service can sometimes be

"slow", but with a "laid-back" vibe and "breathtaking view overlooking the harbor", many ask "what's the rush?"

Barndiva ⓜ *American*   25 | 24 | 22 | $50

Healdsburg | 231 Center St. (Matheson St.) | 707-431-0100 |
www.barndiva.com

"A true wine country experience" awaits at this "charming and rustic" Healdsburg American where "knowledgeable" servers deliver "inspiring", "beautifully presented" plates displaying an "imaginative use" of "farm-fresh" ingredients; the "art-filled" interior has a "relaxed" atmosphere and outside is "spacious and gorgeous", so the only "small minus" is tabs that some "wish were more barnlike."

Barney's Gourmet Hamburgers *Burgers*   21 | 16 | 18 | $17

San Rafael | 1020 Court St. (5th Ave.) | 415-454-4594 |
www.barneyshamburgers.com

See review in City of San Francisco Directory.

Bar Terra *American*   ▽ 25 | 24 | 24 | $53

St. Helena | 1345 Railroad Ave. (bet. Adams St. & Hunt Ave.) |
707-963-8931 | www.terrarestaurant.com

Hiro Sone's "creative" à la carte menu features Asian-inflected New American "small plates" that are "excellent" ("as always") along with cocktails "that raise the bar on artisanal mixology" at this "casual" lounge offshoot of St. Helena's more formal Terra restaurant next door; the "lively" atmosphere and "friendly banter" between "knowledgeable" barkeeps and regulars make for a welcome "respite" from the stuffier "wine country" options.

ⓝⓔⓦ Belcampo Meat Co. *American*   - | - | - | I

Larkspur | Marin Country Mart | 2405 Larkspur Landing Circle
(Sir Francis Drake Blvd.) | 415-448-5810 | www.belcampomeatco.com

Meat sourced from its own sustainably run ShastaValley farms draws diners and shoppers to this Marin County Mart hybrid that's part sit-down country cafe and part old-time butcher shop; with choice cuts and cured meats as well as creative American sandwiches, salads, dinners and desserts, the intimate, budget-friendly cafe covers several bases.

Betty's Fish & Chips *British/Seafood*   23 | 13 | 20 | $18

Santa Rosa | 4046 Sonoma Hwy. (Streamside Dr.) | 707-539-0899

"Take the whole family" to this "folksy" Santa Rosa seafooder with a "long-standing reputation" for some of the "best fish 'n' chips" and "even better pies"; sure, the "kitschy nautical decor" is "nothing to write home about", the space is "small" and tabs are "a little pricey" for the genre, but "friendly" staffers and a "homey atmosphere" still help keep it "busy and crowded."

Bistro des Copains *French*   27 | 21 | 26 | $44

Occidental | 3782 Bohemian Hwy. (bet. Graton & Occidental Rds.) |
707-874-2436 | www.bistrodescopains.com

An "unexpected" "gem" in the "hinterlands of West Sonoma County", this "unpretentious" "locavore" bistro in Occidental charms diners with its "fantastic" Provençal-style "comfort food" and "excellent" wines (including a "bargain" prix fixe and "free corkage" on Thursdays for local bottles); two wood-fired ovens, along with a "friendly" longtime staff that "makes you feel at home", add to the room's "warm", "French countryside" ambiance.

Bistro Don Giovanni *Italian*   25 | 23 | 23 | $46

Napa | 4110 Howard Ln. (bet. Oak Knoll & Salvador Aves.) | 707-224-3300 | www.bistrodongiovanni.com

"Despite all the new upstarts", it's still "sublime" to "sit on the terrace" "surrounded by vineyards" at this "stunningly beautiful" yet "unpretentious" "Italian bistro" in Napa that's "favored by locals" for its "excellent" *cucina*, "good wine list" and "the warmest greeting"; it all comes at a "fair price", though the noise-sensitive note that the "Tuscan-ish" room and "fun bar" can get quite "loud", especially when the "horde of tourists descends."

Bistro Jeanty *French*   27 | 22 | 24 | $55

Yountville | 6510 Washington St. (Mulberry St.) | 707-944-0103 | www.bistrojeanty.com

"No one nails" "French country" like Philippe Jeanty at his Yountville bistro where the "lack of pretentiousness is as delicious as the food"; the "charming" digs might be a bit "cramped" and the "calories will get you to the moon and back", but it remains the "go-to" spot for a "spectacular" wine country meal paired with vins and "friendly service", all "without requiring a second mortgage" – particularly on the "lovely outdoor patio" or at the "community table."

Bistro Ralph *Californian/French*   23 | 18 | 22 | $46

Healdsburg | 109 Plaza St. (bet. Center St. & Healdsburg Ave.) | 707-433-1380 | www.bistroralph.com

"Count on Ralph" Tingle to "mingle with the crowd" at his "classic", "convivial" bistro on Healdsburg Square that's been delivering "consistently well-prepared", "seasonal" French-Cal cuisine, plus a "fantastic Sonoma wine list" and "killer" martinis, since "before all the others came to town"; always "on the money", it's staffed by "the most personable" crew, and "you'll see lots of locals" alongside the "tourists."

Bistro 29 Ⓩ Ⓜ *French*   25 | 21 | 24 | $41

Santa Rosa | 620 Fifth St. (bet. D St. & Mendocino Ave.) | 707-546-2929 | www.bistro29.com

"Outstanding" French cuisine – including buckwheat and sweet crêpes – is served "in an intimate bistro" setting at this Santa Rosa "go-to", where "warm", "attentive" servers and an "excellent-value midweek prix fixe" (Tuesday–Thursday) also work in its favor; add in "affordable prices" and it's "one of the best-kept secrets in Sonoma County."

NEW Blue Barn Gourmet *Californian*   25 | 19 | 19 | $16

Corte Madera | Corte Madera Town Park | 335 Corte Madera Town Ctr. (Madera Blvd.) | 415-927-1104 | www.bluebarngourmet.com
See review in City of San Francisco Directory.

Boon Eat + Drink *Californian*   ▽ 25 | 18 | 21 | $37

Guerneville | 16248 Main St. (bet. 4th & Mill Sts.) | 707-869-0780 | www.eatatboon.com

"By far the hippest" eatery in town, this bistro "rocks Guerneville to a new level" with its "fresh" Californian fare (some featuring produce from their hotel garden nearby) plus local microbrews and a "nice selection of Russian River wines"; the "minimalist" digs with a front patio can get "crowded" and no reservations mean there often can be a "wait", but most surveyors feel it's "an unexpected find" "at a reasonable price."

Boon Fly Café *Californian*　　23 | 19 | 21 | $33

Napa | Carneros Inn | 4048 Sonoma Hwy. (Los Carneros Ave.) | 707-299-4900 | www.thecarnerosinn.com

A "great stop" "between Napa and Sonoma", this "unpretentious" "roadside cafe" offers "inventive", "moderately priced" Californian "comfort food" in Napa's Carneros Inn and makes a "fun place" to "kick back" before or after "wine tasting"; mornings are a "mob scene" due to "amazing brunch" specials like "made-to-order donuts" and "bacon Bloody Marys", but it's open "all day" and run by a "friendly" staff, making it a "satisfying" "alternative to the pricey" wine country options.

Bottega *Italian*　　25 | 24 | 23 | $61

Yountville | V Mktpl. | 6525 Washington St. (Yount St.) | 707-945-1050 | www.botteganapavalley.com

"Diners flock" to this Yountville "rustic Italian" from Michael Chiarello, who "knows how to entertain" and is often around and cooking the "special and creative" fare that "pairs well" with an "extensive" wine list (and "doesn't break the bank"); it's "busy and noisy" in the otherwise "pleasant, warm" indoor-outdoor setting tended by "knowledgeable" servers, and though it's "a tough reservation", even those "normally skeptical of the star-chef scene" "can't wait to go back."

Bouchon *French*　　26 | 23 | 24 | $59

Yountville | 6534 Washington St. (Yount St.) | 707-944-8037 | www.bouchonbistro.com

Thomas Keller's "culinary magic" comes relatively "reasonably priced" at this Yountville "oasis" proffering "carefully prepared", "beautifully presented" French fare that can be paired with "local or French" *vin de carafe*; the dining room and zinc bar area may be "tight", but offer "real bistro atmosphere" while "professional" service completes the "outstanding experience"; P.S. "stock up" on baked goods at its next-door boulangerie.

Brannan's Grill *American*　　19 | 20 | 18 | $36

Calistoga | 1374 Lincoln Ave. (Washington St.) | 707-942-2233 | www.brannansgrill.com

"Sit by the big fireplace" or dine by the "large open windows" "on summer nights" and "watch the tourists go by" this "comfy" New American devotees dub a "Calistoga classic", offering "nice beef, fish and other selections to please every taste"; some say both food and service are "hit-or-miss", but it's still considered one of the area's "better establishments" – with "smooth jazz" some nights.

NEW Bravas Bar de Tapas *Spanish*　　▽ 25 | 20 | 18 | $38

Healdsburg | 420 Center St. (bet. North & Piper Sts.) | 707-433-7700 | www.starkrestaurants.com

Downtown Healdsburg has a "winner" in this Spanish taparia from the team behind Willi's Wine Bar offering a varied selection of both hot and cold small plates (deemed relatively "large" by some) including paper-thin sliced jamón Ibérico, washed down with sangria and Spanish-tinged cocktails; a "to-die-for" back patio helps provides a "beautiful atmosphere", and it all adds up to "good fun."

FOOD | DECOR | SERVICE | COST

Brick & Bottle *Californian*

19 | 18 | 20 | $37

Corte Madera | 55 Tamal Vista Blvd. (Wornum Dr.) | 415-924-3366 | www.brickandbottle.com

"Sincere" service, "reliable" "comfort food" (especially the "divine" pimiento burger) and a "casual" vibe help make this Corte Madera Californian a "regular go-to spot"; even those who dub it "nothing special" appreciate its "vibrant bar area" and moderate prices.

Brix *Californian/French*

22 | 24 | 23 | $55

Napa | 7377 St. Helena Hwy. (Dwyer Rd.) | 707-944-2749 | www.brix.com

A "favorite place to stop while wine tasting", this Napa longtimer garners praise for its "beautiful vineyard setting", "wonderful" view "onto grapevines and hills" and "gorgeous" on-site garden that supplies ingredients for the "elegantly prepared" French-inflected Californian cuisine; "attentive" service further results in a "relaxed atmosphere", and while it's a bit "expensive", most agree it offers "good value for your dollar"; P.S. the arrival of chef David Cruz (ex Ad Hoc) is not reflected in the Food score.

Buckeye Roadhouse *American/BBQ*

25 | 24 | 24 | $48

Mill Valley | 15 Shoreline Hwy. (Hwy. 101) | 415-331-2600 | www.buckeyeroadhouse.com

A Mill Valley "staple" since 1937, this "solid" American is a "reliable" option for "fine cocktails" and a "hearty menu" of "classically prepared" dishes, including "deliciously smoked" babyback ribs and "super" Oysters Bingo; the "upscale log cabin" setting is ideal for "large groups" and "special occasions", and even when "crowded", a "top-notch" staff creates a "welcoming" atmosphere, while valet parking is a bonus; P.S. an adjacent drive-thru coffee kiosk, Buckeye Joe, is open weekdays 6–10 AM.

Bungalow 44 *American*

22 | 21 | 22 | $45

Mill Valley | 44 E. Blithedale Ave. (Sunnyside Ave.) | 415-381-2500 | www.bungalow44.com

"Comfort food meets haute cuisine" at this Mill Valley New American, where "modern versions of great classics" are "hearty" and "flavorful" and service is generally "accommodating"; the "always animated" bar can be a "happening pickup scene" ("lots of cougars" and the male equivalent), but the covered patio can be a "calm" refuge.

Cafe Beaujolais *Californian/French*

26 | 22 | 24 | $53

Mendocino | 961 Ukiah St. (bet. Evergreen & School Sts.) | 707-937-5614 | www.cafebeaujolais.com

"Still a favorite", this "quaint" Mendocino Cal-French delivers "dependably excellent" "seasonal" fare and "local" wines with "outstanding service"; the "homey" Victorian farmhouse setting suits "conversation at lunchtime" (Wednesday–Sunday only) or a "romantic" dinner ("especially" in the "atrium"), all at prices that are "not out of control"; P.S. "homemade breads" from the to-go bakery window are a "treat."

Cafe Citti *Italian*

23 | 16 | 21 | $23

Kenwood | 9049 Sonoma Hwy. (bet. Randolph & Shaw Aves.) | 707-833-2690 | www.cafecitti.com

"While wine tasting in Sonoma", "locals and tourists" make a "quick stop" at this "unpretentious" Kenwood "roadhouse" for "heartwarming" Tuscan "trattoria" fare loaded with "plenty of garlic"; yes, counter "service and decor are minimal" (with patio tables "when it's warm"), but it "simply works" – and it's "priced to please" with no corkage fee to boot.

Cafe La Haye 🈁Ⓜ *American/Californian* | 26 | 20 | 25 | $54 |

Sonoma | 140 E. Napa St. (bet. 1st & 2nd Sts.) | 707-935-5994 | www.cafelahaye.com

"Tiny but mighty", this Cal-American "gem" "just off the square" in Sonoma is a "foodie" favorite for its "limited menu" of "consistently outstanding", "creatively prepared" dishes that come from a kitchen so "little" you'll wonder "how they do it"; the "gracious" staff is "always welcoming", and the lack of a "bar scene" in the "spare", "intimate" space ensures the "focus is on the food"; P.S. "reservations are a must."

NEW Café Lucia *Portuguese* | - | - | - | M |

Healdsburg | 235 Healdsburg Ave. (Matheson St.) | 707-431-1113 | www.cafelucia.net

"Don't miss" this Healdsburg cafe from Manuel Azevedo (LaSalette) and his sister, Lucia, urge early fans of its affordable, "interesting and delicious" contemporary Portuguese cuisine blending "tradition with modern touches" and locally sourced ingredients, complemented by a selection of Iberian and Sonoma wines; tucked away down a pedestrian alley, the high-ceilinged dining room opens onto an all-seasons courtyard filled with trees, tiny white lights and piped-in traditional fado music.

Campo Fina *Italian/Pizza* | - | - | - | M |

Healdsburg | 330 Healdsburg Ave. (bet. North & Plaza Sts.) | 707-395-4640 | www.campo-fina.com

This casual, all-day Healdsburg Italian from the Scopa folks ("so it has to be good!") turns out "outstanding" wood-oven-fired pizzas and "creative" Italian cicchetti (small plates), complemented by affordable Boot and wine country vino, local brews and wine cocktails; the dining room's exposed-brick walls, red leather booths and reclaimed fixtures pay homage to its past as a turn-of-the-century saloon, but what makes the joint truly "special" is its large covered back patio where diners can try their hand at bocce.

Carneros Bistro & Wine Bar *Californian* | ▽ 24 | 22 | 24 | $50 |

Sonoma | The Lodge at Sonoma | 1325 Broadway (bet. Clay St. & Leveroni Rd.) | 707-931-2042 | www.thelodgeatsonoma.com

"Uniformly excellent" "upscale" fare and locally procured wines from an extensive list are delivered by an "exceedingly attentive and pleasant" staff at this "understated" Sonoma Californian that's "unusually great for being in a hotel"; other assets include an "elegant" dining room that opens onto an organic herb garden.

C Casa *Mexican* | 25 | 16 | 18 | $20 |

Napa | Oxbow Public Mkt. | 610 First St. (bet. Silverado Trail & Soscol Ave.) | 707-226-7700 | www.myccasa.com

Fans cheer "holy taco!" for the "imaginative", "fabulously prepared" offerings at this Napa counter-serve "tucked away" in the Oxbow Public Market that also dishes other "gourmet Mexican street food" (including breakfast fare); finding a seat can sometimes be a "challenge" and diners seesaw on the cost – is it "cheap" or "a little pricey"? – but given the "fresh, interesting flavors", most can't help going "back for more."

Celadon *American/Eclectic*

25 | 21 | 24 | $50

Napa | The Historic Napa Mill | 500 Main St. (5th St.) | 707-254-9690 | www.celadonnapa.com

Greg Cole's Napa "institution" (and sibling of Cole's Chop House) is where "locals go to eat" "luscious" American-Eclectic "gourmet comfort food" in the "rejuvenated river area"; whether you sit near the fire pit on the "airy" patio or in the "cozy" dining room of the historic building, it's a "great all-around experience" replete with "wonderful" wines and the "generous host" himself, who "always takes time" with the "efficient" staff to "make sure everything is perfect."

Central Market *Californian/Mediterranean*

25 | 21 | 24 | $40

Petaluma | 42 Petaluma Blvd. N. (Western Ave.) | 707-778-9900 | www.centralmarketpetaluma.com

"Original" Cal-Med "slow food" is the focus of the "brilliantly prepared", "locally sourced" menu, bolstered by "wonderful" wine pairings, at this "Petaluma gem" from "gracious host-chef-owner" Tony Najiola; a few "wish the atmosphere were a bit less casual", but since it's "not too darn expensive for fine dining", most are happy to keep it a Sonoma County "secret" – the kind of place where "chefs dine on their nights off."

NEW Chalkboard Bistro & Wine Bar *American*

- | - | - | M

Healdsburg | Hotel Les Mars | 29 North St. (Healdsburg Ave.) | 707-473-8030 | www.chalkboardhealdsburg.com

Situated inside Healdsburg's Hotel Les Mars, this elegant bistro and wine bar in the former Cyrus space offers moderately priced American small plates with a local, seasonal twist, much of which comes from its own dedicated garden; arched ceilings, white walls and natural light give the roomy restaurant an airy feel, and seating options include a large communal table crafted from old-growth oak.

Charcuterie *French*

20 | 17 | 21 | $34

Healdsburg | Healdsburg Plaza | 335 Healdsburg Ave. (Plaza St.) | 707-431-7213 | www.charcuteriehealdsburg.com

"If pork is your thing", this "good-value" pig-themed "French country" bistro "on the Healdsburg square" offers "consistently" "creative (and distinctly" Gallic) preparations that "change frequently", all served up by "friendly and unpretentious" staffers; while "portions are large", the quarters can come off as "cramped", still, the place exudes a "comfort feel."

Cheesecake Factory *American*

16 | 17 | 16 | $29

Corte Madera | The Village at Corte Madera | 1736 Redwood Hwy. (Tamalpais Dr.) | 415-945-0777 | www.thecheesecakefactory.com

See review in City of San Francisco Directory.

Cheese Steak Shop *Cheesesteaks*

22 | 12 | 19 | $11

Santa Rosa | 750 Stony Point Rd. (Sebastopol Rd.) | 707-527-9877 | www.cheesesteakshop.com

See review in City of San Francisco Directory.

	FOOD	DECOR	SERVICE	COST

Chinois *Asian* ▽ 25 | 24 | 24 | $35

Windsor | 186 Windsor River Rd. (Bell Rd.) | 707-838-4667 |
www.chinoisbistro.com

There's "something to please everyone" at this upscale Asian-fusion bistro in "unassuming" Windsor presenting a "mix of dim sum", Chinese and Southeast Asian cuisines "all rolled into one"; the fare is "light and bright" with "flavors" that "just shine", especially when served with soju, sake and a serious wine list by a skilled staff in a room appointed with authentic Eastern furnishings; P.S. lunch served weekdays only.

Cindy Pawlcyn's Wood Grill & 22 | 20 | 22 | $50
Wine Bar Ⓜ *American*
(fka Brassica)

St. Helena | 641 Main St. (bet. Grayson Ave. & Vidovich Ln.) | 707-963-0700 |
www.cindypawlcynsgrill.com

Fans of chef-owner Cindy Pawlcyn are "excited" by her revamp of this St. Helena venue (fka Go Fish and briefly Brassica), now dishing out an all-American roundup of burgers, pizzas, "don't-miss" eggplant fries and other "comfort food" that – with local wines including those from small-production winemakers – makes for "full, satisfied bellies"; the country-modern setting offers "wine country atmosphere" and is "open and airy" inside or out on a back patio that occasionally offers live music.

Cindy's Backstreet Kitchen *Californian* 24 | 21 | 24 | $45

St. Helena | 1327 Railroad Ave. (bet. Adams St. & Hunt Ave.) |
707-963-1200 | www.cindysbackstreetkitchen.com

"Napa stalwart chef" Cindy Pawlcyn (Mustards) oversees this "idiosyncratic" St. Helena "country kitchen", turning out a "variety" of "well-done" Californian dishes that make for an "utterly delightful" (and "decently priced") "wine country lunch" or "unpretentious" evening – "especially in the summer under the fig tree"; while wayfarers call it a "must-stop", the "homey vibe", "chatty" bar scene and "spot-on service" keep it a "big hangout for locals" as well.

Cole's Chop House *Steak* 27 | 24 | 25 | $69

Napa | 1122 Main St. (bet. 1st & Pearl Sts.) | 707-224-6328 |
www.coleschophouse.com

"As good as any NY steakhouse" but "with a Napa Valley twist", this "classic" "carnivore heaven" from Greg Cole (Celadon) proffers "big portions" of "top-notch" meat "cooked to your exact specifications" and paired "wonderfully with those great big Napa cabs"; set in a "landmark building", it boasts a "fine ambiance" and "service to match", so "high prices" aren't exactly a surprise.

Cook St. Helena *Italian* 26 | 18 | 23 | $45

St. Helena | 1310 Main St. (Hunt Ave.) | 707-963-7088 |
www.cooksthelena.com

"Eat well with locals" at this St. Helena Italian turning out "pasta done right" and other "well-prepared", "locally sourced" eats via "friendly" servers; the storefront setting is "tiny", so expect "insanely crowded conditions", especially since such "quality" meals rarely come so "reasonably priced."

Copita *Mexican*

▽ 24 | 22 | 22 | $40

Sausalito | 739 Bridgeway (Anchor St.) | 415-331-7400 |
www.copitarestaurant.com

Both "foodies" and "families" "love" this "real-deal" Downtown
Sausalito Mexican cantina and tequileria from cookbook author
Joanne Weir and restaurateur Larry Mindel (Poggio, Il Fornaio) where
the "fresh, inspired" meals might start with "killer" margaritas before
"awesome pork belly tacos" and other "flavorful small plates"; the
"casual" space features a bar, wood-fired rotisserie and a patio where
you can "feel the breeze" and "people-watch."

Cucina Paradiso ⑤ *Italian*

27 | 23 | 26 | $37

Petaluma | 114 Petaluma Blvd. N. (bet. Washington St. & Western Ave.) |
707-782-1130 | www.cucinaparadisopetaluma.com

"Be ready for an old-school Italian welcome" to go along with the "terrific pastas", "homemade baked bread", "locally grown vegetables"
and "affordable" wines being served at this "excellent" Petaluma trattoria dubbed "authentic in the best sense of the word"; "lunch or dinner, this place rocks" insist fans, even more so since settling into its
"larger", more "sophisticated" Downtown digs.

Della Fattoria Downtown

26 | 18 | 20 | $24

Café *Bakery/Eclectic*

Petaluma | 141 Petaluma Blvd. N. (bet. Washington St. & Western Ave.) |
707-763-0161 | www.dellafattoria.com

"Excellent" pastries, "amazing, fresh country dishes" and "outstanding" coffee keep this Petaluma Eclectic bakery "always jammed" at
"breakfast or lunch", though some "truly enjoy the dinners" on Friday
nights; a "friendly" staff oversees the colorful space, and "nobody
leaves without a loaf of chewy bread tucked under their arm"; P.S. watch
for Ranch Dinners offered at its nearby private farm.

Della Santina's *Italian*

24 | 22 | 23 | $41

Sonoma | 133 E. Napa St. (bet. 1st & 2nd Sts.) | 707-935-0576 |
www.dellasantinas.com

Enoteca Della Santina Ⓜ *Italian*

Sonoma | 127 E. Napa St. (bet. 1st & 2nd Sts.) | 707-938-4200 |
www.enotecanextdoor.com

"Just off the square in historic Sonoma" lies this "family-run" trattoria (and adjoining enoteca) where they "greet you with a warm
welcome" and send out "well-presented", "homestyle" meals that
"only mama knows how to cook"; with "fair prices" it's a "local and
visitor favorite", especially in the outdoor courtyard that's "delightful
on a warm day."

Diavola Pizzeria & Salumeria *Italian*

26 | 20 | 21 | $34

Geyserville | 21021 Geyserville Ave. (Hwy. 128) | 707-814-0111 |
www.diavolapizzeria.com

"Unreal pizzas", "don't-miss" salumi and other "simple yet extraordinary" dishes make for a "sophisticated but casual meal" at this
"worth-the-schlep" Geyserville Italian set in an early-1900's building;
service gets few complaints, and with "reasonable" prices, it's a "wine
country bargain", just "expect to wait" because it's small and "always
crowded with locals."

	FOOD	DECOR	SERVICE	COST

Dipsea Cafe   *Diner/Greek*   18 | 14 | 18 | $22

Mill Valley | 200 Shoreline Hwy. (Almonte Blvd.) | 415-381-0298 | www.dipseacafe.com

On weekends there's "always a line out the door" for the "highly addictive" "hearty" breakfasts at this "cheery" Mill Valley American diner that adds Greek specialties at dinner (offered Wednesday–Sunday only); some are turned off by the "noisy" environs and somewhat "spotty" service, adding it's "nothing outstanding", but "sitting outside is pleasant" and "inexpensive" tabs don't hurt either.

Downtown Bakery & Creamery   *Bakery*   26 | 13 | 18 | $15

Healdsburg | 308 Center St. (bet. Matheson & Plaza Sts.) | 707-431-2719 | www.downtownbakery.net

A "hometown institution", this "world-class" bakery/cafe is "worth a special detour" to Healdsburg for "seriously good sticky buns", "don't-miss" donut muffins and other "excellent baked goods", plus "refreshing" ice cream and "simple" breakfasts and lunches (a cafe menu is served Friday–Monday); inside is small, so many "take out to the plaza across the street"; P.S. no credit cards for under $10.

Dry Creek Kitchen   *Californian*   24 | 24 | 23 | $67

Healdsburg | Hotel Healdsburg | 317 Healdsburg Ave. (Matheson St.) | 707-431-0330 | www.charliepalmer.com

"Deliciously prepared" dishes are "elevated by imaginative combinations" and "sing when paired with the Sonoma wines" at this "worth-a-voyage" Healdsburg Californian from chef-restaurateur Charlie Palmer; the "blissful" setting is "exactly what you would want", with "large open doors" and a "vine-draped arbor", and service is "high-quality" too, so while some sniff it's "overpriced and overpraised", more find it a "capital-letter keeper", especially given its "enlightened" vino policy (no corkage on local labels, up to two bottles).

Duck Club   *American*   22 | 24 | 22 | $47

Bodega Bay | Bodega Bay Lodge & Spa | 103 S. Hwy. 1 (Doran Beach Rd.) | 707-875-3525 | www.bodegabaylodge.com

You can "treat someone to an upscale experience without going broke" at this Bodega Bay "high-end" hotel restaurant offering "well-prepared" New American fare in a "quiet, elegant" setting; "nice ocean views" are a bonus ("get a table by the window at sunset").

El Dorado Kitchen   *Californian/Mediterranean*   22 | 23 | 22 | $48

Sonoma | El Dorado Hotel | 405 First St. W. (Spain St.) | 707-996-3030 | www.eldoradosonoma.com

"Solid" Cal-Med cooking "hits the spot" at this dining room in Sonoma's El Dorado Hotel, where the "innovative" offerings are set down by "thoroughly professional" staffers in "sophisticated", contemporary surroundings; it may be a "bit pricey for regular dining", but it's still "worth a stop", "especially when you can be out on the patio."

El Farolito   *Mexican*   23 | 8 | 17 | $10

Rohnert Park | 6466 Redwood Dr. (Laguna Dr.) | 707-588-8013
Santa Rosa | 565 Sebastopol Rd. (Avalon Ave.) | 707-526-7444 ●
www.elfarolitoinc.com

See review in City of San Francisco Directory.

FOOD | DECOR | SERVICE | COST

El Huarache Loco *Mexican*
▽ 21 | 13 | 18 | $12

Larkspur | Marin Country Mart | 1803 Larkspur Landing Circle (Lincoln Village Circle) | 415-925-1403 | www.huaracheloco.com
Marinites praise the "fresh", "uncommon offerings" on the menu of "Mexico City street food", including the namesake huarache dishes (sandal-shaped stuffed tortillas) featuring "smoky, rich" mole, at Veronica Salazar's affordable Larkspur eatery; while the decor and service may not impress, loyalists deem it a "gem"; P.S. find their stall at the Alemany Farmers Market weekends 8 AM–3 PM, or at Marin Country Mart Saturdays 9 AM–2 PM.

El Paseo *Steak*
23 | 25 | 21 | $68

Mill Valley | 17 Throckmorton Ave. (Blithedale Ave.) | 415-388-0741 | www.elpaseomillvalley.com
A woodsy, "romantic" "brick-path" entrance leads to this "lovely", "rustic" American steakhouse in Mill Valley, the brainchild of chef Tyler Florence and Sammy Hagar, serving steaks "dry aged the right way" and more; there's a "happening" bar and patio scene with lots of "people-watching" among a stylish crowd that skews "young" (it feels like a "catalog shoot"), and while some caution that it can get "noisy" and "busy on a Saturday night", most consider it a "fun getaway" – "if you can get in."

NEW Empire Ⓜ *Eclectic*
– | – | – | I

Napa | 1400 First St. (Franklin & School Sts.) | 707-254-8888 | www.empirenapa.com
This upscale cocktail lounge in Downtown Napa specializes in crafted cocktails (including pisco sours) and an inexpensive roundup of Eclectic small plates; the swanky, spacious establishment is open evenings (except Mondays) and features a long bar backed by gleaming organ pipes.

Emporio Rulli *Dessert/Italian*
22 | 20 | 18 | $20

Larkspur | 464 Magnolia Ave. (bet. Cane & Ward Sts.) | 415-924-7478 | www.rulli.com
It's like "taking a short vacation in Italy" at these "bustling" cafes that turn out an "amazing" array of "authentic" pastries, "tasty" panini sandwiches and "strong" coffee drinks from "well-trained baristas"; the "bustling" Larkspur original is "cozy", Union Square offers "excellent people-watching on the square" and the SFO branches are an "escape from fast food."

Étoile *Californian*
26 | 26 | 26 | $93

Yountville | Domaine Chandon Winery | 1 California Dr. (Rte. 29/ St. Helena Hwy.) | 707-944-2892 | www.chandon.com
"Very fine dining" is bolstered by a "welcoming, professional" staff at this Yountville Californian on the grounds of the Domaine Chandon Winery; while it's an expensive outing, those who tout the trio of "food, wine and scenery" ask "what could be better?"; P.S. closed Tuesday–Wednesday.

Farm Ⓜ *American*
24 | 26 | 24 | $62

Napa | Carneros Inn | 4048 Sonoma Hwy. (Los Carneros Ave.) | 707-299-4883 | www.thecarnerosinn.com
"Perfect after a long day of wine tasting", this "soaring" space in Napa delivers "delightful" New American fare matched by a "deep" selection

of vino; with its "beautiful modern decor", "fabulous fire-pit lounge area" and service that "excels", many overlook the upscale tabs.

Farmhouse Inn & Restaurant *Californian* 27 | 25 | 26 | $90

Forestville | Farmhouse Inn | 7871 River Rd. (Wohler Rd.) | 707-887-3300 | www.farmhouseinn.com

Set in a "beautiful" restored farmhouse, this "romantic" Forestville Californian offers "out-of-this-world" prix fixe dinners showcasing "farm-fresh local ingredients" plus a "first-class wine selection" overseen by a master sommelier with service that "never misses a beat"; it's a "wonderful weekend retreat" ("even better if you can nab a room at the inn") but priced for "special occasions", so "bring your wallet, your wife's purse – and your children's piggy bank"; P.S. open Thursday–Monday only.

🆕 Farmshop *American* - | - | - | M

Larkspur | Marin Country Mart | 2233 Larkspur Landing Circle | 415-755-6700 | www.farmshopla.com

This Marin County Mart outpost of an LA-based restaurant led by Thomas Keller's former culinary director offers a moderately priced New American menu, on-tap wine and beer and an ambitious cocktail list; an expansive dining area, open kitchen, outdoor patio and bustling bar area are decorated with tiles and rich splashes of color.

Farmstead *American/Californian* 22 | 23 | 21 | $48

St. Helena | 738 Main St. (Charter Oak Ave.) | 707-963-9181 | www.longmeadowranch.com

"As the name would suggest", this Cal–New American in St. Helena serves "satisfying" "farm-to-table" "comfort food" offered in a "bright" and "airy" "barnlike" setting that works for both a "large family meal or more intimate couples dinner"; it's not cheap and a few gripe "quiet tables are hard to come by", but "charming" service, a "sane corkage policy" ($2 donated to charity) and a "huge garden for summer and fall dining" help keep it a Napa "go-to."

🆕 Fast Food Français *American/French* - | - | - | I

Sausalito | 39 Caledonia St. (Johnson St.) | 415-887-9047 | www.eatf3.com

American comfort food with a French twist is the come-on at this inexpensive all-day quick-service stop in Downtown Sausalito from the team behind Le Garage Bistro and L'Appart Resto; despite the name, it's a fairly chic venue outfitted with a long wooden communal table, Edison-style light fixtures, French language newsprint on the walls and a full bar that serves vins and cocktails.

Fatted Calf *Sandwiches* 26 | 16 | 22 | $20

Napa | Oxbow Public Mkt. | 644 First St. (bet. Silverado Trail & Soscol Ave.) | 707-256-3684 | www.fattedcalf.com

See review in City of San Francisco Directory.

Fig Cafe & Winebar *French* 26 | 20 | 24 | $38

Glen Ellen | 13690 Arnold Dr. (O'Donnell Ln.) | 707-938-2130 | www.thefigcafe.com

Locals "hate that more out-of-towners are learning about" this "casual" onetime "hidden treasure" (sister to Girl & the Fig) in Glen Ellen, where the "fantastic" French "comfort food" is "wine country fare at its best", service is "attentive" and prices are "fair"; it stocks "interesting" vinos but many "bring their own sips" due to "free corkage", which means "the only downside is no-reservations, so come prepared to wait."

Fish ⊘ *Seafood*

24 | 14 | 15 | $33

Sausalito | 350 Harbor Dr. (Gates 5 Rd.) | 415-331-3474 | www.331fish.com

Fans suggest you "go fish" at this "bare-bones" midpriced Sausalito shack "overlooking the harbor", where "some of the cleanest, freshest catch anywhere" gets a further boost from a "thoughtful wine and beer list"; "you seat yourselves on picnic tables inside or out", and though it can be a "drag to stand in line to order" and many "hate that it's cash-only", at least patrons "feel great about the whole experience" given its dedication to "sustainable, locally sourced" ingredients.

Fish Story *Seafood*

19 | 20 | 19 | $45

Napa | Napa Riverfront | 790 Main St. (3rd St.) | 707-251-5600 | www.fishstorynapa.com

"Solidly executed" fin fare made with sustainable seafood (a "big plus") and an "inviting" locale on the Napa riverfront mean there's "nothing fishy" about this "wine country delight"; most concede it's "value-priced for the area" and "worth a visit"; P.S. the arrival of chef Scott Ekstrom (ex Angèle) is not reflected in the Food score.

Flavor *Californian/Eclectic*

22 | 20 | 21 | $30

Santa Rosa | 96 Old Courthouse Sq. (bet. 3rd & 4th Sts.) | 707-573-9600 | www.flavorbistro.com

This "local favorite" "bustling" Santa Rosa bistro situated "right on old courthouse square" dishes out a "wide-ranging" Cal-Eclectic menu filled with "consistently good comfort food"; a few surveyors grumble that the offerings are "not very imaginative", but regulars are charmed by the generally "congenial service", "decent prices" and "pleasant setting."

Forchetta/Bastoni *Italian/SE Asian*

∇ 19 | 21 | 17 | $29

Sebastopol | Sonoma Plaza | 6948 Sebastopol Ave. (Bodega Ave.) | 707-829-9500 | www.forchettabastoni.com

A "hip scene for Sebastopol", this "interesting-concept" place with a "cool" look holds two restaurants under one roof, so "you need to choose Italian or Southeast Asian before you sit down"; still, some call the midpriced bites "mediocre at best" and find it best for a "fun drink at the bar."

Frantoio *Italian*

22 | 22 | 22 | $45

Mill Valley | 152 Shoreline Hwy. (Hwy. 101) | 415-289-5777 | www.frantoio.com

It's "reliable in every way" say loyalists of this moderate Mill Valley Italian where the "classics never fail", service is mostly "attentive" and the operational olive oil press is "a sight to see"; the Tuscan-themed space is also "attractive" (if occasionally "noisy"), so it's an easy "go-to" that's "nice enough" for "special events."

Fremont Diner *Diner*

24 | 16 | 19 | $22

Sonoma | 2698 Fremont Dr. (Central Ave.) | 707-938-7370 | www.thefremontdiner.com

"Imaginative twists" elevate "down-home" "diner favorites" to "simply fabulous" proportions at this Sonoma "roadside find", where a "friendly" staff keeps watch over the "small", "funky" space and outdoor patio; it's often "crowded" (and "justifiably so") so "get there early" advise fans, and those who wished they'd "extend their operating hours" will be glad dinner is now served till 9 PM Thursday–Sunday (other days it closes at 3 PM).

French Blue ⓜ American — ▽ 20 | 26 | 20 | $42

St. Helena | 1429 Main St. (bet. Adams & Pine Sts.) | 707-968-9200 | www.frenchbluenapa.com

"Comfortable elegance" sets the tone at this "beautiful addition to St. Helena" serving an all-day American menu based on locally farmed ingredients; while some suggest the service and slightly expensive eats "need improvement", many agree the "ambiance and decor alone are worth a visit" – and "day drinking on the patio" isn't bad either; P.S. closed Monday–Tuesday.

French Garden French — 22 | 21 | 21 | $39

Sebastopol | 8050 Bodega Ave. (Pleasant Hill Ave.) | 707-824-2030 | www.frenchgardenrestaurant.com

From "foodies to grannies" there's "something for everyone" at this "affordably priced" French bistro on the "outskirts of Sebastopol" where the "true farm-to-table cuisine" features produce from its own garden; other pluses include "quality" service and a "spacious patio" perfect for "lingering."

French Laundry American/French — 28 | 27 | 28 | $297

Yountville | 6640 Washington St. (Creek St.) | 707-944-2380 | www.frenchlaundry.com

"The best French restaurant isn't in Paris, it's in Yountville" declare fans of Thomas Keller and his "iconic" stone farmhouse surrounded by organic gardens, "where no urge or whim goes unattended" by an "impeccable staff" delivering "astounding" French-American tasting menus that merge "art and science" and are matched with "superb" wine pairings; it's also "over the top in formality" and price, and "almost impossible" to get a reservation, but those who do insist "every foodie must try it once" (and "ask for a tour of the kitchen").

Fumé Bistro & Bar American — 22 | 18 | 22 | $41

Napa | 4050 Byway E. (Avalon Ct.) | 707-257-1999 | www.fumebistro.com

So far "tourists have missed" this Napa "locals' hangout", a "reliable wine country haunt" where the "solid" American fare is "priced reasonably" and set down by "friendly" servers; not everyone's a fan of the artwork-enhanced surrounds, but it still has a "warm ambiance", and the "lively bar scene" helps.

Gary Chu's ⓜ Chinese — 24 | 21 | 21 | $30

Santa Rosa | 611 Fifth St. (bet. D St. & Mendocino Ave.) | 707-526-5840 | www.garychus.com

For some of the "best Chinese in Sonoma County", diners hit up this midpriced Santa Rosa "favorite", where the "flavors meld perfectly" and many of the "delicious" dishes feature "interesting twists"; modern stylings contribute to a "pleasant atmosphere" and service gets few complaints, plus loyalists point out it's "been here for a long time so it must be doing something right."

	FOOD	DECOR	SERVICE	COST

Girl & the Fig *French*

| | 24 | 21 | 22 | $45 |

Sonoma | Sonoma Hotel | 110 W. Spain St. (1st St.) | 707-938-3634 | www.thegirlandthefig.com

A wine country "icon" right "in the heart of Sonoma square", this bistro from restaurateur Sondra Bernstein "shows no signs of getting tired" say fans citing the "imaginative" "Provence-inspired" creations "prepared simply and well", plus "swoon"-worthy cocktails and a "great selection" of wines "filled with Rhône varietals"; the "convivial" room can get "noisy", but the outdoor patio is "charming", and with "friendly" service and "value" tabs (at least for the area), it's still a "standout."

Glen Ellen Inn *Californian*

| | ∇ 23 | 21 | 24 | $42 |

Glen Ellen | 13670 Arnold Dr. (Warm Springs Rd.) | 707-996-6409 | www.glenelleninn.com

"Well off the beaten path", this Glen Ellen Californian run by a husband-and-wife team is a "real find", offering "creative, high-quality" dishes, including many with a French accent; the "charming", homey surrounds are ripe for "romance" and service is "attentive" too.

Glen Ellen Star *American*

| | ∇ 27 | 19 | 21 | $46 |

Glen Ellen | 13648 Arnold Dr. (Warm Springs Rd.) | 707-343-1384 | www.glenellenstar.com

Dubbed "a little heavenly outpost in the middle of tiny Glen Ellen", this "wine country gem" is a "find" for "innovative" wood-fired American fare and local wines (including a couple on tap) as well as imports; service is solid while an enclosed patio enhances the farmhouse setting ("no decor, but that's the charm"), and housemade ice cream tops it all off.

Goose & Gander ● *American*

| | ∇ 22 | 22 | 20 | $51 |

St. Helena | 1245 Spring St. (Oak Ave.) | 707-967-8779 | www.goosegander.com

Called a "worthy replacement for the lamented Martini House", this Downtown St. Helena American provides "well-executed", upscale gastropub fare in a "beautiful" Arts and Crafts space with "lovely" outdoor dining; for those who find the food and service merely "good", the "inventive", "perfectly balanced" cocktails are the "real standout."

Gott's Roadside *Diner*

| | 22 | 15 | 17 | $19 |

Napa | Oxbow Public Mkt. | 644 First St. (bet. Silverado Trail & Soscol Ave.) | 707-224-6900
St. Helena | 933 Main St. (bet. Charter Oak Ave. & Mitchell Dr.) | 707-963-3486
www.gotts.com

"A 21st-century version of a 1950s burger joint", this "self-serve" trio with "epic lines" puts a "gourmet twist" on everything, adding "amazing" ahi poke tacos and "top-notch wines" to "traditional diner" standards; though it's relatively "pricey", you "gott-sa try it" insist fans, who are "childishly happy" on "sunny days" sitting at "picnic tables on the lawn" in St. Helena (the Napa and SF spin-offs have indoor seating too).

Graffiti *Eclectic*

| | ∇ 25 | 25 | 23 | $35 |

Petaluma | 101 Second St. (C St.) | 707-765-4567 | www.graffitipetaluma.com

An "excellent location overlooking the Petaluma River" makes this midpriced Eclectic a "fantastic place to eat" say fans who also cheer the "creative" cooking, including "many small dishes and interesting large plates"; a "warm and efficient" crew tends to diners in the dining room or out on the patio that's especially "great in good weather", so the few who grumble it "never seems to wow" are in the minority.

Hana Japanese Restaurant *Japanese*   26 | 17 | 24 | $48

Rohnert Park | 101 Golf Course Dr. (Roberts Lake Rd.) | 707-586-0270 | www.hanajapanese.com

"Don't miss the sushi" at this Rohnert Park Japanese where "genius" chef-owner Ken Tominaga "makes sure every dish is of top quality", from "pristine raw fish" that's "beautifully arranged and served", to the "well-prepared" cooked items, all of which are complemented by a "wide selection of sake" and set down by "attentive" staffers; yes, it's in the "oddest" strip-mall location, the decor is somewhat "nonexistent" and it's "not cheap", but most are still happy to pay for such a "memorable" experience.

Harvest Moon Café *Californian/Mediterranean*   25 | 18 | 22 | $46

Sonoma | 487 First St. W. (Napa St.) | 707-933-8160 | www.harvestmooncafesonoma.com

"Delightful memories" are made at this "little jewel on the Sonoma Square", where a husband-and-wife team provides "friendly, attentive" service while turning out "sublime", "reasonably priced" Cal-Med dinners based on "whatever is fresh that day"; the "casual", "homey" interior is somewhat "cramped", so insiders head for the "pleasant" back garden that's like "a bit of Provence."

Healdsburg Bar & Grill *American*   19 | 17 | 19 | $29

Healdsburg | 245 Healdsburg Ave. (bet. Matheson & Mill Sts.) | 707-433-3333 | www.healdsburgbarandgrill.com

Despite its Douglas Keane (of the shuttered Cyrus) pedigree, "don't expect haute cuisine" at this "super-casual" bar and grill in Healdsburg, where "inspired" midpriced American pub grub – including a "great burger" – is served by an "exceptionally nice" staff in a kid-friendly setting; something of the local *Cheers,* it's a natural to "watch the game" or linger at lunchtime "on the patio", and there's a "pretty good wine list" to boot.

Hog Island Oyster Co. & Bar *Seafood*   26 | 18 | 20 | $36

Napa | Oxbow Public Mkt. | 610 First St. (bet. Silverado Trail & Soscol Ave.) | 707-251-8113 | www.hogislandoysters.com
See review in City of San Francisco Directory.

Hopmonk Tavern *Eclectic*   19 | 18 | 20 | $26

Novato | Vintage Oaks Shopping Ctr. | 224 Vintage Way (Rowland Blvd.) | 415-892-6200
Sebastopol | 230 Petaluma Ave. (bet. Burnett St. & Fannen Ave.) | 707-829-7300
Sonoma | 691 Broadway (Andrieux St.) | 707-935-9100
www.hopmonk.com

"Everybody finds something they like" among the "reasonably priced" Eclectic pub food, but it's the "fine selection of local and imported beers" that really draws "lively, young" types to these "hangouts" from Dean Biersch of Gordon Biersch; the atmosphere's particularly "wonderful in summer" on the "super" fire pit-blessed patio and downright "funky" on the weekends thanks to the "fantastic sounds" of local bands.

Hot Box Grill M *Californian*

▽ 25 | 15 | 22 | $45

Sonoma | 18350 Hwy. 12 (Boyes Blvd.) | 707-939-8383 |
www.hotboxgrill.com

The "dining room looks ordinary, but the food is certainly not" at this Boyes Hot Spring Californian from a former Cafe La Haye chef, who whips up an "amazing", "innovative" chalkboard menu of "rich" fare; some find the prices "steep considering the neighborhood", but for others, it's "the find of the decade."

Hurley's Restaurant *Californian/Mediterranean*
23 | 21 | 23 | $50

Yountville | 6518 Washington St. (bet. Humboldt & Yount Sts.) |
707-944-2345 | www.hurleysrestaurant.com

"You always feel welcome" at this Yountville site where chef Bob Hurley prepares "consistent" Californian cuisine with a "flavorful" Mediterranean twist (game preparations are particularly "wonderful"); diners feel prices are relatively "reasonable", especially the lunch prix fixe, making it a "great place to bring out-of-town guests"; P.S. "love the patio."

Ike's Place *Sandwiches*
25 | 12 | 18 | $12

Santa Rosa | 1780 Mendocino Ave. (Dexter St.) | 707-293-9814 |
www.ilikeikesplace.com

See review in City of San Francisco Directory.

Il Davide *Italian*
23 | 20 | 23 | $41

San Rafael | 901 A St. (bet. 3rd & 4th Sts.) | 415-454-8080 |
www.ildavide.net

"Refined" Tuscan fare rife with "unique flavor combinations" comes from chef-owner David Haydon, and a "warm reception" comes from his "superb" staff at this "outstanding" San Rafael ristorante; the "lovely", "lively" atmosphere also pleases, but the best feature may be its "reasonable prices", particularly lunch specials "you can't beat."

Il Fornaio *Italian*
18 | 19 | 18 | $43

Corte Madera | Town Center Corte Madera | 223 Corte Madera Town Ctr.
(Madera Blvd.) | 415-927-4400 | www.ilfornaio.com

See review in City of San Francisco Directory.

In-N-Out Burger ● *Burgers*

23 | 14 | 21 | $9

Mill Valley | 798 Redwood Hwy. (Belvedere Dr.)
Napa | 820 Imola Ave./Hwy. 121 (bet. Gasser Dr. & Soscol Ave.)
800-786-1000 | www.in-n-out.com

See review in City of San Francisco Directory.

Insalata's *Mediterranean*
25 | 23 | 23 | $43

San Anselmo | 120 Sir Francis Drake Blvd. (Barber Ave.) | 415-457-7700 |
www.insalatas.com

Chef-owner Heidi Krahling serves "luscious" Med dishes "usually with local ingredients" and at "fair prices" at this San Anselmo spot; "friendly service", a "well-stocked wine cellar" and an airy, "welcoming" room help make it just the thing for "special occasions", while "interesting takeout" is a boon for "Marin ladies who don't want to cook."

	FOOD	DECOR	SERVICE	COST

Jackson's *Californian*

22 | 22 | 21 | $34

Santa Rosa | 135 Fourth St. (Davis St.) | 707-545-6900 |
www.jacksonsbarandoven.com

"Well-prepared Californian-style bar food" including "delicious" wood-fired pizza is sold for "affordable prices" at this "charming" Santa Rosa "casual spot"; after-work revelers and other scene-seekers go for the "high-energy" atmosphere, especially at the long, "beautiful bar" where "fabulous drinks" are concocted.

Jimtown Store *Deli*

21 | 17 | 17 | $18

Healdsburg | 6706 Hwy. 128 (bet. Alexander Valley & Pitts Rds.) |
707-433-1212 | www.jimtown.com

"On your way to and from the wineries in Alexander Valley", you "must stop" at this "quaint" "old country store" outside of Healdsburg, offering "substantial", "well-prepared" deli sandwiches along with "antiques, collectibles, old-fashioned candy" and "ice cream treats"; hit the "comfortable patio" or, better still, "put together a picnic"; P.S. closes at 5 PM Friday–Sunday, 3 PM Monday, Wednesday and Friday (closed Tuesday).

Joe's Taco Lounge & Salsaria *Mexican*

21 | 19 | 19 | $20

Mill Valley | 382 Miller Ave. (bet. Evergreen & Montford Aves.) |
415-383-8164 | www.joestacolounge.com

This "quirky" taqueria with "an amazing hot sauce collection" is a "Mill Valley favorite" of "just about everyone", dishing out "tasty" "fresh" Mexican fare with a "bucket of beers" sampler or "wine margaritas" to wash it down; "lightning service" and "reasonable prices" keep it packed and "loud as heck", and patrons profess "that's what makes it fun."

John Ash & Co. *Californian*

25 | 25 | 24 | $56

Santa Rosa | 4330 Barnes Rd. (River Rd.) | 707-527-7687 |
www.vintnersinn.com

"Superb food in harmony with glorious decor" distinguishes this "revitalized" Santa Rosa Californian boasting a "romantic setting" "overlooking the vineyards"; the locavore dishes are "beautifully presented" by a "polite, prompt" staff also offering an "extensive" selection of Sonoma-centric vintages, and while it's "expensive", it's deemed "worth it", whether for a "special occasion" or "after a day at the wineries."

Johnny Garlic's *Californian*

19 | 17 | 19 | $29

Windsor | 8988 Brooks Rd. S. (Los Amigos Rd.) | 707-836-8300
Santa Rosa | 1460 Farmers Ln. (Neotomas Ave.) | 707-571-1800
www.johnnygarlics.com

"TV chef" Guy Fieri owns these midpriced Bay Area chain links serving "dependable" Californian cuisine "with flair" in a "fun" "pub-type" atmosphere that can get "a little frenetic"; though some "expect more" "wow", and service varies, "portions are decent" and "all seem to be having a good time"; P.S. "they aren't kidding about the garlic."

Jole *American*

26 | 19 | 22 | $53

Calistoga | Mount View Hotel | 1457 Lincoln Ave. (bet. Fair Way & Washington St.) | 707-942-5938 | www.jolerestaurant.com

"Top-quality local ingredients" are whipped into "innovative" New American small plates offered à la carte or in tasting menus at this "wonderful" Calistoga option with a "cute" "neighborhood feel";

though it's on the "expensive" side, "helpful" service and a selection of small-production wines add value, making it "worth the drive" from afar.

K&L Bistro *French*

25 | 19 | 24 | $46

Sebastopol | 119 S. Main St. (bet. Bodega Ave. & Burnett St.) | 707-823-6614 | www.klbistro.com

"A little bit of Paris" in Sebastapol, this "sophisticated" bistro with "small-town friendliness" is a local "go-to" for "delicious" French fare paired with "excellent" wines; some say they get "a little claustrophobic" inside (there's also a patio), but most don't mind the "small storefront" setting in light of the "reasonable prices", not to mention staffers who serve with "professionalism and good cheer."

Kenwood 🅼 *American/French*

▽ 25 | 23 | 25 | $55

Kenwood | 9900 Sonoma Hwy./Hwy. 12 (Libby Ave.) | 707-833-6326 | www.kenwoodrestaurant.com

Nestled "in the middle of Sonoma Valley's vineyards", this "comfortable" Kenwood "country restaurant" is cited for its "reliable", "delicious" American-French fare, "exceptional wine list" and "high-quality" service; however, it's the "wonderful views" from the patio that really help to make "every visit special."

Kitchen Door *Eclectic*

22 | 18 | 17 | $30

Napa | Oxbow Public Mkt. | 610 First St. (bet. Silverado Trail & Soscol Ave.) | 707-226-1560 | www.kitchendoornapa.com

Todd Humphries (of the defunct Martini House) "has another winner" in this "casual" cafe in Napa's Oxbow Market proffering "innovative" Eclectic eats from a "rustic" "open kitchen" for "down-to-earth prices"; full table service is "a big plus" at brunch, lunch and dinner, both inside and on the "lovely" "deck" overlooking the river.

La Boulange *Bakery*

21 | 17 | 18 | $16

Mill Valley | Strawberry Vill. | 800 Redwood Hwy. (Belvedere Dr.) | 415-381-1260

Novato | Hamilton Mktpl. | 5800 Nave Dr. (bet. Hamilton Pkwy. & Roblar Dr.) | 415-382-8594

www.laboulangebakery.com

See review in City of San Francisco Directory.

La Condesa *Mexican*

▽ 25 | 18 | 19 | $41

St. Helena | 1320 Main St. (bet. Adams St. & Hunt Ave.) | 707-967-8111 | www.lacondesanapavalley.com

"Fantastic", "inventive", somewhat "pricey" Mexican *comida* comes to St. Helena by way of this "friendly", colorful offshoot of an "upscale" Austin hot spot; there's "no shortage of tequila" here – in fact, there's almost "too many to choose from" – the effects of which make it often as "loud" as a "bowling alley."

La Gare 🅼 *French*

26 | 22 | 26 | $44

Santa Rosa | 208 Wilson St. (3rd St.) | 707-528-4355 | www.lagarerestaurant.com

Admirers attest "the beef Wellington is without peer" at this upscale Santa Rosa French where the "extensive" wine list complements "classic cuisine done very well"; "lovely and romantic" with impressive service, it's a "favorite" of those who like an "old-school" touch.

LaSalette *Portuguese*

24 | 19 | 23 | $46

Sonoma | Mercado Ctr. | 452 First St. E. (bet. Napa & Spain Sts.) | 707-938-1927 | www.lasalette-restaurant.com

"Save the airfare to Portugal" suggest fans of this "lovely", "friendly oasis" "tucked away" "off the square" in Sonoma, where chef-owner Manny Azevedo cooks "eye-opening" Portuguese dishes "in an open oven" and staffers "seem to genuinely care"; prices won't break the bank, while the space is "cramped" but "pleasant", making "outside on the patio" the seating of choice "in good weather."

La Taquiza *Mexican*

▽ 27 | 15 | 18 | $13

Napa | 2007 Redwood Rd. (Solano Ave.) | 707-224-2320 | www.lataquizanapa.com

A former French Laundry baker and his wife are behind this "simple" Mexican take-out taqueria in Napa, where nearly everything on the fish-centric menu is so "wonderfully fresh" and "authentic", you "could be sitting on the pier in Ensenada"; though word is "the service and the decor are not so great", at least you can get in and out "quick."

La Toque *French*

27 | 24 | 26 | $100

Napa | Westin Verasa Napa | 1314 McKinstry St. (bet. 1st St. & Soscol Ave.) | 707-257-5157 | www.latoque.com

Patrons profess that Ken Frank's "special-occasion" New French inside the Westin Verasa remains "one of the finest places in Napa Valley" to "splurge" on "exceptional" "tasting menus" featuring "plenty of choices" and matched with "superb" wines by sommeliers who navigate an international list; the main dining room offers a "quiet ambiance" and "understated elegance", while those feeling especially flush might book the chef's table in the kitchen; P.S. the adjacent Bank Bar offers a less-expensive menu throughout the day.

Ledford House *Californian/Mediterranean*

▽ 26 | 26 | 24 | $44

Albion | 3000 N. Hwy. 1 (Spring Grove Rd.) | 707-937-0282 | www.ledfordhouse.com

At this place that's "perched on a bluff" in Albion on the Mendocino coast, husband-and-wife chef-owners "make sure you're happy" with "fabulous" Cal-Med fare, matched with area wines and "wonderful" service; insiders are "there by sunset" for the most "panoramic views", though the "lovely room" and nightly live music are their own draws – no wonder it's always full of folks celebrating "special occasions."

Left Bank *French*

20 | 21 | 19 | $40

Larkspur | Blue Rock Inn | 507 Magnolia Ave. (Ward St.) | 415-927-3331 | www.leftbank.com

"Dependable" brasserie fare at moderate prices is the deal at this "bustling", "family-friendly" French trio (co-owned by La Folie chef Roland Passot) boasting "attractive decor"; service can be either "prompt" or "slow" depending on the staffer (though most are "friendly"), but each branch has outdoor seating that's indisputably "relaxing."

Le Garage *French*

23 | 20 | 22 | $42

Sausalito | 85 Liberty Ship Way (Marinship Way) | 415-332-5625 | www.legaragebistrosausalito.com

Take your "taste buds for service" at this slightly pricey converted repair shop "on the water in Sausalito", where "accented" staffers in "auto-repair overalls" deliver "fantastic" French bistro fare; true, it "gets loud when it's full (and it's usually full)", but everyone loves when "the weather's warm" and the steel-and-glass doors are rolled up, allowing an unobstructed "view of the yachts" at the Schoonmaker Point Marina.

Lincoln Park Wine Bar *Californian* — | — | — | I

San Anselmo | 198 Sir Francis Drake Blvd. (bet. Bank St. & Barber Ave.) | 415-453-9898 | www.lincolnparkwine.com
Chef Steve Simmons (Lark Creek Inn, Bubba's Diner) helms this farm-to-table bistro and wine bar in San Anselmo offering a gently priced, compact menu of Californian 'medium' plates and small-scale, sustainable regional wines (available on tap, in carafe and glass), most of which is sourced from within 60 miles; customers can dine at the marble bar in the front or in the dining room that's outfitted with tufted banquettes and industrial-style lights.

Little River Inn Restaurant *Californian/Seafood* 24 | 23 | 24 | $46

Little River | Little River Inn | 7901 N. Hwy. 1 (bet. Little River-Airport & Park Rds.) | 707-937-5942 | www.littleriverinn.com
Travelers "escaping" to Mendocino "love the atmosphere" at this Little River locale, where the dining room has "beautiful" garden views and the bar overlooking the ocean is "perfect for slurping down some oysters at sunset"; offering "excellent" Californian seafood, "amazing" breakfasts and "accommodating" service at slightly upscale tabs, it comes through as a real "home away from home."

Lococo's Cucina Rustica Ⓜ *Italian* 25 | 20 | 23 | $37

Santa Rosa | 117 Fourth St. (Wilson St.) | 707-523-2227 | www.lococos.net
As "perfect for a romantic evening" as it is for "families needing a night out without breaking the bank", this "cute" Downtown Santa Rosa ristorante dishes out "fabulous", "rich" fare including "fine pastas"; "accommodating" staffers "add to your dining pleasure", but just bear in mind that it's quite "popular", thus "frenetic" and "difficult to get into on weekends."

MacCallum House Restaurant & Grey Whale Bar *Californian* 24 | 24 | 21 | $56

Mendocino | MacCallum House Inn | 45020 Albion St. (bet. Kasten & Lansing Sts.) | 707-937-5763 | www.maccallumhouse.com
"Take a break from those gorgeous Pacific vistas" nearby to focus on the "creative", "indulgent" fare and "interesting" cocktails offered at this "intimate" Californian in a "Victorian marvel"–cum-B&B "in the heart of beautiful Mendocino"; while service might be a bit "uneven", overnight guests (and in-the-know locals) contend the breakfast is "worth rising" for; P.S. a table "near the fireplace" is particularly "romantic."

Madrona Manor Restaurant Ⓜ *American/French* 27 | 26 | 27 | $105

Healdsburg | Madrona Manor | 1001 Westside Rd. (Dry Creek Rd.) | 707-433-4231 | www.madronamanor.com
Count on a "memorable dining experience" – with "professional" service and a "massive price tag" to match – at this "charming" Healdsburg restaurant and country inn set in a "beautiful old mansion" surrounded by "estate gardens" where antique furnishings are the backdrop for

"fantastic" "modern", candlelit New American–French prix fixes highlighting "local wines" and produce ("the gardener's name is even on the menu"); a few find it a "touch too formal", but concede "if you want "froufrou" in Sonoma, "they do it right"; P.S. closed Monday and Tuesday.

Marché aux Fleurs 🗷Ⓜ *French*   25 | 23 | 25 | $55

Ross | 23 Ross Common (Lagunitas Rd.) | 415-925-9200 | www.marcheauxfleursrestaurant.com

"Seasonal, artistically presented", "Provençal-style French food" is a "pure delight" at this "convivial" Ross "jewel" owned by "wonderful people"; though a tad "expensive", it's a winner for "romantic evenings", especially if you enjoy "outdoor dining in the summer."

Marinitas ● *Mexican/Pan-Latin*   21 | 20 | 19 | $32

San Anselmo | 218 Sir Francis Drake Blvd. (Bank St.) | 415-454-8900 | www.marinitas.net

A "contemporary" mix of "upscale" Mexican–Pan-Latin eats starring "tasty" Argentinean steak and ceviche is washed down with "great margaritas" at this San Anselmo cantina (an Insalata's sibling) with a "pleasant, dimly lit atmosphere" and "friendly staff"; it's usually "impossible to carry on a conversation in normal tones", but "most people come for the fun", "uplifting" "party scene" anyway.

Market *American*   22 | 20 | 22 | $45

St. Helena | 1347 Main St. (bet. Adams & Spring Sts.) | 707-963-3799 | www.marketsthelena.com

Both visitors on "a Sunday drive in wine country" and "fiercely loyal" St. Helena locals say "this place never fails to delight", with "flavorful, well-prepared" Traditional American comfort food that's "fairly priced for the quality"; bedecked with "stone walls and rich woodwork", the room is often "fully booked", but the "staff handles it well"; P.S. the "old-time-y bar" and no corkage fees are "added attractions."

Mateo's Cocina Latina *Mexican*   22 | 20 | 19 | $38

Healdsburg | 214 Healdsburg Ave. (Mill St.) | 707-433-1520 | www.mateoscocinalatina.com

"Forget about burritos", "inspired impresario" Mateo Granados (ex Dry Creek Kitchen) is "redefining Mexican cooking" at his "hip" midpriced eatery in Healdsburg where "inventively presented", locally sourced Yucatán cuisine and "tongue-tingling" sauces meet in "revelatory ways"; the garden "patio" and "excellent" tequila bar menu are nice perks.

Meadowood, The Grill *Californian*   22 | 21 | 22 | $53
(aka The Grill at Meadowood)

St. Helena | Meadowood Napa Valley | 900 Meadowood Ln. (Silverado Trail) | 707-968-3144 | www.meadowood.com

Those looking for a "relaxing" "getaway" are drawn to the "low-key elegance" and "fantastic" fairway "views" that surround this "casual" "country club"–esque Californian grill at St. Helena's Meadowood resort, where a "friendly" staff serves breakfast through dinner; "while it pales in comparison" to the experience at its high-end upstairs sibling, if you can "grab a table on the veranda", it makes for a "memorable meal."

Meadowood, The Restaurant ⌧ *Californian*   27 | 27 | 27 | $293
(aka The Restaurant at Meadowood)

St. Helena | Meadowood Napa Valley | 900 Meadowood Ln. (Silverado Trail) | 707-967-1205 | www.therestaurantatmeadowood.com

"Unforgettable" is how fans describe the "singular experience" of dining at this special-occasion standout in St. Helena's Meadowood resort, where Christopher Kostow's "innovative", bespoke tasting menus are paired with California wines and enhanced by "amazing presentations" and service to match, plus "serene" views overlooking croquet fields and fairways; the initiated swear it's worth the "stratospheric prices" to "experience at least once"; P.S. the new bar lounge serves a more affordable three-course menu.

Mendo Bistro *American*   25 | 20 | 24 | $40

Fort Bragg | The Company Store | 301 N. Main St. (Redwood Ave.) | 707-964-4974 | www.mendobistro.com

Chef Nicholas Petti's surprisingly "creative" New American in "remote" Fort Bragg is "worth the trip" for its "fresh" seafood selections ("prepared almost any way you like") and "the best crab cakes in Northern California" (when in season); "affordable" "Mendocino wines", a "caring staff" and a "beautiful view" of Downtown from the "high-ceilinged" former Company Store make the experience especially "memorable."

Mendocino Café *Eclectic*   20 | 16 | 20 | $27

Mendocino | 10451 Lansing St. (Albion St.) | 707-937-6141 | www.mendocinocafe.com

"Comfortable and cozy", this affordable low-key cafe in "pricey Mendocino" offers a "broad menu" of mostly "organic" Eclectic eats (like the "yummy" Thai burrito); a few wonder whether the fare should be described as "fusion or confusion", but who cares when you can "grab a seat on the deck" and enjoy "breathtaking views" over the water.

Miller's East Coast Delicatessen *Deli/Jewish*   20 | 12 | 17 | $19

San Rafael | Montecito Shopping Ctr. | 421 Third St. (Grand Ave.) | 415-453-3354 | www.millersdelisf.com

See review in City of San Francisco Directory.

Model Bakery *Bakery*   23 | 13 | 18 | $15

Napa | Oxbow Public Mkt. | 644 First St. (bet. Silverado Trail & Soscol Ave.) | 707-963-8192

St. Helena | 1357 Main St. (bet. Adams & Spring Sts.) | 707-963-8192
www.themodelbakery.com

Although these "low-key" St. Helena–Napa "coffee stops" are "primarily" "neighborhood" bakeries, they also offer reasonably priced fare for a "casual breakfast or lunch", including "great tartine sandwiches", "tasty pizzas" and "delicious" pastries; "service can be slow" and the Main Street original has more "local ambiance", but both bake up their "famous" English muffins that are "out of this world."

Monti's Rotisserie &   22 | 20 | 21 | $37
Bar *American/Mediterranean*

Santa Rosa | Montgomery Village Shopping Ctr. | 714 Village Ct. (Patio Ct.) | 707-568-4404 | www.starkrestaurants.com

"Creative food *can* be had in a shopping center" attest fans of this "neighborhood restaurant" in Santa Rosa, where the midpriced New

American–Med fare is "dependably delicious" and delivered by a "willing staff"; dining "near the wood-fired oven" (where "fantastic" "nightly rotisserie specials" are cooked) in the terra-cotta, wood and wrought-iron–accented interior is "cozy" on "winter nights", while a patio beckons when the weather's warm.

Morimoto Napa *Japanese*

25 | 23 | 22 | $73

Napa | 610 Main St. (5th St.) | 707-252-1600 | www.morimotonapa.com

Like "your typical Morimoto" kitchen, even basic dishes such as "toro tartare" and "tableside tofu" are "turned into creative" "masterpieces" at this "hip" riverfront Japanese in Downtown Napa that lures star-struck "tourists" with "beautifully presented", "haute" seafood and "one-of-a-kind drinks" in *Architectural Digest*–worthy surroundings; some prefer to "eat out on the terrace" to escape the "rowdy, loud bar scene" and say service is not up to "*Iron Chef*" standards, but most contend it "almost lives up to the incredible hype" so long as diners have the main ingredient – "moolah!"

Murray Circle *Californian*

23 | 25 | 23 | $64

Sausalito | Cavallo Point Resort in Fort Baker | 602 Murray Circle (East Rd.) | 415-339-4750 | www.murraycircle.com

"Ask for a table at the window" (or outside) to take in the "extraordinary" Golden Gate views at this Sausalito Californian "housed in renovated army officers' quarters"; the service enhances the "elegant" atmosphere, and while the "small portions" range from "brilliant" to "fussy", many agree it's "not cheap but worth it."

Mustards Grill *American/Californian*

25 | 21 | 23 | $51

Yountville | 7399 St. Helena Hwy./Hwy. 29 (bet. Oakville Grade Rd. & Washington St.) | 707-944-2424 | www.mustardsgrill.com

"Lots of local color" goes into the "bustling, casual" scene and "first-rate" Cal-New American fare by chef-owner Cindy Pawlcyn at this "unassuming"-looking "Napa Valley classic", an "upscale diner" outside Yountville; "friendly" service and a "spectacular" lemon-lime tart (with "mile-high meringue") complete the "real California" experience; P.S. reservations recommended.

Napa Valley Wine Train *Californian*

20 | 25 | 23 | $148

Napa | 1275 McKinstry St. (bet. 1st St. & Soscol Ave.) | 707-253-2111 | www.winetrain.com

"Having a meal while rolling through vineyards" is a "wonderful experience" for guests who savor the "great scenery" while dining on Californian food and wine on this "classic train"; the service is pleasant too, though critics say the cooking is "not up to par" for the price.

Nick's Cove *Californian*

21 | 21 | 20 | $44

Marshall | Nick's Cove & Cottages | 23240 Hwy. 1 (Snake Rd.) | 415-663-1033 | www.nickscove.com

Since the 1930s, travelers "driving up the coast" on Route 1 have visited this all-day waterside Marshall fish house (with cottages for overnight guests), considered a "find" for "fresh" seafood in a "lovely" setting; loyalists praise the "terrific" barbecue oysters and "excellent" Crab Louie, and say the space has "great views of Tomales Bay" while retaining its "local feel"; P.S. midweek specials include a $25 prix fixe and half-priced Wine Wednesdays.

	FOOD	DECOR	SERVICE	COST

955 Restaurant ⓜ *American/French*   25 | 21 | 23 | $46

Mendocino | 955 Ukiah St. (School St.) | 707-937-1955 |
www.955restaurant.com

Despite its off-the-beaten-path address, this longtime Mendocino "locals' secret" draws them in with "creative", reasonably priced New American–French fare and a staff overseen by husband-and-wife "owner-operators"; additionally, "no one is in a hurry" here, which always makes for a "relaxing atmosphere" in the "peaceful and beautiful" setting.

Norman Rose Tavern *American*   20 | 19 | 20 | $35

Napa | 1401 First St. (Franklin St.) | 707-258-1516 |
www.normanrosenapa.com

At this "clubbyish" American gastropub in Downtown Napa, the "hard-to-beat" burgers and other midpriced locally sourced bar food are paired with "good wine" and suds, helping to "keep this place jam-packed daily" and into the night; while some feel service could use some work, the "nice atmosphere" helps make it a "go-to" for many.

NEW Odalisque   - | - | - | I

Cafe ⓢⓜ *Californian/Mediterranean*

San Rafael | 1335 Fourth St. (D St.) | 415-460-1335 |
www.odalisquecafe.com

Inspired by the famous French painting La Grande Odalisque, this gathering place in Downtown San Rafael turns out a regularly changing menu of affordable, locally sourced Californian-Mediterranean large and small plates, along with a brief slate of wines; in keeping with the arty theme, the spacious setting (formerly a turn-of-the-century opera house) is filled with exposed-brick walls, salvaged wood and rotating art displays.

Oenotri *Italian*   24 | 20 | 21 | $51

Napa | Napa Sq. | 1425 First St. (bet. Franklin & School Sts.) | 707-252-1022 |
www.oenotri.com

The Oliveto alums behind this "trendy" Southern Italian let their "roots show" with "creative pastas", "killer pizza" and "salumi plates", made in an "open kitchen" and paired with "interesting" Boot vinos; it's "on the expensive side" for "small portions" and often so "crowded" it can be "hard to have a conversation", but many say this bit of "Naples" in Napa is still "worth the trip."

Osake ⓢ *Californian/Japanese*   25 | 20 | 23 | $38

Santa Rosa | 2446 Patio Ct. (Farmers Ln.) | 707-542-8282 |
www.garychus.com

Chef-owner Gary Chu "cheerfully prepares sushi" that "could not be fresher" while "hobnobbing with the locals" at this longtime Cal-Japanese in Santa Rosa; with a "really nice ambiance", "reasonable prices" and Sonoma County wines, regulars rave "who could ask for more?"

Osteria Stellina *Italian*   24 | 18 | 21 | $43

Point Reyes Station | 11285 Hwy. 1 (bet. 2nd & 3rd Sts.) | 415-663-9988 |
www.osteriastellina.com

The kind of "place a traveler dreams of finding", this "unpretentious" Italian in "bucolic" Point Reyes Station transforms ingredients from

FOOD DECOR SERVICE COST

"local waters" and "surrounding farms" into "delicious", "rustic" dishes ("get the goat") paired with "outstanding" wine; true, the "ordinary"-looking room can get "crowded" and "super loud", but "fair prices" and "pleasant" service compensate.

Oxbow Wine Merchant *Californian/Mediterranean*

▽ 21 | 19 | 22 | $31

Napa | Oxbow Public Mkt. | 610 First St. (bet. Silverado Trail & Soscol Ave.) | 707-257-5200 | www.oxbowwinemerchant.com
Located in Oxbow Public Market, this shop/restaurant doles out "tastings" of an "amazing" wine, cheese and cured meats inventory, as well as more substantial Cal-Med "small plates" throughout the day; while it may be a "little too pricey" for an order-at-the-counter place, the outdoor seating on the Napa River adds to the appeal.

Pacific Catch *Seafood*

22 | 17 | 20 | $26

Corte Madera | Town Center Corte Madera | 133 Corte Madera Town Ctr. (Madera Blvd.) | 415-927-3474 | www.pacificcatch.com
See review in City of San Francisco Directory.

NEW The Parish Cafe M *Cajun/Creole*

- | - | - | I

Healdsburg | 60 Mill St. (Healdsburg Ave.) | 707-431-8474 | www.theparishcafe.com
Just a few blocks off Healdsburg's plaza, this daytimer offers New Orleans breakfast and lunch fixings including shrimp and grits, fried seafood platters and a variety of po' boy sandwiches on crunchy baguette specially made by local Costeaux Bakery, all served in a small room (with additional seating on the porch) that hums with Preservation Hall style music; there are also light-as-air beignets plus café au lait made with real chicory; P.S. open Wednesday–Sunday, 9 AM–3 PM.

Pasta Pomodoro *Italian*

18 | 16 | 19 | $22

Mill Valley | Strawberry Vill. | 800 Redwood Hwy. (Belvedere Dr.) | 415-388-1692
Novato | Vintage Oaks at Novato | 140 Vintage Way (Rowland Blvd.) | 415-899-1861
www.pastapomodoro.com
See review in City of San Francisco Directory.

NEW The Pear *Cajun/Southern*

- | - | - | M

Napa | 720 Main St. (3rd St.) | 707-256-3900 | www.thepearsb.com
Bringing a taste of New Orleans and the Deep South to Downtown Napa, this regional American bistro overlooking the revitalized riverfront (run by The Peasant and The Pear folks) has devotees "delightfully surprised" by its moderately priced comfort food like fried pickles, po 'boys and chicken and waffles ("they have an amazing way with fried food"), and the staff's "fantastic."

Pearl ⑤M *Californian*

▽ 22 | 16 | 21 | $40

Napa | 1339 Pearl St. (bet. Franklin & Polk Sts.) | 707-224-9161 | www.therestaurantpearl.com
The kitchen "excels" at "pork chops, chicken verde" and other "enjoyable" Californian fare at this Downtown Napa "sleeper" that's "mostly frequented by locals"; boasting a "nice ambiance", "solid value" and "excellent" service, it's a "special place" that's especially comfortable in winter "when there are fewer folks."

	FOOD	DECOR	SERVICE	COST

Pearl's Phat Burgers *Burgers*
23 | 12 | 19 | $13

Mill Valley | 8 E. Blithedale Ave. (Throckmorton Ave.) | 415-381-6010 | www.pearlsdeluxe.com
See review in City of San Francisco Directory.

Peter Lowell's *Italian*
▽ 22 | 16 | 16 | $31

Sebastopol | 7385 Healdsburg Ave. (Florence Ave.) | 707-829-1077 | www.peterlowells.com
"Interesting creations" of "healthy food" anchor this "popular" Sebastopol hangout serving midpriced, organic "farm-to-table" Italian-inspired fare and "local" biodynamic wines; regulars warn "don't eat here if you're in a hurry" (service can be "on the slow side") and wish the "modern" LEED-certified space would "expand" as "seating is very limited", though there's also a "beautiful patio."

Piatti Ristorante & Bar *Italian*
21 | 21 | 21 | $38

Mill Valley | 625 Redwood Hwy. (Hamilton Dr.) | 415-380-2525 | www.piatti.com
See review in City of San Francisco Directory.

Piazza D'Angelo *Italian*
20 | 19 | 20 | $40

Mill Valley | 22 Miller Ave. (bet. Sunnyside & Throckmorton Aves.) | 415-388-2000 | www.piazzadangelo.com
Near town square in Mill Valley, this "happening" Italian is a "longtime local favorite", with "satisfying" renditions of the classics (including "wood-fired pizza") that come with tabs that "aren't over the top"; while a "packed" bar offers "great people-watching", a "super" staff oversees the "ever-crowded", oft-"noisy" dining room, bedecked with a "wood-burning fireplace."

Pica Pica Maize Kitchen *Venezuelan*
21 | 14 | 18 | $15

Napa | Oxbow Public Mkt. | 610 First St. (bet. Silverado Trail & Soscol Ave.) | 707-251-3757 | www.picapicakitchen.com
"Fresh Venezuelan street fare" is the "unusual" specialty at these casual spots in San Francisco's Mission and Castro districts plus the Napa Oxbow Market, where "arepas" – "little corn pillows of goodness" with meat or vegetable fillings – and "maize'wiches" made with sweet-corn bread "provide a break from tacos and burritos"; though service can be uneven, there's "great value" to be had, and newcomers "can't wait to go back."

Picco *Italian*
26 | 21 | 22 | $51

Larkspur | 320 Magnolia Ave. (King St.) | 415-924-0300 | www.restaurantpicco.com
Central Marin locals frequent this Larkspur Cal-Italian "go-to" "with a tableful of friends" to "try everything" from the menu of "innovative small plates"; despite the "thirsty and hungry" crowds, service is "excellent", and while the "bustling" "bar scene" lends a "roadhouse" vibe, this "casual eatery" is still a tad more serious than the popular sister "pizzeria next door."

Pine Cone Diner ⊘ *Diner*
▽ 20 | 15 | 16 | $16

Point Reyes Station | 60 Fourth St. (B St.) | 415-663-1536
Once a truck stop, this updated "everyday diner" in Point Reyes Station uses largely organic, local ingredients in its American breakfasts and

lunches, featuring specialties like housemade corned beef hash; it's "all quite tasty" and affordable, even if not everyone warms up to the service or "greasy-spoon" menu.

Pizza Antica *Pizza* 22 | 17 | 19 | $26

Mill Valley | Strawberry Vill. | 800 Redwood Hwy. (Belvedere Dr.) | 415-383-0600 | www.pizzaantica.com
See review in South of San Francisco Directory.

NEW Pizzalina *Pizza* - | - | - | I

San Anselmo | Red Hill Shopping Ctr. | 914 Sir Francis Drake Blvd. (Sunny Hills Dr.) | 415-256-9780 | www.pizzalina.com
"Delicious", "creative" wood-fired Neapolitan pizzas and other rustic Italian dishes incorporating local ingredients fill the menu at this reasonably priced, "family-friendly" all-day San Anselmo haunt, which also offers beer and wine on tap and by the bottle; the warm and welcoming interior features big windows and upscale rustic decor with white walls, wood accents and marble fixtures.

Pizzando *Californian/Pizza* - | - | - | M

Healdsburg | h2hotel | 301 Healdsburg Ave. (Matheson St.) | 707-922-5233 | www.pizzandohealdsburg.com
Situated just off the Healdsburg plaza in the h2hotel, this casual Spoonbar spin-off overseen by chef Louis Maldonado serves an all-day menu of midpriced market-driven items including pizzas, housemade pastas and rustic grilled meats; the tiny, ultramodern space is outfitted with copper counters and a Mugnaini wood-fired oven, plus a bar that specializes in Italian wines, carbonated cocktails and spirit-based aperitivi; P.S. open late on summer Saturdays for snacks.

Pizzeria Picco *Pizza* 26 | 14 | 18 | $28

Larkspur | 316 Magnolia Ave. (King St.) | 415-945-8900 | www.pizzeriapicco.com
Larkspur's "secret is out" about this "tiny", "upscale pizzeria" (the next-door sib to Picco) cranking out "truly divine", "Neapolitan"-by-way-of-Californian "wood-fired pizzas" and "amazingly fresh" salads, capped off by equally "crave-worthy" wines and "soft-serve" (drizzled with "olive oil or chocolate dipped"); despite being "mobbed" by "hungry people" "waiting patiently" to nab a "barstool" or sidewalk table, staffers "handle the crowds well", though many regulars just grab a "frozen" pie "to take home."

Pizzeria Tra Vigne *Pizza* 22 | 17 | 18 | $27

St. Helena | Inn at Southbridge | 1016 Main St. (bet. Charter Oak Ave. & Mitchell Dr.) | 707-967-9999 | www.pizzeriatravigne.com
"In the land of the pretentious meal", this Downtown St. Helena Italian is a "casual", "not-too-pricey" alternative that "never disappoints" with its "wonderful pizzas", pastas and salads; since the roomy space is often "full of local families", it can get "noisy", but service is "friendly" and the "outdoor dining is very pleasant", "particularly in summer", while a "good choice of draft beers" and "no-corkage" policy sweeten the deal.

NEW The Plant Cafe Organic *Health Food* 22 | 19 | 18 | $26

Mill Valley | Strawberry Village Shopping Ctr. | 800 Redwood Hwy. (Belvedere Dr.) | 415-388-8658 | www.theplantcafe.com
See review in City of San Francisco Directory.

NORTH OF SAN FRANCISCO

FOOD | DECOR | SERVICE | COST

Poggio _Italian_   25 | 25 | 23 | $47

Sausalito | Casa Madrona | 777 Bridgeway (Bay St.) | 415-332-7771 |
www.poggiotrattoria.com

It's "one of the first places tourists see as they leave the ferry landing",
but this trattoria right on Sausalito's main drag is also "popular with locals" enamored of the "garden-inspired", "wood-fired" offerings, both
inside the "supremely comfortable" dining room and "on the sidewalk"
where you can "watch the world go by"; "knowledgeable" service and a
"wonderful wine list" complete a package that has fans returning "again
and again"; P.S. a chef change may not be reflected in the Food score.

Press _American/Steak_   26 | 24 | 24 | $74

St. Helena | 587 St. Helena Hwy. S. (White Ln.) | 707-967-0550 |
www.pressthelena.com

"Carnivores" rave about this St. Helena American's "exceptional"
"charred red meat" plus sides "on a par with any steakhouse" and
"big", all-Napa reds (including "old vintages") from an impressive cellar; a full-court press of "attentive" servers work the "beautiful", modern farmhouse-style quarters, and while regulars advise "take your
cholesterol pills and your wallet", thrifty sorts seek out "the bar menu
for a lighter tab."

NEW Pub Republic ◑ _Pub Food_   - | - | - | M

Petaluma | 3120 Lakeville Hwy. (McDowell Blvd.) | 707-782-9090 |
www.pubrepublicusa.com

Part urban pub, part family-friendly haunt, this casual and classy
American is making its mark on the Petaluma dining scene with
sustainably raised, reasonably priced steaks, seafood, burgers and
small plates, plus rotating taps on draft; a long wooden bar, tables
and comfy booths fill the lively dining room, where wood floors and
stone accents impart a rustic feel and high ceilings enhance the
sense of openness.

The Q Restaurant & Bar _American/BBQ_   22 | 18 | 21 | $33
(fka Barbers Q)

Napa | Bel Aire Plaza | 3900 Bel Aire Plaza (bet. Baxter Ave. & Trancas St.) |
707-224-6600 | www.barbersq.com

A "reliable go-to" when you have a 'cue "craving", this Napa joint delivers "consistently good" BBQ and other "down-home" American eats
bolstered by "local wine pairings"; its "relaxed" "strip-mall" setting is
"pleasant" enough, service gets solid marks and prices are "reasonable", so it's a "locals' spot" that also appeals as a "place to bring the
kids when visiting wine country."

Ravenous Cafe Ⓜ _American_   22 | 18 | 20 | $42

Healdsburg | 117 North St. (bet. Center St. & Healdsburg Ave.) |
707-431-1302

"Back in its original setting next to the Raven Theater", this Healdsburg
"perennial favorite" relocated to its former "cubbyhole" with only
eight tables is still serving up a full-fledged, daily changing "handwrit-
ten menu" of "fantastic", "fresh" New American eats (some old favorites and some new ones), along with "terrific wines" and "warm
vibes", all at a "reasonable price"; P.S. open Wednesday–Sunday for
lunch and dinner plus Sunday brunch.

FOOD DECOR SERVICE COST

Redd *Californian*
27 | 22 | 25 | $71

Yountville | 6480 Washington St. (Oak Circle) | 707-944-2222 | www.reddnapavalley.com

For "serious" "fine dining" in Yountville "without being pretentious", Richard Reddington's "sleek", "modern" Californian offers "innovative", "eye-catching" cuisine incorporating "Asian flavors" and complemented by a "deep" but not "preciously priced" wine list; perks like extended bar hours, "lovely outdoor" seating and Sunday brunch have fans calling it a "favorite."

Redd Wood *Italian/Pizza*
25 | 22 | 22 | $49

Yountville | 6755 Washington St. (bet. Burgundy Way & Madison St.) | 707-299-5030 | www.redd-wood.com

It's "no surprise" that Richard Reddington's "casual" Italian "just down the street" from his more formal Redd is a "spectacular" addition to Yountville's restaurant scene, especially given the "excellent" pizzas fresh "out of the wood-burning oven", handmade pastas, salumi and other expertly prepared, "soulful" dishes accompanied by affordable local wines; understandably, tables in the "cozy" room overlooking the kitchen or on the "patio" are tough to score.

The Restaurant *American/Eclectic*
∇ 22 | 19 | 23 | $55

Fort Bragg | 418 N. Main St. (bet. Laurel & Pine Sts.) | 707-964-9800 | www.therestaurantfortbragg.com

Around "since 1973", this "neighborhood" "hidden gem" has been offering "surprisingly fine dining" in the "small town" of Fort Bragg; the husband-and-wife owners "provide outstanding service" along with "reliably good" (if not cheap) Eclectic–New American dinners in a "charming" dining room filled with "beautiful original oil paintings" by noted local artist Olaf Palm; P.S. closed Tuesday–Wednesday.

Restaurant at Stevenswood *American*
∇ 24 | 21 | 20 | $62

Little River | Stevenswood Lodge | 8211 Shoreline Hwy./N. Hwy. 1 (1 mi. south of Mendocino) | 707-937-2810 | www.stevenswood.com

Situated in a Little River forest resort on the Mendocino coast, this "beautiful" New American presents a "small" but "excellent" menu of "brilliantly prepared and presented" fare; the "intimate" woodsy dining room, overseen by a "kind" staff "gets all the details right" from a roaring fireplace to "lovely background dinner music" to "delicious" breakfasts that "go far beyond" the usual; P.S. dinner is not served Wednesdays.

Risibisi *Italian*
24 | 20 | 22 | $41

Petaluma | 154 Petaluma Blvd. N. (bet. Washington & Western Sts.) | 707-766-7600 | www.risibisirestaurant.com

Serving "satisfying and luxurious" dishes that are a "mashup of California and Italy", this "congenial" Petaluma ristorante features a "cozy", "intimate" space that makes it a "nice choice" for a "quiet, private tête-à-tête"; a "warm" staff that "works very hard to please you" seals the deal – and it's a "good value" to boot.

Rocker Oysterfeller's 🅼 *American/Southern*
∇ 25 | 18 | 22 | $40

Valley Ford | Valley Ford Hotel | 14415 Hwy. 1 (bet. Valley Ford Estero Rd. & School St.) | 707-876-1983 | www.rockeroysterfellers.com

Set in a restored roadside hotel, this "funky" Valley Ford saloon dishes out oysters, po' boys and other "heavenly" Southern comforts with the hospitality to match; it's a "favorite stop" en route to Bodega Bay whether you "eat in the bar" or "outside in the summer", particularly on Thursdays when they offer $1 Tomales Bays; P.S. dinner is served Thursday–Sunday and there's Saturday lunch and Sunday brunch.

Rosso Pizzeria & Mozzarella Bar *Italian/Pizza*   25 | 19 | 23 | $29
Petaluma | 151 Petaluma Blvd. S. (C St.) | 707-772-5177
Rosso Pizzeria & Wine Bar *Italian/Pizza*
Santa Rosa | Creekside Ctr. | 53 Montgomery Dr. (2nd St.) | 707-544-3221
www.rossopizzeria.com

They may be "hard to find", but these pizza tsars in Santa Rosa and Petaluma are "worth the search" for "awesome", "blistered" wood-fired pies made with "top-notch ingredients" and "cracker-thin" crusts; an "outstanding" list of "fairly priced" biodynamic wines and a "friendly, knowledgeable" staff add to the appeal of the "pretty basic" spots, as do "excellent daily specials" that "rarely miss a beat."

Royal Thai *Thai*   ▽ 26 | 19 | 23 | $26
San Rafael | 610 Third St. (Irwin St.) | 415-485-1074 |
www.royalthaisanrafael.com

"Unwavering" for some "three decades", this "pleasant, centrally located, old house" in San Rafael turns out "terrific Thai" that customers call the "best in Marin"; "you could throw a dart at the menu and not go wrong" with offerings like the "yummy pad Thai", curries and crêpes, all "at good prices" and served by a "pleasant, efficient" staff, all adding up to "a winner."

Rustic, Francis's Favorites *Italian*   21 | 25 | 23 | $45
Geyserville | Francis Ford Coppola Winery | 300 Via Archimedes (Souverain Rd.) | 707-857-1400 | www.franciscoppolawinery.com

The "delicious", "creative" Italian dishes, including wood-fired meats and Neapolitan pizzas, are outshined by an "amazing" setting "overlooking the valley and vineyards" at this Geyserville Italian by Francis Ford Coppola; accommodating service, a swimming pool and bocce court are part of the package, and it's "cool" to "see all of Coppola's film goodies" too.

Rutherford Grill *American*   24 | 21 | 23 | $41
Rutherford | 1180 Rutherford Rd. (Hwy. 29) | 707-963-1792 |
www.hillstone.com

Some of the "best comfort food in wine country" (including "knife-and-fork" ribs and "to-die-for" artichokes) and "no corkage fee" make it "hard to drive past" Rutherford's "hopping" member of the Hillstone chain – "high praise when you consider the area"; alas, there's often a "wait for a table", so insiders recommend passing the time sipping a glass from the "nicely priced" reserve wine list – and playing it cool "if a famous vintner is seated beside you at the bar."

Santé *Californian/French*   - | - | - | E
Sonoma | Fairmont Sonoma Mission Inn & Spa | 100 Boyes Blvd. (Sonoma Hwy.) | 707-939-2415 | www.fairmont.com

After a complete renovation, the flagship restaurant and adjacent lobby bar at The Fairmont Sonoma Mission Inn & Spa has reopened, presenting chef Bruno Tison's signature high-end wine country–inspired Cal-French fare along with a vast wine list (more than 500 Sonoma and Napa vinos); the updated dining room is more modern and relaxed, and the new alfresco Santé Terrace offers views on the pool and fire pits.

Sazon Peruvian Cuisine *Peruvian* ▽ 25 | 14 | 21 | $26

Santa Rosa | 1129 Sebastopol Rd. (bet. Burbank & Roseland Sts.) | 707-523-4346 | www.sazonsr.com

"Unique dishes with tons of South American flavor", including ceviches, draw "long lines" to this family-owned Santa Rosa Peruvian in a "small" "storefront" setting; service is generally good, and it's an affordable excursion rewarded with "bold" cooking that's a "great change" of pace.

Scoma's Sausalito *Seafood* 24 | 20 | 22 | $49

Sausalito | 588 Bridgeway (Princess St.) | 415-332-9551 | www.scomassausalito.com

See review in City of San Francisco Directory.

Scopa *Italian* 26 | 18 | 23 | $47

Healdsburg | 109 Plaza St. (bet. Center St. & Healdsburg Ave.) | 707-433-5282 | www.scopahealdsburg.com

"If you want to feel like a local in Healdsburg", make tracks to this "boisterous" Italian hidden "under an old barber shop sign" for "absolutely wonderful" "pizza, pasta and starters" that will "put a smile on your face"; it's "always packed" (so "make a reservation well ahead") and the "tiny, tiny" quarters mean tables are a "bit too tight", but a "delightful staff" smooths over any bumps; P.S. area vintners pour their latest on Winemaker Wednesdays.

Sea Modern Thai Ⓜ *Thai* 26 | 21 | 24 | $32

Petaluma | 500 Petaluma Blvd. S. (G St.) | 707-766-6633
Sea Thai Bistro *Thai*
Corte Madera | 60 Corte Madera (Redwood Ave.) | 415-927-8333 Ⓜ
Santa Rosa | 2323 Sonoma Ave. (Farmers Ln.) | 707-528-8333
www.seathaibistro.com

"Even if you're not that into Thai", fans say "you'll love" this "upscale" North Bay trio that whips up "fabulous" fusion fare with a "modern twist"; "wonderful, warm" service and "sleek" decor help ensure most "come back" for more "adventurous eating"; P.S. fish-phobes take note: the name is an abbreviation for "Southeast Asia."

𝐍𝐄𝐖 Sir & Star Ⓜ *American* - | - | - | M

Olema | Olema Inn | 10000 Sir Francis Drake Blvd. (Hwy. 1) | 415-663-1034 | www.sirandstar.com

Margaret Gradé and Daniel DeLong, the chefs at nearby Manka's Inverness Lodge, are behind this new, hyper-regional Californian with a midpriced menu showcasing ingredients and wines from West Marin (including a Saturday prix fixe); the historic roadhouse is outfitted with taxidermy birds and floor-to-ceiling windows overlooking the gardens.

Solbar *Californian* 26 | 24 | 24 | $58

Calistoga | Solage Resort | 755 Silverado Trail (bet. Brannan St. & Pickett Rd.) | 707-226-0850 | www.solagecalistoga.com

"Super wines" and an "inventive" Californian menu with "something for everybody" ("light for the spa crowd, and hearty for the rest") reveal the chef's French Laundry roots at this "beautiful" "poolside" spot at Calistoga's Solage Resort; inside the "trendy" interior, "young" "glitterati" are attended to by a "knowledgeable" staff, and while romantics profess there's "nothing better than dining on the patio", bottom-line sorts call the prices "most attractive."

Sol Food *Puerto Rican*

24 | 17 | 18 | $18

NEW **Mill Valley** | 401 Miller Ave. (La Goma St.) | 415-380-1986
San Rafael | 811 Fourth St. (bet. Cijos St. & Lincoln Ave.) | 415-451-4765
San Rafael | 901 Lincoln Ave. (3rd St.) | 415-451-4765 ◗
www.solfoodrestaurant.com

Even those who "hate waiting" "will wait" in the sometimes "block-long" lines at these Puerto Rican siblings in San Rafael and Mill Valley, where "consistently" excellent Latin fare includes "tender" chicken thighs (a "sure winner"), Cuban sandwiches and even "excellent" vegan food; "fast" servers sometimes field orders "in line", and while interiors are "not fancy", they're colorful and "comfortable"; P.S. the larger Lincoln Avenue location features live music and an adjacent take-out shop.

Sonoma-Meritage Martini Oyster Bar & Grille *Italian/Seafood*

▽ 19 | 17 | 19 | $43

Sonoma | 165 W. Napa St. (bet. 1st & 2nd Sts.) | 707-938-9430 | www.sonomameritage.com

"For good food and convivial company", locals head to this Northern Italian near Sonoma Plaza serving "well-prepared" fare and featuring oysters (half off during daily happy hours) and other seafood; as for the service and decor, the staff is "friendly and efficient" and the "hand-blown glass fixtures are beautiful."

Spoonbar *Californian*

20 | 23 | 20 | $45

Healdsburg | h2hotel | 219 Healdsburg Ave. (bet. Matheson & Mill Sts.) | 707-433-7222 | www.spoonbar.com

Injecting a little "urban hip" into "Sonoma wine country", this "ultra-modern" Californian in Downtown Healdsburg offers "imaginative", "locally sourced" cuisine, "wonderful cocktails", "friendly service" and a "super-fun atmosphere"; it's a great place to meet up "with friends", especially "in the summer when the windows/doors are open" giving the place "an alfresco feel no matter where you sit."

Stark's Steak & Seafood *Seafood/Steak*

25 | 23 | 22 | $54

Santa Rosa | 521 Adams St. (7th St.) | 707-546-5100 | www.starkrestaurants.com

Carnivores congregate at this "classic" American steak and seafood house with "vintage yet chic" decor, a "go-to spot for special celebrations" in Santa Rosa with "professional" service delivering "dry-aged" beef that "melts in your mouth" and "even better sides"; "it's pricey" alright, but thrifty types can economize at the "amazing happy hour", one of the "best values in town."

Station House Cafe *American*

18 | 15 | 18 | $30

Point Reyes Station | 11180 State Rte. 1 (Mesa Rd.) | 415-663-1515 | www.stationhousecafe.com

"Excellent oysters, burgers and fries" are some of the locally sourced American eats at this "old reliable" that's "perfect for a cool drink" and a bite "after a day of exploring" around Point Reyes Station; though a few diners are disappointed, citing fairly "average", midpriced food, others are appeased by "sitting in the garden" on sunny days and taking in "live music" Sunday evenings; P.S. closed Wednesdays.

St. Orres Restaurant *Californian*

▽ 23 | 26 | 22 | $65

Gualala | St. Orres Hotel | 36601 S. Hwy. 1 (Seaside School Rd.) | 707-884-3335 | www.saintorres.com

Chef/co-owner Rosemary Campiformio continues to ensure everyone is "happy" and well-fed at her "romantic" "Russian-domed" retreat nestled in the "coastal redwoods" of Gualala by delivering "creative" all-inclusive Californian dinners ("wild game dishes are a big favorite") matched by a "thoughtful local wine list"; sure, you'll pay today's prices to dine in a "throwback" "hippie atmosphere", but it's "well worth the trip" for the "unique setting" alone.

Sugo *Italian*

▽ 24 | 19 | 22 | $29

Petaluma | 5 Petaluma Blvd. S. (B St.) | 707-782-9298 | www.sugopetaluma.com

There's "something for everyone" at this "intimate" Petaluman proffering a "well-thought-out menu" of "excellent" Italian fare crafted from "fresh ingredients", plus most everything is made in-house; a "gracious" staff and "reasonable" prices keep patrons smiling in the "contemporary" space (think "cement floors and high ceilings"), as do the movies projected on a wall.

Super Duper *Burgers*

23 | 16 | 19 | $13

Mill Valley | 430 Miller Ave. (Evergreen Ave.) | 415-380-8555 | www.superdupersf.com

See review in City of San Francisco Directory.

Sushi Ran *Japanese*

27 | 22 | 24 | $61

Sausalito | 107 Caledonia St. (bet. Pine & Turney Sts.) | 415-332-3620 | www.sushiran.com

For nearly 30 years, this "authentic Japanese" has been "worth the trip to Sausalito" for its "exquisite-quality", "super-fresh" fish and "so much more" ("even the simplest seafood soba is beauty in a bowl") deftly served in a "serene" setting; "come early" to nab "one of six seats at the sushi bar" or have lunch at the adjacent wine bar with a sake list that's "beyond comparison" – just bank on "spending a pretty penny or two" for an "unforgettable meal."

🆕 Taverna Sofia *Greek/Mediterranean*

– | – | – | M

Healdsburg | 244 Healdsburg Ave. (Matheson St.) | 707-431-1982 | www.tavernasofia.com

Expect "pleasant surprises" at this casual Healdsburg taverna where Greek-born chef-owner Sofia Petridis-Lim relies on a combination of imported and locally sourced organic ingredients to create a midpriced Mediterranean menu including meze, salads, gyros and entrees capped off with fresh-baked sweet pastries; the petite, "bright", white-walled dining room, tucked away behind Copperfield Books, is "fairly plain", but a charming patio painted with a mural of Santorini beckons on sunny days and warm evenings.

Tavern at Lark Creek *American*

21 | 24 | 22 | $43

Larkspur | 234 Magnolia Ave. (Madrone Ave.) | 415-924-7766 | www.tavernatlarkcreek.com

Today's "more casual" "reincarnation of the old" Lark Creek Inn in Larkspur remains a "Marin County favorite" for "family celebrations", while the "sunny" Victorian digs have become "increasingly popular" for its "dependable" New American "tavern food" and "incredible" desserts; "it's a tad more affordable" too, and though service varies, "the atmosphere is unbeatable", particularly outside for "Sunday brunch."

Terra *American*   27 | 25 | 27 | $91

St. Helena | 1345 Railroad Ave. (bet. Adams St. & Hunt Ave.) | 707-963-8931 | www.terrarestaurant.com

Since 1988, Hiro Sone and Lissa Doumani (also of Ame) have made this "original" St. Helena "treasure" "one of the best places to eat in the wine country", thanks to "complex", "distinctive" and downright "amazing" New American tasting menus (his), "to die for" pastries (hers) and an "excellent wine list"; all's presided over by an "impeccable" staff in an "elegant and comfortable" stone farmhouse, while diners desiring à la carte options can find them at the restaurant's Bar Terra next door.

Terrapin Creek Ⓜ *Californian*   ∇ 27 | 20 | 25 | $45

Bodega Bay | 1580 Eastshore Rd. (Hwy. 1) | 707-875-2700 | www.terrapincreekcafe.com

It's "worth the drive out to Bodega Bay" to this "real jewel" that "brings in the crowds" thanks to "utterly charming" chef-owners who "work the floor" and prepare "exceptional", "adventurous" Californian fare "with none of the pretension" or tabs you'd expect; it's a "relaxing" setting with a small patio, and all "so good it's almost a pleasure to pay"; P.S. open Thursday–Sunday.

Tex Wasabi's Rock-N-Roll   19 | 18 | 19 | $34
Sushi-BBQ *BBQ/Japanese*

Santa Rosa | 515 Fourth St. (B St.) | 707-544-8399 | www.texwasabis.com

Popular Food Networker Guy Fieri churns out "unique" "Asian-BBQ fusion" (i.e. "pork sliders and ribs" share the menu with sushi) at this Santa Rosa branch of his modestly priced franchise; the "slick, dark" space attracts fans with "friends and family" who imbibe "yummy drinks", and though some snap it's "more hype than substance", others "get a kick out of it."

The Thomas & Fagiani's Bar ◑ *American*   ∇ 24 | 26 | 23 | $51

Napa | 813 Main St. (3rd St.) | 707-226-7821 | www.thethomas-napa.com

In a setting that's done an "incredible job bringing the old back into the new", this upscale, multilevel Napa locale provides multiple experiences; on the second floor, chef Brad Farmerie (NYC's Public and Saxon + Parole) delivers "visually appealing" American dishes with a "great flavor balance", while the ground-floor bar offers "well-crafted cocktails poured by knowledgeable bartenders" and the rooftop overlooking the river hosts some of the "best terrace dining" in Downtown Napa.

Toast *American*   21 | 16 | 19 | $22

Mill Valley | 31 Sunnyside Ave. (bet. Blithedale & Miller Aves.) | 415-388-2500 | www.toastmillvalley.com
Novato | Hamilton Mktpl. | 5800 Nave Dr. (bet. Hamilton Pkwy. & Roblar Dr.) | 415-382-1144 | www.toastnovato.com

"Just what you want in a neighborhood diner" – "ample portions" of "good ol' American" eats served all day long at "bargain" prices – is what patrons find at this Mill Valley locale and its larger Novato off-

	FOOD	DECOR	SERVICE	COST

shoot; service can be iffy and reviews are mixed on the toast-inspired decor (with pockmarked walls on Nave Drive resembling actual bread), but the lively, "friendly" atmosphere makes it a suitable (if sometimes "noisy") spot to take the "kids."

Tra Vigne *Italian* | 24 | 25 | 23 | $56 |

St. Helena | 1050 Charter Oak Ave. (Main St.) | 707-963-4444 | www.travignerestaurant.com

"There's a reason" this St. Helena Tuscan "treasure" has "been around forever" – it's the "wine country–casual" setting (complete with "delightful" courtyard), servers who "know their stuff" and an "inventive menu" starring "delicious" Northern Italian *cucina* crafted from "fresh local ingredients"; it can be a "little pricey", but the fact there's "no corkage fee" on the first bottle is a "big plus", enabling even spend-thrifts to declare it's "worth the trip."

NEW The Trident *American/Seafood* ▽ | 22 | 26 | 22 | $38 |

Sausalito | 558 Bridgeway (bet. Princess & Richardson Sts.) | 415-331-3232 | www.thetridentsausalito.com

"The setting alone is iconic", having been a rock club and hippie hangout going back to the '60s, but now the main attractions are "wonderful", moderately priced seafood and other American dishes, a "great" preserved interior and one of the "best views in Sausalito"; with a "caring staff", "lively" scene and live music Thursday–Saturday, it's a "favorite" when you want to "enjoy a nice meal, relax" and "watch the boats go by."

Underwood Bar & Bistro  *Mediterranean* | 22 | 21 | 22 | $41 |

Graton | 9113 Graton Rd. (Edison St.) | 707-823-7023 | www.underwoodgraton.com

"After a day" in Sonoma County, this "charming" bistro in "out-of-the-way" Graton is "well worth" seeking out for "unpretentious", reasonably priced Mediterranean fare – and perhaps some fancy cocktails at the "terrific bar"; the "cozy" digs can get "noisy and busy" "even at lunch, when the local wine growers get into their product", but "exceptional service" and late-night hours are pluses.

Uva Trattoria Italiana Ⓜ *Italian* | 19 | 19 | 21 | $35 |

Napa | 1040 Clinton St. (bet. Brown & Main Sts.) | 707-255-6646 | www.uvatrattoria.com

"Great" free "live music" is in the air and "decent" Italian chow (pasta, pizza, etc.) on the plates at this Downtown Napa eatery with an "energetic" vibe; "friendly" servers add to the appeal, as do "reasonable" tabs aided by a BYO policy that waives the corkage on the first bottle.

Volpi's Ristorante & Bar Ⓜ *Italian* ▽ | 22 | 19 | 21 | $32 |

Petaluma | 124 Washington St. (bet. Keller St. & Telephone Alley) | 707-762-2371

Peddling "hearty portions" of "family-style" classics, this "old-world Italian joint" in Petaluma is a "throwback in every way" – and "satisfies" with "every cliché" in the process, from the "checkered tablecloths" to the "speakeasy"-like "bar in back"; "you'll be stuffed when you leave", and the "friendly staff" even busts out "accordion music frequently" to round out the "down-home charm."

	FOOD	DECOR	SERVICE	COST

Water Street Bistro *French*
▽ 23 | 18 | 21 | $28

Petaluma | 100 Petaluma Blvd. N. (Western Ave.) | 707-763-9563 | www.waterstreetbistro.net

"Don't let the low price fool you" – this "terrific local" cafe run by a "wonderful chef"-owner is *the* Petaluma stop for breakfast and lunch", offering "fresh, seasonal" French-inflected fare served by a "knowledgeable staff"; specials frequently "get sold out", and since the "super-homey" setting can get a "bit cramped", regulars vie for tables "on the riverside patio"; P.S. monthly Saturday night dinners require reservations.

Willi's Seafood & Raw Bar *Seafood*
25 | 21 | 21 | $44

Healdsburg | 403 Healdsburg Ave. (North St.) | 707-433-9191 | www.willisseafood.net

"Seafood lovers" descend upon this Healdsburg "pearl" for small bites of "fresh, local" fish, "lobster rolls to die for" and selections from a "great raw bar" (all complemented by "a wine list to match"); "friendly, efficient" servers work the "airy" dining space and "lively bar", but those "tasty" tapas, bivalves and libations can "add up to a hefty check."

Willi's Wine Bar *Eclectic*
25 | 20 | 23 | $47

Santa Rosa | 4404 Old Redwood Hwy. (Ursuline Rd.) | 707-526-3096 | www.williswinebar.net

Despite its "roadhouse" "exterior", locals insist this Eclectic "Santa Rosa gem outshines many of its Napa Valley rivals" with "truly exceptional", "innovative" "small plates" and "memorable" wine pairings; it gets "crowded and noisy", and those "tiny" tidbits "can easily" add up "to a big bill", but it's still an "utterly charming place to pop in for a drink and a bite", especially on the "lovely" patio.

Willow Wood
Market Cafe *Eclectic/Mediterranean*
24 | 20 | 19 | $28

Graton | 9020 Graton Rd. (Edison St.) | 707-823-0233 | www.willowwoodgraton.com

Cranking out possibly "the best brunch/lunch for many miles around", this "adorable" "off-the-beaten-path" country store/cafe with a "nice patio" in Graton is a "great casual place" to "meet and greet in Western Sonoma County"; "despite slightly cramped quarters", the midpriced Eclectic-Med eats are "not your typical boring" choices, and it's a "reliable" alternative to sister Underwood.

Wine Spectator Greystone *Californian*
23 | 23 | 22 | $53

St. Helena | Culinary Institute of America | 2555 Main St. (bet. Deer Park Rd. & Pratt Ave.) | 707-967-1010 | www.ciachef.edu

Home to the CIA in St. Helena, this "beautiful" stone building is "a very special place", where "students" and "seasoned chefs" work side-by-side in an "open kitchen" to turn out "imaginative", "well-prepared" Californian fare that's paired with "playful wine flights"; it's "pricey" considering "it's a training ground" for waiters and cooks, but "lunch on the patio with views of the local vineyards makes any visit to Napa Valley a treat."

Wurst Restaurant *American/Pub Food*
▽ 21 | 15 | 19 | $18

Healdsburg | 22 Matheson St. (Healdsburg Ave.) | 707-395-0214

Fans of wurst call this "sausage heaven" and American pub "the best" thanks to the "Midwest"-made and local dogs (plus a burger that's "da

218

bomb") that are a welcome antidote to Healdsburg's usual "overpriced eats"; it's an "extremely casual", "friendly" spot to "relax and have a beer and a brat", and "when the weather's good" the patio gets "jammed."

Yankee Pier *New England/Seafood* | 19 | 16 | 19 | $35 |

Larkspur | 286 Magnolia Ave. (bet. King St. & William Ave.) | 415-924-7676 | www.yankeepier.com

"Fresh, sustainable" seafood served in a "casual" atmosphere is the hallmark of these "kid-friendly" local chain links in Larkspur and Lafayette; while believers savor the "New England clam shack" fare (including "must-try" lobster rolls and chowder), skeptics call the offerings "pricey for what you get" but the SFO branch "makes a flight delay quite nice."

Zazu M *American/Italian* | 26 | 20 | 24 | $51 |

Sebastopol | 6770 McKinley St. (Willowside Rd.) | 707-523-4814 | www.zazurestaurant.com

Moving from its former Santa Rosa "roadhouse" to larger Sebastopol digs at The Barlow food community center, this "farm-to-table" specialist plans to continue dishing out an "adventurous" New American-Northern Italian menu that'll "knock your socks off", complemented by a "killer" "Sonoma-centric" wine list, all courtesy of chef-owners Duskie Estes and John Stewart (aka "the king and queen of pork"); expect a perhaps even more "convivial" vibe, given the addition of cocktails from a full bar; P.S. scores do not reflect post-move changes.

Zin *American* | 23 | 20 | 23 | $45 |

Healdsburg | 344 Center St. (North St.) | 707-473-0946 | www.zinrestaurant.com

"Consistently delicious", "imaginative" New American fare featuring homegrown produce and housemade condiments comes with a "great wine selection" at this Healdsburg local "favorite"; the "casual, attentive staff" keeps things "cozy" in an "industrial" setting that can get "noisy", but prices are "reasonable in an overpriced neighborhood" and patrons return "again and again."

ZuZu *Spanish* | 24 | 20 | 23 | $44 |

Napa | 829 Main St. (bet. 2nd & 3rd Sts.) | 707-224-8555 | www.zuzunapa.com

Situated on Napa's Riverfront, this "cozy" Spaniard "standby" with a "really nice" staff offers "well-executed tapas" and "outstanding" wines ("many Spanish" varietals "along with Napa bottles") in a "relaxed, casual atmosphere"; it's neither "fine dining" nor cheap, but devotees dub it a "find" that's "well worth" the sometimes "long wait"; P.S. no reservations.

SOUTH OF SAN FRANCISCO

Top Food

28	Sierra Mar	*Cal./Eclectic*
	Cafe Gibraltar	*Med.*
	Evvia	*Greek*
27	La Forêt	*Continental/French*
	Manresa	*American*
	Le Papillon	*French*
	Passionfish	*Cal./Seafood*
26	Marinus	*Californian/French*
	Sent Sovi	*Californian*
	Flea St. Café	*Californian*
	Mingalaba	*Burmese/Chinese*
	Alexander's	*Japanese/Steak*
	Aubergine	*Californian*
	All Spice	*Indian*
	Bistro Moulin	*Euro.*
	Nick's Next Door	*American*
	Baumé	*French*
25	La Costanera	*Peruvian*
	Station 1	*Californian*
	Tamarine	*Vietnamese*

Refuge | *Belgian/Sandwiches*
Roy's at Pebble Beach | *Haw.*
Stella Alpina Osteria | *Italian*
Chantilly | *French/Italian*
Pasta Moon | *Italian*
Sumika | *Japanese*
Ramen Dojo |
    Japanese/Noodle Shop
John Bentley's | *American*
Village Pub | *American*
Plumed Horse | *Californian*
Gochi Japanese | *Japanese*
Dio Deka | *Greek*
Ike's Place | *Sandwiches*
Orenchi Ramen | *Japanese*

24 Jin Sho | *Japanese*
Navio | *American*
Anton & Michel | *Continental*
Bella Vista | *Continental*
Vung Tau | *Vietnamese*
Sushi Sam's Edomata | *Japanese*

Top Decor

29 Sierra Mar

28 Navio
Pacific's Edge
Marinus

27 Roy's at Pebble Beach

26 Shadowbrook Restaurant
Nepenthe
Restaurant at Ventana
Evvia
La Forêt

Manresa

25 Quattro Restaurant & Bar
La Costanera
Madera
Alexander's
Chantilly
Plumed Horse
Aubergine

24 Dio Deka
Anton & Michel

Top Service

27 Sierra Mar
Marinus
Manresa
Baumé
La Forêt*

26 Cafe Gibraltar
Navio
Chantilly
Evvia
Alexander's

Le Papillon
All Spice

25 John Bentley's
Aubergine
Sent Sovi
Bistro Moulin
Station 1
Anton & Michel
Flea St. Café
Quattro Restaurant & Bar

---

* Indicates a tie with restaurant above; excludes places with low votes

TOPS BY CUISINE

AMERICAN
27 Manresa
26 Nick's Next Door
25 John Bentley
   Village Pub
24 Navio

ASIAN
26 Mingalaba
25 Tamarine
24 Vung Tau
23 Koi Palace
   Tai Pan

CALIFORNIAN
28 Sierra Mar
27 Passionfish
26 Marinus
   Sent Sovi
   Flea St. Café

FRENCH
27 La Forêt
   Le Papillon
26 Marinus
   Baumé
25 Chantilly

INDIAN
26 All Spice
24 Saravana Bhavan
   Amber India
23 Roti Indian Bistro
   Shalimar

ITALIAN
25 Stella Alpina Osteria
   Chantilly
   Pasta Moon
24 A Bellagio
   Casanova

JAPANESE
26 Alexander's
25 Sumika
   Ramen Dojo
   Gochi Japanese
   Orenchi Ramen

MED./GREEK
28 Cafe Gibraltar
   Evvia
25 Dio Deka
23 Cetrella
22 71 Saint Peter

MEXICAN
24 La Victoria Taqueria
   Tacolicious
23 Taqueria San Jose
   El Farolito
   Pancho Villa

SEAFOOD
27 Passionfish
24 Flying Fish Grill
   Sardine Factory
23 Old Port Lobster
   Koi Palace

TOPS BY SPECIAL FEATURE

BREAKFAST/BRUNCH
27 La Forêt
24 Navio
   Gayle's Bakery
   Big Sur Bakery
23 Madera

OUTDOOR SEATING
28 Sierra Mar
25 Roy's at Pebble Beach
24 Casanova
23 Madera
22 Sam's Chowder

PEOPLE-WATCHING
28 Evvia
25 Tamarine
   Village Pub
23 Madera
19 Sino

ROMANCE
28 Sierra Mar
27 La Forêt
   Le Papillon
26 Marinus
22 Shadowbrook Restaurant

SINGLES SCENES
25 Tamarine
23 Blowfish Sushi
22 Cascal
20 Straits
19 Sino

SMALL PLATES

25 Tamarine
Gochi Japanese
22 Cascal
20 Straits
19 Sino

VIEWS

28 Sierra Mar
27 La Forêt

25 La Costanera
Roy's at Pebble Beach
24 Pacific's Edge

WINNING WINE LISTS

28 Sierra Mar
27 Passionfish
26 Marinus
25 Plumed Horse
23 Madera

TOPS BY LOCATION

CARMEL/MONTEREY

26 Marinus
Aubergine
Bistro Moulin
24 Anton & Michel
Flying Fish Grill

HALF MOON BAY/COAST

28 Cafe Gibraltar
25 La Costanera
Pasta Moon
24 Navio
23 Caffè Mezza Luna

LOS GATOS/SARATOGA

27 Manresa
26 Sent Sovi
Nick's Next Door
25 Plumed Horse
Dio Deka

MENLO PARK/PALO ALTO

28 Evvia
26 Flea St. Café
Baumé
25 Tamarine
Refuge

PENINSULA

26 Mingalaba
All Spice
25 Refuge
Stella Alpina Osteria
Chantilly

SANTA CRUZ/CAPITOLA

24 Gayle's Bakery
22 Shadowbrook Restaurant
20 Gabriella Café
19 Café Gratitude

Visit zagat.com

Best Buys

Top-rated food $25 and under

1. Mingalaba | *Burmese/Chinese*
2. Refuge | *Belgian/Sandwiches*
3. Ramen Dojo | *Japanese/Noodle Shop*
4. Ike's Place | *Sandwiches*
5. Orenchi Ramen | *Japanese*
6. Vung Tau | *Vietnamese*
7. Dishdash | *Mideastern*
8. Gayle's Bakery | *Bakery*
9. Saravana Bhavan | *Indian*
10. La Victoria Taqueria | *Mexican*
11. Tacolicious | *Mexican*
12. Applewood Pizza | *Pizza*
13. Taqueria San Jose | *Mexican*
14. El Farolito | *Mexican*
15. In-N-Out | *Burgers*
16. Pancho Villa Taqueria | *Mexican*
17. Shalimar | *Indian/Pakistani*
18. Cheese Steak Shop | *Cheesestks.*
19. Patxi's Pizza | *Pizza*
20. Umami Burger | *Burgers*

BEST BUYS BY NEIGHBORHOOD

BURLINGAME/SAN MATEO

26	Mingalaba
25	Ramen Dojo
23	Pancho Villa Taqueria
22	La Corneta
21	La Boulange

MENLO PARK/PALO ALTO

25	Refuge
24	Tacolicious
23	Applewood Pizza
22	Patxi's Pizza
	Umami Burger

MOUNTAIN VIEW/SUNNYVALE

24	Dishdash
	Saravana Bhavan
23	In-N-Out
	Shalimar
22	Cheese Steak Shop

SAN JOSE/SANTA CLARA

25	Ike's Place
	Orenchi Ramen
24	Vung Tau
	La Victoria Taqueria
23	Taqueria San Jose

South of San Francisco

A Bellagio *Italian*   24 | 21 | 23 | $40

Campbell | 33 S. Central Ave. (Orchard City Dr.) | 408-370-7705 | www.abellagio.com

"Slightly old-school with modern sensibilities", this "truly Italian" Campbell trattoria has an "on-point" staff delivering "beautifully plated entrees" in a setting where locals "can actually have a conversation without shouting"; adding to the allure, prices are considered "reasonable" and you can even hit "the terrace with a glass of wine."

Acqua Pazza Ⓜ *Italian*   21 | 19 | 22 | $35

San Mateo | 201 E. Third Ave. (Ellsworth Ave.) | 650-375-0903 | www.acqua-pazza.com

"Authentic" Italian "classics" are on offer at this "reasonably priced" San Mateo trattoria owned by three brothers from Naples; "friendly" servers help create a "warm", "homey feel" in the "lively" bi-level space, so even if a few find the cooking "uninspired", most agree it's generally a "pleasant place to be."

Alexander's Steakhouse *Japanese/Steak*   26 | 25 | 26 | $92

Cupertino | Vallco Shopping Ctr. | 10330 N. Wolfe Rd. (bet. Rte. 280 & Steven's Creek Blvd.) | 408-446-2222 | www.alexanderssteakhouse.com

"Huge" portions of "awesome aged meats" are "grilled to perfection" at this "posh" "temple" to beef that "raises the bar" for carnivores in Cupertino and SoMa; it fuses "Japanese cuisine" with a "classic steakhouse" and service is "exemplary", though diners who haven't "launched a successful IPO" can suffer "sticker shock" from the "über-pricey" tab; P.S. The Sea by Alexander's Steakhouse is in Palo Alto.

All Spice Ⓩ Ⓜ *Indian*   26 | 24 | 26 | $49

San Mateo | 1602 S. El Camino Real (Borel Ave.) | 650-627-4303 | www.allspicerestaurant.com

The menu "sounds so interesting you want to try it all" say devotees of the "exotic", "imaginative" and "delightful" dishes crafted by chef Sachin Chopra at this San Mateo Californian-Indian he runs with his wife, the "gracious and welcoming" Shoshana; a "charming" Victorian house setting with a fireplace and a dash of spice-inspired colors completes the "unique" experience dubbed a "terrific value."

Amarin Thai Cuisine *Thai*   21 | 18 | 18 | $23

Mountain View | 174 Castro St. (bet. Evelyn Ave. & Villa St.) | 650-988-9323 | www.amarinthaicuisine.com

"Consistently good" fare makes this "popular" Mountain View Thai a "go-to" for curries that are "simmered-to-perfection" and other "authentic" dishes made with "well-balanced and flavorful sauces"; service gets mixed marks ("friendly" vs. "flaky") and it can feel "congested" during "rush hour", but "reasonable prices" still ensure it's a "favorite."

Amber Dhara *Indian*   24 | 21 | 21 | $36

Palo Alto | 150 University Ave. (High St.) | 650-329-9644

(continued)

Amber India *Indian*
Mountain View | Olive Tree Shopping Ctr. | 2290 W. El Camino Real (bet. Ortega & Rengstorff Aves.) | 650-968-7511
San Jose | Santana Row | 377 Santana Row (Olsen Dr.) | 408-248-5400

Amber Café *Indian*
Mountain View | 600 W. El Camino Real (View St.) | 650-968-1751
www.amber-india.com

"Excellent" Northern Indian fare makes taste buds "happy" at these midpriced curry outposts known for "outstanding" butter chicken and other "typical dishes prepared with great flavors" and "fabulous" sauces – arguably "best" sampled at the "awesome" lunch buffet at most locations; they tend to draw "crowds" while still offering "attentive" service and decor that ranges from "low-key" (the Café) to "colorful but modern" (Mission) to "Raj fine" (SoMa).

Amici's East Coast Pizzeria *Pizza* | 21 | 16 | 19 | $22 |
Cupertino | 10310 S. De Anza Blvd. (Town Center Ln.) | 408-252-3333
Menlo Park | 880 Santa Cruz Ave. (Evelyn St.) | 650-329-8888
Mountain View | 790 Castro St. (High School Way) | 650-961-6666
Redwood Shores | 226 Redwood Shores Pkwy. (Shoreline Dr.) | 650-654-3333
San Jose | 225 W. Santa Clara St. (Almaden Ave.) | 408-289-9000
San Mateo | 69 E. Third Ave. (bet. El Camino Real & San Mateo Dr.) | 650-342-9392
www.amicis.com
See review in City of San Francisco Directory.

Andre's Bouchée *French* | 24 | 22 | 23 | $58 |
(fka Bouchée)
Carmel | Mission St. (bet. Ocean & 7th Aves.) | 831-626-7880 | www.andresbouchee.com

"A cut above the average", this "French family-owned-and-operated" bistro and wine bar remains "one of the nicest places to eat" in Carmel; the "intimate, inviting atmosphere" sets the stage for enjoying monsieur Andre Lemaire's "fabulously traditional" Gallic fare paired with a "stellar wine list and sommelier" and proffered by "friendly, attentive" garçons.

Anton & Michel Restaurant *Continental* | 24 | 24 | 25 | $60 |
Carmel | Mission St. (bet. Ocean & 7th Aves.) | 831-624-2406 | www.antonandmichel.com

This "elegant", "old-school" Carmel Continental has been serving "deliciously straightforward" fare for more than 30 years in a "lovely old-world setting" replete with "pretty fountains" and working fireplaces; some say the "expert" staff is "stuffy", while others counter "who can resist" the "dining room theater" of "tableside cooking" including rack of lamb, Caesar salad and "flaming desserts"?

Applewood Pizza *Pizza* | 23 | 13 | 17 | $19 |
Menlo Park | 1001 El Camino Real (Ravenswood Ave.) | 650-324-3486 | www.applewoodpizza.com

"Classic sauces", "lots of cheese" and "flavorful toppings in interesting combinations" result in "fully loaded" pies that "satisfy all taste buds" at this "reasonably priced" Menlo Park pizzeria; yes, the "decor leaves something to be desired" and service "could be

FOOD DECOR SERVICE COST

better", but its "selection of beers is hard to match" and prices are quite "reasonable" too.

Arcadia *American*
23 | 21 | 22 | $57

San Jose | San Jose Marriott | 100 W. San Carlos St. (Market St.) | 408-278-4555 | www.michaelmina.net

"Standard upscale" steakhouse fare gets a boost from "well-prepared" New American offerings (lobster pot pie, lamb sliders, charcuterie) at this "opulent" San Jose Marriott eatery from Michael Mina; "attentive" service and "modern" decor add "date"-night appeal, but "bring your credit card" as tabs are a "bit pricey."

Asian Box *Asian*
▽ 19 | 15 | 18 | $14

NEW **Mountain View** | 142 Castro St. (Central Expwy.) | 650-584-3947
Palo Alto | Town & Country Vill. | 855 El Camino Real (Embarcadero Rd.) | 650-391-9305
www.asianboxpaloalto.com

Grace Nguyen (ex Slanted Door) and husband Chad Newton (ex Fish & Farm) peddle "really good", affordable, sustainable Asian street food at these take-out/eat-in/fast-casual eateries in a Palo Alto shopping center and in Mountain View; everything is gluten-free and customizable with a choice of proteins, fixin's and housemade sauces (including the "very hot Hot Box It"), and washed down with Vietnamese iced coffee; P.S. a branch is planned for Macy's Union Square.

Asian Pearl Seafood Restaurant *Chinese*
22 | 17 | 18 | $30

Millbrae | 1671 El Camino Real (bet. Park Blvd. & Park Pl.) | 650-616-8288
The portions are "big" and the dim sum "creative" at this Millbrae Chinese turning out "tasty", "traditional" cuisine delivered by "friendly" (if "slow") servers; some find the decor "lackluster" and note it can get "noisy" (it's "not a date place"), but "affordable" tabs help.

Attic ⌧Ⓜ *Asian*
▽ 20 | 18 | 19 | $31

San Mateo | 234 S. B St. (bet. 2nd & 3rd Aves.) | 650-342-4506 | www.atticrestaurant.com

Locals contend "San Mateo needs more eateries like this" "slightly trendy" Pan-Asian "tucked above" its own "hopping" bar (Under Attic) where revelers can enjoy "great happy-hour drink specials" "before going upstairs" to the main dining room and its "friendly" crew proffering an "interesting mix" of "solid", midpriced "modern" Filipino and Pan-Asian eats; those who've tried it have been "pleasantly surprised."

Aubergine *Californian*
26 | 25 | 25 | $127
(aka L'Auberge Carmel)

Carmel | L'Auberge Carmel | Monte Verde St. (7th Ave.) | 831-624-8578 | www.laubergecarmel.com

"Nothing else comes close" to this "intimate" Carmel Relais & Châteaux "treasure" that's "wonderful in every way", where "truly gifted chef" Justin Cogley crafts "extraordinarily creative", "gorgeous" Californian tasting menus emphasizing "fresh and local ingredients"; "portions are still small" (as is the remodeled jewel-box setting), and "second mortgages might be needed to pay the tab", but the "refined service" enhanced with "spot-on wine parings" from a "stunning" list "rounds out an incredible" "special-occasion dining experience" that's "worth it."

NEW Bantam 🗷 *Californian/Pizza*
— | — | — | M

Santa Cruz | 1010 Fair Ave. | 831-420-0101 |
www.bantam1010.com

This popular husband-and-wife–run Santa Cruz bistro from Chez Panisse and Avanti alums puts an upscale twist on moderately priced seasonal Californian dishes, offering a regularly changing menu of wood-fired pizzas and Mediterranean-influenced starters, salads and entrees incorporating fresh, organic ingredients; the roomy restaurant feels even bigger than it is thanks to open-beamed ceilings and plenty of natural light.

Barbara's Fishtrap 🗷 *Seafood*
21 | 14 | 18 | $25

Princeton by the Sea | 281 Capistrano Rd. (Pacific Coast Hwy.) |
650-728-7049 | www.barbarasfishtrap.com

A "fresh seafood shack, with the emphasis on shack", this "perennial favorite" in Princeton by the Sea dishes out reasonably priced chowder, fish 'n' chips and "everything fried"; though there's "usually a line" ("get there by 11 AM" to "beat the senior crowd"), "the wait isn't too long", and "you can walk by the water" or order from the take-out window for "outdoor picnic table seating"; P.S. cash only.

The Basin *American*
23 | 20 | 23 | $46

Saratoga | 14572 Big Basin Way (5th St.) | 408-867-1906 |
www.thebasin.com

"Kudos" go to this "popular" Saratoga American for its "commitment to sustainable seafood" and organic ingredients plus a "great staff to match"; the menu offers enough "intriguing twists" to keep things "interesting", and if the "cozy" setting gets "a bit loud", the outdoor patio makes an "excellent" choice on a "warm summer night."

Basque Cultural Center 🖾 *French*
20 | 15 | 20 | $31

South San Francisco | Basque Cultural Ctr. | 599 Railroad Ave. (bet. Orange & Spruce Aves.) | 650-583-8091 | www.basqueculturalcenter.com

"For a wonderful cross-cultural experience", "watch jai alai", "enjoy the company of families from the old country" and dig into "huge quantities of very good", "hearty", "family-style" fare served with "big drinks" at this "authentic" Basque "club" in South SF; service is "a bit slow" and it's a little "short on atmosphere", but "high on value" and "fun for a group."

Baumé 🗷🖾 *French*
26 | 23 | 27 | $218

Palo Alto | 201 S. California Ave. (Park Blvd.) | 650-328-8899 |
www.baumerestaurant.com

Bruno Chemel adds a playful touch to the "haute" prix fixe menus at this "imaginative" Palo Alto New French, where "artful and sculptural" dishes that are "clearly labor intensive" can turn diners "from skeptic to fan" with their "intense flavors"; pampered guests declare the "extra special" service and modern space a "treat", just prepare for "very expensive" price tags to match; P.S. open Wednesday–Saturday.

Bella Vista 🗷🖾 *Continental*
24 | 23 | 23 | $59

Woodside | 13451 Skyline Blvd. (5 mi. south of Rte. 92) | 650-851-1229 |
www.bvrestaurant.com

"Tucked away among redwoods", this "romantic", "elegant" Woodside Continental is a "special place" where "outstanding", "old-school"

FOOD DECOR SERVICE COST

fare is ferried by "delightful servers" who help navigate the "impressive" wine list; score "a table by the window" and enjoy the "stunning views" at this "slice of history"; P.S. don't miss the "flawless" dessert soufflés.

Big Sur Bakery &

24 | 17 | 20 | $34

Restaurant *American/Bakery*

Big Sur | 47540 Hwy. 1 (½ mi. south of Pfeiffer State Park) | 831-667-0520 | www.bigsurbakery.com

"A fun place to stop on your way to Big Sur", this "low-key" roadside bakery/restaurant may be known for its "really wonderful" "desserts and pastries", but its "limited" yet "creative" American "comfort-food" menu, including "wood-fired pizzas", is "surprisingly good" too; the indoor/outdoor setting is "rustic" and service is "laid-back", but it offers some of the "best value" around; P.S. no dinner on Mondays.

🆕 Big Sur Roadhouse

- | - | - | M

Restaurant *Cajun/Seafood*

Big Sur | Big Sur Roadhouse | 47080 Hwy. 1 (Pfieffer Rd.) | 831-667-2370 | www.bigsurroadhouse.com

Bringing a taste of NOLA to the PCH, this ambitious all-day roadhouse in Big Sur turns out midpriced coastal Cajun cuisine (think po' boys, seafood gumbo and blackened fish with ingredients sourced from local farmers); the sprawling indoor-outdoor setting includes an airy open dining room and lounge area outfitted with artisanal fixtures and recycled materials, plus two alfresco patios where guests can enjoy the likes of Abita beer or a glass of wine by the fire pits.

Bistro Moulin *European*

26 | 19 | 25 | $47

Monterey | 867 Wave St. (bet. David & Irving Aves.) | 831-333-1200 | www.bistromoulin.com

Providing a "quaint break" from the "nearby Cannery Row" tourist joints, this "charming" European spot "run by the chef and his wife" is the locals' "go-to" place for a "nice dinner out" in Monterey; the "intimate" space may be otherwise "nondescript", but the "fantastic" bistro fare and "excellent" wines, delivered by "an attentive and well-informed" staff, ensure it's "always a treat."

Blowfish Sushi To Die For *Japanese*

23 | 20 | 18 | $41

San Jose | Santana Row | 355 Santana Row (bet. Olin Ave. & Tatum Ln.) | 408-345-3848 | www.blowfishsushi.com

See review in City of San Francisco Directory.

Burger Joint *Burgers*

19 | 15 | 17 | $15

South San Francisco | San Francisco Int'l Airport | Domestic Terminal 2 (Hwy. 101) | 650-821-0582

South San Francisco | San Francisco Int'l Airport | Int'l Terminal, Boarding Area A (Hwy. 101) | 650-821-0582

www.burgerjointsf.com

See review in City of San Francisco Directory.

BurgerMeister *Burgers*

20 | 15 | 17 | $16

Daly City | Westlake Shopping Ctr. | 507 Westlake Ctr. (bet. John Daly Blvd. & Southgate Ave.) | 650-755-1941 | www.burgermeistersf.com

See review in City of San Francisco Directory.

	FOOD	DECOR	SERVICE	COST

Café Brioche *Californian/French* — 21 | 17 | 19 | $32

Palo Alto | 445 S. California Ave. (bet. Ash St. & El Camino Real) | 650-326-8640 | www.cafebrioche-paloalto.com

A "tasty", "something-for-everyone" menu that's part "country French" and part Californian draws a "loyal local clientele" to this "busy" Palo Alto cafe; with "warm" (if occasionally "slow") service, "cozy", "bistro" surrounds and "reasonable prices", it's a "go-to" for a "nice brunch with friends" or a "casual date night."

Cafe Gibraltar ☒ *Mediterranean* — 28 | 24 | 26 | $45

El Granada | 425 Ave. Alhambra (Palma St.) | 650-560-9039 | www.cafegibraltar.com

The drive to El Granada is "more than justified" by "talented" chef and co-owner Jose Luis Ugalde's "simply spectacular", "one-of-a-kind" fusion menus say fans of this Mediterranean where "seasonal", "organic" dishes are creatively presented with "exotic tableware" and coupled with "terrific", "well-priced" wines; factor in "friendly and professional" service and "amazing" Moorish decor (including "low tables" with "pillows" in back and distant ocean views up front) and there's little wonder why this "gem" is deemed by some "the best (somewhat kept) secret on the coast."

Café Gratitude *Vegan* — 19 | 18 | 17 | $23

Santa Cruz | 103 Lincoln Ln. (bet. Cedar St. & Pacific Ave.) | 831-427-9583 | www.cafegratitude.com

See review in East of San Francisco Directory.

Café Rustica ☒ *Californian* — 23 | 19 | 22 | $38

Carmel Valley | 10 Del Fino Pl. (bet. Carmel Valley & Pilot Rds.) | 831-659-4444 | www.caferusticacarmel.com

"Delicious", "well-prepared" plates in "picturesque" digs with a "patio overlooking the beautiful hills" make this "rustic yet refined" Californian a "highlight of Carmel Valley"; service is generally "friendly" and it's "priced right" too, so regulars shrug "what more could you ask for?"

Calafia *Californian* — 20 | 18 | 19 | $32

Palo Alto | Town & Country Vill. | 855 El Camino Real (Embarcadero Rd.) | 650-322-9200 | www.calafiapaloalto.com

Ex-Google chef Charlie Ayers "knows what he's doing" say fans of this "bustling" Californian that "fits the Palo Alto scene" with an "extensive" (if slightly "schizophrenic") menu of "imaginative", "satisfying" dishes, including "healthy" choices and "numerous" vegan options, served by a "friendly, speedy" staff; sure, some find it just "so-so" and complain of "noisy" conditions, but more champion its "casual, comfortable" setting and insist it's "perfect for feeding a mixed group"; P.S. the adjacent market offers grab-and-go items.

NEW Campo 185 *Italian* — ▽ 16 | 15 | 14 | $28

Palo Alto | 185 University Ave. (Emerson St.) | 650-614-1177 | www.campopizzeria.com

Fans call this Palo Altan from the Sam's Chowder House team a "refreshing change from the run-of-the-mill", thanks to its "gourmet" pastas, "thin-crust" pizzas and other Italian fare including a mozzarella bar and "flavorful" sorbets; service is "friendly", and while some say it's not yet "up to par" with its sibling, Osteria Coppa, early adopters insist it keeps "getting better."

Cantinetta Luca *Italian*

21 | 20 | 19 | $51

Carmel | Dolores St. (bet. Ocean & 7th Aves.) | 831-625-6500 | www.cantinettaluca.com

For a "casual yet consistently good" Italian meal, this "lively" Carmel "locals'" "favorite" (with an adjacent "precious food shop", Salumeria Luca) turns out "outstanding" "housemade salumi, crispy pizzas and enveloping pastas"; it's a bit "pricey" and the "rustic" digs with an "open oven in the back" can be "noisy", but everything's "high style – including the decor and clientele."

Casanova *French/Italian*

24 | 24 | 23 | $56

Carmel | Fifth Ave. (bet. Mission & San Carlos Sts.) | 831-625-0501 | www.casanovarestaurant.com

Perhaps the "most romantic place" around, this "quaint" Carmel "favorite" proffers "spectacular" French-Italian fare in "many small dining rooms", including one housing a table from France where Vincent Van Gogh took his meals; ask the "charming" staff for a seat on "the outdoor patio" for "date night" (and never mind the "tourists"); P.S. lunch is less "expensive."

Cascal *Pan-Latin*

22 | 22 | 20 | $36

Mountain View | 400 Castro St. (California St.) | 650-940-9500 | www.cascalrestaurant.com

"Get a large group of friends together" and hit up this "popular" Mountain View Pan-Latin for "interesting", "full-of-flavor" tapas and "bigger entrees" "washed down easily" with "must-have" sangria in a "lively", "colorful" space tended by a "helpful" staff; inside can be "insanely loud" ("bring your megaphone"), but outdoors is "quieter and less crammed", and if penny-pinchers find it a bit "pricey", the "killer happy hour" is a "cheap-ish" alternative.

Cetrella   *Mediterranean*

23 | 23 | 22 | $50

Half Moon Bay | 845 Main St. (Monte Vista Ln.) | 650-726-4090 | www.cetrella.com

This "romantic" "special-occasion spot" centered around a double-sided stone fireplace has "been around Half Moon Bay for a while", drawing in supporters with its "artistically presented" Mediterranean cuisine; an "imaginative wine list" and "bargain" midweek prix fixe add to the appeal, plus there's "live jazz" on Fridays and Saturdays and service is generally "gracious", so surveyors say it's "well worth the drive."

Cha Cha Cha Cuba *Caribbean/Cuban*

22 | 19 | 18 | $27

San Mateo | 112 S. B St. (bet. 1st & 2nd Aves.) | 650-347-2900 | www.chacuba.com

See review in City of San Francisco Directory.

Chantilly   *French/Italian*

25 | 25 | 26 | $67

Redwood City | 3001 El Camino Real (Selby Ln.) | 650-321-4080 | www.chantillyrestaurant.com

"For that special occasion" or big Silicon Valley deal, this upscale Redwood City "classic" offers "beautifully prepared" French and Northern Italian cuisine, served by an "attentive" staff; "you can carry on a conversation" in the white-linen setting, and while a few find it "old-fashioned", others describe it as a "fine experience."

Cheesecake Factory *American* | 16 | 17 | 16 | $29 |

Palo Alto | 375 University Ave. (bet. Florence & Waverly Sts.) | 650-473-9622
San Jose | Westfield Oakridge Shopping Mall | 925 Blossom Hill Rd. (bet. Santa Teresa & Winfield Blvds.) | 408-225-6948
Santa Clara | Westfield Shoppingtown Valley Fair | 3041 Stevens Creek Blvd. (Santana Row) | 408-246-0092
www.thecheesecakefactory.com
See review in City of San Francisco Directory.

Cheese Steak Shop *Cheesesteaks* | 22 | 12 | 19 | $11 |

San Jose | Monterey Plaza | 5524 Monterey Rd. (bet. Blossom Hill & Ford Rds.) | 408-972-0271
Sunnyvale | 832 W. El Camino Real (Hollenbeck Ave.) | 408-530-8159
www.cheesesteakshop.com
See review in City of San Francisco Directory.

Chef Chu's *Chinese* | 22 | 16 | 20 | $28 |

Los Altos | 1067 N. San Antonio Rd. (El Camino Real) | 650-948-2696 | www.chefchu.com
"Year after year", locals return for the "delicious" Chinese fare from chef Lawrence Chu at his "Los Altos institution" that's "family-run" and a family "favorite"; if the "decor is a little dated", "a devoted staff" adds to the "quality value" that "far outshines its surroundings."

Chez Shea *Eclectic* | ▽ 21 | 15 | 17 | $24 |

Half Moon Bay | 408 Main St. (Mill St.) | 650-560-9234 | www.chez-shea.com
"Mediterranean and South American flavors" inform the "unique" Eclectic menu of this Half Moon Bay sibling to Cafe Gibraltar serving "interesting" dishes from "around the world"; "great" prices and a "solid" wine list (with the option to BYO) add to the allure, and while the "small" digs can make it "tough to get in", fans insist it's "well worth trying."

Chez TJ   *French* | 23 | 22 | 23 | $111 |

Mountain View | 938 Villa St. (bet. Bryant & Franklin Sts.) | 650-964-7466 | www.cheztj.com
When "someone else is paying", Mountain View locals choose this "venerable" "special-occasion" prix fixe specialist offering "extremely creative", "three-hour-plus" New French "*gastronomique*" menus" built around "vegetables from the house garden" and "served with precision" in a "romantic" old Victorian "cottage"; acolytes assure "if you're into" "epic" "wine pairings" and savor "very slow" "pacing between courses", the "kitchen wizardry" is "worth the wait"; P.S. an 'abbreviated' menu is also available.

Cin-Cin Wine Bar & Restaurant   *Eclectic* | 24 | 19 | 23 | $40 |

Los Gatos | 368 Village Ln. (Hwy. 9) | 408-354-8006 | www.cincinwinebar.com
Stock up on "hearty little plates" to "share with friends" or "colleagues after work" at this Los Gatos sib to Cascal, a "chic" "neighborhood" Eclectic sporting "flavors from all over the world" matched by a "well-thought-out" wine list; the prices can "sneak up on you", but service is "always pleasant" and the scene "fun and festive", so

be prepared for a "noisy" night out – and the temptation to "nibble off the plates of strangers."

NEW Cindy's Waterfront *American*

- | - | - | M

Monterey | Monterey Bay Aquarium | 886 Cannery Row (Wave St.) | 831-648-4870 | www.montereybayaquarium.org

Napa Valley chef Cindy Pawlcyn lends her touch to this inexpensive full-service, farm-to-table cafe tucked away in the Monterey Bay Aquarium, serving a creative New American menu with a focus on sustainability (all of the seafood adheres to the aquarium's Seafood Watch program); the modern, spacious establishment, which is open to aquarium visitors only, capitalizes on its prime waterfront location with huge windows overlooking the scenic bay.

Cool Café *Californian*

21 | 17 | 16 | $20

Menlo Park | Menlo Business Park | 1525 O'Brien Dr. (bet. Adams Dr. & University Ave.) | 650-325-3665 ⓢ
Stanford | Stanford University Cantor Arts Ctr. | 328 Lomita Dr. (Museum Way) | 650-725-4758 Ⓜ
www.cooleatz.com

These all-organic Californian eateries specialize in "healthy, tasty" fare made with local, sustainably sourced ingredients; the Stanford University location makes a "great getaway in the middle of a school day" or "in between viewing art" at the Cantor Arts Center and is best enjoyed on the outdoor patio overlooking the Rodin sculpture garden, while the Menlo Business Park branch is open weekdays only till 2:30 PM, and if a few find them "a tad pricey" given the "cafeteria"-style setup, more argue that the "quality" makes it "worth the occasional visit."

Counter Palo Alto *Burgers*

22 | 15 | 18 | $19

Palo Alto | 369 S. California Ave. (Ash St.) | 650-321-3900 | www.thecounterburger.com

"Big, messy, exactly-how-you-want-it burgers" star at this "busy" Palo Alto chain link known for a "staggering number of sophisticated toppings" (it's "not for the indecisive"), plus "to-die-for onion strings", "perfectly cooked" sweet potato fries and "thick" shakes; the "attitude-free" staff can be a little "scattered" and you may want to "take earplugs if you're noise-sensitive", but with "fair prices" it's still an "appealing" pick.

Crouching Tiger *Chinese*

22 | 17 | 18 | $19

Redwood City | 2644 Broadway St. (bet. California St. & El Camino Real) | 650-298-8881 | www.crouchingtigerrestaurant.com

"Spicy" Sichuan specialties will make "you sweat" at this Redwood City Chinese where the "consistently tasty" fare is offered at "reasonable prices"; "quick service" and a "comfortable setting" enhanced with paintings up the "family-friendly" appeal.

Curry Up Now *Indian*

▽ 21 | 12 | 16 | $14

San Mateo | 129 S. B St. (bet. 1st & 2nd Aves.) | 650-316-8648
NEW Palo Alto | 321 Hamilton Ave. (Bryant St.) | 650-477-1001
www.curryupnow.com

What started as a "quintessentially trendy" Indian street food truck is now a trio of "not too fancy" brick-and-mortar cafes that "lives up to expectations" for "fresh", "yummy" "fusion"-style fare, including "chicken tikka masala burritos", kathi rolls and more, plus mango lassis to "keep the fire down" after "spicy" dishes; service is "friendly" and the casual digs are usually "buzzing" with fans, while most agree it's a "great value for your money."

Dasaprakash *Indian/Vegetarian*

∇ 22 | 19 | 18 | $20

Santa Clara | 2636 Homestead Rd. (bet. Kiely Blvd. & Layton St.) | 408-246-8292 | www.dasaprakash.com

"Bangalore comes to a Santa Clara strip mall" is how some locals describe this eatery serving "fresh" South Indian vegetarian cuisine full of "complex flavor profiles", including "finger-licking-good" Thali plates, at "low prices"; the space is "pleasant" while the "friendly owner" is "great to chat with", and fans are "happy to go back."

Deetjen's Big Sur Restaurant *Californian*

∇ 24 | 24 | 23 | $49

Big Sur | Deetjen's Big Sur Inn | 48865 Hwy. 1 (30 mi. south of Carmel) | 831-667-2378 | www.deetjens.com

Set in the "historic" Big Sur Inn, this "romantic" Californian offers a "menu that rivals the beauty" of its surroundings, delivering locally sourced fare in an "antiques-filled", candlelit room that exudes a "nostalgic atmosphere"; tabs verge on expensive, but "gourmet-minded travelers" insist it's a "must."

Dio Deka *Greek*

25 | 24 | 23 | $63

Los Gatos | Hotel Los Gatos | 210 E. Main St. (High School Ct.) | 408-354-7700 | www.diodeka.com

There's "not a single blah dish" at this Hotel Los Gatos Greek say fans cheering the "modern take" on "traditional" fare; "friendly" staffers tend to "lots of beautiful people" in the "hustling" "upscale" space, and though tabs are "expensive", many "don't mind paying higher prices" for "special-occasion bliss."

Dishdash 🗷 *Mideastern*

24 | 18 | 20 | $25

Sunnyvale | 190 S. Murphy Ave. (Washington Ave.) | 408-774-1889 | www.dishdash.com

Dish n Dash 🗷 *Mideastern*

Sunnyvale | 736 N. Mathilda Ave. (San Anselmo) | 408-530-9200 | www.dishndashrestaurant.com

"Incredibly flavorful" fare in "generous portions" keeps this Sunnyvale Middle Eastern "packed to the rafters", especially since prices are "reasonable" and "service is generally very friendly and accommodating despite the crowds"; though the "long wait" is a "con", fans advise you just "have another cocktail while you wait" – or head over to its North Mathilda Avenue quick-serve offshoot, a "perfect alternative", with "fresh, filling" fare (wraps, salads, smoothies) fit for an "economy budget."

Donato Enoteca *Italian*

23 | 21 | 22 | $43

Redwood City | 1041 Middlefield Rd. (bet. Jefferson Ave. & Main St.) | 650-701-1000 | www.donatoenoteca.com

You'll feel "close to Tuscany" at this Redwood City Italian where the "passionate" chef-owner creates "deliciously satisfying pizza" and other "consistently good" offerings, including a number of "imaginative", "out-of-the-ordinary" dishes; the staff is "attentive", and while the "relaxing" surroundings are good for "family night", they're also thought to be "romantic" enough for "date night", especially when surveyors are sitting "outdoors under the heated lamps."

Duarte's Tavern _American_ | 22 | 15 | 20 | $29 |

Pescadero | 202 Stage Rd. (Pescadero Creek Rd.) | 650-879-0464 | www.duartestavern.com

For "comfort food at its best" diners "take a step back in time" at this "historic" Pescadero tavern, a "coastal tradition" for "incredible pies", "super-rich" soups (especially the "justly famous" artichoke) and other "tasty" "old-time" American eats, all at moderate prices; service is "personable" and the "knotty-pine-paneled dining room" is joined by an "inviting bar" that's "just the kind of place" to "waste an entire afternoon."

Ebisu ●Ⓜ _Japanese_ | 24 | 18 | 20 | $37 |

South San Francisco | San Francisco Int'l Airport | Terminal G Food Court (Hwy. 101) | 650-588-2549 | www.ebisusushi.com
See review in City of San Francisco Directory.

El Farolito _Mexican_ | 23 | 8 | 17 | $10 |

South San Francisco | 394 Grand Ave. (Maple Ave.) | 650-737-0138 | www.elfarolitoinc.com
See review in City of San Francisco Directory.

Emporio Rulli _Dessert/Italian_ | 22 | 20 | 18 | $20 |

South San Francisco | San Francisco Int'l Airport | Lower Int'l Loop (Hwy. 101) | 888-887-8554

South San Francisco | San Francisco Int'l Airport | Upper Int'l Loop (Hwy. 101) | 888-887-8554 ●
www.rulli.com
See review in North of San Francisco Directory.

Espetus Churrascaria _Brazilian_ | 24 | 21 | 23 | $71 |
(aka Espetus Churrascaria Brazilian Steakhouse)

San Mateo | 710 S. B St. (bet. 7th & 8th Aves.) | 650-342-8700 | www.espetus.com
See review in City of San Francisco Directory.

Evvia _Greek_ | 28 | 26 | 26 | $56 |

Palo Alto | 420 Emerson St. (bet. Lytton & University Aves.) | 650-326-0983 | www.evvia.net

It's "as good as any taverna in Greece" attest fans of Palo Alto's "darling little sister" to SF's Kokkari, which might please "Demeter" (goddess of the harvest) herself along with the power-lunching "tech crowd" and special-occasion celebrants digging into the "fantastic", "inspired" "high-end" Mediterranean cuisine (with requisite "high prices"); a "convivial" (if "noisy") "rustic" setting and "doting" service that's like a "hug" from a "Greek mama" complete the picture.

Fandango _Mediterranean_ | 21 | 21 | 21 | $50 |

Pacific Grove | 223 17th St. (bet. Laurel & Lighthouse Aves.) | 831-372-3456 | www.fandangorestaurant.com

After "many years", this Pacific Grove Mediterranean "still has it" say fans praising its "well-prepared" fare and "killer wine list", both so "extensive" "the only problem is choosing what to eat and drink"; "polished" service and a "charming converted house atmosphere" are additional reasons it remains "popular."

	FOOD	DECOR	SERVICE	COST

SOUTH OF SAN FRANCISCO

Fishwife at Asilomar
Beach *Californian/Seafood*   `22` `16` `21` `$31`
Pacific Grove | 1996½ Sunset Dr. (Asilomar Ave.) | 831-375-7107
Fishwife Seafood Café *Californian/Seafood*
Seaside | 789 Trinity Ave. (Fremont Blvd.) | 831-394-2027
www.fishwife.com

"Locals love" these "low-key" Californians in Pacific Grove and Seaside where you "don't have to dress up" to enjoy the "consistently good" sustainbly caught seafood-focused offerings made more "interesting" by a "Caribbean touch"; "prices are fair", the staff is "friendly" and the "cheerfully decorated" space on Sunset Drive is "close enough to the beach for a nice postprandial stroll", so don't be surprised if it's "crowded."

Flea St. Café Ⓜ *Californian*   `26` `22` `25` `$58`
Menlo Park | 3607 Alameda de las Pulgas (Avy Ave.) | 650-854-1226 | www.cooleatz.com

Still "bringing fresh, local, organic" ingredients "to your table", chef-owner Jesse Ziff Cool works the room at this "inventive" Californian "Menlo Park mainstay", where her "commitment to sustainability" extends even to the recycled-glass bar where "interesting California wines" and farm-fresh cocktails are poured; the "elegant" setting and "top-notch" service make it HQ on the Peninsula for "business dinners" or "bringing your honey", and it's easier to "splurge" knowing it's all "good for the earth."

Flying Fish Grill *Californian/Seafood*   `24` `20` `23` `$46`
Carmel | Carmel Plaza | Mission St. (bet. Ocean & 7th Aves.) | 831-625-1962 | www.flyingfishgrill.com

"One of Carmel's consistent stars", this "serene" Californian from chef/co-owner Kenny Fukumoto "skillfully delivers" "innovative" fin fare with Asian touches by way of "courteous, understated" servers; hidden in the lower level of a shopping plaza, it nonetheless has an "inviting cellar ambiance", and while it's not cheap, the "cozy", "softly lit" environs make for a "welcome escape" from the "hectic" tourist scene.

400 Degrees *Burgers*   `-` `-` `-` `I`
Carmel | Carmel Plaza | Mission St. (7th St.) | 831-244-0040 | www.400degrees.com

"Gourmet burgers" of Angus beef, turkey, portobello mushroom and more are "cooked to order" on a custom-made cast-iron griddle at this Carmel Plaza patty joint (from the folks behind Cantinetta Luca) offering "good, solid food" made with "fresh" ingredients; fries, milkshakes, wine and beer are also delivered with "quick" counter or table service, and the casual, retro booth seating is "fitting for the Carmel area."

Fuki Sushi *Japanese*   `23` `21` `20` `$42`
Palo Alto | 4119 El Camino Real (bet. Arrastradero & Page Mill Rds.) | 650-494-9383 | www.fukisushi.com

"Very fresh" fish has backers calling this "Palo Alto's best sushi place", where the "beautifully prepared" fin fare "melts in your mouth like butter"; cooked Japanese dishes are also offered, and the "pleasantly personal" staff and "traditional setting" including "takami seating"

make for a "nice place to take clients" – but "bring your company credit card" as it's "kind of expensive."

Gabriella Café *Californian/Italian*   20 | 19 | 19 | $40

Santa Cruz | 910 Cedar St. (bet. Church & Locust Sts.) | 831-457-1677 | www.gabriellacafe.com

"Lovely" and "romantic", this longtime "standby" in Santa Cruz serves "classic" Cal-Italian fare in a "tiny", refurbished vintage locale; while the space does get "crowded" (with "tables on top of each other") and some complain the cuisine and service should be better "for the prices", others attest "the food is good, the ambiance makes it better."

Gayle's Bakery & Rosticceria *Bakery*   24 | 14 | 18 | $17

Capitola | Upper Capitola Shopping Ctr. | 504 Bay Ave. (Capitola Ave.) | 831-462-1200 | www.gaylesbakery.com

"People come from miles away" to visit this Capitola bakery/cafe and load up on "upscale picnic" provisions, like "tasty prepared meals", "delicious" sandwiches and "excellent baked goods"; though primarily a "stop-and-go" spot, you can "try to find somewhere to sit" on the enclosed patio – either way you'll be served by "friendly" staffers.

Gochi Japanese Fusion Tapas Ⓢ *Japanese*   25 | 19 | 19 | $40

Cupertino | 19980 Homestead Rd. (bet. Blarney & Heron Aves.) | 408-725-0542 | www.gochifusiontapas.com

The "enormous" menu of "delicious" "izakaya-style" fusion fare is "best enjoyed in groups with a healthy appetite for variety" at this "popular" midpriced Cupertino Japanese offering "traditional" dishes alongside more "interesting" choices, like "awesome pizzas", plus "smooth, sweet sake" and "ice cold beer"; the decor is "authentic" with "lots of tatami-style seating" and service is generally "friendly" (if a little "slow"), so it's "frequently crowded", making reservations "highly recommended."

Grasing's Coastal Cuisine *Californian*   21 | 20 | 22 | $49

Carmel | Sixth Ave. (Mission St.) | 831-624-6562 | www.grasings.com

"Locally sustained" ingredients meet "excellent preparations" at Kurt Grasing's Carmel Californian, where a "great wine list" and "enthusiastic" service add to the appeal; a "bar menu offers more affordable choices" and you can even "bring your dog" to the "beautiful" patio for a "quiet, locals'" experience.

The Grill on the Alley *Steak*   23 | 21 | 21 | $55

San Jose | Fairmont Hotel | 172 S. Market St. (bet. San Carlos & San Fernando Sts.) | 408-294-2244 | www.thegrill.com

"Meat lovers" congregate at this chophouse chain link in San Jose's Fairmont Hotel for "large" cuts in contemporary environs with a "kind of New York vibe"; service is generally "attentive", and though prices seem "set for the expense-account crowd", happy-hour specials in the "comfy, alive" bar are a less-costly alternative.

Hachi Ju Hachi Ⓜ *Japanese*   ▽ 27 | 16 | 24 | $51

Saratoga | 14480 Big Basin Way (3rd St.) | 408-647-2258 | www.hachijuhachi88.com

"Authentic", "humble and honest" Japanese fare – claypot dishes, noodles, teriyaki and a bit of sushi – draws fans to this husband-and-wife-run Saratoga sleeper; the decor is "spartan" and the check will lighten your wallet, but service gets high marks and it's always enjoyable to "sit at the bar" and watch the chef-owner "in action."

Half Moon Bay Brewing
17 | 19 | 17 | $28

Company *Californian/Pub Food*

Half Moon Bay | 390 Capistrano Rd. (Cabrillo Hwy.) | 650-728-2739 | www.hmbbrewingco.com

An "easy place to hang out", this Half Moon Bay stop vends Californian "high-end brewpub" eats and "excellent beers" to a "large après-beach crowd" and "lots of locals"; the interior is "nothing special" and service can be a bit "slapdashy", but sitting outside by the fire pit and "enjoying the ocean view" still can't be beat.

Hong Kong Flower Lounge
21 | 16 | 16 | $29

Restaurant *Chinese*

Millbrae | 51 Millbrae Ave. (bet. Broadway & El Camino Real) | 650-692-6666

Mayflower *Chinese*

Milpitas | Milpitas Sq. | 428 Barber Ln. (Bellew Dr.) | 408-922-2700 www.mayflower-seafood.com

"Delicious dim sum" for "reasonable prices" makes weekends "quite crowded" at these Bay Area siblings, despite waits that can be "long", decor that could use an "update" and a staff that could be "more welcoming"; the full menu features Cantonese dishes with a focus on seafood, and they're also "good for a banquet meal."

Hotaru *Japanese*
21 | 13 | 18 | $24

San Mateo | 33 E. Third Ave. (bet. El Camino Real & San Mateo Dr.) | 650-343-1152 | www.hotarurestaurant.com

There's always a "line out the door" at this "small storefront" Japanese in San Mateo providing a "consistent", "straightforward" selection of sushi, udon, teriyaki, et al.; "the decor is lacking some flair" and the staff makes some feel "rushed", but at the end of the day "no one cares" because it's so "cheap."

Hunan Home's Restaurant *Chinese*
21 | 13 | 19 | $25

Los Altos | 4880 El Camino Real (bet. Jordan Ave. & Los Altos Sq.) | 650-965-8888 | www.hunanhomes.com

Hunan Garden *Chinese*

Palo Alto | 3345 El Camino Real (bet. Fernando & Lambert Aves.) | 650-565-8868 | www.chineserestauranthunangarden.com

See review in City of San Francisco Directory.

Iberia *Spanish*
22 | 19 | 16 | $46

Menlo Park | 1026 Alma St. (bet. Alma Ln. & Ravenswood Ave.) | 650-325-8981 | www.iberiarestaurant.com

Be it "tapas by the fireplace" in "the beautiful bar" or more substantial meals in the dining room or on the patio, fans say this "romantic hideaway in Menlo Park" "consistently provides a fantastic Spanish dining experience"; a few find it "overpriced", but most "would go there again."

Ike's Lair *Sandwiches*
25 | 12 | 18 | $12

NEW **Foster City** | Century Plaza | 1065 E. Hillsdale Blvd. (Foster City Blvd.) | 650-525-1602 | www.ikeslairfostercity.com Ⓢ

Redwood City | 2655 Broadway (El Camino Real) | 650-365-2200 | www.ikeslair.com

(continued)

(continued)

Ike's Place *Sandwiches*
NEW **Cupertino** | 21000 Steven's Creek Blvd. (Stelling Rd.) | 408-861-1000
NEW **Santa Clara** | 2235 The Alameda (Chapman Ct.) | 408-244-2034
Stanford | Stanford University Huang Engineering Ctr. | 475 Via Ortega Dr. (Campus Dr.) | 650-322-1766
www.ilikeikesplace.com
See review in City of San Francisco Directory.

Il Fornaio *Italian*    18 | 19 | 18 | $43
Burlingame | 327 Lorton Ave. (bet. Bellevue & Donnelly Aves.) | 650-375-8000
Carmel | The Pine Inn | Ocean Ave. (bet. Lincoln & Monte Verde Sts.) | 831-622-5100
Palo Alto | Garden Court Hotel | 520 Cowper St. (bet. Hamilton & University Aves.) | 650-853-3888
San Jose | Sainte Claire Hotel | 302 S. Market St. (San Carlos St.) | 408-271-3366
www.ilfornaio.com
See review in City of San Francisco Directory.

Il Postale *Italian*   23 | 18 | 22 | $34
Sunnyvale | 127 W. Washington Ave. (bet. Frances St. & Murphy Ave.) | 408-733-9600 | www.ilpostale.com
At this former Sunnyvale post office, the "sweet, attentive" staff delivers "huge portions" of "luscious Italian"-American fare; the "small" setting "fills up pretty fast" (and gets "loud"), so "be sure you call for a reservation" (accepted only for parties of five or more).

In-N-Out Burger ❂ *Burgers*   23 | 14 | 21 | $9
Millbrae | 11 Rollins Rd. (bet. Adrian Rd. & Millbrae Ave.)
Mountain View | 1159 N. Rengstorff Ave. (Leghorn St.)
Mountain View | 53 W. El Camino Real (bet. Bay St. & Grant Rd.)
San Jose | 550 Newhall Dr. (Coleman Ave.)
San Jose | 5611 Santa Teresa Blvd. (bet. Blossom Hill Rd. & Summerbrook Ln.)
Daly City | 260 Washington St. (Sullivan Ave.)
800-786-1000 | www.in-n-out.com
See review in City of San Francisco Directory.

Izzy's Steaks & Chops *Steak*   22 | 19 | 22 | $45
San Carlos | 525 Skyway Rd. (bet. Airport Way & Monte Vista Dr.) | 650-654-2822 | www.izzyssteaks.com
See review in City of San Francisco Directory.

Jang Su Jang *Korean*   23 | 19 | 19 | $30
NEW **Milpitas** | 269 W. Calaveras Blvd. (Abbott Ave.) | 408-262-3434
Santa Clara | Lawrence Plaza | 3561 El Camino Real (Lawrence Rd.) | 408-246-1212
www.jangsujang.com
Fans assure "you'll always get a great and reliable Korean meal" at this modern-looking Santa Claran (with an unrated Milpitas sibling), offering both "kitchen-cooked" fare and grill-it-yourself barbecue that's perhaps "a little pricier than other places" of its ilk, and "worth it"; though service is "quick", count on "long waits if you don't have a reservation."

Jin Sho *Japanese*

24 | 18 | 18 | $47

Palo Alto | 454 S. California Ave. (bet. Ash St. & El Camino Real) | 650-321-3454 | www.jinshorestaurant.com

"Impeccable" "melt-in-your-mouth" sushi and cooked fare is "expertly prepared" by former Nobu chefs – and "at a price" ("worth it") – at this "modern" Palo Alto Japanese; service can be "a little slow", but that just leaves more time to savor the "highly recommended" omakase, which can be paired with a sake sampler.

John Bentley's *American*

25 | 21 | 25 | $56

Redwood City | 2915 El Camino Real (Selby Ln.) | 650-365-7777 | www.johnbentleys.com

A "tempting array" of "heavenly", "farm-fresh" cuisine makes the "somewhat pricey" tabs "worth it" at this "warm, inviting" Redwood City New American from the eponymous chef-owner; a "terrific" staff and "fine selection of wines" help make it ripe "for that special occasion", but it's also "great for a good meal any time."

Joy Luck Palace *Chinese*

21 | 15 | 15 | $26

Cupertino | 10911 N. Wolfe Rd. (Homestead Rd.) | 408-255-6988

"Arrive early" for lunch, because there's usually "a wait" to get into this Cupertino strip-mall spot, where "dim sum's the treat" and a "ridiculously good value for the price"; "typical Chinese" dinners are also offered in the large space, which features private rooms and "spare but speedy service."

Kabul Afghan Cuisine *Afghan*

24 | 18 | 22 | $30

Burlingame | 1101 Burlingame Ave. (California Dr.) | 650-343-2075
San Carlos | San Carlos Plaza | 135 El Camino Real (bet. F & Holly Sts.) | 650-594-2840
www.kabulcuisine.com

Loyal patrons of "many years" "deeply appreciate" the "fantastic lamb dishes", "wonderful kebabs" and other "exotic", "hearty" Afghan fare prepared at these spots in San Carlos and Downtown Burlingame; the settings are kind of "plain", but that matters not in light of the "fast, friendly service", "generous portions" and "reasonable prices."

NEW Katsu *Japanese*

- | - | - | VE

Los Gatos | 160 W. Main St. (bet. 8th St. & Pennsylvania Ave.) | 408-354-0712 | www.katsulosgatos.com

The name of this high-end Japanese fusioner in Los Gatos refers not to the humble Japanese cutlet but to the chef, Katsuhiko 'Katsu' Hanamure, a Nobu vet; the design is sleek, while the kitchen turns out elaborate omakase and mini-kaiseki dinners, along with luxe à la carte offerings such as a $1,200 appetizer of caviar and gold leaf–topped spiny lobster sashimi dubbed the Decadence Staircase.

The Kitchen ◑ *Chinese*

▽ 23 | 15 | 15 | $32

Millbrae | 279 El Camino Real (bet. La Cruz & Victoria Aves.) | 650-692-9688 | www.thekitchenmillbrae.com

It's a "real winner" say fans of this Millbrae Chinese that dishes up "well-prepared" dim sum (available only at lunch); while the service is "so-so" and the decor not notable, crowds of families on weekends attest to the "excellent" Cantonese cuisine and moderate prices.

	FOOD	DECOR	SERVICE	COST

Koi Palace *Chinese*

	23	18	15	$33

Daly City | Serramonte Plaza | 365 Gellert Blvd. (bet. Hickey & Serramonte Blvds.) | 650-992-9000 | www.koipalace.com

"Packing the house every weekend", this "upscale" Daly City and Dublin duo delivers an "astounding selection" of "to-die-for" dim sum in addition to "stellar seafood" and "elaborate" Cantonese-style banquet dinners in a setting complete with a tranquil koi pond and fish tanks that's nonetheless "a zoo"; waits can be "ridiculous", the "service is spotty" and "it costs more" than some expect, but the "crowds can't be wrong."

Krung Thai *Thai*

	22	16	17	$23

Mountain View | San Antonio Shopping Ctr. | 590 Showers Dr. (bet. California St. & El Camino Real) | 650-559-0366
San Jose | 642 S. Winchester Blvd. (Moorpark Ave.) | 408-260-8224
www.originalkrungthai.com

Fans attest these San Jose and Mountain View twins are among "the best places to go for authentic" Siamese "curries and pad Thai"; since they're "always busy" and can get "very crowded", "friendly" service varies, nonetheless they're "great" for lunch with "business colleagues" or dinner "with friends or family"; P.S. the similarly named New Krung Thai located in San Jose is separately owned.

NEW La Balena Cucina Toscana *Italian*

	–	–	–	E

Carmel | Junipero St. (bet. 5th & 6th Aves.) | 831-250-6295 | www.labalenacarmel.com

At this husband-and-wife-run Carmel Italian, expect pricey Tuscan-style dishes (including handmade pastas) made with local, seasonal ingredients and accompanied by Boot and California wines; the cozy-contemporary space features recycled flooring and tables fashioned from reclaimed shipping crates.

La Bicyclette *French/Italian*

	23	20	21	$38

Carmel | Seventh Ave. (Dolores St.) | 831-622-9899 | www.labicycletterestaurant.com

Turning out "unpretentious", "delicious" fare for three decades, this "cozy" Carmel "gathering spot" is still "hopping", thanks to the "darling" bistro decor, "tasty" pizzas and "authentic and fresh" bread from the word-burning oven, along with an "imaginative menu" of other French-Italian dishes (some of the organic vegetables hail from the local middle school); P.S. the wines are "excellent."

La Bodeguita del Medio ⊠ *Cuban*

	22	19	21	$37

Palo Alto | 463 S. California Ave. (El Camino Real) | 650-326-7762 | www.labodeguita.com

"Popular and trendy", this Palo Alto Cuban transports with "well-prepared" midpriced dishes, "strong" drinks and a cigar lounge that's "as close to Havana heaven as you'll get"; the servers "really care", and Cuban artwork adds ambiance, as do "roomy tables" spaced "far enough" apart for "quiet conversation."

La Boulange *Bakery*

	21	17	18	$16

Burlingame | 1152 Burlingame Ave. (Hatch Ln.) | 650-579-5552
Palo Alto | 151 University Ave. (High St.) | 650-323-3332
www.laboulangebakery.com
See review in City of San Francisco Directory.

La Corneta *Mexican*

22 | 13 | 18 | $12

Burlingame | 1123 Burlingame Ave. (Lorton Ave.) | 650-340-1300
San Carlos | 1147 San Carlos Ave. (Laurel St.) | 650-551-1400
www.lacorneta.com
See review in City of San Francisco Directory.

La Costanera Ⓜ *Peruvian*

25 | 25 | 22 | $50

Montara | 8150 Cabrillo Hwy. (bet. 1st & 2nd Sts.) | 650-728-1600 |
www.lacostanerarestaurant.com
"Go for the incredible views of the ocean, especially as the sun sets"
at this double-decker Montara Peruvian with a "magnificent" location
and "modern design" (but really, it "doesn't need decor"); the high-end,
"delectable" dishes by chef-owner Carlos Altamirano (SF's Piqueo and
Mochica) also "wow", and the service is "solid" too.

La Cumbre Taqueria *Mexican*

20 | 10 | 16 | $11

San Mateo | 28 N. B St. (bet. 1st. & Tilton Aves.) | 650-344-8989
See review in City of San Francisco Directory.

La Fondue *Fondue*

22 | 23 | 21 | $66

Saratoga | 14550 Big Basin Way (4th St.) | 408-867-3332 |
www.lafondue.com
Cheese lovers, carnivores and chocoholics alike are "very fondue this
place" in Saratoga, where diners dip bread, meat, fruit and cake into
tabletop pots; the "two-hour dinner experience" in rooms with "creative", "eclectic decor" is "fun for groups", "older kids" and "date night"
too, and service is "good", but some gripe it's "overpriced" "considering you do all the cooking yourself."

La Forêt Ⓜ *Continental/French*

27 | 26 | 27 | $65

San Jose | 21747 Bertram Rd. (Almaden Rd.) | 408-997-3458 |
www.laforetrestaurant.com
Located only 20 minutes from Downtown San Jose, this historic "special-
occasion" restaurant "surrounded by nature" and a meandering creek
nonetheless "feels so far away" to the Silicon Valley set that finds the "romantic" "country setting" an "excellent choice" for "dinner anytime" (or
a lavish Sunday brunch); the "superb" Continental-French tasting menus
and à la carte offerings are capped off by "amazing" soufflés and impressive wines, with "very formal" service to match.

La Posta Ⓜ *Italian*

▽ 25 | 19 | 21 | $37

Santa Cruz | 538 Seabright Ave. (Watson St.) | 831-457-2782 |
www.lapostarestaurant.com
Behind a modest storefront in Santa Cruz's happening Seabright
neighborhood, this "fantastic" spot doles out "inventive", "superlative"
Italian fare and "outstanding Italian wines" for "reasonable prices";
"wonderful" staffers and a "vibrant bar scene" are draws on any evening, but locals make a point to stop by on Tuesdays for 'neighborhood
nights', featuring a "steal" of a meal deal and live "traditional music."

La Victoria Taqueria *Mexican*

24 | 12 | 16 | $9

Redwood City | 847 Main St. (B'way) | 650-366-1070
San Jose | 131 W. Santa Clara St. (bet. Market & San Pedro Sts.) |
408-993-8230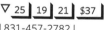

(continued)

(continued)

La Victoria Taqueria

San Jose | 140 E. San Carlos St. (bet. 3rd & 4th Sts.) | 408-298-5335 ●
San Jose | 5015 Almaden Expwy. (Cherry Ave.) | 408-978-7666 ●
www.lavicsj.com

"Apply orange sauce liberally" to your burritos, tacos and "greasy, yummy quesadillas" to get the full experience at this "bargain" Mexican chainlet; it's "nondescript" as looks go, but "nice for the price" and the "late-night" hours at most branches don't hurt either.

LB Steak   *Steak*   22 | 22 | 21 | $60

Menlo Park | 898 Santa Cruz Ave. (University Dr.) | 650-321-8980
San Jose | Santana Row | 334 Santana Row (bet. Stevens Creek Blvd. & Tatum Ln.) | 408-244-1180
www.lbsteak.com

"The cowhide chairs tell you they are serious about their steak" at this "classy, modern" French-flavored meatery duo co-owned by Roland Passot (La Folie) in San Jose's "bustling Santana Row" and Menlo Park, a "go-to" for dates, business meals and "groups"; though the prices are "high", service is "informative" and the "Cal-strong" wine list is "great."

Left Bank   *French*   20 | 21 | 19 | $40

Menlo Park | 635 Santa Cruz Ave. (Doyle St.) | 650-473-6543
San Jose | Santana Row | 377 Santana Row (Olsen Dr.) | 408-984-3500
www.leftbank.com

See review in North of San Francisco Directory.

Le Papillon   *French*   27 | 24 | 26 | $91

San Jose | 410 Saratoga Ave. (Kiely Blvd.) | 408-296-3730 | www.lepapillon.com

It "doesn't look like much from the outside", but "once through the doors", this "phenomenal" "fancy" San Jose stalwart "continues to delight" diners with "inventive" New French prix fixes utilizing "seasonal, fresh" local ingredients plus an "incredible" list of wines (offered by the bottle, half bottle and glass) for pairing; it's a "classy experience" "all the way", including fine service; P.S. à la carte only available during Friday lunch.

Lion & Compass   ⊠ *American*   21 | 19 | 21 | $52

Sunnyvale | 1023 N. Fair Oaks Ave. (Weddell Dr.) | 408-745-1260 | www.lionandcompass.com

"The place to see and be seen in Silicon Valley", this Sunnyvale stalwart "still delivers" "fine" New American fare with "old-school service"; a few ding the "dated" decor, declaring it "detracts from the experience", but it's still a popular place for "business lunches", especially if you're wielding a "corporate credit card."

Liou's House   Ⓜ *Chinese*   ∇ 24 | 9 | 17 | $20

Milpitas | 1245 Jacklin Rd. (Park Victoria Dr.) | 408-263-9888
Hidden in a "humble" strip mall next to a miniature golf course, this affordable off-the-radar spot showcases "authentic" Hunan and Taiwanese specialties by chef James Liou (formerly of Chef Chu's); it's "a level above most of the Chinese places in Milpitas" despite the spare decor.

Little Sheep Mongolian Hot Pot *Mongolian* | 22 | 17 | 16 | $29 |

Cupertino | 19062 Stevens Creek Blvd. (bet. Judy & Tantau Aves.) | 408-996-9919

San Mateo | 215 S. Ellsworth Ave. (bet. 2nd & 3rd Aves.) | 650-343-2566
www.littlesheephotpot.com

"Legions of hungry patrons" line up "to be first" at these Mongolian hot-pot chain links in San Mateo and Cupertino where each table gets a "boiling cauldron" of "rich", "flavorful broth" in which to cook "many different vegetable and meat options" ("satisfying", but maybe "pricey for the amount you get"); though servers are "brisk", they "don't rush you out with the check", meaning it gets and stays "crowded", especially on weekends.

Madera *American* | 23 | 25 | 23 | $69 |

Menlo Park | Rosewood Sand Hill | 2825 Sand Hill Rd. (Hwy. 280) | 650-561-1540 | www.maderasandhill.com

"Silicon Valley" sorts count on this high-end Peninsula New American in the Rosewood Sand Hill Hotel when they want to "impress"; the setting with its "huge fireplace" and views is "gorgeous", the service is strong and it's open all day, though a few find it a bit "pretentious" and feel the food should be more "consistent" to "justify the price."

Manresa Ⓜ *American* | 27 | 26 | 27 | $169 |

Los Gatos | 320 Village Ln. (bet. Santa Cruz & University Aves.) | 408-354-4330 | www.manresarestaurant.com

"Exciting, unexpected and flawless" is how devotees describe the "special experience" at chef-owner David Kinch's Los Gatos New American, where "sublime", "inventive" tasting menus are inspired and sourced from its own biodynamic gardens; the "hours"-long meals served in the "sophisticated" dining room are elevated by "wonderful" wines and service that's like "precision choreography", and though it's all "horribly expensive", there's a lounge menu too; P.S. closed Monday and Tuesday.

Marinus Ⓜ *Californian/French* | 26 | 28 | 27 | $100 |

Carmel Valley | Bernardus Lodge | 415 W. Carmel Valley Rd. (Laureles Grade Rd.) | 831-658-3595 | www.bernardus.com

Diners find "food heaven in Carmel Valley" at this Cal-French in the Bernardus Lodge, where chef Cal Stamenov turns out dinners "perfect" for pairing with bottles from the extensive wine list amid "lovely" surroundings; "superb" service further ensures it's well suited to a "special occasion", though a few critics furrow their brow at the "mega-bill."

Mayfield Bakery & Café *Bakery/Californian* | 20 | 19 | 19 | $35 |

Palo Alto | Town & Country Vill. | 855 El Camino Real (Embarcadero Rd.) | 650-853-9200 | www.mayfieldbakery.com

"On the doorstep of Stanford" in Palo Alto's Town & Country shopping center, this "great little sis to Spruce and Village Pub" turns out "imaginative" Californian dishes from a "beautiful open kitchen"; the dining room, featuring whitewashed wood, can get "noisy" when "crowded", so some suggest "go late" – either way, the staff is "friendly" and fans "highly recommend trying their pastries and bread" from the adjacent bakery.

	FOOD	DECOR	SERVICE	COST

Mezza Luna *Italian* 23 | 21 | 23 | $36

Princeton by the Sea | Princeton Landing Bldg. | 459 Prospect Way (Capistrano Rd.) | 650-728-8108 | www.mezzalunabythesea.com

Caffè Mezza Luna *Italian*

Half Moon Bay | Harbor Vill. | 240 Capistrano Rd. (Pacific Coast Hwy.) | 650-560-0137

It's like "eating in Italy" at this Princeton by the Sea "standby" where the "authentic, mouthwateringly delicious" Southern Italian fare comes at "value" prices; "attentive" staffers and a "casual", fireplace-enhanced setting with harbor views help make it feel like a "retreat", while its Half Moon Bay cafe offshoot serves gelato, pastries, salads and sandwiches.

Mingalaba *Burmese/Chinese* 26 | 16 | 21 | $25

Burlingame | 1213 Burlingame Ave. (bet. Lorton Ave. & Park Rd.) | 650-343-3228 | www.mingalabarestaurant.com

Burlingamers who've braved the nearly "prohibitive lines" outside this "bang-for-your-buck" sibling of SF's Mandalay say they "understand why it's so crowded" once they've tasted its "unbelievable" Chinese cuisine with "delicious" "Burmese twists"; since the "staff is quite knowledgeable" about the "exotic" eats, it's an "outstanding" place to "bring out-of-towners for something they can't get back home."

Mission Ranch Restaurant *American* 20 | 23 | 23 | $48

Carmel | Mission Ranch | 26270 Dolores St. (14th Ave.) | 831-625-9040 | www.missionranchcarmel.com

"You're on Clint Eastwood's turf" at this eatery inside a Carmel hotel, actually a "rambling farmhouse" (restored by the film star) "overlooking the foothills" and a "sheep pasture", where "American comfort food" is served by a "friendly", "experienced" staff; it's quite "popular" and it doesn't take reservations, so it's usually best to "show up early" for drinks at the "lively" piano bar or on the patio where you can "watch the sunset."

Mistral *American/Mediterranean* 22 | 21 | 20 | $40

Redwood Shores | 370-6 Bridge Pkwy. (Marine Pkwy.) | 650-802-9222 | www.mistraldining.com

"Tucked away" in a "pleasant location" in Redwood Shores, this "great neighborhood place" with solid service "never disappoints" for "casual", not-too-pricey New American–Med lunches, brunches and dinners, or just "grabbing a drink"; there's a "nice ambiance" inside, but the "covered, temperature-controlled patio" is the place to be with its "beautiful" views of the lagoon.

Montrio Bistro *American* 23 | 23 | 22 | $49

Monterey | 414 Calle Principal (Franklin St.) | 831-648-8880 | www.montrio.com

"Beautifully crafted" New American fare with Californian, French and Italian influences, "wonderful cocktails" and "a well-considered wine list" keep this "gem" in a "cute, renovated firehouse" in Downtown Monterey "always crowded" (and somewhat "noisy"); factor in "great service" and prices that are only a tad "expensive", and no wonder admirers say they "love everything about this place."

	FOOD	DECOR	SERVICE	COST

Morton's The Steakhouse *Steak* — 23 | 21 | 22 | $80

San Jose | 177 Park Ave. (bet. Almaden Blvd. & Market St.) | 408-947-7000 | www.mortons.com

See review in City of San Francisco Directory.

Mundaka *Spanish* — ▽ 24 | 19 | 23 | $40

Carmel | San Carlos St. (bet. Ocean & 7th Aves.) | 831-624-7400 | www.mundakacarmel.com

It's right "off the main drag" in staid Carmel, but there's "nothing boring" about this "cool" tapas bar presenting a changing slate of "inventive" small plates by local chef Brandon Miller; it's not your typical Spanish fare but the "helpful staff won't steer you wrong", plus "reasonable wine prices", "funky decor" and live music and DJs ensure it's "a party every night"; P.S. coffee and bites are served from 11 AM–5 PM.

Muracci's Japanese Curry & Grill ☒ *Japanese* — 20 | 10 | 16 | $17

Los Altos | 244 State St. (bet. 2nd & 3rd Sts.) | 650-917-1101 | www.muraccis.com

See review in City of San Francisco Directory.

Navio *American* — 24 | 28 | 26 | $78

Half Moon Bay | Ritz-Carlton Half Moon Bay | 1 Miramontes Point Rd. (Hwy. 1) | 650-712-7055 | www.ritzcarlton.com

"Fabulous views with food to match" can be found at this seafood-focused American in the Ritz-Carlton Half Moon Bay, further buoyed by an interior "designed like a ship" and complemented by near-"perfect" service; "when the budget is not restraining", go for an "extraordinary" dinner or "out-of-this-world" Sunday brunch – "it's a beautiful drive and so worth it."

Nepenthe *American* — 18 | 26 | 18 | $38

Big Sur | 48510 Hwy. 1 (bet. Mule Canyon & Rancho Grande Rd.) | 831-667-2345 | www.nepenthebigsur.com

"A total must if you want a true Big Sur experience", this "iconic" stop is the place to "sit on the back deck and hang with a mixture of locals and tourists" while taking in the "stunning" Pacific view; though the midpriced American eats are "forgettable" and the service "average", that's all "irrelevant" given the "spectacularly scenic" locale.

New Krung Thai Restaurant *Thai* — ▽ 25 | 20 | 20 | $27

San Jose | 580 N. Winchester Blvd. (Forest Ave.) | 408-248-3435 | www.newkrungthai.com

"Really tasty" Thai food stands out at this San Jose staple serving "some of the best" curries, among other dishes that may be "a little pricier" than average but "definitely worth it"; it's often "busy" and "loud", but even when full "they usually seat you quickly."

Nick's Next Door ☒ Ⓜ *American* — 26 | 20 | 24 | $49

Los Gatos | 11 College Ave. (Main St.) | 408-402-5053 | www.nicksnextdoor.com

Chef-owner and "gracious host" Nick Difu turns out "creative" New American dishes in a "warm, cozy setting" manned by a "personable" staff at this Los Gatos neighborhood go-to; while it gets "extremely "noisy", fans happily "put up with it" because "neighborhood restaurants don't get better than this"; P.S. reservations are a must.

North Beach Pizza *Pizza*

20 | 12 | 17 | $19

San Mateo | 240 E. Third Ave. (B St.) | 650-344-5000 | www.northbeachpizza.net
See review in City of San Francisco Directory.

Old Port Lobster Shack *Seafood*

23 | 13 | 18 | $29

Portola Valley | 3130 Alpine Rd. (La Mesa Dr.) | 650-561-9500
Redwood City | 851 Veteran's Blvd. (bet. Jefferson Ave. & Middlefield Rd.) | 650-366-2400
www.oplobster.com

When displaced "Maine-iacs" "crave real back-East" "lobstah", this reproduction of a "shack on a wharf" in a "nondescript strip mall" in Redwood City (with a second location in Portola Valley) fits the bill offering lobster rolls filled with "plump, tasty chunks", not to mention "clam chowdah" and "microbrews from New England"; even diehards admit it's "pricey", but "place your order then sit" at the "picnic tables" and "all that's missing" from the mini vacation is the "smell of sea air and swooping seagulls."

O'mei Ⓜ *Chinese*

▽ 24 | 13 | 20 | $29

Santa Cruz | 2316 Mission St. (Fair Ave.) | 831-425-8458

Loyalists "love" the "excellent", spicy Sichuan fare dished out at this casual longtimer in a Santa Cruz strip mall; even though a few note that it's costlier than typical Chinese, it's still wallet-friendly with solid service, and according to some "still better than anything else in town."

Orenchi Ramen Ⓜ⊄ *Japanese*

25 | 13 | 17 | $18

Santa Clara | Lawrence Station Shopping Ctr. | 3540 Homestead Rd. (Lawrence Expwy.) | 408-246-2955 | www.orenchi-ramen.com

"Ramen snobs" "inhale" the "delicious", "perfectly balanced" broth and "fresh noodles" proffered at this Santa Clara Japanese; despite its "unlikely" strip-mall location, it's "extremely popular", so regulars of the spare space warn "arrive early or expect to wait" ("it doesn't take reservations").

Original Joe's ❶ *Italian*
(aka Joe's, OJ's)

22 | 18 | 21 | $33

San Jose | 301 S. First St. (San Carlos St.) | 408-292-7030 | www.originaljoes.com

"Sit at the counter and enjoy the show" at this Downtown San Jose "tradition", where "engaging", "old-world" waiters in tuxes transport "humongous portions" of "hearty", "straight-up" Italian to everyone from "out-of-town guests" to *Mad Men* drinking martinis"; while a few critics argue it's a "bit expensive", longtimers counter that prices are "fair", especially because you'll have "more than enough to take home" – including a side of "nostalgia."

Osteria Ⓩ *Italian*

23 | 16 | 20 | $36

Palo Alto | 247 Hamilton Ave. (Ramona St.) | 650-328-5700
An "old standby" in Palo Alto, this "family-run" Italian has been "consistently good" for decades, turning out "smooth-as-silk" pastas,

"well-made" sauces and other "simple, dependable" Italian fare; it can get "crowded and noisy", with seats packed "so close together" that "some of your clams might creep into your neighbor's fettuccine", but most agree the "food, service and price are right."

Osteria Coppa   *Italian/Pizza*

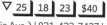

22 | 18 | 19 | $41

San Mateo | 139 S. B St. (bet. 1st & 2nd Aves.) | 650-579-6021 | www.osteriacoppa.com

"Fresh and local whether from the farm or the sea", the "well-prepared" Northern Italian dishes and Neapolitan pizzas satisfy at this slightly upscale San Mateo eatery with an "airy, pleasant" dining room and heated patio; it's "fun to sit at the bar" too, and though it's "loud when packed" and a few call the service and food "hit-or-miss", they concede "when it's good, it's great."

Oswald Restaurant   Ⓜ *American*

∇ 25 | 18 | 23 | $40

Santa Cruz | 121 Soquel Ave. (bet. Front St. & Pacific Ave.) | 831-423-7427 | www.oswaldrestaurant.com

"Hipsters, surfers, professors and over-30s" flock to this "happening place" in Downtown Santa Cruz where an "outstanding" crew proffers "fantastic", ingredient-driven New American plates and "innovative drinks" in a starkly modern setting; it "can be noisy", but the "Wednesday prix fixe" for $29 (the only option that night) is "a steal to say the least"; P.S. open for lunch on Fridays only.

Pacific Catch   *Seafood*

22 | 17 | 20 | $26

Campbell | Pruneyard Shopping Ctr. | 1875 S. Bascom Ave. (Campbell Ave.) | 408-879-9091 | www.pacificcatch.com

See review in City of San Francisco Directory.

Pacific's Edge   *American/French*

24 | 28 | 24 | $79

Carmel | Hyatt Carmel Highlands | 120 Highlands Dr. (Fern Canyon Rd.) | 831-622-5445 | www.pacificsedge.com

"Catch the sunset" for a "magical" experience at this "secluded" spot in the Hyatt Carmel Highlands with a "dramatic oceanfront setting" complemented by a "modern" touch ("you feel as if you're in someone's mansion on Malibu"); while it's quite "expensive", the American-French fare is "delectable" and the service "attentive", and even guests who don't gush about the food find a visit "unforgettable."

Pampas   *Brazilian*

22 | 22 | 21 | $57

Palo Alto | 529 Alma St. (bet. Hamilton & University Aves.) | 650-327-1323 | www.pampaspaloalto.com

"All the perfectly seasoned meat you can eat" comes to your table via "super-friendly" skewer-wielding waiters at this "upscale" Palo Alto Brazilian churrascaria featuring "tender, well-marinated" "rodizio meats" and an "amazing buffet" (get-your-money's-worth types "don't eat for three days before" a meal here, and "skip the salad bar"); "great caipirinhas" and vintages from the "excellent" wine list help "wash down all of that meat", and on Friday–Saturday evenings, a "live band" contributes to the "cool" ambiance.

Pancho Villa Taqueria   *Mexican*

23 | 11 | 17 | $12

San Mateo | 365 S. B St. (bet. 3rd & 4th Aves.) | 650-343-4123 | www.smpanchovilla.com

See review in City of San Francisco Directory.

Parcel 104 *Californian*

23 | 20 | 22 | $64

Santa Clara | Santa Clara Marriott | 2700 Mission College Blvd. (bet. Freedom Circle & Great America Pkwy.) | 408-970-6104 | www.parcel104.com

"Don't be fooled" by a location "hidden" in the Santa Clara Marriott: chef Bradley Ogden's "upscale eatery" "stands out on its own", with "creative", "locally sourced" "seasonal" Californian cuisine and "lovely" wine pairings; the staff is "friendly and helpful", and though the Frank Lloyd Wright–inspired room can feel "cavernous", "noisy" and "busy", it's still a "favorite for business meals" among Silicon Valley sorts – while insiders seek out the "insane happy-hour deals"; P.S. on weekends, it's open for breakfast only.

Passionfish *Californian/Seafood*

27 | 20 | 23 | $46

Pacific Grove | 701 Lighthouse Ave. (Congress Ave.) | 831-655-3311 | www.passionfish.net

"The price is right" and so is the mission behind this "unpretentious" Pacific Grove Californian, a "local favorite" delivering "really delicious and creative" dinners showcasing only sustainable seafood", "local ingredients" and slow-cooked meats; servers "who know what they're doing" "keep guests happy" in the "casual setting" as does the "brilliant, eclectic wine list" say oenophiles, adding that it is "curated with love and intelligence", and priced at near-retail.

Pasta Moon *Italian*

25 | 21 | 23 | $41

Half Moon Bay | 315 Main St. (Kelly St.) | 650-726-5125 | www.pastamoon.com

"Pasta is the strong suit" (natch) at this "romantic" Half Moon Bay "destination", where "farmers, foragers and fishermen" provide the "fresh local ingredients" that go into the "delicious" Italian fare; staffers who "strive to make you feel welcome", along with "reasonable prices" and a "good selection" of "all-Italian wines", help make it a "go-to place" for residents, and "worth the trip" for diners farther afield too.

Pasta Pomodoro *Italian*

18 | 16 | 19 | $22

Redwood City | 490 El Camino Real (Whipple Ave.) | 650-474-2400
San Bruno | Bayhill Shopping Ctr. | 811 Cherry Ave. (San Bruno Ave.) | 650-583-6622
San Jose | 1205 The Alameda (Martin Ave.) | 408-292-9929
San Jose | Camden Park | 2083 Camden Ave. (Union Ave.) | 408-371-2600
San Jose | Santana Row | 378 Santana Row (Olsen Dr.) | 408-241-2200
San Jose | Evergreen Mkt. | 4898 San Felipe Rd. (bet. Paso De Arboles & Yerba Buena Rd.) | 408-532-0271
San Mateo | Bay Meadows | 1060 Park Pl. (Saratoga Dr.) | 650-574-2600
Sunnyvale | 300 W. El Camino Real (Mathilda Ave) | 408-789-0037
www.pastapomodoro.com
See review in City of San Francisco Directory.

Patxi's Pizza *Pizza*

22 | 16 | 18 | $22

(fka Patxi's Chicago Pizza)

Palo Alto | 441 Emerson St. (bet. Lytton & University Aves.) | 650-473-9999
NEW **San Jose** | 3350 Zanker Rd. (Vilaggio St.) | 408-526-1999
www.patxispizza.com
See review in City of San Francisco Directory.

	FOOD	DECOR	SERVICE	COST

Piatti Ristorante & Bar *Italian* | 21 | 21 | 21 | $38 |

Santa Clara | Rivermark Vill. | 3905 Rivermark Plaza (Agnew Rd.) | 408-330-9212 | www.piatti.com

See review in East of San Francisco Directory.

Pizza Antica *Pizza* | 22 | 17 | 19 | $26 |

San Jose | Santana Row | 334 Santana Row (Tatum Ln.) | 408-557-8373 | www.pizzaantica.com

"Lots of families with kids" flock to these suburban Bay Area outposts of the Californian chain of "casual" Italians for "solid salads" and "thin-crust, wood-fired pizzas"; tabs can get "pricey", and since the "noisy", "cavernous" spaces can get "very busy", regulars advise "get there prior to 5 PM" to "avoid a long wait."

The Plant Cafe Organic *Health Food* | 22 | 19 | 18 | $26 |

NEW **Burlingame** | 1395 Burlingame Ave. (Primrose Rd.) | 650-342-0242
South San Francisco | San Francisco Int'l Airport | Domestic Terminal 2 (Hwy. 101) | 650-821-9290
www.theplantcafe.com

See review in City of San Francisco Directory.

Plumed Horse 🅱 *Californian* | 25 | 25 | 24 | $90 |

Saratoga | 14555 Big Basin Way (4th St.) | 408-867-4711 | www.plumedhorse.com

It's "one big wow" "from the moment you walk in" to the "stylish" "modern" digs at this "first-class" Saratoga "special-occasion" Californian; the "top-notch" tasting menus and "constant filling" of your "champagne glass" can add up (you'll likely spend "gobs of money"), but details including an "over-the-top" wine collection stored in a "glass-bottomed" room show they're "trying very hard."

NEW **Puerto 27** *Peruvian* | - | - | - | I |

Pacifica | Pacifica Beach Hotel | 525 Crespi Dr. (Cabrillo Hwy.) | 650-733-7343 | www.puerto27.com

Chef-owner Jose Calvo-Perez, of San Francisco's Fresca and Pasión restaurants, brings fried rice with sea urchin sauce, pork belly with potato stew and other moderately priced Peruvian small plates to Pacifica, pairing them with international wines and pisco cocktails; the airy, two-story restaurant in the Pacifica Beach Hotel features a white stone bar, rich leather barstools and an ocean- and South America-inspired feel.

Quattro Restaurant & Bar *Italian* | 22 | 25 | 25 | $62 |

East Palo Alto | Four Seasons Hotel Silicon Valley | 2050 University Ave. (Woodland Ave.) | 650-470-2889 | www.quattrorestaurant.com

Appealing for a "business lunch or dinner", this "fine" East Palo Alto Italian in the Four Seasons caters to Silicon Valley guests with "very good" food, "innovative" cocktails and a relatively "hip" vibe; though critics call it "too expensive", options like small plates and the Sunday Supper menu go a bit easier on the wallet.

Ramen Dojo *Japanese/Noodle Shop* | 25 | 14 | 16 | $15 |

San Mateo | 805 S. B St. (bet. 8th & 9th Aves.) | 650-401-6568

Serious slurpers line up "before they open" at this "really small" San Mateo noodle shop for arguably "the most" "frickin' delicious" "bowl of ramen" available "outside Japan"; there's little to choose from other than three "different levels of spiciness" and miscellaneous toppings, but service is "super fast" for these "cheap eats"; P.S. closed Tuesdays.

Rangoon Ruby *Burmese*   ▽ 22 | 20 | 21 | $27

Palo Alto | 445 Emerson St. (bet. Lytton & University Aves.) | 650-323-6543

NEW **San Carlos** | 680 Laurel St. (Cherry St.) | 650-592-1852 www.rangoonruby.com

"Tasty" Burmese cooking with lots of vegetarian choices, including "great tea-leaf salad", goes for affordable rates at this Palo Altan with a new San Carlos branch; there's "quick service" at the jade-topped bar, and even if not everyone's "blown away" by the food, the "fun tropical drinks" are a plus.

Refuge *Belgian/Sandwiches*   25 | 15 | 19 | $25

NEW **Menlo Park** | 1143 Crane St. (bet. Oak Grove & Santa Cruz Aves.) | 650-319-8197 Ⓜ

San Carlos | 963 Laurel St. (Morse Blvd.) | 650-598-9813 Ⓢ Ⓜ www.refugesc.com

At this "casual place" in San Carlos and its new Menlo Park sibling, a "simple, perfect" menu "focuses on what they do best" – "thick-cut, housemade" pastrami sandwiches ("take a heart specialist along"), nine-oz. burgers and one of the Peninsula's "best selections of Belgian brews"; the budget-minded call it "rather expensive", but "big portions" and a "small-town-bar" ambiance have out-of-towners sighing "I only wish it were in my neighborhood."

Restaurant at Ventana *Californian*   23 | 26 | 23 | $67

Big Sur | Ventana Inn & Spa | 48123 Hwy. 1 (Coast Ridge Rd.) | 831-667-2331 | www.ventanainn.com

The "wonderful atmosphere" wins out at this "rustic" Big Sur Californian at the Ventana Inn & Spa, ideal for a cozy "dinner on a cold night" or "lunch outside with those spectacular views"; so while the bill may outpace the "really good", locally sourced food, many are pleased with the "excellent" service and call it "one of the best in the area."

Restaurant James Randall Ⓜ *Californian*   ▽ 25 | 21 | 24 | $51

Los Gatos | 303 N. Santa Cruz Ave. (Bachman Ave.) | 408-395-4441 | www.restaurantjamesrandall.com

"There's always something new to try" at this "well-kept secret" in Los Gatos, a "family-run" operation set in a "quaint" "small house" where the "outstanding" eclectic Californian menu "changes" regularly; the price is right, and the adjacent "hip wine bar" hawking "special cocktails" and bar bites makes suburbanites feel like they're "back in civilization"; P.S. open for brunch only on Sunday.

Restaurant Mitsunobu Ⓜ *Japanese*   ▽ 24 | 23 | 26 | $110

Menlo Park | 325 Sharon Park Dr. (Sand Hill Rd.) | 650-234-1084 | www.rmitsunobu.com

"Following the Kaygetsu tradition", this high-end contemporary Japanese situated on the site of that shuttered Menlo Park favorite regales Peninsula diners with "excellent" service and seasonal kaiseki dinners (albeit with a Californian twist) overseen by its predecessor's executive chef; prix fixe and à la carte menus offer sushi, sashimi and cooked small plates, along with an array of premium sakes; P.S. serves lunch Tuesday–Friday.

Rio Grill *Californian*
23 | 20 | 22 | $43

Carmel | Crossroads Shopping Ctr. | 101 Crossroads Blvd. (Rio Rd.) | 831-625-5436 | www.riogrill.com

"After so many years" (since 1983), "locals" and visitors alike are still smitten by this "spirited, breezy" Carmel grill serving "generous portions" of "grilled foods", "great veggies" and other "well-prepared" "Californian cuisine with a Southwestern touch"; patrons look beyond the "shopping-center location", as the "inventive dishes", "awesome" wine selection (listed on an iPad) and "knowledgeable servers" make it "worth returning to again and again."

Roti Indian Bistro *Indian*
23 | 18 | 21 | $30

Burlingame | 209 Park Rd. (bet. Burlingame & Howard Aves.) | 650-340-7684 | www.rotibistro.com

See review in City of San Francisco Directory.

Roy's at Pebble Beach *Hawaiian*
25 | 27 | 24 | $60

Pebble Beach | The Inn at Spanish Bay | 2700 17 Mile Dr. (Palmero Way.) | 831-647-7500 | www.roysrestaurant.com

Like "all Roy's restaurants", this Pebble Beach golf resort locale proffers "outstanding Hawaiian-style" "Asian fusion" delivered by a "super-attentive" staff for "upscale prices", but what really "sets it apart" are the "superlative views over Spanish Bay" visible through "floor-to-ceiling windows" that "make every table" a "choice" one; it's particularly "enchanting" for "lunch followed by a walk on the beach" or by a "fire pit" where you can "catch the bagpiper" "at sundown."

Sakae Sushi Noboru *Japanese*
∇ 25 | 16 | 19 | $68

Burlingame | 243 California Dr. (bet. Burlingame & Howard Aves.) | 650-348-4064 | www.sakaesushi.com

Importing its delicacies from Japan three times a week, this Burlingame sushi joint offers "some of the freshest fish around" matched by top-shelf sakes in a sizable space accented with exposed-brick walls; you can "easily run up" a bill, though some say the "local clientele" "doesn't care about the price."

Sakoon *Indian*
21 | 20 | 18 | $28

Mountain View | 357 Castro St. (bet. California & Dana Sts.) | 650-965-2000 | www.sakoonrestaurant.com

"Savory, satisfying" Indian food "bursts with flavor without being overwhelming" at this modern Mountain View locale with a lively ambiance for "entertaining friends or colleagues"; the service varies and it's somewhat "costly" for its ilk, but the "excellent lunch buffet" is big on value.

Sam's Chowder House *Seafood*
22 | 21 | 20 | $37

Half Moon Bay | 4210 Cabrillo Hwy. N. (Capistrano Rd.) | 650-712-0245 | www.samschowderhouse.com

"Dreamy lobster rolls" and "exceptional clam chowder" make this seafood cliffhanger in Half Moon Bay "feel like the Eastern seaboard", only with "vast views of the Pacific"; a few think it's "a little pricey", but even that "doesn't keep the crowds away" thanks to a patio that's one of the "best places" around for "alfresco dining"; P.S. Sam's Chowdermobile makes stops about town (www.samschowdermobile.com).

Saravana Bhavan *Indian*

24 | 11 | 13 | $14

Sunnyvale | 1305 S. Mary Ave. (Fremont Ave.) | 408-616-7755 | www.saravanaabhavan-ca.com

Customers "craving" "authentic" vegetarian South Indian cuisine, including "fabulous" dosas, head to this inexpensive option that's located "somewhat off the beaten path" in Sunnyvale; on the downside, the place is nothing to look at, and diners might "have to put up with indifferent service."

Sardine Factory *American/Seafood*

24 | 23 | 23 | $62

Monterey | 701 Wave St. (Prescott Ave.) | 831-373-3775 | www.sardinefactory.com

There's still plenty of "history" at this "Cannery Row classic" ("*Play Misty for Me* was filmed here"), but this American seafooder "has had a rebirth" and the "food has become outstanding"; surveyors are attracted to the "many little rooms" (especially the "beautiful atrium" complete with a glass dome) and details like the "ice swans", as well as a "professional staff" that "impresses."

Sawa Sushi ☒ *Japanese*

▽ 23 | 14 | 22 | $106

Sunnyvale | 1042 E. El Camino Real (Henderson Ave.) | 408-241-7292 | www.sawasushi.net

"What a treat!" say those who trumpet the "quality" and "delight" provided by this long-running, high-end Japanese in a Sunnyvale strip mall; private lunches and nightly dinners (especially the ever-changing omakase menu) are "expensive" (and come with "an attitude as well"), but the "interaction" with chef-owner Steve Sawa and the attendant "enlightenment of the senses are worth the small hurdle of getting in" to the minimalist space; P.S. closed Sunday.

NEW The Sea by Alexander's Steakhouse *Seafood*

▽ 23 | 24 | 24 | $115

Palo Alto | Dinah's Garden Hotel | 4269 El Camino Real (Dinah's Ct.) | 650-213-1111 | www.theseausa.com

The "presentation is theater" at this pricey Palo Altan starring "well-executed", sustainably sourced, upscale seafood that might earn a spot in your "taste-bud memory bank"; adding to the attraction, guests are "pleased" by the service, setting and "right-on" wine pairings; P.S. it's also open for lunch Wednesday–Friday.

Sent Sovi Ⓜ *Californian*

26 | 21 | 25 | $85

Saratoga | 14583 Big Basin Way (5th St.) | 408-867-3110 | www.sentsovi.com

Fans say "there is no cozier, friendlier fine dining" in the South Bay than at this "little spot" in Saratoga where "enthusiastic" husband-and-wife chef-owners offer "imaginative" Californian cuisine and "excellent" wines in a "homey" yet "romantic setting"; it's "not inexpensive", but regulars return for the "prix fixe menus" and "special events year-round" that have a "fresh, seasonal focus."

71 Saint Peter ☒ *Californian/Mediterranean*

22 | 20 | 21 | $37

San Jose | San Pedro Sq. | 71 N. San Pedro St. (bet. Santa Clara & St. John Sts.) | 408-971-8523 | www.71saintpeter.com

For an "intimate" dinner, this "charming" Cal-Med bistro in San Jose's San Pedro Square is a midpriced "favorite" that "always delivers" a "delightful dining experience" with "well-prepared", "seasonal" "farm-to-table" fare; if a few find it "nothing too exciting", most maintain that the "beautiful" patio and "above and beyond accommodating" owners make it a "fabulous date-night choice."

Shadowbrook Restaurant *Californian*   22 | 26 | 23 | $50

Capitola | 1750 Wharf Rd. (Lincoln Ave.) | 831-475-1511 | www.shadowbrook-capitola.com

Capitolans take the cable car up to this "magical place" – a "fantasy landscape" holding a "beautifully maintained historic and slightly eclectic building" with a "romantic" ambiance; the Californian fare is "very good" and the service "special", and while it's expensive, the bar menu offers more affordable options; P.S. be sure to "get reservations if you can."

Shalimar *Indian/Pakistani*   23 | 7 | 13 | $16

Sunnyvale | 1146 W. El Camino Real (bet. Bernardo & Grape Aves.) | 408-530-0300 | www.shalimarsv.com

See review in City of San Francisco Directory.

Sierra Mar *Californian/Eclectic*   28 | 29 | 27 | $95

Big Sur | Post Ranch Inn | Hwy. 1 (30 mi. south of Carmel) | 831-667-2200 | www.postranchinn.com

A "bucket-list experience" from start to finish entrances diners "who don't want it to end" when seated in this glassed-in, cliffside aerie "overlooking the Pacific" at Big Sur's Post Ranch Inn, where the "extraordinary architecture" and some of the "best views in California" capture the Bay Area's No. 1 rating for Decor; the setting is a fitting backdrop for "exquisite" (and expensive) Cal-Eclectic cuisine, "world-class wines" and "impeccable" service, and some suggest it's perhaps best appreciated "before sunset" for a "spectacular lunch" or pre-dinner fireside cocktail "on the deck."

Sino *Chinese*   19 | 22 | 17 | $36

San Jose | Santana Row | 377 Santana Row (Olsen Dr.) | 408-247-8880 | www.sinorestaurant.com

A "large, pleasing array of dim sum", "interesting" midpriced Chinese-influenced fare and "excellent" cocktails (both "boozy and nonalcoholic") await the "youngish" set at this Santana Row "scene"; though "service needs some work" and a "nightclub atmosphere" means the "crowded" space gets "noisy", overall it's "a fun place."

Soif Wine Bar *Californian*   ▽ 24 | 20 | 21 | $37

Santa Cruz | 105 Walnut Ave. (Pacific Ave.) | 831-423-2020 | www.soifwine.com

"Delicious" Californian bites that "vary with the season" go with the "great wine tasting and wine buying" at this Santa Cruz bar, restaurant and vino shop (a sib of La Posta); "intimate" and moderately priced, it appeals to "wine and food lovers", and even those who "don't drink alcohol."

Spice Kit Ⓩ *Asian*   19 | 12 | 17 | $14

Palo Alto | 340 S. California Ave. (Birch St.) | 650-326-1698 | www.spicekit.com

See review in City of San Francisco Directory.

Station 1 Restaurant ⓜ *Californian*

25	20	25	$71

Woodside | 2991 Woodside Rd. (Mountain Home Rd.) | 650-851-4988 |
www.station1restaurant.com

Nestled in a "small, rustic" former firehouse, this Woodside Californian offers a "superb" prix fixe menu focused on "seasonal items" that's "always a delightful surprise"; it can be "expensive", especially if you indulge in the "delicious" pre-Prohibition cocktails or pours from the "imaginative" wine list, but "personable" staffers who "remember you after your first visit" help extinguish most concerns.

Stella Alpina Osteria *Italian*

25	21	24	$49

Burlingame | 401 Primrose Rd. (Chapin Ave.) | 650-347-5733 |
www.stellaalpinaosteria.com

"Romantic" sorts smart enough to "make reservations several days ahead" "squeeze into" this "lovely" "neighborhood osteria" in Burlingame for "consistently wonderful" Northern Italian fare prepared with "excellent ingredients" (tip: "don't miss" the "amazing truffle gnocchi" when it's on the menu); tabs can be a "bit pricey", but the "warm, inviting" vibe makes it even more alluring.

St. Michael's Alley ⊠ⓜ *Californian*

22	21	21	$44

Palo Alto | 140 Homer Ave. (High St.) | 650-326-2530 |
www.stmikes.com

"Sitting outside is a delight" at this "off-the-beaten-path" Palo Altan proffering midpriced Californian cuisine with a "twist", though the interior – a collection of "intimate rooms" with "interesting decor" – also has its fans; even the less-impressed agree the "worth-the-wait weekend brunch" served at the eatery's original location (806 Emerson Street) is among the "best in town."

Straits Restaurant *Singaporean*

20	21	18	$36

Burlingame | 1100 Burlingame Ave. (bet. California Dr. & Lorton Ave.) |
650-373-7883
San Jose | Santana Row | 333 Santana Row (bet. Alyssum & Tatum Lns.) |
408-246-6320
www.straitsrestaurants.com
See review in City of San Francisco Directory.

Sumika ⓜ *Japanese*

25	15	19	$41

Los Altos | 236 Central Plaza (bet. 2nd & 3rd Sts.) | 650-917-1822 |
www.sumikagrill.com

The "amazing" skewers "tempt you to order one more (and then one more)" at this "absolutely authentic" yakitori bar in Los Altos, which "grills anything and everything" and serves up Japanese specialties like "oyako-don done right"; there's little decor and spendy tabs ("prices match the quality"), but in-the-know eaters attest it's "worth the effort"; P.S. the secret to the "charcoalicous" taste? "distinctive oak wood" imported from Japan.

The Surf Spot *Eclectic*

-	-	-	M

Pacifica | 4627 Pacific Coast Hwy. (Reina Del Mar Ave.) | 650-355-7873 |
www.surfspoteats.com

Sporting a name and beachy vibe that's inspired by surf destinations around the globe, this casual all-day Pacifica hangout beckons "locals" and families "driving down the coast" with its "delicious" midpriced

	FOOD	DECOR	SERVICE	COST

Eclectic "gourmet comfort food" and good libations; indoors is small, but on a "warm day" the "amazing" outdoor area gets "quite busy" between its fire pits, "outdoor bars", volleyball court, a "grassy hill" where "kids can run around" and a stage for live music on weekends.

Sushi Sam's Edomata 🍣 Ⓜ *Japanese* — 24 | 13 | 18 | $39

San Mateo | 218 E. Third St. (bet. B St. & Ellsworth Ave.) | 650-344-0888 | www.sushisams.com

Fans suggest you "sit at the bar" and "order the omakase (at least 10 pieces)" as Sam "works his magic" at this "reasonably priced" San Mateo sushi joint, which also features a limited menu of cooked Japanese favorites; it's set in a "spartan" space and can be "noisy", but since it offers such "awesome fish" and "delicious" desserts, there are often "lines out the door", so "call ahead to get on the list."

NEW Tacolicious ● *Mexican* — 24 | 19 | 19 | $25

Palo Alto | 632 Emerson St. (bet. Forest & Hamilton Aves.) | 650-838-0500 | www.tacolicious.com

See review in City of San Francisco Directory.

Tai Pan *Chinese* — 23 | 21 | 21 | $36

Palo Alto | 560 Waverley St. (Hamilton Ave.) | 650-329-9168 | www.taipanpaloalto.com

It's "worth the gas money to drive" to Palo Alto swear supporters of this "linen-napkins-and-white-tablecloths" Chinese proffering "authentic" Hong Kong–style chow, including "delicious" dim sum ordered off a menu and "served piping hot from the kitchen" ("no carts"); "professional" servers do the "elegant surroundings" justice, and if the "price is higher" here, it's only because you're paying for "quality."

Tamarine *Vietnamese* — 25 | 22 | 22 | $51

Palo Alto | 546 University Ave. (bet. Cowper & Webster Sts.) | 650-325-8500 | www.tamarinerestaurant.com

"Sit back and be dazzled" at this "inventive" (if "pricey") Palo Alto Vietnamese that attracts a "congenial" crowd with its "beautifully presented" small plates from a menu that "changes regularly" plus "excellent cocktails"; it's "always packed", so "reserve ahead" and don't be surprised if it's "noisy and cramped", but no matter: service that's "attentive without being cloying", "gorgeous design" and that "fabulous" food add up to a "winning combination."

Taqueria San Jose *Mexican* — 23 | 13 | 17 | $11

San Jose | 235 E. Santa Clara St. (6th St.) | 408-288-8616

See review in City of San Francisco Directory.

Taqueria Tlaquepaque *Mexican* — 21 | 11 | 16 | $16

San Jose | 2222 Lincoln Ave. (bet. Curtner & Franquette Aves.) | 408-978-3665

San Jose | 699 Curtner Ave. (Canoas Garden Ave.) | 408-448-1230 🍴

San Jose | 721 Willow St. (Delmas Ave.) | 408-287-9777 Ⓜ

"Faithful fanatics" of "old-school" "Mexican grub" like "chile verde burritos" and "enchiladas suizas" flock to this San Jose trio that's "priced right"; it "may not be the prettiest" and "service is just ok", but you won't care after a round of "addicting" "Mexican beer with tequila" to help wash down the "generous portions."

Tarpy's Roadhouse *American*

24 | 24 | 23 | $38

Monterey | 2999 Monterey Salinas Hwy. (Canyon Del Rey Blvd.) | 831-647-1444 | www.tarpys.com

"Delicious" American "comfort food with a twist" is turned out at this "casual", midpriced "sister restaurant to the Rio Grill" situated in a sprawling "old, restored" stone "roadhouse"; it's "a little out of the way" in Monterey but "worth the drive" for the "quaint" "atmosphere inside or out" plus a "well-stocked" bar and "great wines" that ensure "lots of fun" for brunch, "lunch with girls" or dinner "with family."

Tava Indian Kitchen *Indian*

- | - | - | I

Palo Alto | Town & Country Vill. | 855 El Camino Real (Embarcadero Rd.) | 650-321-8282 | www.tavaindian.com

Expect authentic Indian flavors at these budget-friendly Palo Alto and SoMa quick-grabs offering customize-your-own bowls and 'burroti' wraps (think burritos made with roti bread) made with locally sourced meats and house-roasted spices; seating is limited at both locations.

231 Ellsworth 🗷 *American*

23 | 20 | 22 | $54

San Mateo | 231 S. Ellsworth Ave. (bet. 2nd & 3rd Aves.) | 650-347-7231 | www.231ellsworth.com

Serving New American cuisine for decades, this "special-occasion" Downtown San Mateo destination offers a "terrific" chef's menu in an "intimate setting" suitable for "quiet conversation" or "business meals"; admirers praise the "attentive but not smothering" service, and though some deem it "slightly overpriced", fans keep coming back for the "amazing wine selection" and "elegant yet casual" attitude.

🆕 Umami Burger *Burgers*

22 | 17 | 18 | $22

Palo Alto | 452 University Ave. (bet. Cowper & Waverley Sts.) | 650-321-8626 | www.umamiburger.com

See review in City of San Francisco Directory.

Village Pub *American*

25 | 24 | 24 | $66

Woodside | 2967 Woodside Rd. (Whiskey Hill Rd.) | 650-851-9888 | www.thevillagepub.net

"Rub shoulders with VCs, tech notables" and the "horsey crowd" at this "sumptuous", "hard-to-find" Woodside New American "treat" where "top-flight" food and wine is served by a "welcoming", "down-to-earth" staff; "warm and inviting", it's the "best place around for a celebratory occasion", though "be prepared to pay accordingly."

Viognier 🗷 *Californian/French*

24 | 21 | 23 | $66

San Mateo | Draeger's Mktpl. | 222 E. Fourth Ave. (bet. B St. & Ellsworth Ave.) | 650-685-3727 | www.viognierrestaurant.com

Flush foodies ferret out this "wonderful" Cal-French "fine-dining" spot perched in an "unlikely setting" above a San Mateo gourmet grocer; "haute cuisine with a conscience" ("locally available, sustainable and in season"), a "knowledgeable" staff and "ever-changing" "tasting menus" help patrons "escape the top-of-a-market feel" – as does the "phenomenal" wine list with 1,100-plus selections.

Vung Tau *Vietnamese*

24 | 18 | 18 | $25

Milpitas | Milpitas Green | 1750 N. Milpitas Blvd. (bet. Dixon Rd. & Sunnyhills Ct.) | 408-934-9327

(continued)

Vung Tau

San Jose | 535 E. Santa Clara St. (12th St.) | 408-288-9055
www.vungtaurestaurant.com

"More upscale than the average pho place", this reasonably priced, family-run Vietnamese in San Jose (with a "midrange" outpost in Milpitas, a "budget" locale in Newark and upscale sibling Tamarine in Palo Alto) distinguishes itself with "flavorful, comforting" "traditional" dishes that are "authentic" but made with "an interesting twist"; amid the "simple", "nicely furnished" digs, "friendly" servers are "knowledgeable about portion sizes" and "help steer novice diners in the right direction."

Wakuriya Ⓜ *Japanese*   ▽ 28 | 21 | 28 | $124

(aka Japanese Kitchen Wakuriya)

San Mateo | Crystal Springs Village Shopping Ctr. | 115 De Anza Blvd. (bet. Parrott Dr. & Polhemus Rd.) | 650-286-0410 | www.wakuriya.com

At their "tiny", "haute Japanese" in a San Mateo strip mall, "husband-and-wife duo" Katsuhiro and Mayumi Yamasaki present seasonally changing "kaiseki-style" dinners ("nine delicious courses" of "wow") while making guests "feel like the only ones dining"; it's "hard to get into" (and quite "expensive"), but for such a "memorable experience", it's worth "calling one month in advance", as "reservations are a must"; P.S. open Wednesday–Sunday.

Xanh   *Vietnamese*   21 | 21 | 19 | $34

Mountain View | 110 Castro St. (bet. Evelyn Ave. & Villa St.) | 650-964-1888 | www.xanhrestaurant.com

Even the service is "slick" at this "high-end", "ultramodern" Mountain View Vietnamese, where a "hip" throng assembles to sample "fancy drinks" and an "interesting" menu of "consistently delicious" dishes awash in "explosive and diverse flavors"; if some suggest the "eye-catching" style (e.g. "wall of water") and "clubby vibe" is "over the top" for the "'burbs", they can hit the "bountiful" lunch buffet instead and avoid the "loud" evening scene.

Yankee Pier   *New England/Seafood*   19 | 16 | 19 | $35

South San Francisco | San Francisco Int'l Airport | United Domestic Departure Terminal 3 (Hwy. 101) | 650-821-8938 | www.yankeepier.com

See review in North of San Francisco Directory.

Zibibbo Ⓩ *Mediterranean*   20 | 19 | 19 | $45

Palo Alto | 430 Kipling St. (bet. Lytton & University Aves.) | 650-328-6722 | www.zibibborestaurant.com

This "pleasant" Palo Alto sibling of SF's Restaurant Lulu delivers "solid" "Mediterranean goodies" (including "small plates") to everyone from couples on a "date" to biz types entertaining "clients or potential recruits"; the unimpressed knock a "spacious layout" that can get "noisy" and "inconsistent" service and chow, but for many it remains an "old standby."

INDEXES

LOCATION MAPS

All places are in San Francisco unless otherwise noted (East of San Francisco=E; North of San Francisco=N; South of San Francisco=S).

Special Features

Listings cover the best in each category and include names, locations and Food ratings. Multi-location restaurants' features may vary by branch.

BREAKFAST

(See also Hotel Dining)

Alexis Baking | **Napa/N**	22
Bette's Oceanview | **Berkeley/E**	24
Big Sur | **Big Sur/S**	24
Blackberry Bistro | **Oakland/E**	21
Boulettes Larder/Bouli Bar | **Embarcadero**	25
NEW B. Patisserie | **Pacific Hts**	26
Brenda's | **Civic Ctr**	25
Butler/Chef | **SoMa**	22
Chloe's Cafe | **Noe Valley**	23
NEW Corner Store | **Laurel Hts**	22
Dipsea Cafe | **Mill Valley/N**	18
Downtown Bakery | **Healdsburg/N**	26
Ella's | **Presidio Hts**	21
Emporio Rulli | **Downtown**	22
Fremont Diner | **Sonoma/N**	24
Gayle's Bakery | **Capitola/S**	24
Il Fornaio | **multi.**	18
Jimmy Beans | **Berkeley/E**	20
Jimtown Store | **Healdsburg/N**	21
Kate's Kit. | **Lower Haight**	23
Koi | **Daly City/S**	23
La Boulange | **multi.**	21
La Note | **Berkeley/E**	23
Mama's on Wash. | **N Beach**	24
Mama's Royal | **Oakland/E**	23
Model Bakery | **St. Helena/N**	23
Mo's | **N Beach**	23
903 | **Bernal Hts**	24
Oliveto Cafe | **Oakland/E**	23
NEW Parish Cafe | **Healdsburg/N**	–
Pork Store | **multi.**	19
Rick & Ann's | **Berkeley/E**	23
Rose's Cafe | **Cow Hollow**	22
Sears | **Downtown**	20
Tartine | **Mission**	27
Town's End | **Embarcadero**	21
NEW 20th Century | **Hayes Valley**	–
Venus | **Berkeley/E**	24
Water St. Bistro | **Petaluma/N**	23

Willow Wood | **Graton/N**	24
Zazie | **Cole Valley**	24

BRUNCH

Absinthe | **Hayes Valley**	23
Ahwahnee | **Yosemite/E**	21
Alexis Baking | **Napa/N**	22
Anzu | **Downtown**	23
NEW Backyard | **Forestville/N**	–
Baker St. Bistro | **Marina**	21
Balboa Cafe | **Cow Hollow**	20
Bar Agricole | **SoMa**	22
Bar Jules | **Hayes Valley**	24
Beach Chalet | **Outer Sunset**	16
Bistro Liaison | **Berkeley/E**	23
Boulettes Larder/Bouli Bar | **Embarcadero**	25
Brenda's | **Civic Ctr**	25
Buckeye | **Mill Valley/N**	25
Camino | **Oakland/E**	24
Campton Pl. | **Downtown**	26
Catch | **Castro**	21
Chez Maman | **Potrero Hill**	24
Chloe's Cafe | **Noe Valley**	23
Chow/Park Chow | **multi.**	21
NEW Corner Store | **Laurel Hts**	22
Elite Cafe | **Pacific Hts**	20
Ella's | **Presidio Hts**	21
Epic Roasthse. | **Embarcadero**	22
Erna's Elderberry | **Oakhurst/E**	28
Fandango | **Pacific Grove/S**	21
15 Romolo | **N Beach**	22
Five | **Berkeley/E**	20
Foreign Cinema | **Mission**	24
Fremont Diner | **Sonoma/N**	24
Gabriella Café | **Santa Cruz/S**	20
Garden Ct. | **Downtown**	22
Gayle's Bakery | **Capitola/S**	24
Girl/Fig | **Sonoma/N**	24
Grand Cafe | **Downtown**	20
Greens | **Marina**	25
NEW Hakkasan | **Downtown**	24
NEW Hillside Supper | **Bernal Hts**	–

Insalata's | **San Anselmo/N**	25
Kate's Kit. | **Lower Haight**	23
La Forêt | **San Jose/S**	27
La Note | **Berkeley/E**	23
Lark Creek | **Walnut Creek/E**	23
Liberty Cafe | **Bernal Hts**	22
Luna Park | **Mission**	20
NEW Lungomare | **Oakland/E**	–
Madera | **Menlo Pk/S**	23
Marinitas | **San Anselmo/N**	21
Mayfield | **Palo Alto/S**	20
Mission Bch. Café | **Mission**	24
MoMo's | **S Beach**	19
Navio | **Half Moon Bay/S**	24
NEW Nido | **Oakland/E**	–
Nob Hill Café | **Nob Hill**	22
Nopa | **W Addition**	26
Outerlands | **Outer Sunset**	25
Park Chalet | **Outer Sunset**	16
Piazza D'Angelo | **Mill Valley/N**	20
Picante Cocina | **Berkeley/E**	22
Q Rest./Wine | **Inner Rich**	20
Redd | **Yountville/N**	27
Rick & Ann's | **Berkeley/E**	23
Rio Grill | **Carmel/S**	23
NEW Rosa Mexicano | **Embarcadero**	24
Rose's Cafe | **Cow Hollow**	22
Slow Club | **Mission**	23
SPQR | **Pacific Hts**	25
NEW Stella Nonna | **Berkeley/E**	–
Tarpy's | **Monterey/S**	24
Tav./Lark Creek | **Larkspur/N**	21
1300/Fillmore | **W Addition**	22
Town's End | **Embarcadero**	21
Trader Vic's | **Emeryville/E**	18
Tra Vigne | **St. Helena/N**	24
Universal Cafe | **Mission**	25
Venus | **Berkeley/E**	24
Waterbar | **Embarcadero**	23
Wente Vineyards | **Livermore/E**	25
Willow Wood | **Graton/N**	24
Wise Sons | **Mission**	23
Yank Sing | **SoMa**	26
Zazie | **Cole Valley**	24
Zuni Café | **Hayes Valley**	26

BUSINESS DINING

Alexander's Steak | **multi.**	26
Alfred's Steak | **Downtown**	23
All Spice | **San Mateo/S**	26
Amber India | **multi.**	24
Ame | **SoMa**	26
Americano | **Embarcadero**	20
Anchor & Hope | **SoMa**	21
Anzu | **Downtown**	23
Applewood Rest. | **Guerneville/N**	24
Arcadia | **San Jose/S**	23
Auberge du Soleil | **Rutherford/N**	27
Aubergine | **Carmel/S**	26
Barbacco | **Downtown**	24
Basin | **Saratoga/S**	23
Baumé | **Palo Alto/S**	26
Bella Vista | **Woodside/S**	24
Big Four | **Nob Hill**	24
Bluestem Brass. | **SoMa**	19
Bottega | **Yountville/N**	25
Boulevard | **Embarcadero**	27
Bourbon Steak | **Downtown**	23
Brannan's Grill | **Calistoga/N**	19
Brasserie S&P | **Downtown**	24
Bucci's | **Emeryville/E**	21
Burritt Tavern | **Downtown**	20
Campton Pl. | **Downtown**	26
Chantilly | **Redwood City/S**	25
Chaya | **Embarcadero**	23
Chef Chu's | **Los Altos/S**	22
Chiaroscuro | **Downtown**	25
Cole's Chop | **Napa/N**	27
Cotogna | **Downtown**	26
Credo | **Downtown**	20
Cupola Pizzeria | **Downtown**	21
Dio Deka | **Los Gatos/S**	25
Donato | **Redwood City/S**	23
Epic Roasthse. | **Embarcadero**	22
Evvia | **Palo Alto/S**	28
Fandango | **Pacific Grove/S**	21
Farallon | **Downtown**	25
Fifth Floor | **SoMa**	24
Five | **Berkeley/E**	20
5A5 Steak | **Downtown**	23
Flea St. Café | **Menlo Pk/S**	26
Fleur de Lys | **Downtown**	27
Fuki Sushi | **Palo Alto/S**	23

Restaurant	Location	Rating
Gitane	Downtown	23
Grand Cafe	Downtown	20
Greens	Marina	25
NEW Hakkasan	Downtown	24
Harris'	Polk Gulch	26
House/Prime	Polk Gulch	26
Iberia	Menlo Pk/S	22
Il Fornaio	multi.	18
Izzy's Steak	Marina	22
Jardinière	Civic Ctr	26
Jasper's Corner	Downtown	19
Jin Sho	Palo Alto/S	24
John's Grill	Downtown	21
NEW Katsu	Los Gatos/S	-
Keiko	Nob Hill	27
Kokkari	Downtown	28
Kuleto's	Downtown	23
La Forêt	San Jose/S	27
L'Ardoise	Castro	24
Lark Creek Steak	Downtown	24
LaSalette	Sonoma/N	24
LB Steak	San Jose/S	22
Le Central	Downtown	21
Le Colonial	Downtown	22
Le Papillon	San Jose/S	27
Lion/Compass	Sunnyvale/S	21
Luce	SoMa	21
NEW Lungomare	Oakland/E	-
Madera	Menlo Pk/S	23
Manresa	Los Gatos/S	27
Manzanita	Truckee/E	22
Marinus	Carmel Valley/S	26
MarketBar	Embarcadero	18
Meadowood Grill	St. Helena/N	22
Meritage/Claremont	Berkeley/E	23
Michael Mina	Downtown	27
Mistral	Redwood Shores/S	22
NEW MKT	SoMa	-
MoMo's	S Beach	19
Morton's	multi.	23
Muracci's	Downtown	20
Murray Circle	Sausalito/N	23
NEW M.Y. China	Downtown	19
One Market	Embarcadero	24
Osha Thai	multi.	22
Osteria	Palo Alto/S	23
Ozumo	multi.	25
Palio d'Asti	Downtown	21
Pampas	Palo Alto/S	22
Parallel 37	Nob Hill	24
Pazzia	SoMa	25
Peasant/Pear	Danville/E	23
Perbacco	Downtown	26
Per Diem	Downtown	20
Picco	Larkspur/N	26
Piperade	Downtown	26
Plumed Horse	Saratoga/S	25
Poggio	Sausalito/N	25
Postrio	Downtown	23
Presidio Social	Presidio	19
Press	St. Helena/N	26
Prospect	SoMa	24
Quattro	E Palo Alto/S	22
Quince	Downtown	26
Rest. LuLu	SoMa	21
Rest. Mitsunobu	Menlo Pk/S	24
Rist. Umbria	SoMa	21
RN74	SoMa	22
Roy's	SoMa	24
Ruth's Chris	multi.	24
Saison	SoMa	27
Salt Hse.	SoMa	22
Sam's Grill	Downtown	22
Sanraku	multi.	23
Sardine Factory	Monterey/S	24
Scala's Bistro	Downtown	23
NEW Sea	Palo Alto/S	23
Sens	Embarcadero	20
Sent Sovi	Saratoga/S	26
71 St. Peter	San Jose/S	22
Sino	San Jose/S	19
Solbar	Calistoga/N	26
South Park	SoMa	22
Spruce	Presidio Hts	26
St. Michael's	Palo Alto/S	22
Straits	multi.	20
Tadich Grill	Downtown	24
Thomas & Fagiani's	Napa/N	24
Town Hall	SoMa	23
Townhouse B&G	Emeryville/E	22
Trace	SoMa	22

NEW Tribune Tavern | Oakland/E	-
25 Lusk | SoMa	22
231 Ellsworth | San Mateo/S	23
Vic Stewart's | Walnut Creek/E	24
Village Pub | Woodside/S	25
Viognier | San Mateo/S	24
Waterfront | Embarcadero	21
Wayfare Tav. | Downtown	24
Wexler's | Downtown	23
Yank Sing | SoMa	26
Zadin | Castro	20
Zaré/Fly Trap | SoMa	21
Zazu | Sebastopol/N	26
Zero Zero | SoMa	24
Zibibbo | Palo Alto/S	20
Zuni Café | Hayes Valley	26

CELEBRITY CHEFS

Gastón Acurio	
La Mar | Embarcadero	24
David Bazirgan	
Fifth Floor | SoMa	24
Jan Birnbaum	
Epic Roasthse. | Embarcadero	22
Danny Bowien	
Mission Chinese | Mission	22
Stuart Brioza and Nicole Krasinski	
State Bird | W Addition	26
Wendy Brucker	
Rivoli | Berkeley/E	27
Trattoria Corso | Berkeley/E	25
Paul Canales	
NEW Duende | Oakland/E	23
Michael Chiarello	
Bottega | Yountville/N	25
NEW Coqueta | Embarcadero	-
Lawrence Chu	
Chef Chu's | Los Altos/S	22
Gary Chu's | Santa Rosa/N	24
John Clark and Gayle Pirie	
Foreign Cinema | Mission	24
Machine Coffee | Downtown	-
Showdogs | Downtown	20

Greg Cole	
Celadon | Napa/N	25
Cole's Chop | Napa/N	27
Tom Colicchio	
'Wichcraft | Downtown	18
Jesse Cool	
Cool Café | multi.	21
Flea St. Café | Menlo Pk/S	26
Chris Cosentino	
Boccalone | Embarcadero	25
Incanto | Noe Valley	25
Dominique Crenn	
Atelier Crenn | Marina	27
Gary Danko	
Gary Danko | Fish. Wharf	29
Traci Des Jardins	
Jardinière | Civic Ctr	26
Mijita | multi.	20
Public Hse. | S Beach	17
Greg Dunmore	
Nojo | Hayes Valley	25
Duske Estes and John Stewart	
Zazu | Sebastopol/N	26
Brad Farmerie	
Thomas & Fagiani's | Napa/N	24
Tyler Florence	
El Paseo | Mill Valley/N	23
Wayfare Tav. | Downtown	24
Ken Frank	
Bank Café | Napa/N	23
La Toque | Napa/N	27
Mark Franz	
Farallon | Downtown	25
Waterbar | Embarcadero	23
Ruggero Gadaldi	
Beretta | Mission	24
Delarosa | Marina	21
Pesce | Castro	25
Matt Gandin	
Comal | Berkeley/E	23
Tony Gemignani	
NEW Capo's | N Beach	-
Tony's Coal-Fired | N Beach	24
Tony's Pizza | N Beach	26
Charlie Hallowell	
Boot/Shoe | Oakland/E	24
Pizzaiolo | Oakland/E	26

Bruce Hill	
Bix	**Downtown**	24
Picco	**Larkspur/N**	26
Pizzeria Picco	**Larkspur/N**	26
Zero Zero	**SoMa**	24

Gerald Hirigoyen
Bocadillos	**N Beach**	23
Piperade	**Downtown**	26

Lee Kok Hua
NEW Hakkasan	**Downtown**	24

Joseph Humphrey
Dixie	**Presidio**	20

Todd Humphries
Kitchen Door	**Napa/N**	22

Philippe Jeanty
Bistro Jeanty	**Yountville/N**	27

Laurence Jossel
Nopa	**W Addition**	26
Nopalito	**multi.**	24

Shotaro "Sho" Kamio
Brick/Bottle	**Corte Madera/N**	19
Yoshi's	**multi.**	22

Douglas Keane
Healdsburg B&G	**Healdsburg/N**	19

Hubert Keller
Burger Bar	**Downtown**	20
Fleur de Lys	**Downtown**	27

Loretta Keller
Coco500	**SoMa**	24
NEW Seaglass Rest.	**Embarcadero**	–

Thomas Keller
Ad Hoc	**Yountville/N**	26
Addendum	**Yountville/N**	25
Bouchon	**Yountville/N**	26
French Laundry	**Yountville/N**	28

David Kinch
Manresa	**Los Gatos/S**	27

Christopher Kostow
Meadowood Grill	**St. Helena/N**	22
Meadowood Rest.	**St. Helena/N**	27

Mourad Lahlou
Aziza	**Outer Rich**	26

Dennis Leary
Golden West	**Downtown**	21
Sentinel	**SoMa**	23

Corey Lee
Benu	**SoMa**	27

Dennis Lee
Namu Gaji	**multi.**	24

Louis Maldanado
Pizzando	**Healdsburg/N**	–
Spoonbar	**Healdsburg/N**	20

Tony Mangieri
Una Pizza	**SoMa**	26

Laurent Manrique
NEW Aquitaine	**Downtown**	–

Michael Recchiuti
NEW Chocolate Lab	**Dogpatch**	25

Thomas McNaughton
Central Kitchen	**Mission**	24
Flour + Water	**Mission**	26
Salumeria Deli	**Mission**	–

Michael Mina
Arcadia	**San Jose/S**	23
Bourbon Steak	**Downtown**	23
Michael Mina	**Downtown**	27
RN74	**SoMa**	22

Preeti Mistry
NEW Juhu Beach Club	**Oakland/E**	–

Russell Moore
Camino	**Oakland/E**	24

Masaharu Morimoto
Morimoto	**Napa/N**	25

Nancy Oakes
Boulevard	**Embarcadero**	27
Prospect	**SoMa**	24

Rene Ortiz
La Condesa	**St. Helena/N**	25

Charlie Palmer
Burritt Tavern	**Downtown**	20
Dry Creek	**Healdsburg/N**	24

Roland Passot
La Folie	**Russian Hill**	27
LB Steak	**multi.**	22
Left Bank	**multi.**	20

Daniel Patterson
Coi | **N Beach** 27
Haven | **Oakland/E** 25
Plum | **Oakland/E** 23
Cindy Pawlcyn
Cindy Pawlcyn's | 22
St. Helena/N
Cindy's Backstreet | 24
St. Helena/N
NEW Cindy's Waterfront | -
Monterey/S
Mustards | **Yountville/N** 25
Melissa Perello
Frances | **Castro** 27
Jennifer Petrusky
NEW Empire | **Napa/N** -
Charles Phan
NEW Hard Water | -
Embarcadero
Out the Door | **multi.** 23
Slanted Door | **Embarcadero** 26
NEW South/SFJAZZ | -
Hayes Valley
Yigit Pura
Tout Sweet | **Downtown** -
Richard Reddington
Redd | **Yountville/N** 27
Redd Wood | **Yountville/N** 25
Evan and Sarah Rich
Rich Table | **Hayes Valley** 25
Chad Robertson
Bar Tartine | **Mission** 24
Tartine | **Mission** 27
Judy Rodgers
Zuni Café | **Hayes Valley** 26
Mitchell and Stephen Rosenthal
Anchor & Hope | **SoMa** 21
Salt Hse. | **SoMa** 22
Town Hall | **SoMa** 23
Donna Scala
Bistro Don Giovanni | **Napa/N** 25
Scala's Bistro | **Downtown** 23
Ryan Scott
Market & Rye | **multi.** 19
Joshua Skenes
Saison | **SoMa** 27

Annie Somerville
Greens | **Marina** 25
Hiro Sone
Ame | **SoMa** 26
Bar Terra | **St. Helena/N** 25
Terra | **St. Helena/N** 27
Cal Stamenov
Marinus | **Carmel Valley/S** 26
Craig Stoll
Delfina | **Mission** 26
Locanda | **Mission** 24
Pizzeria Delfina | **multi.** 25
James Syhabout
Commis | **Oakland/E** 27
Hawker Fare | **Oakland/E** 23
Michael Tusk
Cotogna | **Downtown** 26
Quince | **Downtown** 26
Alice Waters
Chez Panisse | **Berkeley/E** 27
Chez Panisse Café | 27
Berkeley/E
Joanne Weir
Copita | **Sausalito/N** 24
Alexander Xalxo
Sakoon | **Mtn View/S** 21
Roy Yamaguchi
Roy's | **SoMa** 24
Roy's | **Pebble Bch/S** 25
Martin Yan
NEW M.Y. China | 19
Downtown
Hoss Zare
Zaré/Fly Trap | **SoMa** 21

CHILD-FRIENDLY
(Alternatives to the usual fast-food places)
Ahwahnee | **Yosemite/E** 21
Alexis Baking | **Napa/N** 22
Alice's | **Noe Valley** 20
Alioto's | **Fish. Wharf** 21
Amici's | **multi.** 21
Aperto | **Potrero Hill** 22
Arcadia | **San Jose/S** 23
Azzurro | **Napa/N** 23
Barbara's Fishtrap | 21
Princeton Sea/S

Barney's | **multi.**	21
Basque Cultural | **S San Francisco/S**	20
Beach Chalet | **Outer Sunset**	16
Bellanico | **Oakland/E**	23
Bette's Oceanview | **Berkeley/E**	24
Bistro Boudin | **Fish. Wharf**	22
Bo's BBQ | **Lafayette/E**	22
Brandy Ho's | **multi.**	20
Brannan's Grill | **Calistoga/N**	19
Buckeye | **Mill Valley/N**	25
Bungalow 44 | **Mill Valley/N**	22
Burger Joint | **Mission**	19
Burma Superstar | **Inner Rich**	25
Cactus Taqueria | **multi.**	21
NEW Capo's | **N Beach**	-
Caspers Hot Dogs | **multi.**	22
Cetrella | **Half Moon Bay/S**	23
Cheesecake Fac. | **multi.**	16
Chenery Park | **Glen Pk**	23
Chow/Park Chow | **multi.**	21
Cindy's Backstreet | **St. Helena/N**	24
NEW Cindy's Waterfront | **Monterey/S**	-
Cook St. Helena | **St. Helena/N**	26
Cool Café | **Stanford/S**	21
Dipsea Cafe | **Mill Valley/N**	18
Duarte's | **Pescadero/S**	22
Eliza's | **Pacific Hts**	22
Ella's | **Presidio Hts**	21
Emmy's Spaghetti | **Bernal Hts**	21
Eric's | **Noe Valley**	22
Fish | **Sausalito/N**	24
Flavor | **Santa Rosa/N**	22
Foreign Cinema | **Mission**	24
400 Degrees | **Carmel/S**	-
Front Porch | **Bernal Hts**	22
Gar Woods | **Carnelian Bay/E**	19
Gioia Pizzeria | **Russian Hill**	25
Giordano | **N Beach**	22
Giorgio's | **Inner Rich**	21
Goat Hill | **Potrero Hill**	22
Gott's Roadside | **multi.**	22
Great Eastern | **Chinatown**	23
Healdsburg B&G | **Healdsburg/N**	19
Henry's Hunan | **multi.**	22
Homeroom | **Oakland/E**	21
Hurley's Rest. | **Yountville/N**	23
Il Fornaio | **multi.**	18
Insalata's | **San Anselmo/N**	25
Jimmy Beans | **Berkeley/E**	20
Jimtown Store | **Healdsburg/N**	21
Joe's Cable Car | **Excelsior**	22
Joe's Taco | **Mill Valley/N**	21
Juan's | **Berkeley/E**	19
Kitchen Door | **Napa/N**	22
Koi | **Daly City/S**	23
Kuleto's | **Downtown**	23
La Boulange | **multi.**	21
La Cumbre | **Mission**	20
La Méditerranée | **multi.**	22
Lark Creek | **Walnut Creek/E**	23
Lark Creek Steak | **Downtown**	24
La Taqueria | **Mission**	25
Left Bank | **multi.**	20
Lers Ros Thai | **multi.**	24
Lo Coco's | **multi.**	22
Lovejoy's Tea | **Noe Valley**	20
Luella | **Russian Hill**	23
Mama's on Wash. | **N Beach**	24
Market | **St. Helena/N**	22
Mifune | **Japantown**	18
Mijita | **multi.**	20
Model Bakery | **multi.**	23
Mo's | **N Beach**	23
Mustards | **Yountville/N**	25
Nepenthe | **Big Sur/S**	18
903 | **Bernal Hts**	24
Norman Rose | **Napa/N**	20
North Bch. Pizza | **multi.**	20
O'mei | **Santa Cruz/S**	24
Original Joe's | **San Jose/S**	22
Osteria Coppa | **San Mateo/S**	22
Pacific Catch | **multi.**	22
Pancho Villa | **multi.**	23
Parada 22 | **Haight-Ashbury**	23
Parcel 104 | **Santa Clara/S**	23
Park Chalet | **Outer Sunset**	16
Pasta Pomodoro | **multi.**	18
Pauline's Pizza/Wine | **Mission**	22
Piatti | **multi.**	21
Picante Cocina | **Berkeley/E**	22
Pizza Antica | **multi.**	22
Pizzeria Delfina | **multi.**	25

Pizzeria Tra Vigne	**St. Helena/N**	22
Q Rest./Wine	**Inner Rich**	20
Quattro	**E Palo Alto/S**	22
R & G Lounge	**Chinatown**	24
Redd Wood	**Yountville/N**	25
Rest. Peony	**Oakland/E**	20
Rick & Ann's	**Berkeley/E**	23
Rosso Pizzeria	**Santa Rosa/N**	25
Roy's	**Pebble Bch/S**	25
Rudy's Can't Fail	**multi.**	19
Rustic	**Geyserville/N**	21
Sam's Chowder	**Half Moon Bay/S**	22
Saul's Rest./Deli	**Berkeley/E**	20
Scoma's	**multi.**	24
Sears	**Downtown**	20
Shen Hua	**Berkeley/E**	22
Showdogs	**Downtown**	20
Super Duper	**multi.**	23
Tacko	**Cow Hollow**	22
Taqueria Can Cun	**multi.**	23
Tarpy's	**Monterey/S**	24
Tommaso's	**N Beach**	24
Ton Kiang	**Outer Rich**	25
Tony's Coal-Fired	**N Beach**	24
Tony's Pizza	**N Beach**	26
Vik's Chaat	**Berkeley/E**	24
Willow Wood	**Graton/N**	24
Wurst Rest.	**Healdsburg/N**	21
Xolo	**Oakland/E**	23
Yankee Pier	**multi.**	19
Yank Sing	**SoMa**	26
Zachary's Pizza	**Oakland/E**	25
Zero Zero	**SoMa**	24

DANCING

Hopmonk Tav.	**multi.**	19
Le Colonial	**Downtown**	22
Luka's Taproom	**Oakland/E**	20
Uva Trattoria	**Napa/N**	19

ENTERTAINMENT

(Call for types and times of performances)

Ahwahnee	**Yosemite/E**	21
Albion River Inn	**Albion/N**	24
Beach Chalet	**Outer Sunset**	16
Big Four	**Nob Hill**	24
Bix	**Downtown**	24
Blowfish Sushi	**San Jose/S**	23

Café Claude	**Downtown**	22
Cascal	**Mtn View/S**	22
Cetrella	**Half Moon Bay/S**	23
NEW Empire	**Napa/N**	–
Everett/Jones BBQ	**Oakland/E**	21
Farm	**Napa/N**	24
Foreign Cinema	**Mission**	24
Garden Ct.	**Downtown**	22
Giordano	**N Beach**	22
Harris'	**Polk Gulch**	26
Hopmonk Tav.	**multi.**	19
La Condesa	**St. Helena/N**	25
La Note	**Berkeley/E**	23
Ledford Hse.	**Albion/N**	26
Marinus	**Carmel Valley/S**	26
Rose Pistola	**N Beach**	21
Sardine Factory	**Monterey/S**	24
NEW South/SFJAZZ	**Hayes Valley**	–
1300/Fillmore	**W Addition**	22
Uva Trattoria	**Napa/N**	19
Yoshi's	**multi.**	22
Zuni Café	**Hayes Valley**	26

FIREPLACES

Ahwahnee	**Yosemite/E**	21
Albion River Inn	**Albion/N**	24
Alexander's Steak	**Cupertino/S**	26
Alex Italian	**Rutherford/N**	24
All Spice	**San Mateo/S**	26
Ame	**SoMa**	26
Anton/Michel	**Carmel/S**	24
Applewood Rest.	**Guerneville/N**	24
Auberge du Soleil	**Rutherford/N**	27
Bella Vista	**Woodside/S**	24
Big Four	**Nob Hill**	24
Bistro Don Giovanni	**Napa/N**	25
Bistro Jeanty	**Yountville/N**	27
Brannan's Grill	**Calistoga/N**	19
Brix	**Napa/N**	22
Buckeye	**Mill Valley/N**	25
Cafe Citti	**Kenwood/N**	23
Café des Amis	**Cow Hollow**	18
Camino	**Oakland/E**	24
Casanova	**Carmel/S**	24
Casa Orinda	**Orinda/E**	20
Cetrella	**Half Moon Bay/S**	23
Chantilly	**Redwood City/S**	25

Chez TJ | **Mtn View/S**	23
Chow/Park Chow | **multi.**	21
Corners Tav. | **Walnut Creek/E**	23
Deetjen's Big Sur | **Big Sur/S**	24
Della Santina | **Sonoma/N**	24
Dio Deka | **Los Gatos/S**	25
Dipsea Cafe | **Mill Valley/N**	18
Duck Club | **Bodega Bay/N**	22
El Dorado | **Sonoma/N**	22
Epic Roasthse. | **Embarcadero**	22
Erna's Elderberry | **Oakhurst/E**	28
Étoile | **Yountville/N**	26
Evvia | **Palo Alto/S**	28
Fandango | **Pacific Grove/S**	21
Farm | **Napa/N**	24
Farmhse. Inn | **Forestville/N**	27
Flavor | **Santa Rosa/N**	22
Fleur de Lys | **Downtown**	27
Flying Fish (Carmel) | **Carmel/S**	24
Foreign Cinema | **Mission**	24
French Laundry | **Yountville/N**	28
Gar Woods | **Carnelian Bay/E**	19
Gayle's Bakery | **Capitola/S**	24
Half Moon Brew | **Half Moon Bay/S**	17
Harris' | **Polk Gulch**	26
House/Prime | **Polk Gulch**	26
Il Fornaio | **multi.**	18
Izzy's Steak | **Marina**	22
John Ash | **Santa Rosa/N**	25
Kenwood | **Kenwood/N**	25
Kokkari | **Downtown**	28
Kuleto's | **Downtown**	23
Lake Chalet | **Oakland/E**	17
La Toque | **Napa/N**	27
LB Steak | **San Jose/S**	22
Ledford Hse. | **Albion/N**	26
Left Bank | **Larkspur/N**	20
Lupa Trattoria | **Noe Valley**	23
MacCallum/Grey Whale | **Mendocino/N**	24
Madera | **Menlo Pk/S**	23
Madrona Manor | **Healdsburg/N**	27
Manresa | **Los Gatos/S**	27
Marinus | **Carmel Valley/S**	26
Meadowood Rest. | **St. Helena/N**	27
Mezza Luna | **Princeton Sea/S**	23

NEW MKT | **SoMa**	-
Murray Circle | **Sausalito/N**	23
Navio | **Half Moon Bay/S**	24
Nepenthe | **Big Sur/S**	18
Nick's Cove | **Marshall/N**	21
Osha Thai | **Embarcadero**	22
Pacific's Edge | **Carmel/S**	24
Parcel 104 | **Santa Clara/S**	23
Piatti | **multi.**	21
Piazza D'Angelo | **Mill Valley/N**	20
Plouf | **Downtown**	22
Plumed Horse | **Saratoga/S**	25
PlumpJack | **Olympic Valley/E**	22
Postino | **Lafayette/E**	24
Press | **St. Helena/N**	26
Prima | **Walnut Creek/E**	26
Ravenous | **Healdsburg/N**	22
Rest./Stevenswood | **Little River/N**	24
Samovar Tea | **Hayes Valley**	20
Santé | **Sonoma/N**	-
Sardine Factory | **Monterey/S**	24
Sierra Mar | **Big Sur/S**	28
NEW Sir & Star | **Olema/N**	-
Skates on Bay | **Berkeley/E**	20
Soule Domain | **Kings Bch/E**	24
Spruce | **Presidio Hts**	26
Stark's Steak/Sea | **Santa Rosa/N**	25
St. Orres | **Gualala/N**	23
Sunnyside Lodge | **Tahoe City/E**	18
Tav./Lark Creek | **Larkspur/N**	21
Terzo | **Cow Hollow**	25
Toast | **Novato/N**	21
Townhouse B&G | **Emeryville/E**	22
Troya | **Inner Rich**	21
Vic Stewart's | **Walnut Creek/E**	24
Village Pub | **Woodside/S**	25
Viognier | **San Mateo/S**	24
Wayfare Tav. | **Downtown**	24
Wine Spectator | **St. Helena/N**	23

GREEN/LOCAL/ORGANIC

Ad Hoc | **Yountville/N**	26
Ajanta | **Berkeley/E**	27
Artisan Bistro | **Lafayette/E**	25
Atelier Crenn | **Marina**	27

La Ciccia | **Noe Valley**	27
La Folie | **Russian Hill**	27
Lalime's | **Berkeley/E**	26
La Posta | **Santa Cruz/S**	25
Lark Creek | **Walnut Creek/E**	23
La Taquiza | **Napa/N**	27
La Toque | **Napa/N**	27
Ledford Hse. | **Albion/N**	26
Local Mission | **Mission**	27
Luella | **Russian Hill**	23
MacCallum/Grey Whale | **Mendocino/N**	24
Madera | **Menlo Pk/S**	23
Madrona Manor | **Healdsburg/N**	27
Magnolia | **Haight-Ashbury**	22
Manresa | **Los Gatos/S**	27
Marché/Fleurs | **Ross/N**	25
Marinitas | **San Anselmo/N**	21
Marinus | **Carmel Valley/S**	26
Market | **St. Helena/N**	22
MarketBar | **Embarcadero**	18
🆕 Marrow | **Oakland/E**	–
Marzano | **Oakland/E**	23
Maverick | **Mission**	24
Meadowood Grill | **St. Helena/N**	22
Meadowood Rest. | **St. Helena/N**	27
Mendo Bistro | **Ft Bragg/N**	25
Mijita | **multi.**	20
Millennium | **Downtown**	26
Montrio Bistro | **Monterey/S**	23
Mustards | **Yountville/N**	25
Navio | **Half Moon Bay/S**	24
Nick's Cove | **Marshall/N**	21
🆕 Nido | **Oakland/E**	–
Nopa | **W Addition**	26
Nopalito | **W Addition**	24
North Bch. Rest. | **N Beach**	24
🆕 Odalisque Cafe | **San Rafael/N**	–
Oliveto Cafe | **Oakland/E**	23
Oliveto Rest. | **Oakland/E**	25
One Market | **Embarcadero**	24
Oola | **SoMa**	21
Osteria Stellina | **Pt Reyes/N**	24
Outerlands | **Outer Sunset**	25
Pacific Catch | **Marina**	22
Pacific's Edge | **Carmel/S**	24

🆕 Padrecito | **Cole Valley**	–
Parallel 37 | **Nob Hill**	24
Parcel 104 | **Santa Clara/S**	23
Passionfish | **Pacific Grove/S**	27
Pauline's Pizza/Wine | **Mission**	22
Pearl | **Napa/N**	22
Peter Lowell | **Sebastopol/N**	22
Piccino | **Dogpatch**	24
Picco | **Larkspur/N**	26
Pizza Antica | **Lafayette/E**	22
Pizzaiolo | **Oakland/E**	26
Pizzeria Picco | **Larkspur/N**	26
Pizzeria Tra Vigne | **St. Helena/N**	22
Pizzetta 211 | **Outer Rich**	26
Plant Cafe | **multi.**	22
Plum | **Oakland/E**	23
Poggio | **Sausalito/N**	25
Press | **St. Helena/N**	26
Prospect | **SoMa**	24
Quince | **Downtown**	26
Radius Rest. | **SoMa**	23
🆕 Ramen Shop | **Oakland/E**	24
Range | **Mission**	27
Ravenous | **Healdsburg/N**	22
Regalito Rosticeria | **Mission**	23
Rest./Stevenswood | **Little River/N**	24
Revival Bar | **Berkeley/E**	22
Richmond | **Inner Rich**	25
Rich Table | **Hayes Valley**	25
Rivoli | **Berkeley/E**	27
Rocker Oysterfeller's | **Valley Ford/N**	25
Saison | **SoMa**	27
🆕 Seaglass Rest. | **Embarcadero**	–
Sebo | **Hayes Valley**	27
Serpentine | **Dogpatch**	23
Sierra Mar | **Big Sur/S**	28
🆕 Sir & Star | **Olema/N**	–
Slanted Door | **Embarcadero**	26
Slow Club | **Mission**	23
Solbar | **Calistoga/N**	26
Spoonbar | **Healdsburg/N**	20
SPQR | **Pacific Hts**	25
Spruce | **Presidio Hts**	26
State Bird | **W Addition**	26

Station 1 | **Woodside/S**	25
St. Orres | **Gualala/N**	23
Super Duper | **multi.**	23
Sutro's | **Outer Rich**	21
Tacubaya | **Berkeley/E**	22
Tamarine | **Palo Alto/S**	25
Tartine | **Mission**	27
Tav./Lark Creek | **Larkspur/N**	21
Terrapin Creek | **Bodega Bay/N**	27
Terzo | **Cow Hollow**	25
Tra Vigne | **St. Helena/N**	24
T Rex | **Berkeley/E**	18
Underdog | **Inner Sunset**	25
Underwood Bar | **Graton/N**	22
Village Pub | **Woodside/S**	25
Viognier | **San Mateo/S**	24
Water St. Bistro | **Petaluma/N**	23
Wente Vineyards | **Livermore/E**	25
Willi's Wine | **Santa Rosa/N**	25
NEW Wine Kitchen | **W Addition**	-
Wise Sons | **Mission**	23
Wolfdale's | **Tahoe City/E**	27
Woodward's Gdn. | **Mission**	24
Xolo | **Oakland/E**	23
Zaré/Fly Trap | **SoMa**	21
Zatar | **Berkeley/E**	24
Zazu | **Sebastopol/N**	26
Zin | **Healdsburg/N**	23
Zuni Café | **Hayes Valley**	26

HISTORIC PLACES

(Year opened; * building)

1800 | Boxing Rm.* | **Hayes Valley**	20
1800 | Central Mkt.* | **Petaluma/N**	25
1800 | Market* | **St. Helena/N**	22
1848 | Cindy's Backstreet* | **St. Helena/N**	24
1848 | La Forêt* | **San Jose/S**	27
1849 | Tadich Grill | **Downtown**	24
1856 | Garden Ct.* | **Downtown**	22
1857 | Little River Inn* | **Little River/N**	24
1860 | Della Fattoria* | **Petaluma/N**	26
1860 | Pizza Antica* | **Lafayette/E**	22
1863 | Cliff Hse. | **Outer Rich**	20

1863 | Sutro's* | **Outer Rich**	21
1864 | Rocker Oysterfeller's* | **Valley Ford/N**	25
1867 | Sam's Grill | **Downtown**	22
1870 | Bottega* | **Yountville/N**	25
1870 | Murray Circle* | **Sausalito/N**	23
1873 | Farmhse. Inn* | **Forestville/N**	27
1875 | La Note* | **Berkeley/E**	23
1876 | Sir & Star* | **Olema/N**	-
1880 | Pianeta* | **Truckee/E**	20
1881 | Il Fornaio* | **Carmel/S**	18
1881 | Madrona Manor* | **Healdsburg/N**	27
1882 | MacCallum/Grey Whale* | **Mendocino/N**	24
1883 | Celadon* | **Napa/N**	25
1884 | Terra* | **St. Helena/N**	27
1886 | Cole's Chop* | **Napa/N**	27
1886 | Mendo Bistro* | **Ft Bragg/N**	25
1886 | Willi's Wine* | **Santa Rosa/N**	25
1888 | Tav./Lark Creek* | **Larkspur/N**	21
1889 | Boulevard* | **Embarcadero**	27
1889 | Pacific Café* | **Outer Rich**	23
1889 | Wine Spectator* | **St. Helena/N**	23
1890 | Chez TJ* | **Mtn View/S**	23
1890 | Eureka* | **Castro**	21
1890 | Scoma's* | **Sausalito/N**	24
1890 | Yankee Pier* | **Larkspur/N**	19
1893 | Cafe Beaujolais* | **Mendocino/N**	26
1893 | Jimtown Store* | **Healdsburg/N**	21
1894 | Duarte's* | **Pescadero/S**	22
1895 | La Posta* | **Santa Cruz/S**	25
1895 | Restaurant* | **Ft Bragg/N**	22
1898 | Slanted Door* | **Embarcadero**	26
1900 | Bar Agricole* | **SoMa**	22
1900 | Bar Tartine* | **Mission**	24
1900 | Cha Cha Cha* | **Mission**	22
1900 | Diavola* | **Geyserville/N**	26
1900 | Emporio Rulli* | **Downtown**	22
1900 | Frances* | **Castro**	27

Year	Restaurant	Location	Rating
1900	French Laundry*	Yountville/N	28
1900	Girl/Fig*	Sonoma/N	24
1900	Pauline's Pizza/Wine*	Mission	22
1904	Bourbon Steak*	Downtown	23
1905	Hopmonk Tav.*	Sebastopol/N	19
1906	AQ*	SoMa	24
1906	Chez Shea*	Half Moon Bay/S	21
1906	Coco500*	SoMa	24
1906	Imperial Tea*	Embarcadero	18
1906	Pork Store*	Haight-Ashbury	19
1906	Wayfare Tav.*	Downtown	24
1907	Tony's Coal-Fired*	N Beach	24
1907	Tony's Pizza*	N Beach	26
1907	Town Hall*	SoMa	23
1908	Bottle Cap*	N Beach	18
1908	John's Grill	Downtown	21
1908	Mezza Luna*	Princeton Sea/S	23
1908	Zaré/Fly Trap*	SoMa	21
1909	Campton Pl.*	Downtown	26
1910	Bull Valley Roadhouse*	Port Costa	-
1910	Catch*	Castro	21
1910	Harris'*	Polk Gulch	26
1910	Rest. LuLu*	SoMa	21
1910	Sasa*	Walnut Creek/E	25
1911	Hotel Mac Rest.*	Richmond/E	22
1911	20th Century*	Hayes Valley	-
1912	Swan Oyster	Polk Gulch	26
1913	Balboa Cafe	Cow Hollow	20
1913	Zuni Café*	Hayes Valley	26
1914	Healdsburg B&G*	Healdsburg/N	19
1914	Wexler's*	Downtown	23
1915	Café des Amis*	Cow Hollow	18
1915	Napa Wine Train*	Napa/N	20
1916	Amer. Grilled*	SoMa	22
1917	Pacific's Edge*	Carmel/S	24
1917	Tarpy's*	Monterey/S	24
1918	St. Francis	Mission	19
1919	Albion River Inn*	Albion/N	24
1919	Sauce*	Hayes Valley	22
1919	Sotto Mare	N Beach	26
1920	Acquerello*	Polk Gulch	28
1920	Albona Rist.*	N Beach	24
1920	Boogaloos*	Mission	20
1920	Commonwealth*	Mission	26
1920	Florio*	Pacific Hts	21
1922	Benu*	SoMa	27
1923	Tribune Tavern*	Oakland/E	-
1924	Big Four*	Nob Hill	24
1925	Alioto's	Fish. Wharf	21
1925	Farallon*	Downtown	25
1925	John Bentley*	Redwood City/S	25
1927	Ahwahnee*	Yosemite/E	21
1927	Bella Vista*	Woodside/S	24
1927	Chop Bar*	Oakland/E	24
1927	Townhouse B&G*	Emeryville/E	22
1928	Alfred's Steak	Downtown	23
1928	Cottonwood*	Truckee/E	20
1928	Elite Cafe*	Pacific Hts	20
1929	Aubergine*	Carmel/S	26
1929	Lucca Deli	Marina	26
1930	Foreign Cinema*	Mission	24
1930	Guamenkitzel*	Berkeley/E	21
1930	Lalime's*	Berkeley/E	26
1930	Lo Coco's*	Oakland/E	22
1930	Ravenous*	Healdsburg/N	22
1930	Soule Domain*	Kings Bch/E	24
1930	Willow Wood*	Graton/N	24
1932	Camino*	Oakland/E	24
1932	Casa Orinda*	Orinda/E	20
1933	Luka's Taproom*	Oakland/E	20
1934	Stark's Steak/Sea*	Santa Rosa/N	25
1935	Tommaso's	N Beach	24
1936	Cafe La Haye*	Sonoma/N	26

Hyatt Carmel Highlands
  Pacific's Edge | **Carmel/S** 24

Inn at Southbridge
  Pizzeria Tra Vigne | 22
  St. Helena/N

Inn at Spanish Bay
  Roy's | **Pebble Bch/S** 25

Inn At The Opera
  Pläj | **Hayes Valley** 24

InterContinental Hotel
  Luce | **SoMa** 21

L'Auberge Carmel
  Aubergine | **Carmel/S** 26

Les Mars, Hotel
  NEW Chalkboard Bistro | -
  Healdsburg/N

Little River Inn
  Little River Inn | **Little River/N** 24

Lodge at Sonoma
  Carneros Bistro | **Sonoma/N** 24

Los Gatos, Hotel
  Dio Deka | **Los Gatos/S** 25

MacCallum House Inn
  MacCallum/Grey Whale | 24
  Mendocino/N

Madrona Manor
  Madrona Manor | 27
  Healdsburg/N

Mandarin Oriental Hotel
  Brasserie S&P | **Downtown** 24

Meadowood Napa Valley
  Meadowood Grill | 22
  St. Helena/N
  Meadowood Rest. | 27
  St. Helena/N

Metropolis, Hotel
  Farmerbrown | **Tenderloin** 21

Mission Ranch
  Mission Ranch | **Carmel/S** 20

Monaco San Francisco, Hotel
  Grand Cafe | **Downtown** 20

Mount View Hotel
  Jole | **Calistoga/N** 26

Mystic Hotel
  Burritt Tavern | **Downtown** 20

Nick's Cove & Cottages
  Nick's Cove | **Marshall/N** 21

Nikko, Hotel
  Anzu | **Downtown** 23

Olema Inn
  NEW Sir & Star | **Olema/N** -

Pacifica Beach Hotel
  NEW Puerto 27 | **Pacifica/S** -

Palace Hotel
  Garden Ct. | **Downtown** 22

Palomar, Hotel
  Fifth Floor | **SoMa** 24

Pine Inn
  Il Fornaio | **Carmel/S** 18

PlumpJack Squaw Valley Inn
  PlumpJack | **Olympic Valley/E** 22

Post Ranch Inn
  Sierra Mar | **Big Sur/S** 28

Prescott Hotel
  Postrio | **Downtown** 23

Ritz-Carlton Half Moon Bay
  Navio | **Half Moon Bay/S** 24

Ritz-Carlton Lake Tahoe
  Manzanita | **Truckee/E** 22

Ritz-Carlton San Francisco
  Parallel 37 | **Nob Hill** 24

Rosewood Sand Hill
  Madera | **Menlo Pk/S** 23

Sainte Claire Hotel
  Il Fornaio | **San Jose/S** 18

San Jose Marriott
  Arcadia | **San Jose/S** 23

Santa Clara Marriott
  Parcel 104 | **Santa Clara/S** 23

Serrano Hotel
  Jasper's Corner | **Downtown** 19

Shattuck Plaza
  Five | **Berkeley/E** 20

Sir Francis Drake Hotel
  Scala's Bistro | **Downtown** 23

Solage Resort
  Solbar | **Calistoga/N** 26

Sonoma Hotel
  Girl/Fig | **Sonoma/N** 24

Stevenswood Lodge
  Rest./Stevenswood | 24
  Little River/N

St. Orres Hotel
  St. Orres | **Gualala/N** 23

St. Regis
  Ame | **SoMa** 26

Taj Campton Pl. Hotel
  Campton Pl. | **Downtown** 26

Truckee Hotel
  Moody's Bistro | **Truckee/E** 23

Valley Ford Hotel
  Rocker Oysterfeller's | **Valley Ford/N** 25

Ventana Inn & Spa
  Rest./Ventana | **Big Sur/S** 23

Villa Florence Hotel
  Kuleto's | **Downtown** 23

Vitale, Hotel
  Americano | **Embarcadero** 20

Westin St. Francis Hotel
  Bourbon Steak | **Downtown** 23

Westin Verasa Napa
  Bank Café | **Napa/N** 23
  La Toque | **Napa/N** 27

W San Francisco
  Trace | **SoMa** 22

Zetta, Hotel
  NEW Cavalier | **SoMa** -

LATE DINING

(Weekday closing hour)

Absinthe | 12 AM | **Hayes Valley** 23
Adesso | varies | **Oakland/E** 22
Alembic | 12 AM | **Haight-Ashbury** 23
Balboa Cafe | varies | **multi.** 20
Bar Agricole | 12:30 AM | **SoMa** 22
Beretta | 12 AM | **Mission** 24
Big Four | 12 AM | **Nob Hill** 24
Bouche | 1 AM | **Nob Hill** 24
Brazen Head | 1 AM | **Cow Hollow** 20
Broken Record | 12 AM | **Excelsior** 24
Brother's Korean | varies | **Inner Rich** 22
Caspers Hot Dogs | 11:30 PM | **Pleasant Hill/E** 22
César | 11:30 PM | **Berkeley/E** 22
Delarosa | 1 AM | **Marina** 21
Don Pisto's | 12:30 AM | **N Beach** 25
El Farolito | varies | **multi.** 23

Emporio Rulli | 12 AM | **S San Francisco/S** 22
15 Romolo | 1:30 AM | **N Beach** 22
Fonda Solana | 12:30 AM | **Albany/E** 22
Gar Woods | 12 AM | **Carnelian Bay/E** 19
Gitane | 1 AM | **Downtown** 23
Globe | 1 AM | **Downtown** 18
Goose & Gander | 12 AM | **St. Helena/N** 22
Great Eastern | 12 AM | **Chinatown** 23
NEW Hard Water | 12 AM | **Embarcadero** -
Hog & Rocks | 12 AM | **Mission** 22
Home of Chicken | varies | **multi.** 19
Hopmonk Tav. | 2 AM | **Novato/N** 19
In-N-Out | varies | **multi.** 23
Katana-Ya | 11:30 PM | **Downtown** 22
King of Thai | varies | **multi.** 21
Kitchen | 1 AM | **Millbrae/S** 23
La Victoria | varies | **San Jose/S** 24
Lers Ros Thai | 12 AM | **Tenderloin** 24
Locanda | 12 AM | **Mission** 24
Lolinda | 1 AM | **Mission** 23
NEW Lucille's Smokehse. | 12 AM | **Concord/E** -
Luka's Taproom | varies | **Oakland/E** 20
Magnolia | 12 AM | **Haight-Ashbury** 22
Maven | 12 AM | **Lower Haight** 18
NEW Mikkeller Bar | varies | **Tenderloin** -
NEW MKT | varies | **SoMa** -
Moody's Bistro | 12 AM | **Truckee/E** 23
Mua Lounge | 12 AM | **Oakland/E** 21
Nihon | 2 AM | **Mission** 21
Nopa | 1 AM | **W Addition** 26
North Bch. Rest. | varies | **N Beach** 24
Oola | 1 AM | **SoMa** 21
Original Joe's | varies | **San Jose/S** 22

Osha Thai | varies | **Tenderloin**	22
Pancho Villa | varies | **Mission**	23
Per Diem | 2 AM | **Downtown**	20
Pi Bar | 12 AM | **Mission**	21
NEW Pub Republic | 1 AM | **Petaluma/N**	–
NEW Ramen Shop | 1 AM | **Oakland/E**	24
Revival Bar | 12 AM | **Berkeley/E**	22
NEW Roka Akor | varies | **Downtown**	–
Rosamunde | 12 AM | **Mission**	22
Rudy's Can't Fail | 1 AM | **multi.**	19
Ryoko's | 2 AM | **Downtown**	25
Sauce | 2 AM | **multi.**	22
Sol Food | 12 AM | **San Rafael/N**	24
Tacolicious | 12 AM | **multi.**	24
Taco Shop/Underdogs | 12 AM | **Outer Sunset**	24
Taqueria Can Cun | varies | **Mission**	23
Thai Hse. | varies | **Tenderloin**	22
Thomas & Fagiani's | 12 AM | **Napa/N**	24
Top Dog | 2 AM | **Berkeley/E**	23
Trace | 2 AM | **SoMa**	22
NEW Trick Dog | 2 AM | **Mission**	–
Tsunami Sushi | 12 AM | **W Addition**	22
NEW The Willows | varies | **SoMa**	–

MEET FOR A DRINK

Abbot's Cellar | **Mission**	20
Absinthe | **Hayes Valley**	23
Adesso | **Oakland/E**	22
Albion River Inn | **Albion/N**	24
Alembic | **Haight-Ashbury**	23
Alexander's Steak | **multi.**	26
Amber Bistro | **Danville/E**	23
Amber India | **multi.**	24
Americano | **Embarcadero**	20
Anchor & Hope | **SoMa**	21
Andalu | **Mission**	21
Anzu | **Downtown**	23
AQ | **SoMa**	24
NEW Aquitaine | **Downtown**	–
A16 | **multi.**	24
Attic | **San Mateo/S**	20

Auberge du Soleil | **Rutherford/N**	27
Balboa Cafe | **multi.**	20
Bank Café | **Napa/N**	23
Bar Agricole | **SoMa**	22
Barbacco | **Downtown**	24
Bar Bocce | **Sausalito/N**	22
Barlata | **Oakland/E**	22
Barndiva | **Healdsburg/N**	25
Bar Terra | **St. Helena/N**	25
Beach Chalet | **Outer Sunset**	16
Bellanico | **Oakland/E**	23
Beretta | **Mission**	24
Betelnut | **Cow Hollow**	24
B44 | **Downtown**	21
Biergarten | **Hayes Valley**	21
Big Four | **Nob Hill**	24
NEW Big Sur Roadhse. | **Big Sur/S**	–
Bistro/Copains | **Occidental/N**	27
Bistro Don Giovanni | **Napa/N**	25
Bix | **Downtown**	24
Bluestem Brass. | **SoMa**	19
Bocadillos | **N Beach**	23
Bottega | **Yountville/N**	25
Bottle Cap | **N Beach**	18
Bouchon | **Yountville/N**	26
Boulevard | **Embarcadero**	27
Bourbon Steak | **Downtown**	23
Boxing Rm. | **Hayes Valley**	20
Brasserie S&P | **Downtown**	24
NEW Bravas Bar/Tapas | **Healdsburg/N**	25
Brazen Head | **Cow Hollow**	20
Brick/Bottle | **Corte Madera/N**	19
Broken Record | **Excelsior**	24
B Star | **Inner Rich**	25
Buckeye | **Mill Valley/N**	25
Bungalow 44 | **Mill Valley/N**	22
Burritt Tavern | **Downtown**	20
Butterfly | **Embarcadero**	23
Café des Amis | **Cow Hollow**	18
Café Rouge | **Berkeley/E**	22
Campanula | **N Beach**	20
Campo Fina | **Healdsburg/N**	–
NEW Campo 185 | **Palo Alto/S**	16
Cantinetta Luca | **Carmel/S**	21
Carneros Bistro | **Sonoma/N**	24
Cascal | **Mtn View/S**	22

Visit zagat.com

SPECIAL FEATURES

Mamacita	**Marina**	24
Manzanita	**Truckee/E**	22
Marica	**Oakland/E**	25
Marinitas	**San Anselmo/N**	21
MarketBar	**Embarcadero**	18
Marzano	**Oakland/E**	23
Mateo's Cocina	**Healdsburg/N**	22
Maven	**Lower Haight**	18
Mayfield	**Palo Alto/S**	20
Meadowood Grill	**St. Helena/N**	22
Meritage/Claremont	**Berkeley/E**	23
Michael Mina	**Downtown**	27
Mission Rock	**Dogpatch**	16
NEW MKT	**SoMa**	-
MoMo's	**S Beach**	19
Moody's Bistro	**Truckee/E**	23
Morimoto	**Napa/N**	25
Mua Lounge	**Oakland/E**	21
Mundaka	**Carmel/S**	24
Murray Circle	**Sausalito/N**	23
Mustards	**Yountville/N**	25
NEW M.Y. China	**Downtown**	19
Naked Lunch	**N Beach**	24
Nettie's Crab	**Cow Hollow**	20
Nick's Cove	**Marshall/N**	21
NEW Nido	**Oakland/E**	-
Nihon	**Mission**	21
Nombe	**Mission**	21
Nopa	**W Addition**	26
Norman Rose	**Napa/N**	20
Oenotri	**Napa/N**	24
Oliveto Cafe	**Oakland/E**	23
One Market	**Embarcadero**	24
Oola	**SoMa**	21
Osteria Coppa	**San Mateo/S**	22
Oswald	**Santa Cruz/S**	25
O3 Bistro	**Civic Ctr**	24
Oxbow Wine	**Napa/N**	21
Oyaji	**Outer Rich**	23
Ozumo	**multi.**	25
NEW Padrecito	**Cole Valley**	-
Palio d'Asti	**Downtown**	21
Parallel 37	**Nob Hill**	24
Parcel 104	**Santa Clara/S**	23
Park Chalet	**Outer Sunset**	16
Park Tav.	**N Beach**	24
Pauline's Pizza/Wine	**Mission**	22

Perbacco	**Downtown**	26
Per Diem	**Downtown**	20
Piazza D'Angelo	**Mill Valley/N**	20
Pi Bar	**Mission**	21
Picán	**Oakland/E**	24
Picco	**Larkspur/N**	26
Pizzando	**Healdsburg/N**	-
Plumed Horse	**Saratoga/S**	25
PlumpJack	**Olympic Valley/E**	22
Poggio	**Sausalito/N**	25
Presidio Social	**Presidio**	19
Press	**St. Helena/N**	26
Prima	**Walnut Creek/E**	26
Prospect	**SoMa**	24
Public Hse.	**S Beach**	17
NEW Pub Republic	**Petaluma/N**	-
NEW Puerto 27	**Pacifica/S**	-
Radius Rest.	**SoMa**	23
Range	**Mission**	27
Rangoon Ruby	**Palo Alto/S**	22
Redd	**Yountville/N**	27
Redd Wood	**Yountville/N**	25
Rest./Ventana	**Big Sur/S**	23
Rest. LuLu	**SoMa**	21
Revival Bar	**Berkeley/E**	22
Rich Table	**Hayes Valley**	25
NEW Rickybobby	**Downtown**	-
Ristobar	**Marina**	20
RN74	**SoMa**	22
Rocker Oysterfeller's	**Valley Ford/N**	25
NEW Roka Akor	**Downtown**	-
NEW Rosa Mexicano	**Embarcadero**	24
Rosamunde	**multi.**	22
Rose Pistola	**N Beach**	21
Rose's Cafe	**Cow Hollow**	22
Rosso Pizzeria	**multi.**	25
Rumbo	**Oakland/E**	19
Rustic	**Geyserville/N**	21
Salt Hse.	**SoMa**	22
Sam's Chowder	**Half Moon Bay/S**	22
Sardine Factory	**Monterey/S**	24
Sens	**Embarcadero**	20
Serpentine	**Dogpatch**	23
Sidebar	**Oakland/E**	22
Sino	**San Jose/S**	19

Skates on Bay | **Berkeley/E**	20
Skool | **Potrero Hill**	23
Slow Club | **Mission**	23
Soif Wine Bar | **Santa Cruz/S**	24
Solbar | **Calistoga/N**	26
Sonoma-Meritage | **Sonoma/N**	19
NEW South/SFJAZZ | **Hayes Valley**	–
Spoonbar | **Healdsburg/N**	20
Spruce | **Presidio Hts**	26
Starbelly | **Castro**	22
Straits | **multi.**	20
St. Vincent Tavern | **Mission**	21
Sunnyside Lodge | **Tahoe City/E**	18
Suppenküche | **Hayes Valley**	23
Surf Spot | **Pacifica/S**	–
Tacolicious | **multi.**	24
Tamarine | **Palo Alto/S**	25
Tav./Lark Creek | **Larkspur/N**	21
Terzo | **Cow Hollow**	25
1300/Fillmore | **W Addition**	22
Thomas & Fagiani's | **Napa/N**	24
Tommy's Mex. | **Outer Rich**	20
Town Hall | **SoMa**	23
Townhouse B&G | **Emeryville/E**	22
Trace | **SoMa**	22
Trader Vic's | **Emeryville/E**	18
Tra Vigne | **St. Helena/N**	24
NEW Tribune Tavern | **Oakland/E**	–
NEW Trick Dog | **Mission**	–
NEW Trident | **Sausalito/N**	22
Tropisueño | **SoMa**	20
25 Lusk | **SoMa**	22
NEW 20 Spot | **Mission**	–
Umami | **Cow Hollow**	25
Underwood Bar | **Graton/N**	22
Uva Enoteca | **Lower Haight**	22
Va de Vi | **Walnut Creek/E**	25
Waterbar | **Embarcadero**	23
Wayfare Tav. | **Downtown**	24
West of Pecos | **Mission**	19
Willi's Seafood | **Healdsburg/N**	25
Willi's Wine | **Santa Rosa/N**	25
NEW The Willows | **SoMa**	–
NEW Wine Kitchen | **W Addition**	–
Wine Spectator | **St. Helena/N**	23
Wood Tav. | **Oakland/E**	26

Xanh | **Mtn View/S**	21
Yoshi's | **W Addition**	22
Zaré/Fly Trap | **SoMa**	21
Zero Zero | **SoMa**	24
Zibibbo | **Palo Alto/S**	20
Zin | **Healdsburg/N**	23
Zuni Café | **Hayes Valley**	26
ZuZu | **Napa/N**	24

NEWCOMERS

Aquitaine | **Downtown**	–
Backyard | **Forestville/N**	–
Bantam | **Santa Cruz/S**	–
Belcampo Meat | **Larkspur/N**	–
Bergerac | **SoMa**	–
Big Sur Roadhse. | **Big Sur/S**	–
B. Patisserie | **Pacific Hts**	26
Bravas Bar/Tapas | **Healdsburg/N**	25
Café Lucia | **Healdsburg/N**	–
Campo 185 | **Palo Alto/S**	16
Capo's | **N Beach**	–
Cavalier | **SoMa**	–
Chalkboard Bistro | **Healdsburg/N**	–
Chocolate Lab | **Dogpatch**	25
Cindy's Waterfront | **Monterey/S**	–
Coqueta | **Embarcadero**	–
Corner Store | **Laurel Hts**	22
Curry Up Now | **Palo Alto/S**	21
Dandelion Chocolate | **Mission**	–
Dante's Table | **Castro**	–
Duende | **Oakland/E**	23
Easy Creole | **Berkeley/E**	–
El Gusano | **Oakland/E**	–
Empire | **Napa/N**	–
Fable | **Castro**	–
Farmshop | **Larkspur/N**	–
Fast Food Français | **Sausalito/N**	–
Forge | **Oakland/E**	–
Grand Lake Kitchen | **Oakland/E**	–
Hakkasan | **Downtown**	24
Hard Water | **Embarcadero**	–
Heyday | **SoMa**	–
Hillside Supper | **Bernal Hts**	–
Hi Lo BBQ | **Mission**	–
Juhu Beach Club | **Oakland/E**	–
Katsu | **Los Gatos/S**	–
Kronnerburger | **Mission**	–

La Balena Cucina	**Carmel/S**	⌐
Lucille's Smokehse.	**Concord/E**	⌐
Lungomare	**Oakland/E**	⌐
Marrow	**Oakland/E**	⌐
Mason Pacific	**Chinatown**	⌐
Mikkeller Bar	**Tenderloin**	⌐
Mill	**W Addition**	⌐
Mission Picnic	**Mission**	⌐
Miss Ollie's	**Oakland/E**	⌐
MKT	**SoMa**	⌐
M.Y. China	**Downtown**	19
Nido	**Oakland/E**	⌐
Odalisque Cafe	**San Rafael/N**	⌐
Padrecito	**Cole Valley**	⌐
Palace	**Mission**	⌐
Parish Cafe	**Healdsburg/N**	⌐
Pear	**Napa/N**	⌐
Pizzalina	**San Anselmo/N**	⌐
Pub Republic	**Petaluma/N**	⌐
Puerto 27	**Pacifica/S**	⌐
Ramen Shop	**Oakland/E**	24
Rickybobby	**Downtown**	⌐
Roka Akor	**Downtown**	⌐
Roku	**Hayes Valley**	⌐
Rosa Mexicano	**Embarcadero**	24
Roxy's Cafe	**Mission**	⌐
Rustic Tavern	**Lafayette/E**	⌐
Schulzies	**Hayes Valley**	⌐
Sea	**Palo Alto/S**	23
Seaglass Rest.	**Embarcadero**	⌐
Shorty Goldstein's	**Downtown**	⌐
Sir & Star	**Olema/N**	⌐
1601 Bar/Kitchen	**SoMa**	⌐
South/SFJAZZ	**Hayes Valley**	⌐
Stella Nonna	**Berkeley/E**	⌐
Sugoi Sushi	**Mission**	⌐
Taverna Sofia	**Healdsburg/N**	⌐
Tomo's Japanese	**Berkeley/E**	⌐
Trattoria/Vittorio	**W Portal**	⌐
Tribune Tavern	**Oakland/E**	⌐
Trick Dog	**Mission**	⌐
Trident	**Sausalito/N**	22
20 Spot	**Mission**	⌐
20th Century	**Hayes Valley**	⌐
The Willows	**SoMa**	⌐
Wine Kitchen	**W Addition**	⌐

OUTDOOR DINING

À Côté	**Oakland/E**	24
Angèle	**Napa/N**	24
Applewood Rest.	**Guerneville/N**	24
Auberge du Soleil	**Rutherford/N**	27
NEW Backyard	**Forestville/N**	⌐
Barbara's Fishtrap	**Princeton Sea/S**	21
Barndiva	**Healdsburg/N**	25
Barney's	**multi.**	21
NEW Big Sur Roadhse.	**Big Sur/S**	⌐
Bistro Aix	**Marina**	23
Bistro Don Giovanni	**Napa/N**	25
Bistro Jeanty	**Yountville/N**	27
Blue Bottle	**SoMa**	24
Bottega	**Yountville/N**	25
Bouchon	**Yountville/N**	26
NEW Bravas Bar/Tapas	**Healdsburg/N**	25
Bucci's	**Emeryville/E**	21
Buckeye	**Mill Valley/N**	25
Cafe Beaujolais	**Mendocino/N**	26
NEW Café Lucia	**Healdsburg/N**	⌐
Casanova	**Carmel/S**	24
Celadon	**Napa/N**	25
Chaya	**Embarcadero**	23
Cheesecake Fac.	**Downtown**	16
Chez Maman	**Potrero Hill**	24
Chez Papa Bistrot	**Potrero Hill**	24
Chloe's Cafe	**Noe Valley**	23
Chow/Park Chow	**multi.**	21
Cindy's Backstreet	**St. Helena/N**	24
Cole's Chop	**Napa/N**	27
Comal	**Berkeley/E**	23
Della Santina	**Sonoma/N**	24
Dopo	**Oakland/E**	25
Dry Creek	**Healdsburg/N**	24
Emporio Rulli	**multi.**	22
Epic Roasthse.	**Embarcadero**	22
Étoile	**Yountville/N**	26
Fish	**Sausalito/N**	24
Flavor	**Santa Rosa/N**	22
Fonda Solana	**Albany/E**	22
Foreign Cinema	**Mission**	24
NEW Forge	**Oakland/E**	⌐
Frantoio	**Mill Valley/N**	22
Fremont Diner	**Sonoma/N**	24

Front Porch | **Bernal Hts** 22

Fumé Bistro | **Napa/N** 22

Gabriella Café | **Santa Cruz/S** 20

Gather | **Berkeley/E** 23

Girl/Fig | **Sonoma/N** 24

Grégoire | **Berkeley/E** 24

Hog Island Oyster | **Embarcadero** 26

John Ash | **Santa Rosa/N** 25

Kenwood | **Kenwood/N** 25

La Mar | **Embarcadero** 24

La Note | **Berkeley/E** 23

LaSalette | **Sonoma/N** 24

Lolinda | **Mission** 23

NEW Lungomare | **Oakland/E** –

Madera | **Menlo Pk/S** 23

Madrona Manor | **Healdsburg/N** 27

Marché/Fleurs | **Ross/N** 25

Murray Circle | **Sausalito/N** 23

NEW Parish Cafe | **Healdsburg/N** –

Pasta Moon | **Half Moon Bay/S** 25

Pazzia | **SoMa** 25

NEW Pear | **Napa/N** –

Piperade | **Downtown** 26

Pizzetta 211 | **Outer Rich** 26

Poggio | **Sausalito/N** 25

Postino | **Lafayette/E** 24

Press | **St. Helena/N** 26

Prima | **Walnut Creek/E** 26

Redd | **Yountville/N** 27

Redd Wood | **Yountville/N** 25

NEW Rosa Mexicano | **Embarcadero** 24

Rose's Cafe | **Cow Hollow** 22

Roy's | **Pebble Bch/S** 25

Rustic | **Geyserville/N** 21

Rutherford Grill | **Rutherford/N** 24

Sam's Chowder | **Half Moon Bay/S** 22

Scoma's | **Sausalito/N** 24

NEW Seaglass Rest. | **Embarcadero** –

Sierra Mar | **Big Sur/S** 28

Slanted Door | **Embarcadero** 26

Sociale | **Presidio Hts** 24

Straits | **San Jose/S** 20

Sushi Ran | **Sausalito/N** 27

Tartine | **Mission** 27

NEW Taverna Sofia | **Healdsburg/N** –

Tra Vigne | **St. Helena/N** 24

Universal Cafe | **Mission** 25

Va de Vi | **Walnut Creek/E** 25

Waterbar | **Embarcadero** 23

Waterfront | **Embarcadero** 21

Wente Vineyards | **Livermore/E** 25

Willi's Seafood | **Healdsburg/N** 25

Willi's Wine | **Santa Rosa/N** 25

Wine Spectator | **St. Helena/N** 23

Zazie | **Cole Valley** 24

Zibibbo | **Palo Alto/S** 20

Zuni Café | **Hayes Valley** 26

PEOPLE-WATCHING

Absinthe | **Hayes Valley** 23

Ace Wasabi's | **Marina** 20

À Côté | **Oakland/E** 24

Amber India | **multi.** 24

Anchor & Hope | **SoMa** 21

Andalu | **Mission** 21

Arcadia | **San Jose/S** 23

A16 | **multi.** 24

Balboa Cafe | **multi.** 20

Bar Agricole | **SoMa** 22

Barbacco | **Downtown** 24

Bar Bocce | **Sausalito/N** 22

Barlata | **Oakland/E** 22

Barndiva | **Healdsburg/N** 25

Beretta | **Mission** 24

Betelnut | **Cow Hollow** 24

Bistro Don Giovanni | **Napa/N** 25

Bistro Jeanty | **Yountville/N** 27

Bix | **Downtown** 24

Blowfish Sushi | **multi.** 23

Bocanova | **Oakland/E** 23

Boogaloos | **Mission** 20

Bottega | **Yountville/N** 25

Bouchon | **Yountville/N** 26

Boulevard | **Embarcadero** 27

Boxing Rm. | **Hayes Valley** 20

Brannan's Grill | **Calistoga/N** 19

Brix | **Napa/N** 22

Bungalow 44 | **Mill Valley/N** 22

Cafe Bastille | **Downtown** 19

Café Claude | **Downtown** 22

NEW Campo 185 | **Palo Alto/S** 16

Cascal | **Mtn View/S** 22

Catch	**Castro**	21	Insalata's	**San Anselmo/N**	25
Central Mkt.	**Petaluma/N**	25	Jardinière	**Civic Ctr**	26
César	**multi.**	22	🆕 Katsu	**Los Gatos/S**	-
Cha Cha Cha	**multi.**	22	Kitchen Door	**Napa/N**	22
Chaya	**Embarcadero**	23	La Mar	**Embarcadero**	24
Chez Panisse	**Berkeley/E**	27	LB Steak	**San Jose/S**	22
🆕 Chocolate Lab	**Dogpatch**	25	Le Central	**Downtown**	21
Cin-Cin Wine	**Los Gatos/S**	24	Left Bank	**Larkspur/N**	20
Comal	**Berkeley/E**	23	Lion/Compass	**Sunnyvale/S**	21
🆕 Coqueta	**Embarcadero**	-	Locanda	**Mission**	24
Corners Tav.	**Walnut Creek/E**	23	Lolinda	**Mission**	23
Cottonwood	**Truckee/E**	20	🆕 Lucille's Smokehse.	**Concord/E**	-
Delarosa	**Marina**	21	
Dio Deka	**Los Gatos/S**	25	🆕 Lungomare	**Oakland/E**	-
Donato	**Redwood City/S**	23	Madera	**Menlo Pk/S**	23
Doña Tomás	**Oakland/E**	22	Magnolia	**Haight-Ashbury**	22
Dosa	**multi.**	23	Mamacita	**Marina**	24
Downtown Bakery	**Healdsburg/N**	26	Manzanita	**Truckee/E**	22
			Marinitas	**San Anselmo/N**	21
🆕 Duende	**Oakland/E**	23	Mario's Bohemian	**N Beach**	19
El Paseo	**Mill Valley/N**	23	MarketBar	**Embarcadero**	18
🆕 Empire	**Napa/N**	-	Mateo's Cocina	**Healdsburg/N**	22
Emporio Rulli	**multi.**	22	Michael Mina	**Downtown**	27
Epic Roasthse.	**Embarcadero**	22	🆕 Mikkeller Bar	**Tenderloin**	-
Evvia	**Palo Alto/S**	28	Mission Rock	**Dogpatch**	16
Farina Foccaccia	**Mission**	22	Moody's Bistro	**Truckee/E**	23
Farina Pizza	**Mission**	20	Morimoto	**Napa/N**	25
Farmstead	**St. Helena/N**	22	Mundaka	**Carmel/S**	24
15 Romolo	**N Beach**	22	Mustards	**Yountville/N**	25
54 Mint	**SoMa**	22	🆕 M.Y. China	**Downtown**	19
Five	**Berkeley/E**	20	Nettie's Crab	**Cow Hollow**	20
5A5 Steak	**Downtown**	23	🆕 Nido	**Oakland/E**	-
Flea St. Café	**Menlo Pk/S**	26	Nihon	**Mission**	21
Flora	**Oakland/E**	23	Nopa	**W Addition**	26
Foreign Cinema	**Mission**	24	Oenotri	**Napa/N**	24
🆕 Forge	**Oakland/E**	-	Oliveto Cafe	**Oakland/E**	23
French Blue	**St. Helena/N**	20	Oswald	**Santa Cruz/S**	25
Frjtz Fries	**Mission**	20	Ozumo	**multi.**	25
Front Porch	**Bernal Hts**	22	🆕 Padrecito	**Cole Valley**	-
Gar Woods	**Carnelian Bay/E**	19	Pampas	**Palo Alto/S**	22
Gather	**Berkeley/E**	23	Park Tav.	**N Beach**	24
Gitane	**Downtown**	23	Picán	**Oakland/E**	24
Goose & Gander	**St. Helena/N**	22	Picco	**Larkspur/N**	26
🆕 Hakkasan	**Downtown**	24	Pizzando	**Healdsburg/N**	-
🆕 Hard Water	**Embarcadero**	-	Plumed Horse	**Saratoga/S**	25
Hog Island Oyster	**Napa/N**	26	Poesia	**Castro**	23
Hopmonk Tav.	**Sebastopol/N**	19	Poggio	**Sausalito/N**	25

SPECIAL FEATURES

NEW Roka Akor | **Downtown**	—
Sam's Grill | **Downtown**	22
NEW Sea | **Palo Alto/S**	23
Sens | **Embarcadero**	20
NEW South/SFJAZZ | **Hayes Valley**	—
Spruce | **Presidio Hts**	26
Tadich Grill | **Downtown**	24
Tony's Pizza | **N Beach**	26
Town Hall | **SoMa**	23
NEW Tribune Tavern | **Oakland/E**	—
Village Pub | **Woodside/S**	25
Viognier | **San Mateo/S**	24
Wayfare Tav. | **Downtown**	24
Zuni Café | **Hayes Valley**	26

PRIVATE ROOMS

(Restaurants charge less at off times; call for capacity)

Absinthe | **Hayes Valley**	23
À Côté | **Oakland/E**	24
Acquerello | **Polk Gulch**	28
Alegrias | **Marina**	22
Alexander's Steak | **Cupertino/S**	26
Alfred's Steak | **Downtown**	23
Andalu | **Mission**	21
Angèle | **Napa/N**	24
Anton/Michel | **Carmel/S**	24
Arcadia | **San Jose/S**	23
Auberge du Soleil | **Rutherford/N**	27
Aubergine | **Carmel/S**	26
Aziza | **Outer Rich**	26
Barndiva | **Healdsburg/N**	25
Basin | **Saratoga/S**	23
BayWolf | **Oakland/E**	26
Bella Vista | **Woodside/S**	24
Big Four | **Nob Hill**	24
Bistro Liaison | **Berkeley/E**	23
Blue Plate | **Mission**	24
Boulettes Larder/Bouli Bar | **Embarcadero**	25
Boulevard | **Embarcadero**	27
Buckeye | **Mill Valley/N**	25
Café Rouge | **Berkeley/E**	22
Carneros Bistro | **Sonoma/N**	24
Casanova | **Carmel/S**	24
Cetrella | **Half Moon Bay/S**	23
Cha Cha Cha | **Mission**	22

Chantilly | **Redwood City/S**	25
Chez TJ | **Mtn View/S**	23
Cindy's Backstreet | **St. Helena/N**	24
Dry Creek | **Healdsburg/N**	24
Erna's Elderberry | **Oakhurst/E**	28
Fandango | **Pacific Grove/S**	21
Farallon | **Downtown**	25
Fifth Floor | **SoMa**	24
Flea St. Café | **Menlo Pk/S**	26
Fleur de Lys | **Downtown**	27
Florio | **Pacific Hts**	21
Foreign Cinema | **Mission**	24
Frantoio | **Mill Valley/N**	22
Gary Chu's | **Santa Rosa/N**	24
Gary Danko | **Fish. Wharf**	29
Grand Cafe | **Downtown**	20
Grasing's Coastal | **Carmel/S**	21
Harris' | **Polk Gulch**	26
Hurley's Rest. | **Yountville/N**	23
Iberia | **Menlo Pk/S**	22
Il Fornaio | **multi.**	18
Incanto | **Noe Valley**	25
Indigo | **Civic Ctr**	20
Insalata's | **San Anselmo/N**	25
Jardinière | **Civic Ctr**	26
John Bentley | **Redwood City/S**	25
Kenwood | **Kenwood/N**	25
Khan Toke | **Outer Rich**	21
Kokkari | **Downtown**	28
La Folie | **Russian Hill**	27
La Forêt | **San Jose/S**	27
Le Colonial | **Downtown**	22
Left Bank | **multi.**	20
Le Papillon | **San Jose/S**	27
Lion/Compass | **Sunnyvale/S**	21
Little River Inn | **Little River/N**	24
MacCallum/Grey Whale | **Mendocino/N**	24
Madrona Manor | **Healdsburg/N**	27
Manresa | **Los Gatos/S**	27
Marinus | **Carmel Valley/S**	26
NEW Mikkeller Bar | **Tenderloin**	—
Millennium | **Downtown**	26
Montrio Bistro | **Monterey/S**	23
Morton's | **Downtown**	23
Navio | **Half Moon Bay/S**	24
North Bch. Rest. | **N Beach**	24

One Market | **Embarcadero**	24
Ozumo | **Embarcadero**	25
Pacific's Edge | **Carmel/S**	24
Palio d'Asti | **Downtown**	21
Parcel 104 | **Santa Clara/S**	23
Passionfish | **Pacific Grove/S**	27
Pauline's Pizza/Wine | **Mission**	22
Perbacco | **Downtown**	26
Pesce | **Castro**	25
Piatti | **Mill Valley/N**	21
Piazza D'Angelo | **Mill Valley/N**	20
Plumed Horse | **Saratoga/S**	25
PlumpJack | **Olympic Valley/E**	22
Poggio | **Sausalito/N**	25
Postino | **Lafayette/E**	24
Postrio | **Downtown**	23
Press | **St. Helena/N**	26
Prima | **Walnut Creek/E**	26
Prospect | **SoMa**	24
R & G Lounge | **Chinatown**	24
Rest. LuLu | **SoMa**	21
Rio Grill | **Carmel/S**	23
NEW Roka Akor | **Downtown**	-
NEW Rosa Mexicano | **Embarcadero**	24
Rose Pistola | **N Beach**	21
Roy's | **SoMa**	24
Ruth's Chris | **Polk Gulch**	24
Sardine Factory | **Monterey/S**	24
Sauce | **Hayes Valley**	22
Scala's Bistro | **Downtown**	23
71 St. Peter | **San Jose/S**	22
Shadowbrook Rest. | **Capitola/S**	22
Slanted Door | **Embarcadero**	26
Soi4 | **Oakland/E**	23
Spruce | **Presidio Hts**	26
St. Orres | **Gualala/N**	23
Straits | **San Jose/S**	20
Tamarine | **Palo Alto/S**	25
Tarpy's | **Monterey/S**	24
Town Hall | **SoMa**	23
Trader Vic's | **Emeryville/E**	18
Tra Vigne | **St. Helena/N**	24
231 Ellsworth | **San Mateo/S**	23
Vic Stewart's | **Walnut Creek/E**	24
Village Pub | **Woodside/S**	25
Viognier | **San Mateo/S**	24

Waterbar | **Embarcadero**	23
Wente Vineyards | **Livermore/E**	25
Yank Sing | **SoMa**	26
Zarzuela | **Russian Hill**	24
Zibibbo | **Palo Alto/S**	20

PRIX FIXE MENUS
(Call for prices and times)

Acquerello | **Polk Gulch**	28
Ad Hoc | **Yountville/N**	26
Ajanta | **Berkeley/E**	27
Alamo Sq. | **W Addition**	22
Amber Bistro | **Danville/E**	23
Auberge du Soleil | **Rutherford/N**	27
Aubergine | **Carmel/S**	26
Aziza | **Outer Rich**	26
Baker St. Bistro | **Marina**	21
Basque Cultural | **S San Francisco/S**	20
Baumé | **Palo Alto/S**	26
Bistro Liaison | **Berkeley/E**	23
Cafe Bastille | **Downtown**	19
Cafe Gibraltar | **El Granada/S**	28
Capannina | **Cow Hollow**	25
Chantilly | **Redwood City/S**	25
Chapeau! | **Inner Rich**	27
Charcuterie | **Healdsburg/N**	20
Chez Panisse | **Berkeley/E**	27
Chez Papa Bistrot | **Potrero Hill**	24
Chez TJ | **Mtn View/S**	23
Cliff Hse. | **Outer Rich**	20
Coi | **N Beach**	27
Commis | **Oakland/E**	27
Dry Creek | **Healdsburg/N**	24
Erna's Elderberry | **Oakhurst/E**	28
Esin | **Danville/E**	26
Espetus | **Hayes Valley**	24
Étoile | **Yountville/N**	26
Farallon | **Downtown**	25
Firefly | **Noe Valley**	24
Fleur de Lys | **Downtown**	27
French Laundry | **Yountville/N**	28
Garibaldis | **Presidio Hts**	24
Gary Danko | **Fish. Wharf**	29
Girl/Fig | **Sonoma/N**	24
Greens | **Marina**	25
Hurley's Rest. | **Yountville/N**	23
Incanto | **Noe Valley**	25

Indigo	**Civic Ctr**	20
Isa	**Marina**	24
Jardinière	**Civic Ctr**	26
Jimmy Beans	**Berkeley/E**	20
Jin Sho	**Palo Alto/S**	24
🆕 Katsu	**Los Gatos/S**	-
Kiss Seafood	**Japantown**	28
La Folie	**Russian Hill**	27
La Forêt	**San Jose/S**	27
Lalime's	**Berkeley/E**	26
Lark Creek Steak	**Downtown**	24
La Toque	**Napa/N**	27
Le Charm Bistro	**SoMa**	22
Ledford Hse.	**Albion/N**	26
Le Papillon	**San Jose/S**	27
Le P'tit Laurent	**Glen Pk**	25
MacCallum/Grey Whale	**Mendocino/N**	24
Madrona Manor	**Healdsburg/N**	27
Manresa	**Los Gatos/S**	27
Marica	**Oakland/E**	25
MarketBar	**Embarcadero**	18
Meadowood Rest.	**St. Helena/N**	27
Mezze	**Oakland/E**	22
Michael Mina	**Downtown**	27
Millennium	**Downtown**	26
MoMo's	**S Beach**	19
Navio	**Half Moon Bay/S**	24
One Market	**Embarcadero**	24
Pacific's Edge	**Carmel/S**	24
🆕 Palace	**Mission**	-
Palio d'Asti	**Downtown**	21
Parcel 104	**Santa Clara/S**	23
Piperade	**Downtown**	26
Plouf	**Downtown**	22
Plumed Horse	**Saratoga/S**	25
Postrio	**Downtown**	23
Quince	**Downtown**	26
Rick & Ann's	**Berkeley/E**	23
Roy's	**SoMa**	24
Saison	**SoMa**	27
Santé	**Sonoma/N**	-
Scala's Bistro	**Downtown**	23
Scoma's	**Fish. Wharf**	24
Sens	**Embarcadero**	20
Sent Sovi	**Saratoga/S**	26
Sierra Mar	**Big Sur/S**	28

Slanted Door	**Embarcadero**	26
Sons/Daughters	**Nob Hill**	26
South Park	**SoMa**	22
St. Orres	**Gualala/N**	23
Tarpy's	**Monterey/S**	24
Ton Kiang	**Outer Rich**	25
Town's End	**Embarcadero**	21
231 Ellsworth	**San Mateo/S**	23
Unicorn	**Downtown**	23
Vik's Chaat	**Berkeley/E**	24
Wakuriya	**San Mateo/S**	28
Waterbar	**Embarcadero**	23
Waterfront	**Embarcadero**	21
Zazie	**Cole Valley**	24
Zibibbo	**Palo Alto/S**	20

QUIET CONVERSATION

Acquerello	**Polk Gulch**	28
Alexander's Steak	**multi.**	26
Alex Italian	**Rutherford/N**	24
All Spice	**San Mateo/S**	26
Andre's Bouchée	**Carmel/S**	24
Anton/Michel	**Carmel/S**	24
Applewood Rest.	**Guerneville/N**	24
Arcadia	**San Jose/S**	23
Atelier Crenn	**Marina**	27
Auberge du Soleil	**Rutherford/N**	27
Aubergine	**Carmel/S**	26
Bacco	**Noe Valley**	23
Baumé	**Palo Alto/S**	26
BayWolf	**Oakland/E**	26
Bella Vista	**Woodside/S**	24
Benu	**SoMa**	27
Bistro Moulin	**Monterey/S**	26
Brasserie S&P	**Downtown**	24
Burritt Tavern	**Downtown**	20
Cafe Jacqueline	**N Beach**	27
Campton Pl.	**Downtown**	26
Casanova	**Carmel/S**	24
Celadon	**Napa/N**	25
Chantilly	**Redwood City/S**	25
Chez Panisse	**Berkeley/E**	27
Chez TJ	**Mtn View/S**	23
Duck Club	**Bodega Bay/N**	22
Farmhse. Inn	**Forestville/N**	27
Fifth Floor	**SoMa**	24
Five	**Berkeley/E**	20

Flea St. Café	**Menlo Pk/S**	26	Boxing Rm.	**Hayes Valley**	20
Fleur de Lys	**Downtown**	27	Café Rouge	**Berkeley/E**	22
French Gdn.	**Sebastopol/N**	22	Central Mkt.	**Petaluma/N**	25
Gary Danko	**Fish. Wharf**	29	Chotto	**Marina**	24
Hotel Mac Rest.	**Richmond/E**	22	Cliff Hse.	**Outer Rich**	20
Keiko	**Nob Hill**	27	El Dorado	**Sonoma/N**	22
Khan Toke	**Outer Rich**	21	Farallon	**Downtown**	25
La Folie	**Russian Hill**	27	Ferry Plaza Seafoods | **Embarcadero**	22
Lalime's	**Berkeley/E**	26		
L'Ardoise	**Castro**	24	Fish Story	**Napa/N**	19
La Toque	**Napa/N**	27	Foreign Cinema	**Mission**	24
Le Papillon	**San Jose/S**	27	Fresca	**Noe Valley**	22
Lovejoy's Tea	**Noe Valley**	20	Glen Ellen Inn	**Glen Ellen/N**	23
Luce	**SoMa**	21	Grand Cafe	**Downtown**	20
Luella	**Russian Hill**	23	**NEW** Hard Water	**Embarcadero**	–
Madrona Manor	**Healdsburg/N**	27	Hog & Rocks	**Mission**	22
Manresa	**Los Gatos/S**	27	Hog Island Oyster	**multi.**	26
Marché/Fleurs	**Ross/N**	25	Ichi Sushi	**Bernal Hts**	27
NEW Mason Pacific	**Chinatown**	–	Lake Chalet	**Oakland/E**	17
Meadowood Rest.	**St. Helena/N**	27	Local's Corner	**Mission**	26
Mescolanza	**Outer Rich**	23	Luka's Taproom	**Oakland/E**	20
Morton's	**multi.**	23	Hong Kong Flower/Mayflower | **Milpitas/S**	21
Murray Circle	**Sausalito/N**	23		
Pacific's Edge	**Carmel/S**	24	Mission Rock	**Dogpatch**	16
Pakwan	**multi.**	23	Monti's	**Santa Rosa/N**	22
Pianeta	**Truckee/E**	20	Nick's Cove	**Marshall/N**	21
Plumed Horse	**Saratoga/S**	25	Rocker Oysterfeller's | **Valley Ford/N**	25
Postino	**Lafayette/E**	24		
Quattro	**E Palo Alto/S**	22	**NEW** Roka Akor	**Downtown**	–
Quince	**Downtown**	26	Sam's Chowder	**Half Moon Bay/S**	22
Rest./Ventana	**Big Sur/S**	23	Saru Sushi	**Noe Valley**	28
Rest. Mitsunobu	**Menlo Pk/S**	24	Skates on Bay	**Berkeley/E**	20
Richmond	**Inner Rich**	25	Slanted Door	**Embarcadero**	26
Sent Sovi	**Saratoga/S**	26	Sonoma-Meritage	**Sonoma/N**	19
Solbar	**Calistoga/N**	26	**NEW** Sugoi Sushi	**Mission**	–
Soule Domain	**Kings Bch/E**	24	Sushi Ran	**Sausalito/N**	27
St. Orres	**Gualala/N**	23	Swan Oyster	**Polk Gulch**	26
Terra	**St. Helena/N**	27	Thomas & Fagiani's	**Napa/N**	24
231 Ellsworth	**San Mateo/S**	23	Walnut Creek Yacht | **Walnut Creek/E**	24
Venticello	**Nob Hill**	23		
			Waterbar	**Embarcadero**	23
RAW BARS			Wayfare Tav.	**Downtown**	24
			Willi's Seafood	**Healdsburg/N**	25
Ame	**SoMa**	26	Woodhouse Fish	**Castro**	22
Anchor Oyster	**Castro**	25	Yankee Pier	**multi.**	19
Bar Crudo	**W Addition**	26	Zibibbo	**Palo Alto/S**	20
Bouchon	**Yountville/N**	26	Zuni Café	**Hayes Valley**	26

SPECIAL FEATURES

ROMANTIC PLACES

Restaurant	Location	Score
Acquerello	**Polk Gulch**	28
Ahwahnee	**Yosemite/E**	21
Albion River Inn	**Albion/N**	24
All Spice	**San Mateo/S**	26
Amber India	**SoMa**	24
Anton/Michel	**Carmel/S**	24
Applewood Pizza	**Menlo Pk/S**	23
Applewood Rest.	**Guerneville/N**	24
Atelier Crenn	**Marina**	27
Auberge du Soleil	**Rutherford/N**	27
Aubergine	**Carmel/S**	26
Aziza	**Outer Rich**	26
Barndiva	**Healdsburg/N**	25
Baumé	**Palo Alto/S**	26
Bella Vista	**Woodside/S**	24
Benu	**SoMa**	27
Big Four	**Nob Hill**	24
Bistro Central	**W Addition**	25
Bistro/Copains	**Occidental/N**	27
Bix	**Downtown**	24
Bottega	**Yountville/N**	25
Boulevard	**Embarcadero**	27
Brix	**Napa/N**	22
Bull Valley Roadhouse	**Port Costa**	-
Cafe Beaujolais	**Mendocino/N**	26
Cafe Jacqueline	**N Beach**	27
NEW Café Lucia	**Healdsburg/N**	-
Casanova	**Carmel/S**	24
Chantilly	**Redwood City/S**	25
Chapeau!	**Inner Rich**	27
Chez Panisse	**Berkeley/E**	27
Chez TJ	**Mtn View/S**	23
Christy Hill	**Tahoe City/E**	23
Coi	**N Beach**	27
Deetjen's Big Sur	**Big Sur/S**	24
Donato	**Redwood City/S**	23
Dry Creek	**Healdsburg/N**	24
Duck Club	**Bodega Bay/N**	22
El Paseo	**Mill Valley/N**	23
NEW Empire	**Napa/N**	-
Epic Roasthse.	**Embarcadero**	22
Erna's Elderberry	**Oakhurst/E**	28
Étoile	**Yountville/N**	26
Fandango	**Pacific Grove/S**	21
Farmhse. Inn	**Forestville/N**	27
Fifth Floor	**SoMa**	24
Flea St. Café	**Menlo Pk/S**	26
Fleur de Lys	**Downtown**	27
French Laundry	**Yountville/N**	28
Gabriella Café	**Santa Cruz/S**	20
Garden Ct.	**Downtown**	22
Gary Danko	**Fish. Wharf**	29
Gitane	**Downtown**	23
Glen Ellen Inn	**Glen Ellen/N**	23
NEW Hakkasan	**Downtown**	24
Harvest Moon	**Sonoma/N**	25
Heirloom	**Mission**	25
Hotel Mac Rest.	**Richmond/E**	22
Incanto	**Noe Valley**	25
Indigo	**Civic Ctr**	20
Jardinière	**Civic Ctr**	26
John Ash	**Santa Rosa/N**	25
John Bentley	**Redwood City/S**	25
Katia's Tea	**Inner Rich**	20
NEW Katsu	**Los Gatos/S**	-
Keiko	**Nob Hill**	27
Khan Toke	**Outer Rich**	21
Kokkari	**Downtown**	28
La Corneta	**Burlingame/S**	22
La Costanera	**Montara/S**	25
La Folie	**Russian Hill**	27
La Forêt	**San Jose/S**	27
Lake Chalet	**Oakland/E**	17
Lalime's	**Berkeley/E**	26
La Mar	**Embarcadero**	24
La Note	**Berkeley/E**	23
L'Ardoise	**Castro**	24
La Toque	**Napa/N**	27
Le Charm Bistro	**SoMa**	22
Le Colonial	**Downtown**	22
Ledford Hse.	**Albion/N**	26
Le Papillon	**San Jose/S**	27
Le P'tit Laurent	**Glen Pk**	25
Little River Inn	**Little River/N**	24
Luce	**SoMa**	21
Luella	**Russian Hill**	23
MacCallum/Grey Whale	**Mendocino/N**	24
Madera	**Menlo Pk/S**	23
Madrona Manor	**Healdsburg/N**	27
Manzanita	**Truckee/E**	22
Marché/Fleurs	**Ross/N**	25
Marinus	**Carmel Valley/S**	26

Matterhorn Swiss | **Russian Hill**	22
Meadowood Rest. | **St. Helena/N**	27
Mescolanza | **Outer Rich**	23
Millennium | **Downtown**	26
Murray Circle | **Sausalito/N**	23
Napa Wine Train | **Napa/N**	20
Navio | **Half Moon Bay/S**	24
Nick's Cove | **Marshall/N**	21
955 Rest. | **Mendocino/N**	25
Pacific's Edge | **Carmel/S**	24
Pampas | **Palo Alto/S**	22
Peasant/Pear | **Danville/E**	23
Pianeta | **Truckee/E**	20
Quince | **Downtown**	26
Rest./Stevenswood | **Little River/N**	24
Rest./Ventana | **Big Sur/S**	23
Risibisi | **Petaluma/N**	24
Roy's | **Pebble Bch/S**	25
Sent Sovi | **Saratoga/S**	26
71 St. Peter | **San Jose/S**	22
Shadowbrook Rest. | **Capitola/S**	22
Sierra Mar | **Big Sur/S**	28
NEW Sir & Star | **Olema/N**	-
Slow Club | **Mission**	23
Solbar | **Calistoga/N**	26
Soule Domain | **Kings Bch/E**	24
St. Michael's | **Palo Alto/S**	22
St. Orres | **Gualala/N**	23
Sunnyside Lodge | **Tahoe City/E**	18
Tav./Lark Creek | **Larkspur/N**	21
Terra | **St. Helena/N**	27
Terzo | **Cow Hollow**	25
1300/Fillmore | **W Addition**	22
Thomas & Fagiani's | **Napa/N**	24
25 Lusk | **SoMa**	22
Venticello | **Nob Hill**	23
Village Pub | **Woodside/S**	25
Viognier | **San Mateo/S**	24
Wente Vineyards | **Livermore/E**	25
Wolfdale's | **Tahoe City/E**	27
Woodward's Gdn. | **Mission**	24
Zaré/Fly Trap | **SoMa**	21
Zarzuela | **Russian Hill**	24

SINGLES SCENES

Ace Wasabi's | **Marina**	20
Amber India | **San Jose/S**	24

Americano | **Embarcadero**	20
Anchor & Hope | **SoMa**	21
Andalu | **Mission**	21
Attic | **San Mateo/S**	20
Balboa Cafe | **multi.**	20
Bar Agricole | **SoMa**	22
Barbacco | **Downtown**	24
Barlata | **Oakland/E**	22
Barndiva | **Healdsburg/N**	25
Beach Chalet | **Outer Sunset**	16
Beretta | **Mission**	24
Bix | **Downtown**	24
Blowfish Sushi | **multi.**	23
Blue Plate | **Mission**	24
Broken Record | **Excelsior**	24
Buckeye | **Mill Valley/N**	25
Bungalow 44 | **Mill Valley/N**	22
Butler/Chef | **SoMa**	22
Butterfly | **Embarcadero**	23
Cafe Bastille | **Downtown**	19
Café Claude | **Downtown**	22
Cascal | **Mtn View/S**	22
Cha Cha Cha | **multi.**	22
Cin-Cin Wine | **Los Gatos/S**	24
NEW Coqueta | **Embarcadero**	-
Cottonwood | **Truckee/E**	20
Dosa | **multi.**	23
Dragonfly | **Truckee/E**	23
NEW Duende | **Oakland/E**	23
E&O Asian Kit. | **Downtown**	21
Elite Cafe | **Pacific Hts**	20
Emmy's Spaghetti | **Bernal Hts**	21
NEW Empire | **Napa/N**	-
15 Romolo | **N Beach**	22
5A5 Steak | **Downtown**	23
Flora | **Oakland/E**	23
Foreign Cinema | **Mission**	24
NEW Forge | **Oakland/E**	-
Frjtz Fries | **Mission**	20
Gar Woods | **Carnelian Bay/E**	19
Gitane | **Downtown**	23
NEW Hakkasan | **Downtown**	24
Half Moon Brew | **Half Moon Bay/S**	17
NEW Hard Water | **Embarcadero**	-
Hog & Rocks | **Mission**	22
Hopmonk Tav. | **multi.**	19

Restaurant	Rating
NEW Katsu | **Los Gatos/S**	–
La Condesa | **St. Helena/N**	25
La Posta | **Santa Cruz/S**	25
Locanda | **Mission**	24
Lolinda | **Mission**	23
Luce | **SoMa**	21
Luna Park | **Mission**	20
NEW Lungomare | **Oakland/E**	–
Magnolia | **Haight-Ashbury**	22
Marlowe | **SoMa**	24
Maven | **Lower Haight**	18
NEW Mikkeller Bar | **Tenderloin**	–
Mission Rock | **Dogpatch**	16
MoMo's | **S Beach**	19
Moody's Bistro | **Truckee/E**	23
Mundaka | **Carmel/S**	24
NEW M.Y. China | **Downtown**	19
Nettie's Crab | **Cow Hollow**	20
Nihon | **Mission**	21
Ozumo | **multi.**	25
NEW Padrecito | **Cole Valley**	–
Parallel 37 | **Nob Hill**	24
Parcel 104 | **Santa Clara/S**	23
Per Diem | **Downtown**	20
Piazza D'Angelo | **Mill Valley/N**	20
PlumpJack | **Olympic Valley/E**	22
Poesia | **Castro**	23
Quattro | **E Palo Alto/S**	22
NEW Rickybobby | **Downtown**	–
NEW Roka Akor | **Downtown**	–
Rose Pistola | **N Beach**	21
Rumbo | **Oakland/E**	19
Serpentine | **Dogpatch**	23
Sino | **San Jose/S**	19
Slow Club | **Mission**	23
Starbelly | **Castro**	22
Straits | **multi.**	20
Tamarine | **Palo Alto/S**	25
Tommy's Mex. | **Outer Rich**	20
NEW Tribune Tavern | **Oakland/E**	–
NEW Trick Dog | **Mission**	–
NEW Trident | **Sausalito/N**	22
Tsunami Sushi | **W Addition**	22
25 Lusk | **SoMa**	22
Umami | **Cow Hollow**	25
Universal Cafe | **Mission**	25
Xanh | **Mtn View/S**	21
Zibibbo | **Palo Alto/S**	20
Zuni Café | **Hayes Valley**	26

SLEEPERS

(Good food, but little known)

Restaurant	Rating
Asmara | **Oakland/E**	26
Bar Terra | **St. Helena/N**	25
Boon Eat/Drink | **Guerneville/N**	25
Chinois | **Windsor/N**	25
Domo Sushi | **Hayes Valley**	27
Emilia's | **Berkeley/E**	27
Encuentro | **Oakland/E**	26
Evan's | **S Lake Tahoe/E**	27
FuseBox | **Oakland/E**	26
Glen Ellen Star | **Glen Ellen/N**	27
Graffiti | **Petaluma/N**	25
Hachi Ju Hachi | **Saratoga/S**	27
Hot Box Grill | **Sonoma/N**	25
Jim's Country | **Pleasanton/E**	26
Kappou Gomi | **Outer Rich**	28
Kenwood | **Kenwood/N**	25
Kiji Sushi Bar | **Mission**	25
La Condesa | **St. Helena/N**	25
La Posta | **Santa Cruz/S**	25
La Taquiza | **Napa/N**	27
Ledford Hse. | **Albion/N**	26
Local's Corner | **Mission**	26
Moki's Sushi | **Bernal Hts**	25
Nama Sushi | **Walnut Creek/E**	27
New Krung Thai | **San Jose/S**	25
Oswald | **Santa Cruz/S**	25
Papito | **Potrero Hill**	26
Rest. James | **Los Gatos/S**	25
Rocker Oysterfeller's | **Valley Ford/N**	25
Royal Thai | **San Rafael/N**	26
Sakae Sushi | **Burlingame/S**	25
Sandbox | **Bernal Hts**	25
Saru Sushi | **Noe Valley**	28
Sazon Peruvian | **Santa Rosa/N**	25
Terrapin Creek | **Bodega Bay/N**	27
To Hyang | **Inner Rich**	25
Truly Med. | **Mission**	26
Wakuriya | **San Mateo/S**	28

TRENDY

Restaurant	Rating
Abbot's Cellar | **Mission**	20
Ace Wasabi's | **Marina**	20

À Côté | **Oakland/E**	24	
Adesso | **Oakland/E**	22	
Amber India | **multi.**	24	
Americano | **Embarcadero**	20	
Anchor & Hope | **SoMa**	21	
AQ | **SoMa**	24	
A16 | **Marina**	24	
Attic | **San Mateo/S**	20	
Balboa Cafe | **Cow Hollow**	20	
Bar Agricole | **SoMa**	22	
Barndiva | **Healdsburg/N**	25	
Bar Tartine | **Mission**	24	
Beast/Hare | **Mission**	23	
Beretta | **Mission**	24	
B44 | **Downtown**	21	
Biergarten | **Hayes Valley**	21	
Bistro Don Giovanni | **Napa/N**	25	
Bix | **Downtown**	24	
Blowfish Sushi | **multi.**	23	
Blue Plate | **Mission**	24	
Bocadillos | **N Beach**	23	
Boot/Shoe | **Oakland/E**	24	
Bottega | **Yountville/N**	25	
Bouchon | **Yountville/N**	26	
Boxing Rm. | **Hayes Valley**	20	
Broken Record | **Excelsior**	24	
B Star | **Inner Rich**	25	
Bungalow 44 | **Mill Valley/N**	22	
Café Rouge | **Berkeley/E**	22	
Cascal | **Mtn View/S**	22	
NEW Cavalier | **SoMa**	–	
Central Kitchen | **Mission**	24	
Cha Cha Cha | **multi.**	22	
NEW Chocolate Lab | **Dogpatch**	25	
Chotto | **Marina**	24	
Coco500 | **SoMa**	24	
Comal | **Berkeley/E**	23	
Commonwealth | **Mission**	26	
NEW Coqueta | **Embarcadero**	–	
Delarosa | **Marina**	21	
Delfina | **Mission**	26	
Doña Tomás | **Oakland/E**	22	
Dosa | **multi.**	23	
NEW Duende | **Oakland/E**	23	
Emmy's Spaghetti | **Bernal Hts**	21	
NEW Empire | **Napa/N**	–	
Farina Foccacia | **Mission**	22	

15 Romolo | **N Beach**	22
5A5 Steak | **Downtown**	23
Flora | **Oakland/E**	23
Flour + Water | **Mission**	26
Fonda Solana | **Albany/E**	22
Foreign Cinema | **Mission**	24
NEW Forge | **Oakland/E**	–
Front Porch | **Bernal Hts**	22
Gitane | **Downtown**	23
NEW Hakkasan | **Downtown**	24
NEW Hard Water | **Embarcadero**	–
Hawker Fare | **Oakland/E**	23
Hog & Rocks | **Mission**	22
Hopmonk Tav. | **multi.**	19
Hopscotch | **Oakland/E**	24
NEW Katsu | **Los Gatos/S**	–
La Mar | **Embarcadero**	24
Locanda | **Mission**	24
Lolinda | **Mission**	23
NEW Lungomare | **Oakland/E**	–
Mamacita | **Marina**	24
Marlowe | **SoMa**	24
Maven | **Lower Haight**	18
Maverick | **Mission**	24
NEW Mikkeller Bar | **Tenderloin**	–
Mission Chinese | **Mission**	22
Morimoto | **Napa/N**	25
Mustards | **Yountville/N**	25
NEW M.Y. China | **Downtown**	19
Namu Gaji | **Mission**	24
Nihon | **Mission**	21
Nopa | **W Addition**	26
Osha Thai | **multi.**	22
Ozumo | **multi.**	25
NEW Padrecito | **Cole Valley**	–
Park Tav. | **N Beach**	24
Piazza D'Angelo | **Mill Valley/N**	20
Picán | **Oakland/E**	24
Picco | **Larkspur/N**	26
Pizzeria Delfina | **Mission**	25
Pizzeria Picco | **Larkspur/N**	26
Plum | **Oakland/E**	23
Postrio | **Downtown**	23
NEW Ramen Shop | **Oakland/E**	24
Range | **Mission**	27
Redd | **Yountville/N**	27
Revival Bar | **Berkeley/E**	22

NEW Rickybobby | **Downtown** _-_
RN74 | **SoMa** 22
NEW Roka Akor | **Downtown** _-_
NEW Rosa Mexicano | **Embarcadero** 24
Salt Hse. | **SoMa** 22
Sebo | **Hayes Valley** 27
Serpentine | **Dogpatch** 23
Sidebar | **Oakland/E** 22
Sino | **San Jose/S** 19
Slanted Door | **Embarcadero** 26
Slow Club | **Mission** 23
Solbar | **Calistoga/N** 26
NEW South/SFJAZZ | **Hayes Valley** _-_
Spoonbar | **Healdsburg/N** 20
SPQR | **Pacific Hts** 25
Spruce | **Presidio Hts** 26
Starbelly | **Castro** 22
Straits | **multi.** 20
Tamarine | **Palo Alto/S** 25
Terzo | **Cow Hollow** 25
Thomas & Fagiani's | **Napa/N** 24
Town Hall | **SoMa** 23
NEW Tribune Tavern | **Oakland/E** _-_
NEW Trick Dog | **Mission** _-_
Tsunami Sushi | **W Addition** 22
25 Lusk | **SoMa** 22
Umami | **Cow Hollow** 25
Underwood Bar | **Graton/N** 22
Waterbar | **Embarcadero** 23
West of Pecos | **Mission** 19
Wood Tav. | **Oakland/E** 26
Xanh | **Mtn View/S** 21
Yoshi's | **W Addition** 22
Zero Zero | **SoMa** 24
Zibibbo | **Palo Alto/S** 20
Zuni Café | **Hayes Valley** 26
ZuZu | **Napa/N** 24

VALET PARKING

Absinthe | **Hayes Valley** 23
Ahwahnee | **Yosemite/E** 21
Alexander's Steak | **multi.** 26
Amber Bistro | **Danville/E** 23
Ame | **SoMa** 26
Americano | **Embarcadero** 20
Andalu | **Mission** 21

Anzu | **Downtown** 23
Applewood Rest. | **Guerneville/N** 24
Arcadia | **San Jose/S** 23
Auberge du Soleil | **Rutherford/N** 27
Aubergine | **Carmel/S** 26
Aziza | **Outer Rich** 26
Baker/Banker | **Upper Fillmore** 25
Balboa Cafe | **Cow Hollow** 20
Barbacco | **Downtown** 24
Bar Bocce | **Sausalito/N** 22
Basin | **Saratoga/S** 23
Bellanico | **Oakland/E** 23
Benu | **SoMa** 27
Big Four | **Nob Hill** 24
Bix | **Downtown** 24
Blowfish Sushi | **San Jose/S** 23
Bocanova | **Oakland/E** 23
Boccalone | **Embarcadero** 25
Boulevard | **Embarcadero** 27
Brasserie S&P | **Downtown** 24
Buckeye | **Mill Valley/N** 25
Campton Pl. | **Downtown** 26
Casa Orinda | **Orinda/E** 20
Chantilly | **Redwood City/S** 25
Chaya | **Embarcadero** 23
Cheesecake Fac. | **Santa Clara/S** 16
Cliff Hse. | **Outer Rich** 20
Coi | **N Beach** 27
Cole's Chop | **Napa/N** 27
Cotogna | **Downtown** 26
Crustacean | **Polk Gulch** 25
Cupola Pizzeria | **Downtown** 21
Delica | **Embarcadero** 25
Dio Deka | **Los Gatos/S** 25
Donato | **Redwood City/S** 23
Elite Cafe | **Pacific Hts** 20
NEW Empire | **Napa/N** _-_
Epic Roasthse. | **Embarcadero** 22
Evvia | **Palo Alto/S** 28
Farallon | **Downtown** 25
Farina Foccaccia | **Mission** 22
Fifth Floor | **SoMa** 24
Five | **Berkeley/E** 20
5A5 Steak | **Downtown** 23
Fleur de Lys | **Downtown** 27
Florio | **Pacific Hts** 21
Foreign Cinema | **Mission** 24

NEW Forge | **Oakland/E**	-
Garden Ct. | **Downtown**	22
Garibaldis | **Presidio Hts**	24
Gary Danko | **Fish. Wharf**	29
Grand Cafe | **Downtown**	20
Harris' | **Polk Gulch**	26
House/Prime | **Polk Gulch**	26
Hunan Home's/Gdn. | **Chinatown**	21
Il Fornaio | **multi.**	18
Insalata's | **San Anselmo/N**	25
Jardinière | **Civic Ctr**	26
Kokkari | **Downtown**	28
Kuleto's | **Downtown**	23
La Folie | **Russian Hill**	27
La Fondue | **Saratoga/S**	22
Lake Chalet | **Oakland/E**	17
La Toque | **Napa/N**	27
Le Colonial | **Downtown**	22
Lion/Compass | **Sunnyvale/S**	21
Luce | **SoMa**	21
Luna Park | **Mission**	20
Manzanita | **Truckee/E**	22
Marinus | **Carmel Valley/S**	26
NEW Mason Pacific | **Chinatown**	-
Matterhorn Swiss | **Russian Hill**	22
Maykadeh | **N Beach**	23
Meritage/Claremont | **Berkeley/E**	23
Michael Mina | **Downtown**	27
Millennium | **Downtown**	26
NEW MKT | **SoMa**	-
MoMo's | **S Beach**	19
Morton's | **multi.**	23
Navio | **Half Moon Bay/S**	24
North Bch. Rest. | **N Beach**	24
One Market | **Embarcadero**	24
Osha Thai | **Cow Hollow**	22
Osteria Coppa | **San Mateo/S**	22
Ozumo | **multi.**	25
Pacific's Edge | **Carmel/S**	24
Parallel 37 | **Nob Hill**	24
Parcel 104 | **Santa Clara/S**	23
Park Tav. | **N Beach**	24
Perbacco | **Downtown**	26
Picco | **Larkspur/N**	26
Pizzeria Picco | **Larkspur/N**	26
Pläj | **Hayes Valley**	24
Plant Cafe | **Embarcadero**	22
Plumed Horse | **Saratoga/S**	25
Poggio | **Sausalito/N**	25
Postino | **Lafayette/E**	24
Postrio | **Downtown**	23
Prima | **Walnut Creek/E**	26
Prospect | **SoMa**	24
Quattro | **E Palo Alto/S**	22
Quince | **Downtown**	26
Rest. LuLu | **SoMa**	21
RN74 | **SoMa**	22
NEW Roka Akor | **Downtown**	-
Rose Pistola | **N Beach**	21
Ruth's Chris | **multi.**	24
Santé | **Sonoma/N**	-
Scoma's | **Fish. Wharf**	24
Sierra Mar | **Big Sur/S**	28
Slanted Door | **Embarcadero**	26
Solbar | **Calistoga/N**	26
Spoonbar | **Healdsburg/N**	20
Spruce | **Presidio Hts**	26
Straits | **Downtown**	20
Sunnyside Lodge | **Tahoe City/E**	18
Sutro's | **Outer Rich**	21
Tav./Lark Creek | **Larkspur/N**	21
Terzo | **Cow Hollow**	25
Thanh Long | **Outer Sunset**	26
Town Hall | **SoMa**	23
Townhouse B&G | **Emeryville/E**	22
Trace | **SoMa**	22
Trader Vic's | **Emeryville/E**	18
NEW Trident | **Sausalito/N**	22
25 Lusk | **SoMa**	22
231 Ellsworth | **San Mateo/S**	23
Venticello | **Nob Hill**	23
Waterbar | **Embarcadero**	23
Waterfront | **Embarcadero**	21
Wayfare Tav. | **Downtown**	24
Wente Vineyards | **Livermore/E**	25
Wine Spectator | **St. Helena/N**	23
Yankee Pier | **multi.**	19
Zuni Café | **Hayes Valley**	26

VIEWS

Ahwahnee | **Yosemite/E**	21
Albion River Inn | **Albion/N**	24
Angèle | **Napa/N**	24
Applewood Rest. | **Guerneville/N**	24

Auberge du Soleil	**Rutherford/N**	27	Kenwood	**Kenwood/N**	25
Barndiva	**Healdsburg/N**	25	La Costanera	**Montara/S**	25
Bella Vista	**Woodside/S**	24	La Forêt	**San Jose/S**	27
Big Sur	**Big Sur/S**	24	La Mar	**Embarcadero**	24
NEW Big Sur Roadhse.	**Big Sur/S**	-	Ledford Hse.	**Albion/N**	26
Bistro Boudin	**Fish. Wharf**	22	Lion/Compass	**Sunnyvale/S**	21
Bistro Don Giovanni	**Napa/N**	25	Little River Inn	**Little River/N**	24
Bocanova	**Oakland/E**	23	Lolinda	**Mission**	23
Boulettes Larder/Bouli Bar		25	**NEW** Lungomare	**Oakland/E**	-
Embarcadero			Madera	**Menlo Pk/S**	23
Boulevard	**Embarcadero**	27	Mama's on Wash.	**N Beach**	24
Brick/Bottle	**Corte Madera/N**	19	Marinus	**Carmel Valley/S**	26
Brix	**Napa/N**	22	Meadowood Rest.	**St. Helena/N**	27
Butterfly	**Embarcadero**	23	Meritage/Claremont	**Berkeley/E**	23
Cafe Beaujolais	**Mendocino/N**	26	Mission Rock	**Dogpatch**	16
Cafe Citti	**Kenwood/N**	23	Murray Circle	**Sausalito/N**	23
Cafe Gibraltar	**El Granada/S**	28	Napa Wine Train	**Napa/N**	20
Cafe La Haye	**Sonoma/N**	26	Navio	**Half Moon Bay/S**	24
Café Rustica	**Carmel Valley/S**	23	Nepenthe	**Big Sur/S**	18
Catch	**Castro**	21	Nick's Cove	**Marshall/N**	21
C Casa	**Napa/N**	25	One Market	**Embarcadero**	24
Chaya	**Embarcadero**	23	Ozumo	**Embarcadero**	25
Cheesecake Fac.	**Downtown**	16	Pacific's Edge	**Carmel/S**	24
Chevalier	**Lafayette/E**	25	Park Chalet	**Outer Sunset**	16
Chez TJ	**Mtn View/S**	23	**NEW** Pear	**Napa/N**	-
Christy Hill	**Tahoe City/E**	23	Piatti	**Mill Valley/N**	21
NEW Cindy's Waterfront		-	Picco	**Larkspur/N**	26
Monterey/S			Press	**St. Helena/N**	26
Cucina Paradiso	**Petaluma/N**	27	Rest./Stevenswood		24
Delica	**Embarcadero**	25	**Little River/N**		
Downtown Bakery		26	Rivoli	**Berkeley/E**	27
Healdsburg/N			Roy's	**Pebble Bch/S**	25
Dry Creek	**Healdsburg/N**	24	Rudy's Can't Fail	**Oakland/E**	19
Dynamo Donut	**Marina**	25	Rustic	**Geyserville/N**	21
Epic Roadhse.	**Embarcadero**	22	Rutherford Grill	**Rutherford/N**	24
Erna's Elderberry	**Oakhurst/E**	28	Scoma's	**multi.**	24
Étoile	**Yountville/N**	26	Sierra Mar	**Big Sur/S**	28
Farm	**Napa/N**	24	Slanted Door	**Embarcadero**	26
Farmhse. Inn	**Forestville/N**	27	St. Orres	**Gualala/N**	23
Fish	**Sausalito/N**	24	Sutro's	**Outer Rich**	21
NEW Forge	**Oakland/E**	-	Tony's Pizza	**N Beach**	26
Frascati	**Russian Hill**	25	**NEW** Trident	**Sausalito/N**	22
Gar Woods	**Carnelian Bay/E**	19	Venticello	**Nob Hill**	23
Greens	**Marina**	25	Waterbar	**Embarcadero**	23
Hog Island Oyster	**Embarcadero**	26	Wente Vineyards	**Livermore/E**	25
HRD Coffee/Smokin	**SoMa**	23	Wolfdale's	**Tahoe City/E**	27
Ike's Pl./Lair	**Stanford/S**	25	Zazu	**Sebastopol/N**	26
John Ash	**Santa Rosa/N**	25		

VISITORS ON EXPENSE ACCOUNT

Restaurant	Location	Score
Acquerello	**Polk Gulch**	28
Ahwahnee	**Yosemite/E**	21
Alexander's Steak	**multi.**	26
Alfred's Steak	**Downtown**	23
Ame	**SoMa**	26
Andre's Bouchée	**Carmel/S**	24
Anzu	**Downtown**	23
Applewood Rest.	**Guerneville/N**	24
Arcadia	**San Jose/S**	23
Atelier Crenn	**Marina**	27
Auberge du Soleil	**Rutherford/N**	27
Aubergine	**Carmel/S**	26
Barbacco	**Downtown**	24
Barndiva	**Healdsburg/N**	25
Baumé	**Palo Alto/S**	26
Benu	**SoMa**	27
Bottega	**Yountville/N**	25
Boulevard	**Embarcadero**	27
Bourbon Steak	**Downtown**	23
Brasserie S&P	**Downtown**	24
Burritt Tavern	**Downtown**	20
Campton Pl.	**Downtown**	26
Central Kitchen	**Mission**	24
Chez Panisse	**Berkeley/E**	27
Chez TJ	**Mtn View/S**	23
Coi	**N Beach**	27
Cole's Chop	**Napa/N**	27
Commis	**Oakland/E**	27
Deetjen's Big Sur	**Big Sur/S**	24
Dixie	**Presidio**	20
Dry Creek	**Healdsburg/N**	24
El Paseo	**Mill Valley/N**	23
Epic Roasthse.	**Embarcadero**	22
Erna's Elderberry	**Oakhurst/E**	28
Étoile	**Yountville/N**	26
Evvia	**Palo Alto/S**	28
Farmhse. Inn	**Forestville/N**	27
Fifth Floor	**SoMa**	24
5A5 Steak	**Downtown**	23
Flea St. Café	**Menlo Pk/S**	26
Fleur de Lys	**Downtown**	27
French Laundry	**Yountville/N**	28
Garden Ct.	**Downtown**	22
Gary Danko	**Fish. Wharf**	29
Greens	**Marina**	25
Hachi Ju Hachi	**Saratoga/S**	27
NEW Hakkasan	**Downtown**	24
Hana	**Rohnert Pk/N**	26
Harris'	**Polk Gulch**	26
Jai Yun	**Chinatown**	23
Jardinière	**Civic Ctr**	26
John Ash	**Santa Rosa/N**	25
John Bentley	**Redwood City/S**	25
NEW Katsu	**Los Gatos/S**	-
Keiko	**Nob Hill**	27
Kokkari	**Downtown**	28
NEW La Balena Cucina	**Carmel/S**	-
La Folie	**Russian Hill**	27
La Forêt	**San Jose/S**	27
La Toque	**Napa/N**	27
Madrona Manor	**Healdsburg/N**	27
Manresa	**Los Gatos/S**	27
Manzanita	**Truckee/E**	22
Marinus	**Carmel Valley/S**	26
McCormick/Kuleto	**Fish. Wharf**	21
Meadowood Rest.	**St. Helena/N**	27
Michael Mina	**Downtown**	27
Millennium	**Downtown**	26
Morimoto	**Napa/N**	25
Morton's	**multi.**	23
NEW M.Y. China	**Downtown**	19
Napa Wine Train	**Napa/N**	20
Navio	**Half Moon Bay/S**	24
Oliveto Rest.	**Oakland/E**	25
Ozumo	**multi.**	25
Pacific's Edge	**Carmel/S**	24
Parallel 37	**Nob Hill**	24
Perbacco	**Downtown**	26
Plumed Horse	**Saratoga/S**	25
Press	**St. Helena/N**	26
Prospect	**SoMa**	24
Quince	**Downtown**	26
Redd	**Yountville/N**	27
Rest./Ventana	**Big Sur/S**	23
Rest. Mitsunobu	**Menlo Pk/S**	24
RN74	**SoMa**	22
NEW Roka Akor	**Downtown**	-
Roy's	**SoMa**	24
Roy's	**Pebble Bch/S**	25
Ruth's Chris	**multi.**	24
Saison	**SoMa**	27

Santé	**Sonoma/N**	-⌋
Sawa Sushi	**Sunnyvale/S**	23⌋
NEW Sea	**Palo Alto/S**	23⌋
Sent Sovi	**Saratoga/S**	26⌋
Seven Hills	**Nob Hill**	27⌋
Sierra Mar	**Big Sur/S**	28⌋
Sino	**San Jose/S**	19⌋
Slanted Door	**Embarcadero**	26⌋
Sons/Daughters	**Nob Hill**	26⌋
Spruce	**Presidio Hts**	26⌋
Terra	**St. Helena/N**	27⌋
Town Hall	**SoMa**	23⌋
Village Pub	**Woodside/S**	25⌋
Wakuriya	**San Mateo/S**	28⌋
Waterbar	**Embarcadero**	23⌋
Wayfare Tav.	**Downtown**	24⌋

WINE BARS

All Seasons	**Calistoga/N**	23⌋
Anchor & Hope	**SoMa**	21⌋
Andre's Bouchée	**Carmel/S**	24⌋
NEW Aquitaine	**Downtown**	-⌋
A16	**Marina**	24⌋
Attic	**San Mateo/S**	20⌋
Barbacco	**Downtown**	24⌋
Bar Tartine	**Mission**	24⌋
Bellanico	**Oakland/E**	23⌋
Bocadillos	**N Beach**	23⌋
Burritt Tavern	**Downtown**	20⌋
Cafe Zoetrope	**N Beach**	21⌋
Carneros Bistro	**Sonoma/N**	24⌋
César	**Berkeley/E**	22⌋
NEW Chalkboard Bistro	**Healdsburg/N**	-⌋
Cin-Cin Wine	**Los Gatos/S**	24⌋
Cindy Pawlcyn's	**St. Helena/N**	22⌋
NEW Cindy's Waterfront	**Monterey/S**	-⌋
Copita	**Sausalito/N**	24⌋
Emporio Rulli	**Larkspur/N**	22⌋
Encuentro	**Oakland/E**	26⌋
Della Santina	**Sonoma/N**	24⌋
Enoteca Molinari	**Oakland/E**	22⌋
Étoile	**Yountville/N**	26⌋
15 Romolo	**N Beach**	22⌋
Fig Cafe/Wine	**Glen Ellen/N**	26⌋
Frascati	**Russian Hill**	25⌋
French Blue	**St. Helena/N**	20⌋

FuseBox	**Oakland/E**	26⌋
Glen Ellen Inn	**Glen Ellen/N**	23⌋
Glen Ellen Star	**Glen Ellen/N**	27⌋
Great Eastern	**Chinatown**	23⌋
Grill/Alley	**San Jose/S**	23⌋
Incanto	**Noe Valley**	25⌋
Italian Colors	**Oakland/E**	22⌋
Kuleto's	**Downtown**	23⌋
La Sen Bistro	**Berkeley/E**	23⌋
La Toque	**Napa/N**	27⌋
Liberty Cafe	**Bernal Hts**	22⌋
Maverick	**Mission**	24⌋
Napa Wine Train	**Napa/N**	20⌋
NEW Odalisque Cafe	**San Rafael/N**	-⌋
Oxbow Wine	**Napa/N**	21⌋
Pauline's Pizza/Wine	**Mission**	22⌋
NEW Pear	**Napa/N**	-⌋
Picco	**Larkspur/N**	26⌋
Pizzando	**Healdsburg/N**	-⌋
Prima	**Walnut Creek/E**	26⌋
RN74	**SoMa**	22⌋
Roam	**Pacific Hts**	23⌋
Rosso Pizzeria	**Santa Rosa/N**	25⌋
Rustic	**Geyserville/N**	21⌋
Soif Wine Bar	**Santa Cruz/S**	24⌋
St. Vincent Tavern	**Mission**	21⌋
Sushi Ran	**Sausalito/N**	27⌋
1300/Fillmore	**W Addition**	22⌋
Va de Vi	**Walnut Creek/E**	25⌋
Viognier	**San Mateo/S**	24⌋
Wente Vineyards	**Livermore/E**	25⌋
Willi's Wine	**Santa Rosa/N**	25⌋
NEW Wine Kitchen	**W Addition**	-⌋
Zin	**Healdsburg/N**	23⌋
ZuZu	**Napa/N**	24⌋

WINNING WINE LISTS

Absinthe	**Hayes Valley**	23⌋
À Côté	**Oakland/E**	24⌋
Acquerello	**Polk Gulch**	28⌋
Adesso	**Oakland/E**	22⌋
Albion River Inn	**Albion/N**	24⌋
Alembic	**Haight-Ashbury**	23⌋
Alexander's Steak	**Cupertino/S**	26⌋
Alex Italian	**Rutherford/N**	24⌋
Alioto's	**Fish. Wharf**	21⌋
All Seasons	**Calistoga/N**	23⌋

SPECIAL FEATURES

Girl/Fig | **Sonoma/N**	24
Glen Ellen Inn | **Glen Ellen/N**	23
Glen Ellen Star | **Glen Ellen/N**	27
Goose & Gander | **St. Helena/N**	22
Gott's Roadside | **Napa/N**	22
Grasing's Coastal | **Carmel/S**	21
Greens | **Marina**	25
Heirloom | **Mission**	25
Incanto | **Noe Valley**	25
Indigo | **Civic Ctr**	20
Jardinière | **Civic Ctr**	26
John Ash | **Santa Rosa/N**	25
John Bentley | **Redwood City/S**	25
Jole | **Calistoga/N**	26
Keiko | **Nob Hill**	27
Kenwood | **Kenwood/N**	25
Kokkari | **Downtown**	28
Kuleto's | **Downtown**	23
NEW La Balena Cucina | **Carmel/S**	–
La Ciccia | **Noe Valley**	27
La Condesa | **St. Helena/N**	25
La Folie | **Russian Hill**	27
La Forêt | **San Jose/S**	27
Lalime's | **Berkeley/E**	26
La Mar | **Embarcadero**	24
La Note | **Berkeley/E**	23
Lark Creek Steak | **Downtown**	24
LaSalette | **Sonoma/N**	24
La Toque | **Napa/N**	27
LB Steak | **San Jose/S**	22
Ledford Hse. | **Albion/N**	26
Left Bank | **multi.**	20
Le Papillon | **San Jose/S**	27
Liberty Cafe | **Bernal Hts**	22
Lincoln Park Wine | **San Anselmo/N**	–
Locanda | **Mission**	24
Luce | **SoMa**	21
Luella | **Russian Hill**	23
NEW Lungomare | **Oakland/E**	–
Madera | **Menlo Pk/S**	23
Madrona Manor | **Healdsburg/N**	27
Manresa | **Los Gatos/S**	27
Manzanita | **Truckee/E**	22
Marché/Fleurs | **Ross/N**	25
Marinitas | **San Anselmo/N**	21
Marinus | **Carmel Valley/S**	26
Mateo's Cocina | **Healdsburg/N**	22
Meadowood Grill | **St. Helena/N**	22
Meadowood Rest. | **St. Helena/N**	27
Mendo Bistro | **Ft Bragg/N**	25
Michael Mina | **Downtown**	27
Millennium | **Downtown**	26
Monti's | **Santa Rosa/N**	22
Montrio Bistro | **Monterey/S**	23
Morimoto | **Napa/N**	25
Mundaka | **Carmel/S**	24
Mustards | **Yountville/N**	25
Napa Wine Train | **Napa/N**	20
Navio | **Half Moon Bay/S**	24
Nick's Cove | **Marshall/N**	21
955 Rest. | **Mendocino/N**	25
Nopa | **W Addition**	26
North Bch. Rest. | **N Beach**	24
Oenotri | **Napa/N**	24
Oliveto Cafe | **Oakland/E**	23
Oliveto Rest. | **Oakland/E**	25
One Market | **Embarcadero**	24
Oxbow Wine | **Napa/N**	21
Pacific's Edge | **Carmel/S**	24
Palio d'Asti | **Downtown**	21
Pampas | **Palo Alto/S**	22
Parallel 37 | **Nob Hill**	24
Passionfish | **Pacific Grove/S**	27
Perbacco | **Downtown**	26
Pianeta | **Truckee/E**	20
Picán | **Oakland/E**	24
Piccino | **Dogpatch**	24
Picco | **Larkspur/N**	26
Piperade | **Downtown**	26
Pizzeria Picco | **Larkspur/N**	26
Plumed Horse | **Saratoga/S**	25
PlumpJack | **Olympic Valley/E**	22
Poggio | **Sausalito/N**	25
Postrio | **Downtown**	23
Press | **St. Helena/N**	26
Prima | **Walnut Creek/E**	26
Prospect | **SoMa**	24
Quince | **Downtown**	26
Range | **Mission**	27
Redd | **Yountville/N**	27
Redd Wood | **Yountville/N**	25
Rest./Ventana | **Big Sur/S**	23

WORTH A TRIP

Cuisines

Includes names, locations and Food ratings.

AFGHAN

Helmand Palace	**Russian Hill**	23
Kabul Afghan	**multi.**	24

AMERICAN

Ad Hoc	**Yountville/N**	26
Ahwahnee	**Yosemite/E**	21
Ame	**SoMa**	26
Amer. Grilled	**multi.**	22
Anchor & Hope	**SoMa**	21
Arcadia	**San Jose/S**	23
Baker/Banker	**Upper Fillmore**	25
Balboa Cafe	**multi.**	20
Bar Jules	**Hayes Valley**	24
Barndiva	**Healdsburg/N**	25
Bar Terra	**St. Helena/N**	25
Basin	**Saratoga/S**	23
Beach Chalet	**Outer Sunset**	16
NEW Belcampo Meat	**Larkspur/N**	-
Benu	**SoMa**	27
Big Four	**Nob Hill**	24
Big Sur	**Big Sur/S**	24
NEW Big Sur Roadhse.	**Big Sur/S**	-
Bi-Rite	**W Addition**	27
Bix	**Downtown**	24
Blue Plate	**Mission**	24
Bluestem Brass.	**SoMa**	19
Bottle Cap	**N Beach**	18
Boudin Sourdough	**multi.**	21
Boulettes Larder/Bouli Bar	**Embarcadero**	25
Boulevard	**Embarcadero**	27
Bourbon Steak	**Downtown**	23
Brannan's Grill	**Calistoga/N**	19
Brazen Head	**Cow Hollow**	20
Buckeye	**Mill Valley/N**	25
Bull Valley Roadhouse	**Port Costa**	-
Bungalow 44	**Mill Valley/N**	22
Bureau 510	**Emeryville/E**	-
Burritt Tavern	**Downtown**	20
Cafe La Haye	**Sonoma/N**	26
Campanula	**N Beach**	20
Celadon	**Napa/N**	25

NEW Chalkboard Bistro	**Healdsburg/N**	-
Cheesecake Fac.	**multi.**	16
Chenery Park	**Glen Pk**	23
Chloe's Cafe	**Noe Valley**	23
Chow/Park Chow	**multi.**	21
Cindy Pawlcyn's	**St. Helena/N**	22
Citizen's Band	**SoMa**	22
Commis	**Oakland/E**	27
Commonwealth	**Mission**	26
Corners Tav.	**Walnut Creek/E**	23
NEW Corner Store	**Laurel Hts**	22
Duarte's	**Pescadero/S**	22
Duck Club	**Bodega Bay/N**	22
Elite Cafe	**Pacific Hts**	20
Ella's	**Presidio Hts**	21
Esin	**Danville/E**	26
Eureka	**Castro**	21
Evan's	**S Lake Tahoe/E**	27
NEW Fable	**Castro**	-
Farm	**Napa/N**	24
NEW Farmshop	**Larkspur/N**	-
NEW Fast Food Français	**Sausalito/N**	-
15 Romolo	**N Beach**	22
Fifth Floor	**SoMa**	24
Five	**Berkeley/E**	20
5A5 Steak	**Downtown**	23
Flea St. Café	**Menlo Pk/S**	26
Flora	**Oakland/E**	23
NEW Forge	**Oakland/E**	-
French Blue	**St. Helena/N**	20
French Laundry	**Yountville/N**	28
Fumé Bistro	**Napa/N**	22
Gary Danko	**Fish. Wharf**	29
Glen Ellen Star	**Glen Ellen/N**	27
Goose & Gander	**St. Helena/N**	22
Hayes Valley Bakeworks	**Hayes Valley**	21
Healdsburg B&G	**Healdsburg/N**	19
NEW Hillside Supper	**Bernal Hts**	-
Hog & Rocks	**Mission**	22
Homeroom	**Oakland/E**	21
Hopmonk Tav.	**multi.**	19

CUISINES

Restaurant	Rating
Hopscotch | **Oakland/E**	24
Hotel Mac Rest. | **Richmond/E**	22
House/Prime | **Polk Gulch**	26
Il Postale | **Sunnyvale/S**	23
Indigo | **Civic Ctr**	20
In-N-Out | **multi.**	23
Jasper's Corner | **Downtown**	19
John Bentley | **Redwood City/S**	25
Jole | **Calistoga/N**	26
Lark Creek | **Walnut Creek/E**	23
Liberty Cafe | **Bernal Hts**	22
Lion/Compass | **Sunnyvale/S**	21
Lucca Deli | **Marina**	26
Luce | **SoMa**	21
Luna Park | **Mission**	20
Madera | **Menlo Pk/S**	23
Madrona Manor | **Healdsburg/N**	27
Magnolia | **Haight-Ashbury**	22
Mama's on Wash. | **N Beach**	24
Mama's Royal | **Oakland/E**	23
Manresa | **Los Gatos/S**	27
Marica | **Oakland/E**	25
Market | **St. Helena/N**	22
MarketBar | **Embarcadero**	18
NEW Marrow | **Oakland/E**	-
NEW Mason Pacific | **Chinatown**	-
Maven | **Lower Haight**	18
Maverick | **Mission**	24
Mendo Bistro | **Ft Bragg/N**	25
Mendo Café | **Mendocino/N**	20
Michael Mina | **Downtown**	27
NEW Mikkeller Bar | **Tenderloin**	-
Mission Cheese | **Mission**	22
Mission Ranch | **Carmel/S**	20
Mistral | **Redwood Shores/S**	22
MoMo's | **S Beach**	19
Monti's | **Santa Rosa/N**	22
Moody's Bistro | **Truckee/E**	23
Mo's | **multi.**	23
Mua Lounge | **Oakland/E**	21
Mustards | **Yountville/N**	25
Navio | **Half Moon Bay/S**	24
Nepenthe | **Big Sur/S**	18
Nick's Next Door | **Los Gatos/S**	26
955 Rest. | **Mendocino/N**	25
Nojo | **Hayes Valley**	25
Norman Rose | **Napa/N**	20
NEW Odalisque Cafe | **San Rafael/N**	-
Original Joe's | **N Beach**	21
Oswald | **Santa Cruz/S**	25
Outerlands | **Outer Sunset**	25
Pacific's Edge | **Carmel/S**	24
Pappo | **Alameda/E**	23
Parallel 37 | **Nob Hill**	24
Park Tav. | **N Beach**	24
Per Diem | **Downtown**	20
Pork Store | **multi.**	19
Postrio | **Downtown**	23
Presidio Social | **Presidio**	19
Press | **St. Helena/N**	26
Prospect | **SoMa**	24
Q Rest./Wine | **Inner Rich**	20
Radish | **Mission**	18
Range | **Mission**	27
Ravenous | **Healdsburg/N**	22
Restaurant | **Ft Bragg/N**	22
Rest./Stevenswood | **Little River/N**	24
Rick & Ann's | **Berkeley/E**	23
Rotunda | **Downtown**	21
Rudy's Can't Fail | **multi.**	19
NEW Rustic Tavern | **Lafayette/E**	-
Rutherford Grill | **Rutherford/N**	24
Saison | **SoMa**	27
Salt Hse. | **SoMa**	22
Sardine Factory | **Monterey/S**	24
Sauce | **multi.**	22
Saul's Rest./Deli | **Berkeley/E**	20
Serpentine | **Dogpatch**	23
Shadowbrook Rest. | **Capitola/S**	22
NEW Sir & Star | **Olema/N**	-
Skates on Bay | **Berkeley/E**	20
Slow Club | **Mission**	23
Sons/Daughters | **Nob Hill**	26
Soule Domain | **Kings Bch/E**	24
NEW South/SFJAZZ | **Hayes Valley**	-
Southie | **Oakland/E**	24
Spruce | **Presidio Hts**	26
Stark's Steak/Sea | **Santa Rosa/N**	25
State Bird | **W Addition**	26
Station Hse. | **Pt Reyes/N**	18
NEW Stella Nonna | **Berkeley/E**	-

Tarpy's | **Monterey/S**	24
Tav./Lark Creek | **Larkspur/N**	21
Terra | **St. Helena/N**	27
3rd St. Grill | **SoMa**	23
Thomas & Fagiani's | **Napa/N**	24
Toast | **multi.**	21
Town Hall | **SoMa**	23
Town's End | **Embarcadero**	21
Trace | **SoMa**	22
NEW Trident | **Sausalito/N**	22
25 Lusk | **SoMa**	22
NEW 20 Spot | **Mission**	-
231 Ellsworth | **San Mateo/S**	23
Universal Cafe | **Mission**	25
Village Pub | **Woodside/S**	25
Wayfare Tav. | **Downtown**	24
NEW The Willows | **SoMa**	-
NEW Wine Kitchen | **W Addition**	-
Woodward's Gdn. | **Mission**	24
Wurst Rest. | **Healdsburg/N**	21
Zazu | **Sebastopol/N**	26
Zin | **Healdsburg/N**	23

ARGENTINEAN

Lolinda | **Mission**	23

ASIAN

Asian Box | **multi.**	19
Bridges | **Danville/E**	23
B Star | **Inner Rich**	25
Butterfly | **Embarcadero**	23
Chinois | **Windsor/N**	25
Chubby Noodle | **N Beach**	24
Dragonfly | **Truckee/E**	23
E&O Asian Kit. | **Downtown**	21
Flying Fish (Carmel) | **Carmel/S**	24
Forchetta/Bastoni | **Sebastopol/N**	19
Hawker Fare | **Oakland/E**	23
House | **N Beach**	27
Imperial Tea | **Embarcadero**	18
O3 Bistro | **Civic Ctr**	24
Spice Kit | **multi.**	19
Unicorn | **Downtown**	23

AUSTRIAN

Leopold's | **Russian Hill**	23

BAKERIES

Alexis Baking | **Napa/N**	22
Arizmendi | **multi.**	25
Bakesale Betty | **Oakland/E**	26
Big Sur | **Big Sur/S**	24
Bi-Rite | **multi.**	27
NEW B. Patisserie | **Pacific Hts**	26
Charles Chocolate | **Mission**	-
Craftsman & Wolves | **Mission**	25
Della Fattoria | **Petaluma/N**	26
Downtown Bakery | **Healdsburg/N**	26
Dynamo Donut | **multi.**	25
Emporio Rulli | **multi.**	22
Gayle's Bakery | **Capitola/S**	24
Golden West | **Downtown**	21
Hayes Valley Bakeworks | **Hayes Valley**	21
La Boulange | **multi.**	21
Liberty Cafe | **Bernal Hts**	22
Mama's on Wash. | **N Beach**	24
Mayfield | **Palo Alto/S**	20
NEW Mill | **W Addition**	-
Model Bakery | **multi.**	23
Sandbox | **Bernal Hts**	25
Sentinel | **SoMa**	23
Tartine | **Mission**	27
Town's End | **Embarcadero**	21
NEW 20th Century | **Hayes Valley**	-

BARBECUE

Addendum | **Yountville/N**	25
Baby Blues BBQ | **Mission**	21
Bo's BBQ | **Lafayette/E**	22
B-Side BBQ | **Oakland/E**	23
Buckeye | **Mill Valley/N**	25
Catheads BBQ | **SoMa**	22
Everett/Jones BBQ | **multi.**	21
NEW Hi Lo BBQ | **Mission**	-
HRD Coffee/Smokin | **N Beach**	23
NEW Lucille's Smokehse. | **Concord/E**	-
Memphis Minnie's | **Lower Haight**	20
My Tofu | **Inner Rich**	23
Old Port Lobster | **multi.**	23
Q Rest. | **Napa/N**	22
Southpaw BBQ | **Mission**	20
Tex Wasabi's | **Santa Rosa/N**	19

CUISINES

T Rex | **Berkeley/E** 18

Wexler's | **Downtown** 23

BELGIAN

Frjtz Fries | **Mission** 20

Refuge | **multi.** 25

BRAZILIAN

Espetus | **multi.** 24

Pampas | **Palo Alto/S** 22

BRITISH

Betty's Fish | **Santa Rosa/N** 23

NEW Cavalier | **SoMa** –

NEW Tribune Tavern | **Oakland/E** –

BURGERS

Balboa Cafe | **multi.** 20

Barney's | **multi.** 21

Burger Bar | **Downtown** 20

Burger Joint | **multi.** 19

BurgerMeister | **multi.** 20

Counter Palo Alto | **Palo Alto/S** 22

400 Degrees | **Carmel/S** –

Healdsburg B&G | **Healdsburg/N** 19

In-N-Out | **multi.** 23

Joe's Cable Car | **Excelsior** 22

NEW Kronnerburger | **Mission** –

Mo's | **multi.** 23

900 Grayson | **Berkeley/E** 24

Pearl's Deluxe/Phat | **multi.** 23

NEW Pub Republic | **Petaluma/N** –

Roam | **multi.** 23

Super Duper | **multi.** 23

Trueburger | **Oakland/E** 21

Umami Burger | **multi.** 22

BURMESE

Burma Superstar | **multi.** 25

Burmese Kit. | **Tenderloin** 22

Mandalay | **Inner Rich** 25

Mingalaba | **Burlingame/S** 26

Nan Yang | **Oakland/E** 22

Rangoon Ruby | **multi.** 22

Yamo | **Mission** 22

CAJUN

Angeline's LA Kit. | **Berkeley/E** 24

NEW Big Sur Roadhse. | **Big Sur/S** –

Boxing Rm. | **Hayes Valley** 20

Cajun Pacific | **Outer Sunset** 23

NEW Easy Creole | **Berkeley/E** –

Elite Cafe | **Pacific Hts** 20

NEW Hard Water | **Embarcadero** –

NEW Parish Cafe | **Healdsburg/N** –

NEW Pear | **Napa/N** –

CALIFORNIAN

Abbot's Cellar | **Mission** 20

Actual Cafe | **Oakland/E** 22

Ahwahnee | **Yosemite/E** 21

Albion River Inn | **Albion/N** 24

All Seasons | **Calistoga/N** 23

All Spice | **San Mateo/S** 26

Amber Bistro | **Danville/E** 23

Anzu | **Downtown** 23

Applewood Rest. | **Guerneville/N** 24

AQ | **SoMa** 24

Artisan Bistro | **Lafayette/E** 25

Asena | **Alameda/E** 26

Auberge du Soleil | **Rutherford/N** 27

Aubergine | **Carmel/S** 26

NEW Backyard | **Forestville/N** –

NEW Bantam | **Santa Cruz/S** –

Bar Agricole | **SoMa** 22

BayWolf | **Oakland/E** 26

Beast/Hare | **Mission** 23

NEW Big Sur Roadhse. | **Big Sur/S** –

Bistro Aix | **Marina** 23

Bistro Boudin | **Fish. Wharf** 22

Bistro Ralph | **Healdsburg/N** 23

Blue Barn | **Corte Madera/N** 25

Blue Barn | **Marina** 25

Blue Bottle | **multi.** 24

Boon Eat/Drink | **Guerneville/N** 25

Boon Fly | **Napa/N** 23

Bouche | **Nob Hill** 24

Brasserie S&P | **Downtown** 24

Brick/Bottle | **Corte Madera/N** 19

Bridges | **Danville/E** 23

Brix | **Napa/N** 22

Bucci's | **Emeryville/E** 21

Butterfly | **Embarcadero** 23

Cafe Beaujolais | **Mendocino/N** 26

Café Brioche | **Palo Alto/S** 21

Cafe La Haye	**Sonoma/N**	26
Café Rouge	**Berkeley/E**	22
Café Rustica	**Carmel Valley/S**	23
Calafia	**Palo Alto/S**	20
Camino	**Oakland/E**	24
Campton Pl.	**Downtown**	26
Carneros Bistro	**Sonoma/N**	24
Central Kitchen	**Mission**	24
Central Mkt.	**Petaluma/N**	25
Chez Panisse	**Berkeley/E**	27
Chez Panisse Café	**Berkeley/E**	27
Chop Bar	**Oakland/E**	24
Christy Hill	**Tahoe City/E**	23
Cindy's Backstreet	**St. Helena/N**	24
Cliff Hse.	**Outer Rich**	20
Coco500	**SoMa**	24
Coi	**N Beach**	27
Cool Café	**multi.**	21
Deetjen's Big Sur	**Big Sur/S**	24
Dragonfly	**Truckee/E**	23
Dry Creek	**Healdsburg/N**	24
El Dorado	**Sonoma/N**	22
Erna's Elderberry	**Oakhurst/E**	28
Étoile	**Yountville/N**	26
Farmhse. Inn	**Forestville/N**	27
Farmstead	**St. Helena/N**	22
Fishwife	**multi.**	22
Five	**Berkeley/E**	20
Flavor	**Santa Rosa/N**	22
Flea St. Café	**Menlo Pk/S**	26
Fleur de Lys	**Downtown**	27
Flying Fish (Carmel)	**Carmel/S**	24
Foreign Cinema	**Mission**	24
Frances	**Castro**	27
Frascati	**Russian Hill**	25
Gabriella Café	**Santa Cruz/S**	20
Garden Ct.	**Downtown**	22
Garibaldis	**Presidio Hts**	24
Gar Woods	**Carnelian Bay/E**	19
Gather	**Berkeley/E**	23
Gioia Pizzeria	**Russian Hill**	25
Glen Ellen Inn	**Glen Ellen/N**	23
Globe	**Downtown**	18
Grasing's Coastal	**Carmel/S**	21
Half Moon Brew	**Half Moon Bay/S**	17
Harvest Moon	**Sonoma/N**	25
Haven	**Oakland/E**	25
Heirloom	**Mission**	25
NEW Heyday	**SoMa**	-
Hot Box Grill	**Sonoma/N**	25
Hurley's Rest.	**Yountville/N**	23
Jackson's	**Santa Rosa/N**	22
Jardinière	**Civic Ctr**	26
John Ash	**Santa Rosa/N**	25
Johnny Garlic's	**multi.**	19
Kenwood	**Kenwood/N**	25
Lake Chalet	**Oakland/E**	17
Lalime's	**Berkeley/E**	26
La Sen Bistro	**Berkeley/E**	23
Ledford Hse.	**Albion/N**	26
Lincoln Park Wine	**San Anselmo/N**	-
Little River Inn	**Little River/N**	24
Local Mission	**Mission**	27
Luella	**Russian Hill**	23
Luka's Taproom	**Oakland/E**	20
MacCallum/Grey Whale	**Mendocino/N**	24
Manzanita	**Truckee/E**	22
Marinus	**Carmel Valley/S**	26
Marlowe	**SoMa**	24
Mayfield	**Palo Alto/S**	20
Meadowood Grill	**St. Helena/N**	22
Meadowood Rest.	**St. Helena/N**	27
Meritage/Claremont	**Berkeley/E**	23
Mezze	**Oakland/E**	22
Mission Bch. Café	**Mission**	24
NEW MKT	**SoMa**	-
Montrio Bistro	**Monterey/S**	23
Murray Circle	**Sausalito/N**	23
Mustards	**Yountville/N**	25
Napa Wine Train	**Napa/N**	20
Nick's Cove	**Marshall/N**	21
900 Grayson	**Berkeley/E**	24
Nopa	**W Addition**	26
NEW Odalisque Cafe	**San Rafael/N**	-
One Market	**Embarcadero**	24
Oola	**SoMa**	21
Osake	**Santa Rosa/N**	25
Oxbow Wine	**Napa/N**	21
NEW Palace	**Mission**	-
Parcel 104	**Santa Clara/S**	23
Park Chalet	**Outer Sunset**	16

Passionfish | **Pacific Grove/S**	27
NEW Pear | **Napa/N**	-
Pearl | **Napa/N**	22
Peasant/Pear | **Danville/E**	23
Piccino | **Dogpatch**	24
Picco | **Larkspur/N**	26
Pizzando | **Healdsburg/N**	-
Pläj | **Hayes Valley**	24
Plow | **Potrero Hill**	26
Plum | **Oakland/E**	23
Plumed Horse | **Saratoga/S**	25
PlumpJack | **Olympic Valley/E**	22
Quince | **Downtown**	26
Radius Rest. | **SoMa**	23
Redd | **Yountville/N**	27
Rest./Ventana | **Big Sur/S**	23
Rest. James | **Los Gatos/S**	25
Revival Bar | **Berkeley/E**	22
Richmond | **Inner Rich**	25
Rich Table | **Hayes Valley**	25
Rio Grill | **Carmel/S**	23
Rivoli | **Berkeley/E**	27
Santé | **Sonoma/N**	-
NEW Seaglass Rest. | **Embarcadero**	-
Sent Sovi | **Saratoga/S**	26
71 St. Peter | **San Jose/S**	22
Sidebar | **Oakland/E**	22
Sierra Mar | **Big Sur/S**	28
Soif Wine Bar | **Santa Cruz/S**	24
Solbar | **Calistoga/N**	26
Spoonbar | **Healdsburg/N**	20
Starbelly | **Castro**	22
Station 1 | **Woodside/S**	25
Stinking Rose | **N Beach**	20
St. Michael's | **Palo Alto/S**	22
St. Orres | **Gualala/N**	23
Straw | **Hayes Valley**	20
St. Vincent Tavern | **Mission**	21
Sutro's | **Outer Rich**	21
Terrapin Creek | **Bodega Bay/N**	27
Townhouse B&G | **Emeryville/E**	22
Venus | **Berkeley/E**	24
Viognier | **San Mateo/S**	24
Waterfront | **Embarcadero**	21
Wente Vineyards | **Livermore/E**	25
Wine Spectator | **St. Helena/N**	23

Wolfdale's | **Tahoe City/E**	27
Wood Tav. | **Oakland/E**	26
Woodward's Gdn. | **Mission**	24
Zaré/Fly Trap | **SoMa**	21

CAMBODIAN

Angkor Borei | **Bernal Hts**	23

CARIBBEAN

Cha Cha Cha | **multi.**	22
Fishwife | **multi.**	22
Front Porch | **Bernal Hts**	22
NEW Miss Ollie's | **Oakland/E**	-

CHEESE SPECIALISTS

Cheese Board | **Berkeley/E**	26
Mission Cheese | **Mission**	22

CHEESESTEAKS

Cheese Steak | **multi.**	22

CHICKEN

Bund Shanghai | **Chinatown**	24
Goood Frikin' | **Mission**	20
Home of Chicken | **multi.**	19

CHINESE

(* dim sum specialist)

Alice's | **Noe Valley**	20
Asian Pearl | **Millbrae/S**	22
Betelnut | **Cow Hollow**	24
Brandy Ho's | **multi.**	20
Bund Shanghai | **Chinatown**	24
Chef Chu's | **Los Altos/S**	22
Crouching Tiger | **Redwood City/S**	22
East Ocean Seafood* | **Alameda/E**	23
Eliza's | **Pacific Hts**	22
Eric's | **Noe Valley**	22
Fang | **SoMa**	22
Gary Chu's | **Santa Rosa/N**	24
Good Luck* | **Inner Rich**	21
Great Eastern* | **Chinatown**	23
NEW Hakkasan | **Downtown**	24
Henry's Hunan | **multi.**	22
Hong Kong East | **Emeryville/E**	22
Hong Kong Flower/Mayflower* | **multi.**	21
Hong Kong Lounge* | **multi.**	24
House/Nanking | **Chinatown**	22

Hunan Home's/Gdn.	multi.	21
Imperial Tea	Berkeley/E	18
Jai Yun	Chinatown	23
Joy Luck Palace	Cupertino/S	21
Just Wonton	Outer Sunset	20
Kingdom/Dumpling	Parkside	22
Kitchen*	Millbrae/S	23
Koi*	multi.	23
Liou's Hse.	Milpitas/S	24
Mingalaba	Burlingame/S	26
Mission Chinese	Mission	22
NEW M.Y. China	Downtown	19
O'mei	Santa Cruz/S	24
Oriental Pearl*	Chinatown	23
R & G Lounge	Chinatown	24
Rest. Peony*	Oakland/E	20
San Tung	Inner Sunset	24
Shen Hua	Berkeley/E	22
Sino*	San Jose/S	19
Tai Pan*	Palo Alto/S	23
Ton Kiang*	Outer Rich	25
Yank Sing*	SoMa	26
Yuet Lee	Chinatown	20
Z & Y	Chinatown	25

COFFEEHOUSES

Blue Bottle	multi.	24
Dynamo Donut	multi.	25
Emporio Rulli	multi.	22
Java Beach	Outer Sunset	20
Machine Coffee	Downtown	-
NEW Mill	W Addition	-

CONTINENTAL

Anton/Michel	Carmel/S	24
Bella Vista	Woodside/S	24
La Forêt	San Jose/S	27

CREOLE

Angeline's LA Kit.	Berkeley/E	24
Boxing Rm.	Hayes Valley	20
Brenda's	Civic Ctr	25
Cajun Pacific	Outer Sunset	23
NEW Easy Creole	Berkeley/E	-
NEW Hard Water	Embarcadero	-
NEW Parish Cafe	Healdsburg/N	-

CUBAN

| Cha Cha Cha | San Mateo/S | 22 |
| La Bodeguita/Medio | Palo Alto/S | 22 |

DELIS

AK Subs	SoMa	22
Bi-Rite	W Addition	27
Boccalone	Embarcadero	25
Deli Board/1058	SoMa	23
4505 Meats	multi.	26
NEW Grand Lake Kitchen	Oakland/E	-
Jimtown Store	Healdsburg/N	21
Lucca Deli	Marina	26
Machine Coffee	Downtown	-
Market & Rye	multi.	19
Miller's East	multi.	20
Salumeria Deli	Mission	-
Wise Sons	multi.	23

DESSERT

Bi-Rite	Mission	27
NEW B. Patisserie	Pacific Hts	26
Cafe Jacqueline	N Beach	27
Charles Chocolate	Mission	-
Cheesecake Fac.	multi.	16
Chile Pies	multi.	22
NEW Chocolate Lab	Dogpatch	25
Craftsman & Wolves	Mission	25
NEW Dandelion Chocolate	Mission	-
Downtown Bakery	Healdsburg/N	26
Emporio Rulli	multi.	22
Gayle's Bakery	Capitola/S	24
Glen Ellen Star	Glen Ellen/N	27
Sandbox	Bernal Hts	25
NEW Schulzies	Hayes Valley	-
Tartine	Mission	27
Tout Sweet	Downtown	-

DINER

Bette's Oceanview	Berkeley/E	24
Dipsea Cafe	Mill Valley/N	18
Fremont Diner	Sonoma/N	24
Gott's Roadside	multi.	22
HRD Coffee/Smokin	SoMa	23
Jimmy Beans	Berkeley/E	20
Pine Cone Diner	Pt Reyes/N	20

CUISINES

Rudy's Can't Fail | **multi.** 19
Saul's Rest./Deli | **Berkeley/E** 20
Sears | **Downtown** 20
St. Francis | **Mission** 19

ECLECTIC

Alembic | **Haight-Ashbury** 23
Andalu | **Mission** 21
NEW Bergerac | **SoMa** -
Celadon | **Napa/N** 25
Chez Shea | **Half Moon Bay/S** 21
Cin-Cin Wine | **Los Gatos/S** 24
NEW Cindy's Waterfront | **Monterey/S** -
Cottonwood | **Truckee/E** 20
Della Fattoria | **Petaluma/N** 26
NEW Empire | **Napa/N** -
Firefly | **Noe Valley** 24
Flavor | **Santa Rosa/N** 22
Graffiti | **Petaluma/N** 25
Kitchen Door | **Napa/N** 22
La Fondue | **Saratoga/S** 22
Mendo Café | **Mendocino/N** 20
NEW Mikkeller Bar | **Tenderloin** -
Pomelo | **multi.** 24
Radish | **Mission** 18
Restaurant | **Ft Bragg/N** 22
NEW Roxy's Cafe | **Mission** -
Samovar Tea | **multi.** 20
Sierra Mar | **Big Sur/S** 28
SoMa StrEAT | **SoMa** 23
Surf Spot | **Pacifica/S** -
NEW Trick Dog | **Mission** -
Va de Vi | **Walnut Creek/E** 25
Willi's Wine | **Santa Rosa/N** 25
Willow Wood | **Graton/N** 24

ETHIOPIAN

Addis Ethiopian | **Oakland/E** 25
Asmara | **Oakland/E** 26

EUROPEAN

Bar Tartine | **Mission** 24
Bistro Moulin | **Monterey/S** 26
Café Rustica | **Carmel Valley/S** 23
Tout Sweet | **Downtown** -

FILIPINO

Attic | **San Mateo/S** 20

FONDUE

La Fondue | **Saratoga/S** 22

FRENCH

À Côté | **Oakland/E** 24
Angèle | **Napa/N** 24
NEW Aquitaine | **Downtown** -
Atelier Crenn | **Marina** 27
Auberge du Soleil | **Rutherford/N** 27
Bank Café | **Napa/N** 23
Basque Cultural | **S San Francisco/S** 20
Baumé | **Palo Alto/S** 26
Bistro Aix | **Marina** 23
Bistro 29 | **Santa Rosa/N** 25
Bix | **Downtown** 24
Bouche | **Nob Hill** 24
Brix | **Napa/N** 22
Cafe Beaujolais | **Mendocino/N** 26
Café Claude | **Downtown** 22
Café des Amis | **Cow Hollow** 18
Cafe Jacqueline | **N Beach** 27
Casanova | **Carmel/S** 24
Chantilly | **Redwood City/S** 25
Chaya | **Embarcadero** 23
Chevalier | **Lafayette/E** 25
Chez TJ | **Mtn View/S** 23
Christy Hill | **Tahoe City/E** 23
Coi | **N Beach** 27
Erna's Elderberry | **Oakhurst/E** 28
NEW Fast Food Français | **Sausalito/N** -
Fifth Floor | **SoMa** 24
Fig Cafe/Wine | **Glen Ellen/N** 26
Fleur de Lys | **Downtown** 27
French Laundry | **Yountville/N** 28
Garçon | **Mission** 22
Gitane | **Downtown** 23
Grand Cafe | **Downtown** 20
Grégoire | **multi.** 24
Isa | **Marina** 24
Jardinière | **Civic Ctr** 26
Keiko | **Nob Hill** 27
Kenwood | **Kenwood/N** 25
La Bicyclette | **Carmel/S** 23
La Boulange | **multi.** 21
La Folie | **Russian Hill** 27

La Forêt	**San Jose/S**	27
La Gare	**Santa Rosa/N**	26
La Note	**Berkeley/E**	23
La Sen Bistro	**Berkeley/E**	23
La Toque	**Napa/N**	27
Le Colonial	**Downtown**	22
Le Papillon	**San Jose/S**	27
Luka's Taproom	**Oakland/E**	20
Luna Park	**Mission**	20
Madrona Manor	**Healdsburg/N**	27
Manzanita	**Truckee/E**	22
Marché/Fleurs	**Ross/N**	25
Marinus	**Carmel Valley/S**	26
955 Rest.	**Mendocino/N**	25
Pacific's Edge	**Carmel/S**	24
Quince	**Downtown**	26
Rest. LuLu	**SoMa**	21
RN74	**SoMa**	22
Santé	**Sonoma/N**	-
NEW Sir & Star	**Olema/N**	-
NEW 1601 Bar/Kitchen	**SoMa**	-
Sonoma-Meritage	**Sonoma/N**	19
South Park	**SoMa**	22
Vanessa's Bistro	**multi.**	23
Viognier	**San Mateo/S**	24

FRENCH (BISTRO)

Alamo Sq.	**W Addition**	22
Andre's Bouchée	**Carmel/S**	24
Artisan Bistro	**Lafayette/E**	25
Baker St. Bistro	**Marina**	21
Bistro Central	**W Addition**	25
Bistro/Copains	**Occidental/N**	27
Bistro Jeanty	**Yountville/N**	27
Bistro Liaison	**Berkeley/E**	23
Bistro Ralph	**Healdsburg/N**	23
Bodega Bistro	**Tenderloin**	24
Bouchon	**Yountville/N**	26
Butler/Chef	**SoMa**	22
Cafe Bastille	**Downtown**	19
Café Brioche	**Palo Alto/S**	21
Chapeau!	**Inner Rich**	27
Charcuterie	**Healdsburg/N**	20
Chez Maman	**multi.**	24
Chez Papa Bistrot	**Potrero Hill**	24
Chouchou	**Forest Hills**	19
French Gdn.	**Sebastopol/N**	22

Fringale	**SoMa**	25
Gamine	**Cow Hollow**	24
Girl/Fig	**Sonoma/N**	24
K&L Bistro	**Sebastopol/N**	25
L'Ardoise	**Castro**	24
Le Central	**Downtown**	21
Le Charm Bistro	**SoMa**	22
Le Garage	**Sausalito/N**	23
Le P'tit Laurent	**Glen Pk**	25
Plouf	**Downtown**	22
Water St. Bistro	**Petaluma/N**	23
Zazie	**Cole Valley**	24

FRENCH (BRASSERIE)

Absinthe	**Hayes Valley**	23
Florio	**Pacific Hts**	21
Left Bank	**multi.**	20

GASTROPUB

Alembic	Eclectic	**Haight-Ashbury**	23
Bar Agricole	Cal.	**SoMa**	22
NEW Cavalier	British	**SoMa**	-
Corners Tav.	Amer.	**Walnut Creek/E**	23
Goose & Gander	Amer.	**St. Helena/N**	22
Magnolia	Southern	**Haight-Ashbury**	22
NEW Mikkeller Bar	Eclectic	**Tenderloin**	-
Norman Rose	Amer.	**Napa/N**	20
Public Hse.	Pub	**S Beach**	17
Salt Hse.	Amer.	**SoMa**	22
Sidebar	Cal.	**Oakland/E**	22
NEW Tribune Tavern	British	**Oakland/E**	-

GERMAN

Biergarten	**Hayes Valley**	21
Guamenkitzel	**Berkeley/E**	21
Rosamunde	**multi.**	22
Schmidt's	**Mission**	22
Suppenküche	**Hayes Valley**	23
Walzwerk	**Mission**	21

GREEK

Dio Deka	**Los Gatos/S**	25
Dipsea Cafe	**Mill Valley/N**	18
Evvia	**Palo Alto/S**	28

CUISINES

Farina Pizza | S | **Mission**	20	Pasta Moon | **Half Moon Bay**/S	25
54 Mint | **SoMa**	22	Pasta Pomodoro | **multi.**	18
Florio | **Pacific Hts**	21	Perbacco | **Downtown**	26
Flour + Water | **Mission**	26	Pesce | N | **Castro**	25
Forchetta/Bastoni | **Sebastopol**/N	19	Peter Lowell | **Sebastopol**/N	22
Frantoio | N | **Mill Valley**/N	22	Piatti | **multi.**	21
Gabriella Café | **Santa Cruz**/S	20	Piazza D'Angelo |	20
Gialina | **Glen Pk**	25	**Mill Valley**/N	
Globe | **Downtown**	18	Piccino | **Dogpatch**	24
Ideale Rest. | S | **N Beach**	25	Picco | **Larkspur**/N	26
Il Cane Rosso | **Embarcadero**	23	Pizza Antica | **multi.**	22
Il Davide | **San Rafael**/N	23	Pizzaiolo | S | **Oakland**/E	26
Il Fornaio | **multi.**	18	Pizzeria Picco | S | **Larkspur**/N	26
Il Postale | **Sunnyvale**/S	23	Pizzeria Tra Vigne | **St. Helena**/N	22
Incanto | N | **Noe Valley**	25	Poesia | S | **Castro**	23
Italian Colors | **Oakland**/E	22	Poggio | N | **Sausalito**/N	25
Jackson Fillmore | **Upper Fillmore**	21	Postino | **Lafayette**/E	24
Kuleto's | N | **Downtown**	23	Prima | N | **Walnut Creek**/E	26
NEW La Balena Cucina |	–	Quattro | **E Palo Alto**/S	22
Carmel/S		Quince | **Downtown**	26
La Bicyclette | **Carmel**/S	23	Redd Wood | **Yountville**/N	25
La Ciccia | **Noe Valley**	27	Risibisi | N | **Petaluma**/N	24
La Posta | **Santa Cruz**/S	25	Ristobar | **Marina**	20
Leopold's | **Russian Hill**	23	Rist. Milano | N | **Russian Hill**	24
Locanda | **Mission**	24	Rist. Umbria | N | **SoMa**	21
Lococo's Cucina | **Santa Rosa**/N	25	Riva Cucina | N | **Berkeley**/E	26
Lo Coco's | S | **multi.**	22	Rocco's Cafe | **SoMa**	24
L'Osteria | N | **N Beach**	24	Rose Pistola | **N Beach**	21
NEW Lungomare | **Oakland**/E	–	Rose's Cafe | N | **Cow Hollow**	22
Lupa Trattoria | S | **Noe Valley**	23	Rosso Pizzeria | **multi.**	25
Mario's Bohemian | **N Beach**	19	Rustic | **Geyserville**/N	21
Marzano | **Oakland**/E	23	Scala's Bistro | **Downtown**	23
Mescolanza | N | **Outer Rich**	23	Scopa | **Healdsburg**/N	26
Mezza Luna | S | **multi.**	23	Seven Hills | **Nob Hill**	27
Mozzeria | **Mission**	21	Sociale | N | **Presidio Hts**	24
Nob Hill Café | **Nob Hill**	22	Sonoma-Meritage | N | **Sonoma**/N	19
North Bch. Rest. | N | **N Beach**	24	Sotto Mare | **N Beach**	26
Oenotri | S | **Napa**/N	24	SPQR | **Pacific Hts**	25
Oliveto Cafe | **Oakland**/E	23	Stella Alpina Osteria |	25
Oliveto Rest. | **Oakland**/E	25	**Burlingame**/S	
Original Joe's | **San Jose**/S	22	Stinking Rose | **N Beach**	20
Original Joe's | **N Beach**	21	Sugo | **Petaluma**/N	24
Osteria | **Palo Alto**/S	23	Tommaso's | S | **N Beach**	24
Osteria Coppa | N | **San Mateo**/S	22	Tony's Coal-Fired | **N Beach**	24
Osteria Stellina | **Pt Reyes**/N	24	Tony's Pizza | S | **N Beach**	26
Palio d'Asti | **Downtown**	21	Tratt. Contadina | **N Beach**	24
Pane e Vino | **Cow Hollow**	23	Trattoria Corso | N | **Berkeley**/E	25

CUISINES

NEW Trattoria/Vittorio | S | **W Portal**	—
Tratt. La Sicil. | S | **Berkeley/E**	24
Tra Vigne | N | **St. Helena/N**	24
Uva Enoteca | **Lower Haight**	22
Uva Trattoria | **Napa/N**	19
Venticello | N | **Nob Hill**	23
Volpi's Rist. | **Petaluma/N**	22
Zazu | N | **Sebastopol/N**	26
Zero Zero | **SoMa**	24

JAPANESE

(* sushi specialist)

Ace Wasabi's* | **Marina**	20
Alexander's Steak | **multi.**	26
Anzu* | **Downtown**	23
Ariake* | **Outer Rich**	25
Blowfish Sushi* | **multi.**	23
Chaya | **Embarcadero**	23
Cha-Ya Veg.* | **multi.**	22
Chotto | **Marina**	24
Delica* | **Embarcadero**	25
Domo Sushi* | **Hayes Valley**	27
Ebisu* | **multi.**	24
Eiji* | **Castro**	25
Fuki Sushi* | **Palo Alto/S**	23
Gochi | **Cupertino/S**	25
Hachi Ju Hachi* | **Saratoga/S**	27
Hamano Sushi* | **Noe Valley**	21
Hana* | **Rohnert Pk/N**	26
Hopscotch | **Oakland/E**	24
Hotaru* | **San Mateo/S**	21
Hotei* | **Inner Sunset**	19
Ichi Sushi | **Bernal Hts**	27
Ippuku | **Berkeley/E**	24
Izakaya Sozai | **Inner Sunset**	23
Izakaya Yuzuki | **Mission**	24
Jin Sho* | **Palo Alto/S**	24
Joshu-ya Brass.* | **Berkeley/E**	25
Kabuto* | **Outer Rich**	26
Kappou Gomi | **Outer Rich**	28
Katana-Ya | **Downtown**	22
NEW Katsu | **Los Gatos/S**	—
Keiko | **Nob Hill**	27
Ken Ken | **Mission**	21
Kiji Sushi Bar* | **Mission**	25
Kirala* | **Berkeley/E**	25
Kiss Seafood* | **Japantown**	28

Koo* | **Inner Sunset**	26
Men Oh Tokushima | **multi.**	—
Mifune | **Japantown**	18
Moki's Sushi* | **Bernal Hts**	25
Morimoto* | **Napa/N**	25
Moshi Moshi | **Dogpatch**	23
Muracci's | **multi.**	20
Nama Sushi | **Walnut Creek/E**	27
Nihon* | **Mission**	21
903 | **Bernal Hts**	24
Nojo | **Hayes Valley**	25
Nombe | **Mission**	21
Orenchi Ramen | **Santa Clara/S**	25
Osake* | **Santa Rosa/N**	25
Oyaji* | **Outer Rich**	23
Ozumo* | **multi.**	25
Ramen Dojo | **San Mateo/S**	25
NEW Ramen Shop | **Oakland/E**	24
Ramen Underground | **Downtown**	19
Rest. Mitsunobu | **Menlo Pk/S**	24
NEW Roka Akor | **Downtown**	—
NEW Roku | **Hayes Valley**	—
Ryoko's* | **Downtown**	25
Sakae Sushi* | **Burlingame/S**	25
Sanraku* | **multi.**	23
Saru Sushi | **Noe Valley**	28
Sasa | **Walnut Creek/E**	25
Sawa Sushi | **Sunnyvale/S**	23
Sebo* | **Hayes Valley**	27
NEW Sugoi Sushi* | **Mission**	—
Sumika | **Los Altos/S**	25
Sushi Bistro | **multi.**	23
Sushi Ran* | **Sausalito/N**	27
Sushirrito* | **multi.**	20
Sushi Sam's | **San Mateo/S**	24
Sushi Zone* | **Castro**	27
Tataki* | **multi.**	24
Tex Wasabi's | **Santa Rosa/N**	19
NEW Tomo's Japanese | **Berkeley/E**	—
Tsunami Sushi* | **multi.**	22
2G Japanese | **Civic Ctr**	22
Umami* | **Cow Hollow**	25
Uzen* | **Oakland/E**	24
Wakuriya | **San Mateo/S**	28
Yoshi's* | **multi.**	22
Zushi Puzzle* | **Marina**	27

JEWISH

Miller's East	**multi.**	20
NEW Shorty Goldstein's | **Downtown**	-
Wise Sons	**multi.**	23

KOREAN

(* barbecue specialist)

Brother's Korean* | **Inner Rich**	22
FuseBox | **Oakland/E**	26
Han IL Kwan | **Outer Rich**	24
HRD Coffee/Smokin* | **multi.**	23
Jang Su Jang* | **multi.**	23
My Tofu | **Inner Rich**	23
Namu Gaji | **multi.**	24
Ohgane Korean | **multi.**	22
San Tung | **Inner Sunset**	24
To Hyang | **Inner Rich**	25

MEDITERRANEAN

Absinthe | **Hayes Valley**	23
À Côté | **Oakland/E**	24
Arlequin Cafe | **Hayes Valley**	20
Asena | **Alameda/E**	26
BayWolf | **Oakland/E**	26
Cafe Gibraltar | **El Granada/S**	28
Café Rouge | **Berkeley/E**	22
Camino | **Oakland/E**	24
Campton Pl. | **Downtown**	26
Central Mkt. | **Petaluma/N**	25
Cetrella | **Half Moon Bay/S**	23
Chez Panisse | **Berkeley/E**	27
Chez Panisse Café | **Berkeley/E**	27
Coco500 | **SoMa**	24
El Dorado | **Sonoma/N**	22
Esin | **Danville/E**	26
Fandango | **Pacific Grove/S**	21
Foreign Cinema | **Mission**	24
Frascati | **Russian Hill**	25
Garibaldis | **Presidio Hts**	24
Harvest Moon | **Sonoma/N**	25
Heirloom | **Mission**	25
Hurley's Rest. | **Yountville/N**	23
Insalata's | **San Anselmo/N**	25
Lalime's | **Berkeley/E**	26
La Méditerranée | **multi.**	22
Ledford Hse. | **Albion/N**	26
Luella | **Russian Hill**	23
Mezze | **Oakland/E**	22

Mistral | **Redwood Shores/S**	22
Monti's | **Santa Rosa/N**	22
Oxbow Wine | **Napa/N**	21
Peasant/Pear | **Danville/E**	23
Rest. LuLu | **SoMa**	21
Rivoli | **Berkeley/E**	27
Sens | **Embarcadero**	20
71 St. Peter | **San Jose/S**	22
Sidebar | **Oakland/E**	22
NEW Taverna Sofia | **Healdsburg/N**	-
Terzo | **Cow Hollow**	25
Truly Med. | **Mission**	26
Underwood Bar | **Graton/N**	22
Wente Vineyards | **Livermore/E**	25
Willow Wood | **Graton/N**	24
Zaré/Fly Trap | **SoMa**	21
Zatar | **Berkeley/E**	24
Zibibbo | **Palo Alto/S**	20
Zuni Café | **Hayes Valley**	26

MEXICAN

Cactus Taqueria | **multi.**	21
Cancun | **Berkeley/E**	22
C Casa | **Napa/N**	25
Chilango | **Castro**	22
Colibrí | **Downtown**	23
Comal | **Berkeley/E**	23
Copita | **Sausalito/N**	24
Doña Tomás | **Oakland/E**	22
Don Pisto's | **N Beach**	25
El Farolito | **multi.**	23
NEW El Gusano | **Oakland/E**	-
El Huarache Loco | **multi.**	21
El Metate | **Mission**	23
Gracias | **Mission**	24
Joe's Taco | **Mill Valley/N**	21
Juan's | **Berkeley/E**	19
La Condesa | **St. Helena/N**	25
La Corneta | **multi.**	22
La Cumbre | **multi.**	20
La Taqueria | **Mission**	25
La Taquiza | **Napa/N**	27
La Victoria | **multi.**	24
Little Chihuahua | **multi.**	21
Loló | **Mission**	25
Mamacita | **Marina**	24
Marinitas | **San Anselmo/N**	21

CUISINES

Mateo's Cocina | **Healdsburg/N**	22
Mijita | **multi.**	20
Nick's Crispy | **Russian Hill**	21
NEW Nido | **Oakland/E**	-
Nopalito | **multi.**	24
NEW Padrecito | **Cole Valley**	-
Pancho Villa | **multi.**	23
Papalote Mex. | **multi.**	22
Papito | **Potrero Hill**	26
Picante Cocina | **Berkeley/E**	22
Regalito Rosticeria | **Mission**	23
NEW Rosa Mexicano | **Embarcadero**	24
Tacko | **Cow Hollow**	22
Tacolicious | **multi.**	24
Taco Shop/Underdogs | **Outer Sunset**	24
Tacubaya | **Berkeley/E**	22
Tamarindo | **Oakland/E**	25
Taqueria Can Cun | **multi.**	23
Taqueria San Jose | **multi.**	23
Taqueria Tlaquepaque | **San Jose/S**	21
3rd St. Grill | **SoMa**	23
Tommy's Mex. | **Outer Rich**	20
Tropisueño | **SoMa**	20
Xolo | **Oakland/E**	23

MIDDLE EASTERN

Dishdash | **Sunnyvale/S**	24
Goood Frikin' | **Mission**	20
La Méditerranée | **multi.**	22
Saha | **Nob Hill**	24
Truly Med. | **Mission**	26

MONGOLIAN

Little Sheep | **multi.**	22

MOROCCAN

Aziza | **Outer Rich**	26

NEPALESE

Little Nepal | **Bernal Hts**	23

NEW ENGLAND

Yankee Pier | **multi.**	19

NOODLE SHOPS

Hotei | **Inner Sunset**	19
King of Thai | **multi.**	21

Men Oh Tokushima | **multi.**	-
Osha Thai | **multi.**	22
Ramen Dojo | **San Mateo/S**	25
NEW Ramen Shop | **Oakland/E**	24
Ramen Underground | **Downtown**	19
San Tung | **Inner Sunset**	24

NUEVO LATINO

Destino | **Castro**	22
Pasión | **Inner Sunset**	25

PACIFIC RIM

Pacific Catch | **multi.**	22

PAKISTANI

Chutney | **Tenderloin**	25
Pakwan | **multi.**	23
Shalimar | **multi.**	23

PAN-LATIN

Bocanova | **Oakland/E**	23
Cascal | **Mtn View/S**	22
César | **Oakland/E**	22
Fonda Solana | **Albany/E**	22
Marinitas | **San Anselmo/N**	21
Rumbo | **Oakland/E**	19

PERSIAN

Maykadeh | **N Beach**	23
Zaré/Fly Trap | **SoMa**	21

PERUVIAN

Fresca | **multi.**	22
La Costanera | **Montara/S**	25
La Mar | **Embarcadero**	24
Limón | **multi.**	24
Mochica | **SoMa**	24
Pasión | **Inner Sunset**	25
Piqueo's | **Bernal Hts**	26
NEW Puerto 27 | **Pacifica/S**	-
Sazon Peruvian | **Santa Rosa/N**	25

PIZZA

Amici's | **multi.**	21
Applewood Pizza | **Menlo Pk/S**	23
Arinell Pizza | **multi.**	23
Arizmendi | **multi.**	25
Azzurro | **Napa/N**	23
NEW Bantam | **Santa Cruz/S**	-

Bar Bocce	**Sausalito/N**	22
Beretta	**Mission**	24
Boot/Shoe	**Oakland/E**	24
Cafe Zoetrope	**N Beach**	21
Campo Fina	**Healdsburg/N**	-
NEW Capo's	**N Beach**	-
Cheese Board	**Berkeley/E**	26
Cupola Pizzeria	**Downtown**	21
NEW Dante's Table	**Castro**	-
Delarosa	**Marina**	21
Diavola	**Geyserville/N**	26
Emilia's	**Berkeley/E**	27
Farina Foccaccia	**Mission**	22
Farina Pizza	**Mission**	20
Flour + Water	**Mission**	26
NEW Forge	**Oakland/E**	-
Gialina	**Glen Pk**	25
Gioia Pizzeria	**multi.**	25
Giorgio's	**multi.**	21
Goat Hill	**multi.**	22
Golden Boy	**N Beach**	24
Little Star	**multi.**	25
Lo Coco's	**multi.**	22
Marzano	**Oakland/E**	23
Mozzeria	**Mission**	21
North Bch. Pizza	**multi.**	20
Palio d'Asti	**Downtown**	21
Patxi's Pizza	**multi.**	22
Pauline's Pizza/Wine	**Mission**	22
Pazzia	**SoMa**	25
Pi Bar	**Mission**	21
Pizza Antica	**multi.**	22
Pizzaiolo	**Oakland/E**	26
NEW Pizzalina	**San Anselmo/N**	-
Pizzando	**Healdsburg/N**	-
Pizzeria Delfina	**multi.**	25
Pizzeria Picco	**Larkspur/N**	26
Pizzeria Tra Vigne	**St. Helena/N**	22
Pizzetta 211	**Outer Rich**	26
Postrio	**Downtown**	23
Ragazza	**W Addition**	25
Redd Wood	**Yountville/N**	25
Rosso Pizzeria	**multi.**	25
Rustic	**Geyserville/N**	21
Source	**Potrero Hill**	24
Starbelly	**Castro**	22

Tommaso's	**N Beach**	24
Tony's Coal-Fired	**N Beach**	24
Tony's Pizza	**N Beach**	26
Una Pizza	**SoMa**	26
Zachary's Pizza	**multi.**	25
Zero Zero	**SoMa**	24

POLYNESIAN

Trader Vic's	**Emeryville/E**	18

PORTUGUESE

NEW Café Lucia	**Healdsburg/N**	-
Iberia	**Menlo Pk/S**	22
LaSalette	**Sonoma/N**	24

PUB FOOD

NEW Bergerac	**SoMa**	-
Biergarten	**Hayes Valley**	21
Half Moon Brew	**Half Moon Bay/S**	17
Public Hse.	**S Beach**	17
NEW Pub Republic	**Petaluma/N**	-
NEW Rickybobby	**Downtown**	-
Wurst Rest.	**Healdsburg/N**	21

PUERTO RICAN

Parada 22	**Haight-Ashbury**	23
Sol Food	**multi.**	24

RUSSIAN

Katia's Tea	**Inner Rich**	20

SALVADORAN

Balompie Café	**multi.**	23

SANDWICHES

(See also Delis)

AK Subs	**SoMa**	22
Amer. Grilled	**multi.**	22
Bakesale Betty	**Oakland/E**	26
Bocadillos	**N Beach**	23
Boccalone	**Embarcadero**	25
Boudin Sourdough	**multi.**	21
Café Bunn	**Inner Rich**	23
Cheese Steak	**multi.**	22
Craftsman & Wolves	**Mission**	25
Fatted Calf	**multi.**	26
4505 Meats	**multi.**	26
Gayle's Bakery	**Capitola/S**	24
Giordano	**multi.**	22

Giorgio's | **multi.**	21
Golden West | **Downtown**	21
NEW Heyday | **SoMa**	-
Ike's Pl./Lair | **multi.**	25
Java Beach | **Outer Sunset**	20
Jimtown Store | **Healdsburg/N**	21
Lucca Deli | **Marina**	26
Machine Coffee | **Downtown**	-
Mario's Bohemian | **N Beach**	19
Market & Rye | **multi.**	19
NEW Marrow | **Oakland/E**	-
Melt | **multi.**	17
NEW Mission Picnic | **Mission**	-
Model Bakery | **multi.**	23
Naked Lunch | **N Beach**	24
903 | **Bernal Hts**	24
Refuge | **multi.**	25
Saigon Sandwiches | **Tenderloin**	25
Salumeria Deli | **Mission**	-
Sentinel | **SoMa**	23
Southie | **Oakland/E**	24
Spice Kit | **multi.**	19
Straw | **Hayes Valley**	20
Sweet Woodruff | **Nob Hill**	24
Deli Board/1058 | **SoMa**	23
Tony's Coal-Fired | **N Beach**	24
'Wichcraft | **Downtown**	18
Yellow Sub | **Inner Sunset**	23

SCANDINAVIAN

Pläj | **Hayes Valley**	24

SEAFOOD

Alamo Sq. | **W Addition**	22
Alioto's | **Fish. Wharf**	21
Anchor & Hope | **SoMa**	21
Anchor Oyster | **Castro**	25
Barbara's Fishtrap | **Princeton Sea/S**	21
Bar Crudo | **W Addition**	26
Betty's Fish | **Santa Rosa/N**	23
NEW Big Sur Roadhse. | **Big Sur/S**	-
Cajun Pacific | **Outer Sunset**	23
Catch | **Castro**	21
NEW Cindy's Waterfront | **Monterey/S**	-
Crab Hse. | **Fish. Wharf**	23
Dante's Weird Fish | **Mission**	22

Dead Fish | **Crockett/E**	21
East Ocean Seafood | **Alameda/E**	23
Farallon | **Downtown**	25
Ferry Plaza Seafoods | **Embarcadero**	22
Fish | **Sausalito/N**	24
Fish Story | **Napa/N**	19
Fishwife | **multi.**	22
Flying Fish (Carmel) | **Carmel/S**	24
Great Eastern | **Chinatown**	23
Half Moon Brew | **Half Moon Bay/S**	17
Hayes St. Grill | **Hayes Valley**	23
Hog & Rocks | **Mission**	22
Hog Island Oyster | **multi.**	26
Hong Kong Flower/Mayflower | **multi.**	21
Hunan Home's/Gdn. | **Los Altos/S**	21
John's Grill | **Downtown**	21
Koi | **Daly City/S**	23
Lake Chalet | **Oakland/E**	17
La Mar | **Embarcadero**	24
Little River Inn | **Little River/N**	24
Local's Corner | **Mission**	26
Marica | **Oakland/E**	25
McCormick/Kuleto | **Fish. Wharf**	21
Mendo Bistro | **Ft Bragg/N**	25
Mission Rock | **Dogpatch**	16
Nettie's Crab | **Cow Hollow**	20
Old Port Lobster | **multi.**	23
Pacific Café | **Outer Rich**	23
Pacific Catch | **multi.**	22
Passionfish | **Pacific Grove/S**	27
Pesce | **Castro**	25
Plouf | **Downtown**	22
PPQ Dungeness | **Outer Rich**	24
Sam's Chowder | **Half Moon Bay/S**	22
Sam's Grill | **Downtown**	22
Sardine Factory | **Monterey/S**	24
Scoma's | **multi.**	24
NEW Sea | **Palo Alto/S**	23
Skates on Bay | **Berkeley/E**	20
Skool | **Potrero Hill**	23
Sonoma-Meritage | **Sonoma/N**	19
Sotto Mare | **N Beach**	26

Stark's Steak/Sea | **Santa Rosa/N**	25
Sunnyside Lodge | **Tahoe City/E**	18
Swan Oyster | **Polk Gulch**	26
Tadich Grill | **Downtown**	24
NEW Trident | **Sausalito/N**	22
Walnut Creek Yacht | **Walnut Creek/E**	24
Waterbar | **Embarcadero**	23
Waterfront | **Embarcadero**	21
Willi's Seafood | **Healdsburg/N**	25
Woodhouse Fish | **multi.**	22
Yankee Pier | **multi.**	19

SINGAPOREAN

Straits | **multi.**	20

SMALL PLATES

(See also Spanish tapas specialist)

À Côté | French/Med. | **Oakland/E**	24
Adesso | Italian | **Oakland/E**	22
Andalu | Eclectic | **Mission**	21
Barbacco | Italian | **Downtown**	24
Barlata | Spanish | **Oakland/E**	22
Bar Terra | Amer. | **St. Helena/N**	25
Campanula | Amer. | **N Beach**	20
Cascal | Pan-Latin | **Mtn View/S**	22
César | Pan-Latin/Spanish | **multi.**	22
Cha Cha Cha | Carib. | **multi.**	22
Chez Shea | Eclectic | **Half Moon Bay/S**	21
Gochi | Japanese | **Cupertino/S**	25
Izakaya Sozai | Japanese | **Inner Sunset**	23
Jole | Amer. | **Calistoga/N**	26
Oxbow Wine | Cal. | **Napa/N**	21
Park Chalet | Amer. | **Outer Sunset**	16
Pauline's Pizza/Wine | Pizza | **Mission**	22
Picco | Italian | **Larkspur/N**	26
Piqueo's | Peruvian | **Bernal Hts**	26
Ristobar | Italian | **Marina**	20
Sino | Chinese | **San Jose/S**	19
Starbelly | Cal. | **Castro**	22
Straits | Singapor. | **multi.**	20
Tamarine | Viet. | **Palo Alto/S**	25
Terzo | Med. | **Cow Hollow**	25

Va de Vi | Eclectic | **Walnut Creek/E**	25
Willi's Seafood | Seafood | **Healdsburg/N**	25
Willi's Wine | Eclectic | **Santa Rosa/N**	25
NEW Wine Kitchen | Amer. | **W Addition**	-

SOUL FOOD

Auntie April's | **Bayview**	24
Broken Record | **Excelsior**	24
Brown Sugar | **Oakland/E**	26
Elite Cafe | **Pacific Hts**	20
Farmerbrown | **multi.**	21
Hard Knox | **multi.**	21
Home of Chicken | **multi.**	19
Picán | **Oakland/E**	24
1300/Fillmore | **W Addition**	22

SOUTH AMERICAN

Balompie Café | **multi.**	23

SOUTHERN

Blackberry Bistro | **Oakland/E**	21
Brenda's | **Civic Ctr**	25
Broken Record | **Excelsior**	24
Brown Sugar | **Oakland/E**	26
Dixie | **Presidio**	20
Front Porch | **Bernal Hts**	22
Hard Knox | **multi.**	21
Home of Chicken | **multi.**	19
Jim's Country | **Pleasanton/E**	26
Kate's Kit. | **Lower Haight**	23
NEW Lucille's Smokehse. | **Concord/E**	-
Magnolia | **Haight-Ashbury**	22
NEW Pear | **Napa/N**	-
Picán | **Oakland/E**	24
Rocker Oysterfeller's | **Valley Ford/N**	25
Southpaw BBQ | **Mission**	20
1300/Fillmore | **W Addition**	22

SOUTHWESTERN

Boogaloos | **Mission**	20
Green Chile Kitchen | **W Addition**	22
Rio Grill | **Carmel/S**	23
West of Pecos | **Mission**	19

CUISINES

SPANISH

(* tapas specialist)

Alegrias* | **Marina**	22
Barlata* | **Oakland/E**	22
B44* | **Downtown**	21
Bocadillos* | **N Beach**	23
NEW Bravas Bar/Tapas | **Healdsburg/N**	25
Canela Bistro* | **Castro**	23
César* | **Berkeley/E**	22
Contigo* | **Noe Valley**	25
NEW Coqueta | **Embarcadero**	-
NEW Duende | **Oakland/E**	23
Esperpento* | **Mission**	22
Gitane | **Downtown**	23
Iberia | **Menlo Pk/S**	22
Mundaka* | **Carmel/S**	24
Piperade | **Downtown**	26
Zarzuela* | **Russian Hill**	24
ZuZu* | **Napa/N**	24

SRI LANKAN

NEW 1601 Bar/Kitchen | **SoMa**	-

STEAKHOUSES

Alexander's Steak | **multi.**	26
Alfred's Steak | **Downtown**	23
Arcadia | **San Jose/S**	23
Bluestem Brass. | **SoMa**	19
Bourbon Steak | **Downtown**	23
Casa Orinda | **Orinda/E**	20
Cole's Chop | **Napa/N**	27
Dead Fish | **Crockett/E**	21
El Paseo | **Mill Valley/N**	23
Epic Roasthse. | **Embarcadero**	22
Espetus | **San Mateo/S**	24
5A5 Steak | **Downtown**	23
Grill/Alley | **San Jose/S**	23
Harris' | **Polk Gulch**	26
House/Prime | **Polk Gulch**	26
Izzy's Steak | **multi.**	22
John's Grill | **Downtown**	21
Lark Creek Steak | **Downtown**	24
LB Steak | **multi.**	22
Lolinda | **Mission**	23
Morton's | **multi.**	23
Press | **St. Helena/N**	26
Ruth's Chris | **multi.**	24

Stark's Steak/Sea | **Santa Rosa/N**	25
Sunnyside Lodge | **Tahoe City/E**	18
Vic Stewart's | **Walnut Creek/E**	24

SWISS

Matterhorn Swiss | **Russian Hill**	22

TEAHOUSES

Imperial Tea | **multi.**	18
Lovejoy's Tea | **Noe Valley**	20
Samovar Tea | **multi.**	20

THAI

Amarin Thai | **Mtn View/S**	21
Anchalee Thai | **Berkeley/E**	23
Bangkok Thai | **multi.**	24
Basil | **SoMa**	24
Khan Toke | **Outer Rich**	21
King of Thai | **multi.**	21
Another Monkey/Koh | **SoMa**	21
Krung Thai | **multi.**	22
Lers Ros Thai | **multi.**	24
Manora's Thai | **SoMa**	23
Marnee Thai | **multi.**	25
New Krung Thai | **San Jose/S**	25
Osha Thai | **multi.**	22
Royal Thai | **San Rafael/N**	26
Sai Jai Thai | **Tenderloin**	24
Sea Thai/Modern | **multi.**	26
Soi4 | **Oakland/E**	23
Thai Hse. | **multi.**	22
Thep Phanom | **Lower Haight**	24

TURKISH

A La Turca | **Tenderloin**	23
Sens | **Embarcadero**	20
Troya | **multi.**	21

VEGETARIAN

(* vegan)

Café Gratitude* | **multi.**	19
Calafia* | **Palo Alto/S**	20
Cha-Ya Veg.* | **multi.**	22
Dante's Weird Fish | **Mission**	22
Dasaprakash* | **Santa Clara/S**	22
Encuentro | **Oakland/E**	26
Gracias* | **Mission**	24
Greens | **Marina**	25

Millennium*	**Downtown**	26
Source	**Potrero Hill**	24
Udupi Palace	**multi.**	23

VENEZUELAN

Pica Pica	**multi.**	21

VIETNAMESE

Bodega Bistro	**Tenderloin**	24
Bun Mee	**Upper Fillmore**	20
Café Bunn	**Inner Rich**	23
Crustacean	**Polk Gulch**	25
Dragon Rouge	**Alameda/E**	24
Le Cheval	**multi.**	21
Le Colonial	**Downtown**	22
Out the Door	**multi.**	23
Pho 84	**Oakland/E**	23
PPQ Dungeness	**Outer Rich**	24
Saigon Sandwiches	**Tenderloin**	25
Slanted Door	**Embarcadero**	26
Sunflower	**multi.**	23
Tamarine	**Palo Alto/S**	25
Thanh Long	**Outer Sunset**	26
Turtle Tower	**multi.**	21
Vanessa's Bistro	**multi.**	23
Vung Tau	**multi.**	24
Xanh	**Mtn View/S**	21
Xyclo	**Oakland/E**	21
Zadin	**Castro**	20

CUISINES

Locations

Includes names, cuisines and Food ratings.

City of San Francisco

AT&T PARK/ SOUTH BEACH

Amici's	*Pizza*	21
Mijita	*Mex.*	20
MoMo's	*Amer.*	19
Public Hse.	*Pub*	17
Tsunami Sushi	*Japanese*	22

BAYVIEW/ HUNTER'S POINT

Auntie April's	*Soul*	24
Limón	*Peruvian*	24

BERNAL HEIGHTS

Angkor Borei	*Cambodian*	23
Balompié Café	*Salvadoran*	23
El Huarache Loco	*Mex.*	21
Emmy's Spaghetti	*Italian*	21
Front Porch	*Carib./Southern*	22
NEW Hillside Supper	*Amer.*	-
Ichi Sushi	*Japanese*	27
Liberty Cafe	*Amer.*	22
Little Nepal	*Nepalese*	23
Moki's Sushi	*Japanese*	25
903	*Japanese/Sandwiches*	24
Piqueo's	*Peruvian*	26
Sandbox	*Bakery*	25

CASTRO

Anchor Oyster	*Seafood*	25
Brandy Ho's	*Chinese*	20
BurgerMeister	*Burgers*	20
Canela Bistro	*Spanish*	23
Catch	*Seafood*	21
Chilango	*Mex.*	22
Chile Pies	*Dessert*	22
Chow/Park Chow	*Amer.*	21
NEW Dante's Table	*Italian*	-
Destino	*Nuevo Latino*	22
Eiji	*Japanese*	25
Eureka	*Amer.*	21
NEW Fable	*Amer.*	-
Frances	*Cal.*	27

Ike's Pl./Lair	*Sandwiches*	25
Kasa Indian	*Indian*	21
La Méditerranée	*Med./Mideast.*	22
L'Ardoise	*French*	24
Pesce	*Italian/Seafood*	25
Pica Pica	*Venez.*	21
Poesia	*Italian*	23
Samovar Tea	*Tea*	20
Starbelly	*Cal.*	22
Super Duper	*Burgers*	23
Sushi Zone	*Japanese*	27
Thai Hse.	*Thai*	22
Woodhouse Fish	*Seafood*	22
Zadin	*Viet.*	20

CHINA BASIN/ DOGPATCH

NEW Chocolate Lab	*Dessert*	25
Hard Knox	*Southern*	21
Mission Rock	*Seafood*	16
Moshi Moshi	*Japanese*	23
Piccino	*Italian*	24
Serpentine	*Amer.*	23

CHINATOWN

Brandy Ho's	*Chinese*	20
Bund Shanghai	*Chinese*	24
Great Eastern	*Chinese*	23
Henry's Hunan	*Chinese*	22
House/Nanking	*Chinese*	22
Hunan Home's/Gdn.	*Chinese*	21
Jai Yun	*Chinese*	23
NEW Mason Pacific	*Amer.*	-
Oriental Pearl	*Chinese*	23
R & G Lounge	*Chinese*	24
Sushirrito	*Japanese*	20
Yuet Lee	*Chinese*	20
Z & Y	*Chinese*	25

COW HOLLOW

Balboa Cafe	*Amer.*	20
Betelnut	*Asian*	24
Brazen Head	*Amer.*	20
Café des Amis	*French*	18
Capannina	*Italian*	25

Gamine | *French*	24
La Boulange | *Bakery*	21
Nettie's Crab | *Seafood*	20
Osha Thai | *Thai*	22
Pane e Vino | *Italian*	23
Patxi's Pizza | *Pizza*	22
Roam | *Burgers*	23
Rose's Cafe | *Italian*	22
Tacko | *Mex.*	22
Terzo | *Med.*	25
Umami | *Japanese*	25
Umami Burger | *Burgers*	22

DOWNTOWN

Alfred's Steak | *Steak*	23
Anzu | *Japanese*	23
NEW Aquitaine | *French*	-
Barbacco | *Italian*	24
B44 | *Spanish*	21
Bix | *Amer./French*	24
Boudin Sourdough | *Amer./Sandwiches*	21
Bourbon Steak | *Steak*	23
Brasserie S&P | *Cal.*	24
Burger Bar | *Burgers*	20
Burritt Tavern | *Amer.*	20
Cafe Bastille | *French*	19
Café Claude | *French*	22
Café Tiramisu | *Italian*	22
Campton Pl. | *Cal./Med.*	26
Cheesecake Fac. | *Amer.*	16
Chiaroscuro | *Italian*	25
Claudine | *French*	22
Colibrí | *Mex.*	23
Cotogna | *Italian*	26
Credo | *Italian*	20
Cupola Pizzeria | *Italian/Pizza*	21
E&O Asian Kit. | *Asian*	21
Emporio Rulli | *Dessert/Italian*	22
Farallon | *Seafood*	25
5A5 Steak | *Steak*	23
Fleur de Lys | *Cal./French*	27
Garden Ct. | *Cal.*	22
Giorgio's | *Pizza*	21
Gitane | *French/Spanish*	23
Globe | *Cal./Italian*	18
Golden West | *Bakery/Sandwiches*	21

Grand Cafe | *French*	20
NEW Hakkasan | *Chinese*	24
Henry's Hunan | *Chinese*	22
Il Fornaio | *Italian*	18
Jasper's Corner | *Amer.*	19
John's Grill | *Seafood/Steak*	21
Katana-Ya | *Japanese*	22
King of Thai | *Thai*	21
Kokkari | *Greek*	28
Kuleto's | *Italian*	23
La Boulange | *Bakery*	21
Lark Creek Steak | *Steak*	24
Le Central | *French*	21
Le Colonial | *French/Viet.*	22
Machine Coffee | *Coffee/Sandwiches*	-
Melt | *Sandwiches*	17
Michael Mina | *Amer.*	27
Millennium | *Vegan*	26
Morton's | *Steak*	23
Muracci's | *Japanese*	20
NEW M.Y. China | *Chinese*	19
Osha Thai | *Thai*	22
Palio d'Asti | *Italian*	21
Perbacco | *Italian*	26
Per Diem | *Amer.*	20
Piperade | *Spanish*	26
Plant Cafe | *Health*	22
Plouf | *French*	22
Postrio | *Amer.*	23
Quince | *French/Italian*	26
Ramen Underground | *Japanese/Noodle Shop*	19
NEW Rickybobby | *Pub*	-
NEW Roka Akor | *Japanese*	-
Rotunda | *Amer.*	21
Ryoko's | *Japanese*	25
Sam's Grill | *Seafood*	22
Sanraku | *Japanese*	23
Sauce | *Amer.*	22
Scala's Bistro | *Italian*	23
Sears | *Diner*	20
NEW Shorty Goldstein's | *Deli*	-
Showdogs | *Hot Dogs*	20
Spice Kit | *Asian*	19
Straits | *Singapor.*	20
Super Duper | *Burgers*	23

LOCATIONS

Sushirrito	*Japanese*	20
Tadich Grill	*Seafood*	24
Taqueria Can Cun	*Mex.*	23
Tout Sweet	*Dessert/Euro.*	-
Unicorn	*Asian*	23
Wayfare Tav.	*Amer.*	24
Wexler's	*BBQ*	23
'Wichcraft	*Sandwiches*	18

EMBARCADERO

Americano	*Italian*	20
Blue Bottle	*Cal./Coffee*	24
Boccalone	*Sandwiches*	25
Boudin Sourdough	*Amer./Sandwiches*	21
Boulettes Larder/Bouli Bar	*Amer.*	25
Boulevard	*Amer.*	27
Butterfly	*Asian/Cal.*	23
Chaya	*French/Japanese*	23
NEW Coqueta	*Spanish*	-
Delica	*Japanese*	25
Epic Roasthse.	*Steak*	22
Fatted Calf	*Sandwiches*	26
Ferry Plaza Seafoods	*Seafood*	22
4505 Meats	*Hot Dogs*	26
Gott's Roadside	*Diner*	22
NEW Hard Water	*Cajun/Creole*	-
Hog Island Oyster	*Seafood*	26
Il Cane Rosso	*Italian*	23
Imperial Tea	*Tea*	18
La Mar	*Peruvian/Seafood*	24
MarketBar	*Amer.*	18
Mijita	*Mex.*	20
Namu Gaji	*Asian/Korean*	24
One Market	*Cal.*	24
Osha Thai	*Thai*	22
Out the Door	*Viet.*	23
Ozumo	*Japanese*	25
Plant Cafe	*Health*	22
NEW Rosa Mexicano	*Mex.*	24
NEW Seaglass Rest.	*Cal.*	-
Sens	*Med./Turkish*	20
Slanted Door	*Viet.*	26
Tacolicious	*Mex.*	24
Town's End	*Amer./Bakery*	21
Waterbar	*Seafood*	23
Waterfront	*Cal./Seafood*	21
Wise Sons	*Deli/Jewish*	23

EXCELSIOR/INGLESIDE

Broken Record	*Soul*	24
Henry's Hunan	*Chinese*	22
Ike's Pl./Lair	*Sandwiches*	25
Joe's Cable Car	*Burgers*	22
North Bch. Pizza	*Pizza*	20
Turtle Tower	*Viet.*	21

FISHERMAN'S WHARF

Alioto's	*Italian*	21
Bistro Boudin	*Cal.*	22
Boudin Sourdough	*Amer./Sandwiches*	21
Crab Hse.	*Seafood*	23
Gary Danko	*Amer.*	29
In-N-Out	*Burgers*	23
King of Thai	*Thai*	21
McCormick/Kuleto	*Seafood*	21
Scoma's	*Seafood*	24

FOREST HILLS/ WEST PORTAL/ LAKESHORE/ PARKSIDE

Boudin Sourdough	*Amer./Sandwiches*	21
Chouchou	*French*	19
Fresca	*Peruvian*	22
Kingdom/Dumpling	*Chinese*	22
Market & Rye	*Deli/Sandwiches*	19
Roti Indian	*Indian*	23
NEW Trattoria/Vittorio	*Italian*	-

GLEN PARK

Chenery Park	*Amer.*	23
Gialina	*Pizza*	25
La Corneta	*Mex.*	22
Le P'tit Laurent	*French*	25
Osha Thai	*Thai*	22
Tataki	*Japanese*	24

HAIGHT-ASHBURY/ COLE VALLEY

Alembic	*Eclectic*	23
BurgerMeister	*Burgers*	20
Cha Cha Cha	*Carib.*	22
La Boulange	*Bakery*	21
Magnolia	*Southern*	22
North Bch. Pizza	*Pizza*	20
NEW Padrecito	*Mex.*	-

Parada 22 | *Puerto Rican* 23

Pork Store | *Amer.* 19

Zazie | *French* 24

HAYES VALLEY/ CIVIC CENTER

Absinthe | *French/Med.* 23

Arlequin Cafe | *Med.* 20

Bar Jules | *Amer.* 24

Biergarten | *German* 21

Blue Bottle | *Cal./Coffee* 24

Boxing Rm. | *Cajun/Creole* 20

Brenda's | *Creole/Southern* 25

Chez Maman | *French* 24

Domo Sushi | *Japanese* 27

Espetus | *Brazilian* 24

Fatted Calf | *Sandwiches* 26

Hayes St. Grill | *Seafood* 23

Hayes Valley Bakeworks | *Amer./Bakery* 21

Indigo | *Amer.* 20

Jardinière | *Cal./French* 26

La Boulange | *Bakery* 21

Lers Ros Thai | *Thai* 24

Nojo | *Amer./Japanese* 25

O3 Bistro | *Asian* 24

Patxi's Pizza | *Pizza* 22

Pläj | *Scandinavian* 24

Rich Table | *Cal.* 25

NEW Roku | *Japanese* -

Samovar Tea | *Tea* 20

Sauce | *Amer.* 22

NEW Schulzies | *Dessert* -

Sebo | *Japanese* 27

NEW South/SFJAZZ | *Amer.* -

Straw | *Cal./Sandwiches* 20

Suppenküche | *German* 23

NEW 20th Century | *Bakery* -

2G Japanese | *Japanese* 22

Zuni Café | *Med.* 26

INNER RICHMOND

Bella Trattoria | *Italian* 24

Brother's Korean | *Korean* 22

B Star | *Asian* 25

Burma Superstar | *Burmese* 25

Café Bunn | *Sandwiches/Viet.* 23

Chapeau! | *French* 27

Giorgio's | *Pizza* 21

Good Luck | *Chinese* 21

Katia's Tea | *Russian* 20

King of Thai | *Thai* 21

Mandalay | *Burmese* 25

My Tofu | *Korean* 23

Q Rest./Wine | *Amer.* 20

Richmond | *Cal.* 25

Sushi Bistro | *Japanese* 23

To Hyang | *Korean* 25

Troya | *Turkish* 21

INNER SUNSET

Arizmendi | *Bakery/Pizza* 25

Chow/Park Chow | *Amer.* 21

Ebisu | *Japanese* 24

Hotei | *Japanese* 19

Izakaya Sozai | *Japanese* 23

Koo | *Asian* 26

Marnee Thai | *Thai* 25

Nopalito | *Mex.* 24

Pacific Catch | *Seafood* 22

Pasión | *Nuevo Latino/Peruvian* 25

Patxi's Pizza | *Pizza* 22

Pomelo | *Eclectic* 24

San Tung | *Chinese/Korean* 24

Underdog | *Hot Dogs* 25

Yellow Sub | *Sandwiches* 23

JAPANTOWN

Kiss Seafood | *Japanese* 28

Mifune | *Japanese* 18

LAUREL HEIGHTS/ PRESIDIO HEIGHTS

NEW Corner Store | *Amer.* 22

Ella's | *Amer.* 21

Garibaldi | *Cal./Med.* 24

Hong Kong Lounge | *Chinese* 24

Pasta Pomodoro | *Italian* 18

Sociale | *Italian* 24

Spruce | *Amer.* 26

LOWER HAIGHT

Indian Oven | *Indian* 23

Kate's Kit. | *Southern* 23

Little Chihuahua | *Mex.* 21

Maven | *Amer.* 18

Memphis Minnie's | *BBQ* 20

Rosamunde	*German*	22
Thep Phanom	*Thai*	24
Uva Enoteca	*Italian*	22

MARINA

Ace Wasabi's	*Japanese*	20
Alegrias	*Spanish*	22
Amici's	*Pizza*	21
A16	*Italian*	24
Atelier Crenn	*French*	27
Baker St. Bistro	*French*	21
Barney's	*Burgers*	21
Bistro Aix	*Cal./French*	23
Blue Barn	*Cal.*	25
Chotto	*Japanese*	24
Delarosa	*Italian*	21
Dynamo Donut	*Coffee*	25
Greens	*Veg.*	25
Isa	*French*	24
Izzy's Steak	*Steak*	22
Lucca Deli	*Deli/Sandwiches*	26
Mamacita	*Mex.*	24
Pacific Catch	*Seafood*	22
Plant Cafe	*Health*	22
Ristobar	*Italian*	20
Super Duper	*Burgers*	23
Tacolicious	*Mex.*	24
Zushi Puzzle	*Japanese*	27

MISSION

Abbot's Cellar	*Amer.*	20
Amber India	*Indian*	24
Amer. Grilled	*Amer./Sandwiches*	22
Andalu	*Eclectic*	21
Arinell Pizza	*Pizza*	23
Arizmendi	*Bakery/Pizza*	25
Baby Blues BBQ	*BBQ*	21
Balompie Café	*Salvadoran*	23
Bar Tartine	*Euro.*	24
Beast/Hare	*Amer./Cal.*	23
Beretta	*Italian*	24
Bi-Rite	*Bakery/Ice Cream*	27
Blowfish Sushi	*Japanese*	23
Blue Bottle	*Cal./Coffee*	24
Blue Plate	*Amer.*	24
Boogaloos	*SW*	20
Burger Joint	*Burgers*	19
Central Kitchen	*Cal.*	24

Cha Cha Cha	*Carib.*	22
Charles Chocolate	*Dessert*	-
Cha-Ya Veg.	*Japanese/Vegan*	22
Commonwealth	*Amer.*	26
Craftsman & Wolves	*Bakery/Sandwiches*	25
Curry Up Now	*Indian*	21
NEW Dandelion Chocolate	*Dessert*	-
Dante's Weird Fish	*Seafood*	22
Delfina	*Italian*	26
Dosa	*Indian*	23
Dynamo Donut	*Coffee*	25
El Farolito	*Mex.*	23
El Metate	*Mex.*	23
Esperpento	*Spanish*	22
Farina Foccaccia	*Italian*	22
Farina Pizza	*Italian/Pizza*	20
Flour + Water	*Italian*	26
Foreign Cinema	*Cal./Med.*	24
4505 Meats	*Hot Dogs*	26
Frjtz Fries	*Belgian*	20
Garçon	*French*	22
Giordano	*Sandwiches*	22
Goood Frikin'	*Mideast.*	20
Gracias	*Mex./Vegan*	24
Heirloom	*Cal./Med.*	25
NEW Hi Lo BBQ	*BBQ*	-
Hog & Rocks	*Amer.*	22
Izakaya Yuzuki	*Japanese*	24
Ken Ken	*Japanese/Noodle Shop*	21
Kiji Sushi Bar	*Japanese*	25
NEW Kronnerburger	*Burgers*	-
La Corneta	*Mex.*	22
La Cumbre	*Mex.*	20
La Taqueria	*Mex.*	25
Limón	*Peruvian*	24
Little Chihuahua	*Mex.*	21
Little Star	*Pizza*	25
Local Mission	*Cal.*	27
Local's Corner	*Seafood*	26
Locanda	*Italian*	24
Lolinda	*Argent./Steak*	23
Loló	*Mex.*	25
Luna Park	*Amer./French*	20
Maverick	*Amer.*	24
Mission Bch. Café	*Cal.*	24

Mission Cheese	*Amer.*	22		

Mission Cheese	*Amer.*	22
Mission Chinese	*Chinese*	22
NEW Mission Picnic	*Sandwiches*	–
Mozzeria	*Pizza*	21
Namu Gaji	*Asian/Korean*	24
Nihon	*Japanese*	21
Nombe	*Japanese*	21
Osha Thai	*Thai*	22
Pakwan	*Pakistani*	23
NEW Palace	*Cal.*	–
Pancho Villa	*Mex.*	23
Papalote Mex.	*Mex.*	22
Pauline's Pizza/Wine	*Pizza*	22
Pi Bar	*Pizza*	21
Pica Pica	*Venez.*	21
Pizzeria Delfina	*Pizza*	25
Pork Store	*Amer.*	19
Radish	*Amer.*	18
Range	*Amer.*	27
Regalito Rosticeria	*Mex.*	23
Rosamunde	*German*	22
NEW Roxy's Cafe	*Eclectic*	–
Salumeria Deli	*Deli/Sandwiches*	–
Schmidt's	*German*	22
Slow Club	*Amer.*	23
Southpaw BBQ	*BBQ*	20
St. Francis	*Diner*	19
St. Vincent Tavern	*Cal.*	21
NEW Sugoi Sushi	*Japanese*	–
Sunflower	*Viet.*	23
Sushi Bistro	*Japanese*	23
Tacolicious	*Mex.*	24
Taqueria Can Cun	*Mex.*	23
Taqueria San Jose	*Mex.*	23
Tartine	*Bakery*	27
Thai Hse.	*Thai*	22
NEW Trick Dog	*Eclectic*	–
Truly Med.	*Med.*	26
NEW 20 Spot	*Amer.*	–
Udupi Palace	*Indian/Veg.*	23
Universal Cafe	*Amer.*	25
Walzwerk	*German*	21
West of Pecos	*SW*	19
Wise Sons	*Deli/Jewish*	23
Woodward's Gdn.	*Cal.*	24
Yamo	*Burmese*	22

NOB HILL

Big Four	*Amer.*	24
Borobudur	*Indonesian*	23
Bouche	*Cal./French*	24
Keiko	*French/Japanese*	27
Nob Hill Café	*Italian*	22
Parallel 37	*Amer.*	24
Saha	*Mideast.*	24
Seven Hills	*Italian*	27
Sons/Daughters	*Amer.*	26
Sweet Woodruff	*Sandwiches*	24
Venticello	*Italian*	23

NOE VALLEY

Alice's	*Chinese*	20
Bacco	*Italian*	23
Barney's	*Burgers*	21
Chloe's Cafe	*Amer.*	23
Contigo	*Spanish*	25
Eric's	*Chinese*	22
Firefly	*Eclectic*	24
Fresca	*Peruvian*	22
Hamano Sushi	*Japanese*	21
Henry's Hunan	*Chinese*	22
Incanto	*Italian*	25
La Boulange	*Bakery*	21
La Ciccia	*Italian*	27
Little Chihuahua	*Mex.*	21
Lovejoy's Tea	*Tea*	20
Lupa Trattoria	*Italian*	23
Pasta Pomodoro	*Italian*	18
Patxi's Pizza	*Pizza*	22
Pomelo	*Eclectic*	24
Saru Sushi	*Japanese*	28
Tataki	*Japanese*	24

NORTH BEACH

Albona Rist.	*Italian*	24
Bocadillos	*Spanish*	23
Bottle Cap	*Amer.*	18
BurgerMeister	*Burgers*	20
Cafe Jacqueline	*French*	27
Cafe Zoetrope	*Italian*	21
Campanula	*Amer.*	20
NEW Capo's	*Italian*	–
Chubby Noodle	*Asian*	24
Coi	*Cal./French*	27
Don Pisto's	*Mex.*	25

15 Romolo | *Amer.*	22
Giordano | *Sandwiches*	22
Golden Boy | *Pizza*	24
House | *Asian*	27
HRD Coffee/Smokin | *BBQ/Korean*	23
Ideale Rest. | *Italian*	25
King of Thai | *Thai*	21
La Boulange | *Bakery*	21
L'Osteria | *Italian*	24
Mama's on Wash. | *Amer.*	24
Mario's Bohemian | *Italian/Sandwiches*	19
Maykadeh | *Persian*	23
Mo's | *Amer.*	23
Naked Lunch | *Sandwiches*	24
North Bch. Pizza | *Pizza*	20
North Bch. Rest. | *Italian*	24
Original Joe's | *Amer./Italian*	21
Park Tav. | *Amer.*	24
Rose Pistola | *Italian*	21
Sotto Mare | *Italian/Seafood*	26
Stinking Rose | *Italian*	20
Tacolicious | *Mex.*	24
Taqueria San Jose | *Mex.*	23
Tommaso's | *Italian*	24
Tony's Coal-Fired | *Pizza*	24
Tony's Pizza | *Italian/Pizza*	26
Tratt. Contadina | *Italian*	24

OUTER RICHMOND

Ariake | *Japanese*	25
Aziza | *Moroccan*	26
Cliff Hse. | *Cal.*	20
Han IL Kwan | *Korean*	24
Hard Knox | *Southern*	21
Hong Kong Lounge | *Chinese*	24
Kabuto | *Japanese*	26
Kappou Gomi | *Japanese*	28
Khan Toke | *Thai*	21
Men Oh Tokushima | *Japanese/Noodle Shop*	-
Mescolanza | *Italian*	23
Oyaji | *Japanese*	23
Pacific Café | *Seafood*	23
Pizzetta 211 | *Pizza*	26
PPQ Dungeness | *Seafood/Viet.*	24
Sutro's | *Cal.*	21
Tommy's Mex. | *Mex.*	20

Ton Kiang | *Chinese*	25
Turtle Tower | *Viet.*	21

OUTER SUNSET

Beach Chalet | *Amer.*	16
Cajun Pacific | *Cajun/Creole*	23
Java Beach | *Sandwiches*	20
Just Wonton | *Chinese*	20
King of Thai | *Thai*	21
Marnee Thai | *Thai*	25
North Bch. Pizza | *Pizza*	20
Outerlands | *Amer.*	25
Park Chalet | *Cal.*	16
Taco Shop/Underdogs | *Mex.*	24
Thanh Long | *Viet.*	26

PACIFIC HEIGHTS

NEW B. Patisserie | *Dessert*	26
Elite Cafe | *Amer.*	20
Eliza's | *Chinese*	22
Florio | *French/Italian*	21
La Boulange | *Bakery*	21
Pizzeria Delfina | *Pizza*	25
Roam | *Burgers*	23
SPQR | *Italian*	25
Tataki | *Japanese*	24
Troya | *Turkish*	21
Woodhouse Fish | *Seafood*	22

POLK GULCH

Acquerello | *Italian*	28
Crustacean | *Asian/Viet.*	25
Harris' | *Steak*	26
House/Prime | *Amer.*	26
Kasa Indian | *Indian*	21
Miller's East | *Deli/Jewish*	20
Ruth's Chris | *Steak*	24
Shalimar | *Indian/Pakistani*	23
Swan Oyster | *Seafood*	26

POTRERO HILL

Aperto | *Italian*	22
Chez Maman | *French*	24
Chez Papa Bistrot | *French*	24
Goat Hill | *Pizza*	22
Market & Rye | *Deli/Sandwiches*	19
Papito | *Mex.*	26
Plow | *Cal.*	26
Skool | *Seafood*	23

Source | *Pizza/Veg.* | 24
Sunflower | *Viet.* | 23

PRESIDIO

Dixie | *Southern* | 20
Presidio Social | *Amer.* | 19

RUSSIAN HILL

Frascati | *Cal./Med.* | 25
Gioia Pizzeria | *Cal./Pizza* | 25
Helmand Palace | *Afghan* | 23
La Boulange | *Bakery* | 21
La Folie | *French* | 27
Leopold's | *Austrian* | 23
Luella | *Cal./Med.* | 23
Matterhorn Swiss | *Swiss* | 22
Nick's Crispy | *Mex.* | 21
Rist. Milano | *Italian* | 24
Zarzuela | *Spanish* | 24

SOMA

AK Subs | *Sandwiches* | 22
Alexander's Steak | *Japanese/Steak* | 26
Amber India | *Indian* | 24
Ame | *Amer.* | 26
Amer. Grilled | *Amer./Sandwiches* | 22
Anchor & Hope | *Seafood* | 21
AQ | *Cal.* | 24
Bar Agricole | *Cal.* | 22
Basil | *Thai* | 24
Benu | *Amer.* | 27
NEW Bergerac | *Eclectic/Pub* | -
Blue Bottle | *Cal./Coffee* | 24
Bluestem Brass. | *Amer./Steak* | 19
Butler/Chef | *French* | 22
Catheads BBQ | *BBQ* | 22
NEW Cavalier | *British* | -
Citizen's Band | *Amer.* | 22
Coco500 | *Cal./Med.* | 24
Deli Board/1058 | *Deli/Sandwiches* | 23
Fang | *Chinese* | 22
Farmerbrown | *Soul* | 21
Fifth Floor | *Amer./French* | 24
54 Mint | *Italian* | 22
Fringale | *French/Spanish* | 25
Goat Hill | *Pizza* | 22
Henry's Hunan | *Chinese* | 22
NEW Heyday | *Cal.* | -

HRD Coffee/Smokin | *Diner/Korean* | 23
Another Monkey/Koh | *Thai* | 21
La Boulange | *Bakery* | 21
Le Charm Bistro | *French* | 22
Luce | *Amer.* | 21
Manora's Thai | *Thai* | 23
Marlowe | *Amer./Cal.* | 24
Melt | *Sandwiches* | 17
NEW MKT | *Cal.* | -
Mochica | *Peruvian* | 24
Mo's | *Amer.* | 23
Oola | *Cal.* | 21
Osha Thai | *Thai* | 22
Pazzia | *Pizza* | 25
Pearl's Deluxe/Phat | *Burgers* | 23
Prospect | *Amer.* | 24
Radius Rest. | *Cal.* | 23
Rest. LuLu | *French/Med.* | 21
Rist. Umbria | *Italian* | 21
RN74 | *French* | 22
Rocco's Cafe | *Italian* | 24
Roy's | *Hawaiian* | 24
Saison | *Amer.* | 27
Salt Hse. | *Amer.* | 22
Samovar Tea | *Tea* | 20
Sanraku | *Japanese* | 23
Sentinel | *Sandwiches* | 23
NEW 1601 Bar/Kitchen | *French/Sri Lanken* | -
SoMa StrEAT | *Eclectic* | 23
South Park | *French* | 22
Super Duper | *Burgers* | 23
Sushirrito | *Japanese* | 20
Tava | *Indian* | -
3rd St. Grill | *Amer./Mex.* | 23
Town Hall | *Amer.* | 23
Trace | *Amer.* | 22
Tropisueño | *Mex.* | 20
Turtle Tower | *Viet.* | 21
25 Lusk | *Amer.* | 22
Una Pizza | *Pizza* | 26
NEW The Willows | *Amer.* | -
Wise Sons | *Deli/Jewish* | 23
Yank Sing | *Chinese* | 26
Zaré/Fly Trap | *Cal./Med.* | 21
Zero Zero | *Italian/Pizza* | 24

TENDERLOIN

A La Turca | *Turkish*	23
Bodega Bistro | *Viet.*	24
Burmese Kit. | *Burmese*	22
Chutney | *Indian/Pakistani*	25
Farmerbrown | *Soul*	21
Lers Ros Thai | *Thai*	24
NEW Mikkeller Bar | *Eclectic*	-
Osha Thai | *Thai*	22
Pakwan | *Pakistani*	23
Pearl's Deluxe/Phat | *Burgers*	23
Saigon Sandwiches | *Sandwiches/Viet.*	25
Sai Jai Thai | *Thai*	24
Shalimar | *Indian/Pakistani*	23
Thai Hse. | *Thai*	22
Turtle Tower | *Viet.*	21

UPPER FILLMORE

Baker/Banker | *Amer.*	25
Bun Mee | *Viet.*	20
Dosa | *Indian*	23
Fresca | *Peruvian*	22
Jackson Fillmore | *Italian*	21
La Méditerranée | *Med./Mideast.*	22
Out the Door | *Viet.*	23

WESTERN ADDITION

Alamo Sq. | *French/Seafood*	22
Bar Crudo | *Seafood*	26
Bi-Rite | *Bakery/Ice Cream*	27
Bistro Central | *French*	25
Cheese Steak | *Cheesestks.*	22
Chile Pies | *Dessert*	22
Green Chile Kitchen | *SW*	22
Little Star | *Pizza*	25
NEW Mill | *Bakery/Coffee*	-
Nopa | *Cal.*	26
Nopalito | *Mex.*	24
Papalote Mex. | *Mex.*	22
Ragazza | *Pizza*	25
State Bird | *Amer.*	26
1300/Fillmore | *Soul/Southern*	22
Tsunami Sushi | *Japanese*	22
NEW Wine Kitchen | *Amer.*	-
Yoshi's | *Japanese*	22

East of San Francisco

ALAMEDA

Asena | *Cal./Med.*	26
BurgerMeister | *Burgers*	20
Burma Superstar | *Burmese*	25
Cheese Steak | *Cheesestks.*	22
Dragon Rouge | *Viet.*	24
East Ocean Seafood | *Chinese*	23
King of Thai | *Thai*	21
Pappo | *Amer.*	23
Pearl's Deluxe/Phat | *Burgers*	23

ALBANY

Caspers Hot Dogs | *Hot Dogs*	22
Fonda Solana | *Pan-Latin*	22
Little Star | *Pizza*	25

BERKELEY

Ajanta | *Indian*	27
Anchalee Thai | *Thai*	23
Angeline's LA Kit. | *Cajun/Creole*	24
Arinell Pizza | *Pizza*	23
Bangkok Thai | *Thai*	24
Barney's | *Burgers*	21
Bette's Oceanview | *Diner*	24
Bistro Liaison | *French*	23
BurgerMeister | *Burgers*	20
Cactus Taqueria | *Mex.*	21
Café Gratitude | *Vegan*	19
Café Rouge | *Cal./Med.*	22
Cancun | *Mex.*	22
César | *Spanish*	22
Cha-Ya Veg. | *Japanese/Vegan*	22
Cheese Board | *Pizza*	26
Cheese Steak | *Cheesestks.*	22
Chez Panisse | *Cal./Med.*	27
Chez Panisse Café | *Cal./Med.*	27
Comal | *Mex.*	23
NEW Easy Creole | *Cajun/Creole*	-
Emilia's | *Pizza*	27
Everett/Jones BBQ | *BBQ*	21
Five | *Amer./Cal.*	20
Gather | *Cal.*	23
Guamenkitzel | *German*	21
Gioia Pizzeria | *Pizza*	25
Grégoire | *French*	24
Imperial Tea | *Tea*	18

Ippuku | *Japanese*	24
Jimmy Beans | *Diner*	20
Joshu-ya Brass. | *Japanese*	25
Juan's | *Mex.*	19
Kirala | *Japanese*	25
Lalime's | *Cal./Med.*	26
La Méditerranée | *Med./Mideast.*	22
La Note | *French*	23
La Sen Bistro | *Cal./French*	23
Le Cheval | *Viet.*	21
Lo Coco's | *Italian*	22
Meritage/Claremont | *Cal.*	23
900 Grayson | *Burgers/Cal.*	24
North Bch. Pizza | *Pizza*	20
Picante Cocina | *Mex.*	22
Revival Bar | *Cal.*	22
Rick & Ann's | *Amer.*	23
Riva Cucina | *Italian*	26
Rivoli | *Cal./Med.*	27
Saul's Rest./Deli | *Deli*	20
Shen Hua | *Chinese*	22
Skates on Bay | *Amer.*	20
NEW Stella Nonna | *Amer.*	-
Tacubaya | *Mex.*	22
NEW Tomo's Japanese | *Japanese*	-
Top Dog | *Hot Dogs*	23
Trattoria Corso | *Italian*	25
Tratt. La Sicil. | *Italian*	24
T Rex | *BBQ*	18
Udupi Palace | *Indian/Veg.*	23
Vanessa's Bistro | *French/Viet.*	23
Venus | *Cal.*	24
Vik's Chaat | *Indian*	24
Zachary's Pizza | *Pizza*	25
Zatar | *Med.*	24

CONCORD

Cheese Steak | *Cheesestks.*	22
NEW Lucille's Smokehse. | *BBQ*	-

CROCKETT

Dead Fish | *Seafood*	21

DANVILLE

Amber Bistro | *Cal.*	23
Amici's | *Pizza*	21
Bridges | *Asian/Cal.*	23
Chow/Park Chow | *Amer.*	21

Esin | *Amer./Med.*	26
La Boulange | *Bakery*	21
Peasant/Pear | *Cal./Med.*	23
Piatti | *Italian*	21

DUBLIN

Amici's | *Pizza*	21
Caspers Hot Dogs | *Hot Dogs*	22
Johnny Garlic's | *Cal.*	19
Koi | *Chinese*	23
Ohgane Korean | *Korean*	22
Shalimar | *Indian/Pakistani*	23

EL CERRITO

Pasta Pomodoro | *Italian*	18

EMERYVILLE

Arizmendi | *Bakery/Pizza*	25
Bangkok Thai | *Thai*	24
Bucci's | *Cal./Italian*	21
Bureau 510 | *Amer.*	-
Hong Kong East | *Chinese*	22
Pasta Pomodoro | *Italian*	18
Rudy's Can't Fail | *Diner*	19
Townhouse B&G | *Cal.*	22
Trader Vic's | *Polynesian*	18

FREMONT/NEWARK

Pakwan | *Pakistani*	23
Shalimar | *Indian/Pakistani*	23
Vung Tau | *Viet.*	24

HAYWARD/ UNION CITY

Caspers Hot Dogs | *Hot Dogs*	22
Everett/Jones BBQ | *BBQ*	21
La Victoria | *Mex.*	24
Hong Kong Flower/Mayflower | *Chinese*	21
Men Oh Tokushima | *Japanese/Noodle Shop*	-
Pakwan | *Pakistani*	23

LAFAYETTE

Artisan Bistro | *Cal./French*	25
Bo's BBQ | *BBQ*	22
Cheese Steak | *Cheesestks.*	22
Chevalier | *French*	25
Chow/Park Chow | *Amer.*	21
La Boulange | *Bakery*	21
Patxi's Pizza | *Pizza*	22

LOCATIONS

Pizza Antica	*Pizza*	22
Postino	*Italian*	24
NEW Rustic Tavern	*Amer.*	-
Yankee Pier	*New Eng./Seafood*	19

LAKE TAHOE

Christy Hill	*Cal./French*	23
Cottonwood	*Eclectic*	20
Dragonfly	*Asian/Cal.*	23
Evan's	*Amer.*	27
Gar Woods	*Cal.*	19
Manzanita	*Cal.*	22
Moody's Bistro	*Amer.*	23
Pianeta	*Italian/Med.*	20
PlumpJack	*Cal.*	22
Soule Domain	*Amer.*	24
Sunnyside Lodge	*Seafood/Steak*	18
Wolfdale's	*Cal.*	27

LIVERMORE

| Patxi's Pizza | *Pizza* | 22 |
| Wente Vineyards | *Cal./Med.* | 25 |

OAKLAND

À Côté	*French/Med.*	24
Actual Cafe	*Cal.*	22
Addis Ethiopian	*Ethiopian*	25
Adesso	*Italian*	22
Arizmendi	*Bakery/Pizza*	25
A16	*Italian*	24
Asmara	*Ethiopian*	26
Bakesale Betty	*Bakery*	26
Barlata	*Spanish*	22
Barney's	*Burgers*	21
BayWolf	*Cal./Med.*	26
Bellanico	*Italian*	23
Blackberry Bistro	*Southern*	21
Blue Bottle	*Cal./Coffee*	24
Bocanova	*Pan-Latin*	23
Boot/Shoe	*Italian/Pizza*	24
Breads/India	*Indian*	20
Brown Sugar	*Soul/Southern*	26
B-Side BBQ	*BBQ*	23
Burma Superstar	*Burmese*	25
Cactus Taqueria	*Mex.*	21
Camino	*Cal./Med.*	24
Caspers Hot Dogs	*Hot Dogs*	22
César	*Pan-Latin*	22
Cheese Steak	*Cheesestks.*	22

Chop Bar	*Cal.*	24
Commis	*Amer.*	27
Doña Tomás	*Mex.*	22
Dopo	*Italian*	25
NEW Duende	*Spanish*	23
El Farolito	*Mex.*	23
NEW El Gusano	*Mex.*	-
Encuentro	*Veg.*	26
Enoteca Molinari	*Italian*	22
Everett/Jones BBQ	*BBQ*	21
Flora	*Amer.*	23
NEW Forge	*Amer./Pizza*	-
FuseBox	*Korean*	26
NEW Grand Lake Kitchen	*Deli*	-
Grégoire	*French*	24
Haven	*Cal.*	25
Hawker Fare	*SE Asian*	23
Home of Chicken	*Southern*	19
Homeroom	*Amer.*	21
Hopscotch	*Amer./Japanese*	24
Ike's Pl./Lair	*Sandwiches*	25
In-N-Out	*Burgers*	23
Italian Colors	*Italian*	22
NEW Juhu Beach Club	*Indian*	-
Lake Chalet	*Cal.*	17
Le Cheval	*Viet.*	21
Lo Coco's	*Italian*	22
Luka's Taproom	*Cal./French*	20
NEW Lungomare	*Italian*	-
Mama's Royal	*Amer.*	23
Marica	*Amer./Seafood*	25
NEW Marrow	*Amer.*	-
Marzano	*Italian/Pizza*	23
Mezze	*Cal./Med.*	22
NEW Miss Ollie's	*Carib.*	-
Mua Lounge	*Amer.*	21
Nan Yang	*Burmese*	22
NEW Nido	*Mex.*	-
Ohgane Korean	*Korean*	22
Oliveto Cafe	*Italian*	23
Oliveto Rest.	*Italian*	25
Ozumo	*Japanese*	25
Pasta Pomodoro	*Italian*	18
Pho 84	*Viet.*	23
Picán	*Southern*	24
Pizzaiolo	*Italian/Pizza*	26
Plum	*Cal.*	23

NEW Ramen Shop	*Japanese/Noodle Shop*	24
Rest. Peony	*Chinese*	20
Rosamunde	*German*	22
Rudy's Can't Fail	*Diner*	19
Rumbo	*Pan-Latin*	19
Sidebar	*Cal./Med.*	22
Soi4	*Thai*	23
Southie	*Amer.*	24
Tamarindo	*Mex.*	25
Top Dog	*Hot Dogs*	23
NEW Tribune Tavern	*British*	-
Trueburger	*Burgers*	21
Umami Burger	*Burgers*	22
Uzen	*Japanese*	24
Wood Tav.	*Cal.*	26
Xolo	*Mex.*	23
Xyclo	*Viet.*	21
Yoshi's	*Japanese*	22
Zachary's Pizza	*Pizza*	25

ORINDA

Casa Orinda	*Italian/Steak*	20

PLEASANT HILL

Caspers Hot Dogs	*Hot Dogs*	22
Pasta Pomodoro	*Italian*	18
Zachary's Pizza	*Pizza*	25

PLEASANTON

Cheesecake Fac.	*Amer.*	16
Cheese Steak	*Cheesestks.*	22
Jim's Country	*Southern*	26

PORT COSTA

Bull Valley Roadhouse	*Amer.*	-

RICHMOND

Caspers Hot Dogs	*Hot Dogs*	22
Hotel Mac Rest.	*Amer.*	22

SAN RAMON

Cheese Steak	*Cheesestks.*	22
Pasta Pomodoro	*Italian*	18
Zachary's Pizza	*Pizza*	25

WALNUT CREEK

Breads/India	*Indian*	20
Caspers Hot Dogs	*Hot Dogs*	22
Cheese Steak	*Cheesestks.*	22
Corners Tav.	*Amer.*	23

Home of Chicken	*Southern*	19
Ike's Lair	*Sandwiches*	25
Il Fornaio	*Italian*	18
La Boulange	*Bakery*	21
Lark Creek	*Amer.*	23
Le Cheval	*Viet.*	21
Nama Sushi	*Japanese*	27
Prima	*Italian*	26
Ruth's Chris	*Steak*	24
Sasa	*Japanese*	25
Va de Vi	*Eclectic*	25
Vanessa's Bistro	*French/Viet.*	23
Vic Stewart's	*Steak*	24
Walnut Creek Yacht	*Seafood*	24

YOSEMITE/OAKHURST

Ahwahnee	*Cal.*	21
Erna's Elderberry	*Cal./French*	28

North of San Francisco

BODEGA BAY

Duck Club	*Amer.*	22
Terrapin Creek	*Cal.*	27

CALISTOGA

All Seasons	*Cal.*	23
Brannan's Grill	*Amer.*	19
Jole	*Amer.*	26
Solbar	*Cal.*	26

CORTE MADERA

Blue Barn	*Cal.*	25
Brick/Bottle	*Cal.*	19
Cheesecake Fac.	*Amer.*	16
Il Fornaio	*Italian*	18
Pacific Catch	*Seafood*	22
Sea Thai/Modern	*Thai*	26

FORESTVILLE

NEW Backyard	*Cal.*	-
Farmhse. Inn	*Cal.*	27

GEYSERVILLE

Diavola	*Italian*	26
Rustic	*Italian*	21

GLEN ELLEN/KENWOOD

Cafe Citti	*Italian*	23
Fig Cafe/Wine	*French*	26

LOCATIONS

Glen Ellen Inn | *Cal.* 23
Glen Ellen Star | *Amer.* 27
Kenwood | *Amer./French* 25

GUERNEVILLE

Applewood Rest. | *Cal.* 24
Boon Eat/Drink | *Cal.* 25

HEALDSBURG/ WINDSOR

Barndiva | *Amer.* 25
Bistro Ralph | *Cal./French* 23
NEW Bravas Bar/Tapas | *Spanish* 25
NEW Café Lucia | *Portug.* –
Campo Fina | *Italian/Pizza* –
NEW Chalkboard Bistro | *Amer.* –
Charcuterie | *French* 20
Chinois | *Asian* 25
Downtown Bakery | *Bakery* 26
Dry Creek | *Cal.* 24
Healdsburg B&G | *Amer.* 19
Jimtown Store | *Deli* 21
Johnny Garlic's | *Cal.* 19
Madrona Manor | *Amer./French* 27
Mateo's Cocina | *Mex.* 22
NEW Parish Cafe | *Cajun/Creole* –
Pizzando | *Cal./Pizza* –
Ravenous | *Amer.* 22
Scopa | *Italian* 26
Spoonbar | *Cal.* 20
NEW Taverna Sofia | *Greek/Med.* –
Willi's Seafood | *Seafood* 25
Wurst Rest. | *Amer./Pub* 21
Zin | *Amer.* 23

LARKSPUR

Avatar's | *Indian* 23
NEW Belcampo Meat | *Amer.* –
El Huarache Loco | *Mex.* 21
Emporio Rulli | *Dessert/Italian* 22
NEW Farmshop | *Amer.* –
Left Bank | *French* 20
Picco | *Italian* 26
Pizzeria Picco | *Pizza* 26
Tav./Lark Creek | *Amer.* 21
Yankee Pier | *New Eng./Seafood* 19

MENDOCINO COUNTY

Albion River Inn | *Cal.* 24
Cafe Beaujolais | *Cal./French* 26

Ledford Hse. | *Cal./Med.* 26
Little River Inn | *Cal./Seafood* 24
MacCallum/Grey Whale | *Cal.* 24
Mendo Bistro | *Amer.* 25
Mendo Café | *Eclectic* 20
955 Rest. | *Amer./French* 25
Restaurant | *Amer./Eclectic* 22
Rest./Stevenswood | *Amer.* 24
St. Orres | *Cal.* 23

MILL VALLEY

Avatar's | *Indian* 23
Balboa Cafe | *Amer.* 20
Buckeye | *Amer./BBQ* 25
Bungalow 44 | *Amer.* 22
Dipsea Cafe | *Diner/Greek* 18
El Paseo | *Steak* 23
Frantoio | *Italian* 22
In-N-Out | *Burgers* 23
Joe's Taco | *Mex.* 21
La Boulange | *Bakery* 21
Pasta Pomodoro | *Italian* 18
Pearl's Deluxe/Phat | *Burgers* 23
Piatti | *Italian* 21
Piazza D'Angelo | *Italian* 20
Pizza Antica | *Pizza* 22
Plant Cafe | *Health* 22
Sol Food | *Puerto Rican* 24
Super Duper | *Burgers* 23
Toast | *Amer.* 21

NAPA

Alexis Baking | *Bakery* 22
Angèle | *French* 24
Azzurro | *Pizza* 23
Bank Café | *French* 23
Bistro Don Giovanni | *Italian* 25
Boon Fly | *Cal.* 23
Brix | *Cal./French* 22
C Casa | *Mex.* 25
Celadon | *Amer./Eclectic* 25
Cole's Chop | *Steak* 27
NEW Empire | *Eclectic* –
Farm | *Amer.* 24
Fatted Calf | *Sandwiches* 26
Fish Story | *Seafood* 19
Fumé Bistro | *Amer.* 22
Gott's Roadside | *Diner* 22

Hog Island Oyster | *Seafood* 26

In-N-Out | *Burgers* 23

Kitchen Door | *Eclectic* 22

La Taquiza | *Mex.* 27

La Toque | *French* 27

Model Bakery | *Bakery* 23

Morimoto | *Japanese* 25

Napa Wine Train | *Cal.* 20

Norman Rose | *Amer.* 20

Oenotri | *Italian* 24

Oxbow Wine | *Cal./Med.* 21

NEW Pear | *Cajun/Southern* -

Pearl | *Cal.* 22

Pica Pica | *Venez.* 21

Q Rest. | *Amer./BBQ* 22

Thomas & Fagiani's | *Amer.* 24

Uva Trattoria | *Italian* 19

ZuZu | *Spanish* 24

NOVATO

Hopmonk Tav. | *Eclectic* 19

La Boulange | *Bakery* 21

Pasta Pomodoro | *Italian* 18

Toast | *Amer.* 21

OCCIDENTAL

Bistro/Copains | *French* 27

PETALUMA

Avatar's | *Indian* 23

Central Mkt. | *Cal./Med.* 25

Cucina Paradiso | *Italian* 27

Della Fattoria | *Bakery/Eclectic* 26

Graffiti | *Eclectic* 25

NEW Pub Republic | *Pub* -

Risibisi | *Italian* 24

Rosso Pizzeria | *Italian/Pizza* 25

Sea Thai/Modern | *Thai* 26

Sugo | *Italian* 24

Volpi's Rist. | *Italian* 22

Water St. Bistro | *French* 23

ROSS

Marché/Fleurs | *French* 25

RUTHERFORD

Alex Italian | *Italian* 24

Auberge du Soleil | *Cal./French* 27

Rutherford Grill | *Amer.* 24

SAN ANSELMO

Insalata's | *Med.* 25

Lincoln Park Wine | *Cal.* -

Marinitas | *Mex./Pan-Latin* 21

NEW Pizzalina | *Pizza* -

SAN RAFAEL

Amici's | *Pizza* 21

Arizmendi | *Bakery/Pizza* 25

Barney's | *Burgers* 21

Il Davide | *Italian* 23

Miller's East | *Deli/Jewish* 20

NEW Odalisque Cafe | *Cal./Med.* -

Royal Thai | *Thai* 26

Sol Food | *Puerto Rican* 24

SANTA ROSA/ ROHNERT PARK

Betty's Fish | *British/Seafood* 23

Bistro 29 | *French* 25

Cheese Steak | *Cheesestks.* 22

El Farolito | *Mex.* 23

Flavor | *Cal./Eclectic* 22

Gary Chu's | *Chinese* 24

Hana | *Japanese* 26

Ike's Pl./Lair | *Sandwiches* 25

Jackson's | *Cal.* 22

John Ash | *Cal.* 25

Johnny Garlic's | *Cal.* 19

La Gare | *French* 26

Lococo's Cucina | *Italian* 25

Monti's | *Amer./Med.* 22

Osake | *Cal./Japanese* 25

Rosso Pizzeria | *Italian/Pizza* 25

Sazon Peruvian | *Peruvian* 25

Sea Thai/Modern | *Thai* 26

Stark's Steak/Sea | *Seafood/Steak* 25

Tex Wasabi's | *BBQ/Japanese* 19

Willi's Wine | *Eclectic* 25

SAUSALITO

Avatar's | *Indian* 23

Bar Bocce | *Pizza* 22

Copita | *Mex.* 24

NEW Fast Food Français | *Amer./French* -

Fish | *Seafood* 24

Le Garage | *French* 23

Murray Circle | *Cal.* 23
Poggio | *Italian* 25
Scoma's | *Seafood* 24
Sushi Ran | *Japanese* 27
NEW Trident | *Amer./Seafood* 22

SEBASTOPOL/GRATON

Forchetta/Bastoni | 19
  Italian/SE Asian
French Gdn. | *French* 22
Hopmonk Tav. | *Eclectic* 19
K&L Bistro | *French* 25
Peter Lowell | *Italian* 22
Underwood Bar | *Med.* 22
Willow Wood | *Eclectic/Med.* 24
Zazu | *Amer./Italian* 26

SONOMA

Cafe La Haye | *Amer./Cal.* 26
Carneros Bistro | *Cal.* 24
Della Santina | *Italian* 24
El Dorado | *Cal./Med.* 22
Fremont Diner | *Diner* 24
Girl/Fig | *French* 24
Harvest Moon | *Cal./Med.* 25
Hopmonk Tav. | *Eclectic* 19
Hot Box Grill | *Cal.* 25
LaSalette | *Portug.* 24
Santé | *Cal./French* -
Sonoma-Meritage | 19
  Italian/Seafood

ST. HELENA

Bar Terra | *Amer.* 25
Cindy Pawlcyn's | *Amer.* 22
Cindy's Backstreet | *Cal.* 24
Cook St. Helena | *Italian* 26
Farmstead | *Amer./Cal.* 22
French Blue | *Amer.* 20
Goose & Gander | *Amer.* 22
Gott's Roadside | *Diner* 22
La Condesa | *Mex.* 25
Market | *Amer.* 22
Meadowood Grill | *Cal.* 22
Meadowood Rest. | *Cal.* 27
Model Bakery | *Bakery* 23
Pizzeria Tra Vigne | *Pizza* 22
Press | *Amer./Steak* 26
Terra | *Amer.* 27

Tra Vigne | *Italian* 24
Wine Spectator | *Cal.* 23

VALLEY FORD

Rocker Oysterfeller's | 25
  Amer./Southern

WEST MARIN/OLEMA

Nick's Cove | *Cal.* 21
Osteria Stellina | *Italian* 24
Pine Cone Diner | *Diner* 20
NEW Sir & Star | *Amer.* -
Station Hse. | *Amer.* 18

YOUNTVILLE

Ad Hoc | *Amer.* 26
Addendum | *Amer.* 25
Bistro Jeanty | *French* 27
Bottega | *Italian* 25
Bouchon | *French* 26
Étoile | *Cal.* 26
French Laundry | *Amer./French* 28
Hurley's Rest. | *Cal./Med.* 23
Mustards | *Amer./Cal.* 25
Redd | *Cal.* 27
Redd Wood | *Italian/Pizza* 25

South of San Francisco

BIG SUR

Big Sur | *Amer./Bakery* 24
NEW Big Sur Roadhse. | -
  Cajun/Seafood
Deetjen's Big Sur | *Cal.* 24
Nepenthe | *Amer.* 18
Rest./Ventana | *Cal.* 23
Sierra Mar | *Cal./Eclectic* 28

BURLINGAME

Il Fornaio | *Italian* 18
Kabul Afghan | *Afghan* 24
La Boulange | *Bakery* 21
La Corneta | *Mex.* 22
Mingalaba | *Burmese/Chinese* 26
Plant Cafe | *Health* 22
Roti Indian | *Indian* 23
Sakae Sushi | *Japanese* 25
Stella Alpina Osteria | *Italian* 25
Straits | *Singapor.* 20

CAMPBELL

A Bellagio	*Italian*	24
Pacific Catch	*Seafood*	22

CARMEL/MONTEREY PENINSULA

Andre's Bouchée	*French*	24
Anton/Michel	*Continental*	24
Aubergine	*Cal.*	26
Bistro Moulin	*Euro.*	26
Cantinetta Luca	*Italian*	21
Casanova	*French/Italian*	24
NEW Cindy's Waterfront	*Amer.*	–
Fandango	*Med.*	21
Fishwife	*Cal./Seafood*	22
Flying Fish (Carmel)	*Cal./Seafood*	24
400 Degrees	*Burgers*	–
Grasing's Coastal	*Cal.*	21
Il Fornaio	*Italian*	18
NEW La Balena Cucina	*Italian*	–
La Bicyclette	*French/Italian*	23
Mission Ranch	*Amer.*	20
Montrio Bistro	*Amer.*	23
Mundaka	*Spanish*	24
Old Port Lobster	*Seafood*	23
Pacific's Edge	*Amer./French*	24
Passionfish	*Cal./Seafood*	27
Rio Grill	*Cal.*	23
Roy's	*Hawaiian*	25
Sardine Factory	*Amer./Seafood*	24
Tarpy's	*Amer.*	24

CARMEL VALLEY

Café Rustica	*Cal.*	23
Marinus	*Cal./French*	26

CUPERTINO

Alexander's Steak	*Japanese/Steak*	26
Amici's	*Pizza*	21
Gochi	*Japanese*	25
Ike's Pl./Lair	*Sandwiches*	25
Joy Luck Palace	*Chinese*	21
Little Sheep	*Mongolian*	22

FOSTER CITY

Ike's Pl./Lair	*Sandwiches*	25

HALF MOON BAY/ COAST

Barbara's Fishtrap	*Seafood*	21
Cafe Gibraltar	*Med.*	28
Cetrella	*Med.*	23
Chez Shea	*Eclectic*	21
Duarte's	*Amer.*	22
Half Moon Brew	*Cal./Pub*	17
La Costanera	*Peruvian*	25
Mezza Luna	*Italian*	23
Navio	*Amer.*	24
Pasta Moon	*Italian*	25
Sam's Chowder	*Seafood*	22

LOS ALTOS

Chef Chu's	*Chinese*	22
Hunan Home's/Gdn.	*Chinese*	21
Muracci's	*Japanese*	20
Sumika	*Japanese*	25

LOS GATOS

Cin-Cin Wine	*Eclectic*	24
Dio Deka	*Greek*	25
NEW Katsu	*Japanese*	–
Manresa	*Amer.*	27
Nick's Next Door	*Amer.*	26
Rest. James	*Cal.*	25

MENLO PARK

Amici's	*Pizza*	21
Applewood Pizza	*Pizza*	23
Cool Café	*Cal.*	21
Flea St. Café	*Cal.*	26
Iberia	*Spanish*	22
LB Steak	*Steak*	22
Left Bank	*French*	20
Madera	*Amer.*	23
Refuge	*Belgian/Sandwiches*	25
Rest. Mitsunobu	*Japanese*	24

MILLBRAE

Asian Pearl	*Chinese*	22
Hong Kong Flower/Mayflower	*Chinese*	21
In-N-Out	*Burgers*	23
Kitchen	*Chinese*	23

MILPITAS

Jang Su Jang	*Korean*	23
Liou's Hse.	*Chinese*	24

LOCATIONS

Hong Kong Flower/Mayflower | *Chinese*	21
Vung Tau | *Viet.*	24

MOUNTAIN VIEW

Amarin Thai | *Thai*	21
Amber India | *Indian*	24
Amici's | *Pizza*	21
Asian Box | *Asian*	19
Cascal | *Pan-Latin*	22
Chez TJ | *French*	23
In-N-Out | *Burgers*	23
Krung Thai | *Thai*	22
Sakoon | *Indian*	21
Xanh | *Viet.*	21

PACIFICA/SAN BRUNO

NEW Puerto 27 | *Peruvian*	-
Surf Spot | *Eclectic*	-

PALO ALTO/ EAST PALO ALTO

Amber India | *Indian*	24
Asian Box | *Asian*	19
Baumé | *French*	26
Café Brioche | *Cal./French*	21
Calafia | *Cal.*	20
NEW Campo 185 | *Italian*	16
Cheesecake Fac. | *Amer.*	16
Counter Palo Alto | *Burgers*	22
Curry Up Now | *Indian*	21
Evvia | *Greek*	28
Fuki Sushi | *Japanese*	23
Hunan Home's/Gdn. | *Chinese*	21
Il Fornaio | *Italian*	18
Jin Sho | *Japanese*	24
La Bodeguita/Medio | *Cuban*	22
La Boulange | *Bakery*	21
Mayfield | *Bakery/Cal.*	20
Osteria | *Italian*	23
Pampas | *Brazilian*	22
Patxi's Pizza | *Pizza*	22
Quattro | *Italian*	22
Rangoon Ruby | *Burmese*	22
NEW Sea | *Seafood*	23
Spice Kit | *Asian*	19
St. Michael's | *Cal.*	22
Tacolicious | *Mex.*	24
Tai Pan | *Chinese*	23

Tamarine | *Viet.*	25
Tava | *Indian*	-
Umami Burger | *Burgers*	22
Zibibbo | *Med.*	20

REDWOOD CITY

Chantilly | *French/Italian*	25
Crouching Tiger | *Chinese*	22
Donato | *Italian*	23
Ike's Pl./Lair | *Sandwiches*	25
John Bentley | *Amer.*	25
La Victoria | *Mex.*	24
Old Port Lobster | *Seafood*	23
Pasta Pomodoro | *Italian*	18

REDWOOD SHORES

Amici's | *Pizza*	21
Mistral | *Amer./Med.*	22

SAN BRUNO

Pasta Pomodoro | *Italian*	18

SAN CARLOS/BELMONT

Izzy's Steak | *Steak*	22
Kabul Afghan | *Afghan*	24
La Corneta | *Mex.*	22
Rangoon Ruby | *Burmese*	22
Refuge | *Belgian/Sandwiches*	25

SAN JOSE

Amber India | *Indian*	24
Amici's | *Pizza*	21
Arcadia | *Amer.*	23
Blowfish Sushi | *Japanese*	23
Cheesecake Fac. | *Amer.*	16
Cheese Steak | *Cheesestks.*	22
Grill/Alley | *Steak*	23
Il Fornaio | *Italian*	18
In-N-Out | *Burgers*	23
Krung Thai | *Thai*	22
La Forêt | *Continental/French*	27
La Victoria | *Mex.*	24
LB Steak | *Steak*	22
Left Bank | *French*	20
Le Papillon | *French*	27
Morton's | *Steak*	23
New Krung Thai | *Thai*	25
Original Joe's | *Italian*	22
Pasta Pomodoro | *Italian*	18

Patxi's Pizza | *Pizza* 22

Pizza Antica | *Pizza* 22

71 St. Peter | *Cal./Med.* 22

Sino | *Chinese* 19

Straits | *Singapor.* 20

Taqueria San Jose | *Mex.* 23

Taqueria Tlaquepaque | *Mex.* 21

Vung Tau | *Viet.* 24

SAN MATEO

Acqua Pazza | *Italian* 21

All Spice | *Indian* 26

Amici's | *Pizza* 21

Attic | *Asian* 20

Cha Cha Cha | *Carib./Cuban* 22

Curry Up Now | *Indian* 21

Espetus | *Brazilian* 24

Hotaru | *Japanese* 21

La Cumbre | *Mex.* 20

Little Sheep | *Mongolian* 22

North Bch. Pizza | *Pizza* 20

Osteria Coppa | *Italian/Pizza* 22

Pancho Villa | *Mex.* 23

Pasta Pomodoro | *Italian* 18

Ramen Dojo | 25
    Japanese/Noodle Shop

Sushi Sam's | *Japanese* 24

231 Ellsworth | *Amer.* 23

Viognier | *Cal./French* 24

Wakuriya | *Japanese* 28

SANTA CLARA

Cheesecake Fac. | *Amer.* 16

Dasaprakash | *Indian/Veg.* 22

Ike's Pl./Lair | *Sandwiches* 25

Jang Su Jang | *Korean* 23

Orenchi Ramen | *Japanese* 25

Parcel 104 | *Cal.* 23

Piatti | *Italian* 21

SANTA CRUZ/APTOS/ CAPITOLA/SOQUEL

NEW Bantam | *Cal./Pizza* -

Café Gratitude | *Vegan* 19

Gabriella Café | *Cal./Italian* 20

Gayle's Bakery | *Bakery* 24

La Posta | *Italian* 25

O'mei | *Chinese* 24

Oswald | *Amer.* 25

Shadowbrook Rest. | *Cal.* 22

Soif Wine Bar | *Cal.* 24

SARATOGA

Basin | *Amer.* 23

Hachi Ju Hachi | *Japanese* 27

La Fondue | *Fondue* 22

Plumed Horse | *Cal.* 25

Sent Sovi | *Cal.* 26

SEASIDE

Fishwife | *Cal./Seafood* 22

SOUTH SF/DALY CITY

Basque Cultural | *French* 20

Burger Joint | *Burgers* 19

BurgerMeister | *Burgers* 20

Ebisu | *Japanese* 24

El Farolito | *Mex.* 23

Emporio Rulli | *Dessert/Italian* 22

In-N-Out | *Burgers* 23

Koi | *Chinese* 23

Plant Cafe | *Health* 22

Yankee Pier | *New Eng./Seafood* 19

STANFORD

Cool Café | *Cal.* 21

Ike's Pl./Lair | *Sandwiches* 25

SUNNYVALE

Cheese Steak | *Cheesestks.* 22

Dishdash | *Mideast.* 24

Il Postale | *Italian* 23

Lion/Compass | *Amer.* 21

Pasta Pomodoro | *Italian* 18

Saravana Bhavan | *Indian* 24

Sawa Sushi | *Japanese* 23

Shalimar | *Indian/Pakistani* 23

WOODSIDE

Bella Vista | *Continental* 24

Station 1 | *Cal.* 25

Village Pub | *Amer.* 25

LOCATIONS

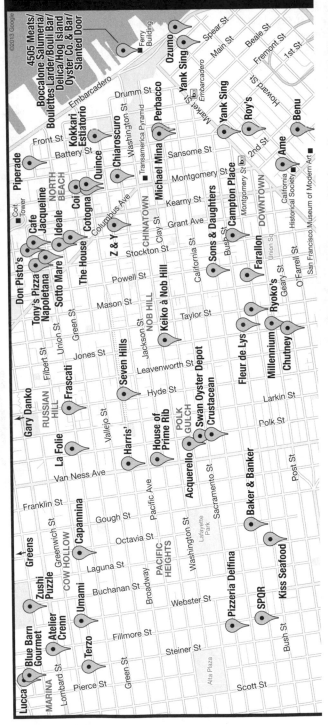

©2013 Google

4505 Meats/
Boccalone Salumeria/
Boulettes Larder/Bouli Bar/
Delica/Hog Island
Oyster Co. & Bar/
Slanted Door

Ferry Building

Ozumo

Spear St

Main St

Beale St

Fremont St

1st St

Yank Sing

Embarcadero

Drumm St

Perbacco

Yank Sing

Howard St

Roy's

Benu

Front St

Kokkari Estiatorio

Chiaroscuro

Washington St

Transamerica Pyramid

Michael Mina

Sansome St

Market St

2nd St

Ame

Battery St

Quince

Montgomery St

California

San Francisco Museum of Modern Art

Piperade

NORTH BEACH

Coit Tower

Cafe Jacqueline

Coi

Cotogna

Columbus Ave

Kearny St

Grant Ave

Clay St

CHINATOWN

Campton Place

Montgomery St

California Historical Society

DOWNTOWN

Ideale

The House

Z & Y

Sons & Daughters

Bush St

Farallon

Union Sq

Don Pisto's

Stockton St

Powell St

O'Farrell St

Tony's Pizza Napoletana

Sotto Mare

Mason St

NOB HILL

Keiko à Nob Hill

Taylor St

Ryoko's

Geary St

Frascati

Union St

Green St

Filbert St

Jones St

Seven Hills

Jackson St

Leavenworth St

Fleur de Lys

Millennium

Chutney

Gary Danko

RUSSIAN HILL

Hyde St

POLK GULCH

Larkin St

La Folie

Vallejo St

Harris'

House of Prime Rib

Swan Oyster Depot

Crustacean

Polk St

Acquerello

Sacramento St

Van Ness Ave

Pacific Ave

Lafayette Park

Post St

Baker & Banker

Franklin St

Capannina

Gough St

Octavia St

Washington St

PACIFIC HEIGHTS

Greens

Greenwich St

Laguna St

Broadway

Pizzeria Delfina

SPQR

Kiss Seafood

Zushi Puzzle

COW HOLLOW

Umami

Buchanan St

Webster St

Bush St

Blue Barn Gourmet

Atelier Crenn

Terzo

Fillmore St

Steiner St

Lucca

MARINA

Lombard St

Pierce St

Green St

Alta Plaza

Scott St

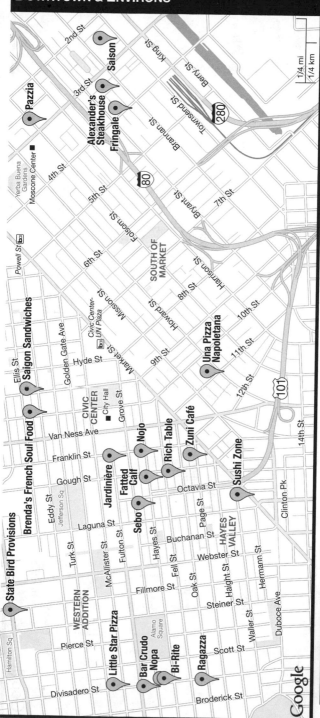

2nd St

Saison

King St

Berry St

3rd St

Pazzia

Alexander's Steakhouse

Fringale

Townsend St

Brannan St

280

4th St

Yerba Buena Gardens
Moscone Center ■

5th St

80

Bryant St

7th St

Folsom St

Powell St

6th St

SOUTH OF MARKET

Harrison St

8th St

Mission St

Howard St

Civic Center-
UN Plaza

9th St

10th St

Una Pizza Napoletana

11th St

Saigon Sandwiches

Golden Gate Ave

Hyde St

Ellis St

Market St

12th St

101

Brenda's French Soul Food

CIVIC CENTER
City Hall ■

Grove St

Zuni Café

14th St

Van Ness Ave

Nojo

Rich Table

Franklin St

Jardinière

Fatted Calf

Sushi Zone

Clinton Pk

Gough St

Octavia St

Eddy St
Jefferson Sq

Laguna St

Sebo

Page St

HAYES VALLEY

State Bird Provisions

Turk St

McAllister St

Fulton St

Hayes St

Fell St

Buchanan St

Webster St

Oak St

Haight St

Hermann St

Duboce Ave

WESTERN ADDITION

Fillmore St

Steiner St

Waller St

Hamilton Sq

Little Star Pizza

Pierce St

Bar Crudo

Alamo Square

Nopa

Bi-Rite

Ragazza

Scott St

Broderick St

Divisadero St

Google

MAPS

1/4 mi
1/4 km

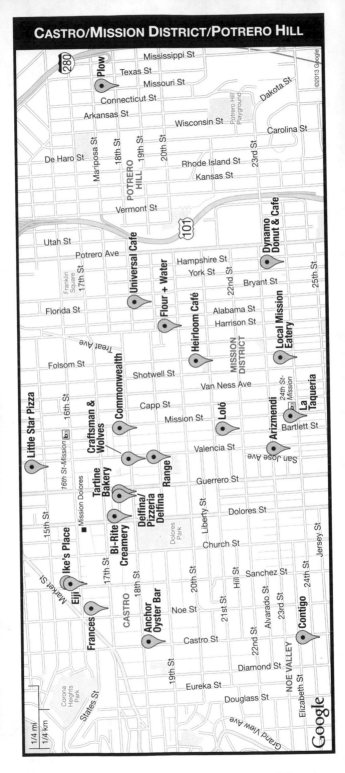

CASTRO/MISSION DISTRICT/POTRERO HILL

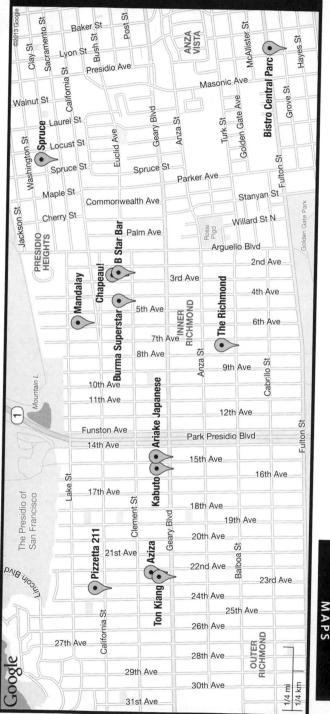

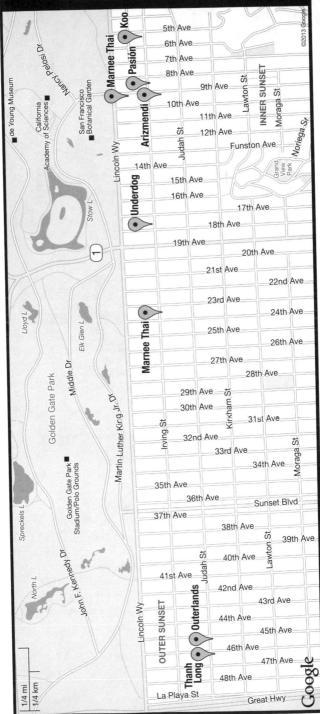

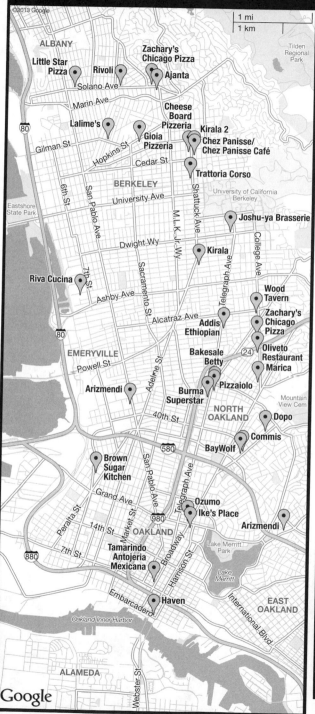

©2013 Google

ALBANY

Little Star Pizza

Rivoli

Zachary's Chicago Pizza

Ajanta

Solano Ave

Marin Ave

80

Lalime's

Cheese Board Pizzeria

Kirala 2

Chez Panisse/ Chez Panisse Café

Gioia Pizzeria

Gilman St

Hopkins St

Cedar St

Trattoria Corso

6th St

San Pablo Ave

BERKELEY

University Ave

University of California Berkeley

M.L.K. Jr. Way

Shattuck Ave

Joshu-ya Brasserie

Eastshore State Park

Dwight Wy

Kirala

College Ave

7th St

Riva Cucina

Sacramento St

Ashby Ave

Telegraph Ave

Wood Tavern

Zachary's Chicago Pizza

Alcatraz Ave

Addis Ethiopian

24

Oliveto Restaurant

Marica

EMERYVILLE

Powell St

Adeline St

Bakesale Betty

Arizmendi

Burma Superstar

Pizzaiolo

NORTH OAKLAND

Mountain View Cem

40th St

Dopo

Commis

580

BayWolf

Brown Sugar Kitchen

Grand Ave

San Pablo Ave

Telegraph Ave

Peralta St

14th St

Market St

980

OAKLAND

Broadway

Ozumo

Ike's Place

Arizmendi

880

7th St

Tamarindo Antojeria Mexicana

Harrison St

Lake Merritt Park

Lake Merritt

Embarcadero

Haven

International Blvd

EAST OAKLAND

Oakland Inner Harbor

Webster St

ALAMEDA

Google

MAPS

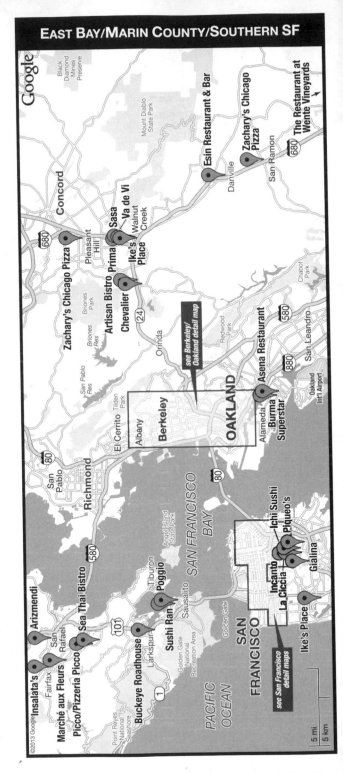

Google

Black Diamond Mines Preserve

Mount Diablo State Park

Esin Restaurant & Bar

Zachary's Chicago Pizza

The Restaurant at Wente Vineyards

680

San Ramon

Concord

Danville

Va de Vi

Sasa

680

Pleasant Hill

Ike's Place

Prima

Walnut Creek

Zachary's Chicago Pizza

Artisan Bistro Chevalier

Briones Park

24

Chabot Park

Asena Restaurant

580

Briones Res

Orinda

Redwood Park

San Leandro

see Berkeley/ Oakland detail map

San Pablo Res

Tilden Park

OAKLAND

880

Oakland Int'l Airport

El Cerrito

Berkeley

Albany

Alameda

Burma Superstar

80

Richmond

San Pablo

SAN FRANCISCO BAY

Ichi Sushi

Piqueo's

80

580

Angel Island State Park

Gialina

Sea Thai Bistro

Tiburon

Incanto

La Ciccia

Arizmendi

Poggio

101

Sausalito

Sushi Ran

Golden Gate

San Rafael

Larkspur

SAN FRANCISCO

Insalata's

Marché aux Fleurs

Picco/Pizzeria Picco

Fairfax

Buckeye Roadhouse

1

Golden Gate National Recreation Area

SAN FRANCISCO

Ike's Place

see San Francisco detail maps

PACIFIC OCEAN

Point Reyes National Seashore

5 mi

5 km

©2013 Google

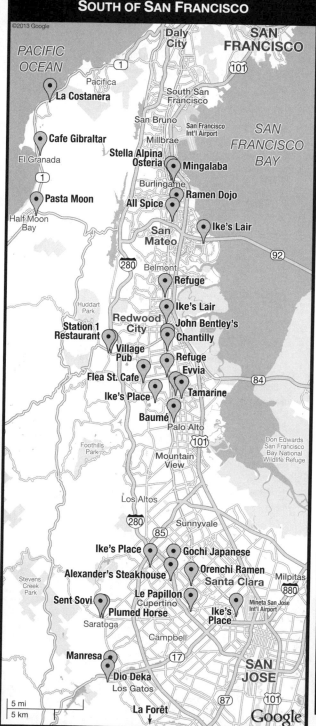

SOUTH OF SAN FRANCISCO

©2013 Google

PACIFIC
OCEAN

SAN
FRANCISCO

Daly
City

La Costanera

Pacifica

South San
Francisco

San Bruno

San Francisco
Int'l Airport

SAN
FRANCISCO
BAY

Cafe Gibraltar

El Granada

Millbrae

Stella Alpina
Osteria

Mingalaba

Burlingame

Ramen Dojo

Pasta Moon

All Spice

Ike's Lair

Half Moon
Bay

San
Mateo

Belmont

Refuge

92

Huddart
Park

Ike's Lair

Station 1
Restaurant

Redwood
City

John Bentley's

Chantilly

Village
Pub

Refuge

Flea St. Cafe

Evvia

84

Ike's Place

Tamarine

Baumé

Palo Alto

Foothills
Park

Mountain
View

Don Edwards
San Francisco
Bay National
Wildlife Refuge

Los Altos

280

Sunnyvale

85

Ike's Place

Gochi Japanese

Alexander's Steakhouse

Orenchi Ramen
Santa Clara

Milpitas

880

Stevens
Creek
Park

Sent Sovi

Le Papillon

Mineta San Jose
Int'l Airport

Plumed Horse

Ike's
Place

Saratoga

Campbell

Manresa

SAN
JOSE

Dio Deka

17

Los Gatos

La Forêt

87

101

5 mi
5 km

Google

MAPS

©2013 Google

Diavola Pizzeria & Salumeria

Geyserville

101

128

R L
Stevenson
State Park

Willi's Seafood
and Raw Bar
Madrona Manor
Restaurant

Scopa
Downtown Bakery & Creamery

Healdsburg

Barndiva

Windsor

Farmhouse
Inn & Restaurant
Forestville

John Ash & Co.

Willi's Wine Bar

Ike's
Place

Sea Thai
Bistro

Zazu

Bistro 29

Osake

Stark's Steak & Seafood
Lococo's Cucina Rustica
La Gare

Santa
Rosa

Rosso Pizzeria &
Wine Bar

Bistro des
Copains

Occidental

K&L Bistro

Sebastopol

101

12

116

Hana Japanese
Restaurant

Rohnert
Park

1

Sea Modern Thai
Rosso Pizzeria & Mozzarella Bar
Central Market
Cucina Paradiso
Della Fattoria Downtown Café

Tomales

Laguna L

Petaluma

Point Reyes
National
Seashore

1

Google

Stafford L

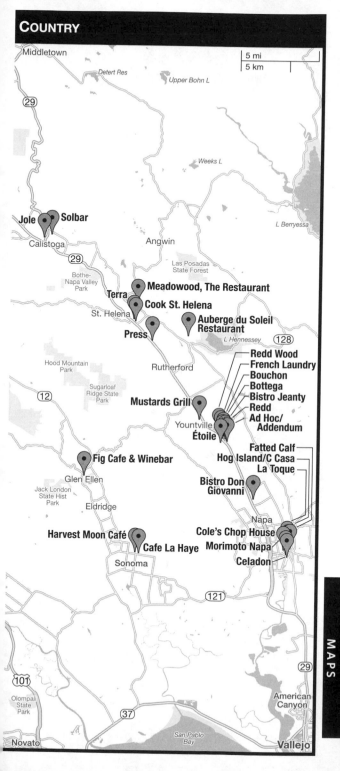

Middletown

Detert Res

Upper Bohn L

5 mi
5 km

29

Weeks L

L Berryessa

Jole **Solbar**

Calistoga

Angwin

29

Las Posadas
State Forest

Bothe-
Napa Valley
Park

Meadowood, The Restaurant

Terra

Cook St. Helena

St. Helena

**Auberge du Soleil
Restaurant**

Press

L Hennessey

128

Hood Mountain
Park

Redd Wood
French Laundry
Bouchon

Rutherford

Bottega
Bistro Jeanty

Sugarloaf
Ridge State
Park

12

Mustards Grill

Redd
Ad Hoc/
Addendum

Yountville

Étoile

Fatted Calf

Fig Cafe & Winebar

Hog Island/C Casa

La Toque

Glen Ellen

**Bistro Don
Giovanni**

Jack London
State Hist
Park

Eldridge

Napa

Cole's Chop House

Harvest Moon Café

Cafe La Haye

Morimoto Napa

Celadon

Sonoma

121

29

MAPS

101

Olompali
State
Park

American
Canyon

37

San Pablo
Bay

Novato

Vallejo

ALPHABETICAL
PAGE INDEX

All places are in San Francisco unless otherwise noted (East of San Francisco=E; North of San Francisco=N; South of San Francisco=S).

Visit zagat.com

351

ALPHA INDEX

Visit zagat.com